DAYS OU

The place to look for places to go

**Top *UK* and *Eire* Visitor
Attractions and Special Events
2004**

www.**daysout*uk***.com

⊠ credits

Days Out *UK*

Days Out *UK*
PO Box 427
Northampton
NN1 3YN

Tel: +44 (0) 1604 622445
Fax: +44 (0) 1604 633866 / 629900

Email: mail@daysoutuk.com
Website: www.daysoutuk.com

ISBN 0-9543899-1- 3
A catalogue record for this book
is available from the British Library

© **Days Out *UK* 2004**
Eighth edition

Database Manager
Leanne Allen

Sales & Administration
Kathy Eele

Design Administration
Helen Dickerson

Designer
Ian Hughes

Photography
All English Heritage and National
Trust properties with pictures are
copyright to their respective libraries
and are used with permission.

Printed and bound by
Newnorth, Bedford

Every effort has been made to
ensure that the information published
is as accurate as possible prior to
publication. A full programme of
verification, directly with the listed
attractions, has been carried out,
however Days Out UK cannot be
held responsible for any errors,
omissions or changes that may have
occurred, or for the consequences of
reliance on the information
published. Days Out UK recommend
that you telephone in advance to
confirm visitor attraction / event
details.

DaYSOUtUK

public holidays 2004

England & Wales

Good Friday	April 9
Easter Monday	April 12
Bank Holiday	May 3
Bank Holiday	May 31
Bank Holiday	Aug 30
Christmas Day	Dec 25
Boxing Day	Dec 26
Bank Holiday	Dec 27
Bank Holiday	Dec 28
New Year Hol 2005	Jan 3

Northern Ireland

St Patrick's Day	Mar 17
Good Friday	April 9
Easter Monday	April 12
Bank Holiday	May 3*
Bank Holiday	May 31
Battle of the Boyne, (Orangemen's Day)	July 12
Bank Holiday	Aug 30
Christmas Day	Dec 25
Boxing Day	Dec 26
Bank Holiday	Dec 27
Bank Holiday	Dec 28
New Year Hol 2005	Jan 3

Scotland

Good Friday	April 9
Bank Holiday	May 3
Bank Holiday	May 31*
Bank Holiday	Aug 2
Christmas Day	Dec 25
Boxing Day	Dec 26*
Bank Holiday	Dec 27
Bank Holiday	Dec 28
New Year Hol 2005	Jan 3
Holiday	Jan 4

Republic of Ireland

St Patrick's Day	Mar 17
Easter Monday	April 12
Public Holiday	May 3
Public Holiday	June 7
Public Holiday	Aug 2
Public Holiday	Oct 25
Christmas Day	Dec 25
St Stephen's Day	Dec 26
Bank Holiday	Dec 27
Bank Holiday	Dec 28
New Year Hol 2005	Jan 3

•Subject to regional and institutional variations

⊙ contents

Harewood House   Museum of Flight   Monkey World   Goonhilly

■ contents

DAYS OUT UK

 Startwater Valley   Painshill Park   Paradise Park   New Pleasurewood Hills

facility symbols

Suitable for pushchairs		Guided tours available	
Baby changing facilities		Photography allowed	
Disabled facilities		Beach/coastal area	
Offering a discount voucher		Credit cards accepted	
No dogs, except guide dogs		Corporate facilities available	
Car parking on site		Wedding ceremonies performe	
Car parking nearby		Educational packs available	
Charged car parking		Celebration catering	
Picnic area		Gift shop	
Light refreshments available		Good weather attraction	
Cafè or restaurant		All weather attraction	
Licensed for alcohol		Allow 1-2 hours for a visit	
National Trust property		Allow half a day for a visit	
National Trust for Scotland		Allow all day for a visit	
English Heritage property		Recommended for adults	
CADW Welsh Historic property		Family friendly	
Historic Scotland		Venue is said to be haunted!	

Bedfordshire

Animal Attractions

Woodside Animal Farm and Leisure Park

Woodside Road Slip End Luton Bedfordshire LU1 4DG

Tel: 01582 841044 Fax: 01582 840626

www.woodsidefarm.co.uk

[From the N: exit M1 J10, follow dual carriageway (A505) to roundabout, take turning for Harpenden (A1081) and follow brown tourist signs for Wildfowl Park. From the S: exit M1 J9, turning N onto the A5 in the direction of Dunstable, turn R onto the B4540 Luton road and follow brown tourist signs for Wildfowl Park. Rail: Luton, then bus service 30, 32, 46 or 231. Plenty of on site parking available]

Woodside Animal Farm is the perfect day out for all the family. With hundreds of animals and birds to see and feed, children are encouraged to get 'touchy-feely' with many of them including rabbits, chicks and owls in the daily 'animal encounter' sessions. There are also flamingoes, llamas, wallabies, goats, snakes, pigs, raccoons, monkeys, cows and iguanas to name a few. Included in the price are tractor rides, bouncy castles, trampolines and the brand new 'Woodside Country Fair', opening Easter 2004. The farm also allows visitors to feed a lot of the animals by selling special pots of feed for them. The kids can wear themselves out in the indoor or outdoor play areas and there's also Farmer Woods 18 hole crazy golf course, sandpit and paddling pool. Woodside runs a number of regular special event days throughout the year including clowns, magicians, reptile celebrities, teddy bears picnics and seaside specials. Visitors can 'pick your own' free range eggs, straight from the hen house, enjoy a delicious meal in the coffee shop and also purchase a wide range of farm produce and souvenirs in our farm shop as well as pets such as rabbits, guinea pigs, hamsters and other small animals. Birthday parties and groups a speciality.

All year Summer Mon-Sat 08.00-18.00, Sun 10.00-18.00, Winter Mon-Sat 08.00-17.00, Sun 10.00-17.00. Please contact farm office for details of Christmas and New Year opening times

A£5.50 C&OAPs£4.50. Group rates available for 20+ people

Discount Offer: One Child Free With Every Full Paying Adult.

Special Events

Sweet & Lollipop Scrambles with Giant Farmer Woods
09/04/2004-27/10/2004
Held on 9 & 11 Apr, 1 June, 22 July, 6 Aug and 27 Oct

Down on the Farm
07/04/2004-13/08/2004
Held on 7 Apr & 13 Aug only. Join in with all the fun with our Old McDonalds themed day

Woodside Easter Treasure Hunts
10/04/2004-12/04/2004
Held on 10 & 12 Apr only. Discover the hidden words and claim your prize plus join our Easter bunny as he searches for eggs

Reptile Celebrities
14/04/2004-26/10/2004
Held on 14 Apr, 27 July, 24 Aug, 26 Oct only. Hands on with snakes, lizards and many other reptiles

Birds of Prey Display with Hawk on the Wild Side
16/04/2004-10/08/2004
Held on 16 Apr & 10 Aug only

Great Gappo
03/05/2004
Magical entertainment and balloons for all the children

Gee jay the Clown
31/05/2004
Fun and entertainment for children of all ages

Tricky Micky
02/06/2004
A day of entertainment for the children

Woodside Treasure Hunt
03/06/2004-28/10/2004
Held on 3 June, 1 Sept & 28 Oct only. Discover the hidden words and claim your prize!

Paint an Animal
04/06/2004-29/10/2004
Held on 4 June & 29 Oct only. Join in the fun and games and paint an animal of your choice. Places for this event are limited

Teddy Bears Picnic
30/07/2004
Half price entry for all children accompanied by their teddy bear. Fun, games and competitions for the best dressed teddy bear. Make sure your teddy knows about it

Smartie Artie
03/08/2004
Fun, games and balloons for all the children

Dallas
17/08/2004
Fun and magical entertainment for all the children

Twilight Walkabout
21/08/2004
Come and watch the animals as they are out to bed. Meet some of our furry friends, also includes evening tractor rides, BBQ and other fun activities

Seaside Special
27/08/2004
Who needs to travel to the coast when you can have all the fun of the seaside at Woodside Farm. Play in the sand, paddle in the pool, watch Punch & Judy, eat candy floss and join in the fun!

Alan Martell with Rufus the Dog
30/08/2004
A wonderful day of entertainment for the children

Pumpkin Hunt
02/10/2004-24/10/2004
Held on 2-3, 9-10, 16-17, 23-24 Oct only. Find the hidden pumpkins around the park. Complete the hunt and win a prize

Halloween Fright Night
30/10/2004
Join in the fun and games if you dare, but watch out for things that go bump in the night!

Special Christmas Activities
04/12/2004-24/12/2004
Visit Father Christmas and join in with the sweet scrambles and Christmas treasure hunts every weekend. Activities also run from 20-24 Dec inclusive

Arts, Crafts & Textiles

Cecil Higgins Art Gallery

Castle Close Castle Lane Bedford Bedfordshire MK40 3RP

Tel: 01234 211222 Fax: 01234 327149

[J13 M1 centre of Bedford just off the River Embankment - signposted. There are public car parks adjacent and the Town Centre is at a walking distance]

Cecil Higgins Art Gallery is situated in an attractive setting beside the beautiful Castle Gardens. Recreated Victorian house including many items from the Handley-Read collection and a fascinating William Burges bedroom. A modern gallery displays an internationally renowned collection of watercolours, prints and drawings, ceramics, glass and lace. There is a charge for guided tours and viewing of reserve collections. Disabled access. Visitors wishing to see particular works are advised to telephone beforehand.

All year Tue-Sat 11.00-17.00, Sun & Bank Hol Mon 14.00-17.00. Closed Good Fri, 25-26 Dec and 1 Jan

A£2.30 C&Concessions£Free, includes a visit to Bedford Museum. Free on Fri and after 16.00 on Tue-Thur

Birds, Butterflies & Bees

Bedford Butterfly Park

Renhold Road Wilden Bedford Bedfordshire
MK44 2PX

Tel: 01234 772770 Fax: 01234 772773

www.bedford-butterflies.co.uk

*[J13 off M1, follow A421 for Bedford, take
bypass towards Cambridge follow signs for
Wilden. Plenty of on site parking]*

For a really enjoyable outing in any weather,
come and visit us at Bedford Butterfly Park.
We're sure you'll have a great time. We have
wild flower meadows outside, and tropical butterflies in our hot house. There are animals, a
playground, a tea room for your lunch and a gift
shop for souvenirs. You'll also find a nature trail,
a room full of creepy crawlies and on weekends
and school holidays there is extra fun for the
kids in our activity barn.

*13 Feb-31 Oct daily 10.00-17.00, 1 Nov-20 Dec
Thur-Fri 10.00-16.00*

A£4.50 C(under3)£Free C£2.75 Family Ticket
(A2+C2) £13.00

**Discount Offer: 25% Discount On
Admission Charges**

Country Parks & Estates

Dunstable Downs

Dunstable Downs Countryside Centre
Whipsnade Road Kensworth Dunstable
Bedfordshire LU6 2TA
Tel: 01582 608489 Fax: 01582 671826
*[J11 M1 Luton, take A505 to Dunstable Town
Centre follow signs for Whipsnade Zoo. Turn L
into Whipsnade Road]*

Commanding outstanding views over the Vale of
Aylesbury and surrounding countryside, 206ha
(510 acres) of grassland and farmland SW of
Dunstable. This local beauty spot offers an
opportunity for many forms of recreation, including walking and kite-flying.
*Downs: All year daily. Countryside Centre & Shop:
1 Apr-31 Oct Tue-Sat 10.00-17.00, Sun 10.00-
18.00, 1 Nov-31 Mar Sat & Sun 10.00-16.00.
Kiosk: All year daily 10.00-dusk. Closed 25 Dec*
Admission Free

Festivals & Shows

Bedford by the Sea

Harpur Square Bedford Bedfordshire
Tel: 01234 343992 Fax: 01234 343992
Bringing the beach to Bedford's Harpur Square!
Giant sand pits, sand castle competitions, inflat-
able volleyball, sand sculpture, fairground rides,
Punch and Judy, fish and chips and many other
seaside attractions for all the family.

July 22-24 2004

Prices vary, please call for details

Bedfordshire Steam and Country Fayre

Old Warden Park nr Biggleswade Bedfordshire
SG18 9EP
Tel: 01462 851711 Fax: 01462 851711
*[2m W on A1 Biggleswade. Free car parking on
site]*

Admission includes entrance to The
Shuttleworth Collection. See steam, tractor and
heavy horse working demonstrations, steam

ploughing, miniature steam, fairground organs, aerobatic display, working crafts, trade and market stalls, motor show, clay pigeon shooting, archery, off-road driving, working dog demonstrations, vintage vehicles, old time fairground and Morris dancing. Plus licensed bar and refreshments.

September 18-19 2004

Prices vary, please call for details

Kensworth Vintage and Classic Car Rally

Dove House Lane Kensworth Dunstable
Tel: 01582 873460 office hours
[0.5m from Whipsnade Zoo or A5, will be signed on day. Free parking available]

A classic vehicle show that attracts hundreds of vehicles, events for the whole family. This is the 9th year and there are 13 classes with awards for 1st and 2nd in each, also autojumble and craft stalls.

September 5 2004 10.00-17.00

A£2.50 C£1.00 OAPs£2.50 Family Ticket £6.50

Luton International Carnival 2004

Luton Bedfordshire LU1 2BQ
[Held in Luton town centre and Wardown Park (New Bedford Road)]

A large street and park based carnival with a spectacular parade.

May 31 2004

Admission Free

Folk & Local History Museums

Bedford Museum

Castle Lane Bedford Bedfordshire MK40 3XD

Tel: 01234 353323 Fax: 01234 273401

www.bedfordmuseum.org

[Bedford Museum is conveniently located close to two town centre car parks and a short walk from Allhallows Bus Station and the Midland Road Railway Station. Limited on site parking]

Embark on a fascinating journey through the human and natural history of North Bedfordshire, pausing briefly to glimpse at wonders from more distant lands. Go back in time to visit the delightful rural room sets and the Old School Museum, where Blackbeard's sword, 'Old Billy' the record breaking longest-lived horse and numerous other treasures and curiosities can be found. Housed in the former Higgins and Sons Brewery, Bedford Museum is situated within the picturesque gardens of Bedford Castle, beside the Great Ouse embankment. The charming courtyard and well laid out galleries provide an excellent setting for the rich and varied nature of the collections. Family activities on selected days. There is a charge for guided tours which must be booked in advance. Facilities for people with disabilities. Museum shop, coffee shop and rooms available for hire.

All year Tue-Sat 11.00-17.00, Sun & Bank Hol Mon 14.00-17.00. Closed Mon, Good Fri, Christmas and New Year

A£2.20 (FREE on Fridays) C(0-17)&Concessions£Free Annual ticket A£8.80

Discount Offer: Two For The Price Of One.

Special Events

Museums and Galleries Month
01/05/2004-31/05/2004
An annual celebration of the UK's museums and galleries

Beekeeping Day
09/05/2004
Discover the fascinating and wonderful world of the honey bee with Bedfordshire Beekeepers Association

Nature Photography Workshop
23/05/2004
An opportunity to learn some of the techniques of wildlife photography with Richard Revels FRPS. Booking essential. Cost: A£35.00

National Archaeology Day
17/07/2004
A fun day of events for families exploring Bedford's past

Art and Craft Exhibition
04/09/2004-03/10/2004
A celebration of English craft skills by Liz Silk, Linda Boy, Jonathon Knight and Felicity Irons displaying their artwork, stained glass, furniture and rushwork

Rangoli Competition and Demonstration
06/11/2004
The museum again hosts the annual Rangoli competition and workshops to celebrate Diwali, in conjunction with the Gujarati Mitra Mandal

Festival Family Day
04/12/2004
Charity event with children's activities and featuring Christmas creches and seasonal traditions from the community

John Dony Field Centre

Hancock Drive Bushmead Luton Bedfordshire LU2 7SF
Tel: 01582 486983 Fax: 01582 422805
[On Bushmead Estate 1.5m N of Luton town centre off A6 to Bedford]

A wealth of wildlife and countryside in and around Luton. A focus for exploring rich landscapes and fascinating plants and animals of the Luton area. Follow 4,000 years of history from Bronze Age burials to the building of the Bushmead estate. Superb photographic displays and large-scale-model of the area. Children's playground nearby.

All year Mon-Fri 09.30-16.45

Admission Free

Gardens & Horticulture

Swiss Garden

Biggleswade Road Old Warden Biggleswade Bedfordshire SG18 9EP

Tel: 01767 626236/627666
[2m W of the A1 signposted from A600]

A charming early 19th century landscaped garden, with plants from all over the world, ponds, bridges, rose arbours, miniature buildings, a grotto and fernery, and a tiny, thatched Swiss Cottage. The adjoining woodland and lakeside picnic area are open all year, and there are good facilities for disabled people. Souvenirs are on sale at the entrance kiosk. Dogs allowed only in the woodland area. The garden may be hired for special events.

All year, Apr-Oct 10.00-17.00, Nov-Mar 10.00-16.00. Closed for Christmas and New Year break, please call for details. Ticket sales and entrance to the garden are from Shuttleworth Collection shop

A£3.00 C&Concessions£2.00 Family Ticket £8.00

Historical

Willington Dovecote and Stables

Willington nr Bedford Bedfordshire MK44 3QG

Tel: 01234 838278

[4m E of Bedford, just N of the Sandy road A603]

A distinctive 16th century stable and stone dovecote, lined internally with nesting boxes for 1,500 pigeons. They are the remains of a historic manorial complex.

1 Apr-30 Sept by appointment only, please call Mrs Endersby on 01234 838278 or write to 21 Chapel Lane, Willington MK44 3QG

£1.00

Military & Defence Museums

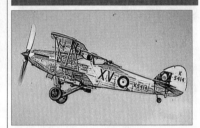

Shuttleworth Collection

Old Warden Aerodrome Biggleswade Bedfordshire SG18 9EP

Tel: 01767 627288 Fax: 01767 627053

www.shuttleworth.org

[2m W on A1 Biggleswade. Plenty of parking on site]

A traditional grass aerodrome, with a world famous collection of aircraft from a 1909 Bleriot to a 1942 Spitfire, plus veteran and vintage motor vehicles and a coachroom of 19th century horse-drawn vehicles all displayed indoors. The aircraft and the vehicles are kept in working order. Please allow a minimum of 2 hrs for your visit.

1 Apr-31 Oct daily 10.00-17.00, Nov & Dec daily 10.00-16.00, Jan & Feb Wed-Sun 10.00-16.00, Mar daily 10.00-16.00. Closed 22 Dec-2 Jan

A£7.50 Accompanied C(0-16)£Free OAP£6.00 Groups of 20+ people: £5.00 School Parties£2.00. Prices on flying days: £15.00 per person

Special Events

The Shuttleworth Indoor Photography Day
24/04/2004

Shuttleworth Air Displays
02/05/2004-05/09/2004
Held on 2 May (Spring Display), 15 May (Evening and Aeromodelling), 6 June (D-Day Anniversary Military Pageant), 19 June (Evening), 27 June (Royal Aeronautical Society and Rolls Royce Garden Party), 4 July (1930s Summer Display), 17 July (Evening), 1 Aug (Military Pageant), 21 Aug (Evening), 5 Sept (Shuttleworth Pageant)

Aero Model Days
16/05/2004-12/09/2004
Held on 16 May, 24-25 July, 7-8 Aug (Sam 35 Aero Modelling), 11 Sept (Aeromodelling and Twilight Sunset Air Display), 12 Sept

Moth Club Charity Flying Weekend
12/06/2004-13/06/2004

Schools Day
16/06/2004

'Kings of Queen - Meatloaf and Cher' Tribute Concert
13/08/2004

The Shuttleworth Collection 'Flying Proms' Concert
14/08/2004

Gala Dinner and Hangar Dance
25/09/2004

Railways

Leighton Buzzard Railway

Page's Park Station Billington Road Leighton Buzzard Bedfordshire LU7 4TN
Tel: 01525 373888 (24hours)
Fax: 01525 377814
www.buzzrail.co.uk

[On A4146 Hemel Hempstead road, near J with A505 Dunstable / Aylesbury road. Plenty of on site parking available. Rail: Leighton Buzzard station 2m. Bus: Arriva service 31 (Luton Airport) links Leighton Buzzard Station, canal and town centre with Stanbridge Road, which is a short walk from Page's Park station along Billington Road]

The Leighton Buzzard Railway lets you experience public transport as it was in the early part of the 20th century, and discover the line's unique history, dating back over 85 years. The 70-minute return journey takes you through the edge of the town and out into the countryside, and features level crossings, sharp curves and steep gradients. Most trains are hauled by an historic steam engine from one of Britain's largest collection of narrow-gauge locomotives.

Sundays 14 Mar-31 Oct, Mondays 12 Apr, 3 & 31 May, 30 Aug, Tuesdays 3-31 Aug, Wednesdays 14 Apr, 2 June-1 Sept, 27 Oct, Thursdays 3 June, 5 Aug-2 Sept, Fridays 9 Apr, Saturdays 10 Apr, 1 & 29 May, 5 June, 7 Aug-11 Sept, 2 Oct. Christmas trains will run in Dec

A£5.50 C(0-2)£Free C£(2-15)£2.50 OAPs£5.00 Day Rover £10.50

Discount Offer: One Child Travels Free With Fare Paying Adult.

Summerfields Miniature Railways

Summerfields Fruit Farm Haynes Bedford Bedfordshire MK45 3BH

Miniature Railways operated by members of Bedford Model Engineering Society. Ground level 0.75 mile, largely steam hauled Elevated 700ft.

Running Days: 11-12 Apr, 3, 30-31 May, 3, 27 June, 4, 18 July, 15, 19, 30 Aug, 5, 19 Sept, 3, 17, 28 Oct. Please call for further details

Ground Level £1.00 or 6 for £5.00, Elevated £0.40

Stately Homes

Woburn Abbey

Woburn Bedfordshire MK17 9WA

Tel: 01525 290666 Fax: 01525 290271

www.woburnabbey.co.uk

[8.5m NW of Dunstable on A4012 J12 or 13 off M1. Rail: Leighton Buzzard Bletchley & Flitwick. Plenty of on site parking]

Set in a beautiful 3,000 acre deer park, Woburn Abbey has been the home of the Dukes of Bedford for nearly 400 years, and is now occupied by the present Duke and his family. The Abbey houses one of the most important private art collections in the world, including paintings by Gainsborough, Reynolds, Van Dyck, Cuyp, and Canaletto, 21 of whose views of Venice hang in the Venetian Room. The tour of the Abbey covers three floors, including the vaults, with 18th Century French and English furniture, silver and a wide range of porcelain on display. Amongst the highlights is the Sèvres dinner service presented to the 4th Duke by Louis XV of France. The Deer Park is home to ten species of deer. Woburn Abbey is also noted for its excellent and unique 40 shop Antiques Centre (including 33 showcases) which has also established an enviable reputation for its in-house catering. We specialise in banqueting, conferences, receptions and company days; the Sculpture Gallery overlooking the Private Gardens provides a splendid setting for Weddings and Wedding Receptions (We hold a Civil Wedding Licence).

1 Jan-12 Mar, House Sat & Sun 11.00-16.00, Park daily 10.00-16.00; 13 Mar-31 Oct daily, House 11.00-16.00 (17.00 Sun & Bank Hols), Park 10.00-17.00. Please call to confirm opening times during Nov & Dec. Antiques Centre: open all year, closed 24-26 Dec

A£9.00 C(5-15)£4.50 OAPs£8.00 Disabled£5.50. Group rates: A£7.50 C£3.50 OAPs£6.50, Abbey only. Cars & motorcycles £2.00, pedestrians & cyclists £1.00, visitors from Safari Park free on production of voucher

Transport Museums

Stondon Transport Museum

Station Road Lower Stondon Henlow Bedfordshire SG16 6JN

Tel: 01462 850339 Fax: 01462 850824

[Just off Hitchin - Bedford Road]

Take a trip down memory lane seeing vehicles from a bygone era. There is always plenty to look at. Over 400 exhibits of cars, motorcycles and other transport, spanning the last 100 years. There is also a full size replica of Captain Cook's ship HMS Endeavour, with conducted daily tours.

All year daily 10.00-17.00. Closed Christmas week, open 1 Jan

A£6.00 C£3.00 OAPs£5.00 Family Ticket (A2+C2) £16.00

Wildlife & Safari Parks

Whipsnade Wild Animal Park

Whipsnade Dunstable Bedfordshire LU6 2LF
Tel: 01582 872171 Fax: 01582 872649
[Just off J9 / 12 M1 and only 20mins from J21 M25]

Set in 600 acres of beautiful parkland, Whipsnade is home to over 2,500 of the world's most incredible creatures. It is one of the largest wildlife conservation centres in Europe.

All year daily from 10.00. Closed 25 Dec

A£13.50 C(3-15)£10.10 OAPs/Students£11.50 Family Ticket (A2+C2 or A1+C3) £42.50

Woburn Safari Park

Woburn Park Woburn Bedfordshire MK17 9QN
Tel: 01525 290407 (10 lines)
Fax: 01525 290489
www.woburnsafari.co.uk

[J13 M1, or leave the A5 at Hockliffe for the A4012. Woburn Safari Park is well signed from these locations. Plenty of parking on site]

Award winning Woburn Safari Park is set in 350 of the 3,000 acres of parkland surrounding Woburn Abbey. The thrill of the Safari Drive, where many animals including tigers and monkeys are just a windscreen's width away, is followed with a full day's fun and animal encounters in the Wild World Leisure Area. At Sea Lion Cove you can see eye to eye with a playful sea lion through the underwater viewing or meet wallabies, squirrel monkey and many other animals. Catch the train, try out the adventure playgrounds or a boat on the lake - it's all included in the entry price. There's a busy programme of animals in action and keeper talks too.

All year 13 Mar-31 Oct daily 10.00-17.00, 6 Nov-12 Mar weekends & Feb half-term only 11.00-15.00

Prices vary according to time of visit. Early Season (13 Mar-28 May, 7 June-21 July): A£13.50 C£10.00 OAPs£10.50. Main Season (29 May-6 June, 2 Sept-31 Oct): A£14.00 C£10.50 OAPs£11.00. High Season (22 July-1 Sept): A£15.50 C£12.00 OAPs£13.00 Family discounts available. Winter Opening (6 Nov-12 Mar): A£8.00 C£7.00 OAPs£7.00

Berkshire

Animal Attractions

Lambourn Trainers Association

Windsor House Crowle Road Lambourn
Hungerford Berkshire RG17 8NR

Tel: 01488 71347 Fax: 01488 72664
www.bloodstocknetwork.com/lta

[M4 J14. Rail: Newbury]

Lambourn Trainers Association will escort visitors around their stables, giving a fascinating insight into the racing world not seen by the public before. Lambourn - Valley of the Racehorse, is highly respected for its enviable record for success, including the winners of the Cheltenham Gold Cup in 2000 and this year of Chieveley Park Stakes and Judd Monte International Stakes York.

All year Mon-Sat 10.00-12.00 by appointment. Closed Bank Hols & Sun

Tours £5.00 + VAT C£Free

Arts, Crafts & Textiles

Stanley Spencer Gallery

High Street Cookham-On-Thames Berkshire
SL6 9SJ
Tel: 01628 471885 Fax: 01628 520537

www.stanleyspencer.org.uk

[Maidenhead 3m, London 28m, Windsor 9m. M4 J7, A4 to Maidenhead bridge, A4094 to Cookham village, there is a car park nearby]

The Stanley Spencer Gallery is unique as the only gallery in Britain devoted exclusively to an artist in the village where he was born and spent most of his life. Set in the heart of the village he immortalised, the gallery occupies the former Victorian Methodist Chapel where Spencer was taken as a child to worship. Not far from Fernley, the house where Spencer was born and lived in Cookham High Street, the gallery was opened in 1962 as a memorial through the effort of the people of Cookham and support from far beyond. The exhibits change during the year and the gallery contains a permanent collection of his work including The Last Supper 1920, Christ Preaching at Cookham Regatta 1959, etc, together with letters, documents, memorabilia, and the pram in which Spencer wheeled his equipment when painting landscapes. It also displays important works on long-term loan, and mounts a winter and summer exhibition each year. Over a thousand works have been shown since the gallery opened.

All year, Easter-Oct daily 10.30-17.30, Nov-Easter Sat Sun & Bank Hol 11.00-16.30, limited opening over Christmas, please call info line. Closed 25 Dec

A£1.00 C£Free Concessions£0.50

Discount Offer: Two For The Price Of One

<u>Special Events</u>

Summer Exhibition - Spencer's Flowers and Gardens Paintings
01/04/2004-31/10/2004

Country Parks & Estates

Wellington Country Park

Odiham Road Riseley Reading Berkshire
RG7 1SP

Tel: 0118 932 6444 Fax: 0118 932 6445

www.wellington-country-park.co.uk

[Signposted off A33. Ample parking on site]

Wellington Country Park, Riseley, near Reading, has 350 acres of wonderful parkland within the Duke of Wellington's estate, providing an ideal venue for a family outing. Explore the nature trails round the lakes. Older children can hire a row boat in season, fish the well-stocked lakes and hit the adventure playground. Younger children will enjoy the lovely sandpit, animal farm and miniature railway. Finish off with a family tournament on the crazy golf course! Acres of space for your own picnics and barbecues, with areas provided. Camping and caravanning site in the park. An ideal touring site for Winchester, Salisbury, Legoland, Windsor and Oxford. Dogs welcomed. Special events throughout the year. Please call for further information.

15 Mar-Nov daily 10.00-17.30 and winter weekends

A£4.80 C£2.50 C(0-5)£Free OAPs£3.80. Group rates available

Discount Offer: Two For The Price Of One

Special Events

Easter Bonanza
11/04/2004-12/04/2004
Bring your decorated eggs and take part in our egg rolling competition. Traditional family fun with demonstrations from 'gamegoer' working dogs and falconry displays, ferret and dog racing. Our favourite clown 'Balloonatic' will be here to entertain. Adding to the fun will be a traditional Punch and Judy show

Ahoy There! Annual Boat Jumble
18/04/2004
Come and buy anything from a boat to a bilge pump in the Rally Field. Separate entrance fee of £3.00 applies. Please call Compass Events on 01803 835915 for further information. There will also be a display of classic motor boats on the large lake

Animal Fun Day
03/05/2004
A great day out for humans and animals alike! Bring your dog along and enter him into the fun dog show or place a bet on the ferret racing. Meet the 'Dulux' dog, wear a snake around your neck with Reptiles R Us, learn and be entertained by The Sheep Show, a fascinating live sheep shearing demonstration, meet 'Nobby', 'Susie' and their woolly friends. Why not bring a picnic or use one of our barbecue areas

May Fair
30/05/2004
A real country day out at the Park! Come and buy traditional country fayre from the many craft, food and plant stalls. A visiting sheep and arable farmer will be here to show you a display with sheep, geese and up to five dogs. You will see the commitment of a working sheepdog doing its daily work or watch the spectacular heavy horse demonstrations. Bodging and fly fishing displays will also be at the Park

Half Term Week
31/05/2004-04/06/2004
Daily creative activities. A fun puppet theatre for children will be attending the Park on Wed-Fri with two shows per day. Facepainting will take place on Mon, Wed & Fri

Marvellous Music in the Park
25/06/2004-27/06/2004
Three fab evenings of music and fun in the spectacular 80 acre Waterloo Meadow. Fri - Counterfeit Stones, Sat - Sailor & Bjorn Again, Sun - classical evening. Bring a picnic and blanket and enjoy a beautiful summer evening listening to music at the Park. Presented by Marvellous Festivals. Call to book

Independence Fun Day
04/07/2004
Line dancing, barn dancing, drum majorettes and rag a jazz trio to get you into the American spirit. See if you can stay seated on the rodeo bull. A truly star spangled day!

Puppy Dog Picnic
11/07/2004
Enjoy doggy demonstrations with the Guide Dog for the Blind puppy walkers. Bring your own puppy dog and enter it into one of the fun show classes. Free dog care and advice. Also dog chipping is offered at a special reduced rate. Fun activities available for children

Fun Activities Day
08/08/2004
Calling all heroes and superstars, come along to the Park and have a go at laser clay shooting, archery, a game of gladiator jousting, test your strength with a bungee run and many more fun activities

Kids Fun Day
30/08/2004
Come along kids and have a blast! Join in this fun day before you have to return to school. A mass of giant inflatables will be here for you to play on to your heart's content. With face painting and much more, what a way to end your summer hols!

Newfoundland Weekend
04/09/2004-05/09/2004
Members of the Newfoundland Club from across the country bring their superb dogs to participate in games, knock-out competitions, carting and a swimming gala. All other breeds of dog are welcome to this lovely event

South East Caravan Show
18/09/2004-26/09/2004
Hosted by local dealer Berkshire Caravans and held in our Rally Field. Special admission fee to the Park for Show visitors. Please telephone 0118 988 8111 for details

Really Wild Week
25/10/2004-29/10/2004
Hold a slithery snake or stroke a lizard. Puppet theatre with Mr Chris and his Scary Haunted Castle Show on Mon, Wed & Fri. Pumpkin carving, painting and seasonal craft activities run daily from 13.00-16.00

Firework Fiesta
06/11/2004
Our fantastic annual firework display, organised by the Lodden Lions Club and hosted in the Park. Barbecues, hot food and sparklers will be on offer. Please call for advance tickets

Festivals & Shows

Bracknell Festival

South Hill Park Ringmead Bracknell Berkshire RG12 7PA
Tel: 01344 484858 Fax: 01344 411427
[J3 M3; J10 M4, follow signs showing comedy mask or for the Arts Centre]

A three day feast of music on three stages, featuring local, national and international acts covering jazz, folk, blues, world music plus children's entertainment, street theatre, workshops. *July 2-4 2004*

Newbury Spring Festival

Newbury Berkshire
Tel: 01635 32421 Fax: 01635 528690
[J13 M4 to Winchester. Rail: Newbury]

Within the West Berkshire region the Newbury International Spring Festival has become a unique and eagerly awaited annual highlight of the arts and social calendar. The Festival has gained a reputation for artistic excellence and is now placed at the forefront of European festivals. Two packed weeks during May provide the finest artistic entertainment from music to the visual arts, hosted at a variety of beautiful venues in Newbury and the surrounding area. The diversity of events on offer draws a large audience from all over the country with many performances selling out well in advance. For further information please contact 01635 32421. Some venues have limited wheelchair access, please telephone first.
May 8-22 2004, various performances.
Prices vary, please call for details. Tickets from The Box Office 01635 522733

Reading Festival 2004

Littlejohn Farm Richfield Avenue Reading Berkshire RG3 1LQ

Tel: 020 8961 5490 Fax: 020 8961 5743
[Traffic arriving from E take J10 M4, from the W take J12 M4, follow festival signs]

The varied and vibrant bill just gets bigger and better at the Reading and Leeds Festival double header over the August Bank Holiday weekend.
August 27-29 2004 (subject to licence)
Prices to be confirmed. Please note, tickets are subject to booking fee. Available from Ticketmaster outlets, selected HMV stores and usual agents

Royal Windsor Horse Show 2004

RWHS Office The Royal Mews Windsor Castle Windsor Berkshire SL4 1NG
Tel: 01753 860280 venue Fax: 01753 830564
[J5 M4, B470 to Windsor RAC signposted]

The UK's largest outdoor equestrian event- a great show of equestrian and country life for all the family. Brings together top International Show Jumping, Carriage Driving, Dressage and Showing. The Country Life displays and demonstrations combined with the shopping village and the Victorian funfair are just some of the attractions which make it a perfect family day out. Set against the backdrop of Windsor Castle this is the ultimate sporting and country experience for all the family.

May 12-16 2004
Prices to be confirmed, for information please call 020 7370 8202

Wokingham May Fayre

Wokingham Town Centre Wokingham Berkshire RG40 1AS
Tel: 01344 423147 Fax: 01344 423147
[J10 M4, A329 Wokingham to town centre]
The May Fayre is an annual event on the May Bank Holiday Monday organised by Wokingham Lions Club. A street market with 150 stalls, music and entertainment from an open-air stage. Entry and parking are free. A Country Fair on Elms Field has farm animals and small mammals. A children's fun fair operates and refreshments are available, a working Craft Fair, exhibition and flower display can be found in the Town Hall. Thousands of families enjoy the day as a low-cost event, raising funds for local charities.
May 3 2004, 10.00-17.00
Admission Free. Free programme and parking

WOMAD

Rivermead Leisure Complex Richfield Avenue Reading Berkshire RG1 8EQ
Tel: 0118 939 0930 Fax: 0118 939 0751
[M40, B4009, B481. BR: Reading]

WOMAD returns to Rivermead in Reading in July 2004 for three days of inspirational music, arts and dance from around the world.
July 23-25 2004
Ticket prices to be confirmed

Gardens & Horticulture

Savill Garden - Windsor Great Park

Wick Lane Englefield Green Nr. Windsor Surrey TW20 0UU
Tel: 01753 847518 Fax: 01753 847536
[Approach from A30 via Wick Road / Wick Lane, Englefield Green. Rail: Egham]

This world renowned 35 acre woodland garden within Windsor Great Park was created in 1932 by Sir Eric Savill. His expert knowledge of horticulture, ability and imagination enabled him to plant and design spectacular spring displays, formal rose gardens and herbaceous borders for Summer, fiery colours for Autumn and misty vistas for winter

Mar-Oct daily 10.00-18.00. Nov-Feb daily 10.00-16.00. Closed 25-26 Dec
A£5.50/£4.50/£3.50 C(6-16)£2.50/£1.50/£1.25

Roman Era

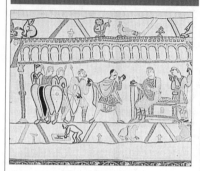

Museum of Reading

The Town Hall Blagrave Street Reading
Berkshire RG1 1QH

Tel: 0118 939 9800 Fax: 0118 939 9881

www.readingmuseum.org

*[Located in the Town Hall in Reading Town
Centre. A couple of minutes walk from Rail:
Reading Station. The entrance is on Blagrave
Street near to the rear of Marks & Spencer]*

Handle real museum objects in the Box Room
when you visit the fully refurbished Museum of
Reading! See Britain's Bayeux Tapestry and visit
the Roman Silchester Gallery. Seven exciting
new galleries including a stunning Victorian Art
Gallery housing Reading's nationally significant
art collection, the world's first biscuit manufacturers Huntley and Palmers, the Green Space
environment gallery and much more. Children's
holiday activities and special events - please call
for details.

*All year Tue-Sat 10.00-16.00, Sun and Bank Hol
11.00-16.00*

Admission Free

Science - Earth & Planetary

The Look Out Discovery Centre

Nine Mile Ride Bracknell Berkshire RG12 7QW

Tel: 01344 354400 Fax: 01344 354422
www.bracknell-forest.gov.uk/lookout

*[J10 M4, J3 M3 off the A322 on B3430. Rail:
Bracknell. Ample parking on site]*

The Look Out Discovery Centre in Bracknell is a
great day out for all ages. The main attraction is
an exciting hands on, interactive science and
nature exhibition that offers over 70 bright and
fun filled exhibits within five themed zones; Light
and Colour, Sound and Communication, Forces
and Movement, Woodland and Wildlife and
Body and Perception. Come and launch the hot
air balloon, freeze your shadow on the wall or
climb through a giant mole hole. In the surrounding 2,600 acres of Crown Estate woodland, visitors can enjoy nature walks, cycle trails,
a picnic area and a child's play area. With child
and adult mountain bike hire (or bring your
own), Coffee Shop, Gift Shop and Tourist
Information Centre, this offers an action packed
day for the whole family at very reasonable
prices.

All year daily 10.00-17.00. Closed Christmas

A£4.80 C£3.20 Concessions£3.20 Family
Ticket £12.80

Discount Offer: One Child Free With A Full Paying Adult

Spectator Sports

Ascot Racecourse

High Street Ascot Berkshire SL5 7JX

Tel: 01344 876876 Fax: 01344 626299

[Close to M3, M4, M40 and M25]

Ascot is the world's most famous racecourse, renowned internationally as the home of thrilling horseracing, fantastic free attractions and superb family entertainment. Set amid the beautiful surroundings of Windsor Great Park, there's 27 days of the finest Flat and National Hunt racing to enjoy throughout the year.
Call for details of meetings
A£7.00-£54.00

Newbury Racecourse

Newbury Berkshire RG14 7NZ

Tel: 01635 40015 Fax: 01635 528354

[J13 M4. Rail: Newbury racecourse station]

Enjoy midweek and weekend racing at Newbury Racecourse all year round. Flat racing from April to October, National Hunt racing from November to March.

Please call for fixture list

Members: A£16.00-£40.00. Grandstand: A£10.00-£20.00. Picnic Enclosure: A£5.00 C(accompanied 17 and under)£Free

Sport & Recreation

Coral Reef Water World

Nine Mile Ride Bracknell Berkshire RG12 7JQ

Tel: 01344 862525 Fax: 01344 869146

www.bracknell-forest.gov.uk/coralreef

[From J3 M3, follow the A322 to Bracknell for 3.7m, from J10 M4 follow the A329 to Bracknell, then follow A322 to Bagshot for 4.1m. Plenty of on site parking]

Fun at Coral Reef - so let the water excitement start here. Coral Reef Bracknell's Water World is a tropical paradise providing fun for all the family. There are three giant water slides and other water features including the wild water rapids, erupting volcano, firing cannons, squirting snakes and bubbling spas. After all this fun why not visit our air-conditioned restaurant on the first floor with views over the pool. Sauna World is available to over 18s only so you can relax in the tranquil surroundings of a Saunarium (a mix of dry and wet heat), two saunas and our two tier steam room. There is a cool pool and footspa to invigorate the whole body. Light refreshments are also available in Sauna World. Coral Reef is open all year round, please contact reception on 01344 862525. Please note that at all times there is a maximum of two children under 8 years to one adult (over 18).

All year Mon 10.30-21.00, Tue-Fri 10.30-21.45, Weekends 09.00-17.45. Please note Wed & Fri 19.00-21.45 over 21's only. Early Bird sessions

Mon-Fri 06.30-9.30 exluding Bank Hol. Term Time Only: Mon-Fri 10.30-15.30 is special Parent & Toddler Sessions

Off peak sessions Mon-Fri 10.30-15.30 (term time): A&C£3.20 C(0-4)£Free, Peak times Mon-Fri 15.30-21.00/21.45 & Weekends 09.00-17.45: A£5.70 C£4.00 C(0-4)£Free. Disabled, over 50's and party rates available. Please telephone venue for price change after Apr 2004

Theme & Adventure Parks

Go Ape! High Wire Forest Adventure

The Look Out Discovery Centre Nine Mile Ride Bracknell Berkshire RG12 7QW

Tel: 0870 420 7876

www.goape.cc

[M3 J3 or M4 J10]

Rural Tourist Attraction of the Year 2003 - NFU Countryside Awards. Designed to appeal to all ages Go Ape! is an extreme, high wire aerial adventure course of some 35 zip slides, scramble nets and hanging rope bridges - at heights

of almost 30ft off the forest floor. Not for the faint hearted, Go Ape! is a thrilling test of agility, courage and determination. Minimum age 10 years, minimum height 1m40cm / 4ft7inch. Under 18s must be accompanied by a participating adult.

Opens Easter 2004. Apr-Oct daily, Nov-Mar weekends only, also open by prior arrangement. Please call information line or check the website for details

A(18+)£16.00 C(10-17)£11.00

LEGOLAND Windsor

Winkfield Road Windsor Berkshire SL4 4AY

Tel: 08705 040404 Fax: 01753 626300

www.legoland.co.uk

[On B3022 Windsor - Ascot road, well signposted from M4 & M3]

Ask yourself what children want from a day out. Then come and see the answer in action at LEGOLAND® Windsor. Here you'll find excitement, stimulation and fun in an environment where children are firmly in control and loving every minute of it. Come and ride our brand new Jungle Coaster in the Park's latest activity area, Adventure Land. The new coaster will be the fastest, coolest ride in the Park with 400 metres of track, a highest point of 16 metres and a top speed of 60km! Guests can climb

inside life-size LEGO vehicles and act as 'test drivers' as they race along a wild roller coaster track. It's a thrilling, turbo-force experience with hair-raising turns and lots of sharp bends! You can also drive a car, pan for gold, brave the Pirate Falls or explore Miniland made from millions of LEGO® bricks. With over 50 rides, shows and attractions, all set in 150 acres of beautiful parkland, LEGOLAND offers a full and exciting day out for children aged 2 to 12 and their families. It is more fun than you can imagine. For further information or to book, call 08705 040404.

20 Mar-31 Oct daily, (closed Tue & Wed Sept-Oct). Opening times vary, please call 08705 040404 for more information

Peak: A£23.00 C(0-2)£Free C(3-15)£21.00 OAPs£21.00. Off Peak: A£21.00 C(0-2)£Free C(3-15)£19.00 OAPs£19.00. For further information on ticket prices and bookings please call 08705 040404

Discount Offer: Save Up To £25.00. This voucher entitles a maximum of 5 people, £5.00 off full admission price to LEGOLAND Windsor.

Wildlife & Safari Parks

Beale Park

Lower Basildon Reading Berkshire RG8 9NH

Tel: 0118 984 5172 Fax: 0118 984 5171

www.bealepark.co.uk

[Signposted from J12 M4, follow brown tourist signs. Plenty of on site parking]

This glorious Thameside Wildlife and Leisure Park has something for everyone. Unique collection of rare and endangered birds, Pets Corner, Deer Park, paddling pools, huge adventure playground, gardens, trails, education department, narrow gauge railway, picnic areas, Model boat collection, shops, cafeteria, fishing and much more.

Mar-end Oct daily 10.00-18.00 (or dusk), Nov-Dec daily 10.00-17.00

A£6.00 C£4.00

Discount Offer: One Child Free With One Adult Paying Full Admission Price

Buckinghamshire

Animal Attractions

Odds Farm Park Rare Breeds Centre

Wooburn Common High Wycombe
Buckinghamshire HP10 0LX
Tel: 01628 520188 Fax: 01628 520188
[J2 M40 then A40 from Beaconsfield and J7 M4 then A355 Beaconsfield]

Created with children in mind, lots of opportunities to observe traditional farm animals and rare breeds closely in an enjoyable atmosphere. regular new arrivals. Hands-on activities, bottle feeding lambs, piggies tea time, and goat show. Indoor playbarn, adventure play area, large sandpit, tea room and gift shop.
All year daily, 14 Feb-2 July 10.00-17.30, 3 July-5 Sept 10.00-18.00, 6 Sept-1 Nov 10.00-17.30, 2 Nov-11 Feb 10.00-16.30. Closed 20 Dec-2 Jan
A£6.00 C(under2)£Free C(2-16)£5.00
OAPs£5.00

Arts, Crafts & Textiles

Fenny Lodge Gallery

76 Simpson Road Fenny Stratford Bletchley
Milton Keynes Buckinghamshire MK1 1BA

Tel: 01908 639494 Fax: 01908 648431

[M1 J13, take A421 towards Milton Keynes. Follow brown tourist signs on V4 and Watling Street at Fenny Stratford]

On the banks of the Grand Union Canal, in an attractive 18th century cottage, Fenny Lodge Gallery invites you to browse or buy. From £10 to £2,000, there's an extensive selection of works of art by contemporary artists and makers, well-known and rising stars, from modern to traditional in style, displayed around 29 walls, nine display cabinets and countless shelves, mantelpieces and window sills in seven rooms - to show you how they would look in your home or office. *All year Mon-Sat 09.00.17.00. Closed Sun and occasional Bank Hol*
Admission Free

Milton Keynes Gallery

900 Midsummer Boulevard Central Milton Keynes Buckinghamshire MK9 3QA
Tel: 01908 676900 Fax: 01908 558308
[From M1 exit at J14, follow signs for Central MK. From A5, exit at A509 Portway Junction, follow Central MK signs]

Milton Keynes Gallery is a purpose-built public contemporary art gallery. Designed by architects Blonski Heard, it opened in October 1999 with 'The Rudimentary Pictures' by Gilbert and George. MK G aims to 'bring new art to new audiences' and presents 8-10 free exhibitions a year. Solo, group and touring exhibitions present works in all media, including painting, sculpture, photography, printmaking and installation.
All year Tue-Sat 10.00-17.00, Sun 11.00-17.00. Closed 24-26 Dec, 1 Jan, Good Fri & Bank Hol Mons
Admission Free

Caverns & Caves

Hellfire Caves

West Wycombe High Wycombe
Buckinghamshire HP14 3AJ

Tel: 01494 533739 Fax: 01494 471617

[On A40. Bus: Green Line No.290 from Victoria to Oxford. Rail: High Wycombe]

Entrance to Hellfire Caves is halfway up the hill beneath the Parish Church and the mausoleum of the Dashwood family. The caves were dug between 1748-1754. Massive entrance facade with flint walls, quarter mile tunnel leading into caves, small caverns with colourful tableaux and sound effects.
All year Mar-Oct daily 11.00-17.30, Nov-Feb Sat & Sun 13.00-17.00

A£4.00 C&OAPs£3.00 Students£3.00 Family Ticket (A2+C3) £12.00

Country Parks & Estates

Emberton Country Park

Emberton Nr Olney Buckinghamshire
MK46 5DB
Tel: 01234 711575 Fax: 01234 711575
*[Leave M1 at J14 and take A509 going N.
Emberton Country Park is just 1m before village of
Olney]*

The park opened in 1965, originally a gravel
works, now transformed into an attractive parkland setting covering 205 acres which welcomes the visitor and encourages peace and
relaxation. The park caters for a wide range of
uses and interests including caravanning and
camping with 200 touring and 115 static pitches, fishing, sailing, walking, picnicking and lots
more. You will find this to be an ideal location
for a day visit, weekend break or a longer holiday.
*All year daily with access through a coin or card
controlled barrier*
Park admission £3.00 per vehicle

Festivals & Shows

Olney Pancake Race

Olney Buckinghamshire

Tel: 01234 711392 Fax: 01234 241519

[A509 Olney Town Centre. Rail: Milton Keynes]

Warning bells are rung from the church steeple
and local townswomen race with frying pans
from Market Square to the Church where the
Shriving service begins. Street entertainment in
the town centre & childrens races prior to the
main event.
Shrove Tuesday 2005
Admission Free

Folk & Local History Museums

Amersham Museum

49 High Street Amersham Buckinghamshire
HP7 0QE
Tel: 01494 723700
*[In the centre of the old town, a short walk from
the Market Hall, oppostie the King's Arms, sign-
posted from car park and in the street]*

Housed in part of a medieval hall house c1450
which still contains much of the original timber
framing and the original open hearth. The displays are of local history ranging from fossil and
Roman finds to artefacts of more recent date. It
is a small collection but an expanding one
which also includes dairying bygones and
smocks, wheelwright and other tools, lacemak-
ing and straw plait work, material relating to
Amersham's Second World War naval connections, items of clothing, old sewing machines,
brewery history and a variety of maps, photographs and charts.
*Easter-end Oct Sat, Sun & Bank Hol Mon 14.00-
16.30 also each Wed & Thur 14.00-16.30 from
June-Sept*
A£1.00 C(0-16)£Free

Bucks County Museum and The Roald Dahl Children's Gallery

Church Street Aylesbury Buckinghamshire
HP20 2QP

Tel: 01296 331441 Fax: 01296 334884

www.buckscc.gov.uk/museum

[Near St Mary's Church, at top of Market Square]

You really can awaken your senses at this award-winning Museum with its innovative touchable displays about Buckinghamshire, exciting programme of family exhibitions, and regular events and activities. Touch a real mammoth's tooth; test your knowledge of fossils; and make friends with Tim Burr the wooden man. Also on site is The Roald Dahl Children's Gallery, a unique hands on gallery where children can enter James' Giant Peach, discover Willy Wonka's inventions, crawl through Mr Fox's tunnel, ride in the Great Glass Elevator and let their imaginations run wild! Plus garden, café, shop, meeting rooms. Telephone for details and bookings.

All year Mon-Sat 10.00-17.00, Sun 14.00-17.00. During Buckinghamshire term time The Roald Dahl Gallery is open exclusively to schools from 10.00-15.00 and then open to the public 15.00-17.00. As the Dahl Gallery is very popular and entrance is limited, pre-booking is advised

Dahl Gallery: A£3.50 C(3-16)£2.75 C(Under 3)£Free. Museum only: Admission Free

Special Events

A History of Photography
12/06/2004-10/10/2004
Discover 150 years of portrait photography with images as wide ranging as Oscar Wilde, Mick Jagger and Queen Victoria

Roald Dahl Festival
26/06/2004
One day festival and family fun day celebrating the work of Roald Dahl

The English Civil War
27/11/2004-27/02/2005
A spectacular collection of 17th century portraits, miniatures and costumes that tell the story of the English Civil War

Cowper and Newton Museum

Orchard Side Market Place Olney
Buckinghamshire MK46 4AJ

Tel: 01234 711516

www.cowperandnewtonmuseum.org

[Olney N of Newport Pagnell via A509]

Not every museum can boast of having a former slaver turned evangelical preacher who also wrote world-famous hymns as one of its main raison d'etre. He became good friends with a poet who lived in the present buildings of the Cowper & Newton Museum. The slaver, John Newton and William Cowper, the international poet who was also a translator of Homer and a progressive gardener lived very close to one another in Olney. The Museum also boasts of having a nationally renowned lace collection, dinosaur bones, a costume gallery and trade rooms housing a collection of Olney's social history from the early 18th century. Another bonus is that of having extensive gardens which are home to 18th century or earlier plants. The Museum is of early Georgian origins.

1 Mar-23 Dec Tue-Fri 10.00-13.00 & 14.00-17.00, Sat 10.00-17.00. Also open Sun in June, July & Aug plus Bank Hol Mons & Shrove Tue 14.00-17.00. Closed Good Fri

A£3.00 C(5-18)£1.50 Concessions£2.00 Family Ticket £7.50. Groups rates available for 12+ people. Gardens only: £1.00

Heritage & Industrial

Milton Keynes Museum

Stacey Hill Farm McConnell Drive Wolverton
Milton Keynes Buckinghamshire MK12 5EL
Tel: 01908 316222 Fax: 01908 319148

[Access off Milton Keynes Grid Road H2 Millers Way]

A visit to Milton Keynes Museum whisks you back through 200 years of local and national history. Victorian and Edwardian room setting. An extensive collection of industrial, agricultural and domestic items including tractors, implements, stationary engines, printing and telephone equipment.

1 Apr-31 Oct Wed-Sun 11.00-16.30, Nov-Apr Sat-Sun 11.00-16.30

A£3.50 Concessions£2.50 Family Ticket £8.00

Historical

Stowe House (Stowe School)

Buckingham Buckinghamshire MK18 5EH

Tel: 01280 818280 / 818282

Fax: 01280 818186

www.stowe.co.uk

[4m N of Buckingham town]

Set in the National Trust's Landscape Gardens, Stowe House is a major work of architecture on an immense and palatial scale that has inspired and contains the work of a number of leading 18th century designers including Vanbrugh, Adam, Gibbs, Kent and Soane. The Stowe House Preservation Trust was established in 1997 to restore and preserve it for the benefit of the public and the nation. The House has been a major public school since 1923. The House is licensed for civil weddings and is also available to hire for private and corporate functions.

24-25 Jan, 7-8 & 14-15 Feb, 13-14 Mar, Sat & Sun for guided tour only at 14.00, 27 Mar-25 Apr Wed-Sun 12.00-17.00 with guided tour at 14.00, 30 May-6 June Wed-Sun guided tours only at 14.00, 7 July-4 Sept Wed-Sun (plus Aug Bank Hol Mon) 12.00-17.00 with guided tour at 14.00, 2 Sept-17 Oct Wed-Sun guided tours only at 14.00, 20-21 Nov, 11-19 Dec Sat & Sun guided tours only at 14.00. Group visits are available by arrangement throughout the year. Opening times may vary, please call 01280 818280 / 818282 to confirm

A£2.00 C(under16)£1.00. Guided tours: A£3.00 C(under16)£1.50

Special Events

Plant Fair
18/04/2004

Stowe Opera (Carmen)
31/07/2004-08/08/2004

Stowe Christmas Fayre
23/10/2004-24/10/2004

Waddesdon Manor

Aylesbury Buckinghamshire HP18 0JH

Tel: 01296 653211 Fax: 01296 653208

www.waddesdon.org.uk

[At W end of Waddesdon village, 6m NW of Aylesbury on Bicester Road A41. Plenty of on site parking. Bus: Red Rover 1, 15, 16 from Aylesbury]

Waddesdon Manor was built (1874-89) for Baron Ferdinand de Rothschild to display his vast collection of 18th century art treasures, which include French Royal furniture, Savonnerie carpets and Sèvres porcelain as well as important portraits by Gainsborough and Reynolds. It has one of the finest Victorian Gardens in Britain, a fully stocked Rococo-style aviary, wine cellars, shops and licensed restaurants. Many events are organised throughout the year. For more information please call the Booking Office on 01296 653226.

Garden, Aviary, Manor & Stables, Restaurants, Gift & Wine Shops: 3 Mar-31 Oct Wed-Sun & Bank Hol Mons 10.00-17.00, 3 Nov-23 Dec Wed-Sun & Mon 20-Tues 21 Dec 11.00-17.00. House & Wine Cellars: 31 Mar-31 Oct Wed-Sun & Bank Hol Mons 11.00-16.00, (Part of House open) 17 Nov-23 Dec Wed-Sun & Mon 20-Tues 21 Dec 13.00-17.00. Bachelors' Wing: Wed-Fri 11.00-16.00 when house open (space is limited and access cannot be guaranteed)

House & Grounds: A£11.00 C(5-16)£8.00. Grounds only: A£4.00 C(5-16)£2.00 Bachelors' Wing £1.00. NT Members £Free. Timed tickets to the House can be purchased on site or reserved up to 24 hours in advance by telephoning 01296 653226. Advance booking fee: £3.00 per transaction

Special Events

Easter Walks
11/04/2004-18/04/2004
Held on 11 & 18 Apr. Enjoy a walk with a member of Waddesdon's Gardens Team. End the morning with a revitalising drink and homemade biscuits at the Manor. Time: 11.00-12.00 Cost: A£9.00 C£4.50. Booking essential

Summer Menu Mastercladd
20/04/2004
Time: 10.00-15.00 Cost: £55.00 (includes coffee on arrival, three course set lunch and wine)

Manor Restaurant Open For Dinner
24/04/2004-18/12/2004
Held on 24 Apr, 29 May, 19 June, 24 July, 28 Aug, 25 Sept, 23 Oct, 27 Nov, 18 Dec. Menus based on seasonal ingredients, and explore our award winning wine list. Time: 19.00-22.30, last orders taken at 21.15. Reservations essential

Spotlight On Bordeaux
24/04/2004
During this tasting the discussion of vintage, quality and price as well as the importance of the futures market will be covered. Time: 10.30-12.30. Cost: £50.00 (includes coffee on arrival and all wines) £70.00 (includes coffee on arrival, all tasting wines and a three course set lunch)

Autumn Menu Masterclass
27/04/2004
Time: 10.00-15.00 Cost: £55.00 (includes coffee on arrival, three course set lunch and wine)

Museums And Galleries Month
01/05/2004-30/05/2004
Secrets and Surprises at Waddesdon. Clocks, boxes, desks and tables are shown to reveal their secrets. Normal admission charges apply

The Tulip
07/05/2004
According to Anna Pavord, the tulip is the sexiest, most capricious and intriguing flower on earth. The day includes a walk in the gardens with Anna. Time: 10.30-16.00 Cost: £85.00 (includes morning coffee, lunch and afternoon tea)

Fine Food, Wine And Spirits Fair
08/05/2004-09/05/2004
Come to our exciting new venue at The Stables where over 25 producers from across the country will be selling the best food, wines and spirits. Time: 10.00-17.00

Introduction To Wine Tasting
08/05/2004-06/11/2004
Held on 8 May, 19 June, 3 July, 7 Aug, 4 Sept, 2 Oct, 6 Nov. Waddesdon's Master of Wine, Marcia Waters, uses six wines to introduce guests to the pleasures of wine tasting. Time: 10.30-12.30. Cost: £30.00 (includes coffee/tea on arrival and all wines) £50.00 also includes a set three course lunch)

Guided Tour Of The House - Ground Floor
15/05/2004-04/09/2004
Held on 15 May, 12 June, 4 Sept. An escorted tour led by Waddesdon Manor Guides. Time: 10.45-12.00. Cost: £16.00 (including entry charge)

Guided Tour Of The House - 1st Floor And Bachelors' Wing
22/05/2004-11/09/2004
Held on 22 May, 26 June, 11 Sept. An escorted tour led by Waddesdon Manor Guides. Time: 10.45-12.00. Cost: £16.00 (including entry charge)

Rules Made To Be Broken
22/05/2004-13/11/2004
Held on 22 May and 13 Nov. Why should a vin de pays be more expensive than an appellation contrôlée? Time: 10.30-12.30. Cost: £50.00 (includes coffee on arrival and all wines), £70.00 (as above plus 3 course lunch)

Race For Life
23/05/2004
A series of events held across the UK in aid of Cancer Research UK. Waddesdon Estate is the venue again for one of these events which aim to bring up to 2000 women together to walk, run or jog 5km. To register online: www.raceforlife.co.uk. Registration forms available from Tesco, or by calling 08705 134314. Time: 11.00

Half-Term Children's Activities
26/05/2004-30/05/2004

Great Wines From Down Under
29/05/2004
John Thoroughgood, Director of Lay & Wheeler, will lead this tasting of the top wines from Australia and New Zealand. Time: 10.30-16.00 Cost: £125.00

Container Gardening
03/06/2004
Learn about container gardening with Len Bellis, Manager of the Waddesdon Plant Centre. Time: 13.30-16.00 Cost: £25.00 (includes all materials and afternoon tea) £45.00 (plus 3 course lunch)

Louis Vuitton Event
05/06/2004
Britain's premier classic car competition, the Louis Vuitton Classic. In its 14th year, the Louis Vuitton Classic also celebrates the 150th anniversary of the house of Louis Vuitton. Come and see some of the most beautiful classic cars in the world.

Rothschild Wine Day
11/06/2004-22/10/2004
Held on 11 June, 16 July, 3 & 24 Sept, 8 & 22 Oct. Ben Howkins leads a tutored tasting of eight Rothschild wines. Time: 10.15-16.00. Tickets: £90.00

Early Morning Wildlife Walk
12/06/2004-14/08/2004
Held on 12 & 19 June, 7 & 14 Aug. Catch a glimpse of Waddesdon's wildlife and hear the morning chorus. Time: 06.30-08.30. Cost: £14.00 (including breakfast)

Summer's Evening In The Gardens
19/06/2004
The gardens will stay open until 22.00 to allow you to enjoy the unique atmosphere of Waddesdon on a summer's evening.

Father's Day
20/06/2004
A day for every member of the family! A collection of cars from the Vintage Sports Car Club in front of the House, special Father's Day lunch in the Manor Restaurant, and an informal wine tasting (charged) in the Cellars. Time: 10.00-17.00

Family Walks
04/07/2004-25/07/2004
Held on 4, 11, 18, 25 July. Enjoy a leisurely stroll with members of the Gardens Team and learn more about the Manor grounds. Time: 12.00-13.00

Performing Arts Orchestra Music From The Movies
10/07/2004
The Performing Arts Symphony Orchestra and singer Mary Carewe perform some of the greatest music from the silver screen. Time:18.00 for 20.00 Costs: Tickets in advance A£20.50 C£13.00

Baron Ferdinand's House Party
17/07/2004
Every summer Baron Ferdinand opened his doors to the cream of London society. Follow in their footsteps with a guided tour of the House and enjoy a special four course menu. Time: 18.30-23.00 Cost: £85.00

A Summer's Afternoon In A Rothschild Garden
29/07/2004
In celebration of the bicentenary of the RHS, Kate Garton will give a lecture on The Rothschild Gardens. Time: 14.00-18.30 Cost: £30.00 (includes afternoon tea, champagne, canapés and a guided tour of the gardens)

Champagne On The Parterre
31/07/2004
The Parterre is the perfect setting for this popular, annual event. Time: 18.30-20.30. Cost: £25.00 tasting & champagne reception. Early booking recommended

Children In The Garden
01/08/2004-29/08/2004
Held on 1, 8, 15, 22, 29 Aug. The largest bird at Waddesdon is not in the Aviary and not all flowers smell sweet! Time: 12.00-13.00. Cost: C£Free

Onatti Theatre Present - The Way Of The World By William Congreve
05/08/2004-07/08/2004

A highly entertaining and witty comedy. Please bring a picnic and a chair. Time: 19.00-22.00. Cost: £12.50

Children In The House
07/08/2004-28/08/2004
Held on 7, 14, 21, 28 Aug. Each Saturday in August there is a Children's Tour in the House. Time: 10.45-11.15. Cost: C£Free

Children's Day
14/08/2004
Enjoy a traditional children's fair, Punch and Judy and other activities on the North Front. Time: 11.00-15.00.

Discovering Waddesdon Study Day
21/09/2004
Participants will have access to unrivalled fine and decorative arts; 18th century French furniture, porcelain and drawings, and the opportunity to explore them with distinguished experts. Time: 10.00-16.00. Cost: £125.00 (includes coffee on arrival, two course lunch with wine and afternoon tea)

NGS Manor Gardens And Water Garden Open Day
22/09/2004
Open in aid of the National Garden Scheme. Time: 10.00-17.00. Cost: A£6.00 C£3.00

Gift Shop Sale
29/09/2004-24/10/2004
Many items at bargain prices!

Bucks Garden Trust
02/10/2004
The first of the autumn talks features archaeologist, Brian Dix, looking at the role of garden archaeology. Time: 14.30. Cost: £9.00 (includes tea and biscuits).

Dinner With The King: The George III Silver Service
07/10/2004
This day is a rare opportunity for a close look at the Service. Time: 10.30-16.00. Cost: £60.00 (includes morning coffee, lunch and afternoon tea)

Clocks And Automata
14/10/2004
Jonathan Betts, Curator of Horology at the National Maritime Museum, and noted expert in the field, will examine the history of clockwork automata and lead a close examination session. Time: 10.30-16.00. Cost: £60.00 (includes morning coffee, lunch and afternoon tea)

Bucks Garden Trust Gala Event
16/10/2004
An event, featuring a tour of Waddesdon's gardens, a lecture by Melanie Aspey, and drinks in the Wine Cellars followed by a two course dinner. Time: 15.00-22.00. Cost: £45.00

Recreating The Red Book: Ferdinand And The Art Of Victorian Interior Decoration
21/10/2004
Matthew Hirst, Curator and specialist in 19th-century interiors, will explore the original appearance and arrangement of Waddesdon in Ferdinand's day, recorded in his Red Book of 1897. Time: 10.30-16.00. Cost: £60.00 (includes morning coffee, lunch and afternoon tea)

Half-Term Children's Activities
27/10/2004-31/10/2004

A Cabinet Of Curiosities:
28/10/2004
Discovering the Renaissance through the Bachelors' Wing collections. Time: 10.30-16.00 Cost: £60.00 (including morning coffee, lunch and afternoon tea)

Floodlit Opening
30/10/2004
The House is bathed in light, inside and out, taking on the atmosphere of a great house party. Please bring a torch. Pre-booking essential. Time: From 18.00 Cost: Wine Tasting: £10.00 Buffet Supper: £23.50 Candlelit Dinner: £40.00 (includes canapés and three course dinner with coffee

Bucks Garden Trust
30/10/2004
John Harris looks at the changing fate of the country house throughout Europe since World War II. Time: 14.30 Cost: £9.00 (includes tea and biscuits)

Christmas Gift And Wine Shops
03/11/2004-23/12/2004
Decorated and open for Christmas shopping.

A Celebration Of Craft And Design
05/11/2004-07/11/2004
Come to this Christmas Fair with a difference! Something for all tastes and budgets. Time: 10.00-17.00

A Celebration Of Contemporary Designer Crafts
10/11/2004-21/11/2004
(Excluding Mon & Tue). An exhibition and sale of exquisite, innovative and distinguished gifts made

by professional crafts people from the
Gloucestershire Guild of Craftsmen. Time: 10.30-
17.00

Tips And Tipples
12/11/2004-10/12/2004
*Held on 12, 19, 26 Nov, 3, 10 Dec.
Demonstrations and hints for impressive entertaining over the Christmas season. Time: 10.30-
12.00. Cost: £16.00 (includes morning coffee,
food and wine tastings and entry to grounds)*

A European Christmas
17/11/2004-23/12/2004
*The East Wing of the House opens decorated for
Christmas.Time: 13.00-17.00*

Fit For a King
18/11/2004
*Dr Ulrich Leben, Associate Curator of Furniture,
leads a day examining the stunning and surprising
royal furniture brought together by Baron
Ferdinand and his family. Time: 10.30-16.00 Cost
£60.00 (includes morning coffee, lunch and afternoon tea)*

Decorations For Christmas Celebrations
20/11/2004
*Stephen Crisp, garden designer, lecturer and
Head Gardener at the American Ambassador's
residence in London, demonstrates ideas for decorating your home for Christmas. Time: 10.30-
16.00 Cost: £85.00 (includes materials, morning
coffee, lunch and afternoon tea)*

Putting The House To Bed
25/11/2004
*The day will offer a glimpse of what goes on
behind closed doors during the annual winter
clean. Time: 10.30-16.00 Cost: £60.00 (includes
morning coffee, lunch and afternoon tea)*

An Intimate Eye
03/12/2004
*Dutch paintings of the Golden Age. Time: 10.30-
16.00 Cost: £60.00 (includes morning coffee,
lunch and afternoon tea)*

Military & Defence Museums

Bletchley Park Museum

The Mansion Bletchley Park, Wilton Avenue
Bletchley Milton Keynes Buckinghamshire
MK3 6EB

Tel: 01908 640404 Fax: 01908 274381

www.bletchleypark.org.uk

*[300yds from Bletchley Station. Limited parking
on site, free parking at station]*

Bletchley Park was until recently "Britain's Best
Kept Secret", as the centre of WWII codebreaking the secrecy of its location was vital for security. It was here that coded messages from the
military cypher machine Enigma were studied
and decoded often providing vital information in
advance of military operations. See the Turing
Bombe which was developed to assist in this
and follow the unravelling of a German coded
message in our cryptology trail. Colossus, the
world's first large electronic valve computer and
forerunner of today's computer technology, was
developed to help break into Hitler's messages
to his generals, see the replica standing where
one of the original machines worked. Many
other exhibitor groups use the facilities at
Bletchley Park. You can see everything from aircraft recovery to WWII re-enactments, comput-
ers, uniforms, model railway layouts, model
boats, military vehicles, period toys and a
superb collection of Churchill memorabilia.

*From 2 Jan Sat-Sun 10.30-17.00, Mon-Fri after-
noons from 12.30 for a single guided tour at
14.00. Group visits welcome on any day by
appointment*

A£10.00 C(under8)£Free C&Concessions£8.00
Family Ticket £25.00, Free guided tour

Model Towns & Villages

Bekonscot Model Village

Warwick Road Beaconsfield HP9 2PL
Tel: 01494 672919 Fax: 01494 675284
www.bekonscot.com

[2.7m from J2 M40, signposted, 4m from J16 M25]

BE A GIANT in a miniature wonderland where nobody grows up. This magical haven depicts rural England in the 1930s where time has stood still in this wonderland of nostalgic make-believe. The miniature static population enjoy the fun of the fair, visiting the zoo, or lazily watch the cricket match, as yet unconcerned by the growing shadows of mass unemployment, poverty and impending war. Among the interesting buildings there are castles, a Tudor house, thatched cottages, and a copy of Enid Blyton's house 'Green Hedges'. There is an excellent Gauge 1 Model Railway and many moving models, as well as a new 7 1/4 miniature railway at a small extra charge, running during Buckinghamshire school holidays and weekends. A delight for all the family. Children's parties. Play area, souvenir shop, refreshment kiosk, picnic area.

14 Feb-31 Oct daily 10.00-17.00
A£5.30 C£3.20 OAPs&Students£4.00. Groups of 13+ A£4.50 C£3.00. Special rates for school groups

Discount Offer: One Child Free. With One Full Paying Adult.

Bletchley Park Museum

Bletchley Park was until recently "Britain's Best Kept Secret", as the centre of WWII codebreaking the secrecy of its location was vital for security. It was here that coded messages from the military cypher machine Enigma were studied and decoded often providing vital information in advance of military operations.

Bletchley, Buckinghamshire MK3 6EB
Tel: 01908 640404 www.bletchleypark.org.uk

Police, Prisons & Dungeons

Old Gaol Museum

Market Hill Buckingham Buckinghamshire
MK18 1JX

Tel: 01280 823020 Fax: 01280 823020

The landmark building of Buckingham town
centre. Restored by the Buckingham Heritage
Trust, it contains a fascinating fully registered
Museum, which reflects various aspects of
Buckingham's past - including its military history,
and presents the story of the Old Gaol with an
audio-visual display.

All year Mon-Sat 10.00-16.00. Closed Sun

A£1.50 C&OAPs£1.00

Sport & Recreation

Wycombe Summit Ski and Snowboard Centre

Abbey Barn Lane High Wycombe
Buckinghamshire HP10 9QQ

Tel: 01494 474711 Fax: 01494 443757

*[Between J3/4 of M40 just 30mins from London.
Plenty of parking on site]*

England's longest slope and world class ski and
snowboard school, Wycombe Summit is suitable for experts and beginners alike. 300m main
slope, 100m trainer slope and several nursery
areas with three lifts, all floodlit and fully lubricat-
ed.
All year, call for times. Closed Christmas Day
1 Hour from: A£11.50-£14.00
C(under16)£10.00-£12.00. All day from:
A£14.00-£27.50 C£12.00-£24.00. Lessons are
extra, please call for details

Theme & Adventure Parks

Gulliver's Land

Livingstone Drive Newlands Milton Keynes
Buckinghamshire MK15 ODT
Tel: 01908 609001 Fax: 01908 609101
[J14 M1. Follow signposts]

Gulliver's Land offers you and your family a day
out of this world. Let us transport you away
from the day to day worries into a world of wonder and fantasy. Enjoy the sounds of laughter
and fun in Toy Land, mosey on down into
Discovery Bay with its fortress and jail or down
into the jungles into Adventure Land.
*3-18 & 24-25 Apr, 1-3, 8-9, 12-14, 15-16, 19-
21, 22-23, 26-31 May, 1-6, 8-13, 15-30 June,
1-31 July, 1-31 Aug, 1-5, 11-12, 18-19, 25-26
Sept, 2-3, 9-10, 16-17, 23-30 Oct, 27-28 Nov,
4-5, 9-12, 15-19, 21-23 Dec. Park opens from
10.00/10.30*
A&C£10.30 C(under 90cm tall)£Free

Transport Museums

Buckinghamshire Railway Centre

Quainton Road Station Quainton Aylesbury
Buckinghamshire HP22 4BY

Tel: 01296 655450 Fax: 01296 655720

www.bucksrailcentre.org.uk

[6m N of Aylesbury, 15m from Milton Keynes, 10m from Bicester, 20m from Oxford and Watford and 25m from Luton. Off A41 Aylesbury / Bicester road signposted from A41 at Waddesdon & A413 at Whitchurch. Plenty of free on site parking]

In this working steam museum visitors can experience the age of steam, riding behind full-sized steam locomotives in old-style carriages and travelling on the extensive miniature railway. Among the collection of over 35 locomotives and numerous carriages and wagons are items from South Africa, the USA and Egypt as well as the UK.

Mar-Oct Wed-Sun & Bank Hol Mons 10.30-17.30 (16.30 weekdays) for viewing. Train rides available on Sun & Bank Hol Mons plus Wed in School Hols

Bank Hol Weekends: A£7.00 C&OAPs£5.00 FamilyTicket (A2+C4) £20.00. Steaming Open Days: A£6.00 C&OAPs £4.00 Family Ticket (A2+C4) £18.00. Static Viewing Days: A£3.00 C&OAPs£2.00. Day Out With Thomas Events: A£8.00 C(2+)£6.00. Santa's Magic Steamings: Special prices apply

Special Events

Days Out with Thomas
10/04/2004-12/04/2004

May Day Weekend
02/05/2004-03/05/2004

Spring Bank Holiday Weekend
30/05/2004-31/05/2004

Miniature Traction Engine Rally
05/06/2004-06/06/2004

Days Out with Thomas
09/07/2004-11/07/2004

200th Anniversary of Railways
28/08/2004-29/08/2004

Veteran and Vintage Car Rally
30/08/2004

Day Out with Thomas
11/09/2004-12/09/2004

Traction Engine Rally
18/09/2004-19/09/2004

Santa's Magic Steaming
27/11/2004-28/11/2004

Santa's Magic Steaming
04/12/2004-19/12/2004

Cambridgeshire

Agriculture / Working Farms

Sacrewell Farm and Country Centre

Thornhaugh Peterborough Cambridgeshire
PE8 6HJ

Tel: 01780 782254 Fax: 01780 781370

www.sacrewell.org.uk

[Situated just E of the A1/A47 intersection, clearly signposted on approaching the intersection from either direction on both the A1 and A47. Plenty of parking on site]

Hidden deep in the heart of the countryside nestles a country farm and 18th century watermill where the treasures of farming and country life lie waiting to be discovered. Sacrewell has always had that special magic for young and old alike. With everything from a working watermill to farm animals and play areas, there is something for all to explore at Sacrewell. In the Miller's Kitchen you will find delicious home-cooked meals and refreshments to tempt you, and a shop to browse for souvenirs or gifts. All aspects of farming and country life through the ages are here to discover at Sacrewell: friendly farm animals and pet village; tractor rides; children's play areas and mini-maze; 18th century working watermill and mill house; farm bygones, gardens and farm trails; excellent home cooked food from the Miller's Kitchen and gift shop; special events held throughout the year; birthday parties and function rooms; camping and caravanning facilities with electric hook-ups, showers and toilets; caravan rally site.

All year daily, Mar-Sept 09.30-17.00, Oct-Dec 10.00-16.00. Closed 24 Dec-1 Jan

A£4.00 C£2.50 OAPs£3.00 Family Ticket £10.50. Group discounts available for 10+ people

Discount Offer: One Child Free With Every Full Paying Adult

Special Events

Easter Egg Hunts and Chicks
03/04/2004-18/04/2004
Take the tractor ride to the Enchanted Wood to hunt for eggs. See the newly hatched chicks

Easter Lunch
11/04/2004
Treat yourself to a special Easter lunch in the Miller's Kitchen

Spinners and Weavers
01/05/2004-05/06/2004
Held on 1 May & 5 June only. Spinning and weaving demonstrations

A1 Festival of Music and Dance
11/06/2004-13/06/2004
This will be the fourth year Sacrewell has hosted this event. The festival will produce some of the finest folk-playing musicians in the country. Three days of fantastic Blue Grass music, dance and much more

Miniature Steam Rally and Model Engineers Fair
17/07/2004-18/07/2004
Miniature steam engines, model boats and planes. Plenty of action and loads to see and do

Handmade 2004
24/09/2004-26/09/2004
'A Show of Skills'. From the organiser of the 'Fruits of the Forest' show this new exciting event plans to showcase handmade crafts, skills, demonstrations and much more

Spooky Spectacular Halloween Half Term
23/10/2004-31/10/2004
Experience the Ghost Buster Special Ride and the Haunted House Tour. Spooky gifts will be available in the shop

Winter Wonderland
27/11/2004-23/12/2004
The magic of Christmas at Sacrewell. See the nativity scene with real animals and take a sleigh ride to the Winter Wonderland barn and Santa's Grotto

Arts, Crafts & Textiles

Kettle's Yard

Castle Street Cambridge Cambridgeshire
CB3 0AQ
Tel: 01223 352124 Fax: 01223 324377
*[From S, M11 J13. From N, from A14 take
A1307 to Castle Street]*

For sixteen years, Kettle's Yard was the home of
Jim Ede, a former curator at the Tate Gallery,
London, and his wife, Helen. It houses Ede's
collection of art, mostly of the first half of the
twentieth century. The collection includes paint-
ings by Ben and Winifred Nicholson, Alfred
Wallis, Christopher Wood, David Jones, Joan
Miro and many others, along with sculpture by
artists including Henri Gaudier-Brzeska,
Constantin Brancusi, Henry Moore and Barbara
Hepworth.

*House: All year, 10 Apr-29 Aug Tue-Sun & Bank
Hol Mons 13.30-16.30, winter Tue-Sun & Bank
Hol Mons 14.00-16.00. Gallery: Tue-Sun & Bank
Hol Mons 11.30-17.00*
Admission Free

Stained Glass Museum

The South Triforum Ely Cathedral Ely
Cambridgeshire CB7 4DL
Tel: 01353 660347 Fax: 01353 665025
[Off A10 Ely Cathedral]

An exhibition of over one hundred original
stained glass panels rescued from redundant
churches, illustrating the history of this ancient
craft from medieval to modern times. A unique,
national collection of exceptional quality displayed at eye level enabling visitors to study the
glass at close quarters.

*All year daily Mon-Fri 10.30-17.00, Sat & Bank
Hol 10.30-17.30, Sun 12.00-18.00, Sun closing
in Winter 16.30. Closed 25-26 Dec and Good Fri*
A£3.50 C&Concessions£2.50 Family Ticket
(A2+C2)£7.00

Birds, Butterflies & Bees

Raptor Foundation

The Heath St. Ives Road Woodhurst
Cambridgeshire PE28 3BT

Tel: 01487 741140 Fax: 01487 841140

www.raptorfoundation.org.uk

*[From the A14 exit at St. Ives follow the ring road,
follow signs to Industrial Estate, R turn onto the
B1040 to Somersham follow brown tourist sign.
From A1 exit at Huntingdon, follow signs to St.
Ives, then B1040 to Somersham, follow brown
tourist signs. Plenty of on site parking available]*

The Raptor Foundation is a unique and exciting
place for children and adults alike to meet and
learn about owls, falcons, hawks and buzzards.
Located in 30 acres, the Foundation is home to
over 300 raptors and more than 25 species,
many threatened or endangered. The
Foundation also provides medical care for
injured raptors, returns rehabilitated birds to the
wild, provides sanctuary for unreleasable raptors, breeds permanently injured raptors so that
the offspring may take their place in the wild
and provides research into environmental prob-
lems and conservation matters. Also on site is a
tea room, gift shop, exhibition room and camp
site. Guided tours, membership, adoption, hunting days and meet the bird days available on
request.

*All year daily 10.00-17.00. Flying displays at
12.00, 14.00 & 16.00*

A£3.50 C£2.00 OAPs£2.50. Private groups welcome. Registered Charity No. 1042085. All proceeds contribute to the care and rehabilitation
of injured birds of prey

**Discount Offer: One Child Free With
Two Adults**

Festivals & Shows

15th Cambridge International Concert Series 2003-2004

Cambridge Corn Exchange Wheeler Street
Cambridge CB2 3QE
Tel: 01223 357851 Fax: 01223 329074
[Located in the centre of Cambridge directly behind the Guildhall, in the Market Square. For the nearest parking, follow signs to Lion Yard Car Park. Rail: Cambridge, 20mins]

Once again the series is truly international, featuring not only the very best of Britain's orchestras but also outstanding orchestras from Germany and Russia, two countries with a magnificent musical heritage. The Berlin Symphony and the Moscow Radio Symphony Orchestra both make welcome return visits to the Corn Exchange, while the Philharmonia and that most international of bands, the European Union Chamber Orchestra, are back after long absences. Making its International Series debut is Cambridge's own Britten Sinfonia, a development which recognises the orchestra's burgeoning national reputation.
October 9 2003-May 21 2004
Individual Concerts: £5.00-24.50

BMF Show

East of England Showground Oundle Road
Alwarton Peterborough Cambridgeshire
PE2 6XE
Tel: 0116 254 0666
[From A1 S take the Peterborough Alwalton turn, showground on R. From A1 N take the Peterborough S junction, follow the A605 to the roundabout. Take the fourth exit and follow signs to the showground]

The BMF Show is an event that for tens of thousands of people has become a firm fixture in the biking calendar. Already the biggest show of its type in Europe, it's an outdoor event that buzzes with bikes from dawn 'til dusk! BMW;

Honda; Kawasaki; KTM; Suzuki; Triumph; Yamaha; Hein Gericke; Frank Thomas and Phoenix Distribution (better known as Belstaff and Arai distributors), are just some of the big names already signed up to this annual feast of all that's best in biking. Children under 14 years old must be accompanied by an adult.
May 22-23 2004, 09.00-17.00
A£13.00 Pre-booked A£11.00 C(under14)£Free
OAPs£5.00 (proof required)

Cambridge Summer Music Festival

Cambridge Cambridgeshire CB3 0AQ
Tel: 01223 894161 Fax: 01223 892945
[Over 20 city centre venues including: King's College Chapel, Great St. Mary's Church, The Catholic Church and Kettle's Yard]

Cambridge's month long classical music festival celebrates its twenty fifth year in 2004. The Festival will be packed with a wide variety of performances by artists and groups of national and international standing including Julian Lloyd Webber, The Academy of Ancient Music and Maria Ewing. The city's most historic and famous buildings will play host to the Festival, which will include a series of lunchtime events, evening and twilight concerts presenting all kinds of classical music.
July 16 - August 14 2004
Prices vary according to event. Tickets and reservations are available from Cambridge Arts Theatre Box Office, 6 St Edward's Passage, Cambridge, CB2 3PJ, open Mon-Sat 10.00-19.00 or by telephone on 01223 503333

East of England Showground

Oundle Road Alwalton Peterborough
Cambridgeshire PE2 6XE
Tel: 01733 234451 Fax: 01733 370038
[5m from BR: Peterborough. 5m W of Peterborough just off A1]

Major showground holding many events throughout the year. See Special Events
All year - see events for major shows

Special Events

Giant Plant and Shrub Sale
09/04/2004-12/04/2004

National Motorhomes Show
23/04/2004-25/04/2004

Truckfest
02/05/2004-03/05/2004

Garden Show
07/05/2004-09/05/2004

BMF Show
22/05/2004-23/05/2004

Giant Plant and Shrub Sale
28/05/2004-31/05/2004

East of England Country Show
18/06/2004-20/06/2004

Eastern Homebuilding and Renovating Show
03/07/2004-04/07/2004

Woodworking and Power Tool Show
17/07/2004-18/07/2004

East of England Championship Dog Show
20/07/2004-22/07/2004

Ponies (UK) Summer Championships
17/08/2004-21/08/2004

British Show Ponies Championship Show
27/08/2004-31/08/2004

The Land Rover Show
11/09/2004-12/09/2004

BMF Tail End Event
18/09/2004-19/09/2004

Antiques Fair
01/10/2004-20/10/2004

East of England Autumn Show
10/10/2004

Giant Plant and Shrub Sale
22/10/2004-24/10/2004

East of England Christmas Festival
13/11/2004-14/11/2004

Ely Folk Weekend

Ely Cambridgeshire
Tel: 01353 664706
[20mins from A14 and M11]

The 19th Ely Folk Weekend combines an impressive guest list and programme of workshops, concerts, displays, ceilidhs and children's entertainment.
July 9-11 2004

Peterborough Beer Festival 2004

Peterborough River Embankment Peterborough Cambridgeshire
Tel: 07900 056940
27th year of the largest beer festival under canvas in the UK. Mainly pub opening hours, families welcome lunch sessions. Live music featured every evening, plus quiet area. Over 150 Real Ales, plus Cider, Perry and Wine, plus Continental Beers.
August 24-29 2004
A£2.00-£4.00. Free to CAMRA members. Tickets available at the event

Peterborough Festival

Peterborough Cambridgeshire
The Peterborough Festival is now approaching its sixth year and is recognised regionally and nationally as a major event. Featuring within the theme of 'Italia', from the Roman Empire to the modern day, will be the Mayor's Parade and Carnival, Party in the Park, The City of Birmingham Symphony Orchestra, a Roman Exhibition and Roman Enactments, film and theatre events, sporting events, an Italian Cultural Weekend, lunchtime recitals, Literature events, Toga parties, an outdoor concert with 'BUSTED' and much more.
June 26-July 11 2004

Stilton Cheese Rolling 2004

High Street Stilton Peterborough
Cambridgeshire
Tel: 01733 241206
[8m S of Peterborough off A1 at Norman Cross. Rail: Peterborough / Huntingdon. Follow signs for Stilton]

The days starts with the May Queen's procession and traditional dancing. There are stalls, refreshments, four public houses, food, side shows, fairground rides, street entertainers. At noon weirdly dressed teams of four persons roll wooden 'Stilton Cheeses' down the wide, straight Roman road that is the High Street to win a whole Stilton cheese and beer to wash it down with! A free day out with something for all ages.
May 3 2004
Admission Free

Wisbech Rose Fair

St Peter and St Paul Church Church Terrace
Wisbech Cambridgeshire PE13 1BJ
Tel: 01945 461393
[A47 E or W. A17, A1 from N, A10 from S]

One of the largest flower festivals in East Anglia. See exotic blooms and traditional English blooms brought together in a themed display set against the backdrop of St Peter and St Pauls Church. Visit the gardens and browse among stalls. Refreshments available.
June 30-July 4 2004 09.30-20.30
Admission Free

Folk & Local History Museums

Ramsey Rural Museum

Wood Lane Ramsey Cambridgeshire PE26 2XA
Tel: 01487 814304 / 815715
[A141 from Huntingdon then B1040, or B660 from A1. In both cases, follow signs for Ramsey. Museum is situated just beyond duck pond and parish church]

Ramsey Museum is housed in mainly 17th cen-

tury farm buildings and covers a 2.5 acre site set in open countryside. The collections illustrate all aspects of Fenland life and include a wide variety of well-restored agricultural machinery, trades, crafts and domestic bygones. Visit the Chemists Shop, Cobblers and Blacksmith's Forge.
Apr-end Sept Thur 10.00-17.00, Sun & Bank Hols 14.00-17.00.
A£2.00 C(under5)£Free C£1.00 OAPs£1.00

Food & Drink

Chilford Hall Vineyard

Chilford Hall Balsham Road Linton Cambridge
Cambridgeshire CB1 6LE

Tel: 01223 895600 Fax: 01223 895605

www.chilfordhall.co.uk

[Signs from the A11 or the A1307. Chilford Halls are just off the B1052 between Linton / Balsham. Plenty of parking on site]

Taste and buy award winning wines from the largest vineyard in Cambridgeshire. See the grapes growing in the 18 acre vineyard and take a winery tour to learn how English wine is made and appreciate the subtle difference between each of the Chilford quality wines.

1 Mar-31 Oct daily 11.00-17.30

A£4.50 C£Free. Group rates 15+ £3.75

Discount Offer: Two For The Price Of One.

<u>Special Events</u>

English Wine Week
29/05/2004-06/06/2004

Chilford Hall & Cambridge Evening News
Wedding Fair
03/10/2004

Mind, Body and Soul Exhibition
23/10/2004-24/10/2004

Eastern Events Quality Craft Show
29/10/2004-31/10/2004

Grosvenor Exhibitions Quilt Fair
12/11/2004-14/11/2004

Gardens & Horticulture

Cambridge University Botanic Garden

Cory Lodge Bateman Street Cambridge
Cambridgeshire CB2 1JF

Tel: 01223 336265 Fax: 01223 336278

www.botanic.cam.ac.uk

[1m S of city centre]

The Cambridge University Botanic Garden was opened on its present site in 1846 and now holds a treasure trove of 8,000 plant species. The Grade II* heritage landscape includes the Rock Garden, the Winter and Autumn Gardens, Scented Garden and Herbaceous Beds, tropical rainforest and seasonal displays in the Glasshouses, the historic Systematic Beds, an excellent collection of British wild plants and the finest display of trees in the East of England. The Botanic Garden has been designed for year-round interest and some part will be looking wonderful or smelling gorgeous whenever you visit. But the Garden is much more than just a beautiful green space. It is here to celebrate the plants themselves. Throughout your visit you will experience the exuberance and diversity of plant life and witness the beauty of flowers, the patterns and textures of leaves, and the rich surfaces of trunks and branches. Enjoy it!

All year daily. Summer: 10.00-18.00. Winter: 10.00-16.00 Glasshouses: All year daily 10.00-15.45. Please call for Christmas and New Year details. Café/Resturant & Gift Shop Mar-Oct

A£2.50 C£2.00. Season tickets available

Historical

Oliver Cromwell's House

29 St. Mary's Street Ely Cambridgeshire
CB7 4HF

Tel: 01353 662062 Fax: 01353 668518

www.eastcambs.gov.uk

[In the heart of the city, a short walk from major car-parks. Signposted]

Oliver Cromwell and his family moved here in 1636 and remained in Ely for some ten years. The 13th century house has been beautifully restored. Period rooms, sets, exhibitions and videos give insight into 17th century domestic life, the fascinating character of Oliver Cromwell and the Fen Drainage story. Exhibitions. Now features haunted bedroom complete with ghost. Special features for children. Toilets nearby with baby changing facilities.

Apr-Oct daily 10.00-17.30, Nov-Mar Mon-Fri 11.00-16.00, Sat 10.00-17.00, Sun 11.00-16.00

A£3.75 C£2.50 Concessions£3.25

Discount Offer: One Child Free With A Full Paying Adult

Military & Defence Museums

Imperial War Museum, DUXFORD

Imperial War Museum Duxford Cambridge Cambridgeshire CB2 4QR
Tel: 01223 835000 Fax: 01223 837267
[Off J10 M11 on A505 Royston - Newmarket road]

Europe's top aviation museum with nearly 200 aircraft on display including Spitfires, Concorde and a Harrier Jet. See the dramatic display of tanks and military vehicles in the Land Warfare Hall. There are pleasure flights available during summer. Airshows at Duxford are World famous.
All year daily Summer 10.00-18.00, Winter 10.00-16.00. Closed 24, 25 & 26 Dec
A(19-59)£10.00 C(under15)£Free OAPs£8.00 Concessions£6.00

Places of Worship

Ely Cathedral

Chapter House The College Ely Cambridgeshire CB7 4DL

Tel: 01353 667735 Fax: 01353 665658

[A10. Limited on site parking]

The octagon tower of Ely Cathedral can be seen for miles as it rises above the surrounding flat fenland. The magnificent cathedral was founded by St Etheldreda in 673 but the present church is now mostly 12th century.

Summer Mon-Sat 07.00-19.00, Winter Mon-Sat 07.30-18.00, Sun 07.30-17.00

A£4.80 C£Free Concessions£4.20

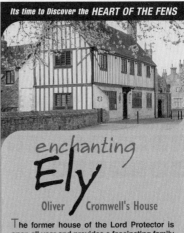

Peterborough Cathedral

Minster Precincts Peterborough Cambridgeshire
PE1 1XS

Tel: 01733 343342 Fax: 01733 552465

www.peterborough-cathedral.org.uk

*[A1, on the J with A605 / A47, follow City Centre
signs]*

Visit Peterborough Cathedral - "an undiscovered
gem" - one of the finest Norman buildings in
England. Magnificent West Front, unique
medieval painted ceiling, fine fan vaulting, burial
place of two queens and much more. Excellent
visitors exhibition in the Cathedral; guided tours
available to book in advance. The Cathedral's
Beckets Restaurant, Gift and Book Shop and
the City Tourist Information Centre are all in the
Minster Precincts.

*All year Mon-Fri 09.00-17.15, Sat 09.00-16.45 &
Sun 12.00-16.45*

Donations are politely requested, A£3.00
Concessions£2.00 suggested

Exhibition & Visitor Centres

Eric Young Orchid Foundation

La Rue du Moulin du Ponterrin Trinity Jersey Channel Islands JE3 5HH

Tel: 01534 861963 Fax: 01534 863293

www.ericyoungorchidfoundation.co.uk

[From St Helier ring road, choose A7 or A8 and follow signs to Victoria Village and then specific signs to Orchid Foundation. Plenty of on site parking available]

Since mankind first became fascinated by beautiful things, orchids have exerted a potent allure for the 'Royal Family of Plants', comprising more than 20,000 species. They achieve a diversity of beauty, colour and form that is an expression of nature's genius to dazzle and enthral. One of the finest collections of orchids in the world is to be found at the Eric Young Orchid Foundation, housed in a purpose-built nursery and exhibition complex - a visual enchantment and a unique experience.

All year Wed-Sat 10.00-16.00

A£2.50 C£1.00 OAPs/Students£1.50

Festivals & Shows

Early Summer Rose and Flower Festival

Various venues Jersey Channel Islands
Tel: 01534 500723 Fax: 01534 500899
The Jersey Rosarians and the Royal Jersey Horticultural Society join together to celebrate all things floral with a full programme of displays, demonstrations, open gardens and environmental walks and talks.
June 10-13 2004
Prices vary according to event attended

Jersey Battle of Flowers and Moonlight Parade

Meadow Bank St. Lawrence Jersey Channel Islands JE3 1EE
Tel: 01534 639000 Fax: 01534 768985
An internationally renowned parade traditionally held on the second Thursday of August. The Battle features dozens of flower-festooned floats, musicians, dancers and carnival queens providing a tremendous holiday spectacle for the thousands of visitors to the Island each year. The Moonlight Parade sees many of the previous days exhibits illuminated and following the same course as the main Battle of Flowers Parade along Victoria Avenue. There is also a fireworks display.
August 12-13 2004, Thur from 12.30, Fri 19.30
Day Parade: £18.00 or £14.00. Night Parade: £18.00. Combined Day & Night Ticket: £28.00 or £32.00

Jersey Festival of Motoring

Jersey Channel Islands
Tel: 01534 863424 Fax: 01534 863424
Seafront sprints, concours, cavalcades, closed-road hill climbs and static displays give participants and spectators the opportunity to come together in an extravaganza of motoring from yesterday - look out for vintage Lagondas, Porsches, Lotus, Austins, Aston Martin, Bentleys and Sunbeams.
June 4-6 2004
Call 01534 863424 for details

Jersey International Choir Festival

Jersey Channel Islands
Tel: 01534 864014 Fax: 01534 862667
Visiting choirs from Europe and beyond participate in numerous concerts and competitions
throughout the Festival. In addition, it is hoped
to incorporate a Male Voice Choir Surgery
which will comprise of workshops by numerous
experts specifically aimed at male voice choirs.
The Senior Youth Orchestra of the Prague
Conservatoire will be in attendance throughout
the Festival.
October 7-10 2004
Please call for further details

Jersey Revels

Various venues Jersey Channel Islands JE1
In 2004 Jersey celebrates 800 years of alle-
giance to the Crown. Mount Orgueil Castle will
be the focal point for celebrations extending on
to the Castle Green, pier and main coast road.
Professional re-enactors will perform. The highlights will include demonstrations of medieval
crafts, a siege of the Castle, jousting on the
Green, falconry, medieval market and ships in
the harbour. An event unparalleled in Jersey,
engaging the whole community.
June 25-27 2004

La Fete de Noue (Christmas Festival)

Jersey Channel Islands
Tel: 01534 500700 Fax: 01534 500899
Help celebrate the run up to the festive season
with a number of activities arranged, including
late night shopping, in-store activities, traditional
craft market, al fresco street entertainment and
horse-drawn carriage rides.
November 27-December 5 2004
Admission Free

Spring Country Fayre

Jersey Channel Islands JE1
Come along to this traditional country fayre with
its full entertainment programme for all the family. Activities include cattle shows, a country craft
show, ring events, food tasting and traditional
country games.
May 29-31 2004

Spring Garden Festival

Jersey Channel Islands
Tel: 01534 500700 Fax: 01534 500899
Come and experience the magic of springtime
in Jersey with a series of guided environmental
walks such as the Dawn Chorus Walk, and
open gardens in the company of some of the
UK's top gardening experts. The week starts off
with the Royal Jersey's Horticultural Society's
wonderful spring show.
March 26 - April 4 2004
Admission Free

Spring Walking Week

Jersey Channel Islands
Tel: 01534 500700 Fax: 01534 500899
Watch Jersey's history and heritage unfold
through a week of escorted walks including the
unique 'Around Island' walk, 'Moon Walks' and
much more. The walks are suitable for all age
groups and abilities.
May 15-22 2004
Please call for further details

Summer Walking Week

Jersey Channel Islands
Tel: 01534 500700 Fax: 01534 500899
Celebrate the summer in Jersey by participating
in a full programme of unique countryside,
coastal and history walks. New for 2004 is the
'Jersey Flag' walk which guides visitors to all
four corners of the Island mirroring our unique

flag and bringing to life our unique 800 year relationship with England.
July 10-11 2004

Time Travellers

La Hougue Bie Museum La Route de la Hougue Bie St Saviour Jersey Channel Islands JE2 7UA
Tel: 01534 633300
Visitors to the Neolithic site of La Hougue Bie will discover the way of life, not only of Neolithic man, but also of his counterparts at other great moments in the life of this ancient monument. Re-enactments of Neolithic man are held at this Heritage Site of Special Interest.
June 1-6 2004
A£4.95 C(0-9)£Free Concessions£4.20

Folk & Local History Museums

Battle of Flowers Museum

La Robeline Le Mont Des Corvees St. Ouen Jersey Channel Islands JE3 2ES
Tel: 01534 482408
[Plenty of on site parking available]
The Battle of the Flowers Museum presents the show of the year. So why not come on safari with us, see a wonderland of animals, meet the zebras, lions and the 101 Dalmations, and lots of other interesting exhibits. Kids will love it here, a great show to suit all ages!
Easter-end Oct daily 10.00-17.00. Closed winter months
A£3.50 C£2.00 OAPs£3.25

Gardens & Horticulture

Jersey Lavender Farm

La Rue du Pont Marquet St. Brelade Jersey Channel Islands JE3 8DS
Tel: 01534 742933 Fax: 01534 745613
[Plenty of parking on site]
Visitors can see the complete process of laven-der production from cultivation through to harvesting and distillation to the bottling, labelling and packaging of the final product. Other herbs are distilled before and after the lavender harvest. There is an explanatory video presentation, a herb garden and plant sales area.
10 May-18 Sept Mon-Sat 10.00-17.00
A£3.10 C(0-14)£Free

Heritage & Industrial

Pallot Steam Museum

Rue de Bechet Trinity Jersey Channel Islands JE3 5BE
Tel: 01534 865307 Fax: 01534 864248
[Turn off the A9/A8. Plenty of on site parking]

Step back in time and enjoy a fascinating collection of steam engines, vintage vehicles and bicycles, tractors, agricultural implements, and other machinery, together with a variety of organs, including a pipe church and Compton theatre organ, housed in this absorbing, recently built Museum. Among the collection are two Marshall steam rollers from 1922 and 1925, a superbly restored 1904 Ransomes traction engine and a rare Merlin portable from 1924. Train rides in Victorian carriages hauled by steam locomotive may be taken on certain days.
Apr-Oct Mon-Sat 10.00-17.00. Closed Sun & Good Fri
A£3.50 C(under5)£Free C(5+)£1.50 OAPs£3.00

Historical

Castle Cornet

Castle Emplacement St. Peter Port Guernsey Channel Islands GY1 1AU
Tel: 01481 721657 Fax: 01481 714021
[Town centre location, 5mins walk from the bus terminal]

This magnificent Castle spans eight centuries and its buildings now house several updated museums, a tea room, shop, and four period gardens. The Maritime Museum traces the history of Guernsey's sea trade routes, The Story of Castle Cornet tells the story of The Castle, the Royal Guernsey Militia Museum and the 201 Squadron Museum offer a unique insight into aspects of military history.

Easter-Sept daily 10.00-17.00. Gift Shop open May-Sept
A£6.00 C£Free OAPs£4.00. Joint Ticket with Fort Grey & Guernsey Museum: A£9.00 C£Free OAPs£5.00. Students in full time education £Free

Sausmarez Manor

St. Martin Guernsey Channel Islands GY4 6SG

Tel: 01481 235571 Fax: 01481 235572

www.guernsey.org/sausmarez

[Venue is signposted. Plenty of on site parking available]

The Manor has been owned by the same family for seven centuries. On the estate there is one of the largest collection of dolls houses in Britain, Guernsey's largest pitch and putt course, a recommended sub tropical wild woodland garden, an Egon Ronay tea room. A children's play area, a copper and silver smiths and one of the most comprehensive sculpture parks in Britain. 2004 celebrates 750 years of the Family's connection with the House and the 290th Anniversary of the death of the 1st Governor of New York who owned the property for some time. He was also Governor of nine of the original states.

House: Easter-May, Sept & Oct 10.30 & 11.30, June-Aug 10.30, 11.30 & 14.00. Dolls Houses,

Pitch & Putt Gardens & Sculpture Park: Easter-Oct check for details in winter months

A£5.00 C£3.00 OAPs£3.50. Group rates available

Discount Offer: Two For The Price Of One. In Sculpture Park And Woodland Garden

Military & Defence Museums

Channel Island Military Museum

La Grande Route des Mielles St Ouen Jersey Channel Islands JE3 2FN
Tel: 01534 723136
[At Northern end of the 5m road directly behind the Jersey Woollem Mills and opposite Jersey Pearl]

The Museum is housed in a former German bunker and contains the best collection of German, British and Civilian occupation items. This is a fascinating insight into the long gone dark distant days of German rule. On display visitors will see an Enigma decoding machine as well as military motorcycles and many civilian items made at the time.

5 Apr-31 Oct daily 10.00-17.00
A£3.00 C£1.00. Group rates available, please call for details

Science - Earth & Planetary

Treasures of the Earth

La Route De L'etacq St. Ouen Jersey Channel Islands JE3 2FD

Tel: 01534 484811 Fax: 01534 483394

An exhibition of a beautiful and bizarre collection of gems, rocks, fossils and minerals. There is a workshop, cutting gemstones, goldsmiths, shop and Art Gallery.

Mar-Nov daily 09.30-17.00. Closed Dec, Jan & Feb

A£3.00 C£1.75 OAPs£2.50

Zoos

Jersey Zoological Park - Durrell Wildlife Conservation Trust

La Profonde Rue Trinity Jersey Channel Islands JE3 5BP

Tel: 01534 860000 Fax: 01534 860001

[Signposted 4m N of St Helier]

Jersey Zoo offers visitors an extraordinary experience. Green open spaces, free-living animals and an exciting programme of visitor activities encourage the discovery of how this world leader in wildlife conservation is helping to save animals from extinction. First Impressions, an exciting multi-species habitat, provides visitors with a dramatic first impression of wildlife conservation at work.

All year daily 9.30-18.00 in summer, 9.30-17.00 in winter. Closed 25 Dec

A£9.95 C(4-16)£7.25 OAPs£8.35 Students(17-22)£8.35

Cheshire

Arts, Crafts & Textiles

Blakemere Craft Centre

Chester Road Sandiway Northwich Cheshire
CW8 2EB
Tel: 01606 883261 Fax: 01606 301495
[R on J of A49 / A556]

Set in Cheshire's countryside, Blakemeres' 30
craft shops offer individually handcrafted items
within an Edwardian Stable Block. Visit our
weekend craft fayre with 12 stalls or our
Children's Playbarn, Aquatic and Falconry
Centre plus large Garden Centre.
*All year Tue-Fri 10.00-17.00, Sat-Sun 10.00-
17.50. Closed Mon except Bank Hols*
Admission Free

Costume & Jewellery Museums

**Hat Works - The Museum of
Hatting, Stockport**

Wellington Mill Wellington Road South

Stockport Cheshire SK3 0EU

Tel: 0161 355 7770 Fax: 0161 480 8735

www.hatworks.org.uk

*[Wellington Mill's landmark chimney is highly visible
from all the main routes into Stockport and is
located on the main throughfare, the A6
Wellington Road South. It is opposite the bus station, close to the railway station, only 2mins walk
away from Merseyway Shopping Centre and
other town centre shops. Parking: A range of
inexpensive parking facilities are available in and
around Stockport town centre. The nearest car
parks are: Heaton Lane, Mersey Way and Grand
Central]*

The UK's first and only museum dedicated to
the exciting world of hats and hat making.
Learn about Stockport's historic links with hatting and how the industry flourished employing
over 4,500 people by the end of the 19th century. Take a step back in time to Hope Street
with a glimpse into a Hatter's Cottage, marvel at
the machines restored to full working order -
giving a noisy and thrilling encounter with the
town's industrial past. Interactive demonstrations reveal the art and mystery of hat making.
The stunning display of hats from the early
1800s to modern day. There's so much to see
and do, it is simply brimming over! Educational
Sessions: linked to Key Stages 1 & 2 with a
dedicated Education Suite, details available
upon request. The Level 2 Internet Café is open
to all, visitor to the museum or not! Relax in styl-
ish surroundings and choose from a range of
coffees, pastries or light lunches.

*All year daily Mon-Sat 10.00-17.00, Sun 11.00-
17.00. Closed 25-26 Dec & 1 Jan*

A£3.95 C£2.50 Concessions£2.50 Family
Ticket (A2+C2) £11.00. Group discounts available, please call for details

**Discount Offer: Two For the Price of
One. Not Valid For Special Events**

Special Events

Easster Egg Painting and Bonnet Making
05/04/2004-16/04/2004

Country Parks & Estates

Tatton Park

Knutsford Cheshire WA16 6QN

Tel: 01625 534400 / 534435 info

Fax: 01625 534403

www.tattonpark.org.uk

[2m NE of Knutsford, 12m S of Manchester city centre, grid ref. SJ 755810. Tatton Park is signposted on and from the M6 J19, and M56 J7. Signposted on and from the A556 and A50. Plenty of on site parking. Rail: Knutsford or Altrincham station, then Taxi. Temporary helicopter landing facilities can be arranged, grid ref SJ 6747816]

Magnificent grounds, superb gardens, lakes, a Tudor Old Hall and a Neo-classical Mansion make Tatton Park one of England's finest country estates. Visit the gardens with 50 acres of exotic trees and plants from all over the world; the Mansion with its collection of treasurers; the Tudor Old Hall where you are guided through the smoky shadows of the 16th century through time or see the rare breeds of animals at the Home Farm. Garden, Gift and Speciality Food Shops offer a variety of estate and local produce and gift wear. Special events most weekends including the Hallé Firework concert and the RHS Flower Show (Park entry fee applies). Managed and financed by Cheshire County Council.

High Season: Apr-Sept, Park & Restaurant daily, Attractions Tue-Sun, Tudor Old Hall Sat. Low Season: Oct-Mar, Park & Gardens Tue-Sun only, Farm Sat-Sun. Please call for details of specific opening times

Mansion, Gardens, Tudor Old Hall or Farm: A£3.00 C(4-15)£2.00 Family Ticket (A2+C3) £8.00, Group rates (12+): A£2.40 C£1.60. Discovery Saver Ticket (valid for one visit to any two attractions excl. car charge): A£4.60 C£2.60 Family Ticket £12.80, Group rates: A£3.80 C£2.10. Car Entry to Park: £3.90

Festivals & Shows

Bawming of the Thorn

Appleton Thorn Village Hall Appleton Thorn Warrington Cheshire WA4 4RW
Tel: 01925 266764 Fax: 01925 861737
[M6, follow signs to Thorn Cross]

The Thorn was planted by Adam de Dutton, a Crusader in the 12th century. Bawming or decorating a tree was once widespread but now only Appleton Thorn holds this ceremony. Procession starts at 12.45 from Appleton Thorn Village Hall. Bawming ceremony at the tree in the centre of the village. Dance and song, school fete, sing "Bawming Song" parade, rides, games and afternoon teas. Culminates in a barbecue, bring your own meat, bread and salad provided.
June 19 2004
Admission Free

Knutsford Royal May Day

Knutsford Cheshire WA16 6TA
Tel: 01270 500534
[J19 off M6 - follow signs for the town centre. Activities take place on the Heath with limited parking on site. Further parking available in the Town Cente]

Royal May Day in Knutsford is an annual event which dates back to 1864. The modern day festivals still recreate the customs upon which it is based, including unique traditions such as 'sanding' the streets. May Day in Knutsford earned its 'Royal' title in 1887 courtesy of the then Prince and Princess of Wales and today attracts thousands of visitors every year. The procession of children, bands, Morris dancers and decorated horses proceeds round the town to the heath where the May Queen is crowned. This a traditional event attended by local dignitaries and old characters.

May 1 2004
Admission Free

Middlewich Folk and Boat Festival 2004

Market Field and Middlewich Town Middlewich Cheshire
Tel: 01606 836896 after 18.00
[2m from M6 J18]

The 14th Middlewich Folk and Boat Festival has 15 fringe venues and a mainstage marquee offering a huge variety of musical events in and around the town centre. International stars of stage and screen perform alongside some of the best musicians, singers and dancers in the UK. Not just a 'folk' festival but a unique community experience. Free canal boat rally and children's entertainment.

June 18-20 2004, Fri 22.00-1.00 Sat and Sun 10.00-23.30

Most events free. Main stage weekend ticket prices have yet to be confirmed

Folk & Local History Museums

Stockport Museum

Vernon Park Turncroft Lane Stockport Cheshire SK1 4AR

Tel: 0161 474 4460 Fax: 0161 474 4449

[1m from town centre - follow signposts]

Displays on the history of Stockport from Pre-historic times to the present, and the Green

Gallery - a display on the local environment. "Hidden Treasures" in the basement.

Apr-Oct daily 13.00-17.00, Nov-Mar Sat & Sun only 13.00-16.00

Admission Free

Warrington Museum and Art Gallery

Museum Street Warrington Cheshire WA1 1JB

Tel: 01925 442733 Fax: 01925 443257

[Near shopping centre]

Collections of Egyptology, ethnology, geology, archaeology and natural history. Temporary exhibitions on local history. Art galleries present special exhibitions programme. The museum also houses a selection of the town's fine collection of oil paintings and watercolours.

All year Mon-Fri 10.00-17.00, Sat 10.00-16.30. Closed Bank Hols

Admission Free

Gardens & Horticulture

Cholmondeley Castle Garden

Cholmondeley Malpas Cheshire SY14 8AH

Tel: 01829 720383 Fax: 01829 720877

www.cholmondeleycastle.co.uk

[Off A49 Whitchurch / Tarporley road. Rail: Crewe. Plenty of on site parking]

Extensive ornamental gardens dominated by a romantic Gothic Castle, built in 1801 of local sandstone. Beautiful Temple water garden, rose garden and many mixed borders. Lakeside picnic area, children's play areas, rare breeds of farm animals including Llamas, children's corner with rabbits, chickens and free flying aviary birds. Ancient private Chapel in the park. Gift shop and tea room. Plants for sale. Castle not open to the public except for groups by prior arrangement.

4 Apr-26 Sept, Wed, Thurs, Sun & Bank Hols 11.30-17.00. Open Good Fri, Easter Sun & Easter Mon. Also open for Autumn Tints on some Sun in Oct, please call for details

A£3.50 C£1.50. Group rates (25+): A£3.00 C£1.00

Special Events

Classic Car Rally
09/05/2004

Stately Car Boot Sale
23/05/2004

Jazz in the Temple Garden
31/05/2004

National Garden Scheme
07/07/2004

Rare Plant Fair
11/07/2004

Firework Concert Spectacular
17/07/2004

Rain or Shine Theatre Company
13/08/2004

Jazz in the Temple Garden
30/08/2004

Classic Car Rally
05/09/2004

Norton Priory Museum and Gardens

Tudor Road Manor Park Runcorn Cheshire WA7 1SX

Tel: 01928 569895

www.nortonpriory.org

[M56 J11 turn for Warrington follow Norton Priory signs. From all other directions follow the 'all other' Runcorn traffic then for Norton Priory. Plenty of on site parking available]

38 acres of peaceful woodland include a beautiful, award-winning Walled Garden, remains of a medieval priory, a museum to tell the story of the site, plus much more. National Collection of Cydonia Oblonga. The 600 year old statue of St Christopher returned in 1999. Please phone or visit our website for up-to-date information prior to visit.

Apr-Oct Mon-Fri 12.00-17.00, Weekends & Bank Hol 12.00-18.00, Nov-Mar daily 12.00-16.00. Closed 24-26 Dec & 1 Jan

A£4.25 C(under5)£Free Concessions£2.95 Family Ticket (A2+C3) £10.00. Group discount available

Discount Offer: Two For The Price Of One Full Paying Adult.

Stapeley Water Gardens

London Road Stapeley Nantwich Cheshire
CW5 7LH
Tel: 01270 628628 Fax: 01270 624188
[J16 M6 1m S of Nantwich on A51 to Stone follow brown tourist signs]

There is something for everyone at the World's largest water garden centre. Display gardens and pools with the National Collection of water lilies in bloom during the summer. The Palms Tropical Oasis is a huge glasshouse home to tropical plants, fish, birds and animals.
Summer (Mid Mar-Mid Sept): Garden & Angling Centres: Mon-Sat 09.00-18.00, Wed open until 20.00. Bank Hol 10.00-18.00, Sun 10.00-16.00, Palms Tropical Oasis: daily 10.00-18.00. Winter: Garden & Angling Centres: Mon-Sat 09.00-17.00, (Angling Centre: Wed open till 20.00), Bank Hol 10.00-17.00, Sun 10.00-16.00. Palms Tropical Oasis: daily 10.00-17.00. Closed 25 Dec except for booked lunches. Garden & Angling Centres also closed Easter Sunday.
The Palms Tropical Oasis: A£4.35 C£2.50
OAPs£3.90

Historical

Adlington Hall

Mill Lane Adlington Macclesfield Cheshire
SK10 4LF

Tel: 01625 820875 Fax: 01625 828756

www.adlingtonhall.com

[5m N of Macclesfield on the Stockport / Macclesfield road (A523). Rail: Adlington 0.5m, Macclesfield and Wilmslow both 5m. Plenty of on site parking available]

The Cheshire Manor home of the Leghs since 1315. The Great Hall was built between 1450 and 1505, the Elizabethan 'Black and White' in 1581 and the Georgian South Front in 1757. An organ (played by Handel) was installed in 1670. Follies include a Chinese bridge, Temple to Diana, T'ing House and Shell Cottage. Garden features include a maze, rose garden, Father Tiber water garden and penstemon garden. Disabled access limited, please call for details.

All year Mon-Fri to groups by prior arrangement. Public opening June-Aug 2004 Wed 14.00-17.00

A£5.00 C£2.00. Group rates (20+) £4.00

Discount Offer: One Child Free With Two Full Paying Adults

Special Events

Nurseryman's Plant Fair
09/05/2004
Time: 10.30-16.30. Tickets: Plant Fair A£2.50 C(under16)£Free, House A£2.50 C£2.00

National Gardens Scheme
13/06/2004
Time: 13.30-17.00. Tickets: Garden A£3.00 C£0.50, House A£2.00 C£1.00

Charity Open Day
18/07/2004
Time: 13.30-17.00. Tickets: Garden A£2.50 C£0.50, House A£2.50 C£1.00

Garden open in aid of the Red Cross
15/08/2004
Time: 13.30-17.00. Tickets: Garden A£2.50 C£0.50, House A£2.50 C£1.00

Arley Hall and Gardens

Arley Nr Great Budworth Northwich Cheshire
CW9 6NA
Tel: 01565 777353 Fax: 01565 777465
[5m N of Northwich, 6m W of Knutsford]

The Hall, built about 1840 is an example of early
Victorian Jacobean style. Private Chapel
designed by Anthony Salvin and fifteenth century cruck barn. Voted one of the top 50 gardens
with beautiful parkland, many unique features,
the double herbaceous border, Ilex columns, a
large variety of plants, exotic trees and shrubs
and over 200 varieties of Rhododendron.
*3 Apr-26 Sept Tue-Sun & Bank Hol Mon 11.00-
17.00, Oct Sat & Sun 11.00-17.00. Hall: Tue &
Sun only 12.00-17.00*
Gardens: A£4.50 C(under 5)£Free C(5-15)£2.00
Family Ticket (A2+C2)£11.25 OAPs£3.90. Hall:
A£2.50 C(under 5)£Free C(5-15)£1.00
OAPs£2.00

Gawsworth Hall

Church Lane Gawsworth Macclesfield Cheshire
SK11 9RN
Tel: 01260 223456 Fax: 01260 223469
*[2.5m S of Macclesfield on A536. Rail:
Macclesfield]*

This fine Tudor black & white manor house was
the birthplace of Mary Fitton (supposedly the
Dark Lady of Shakespeare's sonnets). Pictures
and armour can be seen in the house, which
also has a tilting ground, thought to be a rare
example of an Elizabethan pleasure garden.
*8 Apr-29 Sept Sun-Wed 14.00-17.00, 14 June-
31 July daily 14.00-17.00*
A£5.00 C£2.50

Lyme Park

Lyme Park Disley Stockport Cheshire SK12 2NX

Tel: 01663 762023 / 766492
Fax: 01663 765035
*[On A6, 6.5m SE of Stockport, 17m NW of
Buxton. House & car park 1m from entrance. Rail:
Disley]*

Originally a Tudor house, Lyme was transformed
by the Venetian architect Leoni into an Italianate
palace. Some of the Elizabethan interiors survive and contrast dramatically with later rooms.
The state rooms are adorned with Mortlake
tapestries, Grinling Gibbons wood-carvings and
an important collection of English clocks. 6.8ha
(17 acre) Victorian garden.
*House: 29 Mar-30 Oct Mon-Tue, Fri-Sun 13.00-
17.00. Park: 1 Apr-31 Oct daily 08.00-20.30, 1
Nov-31 Mar daily 08.00-18.00. Garden: 29 Mar-
30 Oct Mon-Tue, Fri-Sun 11.00-17.00 Wed-Thur
13.00-17.00, 1 Nov-18 Dec Sat & Sun 12.00-
15.00. Open Bank Hol Mons*
House & Garden: A£5.80 C£2.90 Family Ticket
£12.50. Garden only: A£2.70 C£1.40. House
only: A£4.20 C£2.10. Park: £3.80 per car

Railways

Brookside Miniature Railway

Brookside Garden Centre Macclesfield Road
Poynton East Cheshire SK12 1BY

Tel: 01625 872919 Fax: 01625 859119

*[Located in Poynton in North East Cheshire along-
side the A523 - Macclesfield road. Plenty of free
parking on site for cars and coaches. Access,
together with all facilities, provided for disabled
visitors]*

Newly extended, the ever popular Brookside
Line is now nearly half a mile long. Attention to
detail and authenticity is amazing. The seven
and quarter inch gauge line takes in gradients
and cuttings, three river bridges and two tunnels - every inch of it is sheer delight. Steam

and diesel engines draw up to 50 passengers at a time round the Garden Centre's landscaped maze of beautiful rockeries, flower beds and winding pathways. The unmissable West Country style Station has three canopied platforms with an assortment of rail artefacts. Catering for all gardeners the Showsite stocks a hugely varied range of plants; also there's a comprehensive Aquatics Centre with giant Koi Carp, a Craft Centre including a Model Shop and a working Pottery where 'hands-on' courses can be arranged.

All year Sat & Sun, Apr-Sept Wed, daily July & Aug 11.00-16.30. Also open most school holidays

Train: A£1.00 C£0.50 C(0-2)£Free

Discount Offer: Two For One. Two People Can Ride For The Price Of One

Roman Era

Dewa Roman Experience

Pierpoint Lane Chester Cheshire CH1 1NL
Tel: 01244 343407 Fax: 01244 343407
[Off Bridge St]

Stroll along reconstructed streets experiencing the sights, sounds and smells of Roman Chester. From this you return to the present day on an extensive archaeology 'dig' where you can discover Roman, Saxon and medieval remains beneath Chester.
All year daily 09.00-17.00, Sun 10.00-17.00. Opening times in winter vary
A£4.25 C£2.50 OAPs£3.75 Family Ticket £12.00

Science - Earth & Planetary

Catalyst: Science Discovery Centre

Mersey Road Widnes Cheshire WA8 0DF
Tel: 0151 420 1121 Fax: 0151 495 2030
[Follow road signs to Widnes (S) and then tourism signs, signposted from J7 M62 and J12 M56]

Discover the science and technology behind the chemical industry with over 100 interactive exhibits. Explore the impact of chemicals in everyday life through scenes from the past, hands-on exhibits and multimedia programmes.
All year Tue-Fri & Bank Hol Mon 10.00-17.00, Sat & Sun 11.00-17.00. Closed 24-26 Dec & 1 Jan
A£4.95 C£3.50 Family Ticket (A2+C2) £14.95 Concessions£3.95

Discount Offer: One Child Free With A Full Paying Adult.

Sealife Centres & Aquariums

Blue Planet Aquarium

Longlooms Road Cheshire Oaks Ellesmere Port Cheshire CH65 9LF

Tel: 0151 357 8800 Fax: 0151 356 7288

www.blueplanetaquarium.com

[J10 M53, signposted. Easy to find from M6 & M56. Plenty of on site parking available]

Blue Planet Aquarium is an experience you'll never forget. A fascinating underwater world of colours and close encounters. A voyage of discovery through rivers and reefs to where our divers hand feed the sharks. Glide through the most spectacular safari and be surrounded by a carnival of Caribbean fish, including one of the largest collections of sharks in Europe!!! Special events held throughout the year, please call 0151 357 8804 for details.

All year daily from 10.00. Please call to check closing times as these may vary. Closed 25 Dec

A£8.95 C(3-15)£6.50 C(under3)£Free Concessions£6.95 Family Ticket (A2+C2) £30.00

Stately Homes

Social History Museums

Bramall Hall

Bramhall Park Bramhall Cheshire SK7 3NX

Tel: 0161 485 3708 Fax: 0161 486 6959

**www.stockport.gov.uk/tourism/bramall/def
ault.asp**

*[4m S of Stockport off the A5102, 10mins from
Stockport town centre. Ample on site parking
available]*

Magical Tudor House set in 70 acres of parkland. House contains 16th century wall paintings, Elizabethan plaster ceilings, Victorian
kitchens and Servants' quarters. Available for
civil marriages and corporate entertaining.
Wheelchair and pushchair access limited to
ground floor only. Photography (but not flash)
permitted.

*Jan-Easter, Weekends and New Years Day
13.00-16.00. Good Fri-30 Sept Mon-Sat 13.00-
17.00, Sun & Bank Hol 11.00-17.00. 1 Oct-31
Dec Tue-Sat 13.00-16.00, Sun 11.00-16.00.
Closed 25 & 26 Dec*

A£3.95 C&OAPs£2.50. Groups call for details

**Discount Offer: Free Adult Or Child
With A Full Paying Adult.**

Stockport Air Raid Shelters

61 Chestergate Stockport Cheshire SK1 1NE

Tel: 0161 474 1940 Fax: 0161 474 1942

www.stockport.gov.uk/Shelters/index.htm

[M60, J1, A6. Rail: Stockport, 10mins]

First-hand experience of daily life in 1940s, war-
torn Britain. A labyrinth of tunnels under part of
the town centre provided shelter - and a way of
life - for Stockport and Manchester families
through the dark days of the Blitz. Take time to
wonder how everyone managed with those
bunks and benches; lights and sounds; toilet
arrangements and Red Cross facilities. Explore
authentic reconstructions in a core area of
sandstone tunnels. Sense the immense network
of structure; the thousands of people; their con-
cern and determination. Audio-experience the
sounds of 1940 - the historical context, the
songs and the reminiscences. Reflect on the
complexities of conflict in the 'Web of War' exhibition. Admire the contributions of Wardens,
WVS and other volunteers, experience the
atmosphere and respect the memories as you
stroll through the tunnels.

*All year daily Mon-Sat 11.00-17.00 Sun 13.00-
17.00. Open Bank Holidays except Christmas
Day, Boxing Day and New Years Day*

A£3.95 C£2.50 Concessions£2.95 Family
Ticket (A2+C2) £11.00

**Discount Offer: Two For The Price Of
One.**

Dunham Massey Hall, Garden and Park

The National Trust Dunham Massey Hall
Altrincham Cheshire WA14 4SJ
Tel: 0161 941 1025 Fax: 0161 929 7508
[3m SW of Altrincham off A56 J19 off M6 J7 off M56]

Three hundred years of history are packed into this friendly country estate but it's still very much alive today. Tour the house on your own and talk to the knowledgeable stewards, or join a guided tour. The beautiful garden is one of the finest in the north-west, with highlights all through the year.

Park, Restaurant and shop: all year daily. House and Garden: 27 Mar-3 Nov. House: Sat-Wed 12.00-17.00 (11.00-17.00 Bank Hol Sun & Mon, also Good Fri). Garden: Open Daily, 11.00-17.30

House & Garden: A£6.00 C£3.00 Family Ticket £15.00. House or Garden: A£4.00 C£2.00

Discount Offer: Up To Three Children Free When Accompanied By Two Full Paying Adults.

Theme & Adventure Parks

Gullivers World

Warrington Cheshire WA5 9YZ

**Tel: 01925 444888 / 230088
Fax: 01925 637354**

[M62, J9 - signposted]

From the very first time you arrive at Gulliver's you will be entering into another world. Unlike most Theme Parks, Gulliver's World is built within a beautiful parkland setting, where much of the fantasy is created by the centuries old trees and beautiful lake which makes up the centre-piece of the park.
Please call for varied opening times.
A/C£9.30 (includes all rides and attractions)
C(under90cm)£Free OAPs£8.30

Transport Museums

Griffin Trust

The Hangars South Road Hooton Park Airfield
Ellesmere Port Cheshire CH65 1BQ
Tel: 0151 327 4701 Fax: 0151 327 4701
[J6 M53 Eastham Oil Terminal exit, near the Vauxhall Car Factory]

This historic site was one home to many aircraft and airmen during its life both as a civil and operational RAF aerodrome. It is now the intention of the Griffin Trust to help the Hooton Park Trust restore the buildings and surrounding area to their original glory, and to create a living record of the past, combining aeronautical aspects with a related display of road transport.
Open by appointment for groups only
A£2.50 C(6-14)£1.50

Mouldsworth Motor Museum

Smithy Lane Mouldsworth Chester Cheshire
CH3 8AR

Tel: 01928 731781
[6m E of Chester off B5393, close to Delamere Forest and Oulton Park Racing Circuit]

Housed in a large Art Deco building close to Delamere Forest, a collection of over 60 motor cars, motorcycles and early bicycles. We also have a fantastic teapot collection. Plenty of activities for children, plus new quiz with prizes.

Feb-end Nov Sun 12.00-17.00, all Bank Hol weekends, July & Aug Wed 13.00-17.00
A£3.00 C£1.50

Zoos

Chester Zoo

Upton-by-Chester Chester Cheshire CH2 1LH

Tel: 01244 380280 Fax: 01244 371273

www.chesterzoo.org

[On the A41 2m N of Chester. Plenty of free on site parking, with car and coach parking available]

Chester Zoo - Always New! New Tsavo Rhino Experience. Spirit of the Jaguar. Two young elephants - Po Chin and Assam. Spectacled bears and miniature monkeys. Twilight Zone Bat Cave, Islands in Danger. Great Gardens. It takes at least five hours to see everything!

All year daily from 10.00. Closed Christmas Day

A£12.00 C(3-15)£9.50 OAPs£9.50 Family Ticket (A2+C2) £39.00. Discounts available for groups of 15+

Cleveland

Agriculture / Working Farms

Newham Grange Leisure Farm

Wykeham Way Coulby Newham Middlesbrough Cleveland TS8 0TG
Tel: 01642 515729 / 300202
Fax: 01642 300276
[A19, A174 Parkway, B1365 to Coulby Newham then signposted]

Newham Grange Leisure Farm is a working farm which is open to the public. It is a recognised Rare Breeds Survival Trust centre with pigs, cattle, sheep, poultry and ponies, café, picnic area, play area and museums.
All year Mar-Sept daily 09.30-17.30, Oct-Feb Sat & Sun only 10.00-16.00
A£2.15 C&OAPs£1.35 Family Ticket £5.90

Discount Offer: One Child Free When Accompanied By A Full Paying Adult. (Not OAP)

Arts, Crafts & Textiles

Billingham Art Gallery

Queensway Billingham Stockton-On-Tees Tees Valley TS23 2LN
Tel: 01642 397590 Fax: 01642 397594
Billingham Art Gallery welcomes local, national and international arts and crafts people, to exhibit their work. From craft to displays of modern art, the gallery offers a varied programme of exhibitions, workshops and crafts fairs to suit everyone.
Mon-Fri 09.00-17.00, Sat 09.00-13.00 & 13.30-17.00, during exhibitions closed Sun and Bank Hols
Admission Free

Festivals & Shows

Billingham International Folklore Festival

Town Centre Billingham Cleveland
Tel: 01642 552663
[A1 (M) for A178 / A19 Teesside and continue to Billingham. Rail: Billingham]

Folklore troupes from across the globe, normally perform in local theatres in the evenings and custom-built 1400 seat outdoor venue for daytime. Culminates with fireworks.
August 7-14 2004
Tickets at various prices available from the Box Office 01642 552663

Hartlepool Horticultural Show

Borough Hall Middlegate Headland Hartlepool Cleveland TS24 0JN
Tel: 01429 266269 Fax: 01429 523477
One of the most popular firework displays in the area. Children's funfair rides/stalls from 16.00, entertainment from 17.00 and the display begins at 18.30. Park & Ride shuttle service available, call for details.
November 6 2004
Admission Free

Hartlepool Maritime Festival 2004

Hartlepool Marina and Historic Quay Hartlepool Cleveland
Tel: 01429 523420 Fax: 01429 523477
[A19: A179 from North A689 from South]

The Hartlepool Maritime Festival will be held on the weekend of 3 and 4 July and will be set against the background of the Marina and the Hartlepool Historic Quay. There will be a programme of maritime themed activities including street theatre, music, re-enactments, water sports, crafts, French market, international cuisine and much, much more.
July 3-4 2004, Sat 12.00-20.00 Sun 12.00-18.00
Admission Free

Hartlepool Music and Arts Festival

Hartlepool Town Hall Theatre Raby Road Hartlepool Cleveland TS24 8AH
Tel: 01429 860663 / 890000
Fax: 01429 864370
HMAF gives the opportunity for amateurs to form an appreciation of artistic standards. It allows the competitors to perform before a different type of audience, and in the near future the opportunity to partake in workshops and master classes and to be assessed, encouraged and inspired by active professionals they would not meet in any other way.
Session Heats: May 7-15 2004. Final: June 12 2004 19.00
Session Heats: (Competitors) £5.00 one entry, £3.00 for any subsequent entry and £2.50 duets (Non-competitors) £3.00
Concessions£2.00. Final: £6.00
Concessions£4.00

Middlesbrough Mela

Albert Park off Linthorpe Road Middlesbrough Cleveland TS5 6HF
Tel: 01642 729138 Fax: 01642 729978
[Follow the AA Mela Car Park signs to direct you to Clairville Common, next to Albert Park]

This year Middlesbrough celebrates its 14th Mela with an exciting programme of performers. Contributing to the unique atmosphere will be fashion, craft and of course food stalls, plus children's entertainment. The Middlesbrough Mela is a blend of popular Asian art forms and activities, concentrating on popular and folk music, dance, eating and entertainment, the fusion of Eastern and Western culture. It's a celebration of the area's cultural diversity in which everyone can share and to which everybody is invited.
July 18 2004
Admission Free

Middlesbrough Music Live

Various venues Middlesbrough Cleveland
Tel: 01642 729138 Fax: 01642 729978
Middlesbrough town centre will once again come alive to the sounds of music of national, regional and local importance. Stages throughout the town with live music and street entertainment on every corner.
May 31 2004
Admission Free

North East Modelling Society - Scale Model Open

Borough Hall Middlegate Headland Hartlepool Cleveland TS24 0JN
Tel: 01429 266269 Fax: 01429 523477
[At Hartlepool Headland 3m from town centre Bus: 5 / 7 / 12. Free car parking]

National event for scale modellers. Over 35 competition classes including aircraft, figures, vehicles and sci-fi with trophies awarded. There will also be a club display and modelling area, war gaming, trade stands and refreshments.
July 10-11 2004, 10.00-16.00
A£1.00 Concessions£0.50

Summer Brass Band Concert Season

Hartlepool Cleveland TS24
Tel: 01429 523420 Fax: 01429 523477
Summer Brass Band Concert of traditional and new music set against the background of either Ward Jackson Park or the Quayside at the Museum of Hartlepool.
Ward Jackson Park: July 18, August 1 & 15 2004. The Quayside: July 25, August 8 & 29 2004
Admission Free

Folk & Local History Museums

Kirkleatham Museum

Kirkleatham Redcar Cleveland TS10 5NW
Tel: 01642 479500 Fax: 01642 474199
Today Kirkleatham Museum is the ideal place
for a grand day out for the whole family. Mum,
Dad, Grandma and Grandad will be fascinated
by local history, WWII memorabilia and the vari-
ety of displays and artefacts. The children will
love the playground, owl centre and the picnic
area.
*All year Apr-Sept Tue-Sun 10.00-17.00, Oct-Mar
Tue-Sun 10.00-16.00. Closed 25 Dec-1 Jan*
Admission Free

Heritage & Industrial

Margrove South Cleveland Heritage Centre

Margrove Park Boosbeck Saltburn-by-the-Sea
Cleveland TS12 3BZ
Tel: 01287 610368 Fax: 01287 610368
[Off the A171 Guisborough to Whitby Road]

This award winning centre on the edge of the
North Yorkshire National Park promotes the
upland, valley and coastal landscapes of South
Cleveland, charting humans' impact on the
environment.
Apr-Sept Wed-Sun 10.00-17.00
Admission Free

Historical

Captain Cook Birthplace Museum

Stewart Park Marton Middlesbrough Cleveland
TS7 6AS
Tel: 01642 515658 Fax: 01642 317419
[3M S on A172 at Stewart Park, Marton]

Discover why Captain Cook is the world's most
famous explorer with a unique insight into his
early life, seafaring career and legacy of his voy-
ages. Experience life below decks for a sailor of
the 18th century. Audio-visual presentations,
hands-on, interactive displays and original
objects. Interesting and fun for all ages.

*All year, Mar-Oct Tue-Sun 10.00-17.30, Nov-Feb
Tue-Sun 09.00-16.00. Closed 25-26 Dec & 1
Jan*

A£2.40 Concessions£1.20 Family Ticket £6.00

Maritime

H M Bark Endeavour

Castlegate Quay Watersports Centre Moat
Street Stockton-On-Tees Cleveland TS18 3AZ

Tel: 01642 676844 Fax: 01642 607171

[Off A66 moored in Castlegate Quay]

At Castlegate Quay there is a splendid reconstruction of Captain Cook's H M Bark
Endeavour, the first ship to travel on a voyage of
discovery to the South Pacific under Captain
Cook's command. Guided tours provide a fascinating insight into life at sea in Captain Cook's
time. Tours last approx. 45 mins. The ship, or
part of the ship, can be hired out for private
events.

*Easter-Nov Mon-Wed 11.00-17.00. Open other
times by appointment*

A£3.00 C£2.00 Concessions £2.50

HMS Trincomalee

Jackson Dock Hartlepool Cleveland TS24 OSQ

Tel: 01429 223193 Fax: 01429 864385

www.hms-trincomalee.co.uk

[Follow brown heritage signs A689 & A19 A1M. Plenty of on site parking available]

HMS Trincomalee, built in 1817, is the oldest ship afloat in the UK and the only surviving example of a commissioned frigate of the Nelson era. The ship is open throughout the year for tours at Hartlepool Historic Quay. The vessel has been skilfully restored in an award-winning project and visitors can now experience life on board the warship nearly two centuries ago. An audio guide system is available and in addition two platform lifts have been installed that assist visitors to explore the three main decks of the vessel. The ship is a popular attraction for families and groups as well as those with a specific maritime interest, and the tour takes about 75 minutes and is suitable for all. In addition to the tours, HMS Trincomalee is often used for filming historical scenes and re-enactments, and is also a superb and popular venue for weddings and functions.

All year daily, Summer from 10.30, Winter from 11.00. Closed Christmas, Boxing Day and New Year's Day

A£4.25 C&Concessions£3.25 Family Ticket (A2+C3) £11.75. Groups 20+ 20% discount. Education groups £1.70

RNLI Zetland Museum

5 King Street Esplanade Redcar Cleveland TS10 3AH
Tel: 01642 494311
[A19 travelling N & S - take A174 to Kirkleatham then A1042 to A1085. Museum is situated on Redcar Esplanade on A1085. Rail: Redcar]

The museum portrays the lifeboat maritime, fishing and local history of the area. The main exhibit is the 'The Zetland' - the oldest lifeboat in the world dating from 1802. There is also a replica of a fisherman's cottage c1900 and almost 2000 other exhibits.
May-Sept Mon-Fri 11.00-16.00, Sat & Sun 12.00-16.00
Admission Free

Nature & Conservation Parks

Nature's World

Ladgate Lane Acklam Middlesbrough Cleveland TS5 7YN
Tel: 01642 594895 Fax: 01642 591224
[Follow Brown tourist signs from A19 onto A174]

Unique environmental attraction featuring a 400 metre working model of the River Tees. Also over 20 acres of organic demonstration gardens, ponds and wildlife areas. 2002 saw the opening of the Ecostructure and Tropical Hydroponicum. Livestock corner and exhibition hall. Tearooms, shop and plant sales areas.
Apr-Sept Mon-Sat 10.00-17.00, Sun 10.00-

18.00. Oct-Mar daily 11.00-15.00
A£4.00 C£2.00 Family Ticket £10.00
Concessions£3.00

Discount Offer: One Child Free When Accompanied By A Full Paying Adult

Railways

Saltburn Cliff Lift

Lower Promenade Saltburn-By-The-Sea
Cleveland TS12 1QX
Tel: 01287 622528
[Take the A174 through Saltburn down the steep bank and turn L into the car park. The lift is opposite the pier]

Opened on 28th June 1884, today it is the oldest remaining waterblance cliff lift in Britain linking Saltburn pier with the town. In 1998 the lift had its main winding wheel replaced for the first time in its 166 year history, as well as the installation of a new hydraulic system. The journey takes approximately 55 seconds!
10 Apr-23 May Sat & Sun 10.00-17.00, 29 May-12 Sept daily 10.00-19.00, 13 Sept-31 Oct Sat & Sun 10.00-17.00
A&C(over5)£0.60 C(under5)£Free OAPs£0.30
Pram £0.25

Science - Earth & Planetary

Dorman Museum

Linthorpe Road Middlesbrough TS5 6LA
Tel: 01642 813781 Fax: 01642 358100
The Dorman Museum houses a huge collection of items from the fantastic to the ordinary, from natural history and geology to social history and Victorian arts and craft. Interesting and fun for all ages and abilities. With five new galleries, there's something for everyone including plenty of hands-on activities, objects and children's trails. Try your hand at experiments involving water, creating a pot, or identifying Linthorpe pottery.
All year Tue-Sun 10.00-17.30. Closed 25-26 Dec & 1 Jan. Please call for details of Bank Hol opening

Admission Free

Sport & Recreation

Albert Park Visitor Centre

Linthorpe Middlesbrough Cleveland TS1 3LB
Tel: 01642 829319 Fax: 01642 827563
Boating and fishing lake, extensive ornamental flower beds, rockery area with water features, play area, 4 bowling greens. 10 hard tennis courts, activity area, changing facilities. Also roller rink, boating lake and teenage play area.
Park: all year daily 07.30-dusk. Visitor Centre: 10.00-20.00
Park: Admission Free. Small charge for other activities

Stewart Park

Ladgate Lane Marton-in-Cleveland
Middlesbrough Cleveland TS7 8AR
Tel: 01642 300202 / 515600
Fax: 01642 300276
[A19, A174 Parkway A172 Stokesley road then signposted]

Captain Cooks Birthplace, Stewart Park offers a wide range of facilities including lakes, arboretum, walks, orienteering course, sculpture trail and picnic areas. Pets Corner which house Llamas, pygmy goats, rabbits, guinea pigs, peafowl, ornamental pheasants and poultry.
All year daily 07.30-dusk. Baby changing facilities and cafe facilities not available on Mondays
Admission Free

Cornwall

Animal Attractions

National Seal Sanctuary

Gweek Helston Cornwall TR12 6UG
Tel: 01326 221874 Fax: 01326 221210
[Follow signs to Helston then to Gweek]

Enjoy a privileged peek into the work of
Europe's busiest seal rescue facility - with more
than 40 abandoned pups cared for in a fully-
equipped hospital and spacious outdoor rehabilitation pools. The Otter Sanctuary, housed in
a fabulous woodland setting in the picturesque
Helford estuary, is a spacious, purpose-built
enclosure for a pair of captive-bred Asian short-
clawed otters
*All year daily, Summer 10.00 onwards, please call
for Winter opening times. Closed Christmas Day*
A£7.50 C(4-14)£5.50 OAPs£6.50

Arts, Crafts & Textiles

Barbara Hepworth Museum and Sculpture Garden

Barnoon Hill St. Ives Cornwall TR26 1AD

Tel: 01736 796226 Fax: 01736 794480

www.tate.org.uk

[Barnoon Hill, St Ives town centre close to Trewyn Gardens]

Sculptures in wood, stone and bronze can be
seen in the late Dame Barbara Hepworth's
house, studio and sub-tropical garden, where
she lived and worked from 1949-75.
Photographs, documents and other memorabilia are also exhibited, as are workshops housing
a selection of tools and some unfinished carvings. The Museum is managed by Tate St Ives.

*All year Mar-Oct daily 10.00-17.30, Nov-Feb Tue-
Sun 10.00-16.30. Closed 24-26 Dec*

A£4.25 Concessions£2.25

Falmouth Art Gallery

Municipal Buildings The Moor Falmouth
Cornwall TR11 2RT

Tel: 01326 313863 Fax: 01326 318608

*[In the central square of the town on the upper
floor of the Passmore Edwards Building above the
library]*

The Gallery's art collection is one of the most
important in Cornwall, and features works by
major British artists, including Sir Alfred
Munnings PRA, Dame Laura Knight RA and
Henry Scott Tuke RA. The gallery also houses
the internationally famous painting 'Lady of
Shalott' by John William Waterhouse RA, and
mounts an exciting programme of temporary
exhibitions.

*All year Mon-Sat 10.00-17.00 including spring
and summer bank holidays*

Admission Free

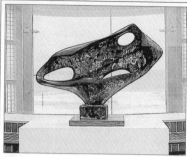

Tate St Ives

Porthmeor Beach St. Ives Cornwall TR26 1TG

Tel: 01736 796226 Fax: 01736 794480

www.tate.org.uk

[Off A30. On foot: the Gallery is within walking distance of St Ives town centre and Porthmeor Beach. Rail: regular train service from London Paddington. Change at St Erth for the branch line to St Ives]

Tate St Ives presents changing displays from the Tate Collection, focusing on the post war modern movement St Ives is famous for. There are also exhibitions of work by contemporary artists. Tate St Ives manages the Barbara Hepworth Museum and Sculpture Garden in St Ives.

All year Nov-Feb Tue-Sun 10.30-16.30, Mar-Oct daily 10.30-17.30. Free gallery talks daily at 14.30

A£4.75 C(under18)&OAPs£Free Concessions£2.50. Joint admission with Barbara Hepworth Museum: A£7.25 Concessions£3.90. Barbara Hepworth Museum only: A£4.50 Concessions£2.25

Special Events

Bernard Leach, Shoji Hamada and Circle
07/02/2004-09/05/2004
Leach travelled to St Ives from Japan with fellow potter Hamada in 1920 to set up the Leach Pottery, which became one of the most celebrated potteries in Britain. This display highlights a selection of works by key figures in the story of the Leach Pottery

Ged Quinn
07/02/2004-09/05/2004
Ged Quinn is the second recipient of the Tate St Ives Artists' Residency Programme based at the
historic Porthmeor Studio. This initiative provides artists with a residency fee and studio space to support the development of their professional practice. Evolving from a spectrum of sources in art history, photographs, memory, newspaper cuttings and books, Quinn's canvases introduce new and universal topics.

Pier Arts Centre Collection
07/02/2004-09/05/2004
Whilst the Pier Arts Centre in Orkney renovates its buildings, Tate St Ives is showing their collection containing particularly fine examples of work by St Ives artists. It was formed by Margaret Gardiner, a close friend and supporter of many of these artists

Karl Weschke: Beneath a Black Sky
07/02/2004-09/05/2004
Celebrating a career that spans over fifty years, this new exhibition, curated by Ben Tufnell, offers an opportunity to see a range of paintings and drawings from the 1950s to the present day. Weschke's work is strongly linked to his immediate environment, where the landscape often becomes a setting for mythic events which dramatise the human condition as a solitary, isolated struggle for survival

Grayson Perry
07/02/2004-09/05/2004
Turner Prize winner Grayson Perry shows a selection of his pots at Tate St Ives, as well as a 'coming out' frock designed by the artist. Perry's work combines the traditions of fine and decorative arts including drawing, embroidery and ceramics, to explore compelling personal and social themes

Mariele Neudecker
22/05/2004-26/09/2004
Mariele Neudecker (b.1965) left Germany in the 1980s and now lived and works in Bristol. She creates landscapes, often evocations of mountain ranges, which are made of fibreglass resin airbrushed with acrylic and placed in glass cases. The essence of her work is an exploration of the territory between reality, imagination, experience and memory, and central to her practice is her interest in German Romanticism

David Nash
22/05/2004-26/09/2004
David Nash (b.1945) has established an international reputation as a sculptor working primarily in wood. He has an interest in ecology and the environment, often utilising fallen or uprooted trees as source material. His sculptures combine the remote, rugged environment of his homeland, North Wales, with the ability to work with the subtle nuances of different woods

Trevor Bell
09/10/2004-09/01/2005

Trevor Bell (b.1930) returned to Cornwall in the 1990s from the United States. His work explores the way the experience of colour and space in painting and that found in the landscape. Although his work does not contain obvious land-scape references, it retains a strong sense of space and atmosphere, emphasised by his use of dramatically shaped canvases

Birds, Butterflies & Bees

Screech Owl Sanctuary

Trewin Farm Nr Indian Queens Goss Moor St Columb Cornwall TR6 6HP
Tel: 01726 860182 Fax: 01726 861545
[From A30, follow A30 until you reach brown signs for Screech Owl Sanctuary. DO NOT follow signs for Indian Queens as we are not in the village]

Visit our centre to see a large collection of owl species from all over the world, and be offered a most unique learning experience in owl con-servation and education. Over 145 birds with 45 different species.
All year daily Mar-end Nov 10.00-18.00, Nov-end Feb 10.00-16.00. Closed 25-26 Dec
A£5.75 C(3-13)£3.95 OAPs£5.25 Family Ticket (A2+C3) £18.00

Discount Offer: One Half Price Entry With This Voucher

Festivals & Shows

Bude Jazz Festival 2004

Bude Cornwall EX23
Tel: 01288 356360 Fax: 01288 356360
[Held at more than 20 venues within Bude. J27 M5, A39 Atlantic Highway between Bideford / Wadebridge. Also A30 Okehampton by-pass via A3072]

200 jazz events in 8 days - all day, every day. 100 bands with leading jazz musicians from all over Britain. 20 different venues hosting jazz events. Four New Orleans style street parades, jazz services. In addition there are some late evening 'Festival Extra' events. Further details available from Bude Visitor Centre, The Crescent, Bude, Cornwall EX23 8LE. Disabled access in most venues, please call for details.
August 28-September 4 2004 12.00-23.30
Stroller tickets for full week £77.50. Gives admission to sessions. Other tickets available

Daphne du Maurier Festival of Arts and Literature 2004

Fowey Cornwall PL23 1AR
Tel: 01726 77477 Box Office
[Fowey and surrounding areas. M5 at Exeter, A38 or A30. Rail: St Austell 9m]

The 8th Daphne du Maurier Festival of Arts and Literature will take place in and around Fowey. The festival is a general arts and literature festi-val, held in memory of Dame Daphne du Maurier, who lived and wrote in the area. Set in Fowey, overlooking the picturesque Fowey Estuary and neighbouring towns, the festival is a sparkling mix of star names, guided walks, talks, drama, community events and free enter-tainment. The combination of professional names and local events make the Daphne du Maurier Festival one of the most popular of its kind in the UK.
May 7-16 2004
Various prices, some venues £Free. Tickets available from Box Office or by post/in person from Daphne du Maurier Literary Centre, 5 South Street, Fowey, Cornwall, PL23 1AR. Or, contact the Box Office at foweytic@visit.org.uk
Festival Information Line (24 hr) 01726 223535

Falmouth Big Green Fair

Falmouth Cornwall
Tel: 01326 377173 Fax: 01326 378587
[Rail: Penmere 1m]

The Big Green Fair is a major community event held in Falmouth on the First Saturday of July. Environmental and Community Groups throughout the county participate in the day's activities which include workshops, stalls, exhibitions, food, fun and entertainment.

July 3 2004

Admission Free if travel by bus, cycle or foot. Full cars free but charges if contain 1-2 people

Fowey Royal Regatta and Carnival

Fowey Cornwall

Tel: 01726 832133

[Fowey. B3269 / A3082 to Fowey. Rail: Par 3m / St Austell 9m. Bus: National Exress St Austell. Hoppa Bus 24 from St Austell]

Includes gig racing, male voice choir, children's entertainment, torchlight procession on river, the Red Arrows and a fireworks carnival. Great fun for all!

August 15-21 2004

Voluntary donation appreciated. C£Free

Gorsedd of Cornwall Annual Assembly of Bards

Truro Cornwall

[Launceston, follow official Gorsedd signposts]

In 2004 the Gorsedd of Cornwall Annual Assembly of Bards will be held in Truro. This is the 76th anniversary of the procession of approximately 250 robed Bards, delegates from Wales and Brittany. Dancers from local primary school. Afternoon ceremony in Cornish language, translation for visitors, presentation of awards and prizes. Initiation of new Bards. Celtic dancing, stalls in the morning and afternoon, evening concerts. Givespero (Evensong) on Sun at 15.00 in a local church. Photography permitted outside the circle only.

September 4 2004

Admission Free

Helston Flora Day

Helston Cornwall TR13 9HQ

Tel: 01326 572082

[Helston town centre. Town centre closed to all traffic from 06.30-early eve]

Continuous programme of dancing. Children's dance featuring over 1000 children dressed in white, the Hal-An-Tow pageant about the history of Helston. Early dance and evening dance. Thousands dance their way through the town in colourful costumes and top hats. You'll find the town decked out with bluebells, gorse, laurel leaves and colourful flags. Watch St George and St Michael slay the Dragon and the Devil, cheered on by a crowd dressed in Lincoln green and Elizabethan robes. The dancers weave in and out of the shops, houses and gardens behind the Helston Band playing the famous Flora Dance tune. The origins of the dance are certainly pre-Christian and are connected with ancient spring festivals all over Europe. Nowadays its ancient intention of ushering in prosperous harvests goes hand in hand with the splash of colour all over the town, the joyous music and high spirits of all involved.

May 8 2004. First dance starts 07.00

Admission Free

Mevagissey Feast Week

Various locations Mevagissey Cornwall

Tel: 01726 842920 / 74014

Fax: 01726 844944 / 74014

A full week of events celebrating the Festival of St Peter, the patron saint of Mevagissey and Fishermen. Events include a Fishing Boat Race, Raft Race, Carnival Procession, Helicopter display, Celebration of Fish Day, choral concerts, brass bands, dancing, sports, crab catching contest, street and children's entertainers. This spectacular festival culminates with a huge firework display set to music around the harbour.

June 27-July 3 2004

Prices vary, please call for details

Polperro Festival 2004

Village Yokel Fore Street Polperro Cornwall
PL13 2QR

Tel: 01503 272129 Fax: 01503 272775

*[Polperro village. A38 to Plymouth follow towards
Liskeard, turn L at Trerulefoot for Looe. Signed
from Looe, use main car park. Rail: Poole]*

Art - music - choirs - poetry - street entertainment - Morrismen - all Public Houses have live
music, varied tastes - Furry Dance and a variety
of other events. Some disabled access.

June 19-27 2004

Events: virtually all £Free

Royal Cornwall Show 2004

The Royal Cornwall Showground Wadebridge
Cornwall PL27 7JE

Tel: 01208 812183 Fax: 01208 812713
*[1.5m W of Wadebridge on the A39. Rail: Bodmin
Parkway]*

The Royal Cornwall Show is today regarded as
one of the last true major agricultural shows in
the UK. Regularly attracting well over 100,000
people, the show boasts over 850 trade stands,
including huge areas of agricultural machinery
and related displays, plus hundreds of competi-
tive classes attracting the very best of British
livestock and horses. Add to this a Flower Show
of national repute, an action-packed main
arena, stage areas and specialist features such
as the NatWest Countryside Area and the
Steam Fair, and you have an event for all the
family. Although now well over 200 years old,
the show is moving ever forward, with new features and exhibits every year.

June 10-12 2004

Prices vary, please call for details

Folk & Local History Museums

Royal Cornwall Museum

River Street Truro Cornwall TR1 2SJ

Tel: 01872 272205 Fax: 01872 240514

www.royalcornwallmuseum.org.uk

[In the centre of Truro]

The museum has a permanent display on the
history of Cornwall from the Stone Age to the
present day, as well as the natural history of
Cornwall, a world famous collection of minerals,
a pre-eminent collection of ceramics, and a
changing display of fine and decorative art. The
museum has a wide range of temporary exhibitions, from photographs to textiles, Old Master
drawings to natural history. Exhibitions held in
the Galleries are subject to admission charges,
those in the Cafe Gallery are free. A Children's
exhibition is held in the summer. Special exhibition for 2004: Travelling Trees: adventure, danger and death in search of perfection; a major
exhibition on 200 years of plant hunting and the
introduction of exotic trees and shrubs into
Cornish gardens. Full supporting programme of
family activities throughout the summer holidays.

All year Mon-Sat 10.00-17.00. Closed Bank Hol

A£4.00 C(Accompanied)£Free
C(Unaccompanied)£0.50 Concessions£2.50
School parties £Free

**Discount Offer: Two Adults For The
Price Of One**

Smugglers at Jamaica Inn

Jamaica Inn Complex Bolventor Launceston
Cornwall PL15 7TS

Tel: 01566 86250 Fax: 01566 86177

www.jamaicainn.co.uk

[On the A30 Launceston / Bodmin road. Plenty of free on site parking]

An attraction in three parts, designed to appeal to all the family. Employing the latest digital technology with traditional methods of interpretation. Visitors are first welcomed with a theatrical presentation of the Jamaica Inn story told in tableaux, light and sound, then on to see one of the finest collections of smuggling relics, dating from past to present. And finally, on to Dame Daphne Du Maurier's life and works including her Sheraton writing desk where she wrote so many of her famous novels.

Mid season daily 10.00-17.00, Summer daily 10.00-19.00, Part Winter 11.00-16.00

Museum Passport: A£3.50 C(under16)£3.00 OAPs£3.00 Family Ticket (A2+C2) £8.95. Coach party rate: £2.50 per person

Gardens & Horticulture

The Lost Gardens of Heligan

Pentewan St. Austell Cornwall PL26 6EN

Tel: 01726 845100 Fax: 01726 845101

www.heligan.com

[Signposted from A390 / B3273. Plenty of parking on site]

Heligan, seat of the Tremayne family for more than 400 years, is one of the most mysterious estates in England. At the end of the nineteenth century its thousand acres were at their zenith, but only a few years after the Great War of 1914 bramble and ivy were already drawing a green veil over this 'Sleeping Beauty'. After decades of neglect, the devastating hurricane of 1990 should have consigned the Lost Gardens of Heligan to a footnote in history. Now, over a decade into what The Times has called 'the garden restoration of the century', the celebrated Lost Gardens extend to two hundred acres of pleasure grounds, productive gardens, lakes, wetlands, ancient broadleaved woodlands, and permanent pasture where the Heligan flock and herd graze the grassland slopes. Heligan is so much more than simply a garden restored; its own special atmosphere encourages both exploration and contemplation, satisfying the broadest range of horticultural interest, while appealing to non-gardeners too.

All year daily, main season 10.00-18.00, winter 10.00-17.00. Closed 24-25 Dec

A£7.50 C£4.00 OAPs£7.00 Family Ticket £20.00. Please note, prior booking is essential for group visits

Trebah Garden

Mawnan Smith Falmouth Cornwall TR11 5JZ

Tel: 01326 250448 Fax: 01326 250781

[From Treliever Cross roundabout at junction of A39 and A394, follow brown and white tourism signs through Mawnan Smith to Trebah]

26-acre sub-tropical ravine garden falling from 18th century house to private beach on the historic Helford River. Cascading water garden has pools full of giant Koi Carp and exotic water plants.

All year daily 10.30-17.00

A£5.00 C£3.00 OAPs£4.50 Disabled£3.00. Group rates: A£4.00 C£2.00 OAPs£4.00 DIsabled£2.00

Heritage & Industrial

Charlestown Shipwreck and Heritage Centre

Quay Road Charlestown St. Austell Cornwall PL25 3NJ

Tel: 01726 69897 Fax: 01726 69897

[1.25m SE A3061 2m from St Austell]

Charlestown is a small and unspoilt village with a unique sea-lock china-clay port. It was purpose built in the 18th century by Charles Rashleigh. The Shipwreck and Heritage Centre houses the largest display of shipwreck artefacts in the UK, along with a series of lifesize tableaux, photographs depicting village life and the great Steam Liners including the 'Titanic'.

1 Mar-31 Oct daily 10.00-17.00 later in high season

A£4.95 C£Free (when accompanied by paying Adult) Concessions £3.45

The history of Cornwall from the Stone Age to the present day

Truro Cornwall TR1 2SJ

Tel: 01872 272205

www.royalcornwallmuseum.org.uk

Historical

Mount Edgcumbe House and Country Park

Cremyll Torpoint Cornwall PL10 1HZ

Tel: 01752 822236 Fax: 01752 822199

www.cornwalltouristboard.co.uk

[On Rame Peninsula via Torpoint Car Ferry from Plymouth. On foot: Ferry - Plymouth to Cremyll. Rail: Plymouth Liskeard. Plenty of on site parking]

Tudor mansion, former home of the Earls of Mount Edgcumbe. Refurbished in 18th century style. Family Treasures. Programme of special exhibitions and events. Features include shell seat in Earls 2 acres garden, historic buildings, formal gardens include Italian, French, English, American and New Zealand sections. One of 3 Grade I listed gardens in Cornwall. 865 acres of country park overlooking Plymouth Sound.

House & Earls Garden: 4 Apr-30 Sept Sun-Thur & Bank Hol Mons 11.00-16.30. Formal Gardens: All year daily 08.00-dusk

House & Gardens: A£4.50 C£2.25 Concessions£3.50 Family Ticket £10.00. Season Ticket £7.50. Country Park: Admission Free

Discount Offer: Two Adults For The Price Of One.

Maritime

National Maritime Museum Cornwall

Discovery Quay Falmouth Cornwall TR11 3QY

Tel: 01326 313388 Fax: 01326 317878

www.nmmc.co.uk

[At the South-Eastern end of Falmouth's harbour front, near the docks, car parking and railway station. Rail: Falmouth]

Whether novice or master mariner, National Maritime Museum Cornwall (NMMC) is a must see visitor destination for all the family. This exciting, multi-award winning Museum has achieved wide national and international acclaim for its architecture, hands-on displays, world-renowned boats and associated video footage, maritime heritage and interactive entertainment. Use the Museum's unique Park & Float/Ride service (summer only) to travel down to the Museum by boat - what better way to arrive at the project than by water? Explore the Tidal Zone, the only one in Europe and one of only three in the world, offering a unique 'fish-eye' view of life under the water and see some of the aquatic visitors to the Museum! Marvel at the views from the 29m Look-out tower, travel through time and explore Cornwall's unique heritage and unravel the mysteries of navigation and meteorology. Complete with waterside cafe, lecture theatre, reference library and shop, NMMC, is a 21st century hands-on attraction that promises to be a great day out.

All year daily 10.00-17.00. Closed Christmas Day and Boxing Day

A£5.90 C(under5)£Free C&Concessions£3.90 Family Ticket £15.50

Nature & Conservation Parks

Eden Project

Bodelva Parr St Austell Cornwall PL26 2SG
Tel: 01726 811911 Fax: 01726 811912
[Off the A390 between St Austell and Liskeard, turn off at St Blazey Gate]

An unforgettable experience in a breathtaking epic location. Eden is a gateway into the fascinating world of plants and people and a vibrant reminder of how we need each other for our mutual survival. Its home is a dramatic global garden the size of thirty football pitches, nestling like a lost world in a crater overlooking St Austell Bay.

All year daily, Nov-Mar 10.00-16.30, Apr-Oct 10.00-18.00. Closed 24-25 Dec

A£12.00 C(5-15)£5.00 C(under5)£Free
OAPs£8.00 Students£6.00 Family Ticket
£30.00

Railways

Bodmin and Wenford Railway

Bodmin General Station Lostwithiel Road Bodmin Cornwall PL31 1AQ
Tel: 0845 125 9678 Fax: 01208 77963
[On the B3268 Lostwithiel road near the centre of Bodmin. From the A30/A38 follow the signs to Bodmin town centre then brown tourist signs to the steam railway]

The Bodmin and Wenford Railway offers a trip into nostalgia with steam trains operating from the historic town of Bodmin through scenic countryside along the preserved six-mile Great Western Railway branch line to Bodmin Parkway (for walks to Lanhydrock House) and Boscarne Junction (for the Camel Trail footpath). Steam locomotives include a newly-restored Great Western Railway prairie tank which returned to steam in 2003.

June-Sept daily, also some days in Apr, May & Oct, please call for a timetable

All Line Ticket (Return): A£9.00 C(under3)£Free C(3-16)£5.00 Family Ticket (A2+C4) £25.00. Bodmin General & Boscarne Junction: A£5.00 C(under3)£Free C(3-16)£3.00 Family Ticket (A2+C4) £15.00. Bodmin General & Bodmin Parkway: A£6.00 C(under3)£Free C(3-16)£3.50 Family Ticket (A2+C4) £17.50

Science - Earth & Pla

Goonhilly Satellite Earth Station Experience

The Visitor Centre Goonhilly Downs Helston Cornwall TR12 6LQ
Tel: 0800 679593 Fax: 01326 221438
www.goonhilly.bt.com
[Goonhilly Downs. 7m from Helston on B3293 St. Keverne Rd]

What is Goonhilly? With over 60 huge dishes, Goonhilly is the largest satellite earth station in the world and makes a dramatic impression on the landscape. The size of the site is equivalent to 160 football pitches. It is able to transmit millions of international phone calls, emails and TV broadcasts to every corner of the globe, via space or through submarine fibre optic cable. The Visitors centre provides a unique opportunity to explore the story of international communities. Using state of the art technology we will take you on a eye-opening journey. Enjoy a fascinating guided tour and visit the Command Complex and see the route that a live TV picture takes to get to the TV in your living room. The Earth Station Experience includes: 3D Virtual Head Creation Display, Free High Speed Internet Access, Big Dish Cafe, Gift Shop, Children's Play Areas. Average visiting time 2-4 hours, but time is not restricted.
Open from 10 Feb 2004, call for opening times
A£5.00 C(5-16)£3.50 C(under5)£Free
OAPs£4.00 Family Ticket £15.00. Group rates (20+): A£4.00 C£2.80 OAPS£3.30 (must be pre-booked)

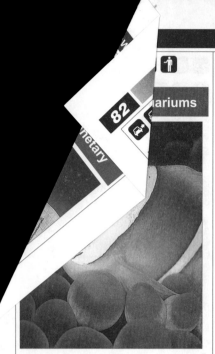

Blue Reef Aquarium

Towan Promenade Newquay Cornwall TR7 1DU

Tel: 01637 878134 Fax: 01637 872578

www.bluereefaquarium.co.uk

[Follow brown tourist signs in town centre, on Towan beach]

Newquay's Blue Reef Aquarium offers visitors a dazzling undersea safari through the oceans of the world. Overlooking the mighty Atlantic Ocean, the aquarium transports visitors to the spectacular 'underwater gardens' of the Mediterranean and the stunning beauty of tropical waters - home to everything from seahorses and puffer fish to living corals and tropical sharks. At its heart is a giant tropical ocean tank where an underwater walkthrough tunnel offers incredibly close encounters with sharks, stingrays and hundreds of colourful reef fish. More than 30 naturally-themed displays reveal the sheer variety of life in the deep from native sharks and rays to the amazing octopus and the bizarre shape-shifting cuttlefish!

All year daily from 10.00. Closed 25 Dec

A£5.50 C(3-16)£3.50 Students&OAPs£4.75 Family Ticket (A2+C2/3) £16.95. Discounts for groups, students, disabled - call for details

Discount Offer: One Child Free With One Full Paying Adult

Special Events

Launch of Blue Reef Nursery
09/04/2004-12/04/2004
The new Blue Reef nursery provides a fascinating insight into the life cycles of marine creatures from around the world. Please call for further details

Shark Awareness Week
29/05/2004-05/06/2004
Shark Week is a celebration of the oceans' greatest predator. Learn the facts behind the fiction and discover why sharks have got lots more to fear from us than we have from them. Regular talks, workshops and feeding demonstrations

Summer Holidays - Family Fun
01/07/2004-31/08/2004
Throughout the summer holidays, Blue Reef is organising a series of fun activities aimed at families. From rockpool encounters to marine themed quiz trails, talks and feeding demonstrations, there's something for visitors of all ages to enjoy

October Half Term Event - Claws
01/10/2004-31/10/2004
From comical hermit crabs and 'fashion conscious' decorator crabs to giant lobsters and the mighty king crab, this exciting feature offers a fascinating insight into the incredible world of crustaceans. Please call for specific dates

Theme & Adventure Parks

Dobwalls Adventure Park

Dobwalls Liskeard Cornwall PL14 6HB
Tel: 01579 320325 / 321129
Fax: 01579 321345
[Venue is 0.5m from A38 follow brown tourist signs]

A 25 acre parking incorporating the Forest Railway - one of Europe's most extensive miniature railroads, outdoor adventure play areas, the Krazee Kavern and Rattlesnake Ranch exciting indoor adventure play (over 12,000 sq ft). John Southern Gallery exhibiting and selling wildlife art by Carl Brenders and Steven Townsend.
Easter-end Oct 10.30-17.00, open most days
Single £8.50 C(under2)£Free Concessions£5.50

Family Ticket (2 people) £16.50, (3 people) £24.50, (4 people) £32.50, (5 people) £40.50

31 Mar-31 Oct; 31 Mar-22 Apr daily 10.00-17.00, 23 Apr-30 May daily 10.30-17.00 (closed 14, 21, 28 May), 31 May-25 July daily 10.00-17.00, 26 July-3 Sept daily 10.00-17.30, 4 Sept-31 Oct 10.00-17.00 (closed 1, 4, 8, 11, 15 Oct)

A(15-54)£9.95 C(under4)£Free C(5-14)£8.95 OAPs(55+)£5.75 A(over80)£Free. Family Ticket (3 people) £9.10per person, (4 people) £9.00p/p, (5 people) £8.80p/p, (6 people) £8.65p/p - one member of each group must be a supervising adult. Afternoon tickets on sale after 14.15 (18.00 during August firework evenings): A£6.95 C£5.95 OAPs£4.50

Special Events

Baloo Party in the Park
07/04/2004-18/04/2004
Excluding Saturdays

Easter Eggsplosion
12/04/2004
Free chocolate eggs for children up to 14 years. Baloo fun, games and prizes all afternoon

Peter Pan
14/04/2004
On stage from 13.30

Penalty Shoot Out Competition
03/05/2004
Children under 11 years admitted free in soccer strip. Must be accompanied by a supervising adult. Cash prizes. Cost: £3.00 per competition entry

Bob the Builder
31/05/2004
On stage from 13.30

Baloo Party in the Park
31/05/2004-06/06/2004
Excluding Saturdays

Ferdi's Birthday Party
02/06/2004
Children under 11 years get in free with a hand drawn colour picture of Ferdi. Best picture competition

Fathers' Day Promotion
20/06/2004
Free admission for Fathers with a full paying child. From 13.30 meet Marge and Homer Simpson

Flambards Experience

Helston Cornwall TR13 0QA

Tel: 01326 573404 Fax: 01326 573344
www.flambards.co.uk

[0.5m S on A3083 from Helston near Redruth or Penzance. Plenty of parking on site. Shaded parking for dogs]

The packed Flambards menu includes the award winning Flambards Victorian Village, a life-size recreation of a lamp-lit village with more than 50 shops, traders and homes. Britain in the Blitz recreates a World War II blitzed street. Family rides include the Thunderbolt, the Hornet Coaster, the Log Flume, and the Extreme Force. The Flambards Formula Circuit, the Weather Forecasting Studio, Cornwall's Science Centre, Sealegs Safari, the Wildlife Encounters Experience and the Gus Honeybun show will keep everybody entertained. With huge undercover areas, superb exhibitions, rides, family shows, live entertainment as published, glorious gardens and spectacular new thrills included in the new Super Family Saver tickets Flambards is - the Best day of the Week, whatever the weather.

Baloo - Party in the Park
18/07/2004-05/09/2004
Excluding Saturdays

Vision
02/08/2004
From 19.30 see popular Cornish band Vision on stage followed by fireworks at approx. 21.30

Peter Pan
04/08/2004
From 13.30 and then party to Baloo from 19.00 and end the evening with fireworks at approx. 21.30

Small Wonder
09/08/2004
Cornish band Small Wonder on stage at 19.30 and then round off the evening with fireworks at approx. 21.30

Loony Tunes
11/08/2004
Bugs Bunny and Daffy Duck are on stage from 13.30, then party in the park with Baloo from 19.00, and finish off the evening with fireworks

David White and the Strangers
16/08/2004
Try your hand at line dancing or just listen to the music of BBC Radio Cornwall's David White and his band the Strangers, followed by fireworks at approx. 21.15. Free entry for Cowboys / Cowgirls (of all ages) after 18.00

Peter Pan
18/08/2004
See Peter Pan from 13.30, party in the park with Baloo at 19.00 and then watch the fireworks

Vision
23/08/2004
See and dance to the Cornish band Vision, and finish the evening with fireworks at approx. 21.15

Snoopy Work Out
25/08/2004
On stage from 13.30 and then party in the park with Baloo from 19.00 before the fireworks at approx. 21.00

Teddy Bears' Picnic
30/08/2004
Free entry to children under 11 years with a Teddy Bear. Best dressed Teddy competition

Small Wonder
01/09/2004
Another chance to see and dance to the great Cornish band Small Wonder, with fireworks at approx. 21.00

Meet Bart and Homer Simpson
19/09/2004
On stage from 13.30

Undivided
10/10/2004
Local band in the restaurant from 12.00-14.30

End of Season Fireworks Show
23/10/2004
Special discounted tickets available in advance. Full entry price on the day. Wizards hat competition at 15.30 for children under 11 years. Party in the park with Baloo from 16.00

Hallowe'en Special
30/10/2004
Get in for £3.00 with your Fireworks ticket. Free lucky bag for each child under 11 years

Last Day of the Season
31/10/2004
Park Return Cardholders special promotion price £1.75. Local Blues Band Me and the Devil play in the restaurant from 12.00-14.30

Zoos

Newquay Zoo

Trenance Gardens Newquay Cornwall TR7 2LZ
Tel: 01637 873342 Fax: 01637 851318
[A30 Indian Queens, A392 to Newquay]

Amongst the exotic lakeside gardens live hundreds of animals from all around the world from small rare monkeys to shy red pandas. Look out for penguins playing in their pool, and glimpse the strange and endangered lemurs and fossa.
Apr-Oct daily 09.30-18.00, Nov-Mar daily 10.00-dusk. Closed 25 Dec
A£6.95 C(3-15)£4.45 OAPs/Students£5.45

County Durham

Animal Attractions

Hall Hill Farm

Lanchester County Durham DH7 0TA
Tel: 01388 731333
*[A691/A68 Farm is located half way between Tow
Law and Lanchester on B6296]*

Family farm set in attractive countryside with
opportunity to see and touch animals at close
quarters. Farm trailer rides, new play area. Farm
tea-shop and children's play area. Rabbit and
chick handling areas plus other new animals
and the chance to try milking our wooden cow.
Special lambing days during April.
*From 3 Apr, daily 10.30-16.00. Please call to
confirm opening from autumn*
A£3.95 C(3-15)£2.95 OAPs£3.20 Family Ticket
(A2+C2) £12.00 Family Season Ticket £43.00

Arts, Crafts & Textiles

The Bowes Museum

Barnard Castle County Durham DL12 8NP

Tel: 01833 690606 Fax: 01833 637163

www.bowesmuseum.org.uk

*[Historic Market Town of Barnard Castle. Parking
on site]*

A great day out for all the family awaits you at
The Bowes Museum. With a variety of activities,
events, superb permanent collection and exhibition programme, there is something for everyone at this world-class visitor attraction. The
Bowes Museum, a grand French-style chateau,
is situated in beautiful parkland with a parterre
garden nestling in the picturesque market town
of Barnard Castle. The Museum has a well-
stocked gift shop and a superb cafe where you
can enjoy a culinary treat made to order from
only the finest local ingredients. The Bowes
Museum can provide everything you need for a
memorable day out. Hope to see you soon!

*All year daily 11.00-17.00. Closed 25-26 Dec &
1 Jan*

A£6.00 C(under16)£Free Concessions£5.00

Special Events

Wedding Belles
24/05/2003-18/04/2004
Two centuries of Bridal Gowns

The John and Josephine Bowes Story
27/01/2004-31/12/2004
*Relive the remarkable story of John and
Josephine Bowes and their ambitious museum
project*

Braids and Beyond
03/04/2004-27/06/2004
*A broad look at narrow wares from The Braid
Society*

Northumbria Gardens Trust
03/04/2004-30/05/2004
*Great gardens of the region; featuring conserva-
tion issues*

Boudin, Monet and the Sea Painters of Normandy
29/05/2004-30/08/2004
*Explores the close relationship between Monet
and Boudin and their work in Normandy from the
1860s. Includes international loans*

Anthony Clark - Contemporary Paintings
12/06/2004-12/09/2004

**Yorkshire Sculptors Group - Mixed Media
Sculpture**
10/07/2004-12/09/2004

Toulouse Lautrec and the Art Nouveau Poster
11/09/2004-09/01/2005
Posters by Toulouse Lautrec and others

Lubaina Himid and Friends
25/09/2004-01/01/2005
*Contemporary work. Exhibition due to run through
to Jan 2005 but specific date has yet to be confirmed*

Heritage & Industrial

Killhope The North of England Lead Mining Museum

Cowshill Weardale County Durham DL13 1AR
Tel: 01388 537505 Fax: 01388 537617
[3m W of Wearhead on A689]

A great day out full of hands-on activities for the whole family. Work as a washerboy and find lead ore, experience the living conditions of Victorian lead miners, and walk the woodland trail. Park Level Mine is an exciting trip deep underground splashing through water by the light of your caplamp.

20-21 Mar, 1 Apr-31 Oct daily 10.30-17.00 (17.30 on Bank Hols and 19 July-1 Sept)
A£4.50 C(4-16)£1.70 Concessions£4.00 Family Ticket (A2+C3) £11.00. With mine: A£6.00 C£3.00 Concessions£5.50 Family Ticket £17.00

Discount Offer: Two For The Price Of One. (Excludes Mine Tour)

Historical

Auckland Castle

Bishop Auckland County Durham DL14 7NR
Tel: 01388 601627 Fax: 01388 609323
[10m SW of Durham and 8m from A1(M)]

Home of the Bishops of Durham for over 800 years, this magnificent building has architecture from the 12th, 14th, 16th and 18th century. Also houses the largest private chapel in Europe and a fine collection of paintings. Group bookings welcome, guided tours available.
Castle: Easter Mon-end Sept Sun & Mon 14.00-17.00, plus Wed during Aug only. Park: open daily 07.00-sunset
A£4.00 C(12-16)&OAPs£3.00 C(0-12)£Free

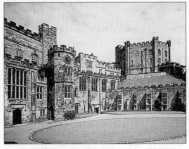

Durham Castle

Palace Green Durham County Durham DH1 3RW

Tel: 0191 334 3800 Fax: 0191 334 3801

www.durhamcastle.com

[Central Durham adjacent to Cathedral. Rail: Durham 0.5m]

Durham Castle, the former home of the Prince Bishops of Durham, was founded in 1072. Since 1832 it has been the foundation College of the University of Durham. With the Cathedral it is a World Heritage Site. During holidays the Castle is a conference and holiday centre and is a superb venue for wedding receptions.

Guided Tours only, Apr-Sept daily 10.00-12.00 & 14.00-16.30, Oct-March Mon, Wed, Sat & Sun 14.00-16.00

A£3.00 C£2.00 Family Ticket £6.50. From 1 July: A£3.50 C£2.50 OAPs£3.00 Family Ticket £8.00. Guide Book £2.50. Group rates: minimum of 10 people, maximum of 40, available on application

Places of Worship

Durham Cathedral

The College Durham County Durham DH1 3EH
Tel: 0191 386 4266 Fax: 0191 386 4267
The cathedral was founded in 1093 as a shrine to St Cuthbert. His bones still rest in his shrine. The cathedral is a remarkable example of Norman architecture set within an imposing site high above the River Wear.
The Cathedral is open for worship and private prayer Mon-Sat 07.30-09.30, Sun 07.45-12.30. The Cathedral closes Mon-Sat 18.15, Sun 17.00 (18.00 Apr-end Sept), extended summer opening 31 May-5 Sept 09.30-20.00. The Cathedral is

not always fully accessible to visitors so please call if you wish to visit on a particular day
Cathedral: no entrance fee but donation requested, some parts charged

Social History Museums

Beamish, The North of England Open Air Museum

Beamish County Durham DH9 0RG
Tel: 0191 370 4000 Fax: 0191 370 4001
[From the N or S - follow the A1(M) to J63, Chester-le-Street exit, 12m N of Durham City, 8m S of Newcastle upon Tyne]

Beamish is unique. It's a living, working experience of life as it was in the Great North in the early 1800s and early 1900s. Take a tram ride into the past to explore the Manor House, go underground at a real 'drift' mine, ride on the amazing steam train and meet the animals at Home Farm. Sample the treats at the Jubilee Sweetshop or visit the Dentist in the Award-winning Town.
Summer daily from 10.00. Closed Mon & Fri in Winter
Summer: A£14.00 C(under5)£Free C(5-16)£7.00 OAPs£11.00. Winter: all £5.00

Theme & Adventure Parks

Diggerland

Riverside Industrial Estate Langley Park County Durham DH7 9TT

Tel: 08700 344437 Fax: 09012 010300

www.diggerland.com

[From the A1(M) J62 head W, following signs to Consett, after 6m turn L at roundabout signed to Langley Park, turn R into Riverside Industrial Estate. Plenty of on site parking available]

All ages will enjoy the opportunity to ride in and drive different types of machines from Dumper-trucks to JCB Mini Diggers and Large Diggers (all under strict supervision). Taking up challenges like fishing ducks out of a pond using a JCB digger and learning about the machines, makes it a fun and informative attraction. There are over 20 different rides and attractions at Diggerland. Birthday parties are catered for, so if you fancy a party with a difference for your young children then contact us for details.

Weekends & Bank Hols and daily during half-term and school holidays 10.00-17.00. Closed Dec, Jan & Feb

A&OAPs£2.50 C(under2)£Free C£2.50 which covers all non-mechanical rides. Group rates (20+): 20% discount. To drive the real diggers costs from £1.00 per ride OR an all day wristband at £18.00

Discount Offer: 1/2 Price Entry For Up To 6 People. (Voucher Applies To Entry Charge Only)

Special Events

Easter Sunday
11/04/2004
Free Easter eggs on arrival for kids

4x4 Off Road Day
17/04/2004
Bring your own 4x4 and tackle the challenge of the custom built Diggerland Off Road course - can you get round it or will you get stuck in the mud? Please call for entry tickets well in advance, numbers strictly limited

Metal Micky's Birthday Party
25/04/2004
Metal Micky is 4 years old. Come and join him for a day of fun and celebration

Stunt Demonstrations
03/05/2004
Amazing Digger stunts from our Dancing Diggers display performed hourly throughout the afternoon

Bob the Builder Day
22/05/2004
Come along dressed as Bob the Builder and enter Diggerland Free. Also a few other Bob surprises!

Fathers Day
20/06/2004
Free admission to Diggerland for all Dads on this special day. Dads are just big kids anyway!

Stunt Demonstrations
04/07/2004
Amazing Digger stunts from our Dancing Diggers display performed hourly throughout the afternoon

Young Driver Experience
15/07/2004
Personal Tuition on, and a great chance to drive a selection of vehicles including Land Rovers and Diggers, for ages 9-16. Can be purchased as a gift. Ring or email well in advance to book. Cost: £49.00. Numbers strictly limited

Diggerland Summer Fete
25/07/2004
Join in our Summer Fete with an all-day Barbeque, face painting and lots more

4x4 Off Road Day
10/10/2004
Bring your own 4x4 and tackle the challenge of the custom built Diggerland Off Road course - can you get round it or will you get stuck in the mud? Please call for entry tickets well in advance, numbers strictly limited

Transport Museums

Darlington Railway Centre and Museum

North Road Station Station Road Darlington County Durham DL3 6ST
Tel: 01325 460532 Fax: 01325 287746
[A1(M) J59 0.75m N of Town Centre off A167 signposted]

Restored Victorian station, dating from 1842, on the original route of the Stockton and Darlington Railway, now a museum devoted to railway heritage of North-East England. Exhibits include Stephenson's "Locomotion" (1825), other steam engines and many smaller exhibits.

All year daily 10.00-17.00. Closed 25-26 Dec & 1 Jan

A£2.20 C(under5)£Free C£1.10 Concessions£1.50

Cumbria

Animal Attractions

Trotters World of Animals

Coalbeck Farm Bassenthwaite Keswick
Cumbria CA12 4RD
Tel: 017687 76239 Fax: 017687 76598
[5m NE of Cockermouth near north end of Bassenthwaite lake]

A world apart from the noisy traffic and hectic city life set amongst lakes and mountains our friendly staff will welcome you. Trotters World of Animals is home to hundreds of friendly animals including lemurs, wallabies and other exotic animals, along with reptiles and birds of prey and our family of gibbons will keep you amused for hours.
All year 15 Feb-1 Nov daily 10.00-17.30, Nov-Jan Sat-Sun 11.00-16.00. Closed 25 Dec & 1 Jan
A£5.25 C(3-14)£3.95

Arts, Crafts & Textiles

Abbot Hall Art Gallery

Kendal Cumbria LA9 5AL
Tel: 01539 722464 Fax: 01539 722494
[J36 M6, signposted on A6 brown museum signs]

One of Britain's finest small art galleries showing changing displays of contemporary art and touring exhibitions. The gallery is housed in a Grade I listed Georgian Villa and the ground floor rooms have been restored to provide a perfect setting for showing the permanent collection of portraits and paintings by George Romney and 18th century furniture
20 Jan-23 Dec Mon-Sat 10.30-16.00 (17.00 Apr-Oct)
Collection only: A£3.75 C&Students£2.75 Family Ticket £11.00. Exhibition (includes entry to Collection): A£4.75 C&Students£3.75 Family Ticket £14.00

Exhibition & Visitor Centres

Rheged - The Village in the Hill

Redhills Penrith Cumbria CA11 0DQ
Tel: 01768 868000 Fax: 01768 868002
[Less than 1m from M6 J40 at Penrith on the A66 in the direction of Keswick]

Named after Cumbria's ancient Celtic Kingdom and recently voted Cumbria's best large visitor attraction 2002, Rheged is located in Europe's largest grass covered building and has something for everyone. Rheged's centrepiece is a giant cinema screen the size of six double decker buses. Enjoy epic adventure family movies shown daily all from the comfort of your own cinema seat, including Rheged - The Movie, a dramatic journey of myths, legends and spectacular new large format family films.
All year daily 10.00-17.30
Giant Movies: A£5.50 C£3.90
OAPs&Students£4.70 Family Ticket
(A2+C3)£16.00. Exhibition price packages available

Festivals & Shows

Brampton Live 2004

William Howard Centre Longtown Road Brampton Cumbria CA8 1AR
Tel: 01228 534664 Fax: 01228 810249
[Brampton is 10m E of Carlisle, off A69 Carlisle to Newcastle road]

The North of England's biggest and best folk/roots music festival with top acts from all over the world. Great mix of music and very family-friendly! Free camping available.
July 16-18 2004, Fri 08.00-23.30, Sat & Sun 12.30-23.30
Tickets are for the festival not individual concerts, therefore tickets allow admission to all stages

Cockermouth Festival 2004

Cockermouth Cumbria CA13 9NP
Tel: 01900 822634 Fax: 01900 822603
[Take A66 from M6 J40 - 31 miles W. Take A595 from Carlisle. Rail: Carlisle / Penrith]

The Festival is a month long event with a programme comprising art, theatre, music, exhibitions, demonstrations, children's shows and story telling. Approximately 100 events in total.
June 26-July 31 2004
Ticket prices vary according to event

Grasmere Lakeland Sports and Show

Grasmere Sportsfield Grasmere Ambleside Cumbria LA22 9PZ
Tel: 015394 32127
[M6 then A592. Rail: Windermere 8m. Plenty of free parking on site]

The world famous lakeland heritage and cultural event. Celebrating 150 years since records began. Features Cumberland and Westmorland Wrestling inc. 11 stone World Championship. Also includes Inter Pub/Club Tug-o-War, Fell Races, Mountain Bike Races, The Scottish Terrier Racing Team, Eagle and Vulture Show, The Adamson Military Band, Gus Darmody (of BBC TV One Man and His Dog fame), Sheepdog Demonstrations, Terrier Show, Trail Hound Puppy Show, Pet Dog Show. Plus Made

in Cumbria Marquee, Crafts Marquee, Fairground, 50+ Trade Stands, Beer Tent and Catering. A great family fun day out.

August 22 2004

A£7.50 C(5-14)£2.50

La'al Cumbrian Beer Festival

The Wasdale Head Inn Wasdale Head Gosfort Cumbria CA20 1EX
Tel: 019467 26229 Fax: 019467 26334
[J43 M6, A595 or J36 M6 A590 / A595 to Gosforth, then 9m]

The Inn is at a crossroads, at one time notorious for smuggling activities. Within the Inn the is a collection of photographs and memorabilia taken by the Keswick Brothers who recorded the birth and development of British rock climbing which was centred upon the Wasdale. The Beer Festival features real ales from Cumbria only.
June 4-6 Fri-Sun 2004
Admission Free

Wordsworth Summer Conference

Prince of Wales Hotel Grasmere Cumbria LA22 9PR
Tel: 015394 35003 Fax: 015394 35748
[S of Grasmere village on the main A591 Kendal Keswick Rd. Rail: Windermere. Bus: 555, hourly. In summer open top bus every 20mins]

The Conference concerns itself with every aspect of Romantic studies and draws scholar students and non-specialist lovers of poetry to the heart of the English Lake District every August. Uniquely, the two-week Conference blends academic activities with the opportunity to get to know the landscape which inspired so much great poetry. It takes place close to Dove Cottage (William and Dorothy's home 1799-1808) and the Wordsworth Museum and Librar (containing 90% of the poet's manuscripts, all c Dorothy's and major holdings of Coleridge, De Quincey and others).

ly 31 - August 14 2004
ease apply for residential costs

Folk & Local History Museums

ullie House Museum and Art Gallery

astle Street Carlisle Cumbria CA3 8TP
el: 01228 534781 Fax: 01228 810249
M6, J4, 43, 44 follow brown signs to city centre ullie House opposite Carlisle Castle]

ward-winning museum and art gallery.
tunning and imaginative displays covering order History from Roman times to the Reivers nd beyond. A rich collection of regional impor-
ance includes archaeology, natural history and
Carlisle's social history. Experience the fantastic
ew underground Millennium Gallery. Many
nteractives to fascinate and delight all ages.

*All year daily Mon-Sat 10.00-17.00, Sun 12.00-
7.00, Sun in July & Aug 11.00-17.00. Closed
5, 26 Dec & 1 Jan*
£5.20 Concessions£3.60/£2.60 Family Ticket
£14.50

Forests & Woods

Whinlatter Forest Park

Braithwaite Keswick Cumbria CA12 5TW
Tel: 017687 78469 Fax: 017687 78049
Near Keswick, the Lake District]

England's only Mountain Forest, and Whinlatter
s one of Britain's Best. Having recently spent
£500,000 redeveloping our facilities, Whinlatter
Forest Park now offers an even better day out
for all the family. Our improved Visitor Centre
offers a larger Forest Shop as well as Siskins
cafe, with new balcony area. A network of forest
walks for all ages and abilities, the popular rabbit run and foxtrot children's trails, adventure
playground and giant badger sett.

*All year daily from dawn to dusk. Visitor Centre:
daily with seasonal variations, 10.00-17.00.
Closed 25 Dec-mid Jan*
Admission Free, Parking charge £1.00 for 1hr,
£3.00 for 4hrs or £4.00 all day

Historical

Dalemain Historic House and Gardens

Dalemain Penrith Cumbria CA11 0HB

Tel: 017684 86450 Fax: 017684 86223

www.dalemain.com

*[M6, J40 2m, between Penrith / Ullswater on the
A592, follow brown signs. Plenty of on site parking available]*

The first thing you'll discover about Dalemain is
that it is not quite what it seems. The impressive
Georgian facade is just that - a facade, added
to the Elizabethan part of the house by Edward
Hasell, in the middle of the eighteenth century.
Behind it lies the real surprise of Dalemain - its
sheer variety. There has been a settlement of
one sort or another on the site since Saxon
times, and the present house has evolved,
rather than simply having been built, with its
shape dictated sometimes by domestic or agricultural demands, sometimes by the fashion of
the day. As a result, some parts of the house
are a glorious confusion of winding passages,
quaint stairways, unexpected rooms - the sort of
house that children love to play in. Indeed part
of the charm of Dalemain is that it is still very
much a family home, still occupied by the Hasell
family who have lived here for more than 300
years. Dalemain has its fair share of grand public
rooms, including the breathtaking Chinese
Room, with its original hand-painted wallpaper,
furniture and fittings. In all rooms you will find
many examples of fine furniture and portraits -
the extent and richness of the collection at
Dalemain is quite exceptional for a house of its
size. Inside the house is the Westmorland and
Cumberland Yeomanry Museum. Outside, in the
courtyard is a Countryside Collection. The 16th
century great barn contains old agricultural
machinery and the Fell Pony Museum, including
a blacksmith's and a saddler's shop. The

delightful gardens have many rare plants and a wonderful collection of over 100 old-fashioned roses. Special care has been taken to make Dalemain not only fascinating for adults, but great fun for children too. They'll be delighted with Mrs Mouse's House and the Old Nursery with its 'baby house', and intrigued by the hiding hole in the housekeeper's room. Enjoy delicious home-made meals and teas beside the log fire in the Mediaeval Hall. An Electric Scooter may be available for use in the Gardens for disabled persons. For further information please contact the Administrator. Member of the Historic Houses Association. Photography is permitted in the Gardens ONLY.

28 Mar-21 Oct Sun-Thur 10.30-17.00, Gardens, Licensed Restaurant & Tea Room, Gift Shop and Agricultural & Countryside Collections (House 11.00-16.00) Sept & Oct 10.30-16.00 (House 11.00-15.00 last admission 14.00) Winter - gardens and Tea Room open please phone for opening times

House & Gardens: A£5.50 C(6-16)£3.50 Family Ticket (A2+any number of own C) £14.50 Wheelchair users£Free. Gardens only: A£3.50 Accompanied C£Free. Group rates during opening hours - House & Gardens: £4.50; Gardens: £3.50. Outside opening hours by arrangement with the Administrator. FREE admission to: Car and coach park, The Mediaeval Hall - Tea Room and licensed Restaurant, the Gift Shop, the Dalemain Plant Centre and The Agricultural and Countryside Collections

Discount Offer: Two For The Price Of One. (House And Gardens). Not Valid For Special Events. Valid Until 21 Oct 2004

Special Events

A Walk Around the Gardens with the Gardener
25/04/2004-04/07/2004
Held on: 25 Apr, 23 May, 13 June & 4 July

National Gardens Scheme Open Day
02/05/2004

Fell Pony Society Stallion Show
15/05/2004

North-West Carriage Driving
16/05/2004

Dalemain Craft Fair

17/07/2004-18/07/2004

Cumbria Classic Car Show
22/08/2004

National Gardens Scheme Open Day
05/09/2004

Plant Fair
12/09/2004

Dove Cottage and The Wordsworth Museum

Dove Cottage Grasmere Ambleside Cumbria LA22 9SH
Tel: 015394 35544 Fax: 015394 35748
[S of Grasmere village, on the main A591 Kendal / Keswick road]

The award-winning museum displays the Wordsworth Trust's unique collections of manuscripts, books and paintings interpreting the life and work of Wordsworth, his family and circle. There is a major exhibition every year. Dove Cottage was William Wordsworth's home from 1799-1808. The garden, "a little nook of mountain-ground," is open when weather permits.
All year daily 09.30-17.30
A£5.95 C£3.00 OAPs£5.30 Concessions£4.60

Guildhall Museum

Green Market Carlisle Cumbria CA3 8JE
Tel: 01228 534781 Fax: 01228 810249
Once the meeting place of Carlisle's eight trade guilds it still has an atmosphere of medieval times. It is an early 15th century building with exposed timber and wattle and daub walls.
Easter-Oct Thur-Sun 13.00-16.00
Admission £Free

Holker Hall and Gardens

Holker Hall Cark in Cartmel Grange-Over-Sands
Cumbria LA11 7PL

Tel: 015395 58328 Fax: 015395 58378

www.holker-hall.co.uk

*[Off A590, follow brown and white signs from M6
J36. Plenty of on site parking]*

At Holker you always feel like a welcome guest
not a tourist. Surrounded by some of the most
spectacular scenery in Cumbria you can wander
freely through this 'best-loved' of stately homes
never impeded by ropes or barriers. 25 acres of
award winning gardens offer rare treats and
allow for personal discoveries. The Lakeland
Motor Museum featuring the Campbell Bluebird
Legend Exhibition and an extensive collection of
transport and motoring memorabilia will enthral
the enthusiast, 2003 marked its 25th
Anniversary. Throughout the year Holker Hall
boasts special events including the highly
acclaimed Holker Garden Festival. The
Courtyard Café will tempt your palate with traditional Cumbrian fare and no trip would be complete without a visit to Holker's gift shop. New
for 2004 will be Food at Holker Hall, a marvellous addition. By prior arrangement, special
guided tours. Tours for the less able, hearing
and sight impaired are available. Awarded the
Family Attraction of the Year by The Good
Britain Guide 2003, we are confident with special family activities, discovery walks, unique
activities for the children at Easter, during the
summer holidays and at Christmas that a day at
Holker will be a day remembered. Photography
permitted, but not in Hall.

*All facilities: 1 Mar-24 Dec daily 10.00-18.00. Hall
& Gardens: 28 Mar-29 Oct Sun-Fri. Alternative
arrangements may be in place on special event
days, please call to confirm*

Hall, Gardens & Lakeland Motor Museum:

A£8.75 C(6-15)£5.00 Family Ticket
(A2+C2)£25.75. Groups of 20+ people welcome

**Discount Offer: One Child Free With
Two Full Paying Adults**

Mirehouse Historic House and
Gardens

Keswick Cumbria CA12 4QE

Tel: 017687 72287 Fax: 017687 75356

www.mirehouse.com

*[M6, J40 signs from A66 3m N of Keswick on
A591. Limited on site parking available. Bus: regular bus service (X4, 555, 73, 73A), for details
please call 0870 608 2 608]*

Simon Jenkins wrote in 'The Times', 'Mirehouse
is more than the sum of its parts. It is the Lake
District with its hand on its heart'. Strong ties of
friendship bound it to Tennyson, Wordsworth
and Southey and it remains a welcoming family
home. In 1999 it was voted 'The Best Property
for Families in the UK' in the NPI Heritage
Awards. Our visitors return for many reasons
including: 'Excellent value', 'staff brilliant, especially with our children', 'could listen to the
pianist all day', 'Magic! Natural playgrounds',
the changing displays in the Poetry Walk, free
children's nature notes regularly updated, an
ancient wildflower meadow and a walled garden. The house is not open every day as it is a
living family home and to conserve the delicate
objects which are on display. The grounds are
open every day, as is the tearoom, known for

generous Cumbrian cooking. Many places for picnics.

Grounds: Apr-Oct daily 10.00-17.30. House: Apr-Oct Sun, Wed (& Fri in Aug) 14.00-17.00

House & Grounds: A£4.60 C£2.30 Family Ticket (A2+C4) £13.80. Grounds only: A£2.20 C£1.10

Discount Offer: Two Full Price Adults For The Price Of One. One Voucher Per Party. Valid Sun, Wed (Also Fri In Aug) Only

Muncaster Castle, Gardens and Owl Centre

Muncaster Castle Ravenglass Cumbria
CA18 1RQ
Tel: 01229 717614 Fax: 01229 717010
[1m S of Ravenglass on A595]

Diverse attractions are offered at this castle, the seat of the Pennington Family since the 13th century. Experience the wild beauty of Muncaster's huge gardens. Check out the wonderful Himalayan Gardens featuring many specimens rarely seen in the West. Talk and Bird Display from the World Owl Trust daily at 14.30 throughout the season. Watch the wild Herons feed at 16.30.

Castle: Early Mar-Early Nov Sun-Fri 12.00-17.00. Gardens & Owl Centre: all year daily 10.30-18.00.
Castle, Gardens & Owl Centre: A£8.50 C(under5)£Free C£5.50 Family Ticket (A2+C2) £23.00. Gardens and Owl Centre: A£6.00 C(under5)£Free C£4.00 Family Ticket £18.00

Maritime

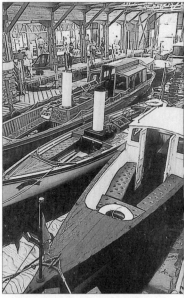

Windermere Steamboats and Museum

Rayrigg Road Windermere Cumbria LA23 1BN

Tel: 015394 45565 Fax: 015394 48769

www.steamboat.co.uk

[0.5m N of Bowness Bay on A592. Plenty of on site parking available]

A unique exhibition of Lake Windermere's nautical heritage. The Museum houses an historic collection of Victorian and Edwardian steam launches and classic motor boats both afloat and on display undercover (including 'Dolly' - the world's oldest surviving mechanically powered boat). Spectacular lakeside setting, premier all-weather attraction. Guided tours of Museum and 'Esperance' (Ransome's inspiration for Captain Flint's houseboat). Exhibition: 'Swallow and Amazons' - 'Model Boats - You Can Do It Too!'. Special events, cruises (weather permitting), shop, tea room, picnic area, model boat pond, disabled facilities.

Mid Mar-beginning Nov daily 10.00-17.00

A£3.50 C£2.00 Family Ticket (A2+C3)£8.50. Group rates available

Discount Offer: Two For The Price Of One

Nature & Conservation Parks

Lake District Visitor Centre at Brockhole

Windermere Cumbria LA23 1LJ

Tel: 01539 446601 Fax: 01539 445555
[On A591 between Windermere/Ambleside]

Outstanding setting on the shores of Lake Windermere. 30 acres of award winning gardens and grounds. Cruises on Lake Windermere, adventure playground, walks, trails, events and activities, two floors of exciting interactive exhibitions, film auditorium and programme.

*Visitor Centre: Apr-Oct daily 10.00-17.00.
Grounds & Gardens: all year daily*

Admission Free

On the Water

Steam Yacht Gondola

Pier Cottage Coniston Cumbria LA21 8AJ

Tel: 015394 41288 Fax: 015394 35353

[Coniston 0.5m to Coniston Pier. Rail: Foxfield / Windermere via vehicle ferry]

Experience the grand Victorian elegance of Gondola and her plush interior. Sailing on beautiful Coniston Water, this re-built steam powered yacht will transport you back to an era of peace and tranquility. Gondola is completely unique and provides an experience which should really not be missed.

*Apr-31 Oct to daily timetable beginning 11.00.
Booking Tel: 015394 41288 or 35599*

Prices & timetable on application

Roman Era

Roman Army Museum

Greenhead Carlisle Cumbria CA6 7JB

Tel: 01697 747485 Fax: 01434 344060

[Greenhead is situated off the A69 Carlisle-Newcastle Upon Tyne road on the B6318 approximately .75m from Hadrians Wall]

Join the Roman Army after watching the recruitment film with audio visual effects. Free family activity sheets. Video films. General display. Education facilities. New Eagle's Eye Film - virtual aerial guided tour of a section of Hadrian's Wall with a virtually reconstructed return flight.

Feb-Mar daily 10.00-17.00, Apr-Sept daily 10.00-18.00, Oct- Nov daily 10.00-17.00

A£3.50 C£2.20 Concessions£3.00 Family Ticket (A2+C2) £13.00

Sport & Recreation

The Sands Centre

The Sands Carlisle Cumbria CA1 1JQ

Tel: 01228 625222 Fax: 01228 625666

[J 44 M6]

Cumbria's largest entertainment venue incorporating a full activities programme for recreation and sports, for all ages.

Reception 09.30-21.30

Individual prices per activity or event

Theme & Adventure Parks

Go Ape! High Wire Forest Adventure

Grizedale Forest Visitor Centre Grizedale Hawkshead Ambleside Cumbria LA22 OQJ

Tel: 0870 420 7876

www.goape.cc

[Near Hawkshead on the Satterthwaite Road]

Rural Tourist Attraction of the Year 2003 - NFU Countryside Awards. Designed to appeal to all ages, Go Ape! is an extreme, high wire aerial adventure course of some 37 zip slides, scramble nets and hanging rope bridges - at heights of up to almost 60 feet off the forest floor. Not for the faint hearted, Go Ape! is a thrilling test of agility, courage and determination. Minimum age 10 years, minimum height 1m 40cm/ 4'7". Under 18s must be accompanied by a participating adult. Booking essential.

Apr-Oct daily, also open Feb half term. Closed Nov-Mar

Standard rates: A(18+)£17.00 C(10-17)£12.00

Zoos

South Lakes Wild Animal Park

Crossgates Dalton-in-Furness Cumbria LA15 8JR
Tel: 01229 466086 Fax: 01229 461310
[M6 J36, A590 to Dalton-in-Furness signposted]

The Lake District's only zoological park, recognised as one of Europe's leading conservation zoos. The rolling 17 acres are home to the rarest animals on earth, they are participants in programmes to save them from almost certain extinction in the wild.

All year daily 10.00-17.00, Winter 10.00-16.30. Closed 25 Dec

A£9.50 C(3-16)£6.00 OAPs£6.00. Winter prices: A£6.00 C£4.00

Derbyshire

Arts, Crafts & Textiles

Derby Museum and Art Gallery

The Strand Derby Derbyshire DE1 1BS
Tel: 01332 716659 Fax: 01332 716670
[M1 / A52 or M1 / A6]

The museum has a wide range of displays, notably of Derby porcelain and of paintings by the local artist Joseph Wright (1734-97). Also antiquities, natural history and militaria, as well as many temporary exhibitions.
All year Mon 11.00-17.00, Tue-Sat 10.00-17.00, Sun & Bank Hol 14.00-17.00. Closed Christmas and New Year
Admission Free

Caverns & Caves

Heights of Abraham - Cable Cars, Caverns and Hilltop Park

Matlock Bath Matlock Derbyshire DE4 3PD

Tel: 01629 582365 Fax: 01629 581128

www.heights-of-abraham.co.uk

[On A6 N of Derby]

A unique Hilltop Park set on top of a dramatic limestone gorge, amid great natural beauty. Ride high above the Derwent Valley in the Cable Cars. Go down two famous Show Caverns, play and picnic areas, 'Who + Why = What' exhibition. Spectacular views, Hi Café and Gift Shops.
14-22 Feb daily 10.00-16.30, 28 Feb-26 Mar

weekends only 10.00-16.30, 27 Mar-31 Oct daily 10.00-17.00

A£8.50 C£5.50 OAPs£6.50. Group rates available for 20+ people: A£7.50 C£4.90 OAPs£5.50

Discount Offer: One Child Free With Full Paying Adult. For The Cable Car & Caverns

Peak Cavern

Peak Cavern Road Castleton Hope Valley Derbyshire S33 8WS

Tel: 01433 620285 Fax: 01433 623229
www.peakcavern.co.uk

[On A625, 15m W of Sheffield, 25m E of Manchester, in centre of Castleton village]

The Peak Cavern is the largest natural cavern in Derbyshire, and has the largest entrance to any cave in Britain. A village once existed inside the cave entrance, built and inhabited by rope makers, who carried out their craft in the cave for over 300 years. Today, ropemaking demonstrations are an integral part of every tour.
Apr-Oct daily 10.00-17.00, Nov-Mar Sat & Sun 10.00-17.00

A£5.50 C(under5)£Free C(5-15)£3.50 Concessions£4.50 Family Ticket (A2+C2) £16.00. Group rates available

Speedwell Cavern

Castleton Hope Valley Derbyshire S33 8WA

Tel: 01433 620512 Fax: 01433 621888

www.speedwellcavern.co.uk

[Off A6187, 0.5m W of Castleton Village]

Visited by boat, this cavern is a vast natural cave and an old lead mine worked in the early 18th century. Parties are taken by guides, who explain the full history and mysteries of this subterranean world 840 feet below the surface.

All year daily, Summer 09.30-17.00, Winter 10.00-16.00

A£6.00 C£4.00 Concessions£5.00. Group rates on application

Poole's Cavern and Buxton Country Park

Green Lane Buxton Derbyshire SK17 9DH

Tel: 01298 26978 Fax: 01298 73563

www.poolescavern.co.uk

[A515 Ashbourne road 15min walk from Buxton town centre]

Limestone rock, water and millions of years created this magnificent natural cavern. Rich in spectacular formations including Derbyshire's largest stalactite and the unique Poached Egg chamber. Set in 100 acres of beautiful woodland with walks to a panoramic viewpoint tower at 1440ft. Please call for information on new, award winning disabled access.

Mar-Oct daily 10.00-17.00 (Group bookings all year round)

A£5.50 C£3.00 Family Ticket £15.00. Concessions and Group rates available

Discount Offer: 20% Off Admission Price With This Voucher

Treak Cliff Cavern

Buxton Road Castleton Hope Valley Derbyshire
S33 8WP

Tel: 01433 620571 Fax: 01433 620519

www.bluejohnstone.com

[Castleton is situated at the centre of the Peak National Park on the A6187. 16m from Sheffield and 29m from Manchester within easy reach of the M1 and M6]

Treak Cliff Cavern at Castleton has been a working Blue John mine since 1750 and open to the public as a visitor attraction since 1935. Visitors can see some of the finest stalactites and stalagmites in the Peak District whilst also experiencing the beauty of Blue John Stone. The largest areas of Blue John stone ever revealed can be fully appreciated by the light of newly installed spotlights. The largest single piece ever discovered can still be seen in situ. This underground wonderland also contains thousands of stalactites and stalagmites plus all kinds of rocks, minerals and fossils. Multi coloured flowstone covers the walls of Aladdin's cave, whilst the most famous formation is The Stork, standing on one leg. The Cavern is enjoyed by visitors of all ages from all over the world. No wheelchair access - walking disabled only. Facilities for partially deaf visitors.

All year, Mar-Oct daily 10.00, last tour 16.20, Nov-Feb daily 10.00, last tour 15.20. Closed 24-25 Dec and 1 Jan (open 1 Jan 2005). Please call for further details of holiday opening times

A£5.80 C(5-16)£3.00 Concessions£5.20 Family Ticket £16.00. Discounts for pre-booked parties

<u>Special Events</u>

Polish Your Own Blue John Stone
03/04/2004-31/10/2004
Held on 3-18 Apr, 29 May-6 June, 24 July-5 Sept and 23-31 Oct

Easter Egg Hunt
10/04/2004
Take a guided tour of the underground and search for eggs. Look out for the Easter Bunny inside the Cavern

Carols by Candlelight
11/12/2004-19/12/2004
Held on 11-12 & 18-19 Dec. Carol singing in a festive underground atmosphere. Admission by ticket only, booked and paid for in advance. Please call 01433 621487 for further details

Exhibition & Visitor Centres

Conkers

Millennium Avenue Rawdon Road Moira
Swadlincote Derbyshire DE12 6GA

Tel: 01283 216633 Fax: 01283 210321

www.visitconkers.com

[M1, M42/A42 and A444. Approx. 30mins from Birmingham, Leicester, Derby and Nottingham. Bus: Regular bus services: Leicestershire 0116 251 1411; Derbyshire 01332 29220; Staffordshire 01785 223344; National Express 0990 808080. Rail: Burton upon Trent, Lichfield, Tamworth, Leicester and Loughborough. Plenty of on site parking available]

CONKERS the 120-acre attraction in The Heart of the National Forest, two award winning buildings linked by a train! Relax and enjoy amazing indoor exhibits and outdoor experiences. Feel a leaf breathe, touch a toad... tackle the assault course or rise to the challenge of Billy Bonkers playpark. Enjoy the Artscape sculpture trail, water play area and Forest Garden. Discover wildlife through the woodland and wetland walks; tree canopy walk way and bird hide. Relax in one of two lakeside restaurants. Enjoy events all year round, explore our innovative education programme and browse in our shops.

All year daily 10.00-18.00

A£5.95 C£3.95 Concession£4.95 Family Ticket (A2+C2) £17.50

Special Events

'A Taste of Africa' Sculpture Exhibition
01/01/2004-31/12/2004
Over 30 magnificent stone sculptures grace the woodland park. Artists represented include Henry Munyaradzi, Amos Supuni and Dominic Benhura. Sculptures available for sale and to commission from Just Zimbabwe - the flouze of stone

East-er Midlands Fine Foods Fayre
09/04/2004-12/04/2004
Featuring the best of the region's fine food and drink products

Metamorphosis
01/05/2004-04/06/2004
An exciting exhibition of contemporary art and sculpture inspired by Conkers' evolution from colliery to award winning attraction. A collaboration by a new group of local artists called Morph. The exhibition takes place in the 'Tree of Life Hall' and is free to Conkers' visitors

Moira Canal Festival 2004 - a bicentenary celebration
15/05/2004-16/05/2004
The main event site is at Moira Furnace, with activities incorporating the length of the canal between the canal basin at Conkers Waterside and Donisthorpe Miner's Welfare. Attractions include boats of all varieties, live steam, music, family entertainment, historic re-enactments, vintage engines, trade and craft stalls. For further information please call 01530 273956

'The Green Team' out of school club
01/06/2004-04/06/2004
Environmental fun and games supervised by our educational rangers. Operates 10.00-16.00 and is suitable for children aged 8-12 years. Cost: C£20.00 per person, per day, including lunch

and Billy Bonkers cap. Pre-booking essential on 01283 213731

Father's Day Assault Course Challenge
20/06/2004

Don Giovanni by the Garden Opera Company
03/07/2004
In the Lakeside Amphitheatre at Conkers Waterside. Tickets: £20.00 per person, call 01283 216633 for details

The Last Night of the Proms
31/07/2004
In the Lakeside Amphitheatre at Conkers Waterside. Please call 01283 216633 for details

Family Learning Day
16/10/2004
Packed with free arts, crafts, environmental and IT workshops

Halloween Spooky Fun
31/10/2004
Ghost walks in the haunted woods if you dare! Storytelling, Halloween disco and fancy dress competition, craft activities. For tickets and further information please call 01283 216633

Rotary Firework Extravaganza
06/11/2004
One of the highlights of the Conkers event calendar. Doors open at 17.00 and tickets include free entrance into exhibits. Main event starts at 19.30. Food, drink and children's entertainment also. Please call 01283 216633 for further information and tickets

Santa Specials
04/12/2004-23/12/2004
Held on 4, 5, 11, 12, 18, 19, 20, 21, 22, 23 Dec only. Take a festive train ride to visit Santa in his woodland Grotto. Enjoy a glass of mulled wine and a minced pie whilst the children visit Santa and reeive a Christmas gift. Pre-booking essential on 01283 216633

Factory Outlets & Tours

Denby Pottery Visitor Centre

Derby Road Denby Ripley Derbyshire DE5 8NX

Tel: 01773 740799 Fax: 01773 740749

www.denbyvisitorcentre.co.uk

[We are next to the Pottery on the B6179, off the A38, 2m S of Ripley and 8m N of Derby. We have parking for 250 cars]

A warm welcome awaits you at Denby Visitor Centre. The centre has an attractive cobbled courtyard with shops, restaurant and play area. Activities include free cookery demonstrations, glass blowing studio and pottery tours. There are lots of bargains on offer in the seconds shop; other shops include gifts, paintings, garden centre and Dartington Crystal. Factory tours are fully guided which gives a refreshing personal touch to the experience. Tours of the working factory run Monday-Thursday at 10.30 and 13.00 (excluding factory holidays), but the new Craftroom Tour is available every day between 11.00-15.00. Here you find out about Denby stoneware past and present then have a go at painting a Denby plate with glaze and making a clay souvenir to take home. This tour is suitable for all ages and can accomodate wheelchairs. Please contact us for information on school holiday activities, special events and factory shop offers.

All year. Factory tours: Mon-Thur 10.30 & 13.00. Craftroom tour daily from 11.00-15.00. Centre open: Mon-Sat 9.30-17.00, Sun 10.00-17.00

Factory tour: A£4.95 C&OAPs£3.95. Craftroom: A£3.50 C&OAPs£2.50

Festivals & Shows

Belper Celebration Arts Fesitval and Carnival

Various venues Belper Derbyshire
Tel: 01773 824527 Fax: 01773 824527
[8m N of Derby on A6. Rail: Belper]

The Carnival Procession through Belper starts from Belper Market Place, and goes down King Street, and along Bridge Street to the Football Ground. This event is followed by an Arts Festival featuring Music, Poetry, Sculptors, Sport and Paintings.
May 15-21 2004
Most events are £Free

Castleton Ancient Garland Ceremony 2004

Castleton Hope Valley Derbyshire S33 8WP
Tel: 01433 621595 Fax: 01433 621767
[A625 from Sheffield, A6 & A6187 from Manchester. Rail: Sheffield / Manchester to Hope]

Ancient fertility rite involving the Garland King who rides on horseback wearing the Garland itself, which is a beehive shaped headdress covered in flowers.
May 29 2004, 18.30-21.00
Admission Free

Dove Holes International Beer and Jazz Festival

Dove Holes Community Hall Dove Holes Buxton Derbyshire
Tel: 01298 814722
[A6 Manchester road out of Buxton]

A festival focusing on New Orleans jazz and real ale. We have top New Orleans style bands with a bar serving around 20 real ales. We provide a campsite for festival patrons and events in the

local pubs over the weekend. Known as "The Small Friendly Festival with the Big Names".
July 2-4 2004
Weekend ticket: A£25.00 in advance

Folk & Local History Museums

Eyam Museum

Hawkhill Road Eyam Hope Valley Derbyshire
S32 5QP

Tel: 01433 631371 Fax: 01433 631371

www.eyam.org.uk

[Off A623 signed R to Eyam on B6521, follow white & brown signs]

Bubonic Plague! Our main theme is the famous outbreak in Eyam in 1665/6. You will see the world-wide spread of plague, leading to its arrival from London in 1665 in a fatally infected bundle of cloth. The awful symptoms are described, and some very strange ancient cures! Carefully researched stories of individual families are graphically told. You see the Rectors Mompesson and Stanley discussing the quarantining of the village, and the dreadful last days of Plague victim John Daniel. We go on to show how the village recovered. Silk, cotton, agriculture, shoes, lead and fluorspar mining, and quarrying played their part in Eyam's subsequent history. We end with a display of fine local minerals and fossils. A 30 seat lecture room is available for talks to pre-booked parties. There is wheelchair access to the ground floor, and a stairlift is available.

30 Mar-7 Nov Tue-Sun & Bank Hol 10.00-16.30

A£1.75 C&OAPs£1.25 Family Ticket £5.00.
Group rates on application

Forests & Woods

Rosliston Forestry Centre

Burton Road Rosliston Swadlincote Derbyshire
DE12 8JX

Tel: 01283 563483 Fax: 01283 563483
www.forestry.gov.uk

[On the Rosliston to Burton road, signposted off the A444 at Castle Gresley. Bus: Arriva 22 from Swadlincote or Burton, Mon-Sat]

Opened in 1994, Rosliston Forestry Centre is being developed by The Forestry Commission and South Derbyshire District Council in partnership with The National Forest Company. The site consists of 154 acres of land containing new community woodlands of conifer and native broadleaf blocks, ponds, gardens, meadows and the Rolls-Royce Greenheart Lake. There is plenty to see and do from quiet places to enjoy the countryside and waymarked trails for all ability levels, to family fun activities like crazy golf, basketball, cycle hire and routes, orienteering, and fishing. For the kids there's also a soft play area and adventure playground. The visitor centre holds a licensed restaurant which caters for parties as well as visitors, craft shops and a classroom used by the on-site education staff, Rascals the after school club and local groups. For details of Rosliston's events programme and other activities please contact the Centre Manager.

All year daily, 08.00-dusk

Admission Free. Some priced attractions and car park charges apply

Heritage & Industrial

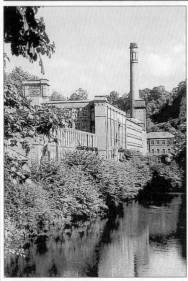

Sir Richard Arkwright's Masson Mills

Working Textile Museum Derby Road Matlock Bath Derbyshire DE4 3PY

Tel: 01629 581001 Fax: 01629 581001

www.massonmills.co.uk

[On the A6 0.5m S of Matlock Bath. Rail: 1m. Bus stop directly outside. Plenty of on site parking available]

Sir Richard Arkwright's Masson Mills were built in 1783 on the banks of the River Derwent at Matlock Bath, Derbyshire. These beautifully restored mills are recognised as perhaps the best example remaining of an eighteen century cotton mill and are the finest and best preserved example of one of Arkwright's mills. They now house a shopping village and a Working Textile Museum where you can experience the genuine atmosphere of the mills by stepping back in time to see authentic historic textile machinery spinning yarn and weaving cloth. Gateway to Derwent Valley Mills World Heritage Site.

Working Textile Museum: All year Mon-Fri 10.00-

16.00 Sat 11.00-17.00 Sun 11.00-16.00. Closed Christmas Day and Easter Day

A£2.50 C(5-16)£1.50 Concessions £2.00 Family Ticket £6.50. School Groups C£1.00. Adult Groups (30+) A£2.00

Discount Offer: Two For The Price Of One

The Silk Mill - Derby's Museum of History and Industry

Silk Mill Lane Derby Derbyshire DE1 3AR
Tel: 01332 255308
[M1/A52, off Full Street]

Displays form an introduction of the industrial history of Derby and Derbyshire. They include railway engineering and power galleries, and a major collection of Rolls Royce aero-engines ranging from an Eagle of 1915 to an RB211 from the first Tristar airliner.
All year Mon 11.00-17.00, Tue-Sat 10.00-17.00, Sun & Bank Hol 14.00-17.00. Closed Christmas & New Year
Admission Free

Historical

Chatsworth

Bakewell Derbyshire DE45 1PP
Tel: 01246 582204 / 565300
Fax: 01246 583536
[8m N of Matlock off B6012. 16m from J29 M1 signposted via Chesterfield. 30m from J19 M6]

Chatsworth is the palatial home of the Duke and Duchess of Devonshire and has one of the richest collections of fine and decorative arts in private hands. Garden with fountain and maze. The park is one of the finest in Britain, laid out by Capability Brown.
17 Mar-19 Dec. House: 11.00-17.30. Garden: 11.00-18.00, June-Aug Garden opens at 10.30.

Farmyard & Adventure Playground: 10.30-17.30
House & Garden: A£9.00 C£3.50
Concessions£7.00 Family Ticket £21.50

Eyam Hall

Eyam Hope Valley Derbyshire S32 5QW
Tel: 01433 631976 Fax: 01433 631603
[Approximately 10m from Sheffield / Chesterfield / Buxton. Eyam Hall is off A623 which runs between Stockport / Chesterfield in centre of village past church]

Robert and Nicola Wright welcome you to their family home, Eyam Hall and hope you will enjoy your visit to this fascinating 17th century house, with its collections of portraits, tapestries, costumes and family memorabilia.
House: July & Aug Wed, Thur, Sun & Bank Hol 11.00-16.00. Craft Centre & Buttery: All year Tue-Sun 10.30-17.00
Craft Centre: Admission Free. House: A£4.75 C£3.50 Concessions£4.25 Family Ticket £15.50. Garden: A£2.00 C£1.00

Melbourne Hall and Gardens

Church Square Melbourne Derbyshire DE73 1EN
Tel: 01332 862502 Fax: 01332 862263
[9m S of Derby on A514]

1133 saw Henry I give the manor of Melbourne to the first Bishop of Carlisle, sold to Sir John Coke (Charles I Secretary of State in 1628) and still owned by his descendants. Converted over time to a grander residence, the home of two Prime Ministers Palmerston and Melbourne, now houses collections of art and antiques with formal gardens laid out in the French style.
Gardens: Apr-Sept Wed, Sat, Sun & Bank Hol Mon 13.30-17.30. House: Aug only Tue-Sat 14.00-17.00. Sun & Bank Hol Mon (No Guided Tours)
House Guided Tour: A£3.00 C£1.50

OAPs£2.50. House: A£2.50 OAPs£2.00 C£1.00. House & Garden: Aug only A£5.00 OAPs£4.00 C£3.00. Garden only: A£3.00 OAPs£2.00 Family Ticket £8.00

Arkwright's Cromford Mill

Mill Road Cromford Matlock Derbyshire DE4 3RQ
Tel: 01629 823256 Fax: 01629 823256
[Turn off A6 at Cromford follow brown tourist signs. Rail: on Derby-Matlock branch line]

The world's first successful water powered cotton spinning mill. Guided tours, shops, restaurant. There is an on going restoration programme and a guide will explain the history and plans for the future.
All year daily 09.00-17.00. Guided tours 09.00-17.00. Closed 25 Dec
Guided tours & exhibitions: A£2.00 C&OAPs£1.50. Mill: Admission Free

Midland Railway - Butterley

Butterley Station Ripley Derbyshire DE5 3QZ

Tel: 01773 747674 /570140 info Fax: 01773 570721
[J28 M1 then A38 to Derby, signposted from the A38]

This centre not only operates a regular steam-train passenger service, but also provides the focal point for an industrial museum project. Amongst new inclusions are the fascinating museum; country park; farm park; narrow gauge, miniature and model railway and much more to provide an interesting and informative day out for the whole family.
Trains operate all year call for timetable
A£7.95 C(0-5)£Free C£4.00 OAPs£6.95

Sporting History Museums

Donington Grand Prix Collection

Donington Park Castle Donington Derby
Derbyshire DE74 2RP

Tel: 01332 811027 Fax: 01332 812829

www.doningtoncollection.com

*[At the Donington Park Grand Prix Circuit, just off
the A453, close to J23a/24 M1 and M42/A42]*

The Donington Grand Prix Collection is the
World's largest collection of Grand Prix racing
cars, with a display of over 130 exhibits con-
tained within five halls, depicting motor sport
history from the early 1900s to the present day.
Cars on display include those driven by 1938
Donington Grand Prix winner Tazio Nuvolari, Sir
Henry Segrave, Sir Stirling Moss OBE, Jim
Clark, Graham Hill, Damon Hill, Nigel Mansell,
Eddie Irvine and many more. These include
Nuvolari's personal 1934 2.9 litre Maserati 8CM,
and the amazing 1936 Alfa Romeo Bimotore,
which features twin engines, with a power out-
put of 500 bhp and a top speed approaching
200mph. The World's largest collection of
McLaren Formula One cars on public display
also features, together with the world's most
complete collection of Vanwalls, a line-up of
Williams cars, and a fabulous display of BRMs.

*All year daily 10.00-17.00. Closed certain days
between Christmas and New Year*

A£7.00 C(0-5)£Free C(6-16)£2.50 Family Ticket
(A2+C3) £14.00 OAPs&Students£5.00

Theme & Adventure Parks

American Adventure

Ilkeston Derbyshire DE7 5SX

Tel: 0845 330 2929 Fax: 01773 716140

www.americanadventure.co.uk

*[6m from J26 M1, Heanor to Ilkeston road
(A6007). Rail: Langley Mill or Derby and
Nottingham]*

With awesome rides, attractions and live shows
The American Adventure is a great family day
out at a price you can afford! 'Swing into action'
at The American Adventure this summer and try
our Missile Rollercoaster, Nightmare Niagara
Log Flume or Rocky Mountains Rapids. We
have something for everyone from gentle children's rides to white knuckle thrill rides. Enjoy all
these rides and lots and lots more!

3 Apr-31 Oct daily from 10.00

A£16.50 C(12&under)£13.50 C(1.01m-
1.22m)£11.99 C(1.0m&below)£Free. Group
rates available on request, call 01773 535301

**Discount Offer: Two For One On Full
Adult Entry Price.**

Gullivers Kingdom Theme Park

Temple Walk Matlock Bath Derbyshire DE4 3PG
Tel: 01925 444888 info line Fax: 01629 57710
[J28 M1 and follow signs. A38 exit M6 towards

Lichfield and follow until signposts]

Plenty of attractions and rides to keep the whole family occupied, including cable car ride, Royal Cave Tour, Wild West Street and Alpine Log Flume.
Please call for varied opening times
A£8.30 C(under90cm)£Free OAPs£7.30

Transport Museums

Crich Tramway Village

Crich Matlock Derbyshire DE4 5DP

Tel: 0870 758 7267 Fax: 01773 852326

www.tramway.co.uk

[J28 M1, signs from A6 and A38, off B5035. Plenty of parking on site]

Crich Tramway Village, offers a family day out in the relaxing atmosphere of a bygone era. Explore the recreated period street with its genuine buildings and features, fascinating exhibitions and most importantly, its trams. Unlimited tram rides are free with your entry fee, giving you the opportunity to fully appreciate Crich Tramway Village and the surrounding countryside. Journey on one of the many beautifully restored vintage trams, as they rumble through the cobbled street past the Red Lion pub and restaurant, exhibition hall, workshops, viewing gallery, children's play and picnic area, before passing beneath the magnificent Bowes-Lyon Bridge. Next it's past the bandstand, through the woods, and then on to Glory Mine taking in spectacular views of the Derwent Valley. New for 2004, Woodland Walk and Sculpture Trail.

4-22 Feb daily 10.30-16.00, 1-31 Mar Sat & Sun 10.30-16.00, 1 Apr-31 Oct daily 10.30-16.00, Nov-19 Dec Sat-Sun 10.30-16.00

A£8.00 C(3-15)£3.50 Family Ticket £20.00 OAPs£6.50. Group rates: A£7.00 C£3.00

OAPs£5.50

Discount Offer: One Child Free With Every Full Paying Adult

Devon

Animal Attractions

Miniature Pony and Animal Farm

Wormhill Farm North Bovey Newton Abbot
Devon TQ13 8RG

Tel: 01647 432400 Fax: 01647 433662

www.miniatureponycentre.com

*[B3212 just 2m W of Moretonhampstead on the
Princetown rd on Dartmoor]*

'Animals + activities + adventure = a fun day
out'. Meet and touch more than 150 animals,
including our famous miniature ponies and donkeys. You will also meet lots of very friendly
pigs, goats, cows, lambs, and new, alpacas
and chipmunks. Also new is Cute 'n' Cuddly,
where you can meet lots of smaller animals,
including rabbits, chinchillas and friends. There
is no better way for the children to be introduced to animals than here. There are supervised pony rides in our new outdoor riding
arena. With at least 9 different free activities
every day, the whole family can really join in.
The activities change according to the season,
so please check the Activities Timetable on the
blackboard when you arrive, and remember, listen for the bell. Older children can choose
between outdoor and indoor adventure play
areas. Younger children can choose between
HorsePlay, our new indoor soft play area, or the
play park beside the picnic area.

*1 Apr-31 Oct daily, 6 Nov-19 Dec Sat & Sun only,
20-24 Dec daily, 10.00-17.00*

A£6.00 C£5.00 OAPs£5.00 Family Ticket
(A2+C2) £20.00

Country Parks & Estates

Escot Country Park and Gardens

Escot Fairmile Nr Exeter Devon EX11 1LU
Tel: 01404 822188 Fax: 01404 822903
[0.5m off the A30 Exeter to Honiton road]

Escot is 220 acres of stunning 18th century
parkland and gardens filled with rare shrubs and
magnificent trees, and teeming with wildlife.
There are otters and wild boar, red squirrels and
in spring and summer, impressive birds of prey
displays. The formal gardens and woodland of
this beautiful estate are being transformed by
Ivan Hicks, one of the foremost landscape gar-
dener-artists of our age.
*Open all year except Christmas Day and Boxing
Day 10.00-18.00 (10.00-17.00 Nov to Easter)*
A£4.95 C(4-15)&OAPs£3.50 C(0-4)£Free Family
of 4 £15.00 (reduced rates available during winter months)

Exhibition & Visitor Centres

High Moorland Visitor Centre

Tavistock Road Princetown Yelverton Devon
PL20 6QF

Tel: 01822 890414 Fax: 01822 890566

[Accessible from Plymouth / Exeter along B3212]

The Centre offers a comprehensive information
service and a good range of books and walking
accessories. There are exciting displays giving a
unique insight into Dartmoor, its landscape and
cultural heritage.

*All year daily, 10.00-17.00 peak season, 10.00-
16.00 off peak. Closed 24, 25, 26 Dec and 1
week in March*

Admission Free

Factory Outlets & Tours

Dartington Crystal

Linden Close Torrington Devon EX38 7AN

Tel: 01805 626242 Fax: 01805 626263

www.dartington.co.uk

[At intersection of routes between Barnstaple, Plymouth, Bideford, Exeter and South Molton, in centre of Torrington. Follow brown tourist signs. Rail: Exeter St. Davids change for Barnstaple, taxis available from here. Plenty of car parking on site]

Dartington Crystal is internationally famous for beautiful, handmade glassware. Visitors to the factory will be fascinated to watch the highly skilled craftsmen blowing and shaping crystal, perfecting an art form of 3,000 years in the making. Discover the history of glass and the unique Dartington story in the popular visitor centre, or have fun and get hands-on in the family activity area. You can also visit our glass, gift and Tarka Mill Shops for great bargains at factory prices or simply relax in our fully licensed Pavilion Café.

All year. Visitor Centre, Factory Tour, Pavilion Café and Shops: Mon-Fri 09.00-17.00, Sat 10.00-17.00, Sun 10.00-16.00 (tours only available Mon-Fri). Please call to confirm details of Christmas, New Year and Bank Hol opening times

A£4.50 C(0-16)£Free OAPs£3.50

Discount Offer: One Adult Free With Each Full Paying Adult

Festivals & Shows

5th North Devon Festival

Tel: 01271 324242
[From the E: M5, J27, A361 A39. From the W/S: A39 up through Bude or the A386 from Okehampton]

The North Devon Festival is rapidly establishing itself as a major UK festival. It is a celebration of the rich and diverse cultural life in North Devon, with a wide range of activities that reflect the character of the region. The festival is probably unique in the UK as it includes not only top quality arts and entertainment, but also many events associated with the people and the place, those things which residents and visitors love about the natural beauty of the area. They include heritage, community, lifestyle, sports and horticultural activities.
June 4-27 2004

Brixham Heritage Festival

Brixham Devon TQ5 9JS
Tel: 01803 858362
The Heritage Festival features live music, car rallies, classic boat rallies and children's entertainment. There will also be two firework displays on the pier with synchronised music, and a photography exhibition and competition. Punch and Judy shows will be there, and the Gloucestershire Youth Jazz Orchestra.
May 29 - June 5 2004
Admission charge for Gourmet Meal, Classic Boat Meal and Greek Night. Other entertainment Free

Hunting of the Earl of Rone

Combe Martin North Devon
Tel: 01271 882366
[On A399 between Ilfracombe and Lynton]

Villagers parade with Grenadiers and a be-ribboned Hobby Horse led by a Fool in a Smock. Spectacle includes drummers, musicians and dancers and on the Mon evening there is a masked person in a sack cloth riding back to front on a donkey - the Earl of Rone. He is shot, revived and finally cast into the sea. Fri eve, starting at Kiln Car Park near seaside at 19.30. Sat, starting from the school at 11.00. Sun,

starting from Sandaway Caravan Park at 13.30.
Mon, starting from Top George Inn at 18.00.
May 28-31 2004
Admission Free

Port of Brixham Trawler Race 2004

Fish Quay Brixham Devon TQ5 8AW
Tel: 01803 883548/07966 230416
Trawler race, music, demonstrations, charity
stalls, children's rides, film show, model boat
race. Navy boat in attendance.
June 19 2004, 10.00 onwards
Admission Free. Programme £1.00

Sidmouth International Festival

Station Road Sidmouth Devon EX10 8NZ
Tel: 01629 760123 Fax: 01629 760777
[J30 M5 then A3052]

The 50th Festival with hundreds of events
including a celebration of the history of the festival. International music and dance spectaculars,
concerts, ceilidhs, workshops, processions,
craft fair and children's festival.
July 31 - August 6 2004
Prices range from A£3.00 C£1.00

Tiverton Spring Festival 2004

Tiverton Devon EX16 6LU
Tel: 01884 258952
Operas, orchestral, street entertainment, drama,
lectures, music and dancing, rock concerts,
exhibitions and much more.
May 8-16 2004
Prices vary. Information available from: Tourist
Information 01884 255827

Heritage & Industrial

Underground Passages

Romangate Passage High Street Exeter Devon
EX4 3PZ
Tel: 01392 665887 Fax: 01392 265695
*[J30 M5, follow signs for Exeter, use city centre
car parks or park and ride scheme]*

A remarkable medieval water system with an
introductory exhibition and video presentation.
Definitely not for those inclined to claustropho-
bia. Britain's only ancient city passageways
open to the public. Guides pass on fascinating
tales and facts, from rats and ghosts to the
financial wheeling and dealing associated with
the provision of water in the city. Not suitable for
children under 5 years old.
*June-Sept & School Hol Mon-Sat 10.00-17.00,
other times Tue-Fri 12.00-17.00 & Sat 10.00-
17.00. Advanced booking advised*
Oct-May: A£3.00 C£2.00 Family Ticket £9.00.
June-Sept: A£3.75 C£2.75 Family Ticket
£11.00

Historical

Berry Pomeroy Castle

Berry Pomeroy Totnes Devon TQ9 6NJ
Tel: 01803 866618
[2.5m E of Totnes off A385]

A romantic late-medieval castle, unusual in
combining the remains of a large castle with a
flamboyant courtier's mansion. It is reputed to
be the most haunted castle in Devon. Tales of
apparitions, kidnappings and other dark deeds
make a haunting experience for visitors. It has a
picnic area of exceptional beauty.
*1 Apr-31 Oct daily 10.00-17.00 (July-Aug 10.00-
18.00, Oct 10.00-16.00)*
A£3.00 C£1.50 Concessions£2.30

Cadhay

Ottery St. Mary Devon EX11 1QT
Tel: 01404 812962 Fax: 01404 812962
[Near J of A30 & B3176]

A mile north west of Ottery, over Cadhay

Bridge, this beautiful Tudor and Georgian house is well worth a visit. It was begun in 1550 and stands around a courtyard.

July-Aug Fri 14.00-18.00, Sun & Mon Bank Hol of late spring and summer

A£5.00 C£2.00

Dartmouth Castle

Castle Road Dartmouth Devon TQ6 0JN
Tel: 01803 833588 Fax: 01803 834445
[1m SE off B3205, narrow approach road]

This brilliantly positioned defensive castle juts out into the narrow entrance of the Dart estuary with the sea lapping at its feet. It was one of the first castles constructed with artillery in mind and has seen 450 years of fortification and preparation for war.

1 Apr-31 Oct daily 10.00-17.00 (July-Aug 10.00-18.00, Oct 10.00-16.00), 1 Nov-31 Mar Sat-Sun 10.00-16.00. Closed 24-26 Dec & 1 Jan

A£3.50 C£1.80 Concessions£2.60

Tiverton Castle

Park Hill Tiverton Devon EX16 6RP
Tel: 01884 253200 / 255200
Fax: 01884 254200
[In Tiverton 7m from J27 M5 A361 to Tiverton - signposted]

Few buildings evoke such immediate feeling of history. Originally built in 1106, rebuilt 14th Century. Many architectural styles. Castle witnessed extremes of peace and turbulence, but is now a peaceful, private house. Fine Civil War Armoury, come and try some on. Beautiful Gardens.

Easter-June & Sept Sun, Thur & Bank Hol Mon 14.30-17.30, July & Aug Sun-Thur 14.30-17.30

A£4.00 C(under 7)£Free C(7-16)£2.00

Torre Abbey Historic House and Gallery

Torre Abbey The Kings Drive Torquay TQ2 5JE

Tel: 01803 293593 Fax: 01803 215948

www.torre-abbey.org.uk

[On Torquay sea front next to the Riviera Centre]

From monastery to Mayor's parlour, Torre Abbey is Torquay's most historic building. Situated by the sea, and surrounded by colourful gardens, the Abbey offers you a delightful visit. Over 20 historic rooms, Monastic ruins, stunning paintings, memorials of crime-writer Agatha Christie, special children's quest.

1 Apr-1 Nov daily 09.30-18.00

A£3.50 C(8-15)£1.70 OAP&Students£3.00 Family Ticket £7.75. Group rates £2.75

Discount Offer: One Child Free. With Every Full Paying Adult

Totnes Castle

Castle Street Totnes Devon TQ9 5NU
Tel: 01803 864406 Fax: 01803 864406
A classic example of the Norman motte-and-bailey castle. Totnes dates from the 11th century. The circular shell-keep is protected by a curtain wall erected in the 13th century and reconstructed in the 14th. Marvellous views from the walls of the keep across the town to the Dart Valley.

1 Apr-31 Oct daily 10.00-17.00, (July-Aug 10.00-18.00, Oct 10.00-16.00)
A£2.00 C£1.00 Concessions£1.50

Mills - Water & Wind

Old Corn Mill and Pottery

Watermouth Road Hele Ilfracombe Devon EX34 9QY

Tel: 01271 863185 Fax: 01271 863185

[Off A399, follow tourist signs]

A unique 16th century watermill that can produce wholemeal flour and muesli. Pottery by Robin Gray or 'you' make a pot on the potters wheel.

Easter or 1 Apr-31 July Mon-Sat 10.00-17.00, 1-31 Aug daily 10.00-18.00, 1 Sept-31 Oct Mon-Sat 10.00-17.00
A£2.50 C(0-4)£Free C£1.50 OAPs£2.00

Nature & Conservation Parks

Gnome Reserve and Wildflower Garden

West Putford Bradworthy Devon EX22 7XE

Tel: 0870 845 9012 Fax: 0870 845 9012

[J27 M5]

A trip to North Devon is not complete without a visit to The Gnome Reserve. Two acres of enchanted woodland with 1,000+ gnomes and pixies to meet: Fish in the Ottery, sit in the circle of imagination or go inside a pixie dwelling. Optional Gnome Hats and Fishing Rods loaned FOC.

21 Mar-31 Oct daily 10.00-18.00

A£2.45 C(3-16)£1.90 C(0-3)£Free OAPs£2.20

On the Water

Grand Western Horseboat Company

The Wharf Canal Hill Tiverton Devon EX16 4HX

Tel: 01884 253345 Fax: 01884 255984

www.horseboat.co.uk

[Situated midway between Exeter and Taunton, 7m from M5 J27. On approaching Tiverton follow brown signs for 'Grand Western Canal'. Plenty of on site parking available. Rail: Tiverton railway station 7m, buses run from Tiverton hourly. Bus: 10min walk from Tiverton Bus Station]

The West Country is privileged to have one of England's few remaining traditional Horse-drawn Barges enchanting thousands of visitors with an experience of peace and tranquillity, now so rarely enjoyed. The Canal dates back to 1814, built primarily for the lime trade. It is now a very beautiful Country Park, its banks and towpath are rich in wildlife. Moorhens, coots, and water voles hide amongst the reeds, while dragonflies skim the surface. Yellow water Iris and white water lilies add unique decoration as the Barge ripples onward, and the only sounds to be heard are bird song, nature and the rhythmic clip-clop of the shire horses hooves. Also canal shop, boat hire and picnics.

Apr-Oct Public trips, operating to a published timetable

A£7.65 C£5.05 for a two and a half hour trip. Group rates available. Trip lengths vary from 1-3 hours, operate to published timetable

Railways

Paignton and Dartmouth Steam Railway

Queens Park Station Torbay Road Paignton Devon TQ4 6AF

Tel: 01803 555872 Fax: 01803 664313

www.paignton-steamrailway.co.uk

[Off the M5 follow either the A380 to Newton Abbot then follow signs for Paignton OR take the A379 coastal road to Paignton]

The holiday line with steam trains running for seven miles in Great Western tradition along the spectacular Torbay Coast to Kingswear, with ferry crossing to Dartmouth. Combined River Excursions available 'The Round Robin' and 'Boat Train'. Special trains run for Dartmouth Regatta and the Red Arrows.

Apr, May & Oct. June-Sept daily

Train only Paignton-Kingswear: A£7.00 C(5-15)£5.00 OAPs£6.50 Family Ticket (A2+C2) £22.00. Train & Ferry to Dartmouth: A£8.50 C£5.80 OAPs£8.00 Family Ticket £26.00. Train, Ferry & 'Boat Train' Cruise: A£13.00 C£9.00 OAPs£12.00 Family Ticket £37.00. Train, Ferry, Cruise & Bus: A£13.50 C£9.00 OAPs£12.50 Family Ticket £39.00

Seaton Tramway

Harbour Road Seaton Devon EX12 2NQ
Tel: 01297 20375 Fax: 01297 625626
[20m SE of Taunton]

Seaton Tramway operates in East Devon's glorious Axe Valley and is noted for panoramic views of the Axe estuary and its wading birds. The tramway originated as a portable system in 1949, evolving into the Eastbourne Tramway in 1954; the move to Seaton occurred in 1970 after closure of the Seaton railway branch.
14-22 Feb daily 10.00-16.00, 28 Feb-28 Mar Sat & Sun 10.00-16.00, 3 Apr-24 July daily 10.00-17.00, 25 July-4 Sept daily 10.00-20.40, 5 Sept-31 Oct daily 10.00-17.00, 6 Nov-19 Dec Sat & Sun 10.00-16.00
Seaton-Colyton Return Tickets: A£5.50 C(4-14)£3.85 OAPs£5.00

Sealife Centres & Aquariums

National Marine Aquarium

Rope Walk Coxside Plymouth Devon PL4 0LF
Tel: 01752 600301 Fax: 01752 600593
www.national-aquarium.co.uk

[Follow signs to City Centre and National Marine Aquarium]

Discover Britain's Biggest Aquarium with Europe's Deepest Tank! Voted 'Aquarium of the Year' and 'Devon Family Attraction of the Year' (Good Britain Guide 2003) the Aquarium is now the largest in the UK and a visit will take you right to the heart of the deep seas. You'll see jewel-bright tropical fish and other marine life around every corner, come face to face with the only real giant squid on exhibit anywhere in this country and meet Snorkel, the turtle with the big personality. Plus enjoy an adrenaline-charged encounter with the world's oldest living predator, the shark, in our massive Mediterranean Tank where Roboshark, from the hit BBC programme 'Smart Sharks', will be swimming alongside four large Sand Tiger sharks. Then return to the surface and pause in the beautiful Maritime Garden, visit our shop and enjoy some refreshments in our restaurant with its panoramic views out over Plymouth Sound.

All year daily 1 Nov-31 Mar 10.00-17.00, 1 Apr-31 Oct 10.00-18.00. Closed Christmas Day

A£8.00 C(4-15)£4.75 Concessions£6.50. Group rates (12+): £6.50 Family Ticket (A2+C2) £23.00, school parties from £3.50

Discount Offer: £1.00 Off A Souvenir Guide.

Stately Homes

Arlington Court

Arlington Barnstaple Devon EX31 4LP
Tel: 01271 850296 Fax: 01271 851108
[8m NE of Barnstaple on A39]

The plain exterior of this house, built in neo-classical style in 1822, does little to prepare the visitor for the astonishing rooms inside. Full of collections for every taste, many amassed by the eccentric and widely travelled Miss Rosalie Chichester, they include displays of model ships, costume, pewter, shells and other fascinating objects.
House: 28 Mar-31 Oct Sun-Fri 11.00-17.00. Garden: 28 Mar-30 June Sun-Fri 10.30-17.00, 1 July-31 Aug daily 10.30-16.30, 1 Sept-31 Oct Sun-Fri 10.30-17.00. Grounds: all year dawn-dusk

A£6.00 C£3.00 Family Ticket £15.00 Gardens & Carriage Collection only: A£4.00 C£2.00. On Sat July-Aug (Gardens & Bat Cave only) A£2.60 C£1.30

Theme & Adventure Parks

Crealy Adventure Park

Sidmouth Road Clyst St Mary Exeter Devon EX5 1DR

Tel: 01395 233200 Fax: 01395 233211

www.crealy.co.uk

[Crealy is Easy to Find - Hard to Leave! We are just 4mins from J30 of the M5, on the Sidmouth Road near Exeter. Approximate driving times: Birmingham: 2hrs 30mins. Bournemouth: 2hrs. Bristol: 1hr 30mins. London: 3hrs. Plymouth: 40mins. Taunton 30mins. Torbay: 30mins. Weymouth: 1hr 25mins. Plenty of on site parking available]

Crealy offers an unforgettable day packed with magic, fun and adventure for all the family, with Tidal Wave log flume, El Pastil Loco Coaster, Queen Bess Pirate Ship, Techno Race Karts, Bumper Boats, Victorian Carousel and huge all weather play areas. Visit the Animal Realm to ride, feed, milk, groom or cuddle the friendliest animals in Devon. Unearth the Farming Realm's adventures and the world's first Sunflower Maze. Crealy's restaurant and food outlets offer great food at even greater prices!

All year, 2 Apr-17 July daily 10.00-17.00, 18 July-31 Aug daily 10.00-18.00, 1 Sept-31 Oct daily 10.00-17.00, 1 Nov-1 Apr Wed-Sun (Mon & Tue during school hols) 10.00-17.00

Admission from £7.75 Four-or-more ticket £7.50 C(Under3)£Free OAPs£5.00. Group rates available

Diggerland

Verbeer Manor Cullompton Devon EX5 2PE
Tel: 08700 344437 Fax: 09012 010300
www.diggerland.com

[Exit M5 J27. Head E on A38 turn R at round-about onto B3181. Diggerland is 3M on L hand side. Plenty of on site parking available]

All ages will enjoy the opportunity to ride in and drive different types of machines from Dumper-trucks to JCB Mini Diggers and Large Diggers (all under strict supervision). Taking up challenges like fishing ducks out of a pond using a JCB digger and learning about the machines, makes it a fun and informative attraction. There are over 20 different rides and attractions at Diggerland. Birthday parties are catered for, so if you fancy a party with a difference for your young children then contact us for details.

Weekends & Bank Hols and daily during half-term and school holidays 10.00-17.00. Closed Dec, Jan & Feb

A&OAPs£2.50 C(under 2)£Free C£2.50 which covers all non-mechanical rides. Group rates for 20+ 20% discount. To drive the real diggers costs from £1.00 per ride OR an all day wrist-band at £18.00

Discount Offer: 1/2 Price Entry For Up To 6 People. (Voucher Applies To Entry Charge Only)

Special Events

Easter Sunday
11/04/2004
Free Easter eggs on arrival for kids

4x4 Off Road Day
17/04/2004
Bring your own 4x4 and tackle the challenge of the custom built Diggerland Off Road course - can you get round it or will you get stuck in the mud? Please call for entry tickets well in advance, numbers strictly limited

Metal Micky's Birthday Party
25/04/2004
Metal Micky is 4 years old. Come and join him for a day of fun and celebration

Bob the Builder Day
22/05/2004
Come along dressed as Bob the Builder and enter Diggerland Free. Also a few other Bob surprises!

Fathers Day
20/06/2004
Free admission to Diggerland for all Dads on this special day. Dads are just big kids anyway!

Stunt Demonstrations
04/07/2004
Amazing Digger stunts from our Dancing Diggers display performed hourly throughout the afternoon

Young Driver Experience
15/07/2004
Held on 15 July & 12 Aug only. Personal Tuition on, and a great chance to drive a selection of vehicles including Land Rovers and Diggers, for ages 9-16. Can be purchased as a gift. Ring or email well in advance to book. Cost: £49.00. Numbers strictly limited

Diggerland Summer Fete
25/07/2004
Join in our Summer Fete with an all-day Barbeque, face painting and lots more

Bob the Builder Day
04/09/2004
Come along dressed as Bob the Builder and enter Diggerland Free. Also a few other Bob surprises!

4x4 Off Road Day
10/10/2004
Bring your own 4x4 and tackle the challenge of the custom built Diggerland Off Road course - can you get round it or will you get stuck in the

mud? Please call for entry tickets well in advance, numbers strictly limited

Wildlife & Safari Parks

Combe Martin Wildlife and Dinosaur Park

Combe Martin Ilfracombe Devon EX34 0NG
Tel: 01271 882486 Fax: 01271 883869
www.dinosaur-park.com

[J27 M5. Go W on A361 towards Barnstaple. Turn R onto A399 following signs for Ilfracombe and Combe Martin. Plenty of on site parking available]

The land that time forgot. A Sub Tropical Paradise with hundreds of birds and animals and the most realistic Dinosaurs on the planet. They move, they roar, they're alive! The UK's only full size animatronic Tyrannosaurus Rex plus Dilophosaurus the Spitting Dinosaur - watch out you may get wet! Wander around 26 acres of beautiful botanical gardens with rare plants, cascading waterfalls and free flying exotic birds. Snow leopards, meerkats, apes and monkeys, sealions, timber wolves, tropical but-

terfly house and much more. Daily falconry displays, sealion shows, lemur encounters, and handling sessions. New for 2004, the UK's only Wolf Education and Research Centre. Spectacular lightshow, destination Mars, a truly out of this world experience! Earthquake Canyon, the most unique train ride in the UK. Experience a gigantic earthquake and survive! A great day out for all of the family. As seen on BBC television.

15 Mar-2 Nov daily from 10.00

A£10.00 C(under3)£Free C(3-15)£6.00 OAPs£7.00 Family Ticket (A2+C2) £29.00. Group rates available, please call for details

Discount Offer: One Child Free With Every Two Paying Adults

Zoos

Paignton Zoo, Environmental Park

Totnes Road Paignton Devon TQ4 7EU
Tel: 01803 697500 Fax: 01803 523457
[1m from Paignton centre, on the A385]

You can cover thousands of miles in just a few hours and on foot, on a worldwide nature trail at Paignton Zoo. Over £6 million has been spent on creating one of the best zoos in the country and giving animals the homes they deserve.

All year daily 10.00-18.00 (dusk in winter)

To 1 Nov: A£8.50 C(3-15)£6.20 OAPs&Students£7.00 Family Ticket (A2+C2) £26.70; 2 Nov-31 Mar: A£6.95 C(3-15)£5.10 OAPs/Students£5.70 Family Ticket (A2+C2) £24.00

Dorset

Agriculture / Working Farms

Farmer Palmer's Farm Park

Wareham Road Organford Poole Dorset
BH16 6EU
Tel: 01202 622022 Fax: 01202 622933
[4m from Poole towards Bere Regis off the A35]

Have an exciting and educational day out.
Famer Palmer and his staff are happy to answer
any questions and welcome groups. In The
Animal Barn you will find goats, lambs to feed,
rare Kune Kune pigs, calves, rabbits and guinea
pigs with hands-on supervised handling at set
times during the day. Burn off some excess
energy in the Under Cover Play Area.
*14-22 Feb daily 10.00-16.00, 23 Feb-19 Mar Sat
& Sun 10.00-16.00, 20 Mar-26 Sept daily 10.00-
17.30, 27 Sept-22 Oct Sat & Sun 10.00-16.00,
23-31 Oct daily 10.00-16.00, 1 Nov-19 Dec Sat
& Sun 10.00-16.00*
A£4.50 C(under2)£Free C£3.75 OAPs£4.00
Family Ticket £15.50

Animal Attractions

Monkey World Ape Rescue Centre

Wareham Dorset BH20 6HH
Tel: 01929 462537 Fax: 01929 405414
www.monkeyworld.org

*[Between Bere Regis and Wool off the A35, sign-
posted from Bere Regis]*

Since Monkey World was set up in 1987, the
internationally-acclaimed ape rescue centre in
Dorset has helped change the lives of thousands of primates from around the world.

Dedicated to educating visitors about ape rescue and animal conservation, Monkey World
works with foreign governments to highlight and
put a stop to the illegal trade of apes from the
wild. Monkey World provides a stable, permanent home for over 160 primates including the
largest group of chimpanzees outside Africa,
the most important group of Borneo orangutans
outside of that country, woolly monkeys,
macaques, gibbons and many more. All of the
primates are able to live naturally, as they would
in the wild, in large enclosures with companion-
ship of their own kind. Visitors can observe the
animals, living in social groups and behaving
naturally, in 67 acres of beautiful woodland - a
unique opportunity to see these fascinating
creatures up close. Keepers hold half-hourly
talks with a chance to ask questions and find
out more about Monkey World's residents who
feature in the hugely popular TV programme
'Monkey Business'. Boasting the largest children's play area on the South Coast, Monkey
World combines animal education with fun
offering woodland walks, a pets corner, cafe,
picnic areas and full disabled facilities.

*All year daily 10.00-17.00, July & Aug 10.00-
18.00. Closed 25 Dec*

A£8.00 C£6.00 Concessions£6.00 Family
Ticket (A1+C2) £18.00, (A2+C2) £24.00. Group
rates available on request. School Parties
C£4.00, Teacher £Free on (1:10) ratio

**Discount Offer: One Child Free With
Two Full Paying Adults.**

Arts, Crafts & Textiles

Russell-Cotes Art Gallery and Museum

East Cliff Bournemouth Dorset BH1 3AA
Tel: 01202 451858 Fax: 01202 451851
*[Signposted off A338, venue on the E side of
Bournemouth Pier]*

The museum was built in 1897 as East Cliff Hall.
Together with a new extension and art galleries
it houses a collection of 17th-20th century
paintings, watercolours, sculpture, ceramics,
furniture and world wide collections.
*All year Tue-Sun 10.00-17.00. Closed 25 Dec &
Good Fri*
Admission Free. Guided tours: £2.00 per person, pre-booking required

Walford Mill Craft Centre

Stone Lane Wimborne Dorset BH21 1NL
Tel: 01202 841400 Fax: 01202 841460
www.walfordmillcrafts.co.uk

[From Wimborne heading N on B3078 turn L at traffic lights into Stone Lane, then 1st R after 100yds. Plenty of parking on site]

Walford Mill aims to show the very best in contemporary craft and design. Every month there is a different exhibition in the gallery, and the shop has a wide range of pottery, textiles, jewellery, wood and metalwork, plus books and cards. It is a converted 18th century mill, set in gardens alongside Walford Bridge over the river Allen. It is a popular attraction both for local residents and for visitors to Dorset.

All year daily Mon-Sat 10.00-17.00, Sun 12.00-17.00. Closed Mon Jan-Mar

Admission Free

Special Events

David Leach
10/04/2004-16/05/2004
Ceramic retrospective touring exhibition

Footsteps - Touring exhibition
22/05/2004-04/07/2004

Quilters Part I
10/07/2004-25/07/2004
C&G Patchwork and Quilting Group

Nature in Clay
31/07/2004-05/09/2004

Ian Gregory and other artists

Exploring Furniture
11/09/2004-24/10/2004
Contemporary furniture

Christmas Exhibition
30/10/2004-24/12/2004
Selling exhibition of mixed contemporary craft work

Festivals & Shows

Bournemouth Live! Music Festival

Bournemouth Tourism Westover Road
Bournemouth Dorset BH1 2BU
Tel: 01202 451700 Fax: 01202 451743
Come and listen to the sounds of summer-Bournemouth Live! Music Festival is Bournemouth's premier free summer event attracting bands from all over Europe to perform concerts in and around the town.
June 27-July 3 2004
Admission Free

Great Days Of Summer

Weymouth Beach Dorset DT4
Tel: 01305 785747 Fax: 01305 788092
Highlight of Weymouth's summer season. Internationally themed fireworks, live music, entertainment, competitions and prizes.
August 2, 9, 18, 23 & 30 2004

Military and Veterans Festival 2004

Weymouth Pavilion The Esplanade Weymouth Dorset DT4 8ED
Tel: 01305 785747 Fax: 01305 761654
[M27 / M3 / M5]

Festival includes major parade with marching bands, historic vehicles, Forces Music Hall, band concerts and international veterans rendezvous.

June 19-25 2004
Admission Free

Possum Fez Week

Portesham Weymouth Dorset DT3 4ET
Tel: 01305 871316
[On A3157 Weymouth - Bridport Rd]

Possum Fez Week is a reconstruction of an old festival held in Dorset. Village crier competition, street fair, craft exhibition and much more.
July 29-August 1 2004
Some events free

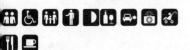

Shaftesbury Summer Festival 2004

Shaftesbury and District Dorset SP7
Tel: 01747 850944 Fax: 01747 850944
[N & S A350, E & W A30]

Including Gold Hill Fair, Shaftesbury Carnival, Gillingham and Shaftesbury Agricultural Show and Shaftesbury and District Arts and Crafts Festival.
June 1-September 30 2004

Weymouth Folk Festival

Pavilion Theatre Weymouth Dorset DT4 8ED
Tel: 01305 783225
The international line up already confirmed includes Show of Hands, Jez Lowe and the Bad Pennies plus Workshops, Concerts, Late Night Sessions, Morris Dancing, Ceilidh, Parades, Folk Village, Dancing, Busking, Pub Sessions, Appalachian Dancing.

May 7-9 2004

Weymouth International Beach Kite Festival

Weymouth Esplanade Weymouth Dorset DT4 8ED
Tel: 01305 785747 Fax: 01305 838556
[M27 / M3 / M5]

With over 500 Kite enthusiasts from all over Britain and around the globe, the Golden Sands of Weymouth will once again play host to this spectacular event. The Skies over Weymouth beach will come to life with an array of Kites in varying colours, shapes and sizes. With over 40,000 spectators expected over the weekend to enjoy and witness this accumulation of colour, this is an event not to be missed.
May 2-3 2004, 10.00-18.00
Admission Free

Weymouth International Firework Displays and Carnival

Weymouth Dorset DT4 8TR
Tel: 01305 785747 Fax: 01305 761654
[M27 / M5 / M3]

Internationally famed fireworks fired from a special floating pontoon in Weymouth Bay. Spectacular views from Weymouth Esplanade. Includes Weymouth Carnival, with the Red Arrows, carnival procession, aerial displays, fun fair and competitions.
August 18 2004
Admission Free

Weymouth International Maritime Modelling Festival

Weymouth Dorset DT4 8ED
Tel: 01305 785747 Fax: 01305 761654

[M5 / M3 / M2.]

Over 1,000 operational models and displays, battleships with live battles, Tall Ships, yacht racing, steam powered, electric speedboats, tug towing, novelty class displays and trawlers, trade stalls and workshops.

July 10-11 2004 10.00-17.00 daily
Admission Free

Weymouth Old Harbour Oyster Festival

Brewers Quay Hope Square Weymouth Dorset DT4 8TR
Tel: 01305 785747 Fax: 01305 761654
[M5 / M3 / M27]

Oyster market, oyster displays and competitions. Full programme of live music, Shire horses, street entertainment, fancy dress, fair, face painting, oyster trail and challenge.

May 30 2004, 10.00-16.00 call for details
Admission Free

Wimborne Folk Festival 2004

Town Centre Wimborne Dorset BH21 1HR
Tel: 01202 743465 Fax: 01202 718488
[A31 from E or W, A350 from N]

One of the largest traditional music and dance festivals, including over 70 dance teams from UK and Europe. Colourful processions, huge craft market, concerts, Ceilidh's, and workshops. Children's entertainment including street theatre, face-painting and musical workshops.

June 11-13 2004, Fri 19.30-Late Sat 10.00-Late Sun 10.30-17.00

Folk & Local History Museums

Tolpuddle Martyrs Museum

TUC Memorial Cottages Tolpuddle Dorchester Dorset DT2 7EH
Tel: 01305 848237
www.tolpuddlemartyrs.org.uk

[Off A35. From Dorchester, Tolpuddle is signposted at Troytown turn off. If you continue further along A35, Museum has brown heritage signpost giving clear directions. From Poole/Bournemouth take A31 then A35 to Dorchester then follow brown heritage signpost]

One dawn, in the bitter February of 1834, six Tolpuddle farm labourers were arrested after forming a trade union. A frightened Squire's trumped up charge triggered one of the most celebrated stories in the history of human rights. Packed with illustrative displays, this new state-of-the-art, interactive exhibition tells the Tolpuddle Martyrs story. Discover why the Judge and Squire were so vindictive - learn who betrayed the Martyrs in the company of Death and the Skeleton - hear about their struggle for survival after transportation to Australia - share the relief of freedom and the pleasure of the homecoming. Call now for a FREE colour brochure.

Apr-Oct Tue-Sat 10.00-17.30, Sun 11.00-17.30 Nov-Mar Tue-Sat 10.00-16.00, Sun 11.00-16.00. Open Bank Holiday Mon, closed other Mon. Closed Christmas-New Year

Admission Free

Special Events

Tolpuddle Martyrs Festival
16/07/2004-18/07/2004

Gardens & Horticulture

Mapperton Gardens

Mapperton Beaminster Dorset DT8 3NR
Tel: 01308 862645 Fax: 01308 863348
[2m SE off A356 & B3163]

Terraced valley gardens surrounding a delightful
Tudor/Jacobean manor house, stable blocks,
and dovecote. There is a 17th century Summer
House, with specimen shrubs and rare trees,
leading to woodland and spring gardens.
Magnificent walks and views.
Mar-Oct daily 14.00-18.00
A£4.00 C(under18)£2.00

Historical

Athelhampton House and Gardens

Athelhampton Dorchester Dorset DT2 7LG
Tel: 01305 848363 Fax: 01305 848135
[Off the A35 1m E of Puddletown, 5m E of Dorchester]

Athelhampton is one of the finest 15th century
manor houses and is surrounded by one of the
great architectural gardens of England. The
house contains many magnificently furnished
rooms. Athelhampton was often visited by
Thomas Hardy.
Mar-Oct Sun-Thur, Nov-Mar Sun, 10.30-17.00
House & Gardens: A£7.75 C£Free OAPs£7.00.
Garden only: £5.50

**Discount Offer: £1.00 Off Adult &
OAPs Admission To House & Garden**

Lulworth Castle and Park

East Lulworth Wareham Dorset BH20 5QS
Tel: 01929 400352 Fax: 01929 400563
[Off B3070]

Beautiful 17th century Castle and Chapel in
delightful parkland. Spectacular views from the
tower, interesting artefacts and displays. Lots
for children, including a special room full of puz-
zles and games, adventure playground, and an
Animal Farm open Easter to September.
*All year Sun-Fri Summer 10.30-18.00, Winter
10.30-16.00. Closed 24 Dec-12 Jan*
A£7.00 C£4.00 Family Ticket (A2+C3) £21.00
Concessions£5.00

Sherborne Castle

off New Road Sherborne Dorset DT9 5NR
Tel: 01935 813182 / 812072
Fax: 01935 816727
*[From Bristol and W via Yeovil & A30; from
Bournemouth & S via Blandford or Dorchester;
from Salisbury & E via A30]*

Built by Sir Walter Raleigh in 1594, the castle
contains a fine collection of pictures, porcelain
and treasurers. The Lakeside gardens were
designed by Capability Brown and extend over
20 acres around a 50 acre lake.
*1 Apr-31 Oct Tue-Thur & Sat-Sun 11.00-16.30
(opens 14.30 Sat). Open Bank Hol Mons*
Castle & Gardens: A£7.00 C(0-15)£Free*
OAPs£6.50. Gardens only: A£3.50 C£Free*.

* 4 children can be admitted by a paying adult

Natural History Museums

Dinosaur Museum

Icen Way Dorchester Dorset DT1 1EW
Tel: 01305 269880 Fax: 01305 268885
[In town centre just off main High East Street]

Britain's original museum devoted to dinosaurs.
Mixes fossils, skeletons, life-size reconstructions
and interactive displays such as the 'feelies'.
This award-winning Museum is great fun!
*Apr-Oct daily 09.30-17.30. Nov-Mar daily 10.00-
16.30. Closed 24-26 Dec*
A£5.50 C£3.95 OAPs&Students£4.75

Sealife Centres & Aquariums

Weymouth Sea Life Park and Marine Sanctuary

Lodmoor Country Park Greenhill Weymouth Dorset DT4 7SX
Tel: 01305 788255 Fax: 01305 760165
www.sealife.co.uk

[On A353. A short walk from public car parks. Plenty of on site parking]

Don't miss the Brand New AmaZone - experience the world's greatest river 'The Amazon' for yourself. The unique atmospheric building gives you the feeling that you are in the heart of the Amazon as you come face to face with Razor-toothed Piranhas, exotic Poison Arrow Frogs, Silver Dollar Fish and the fascinating Tucan Fish. This really is an experience you can't miss, watch out for the regular monsoons though! A small colony of rare Humboldt penguins reside in a new purpose built facility with underwater viewing window. The Otter Sanctuary features the Park's resident Asian Short-Clawed Otters and a newly created retirement facility houses seal pups that are unable to be released into the wild. Enjoy interactive fun and games for all the family at the Shark Academy as you battle to become famous 'shark scholars!' Also features a marine-themed play area with sunken galleon and lighthouse. The Tropical Shark Lagoon houses tropical sharks including black-tipped reef, leopard and nurse sharks and Mysteries of the Deep houses some of the most mysterious creatures. A host more displays pro-vide a fascinating insight into the myriad marine marvels to be discovered beneath the seas, providing close encounters with everything from humble shrimps and starfish to sharks and stingrays.
All year daily from 10.00. Please call for winter opening hours
A£8.95 C(under3)£Free C(3-14)£6.25 OAPs£7.50. Groups 10+ call for details

Discount Offer: £2.00 Off Per Person.

Social History Museums

Dorset County Museum

High West Street Dorchester Dorset DT1 1XA
Tel: 01305 262735 Fax: 01305 257180
A must for anyone interested in the Dorset area and its fascinating archaeology. There are also galleries on geology, Dorset writers, wildlife, Dorchester and temporary exhibitions. Over 20 interactives for children.
All year Mon-Sat 10.00-17.00 and daily July-Sep including Bank Hol. Closed Good Fri & 24-26 Dec
A£4.30 (2 children per accompanying adult £Free) Concessions£3.20

Sport & Recreation

Tower Park Entertainment Centre

Yarrow Road Poole Dorset BH12 4NY
Tel: 01202 723671 infoline

Fax: 01202 722087
www.towerparkcentre.co.uk

Follow signs for Poole town centre, then look for brown and white signs for Tower Park, just off the A3049. Plenty of on site parking]

Tower Park in Poole is the south coast's biggest leisure complex offering entertainment for all the family throughout the year. Tower Park has something for everyone whatever the weather and also hosts regular free family events throughout the year. Located just three miles from the centre of Poole and five miles from Bournemouth. Parking is free! Tower Park includes; Splashdown - the area's only water flume attraction, tel. 01202 716123; Sundown - the latest stand-up tanning units in addition to beauty and massage therapy, tel. 01202 711577; UCI - 10 screen cinema, tel. 08700 102030; Megabowl - with 30 computerised ten-pin bowling lanes, tel. 01202 715907; Gala Clubs - free membership, tel. 01202 739989; Slots - take on the latest challenges in video game technology and fruit machines, tel. 01202 716604; Sticky Mickey - ice creams to snacks and candy, tel. 01202 745745; Exchange Bar & Grill - offers an extensive American style menu, tel. 01202 738308; Pizza Hut - provides the best pizzas and pastas, tel. 01202 718717; Burger King - restaurant and Drive Thru with varied menu and Kids Club meals, tel. 01202 736761; KFC Express - serves up the freshest chicken burgers and meal deals, tel. 01202 717173.

All year daily. Closed 25 Dec. Opening times of individual attractions do vary, please call 01202 723671 for further information

Admission price vary according to season and attraction, please call 01202 723671 for more information

Theme & Adventure Parks

Alice in Wonderland Family Park

Merritown Lane Hurn Christchurch Dorset BH23 6BA
Tel: 01202 483444 Fax: 01202 483444
www.aliceinwonderlandpark.co.uk

[Follow brown signs from Christchurch J with A338 or from Parley Cross. Opposite Bournemouth Airport. Plenty of on site parking available]

This unique Family Park brings Lewis Carroll's world-famous stories to life in acres of themed fun featuring one of the largest mazes in the UK and a host of attractions. Alice and her friends lead the fun with rides including the Runaway Train Rollercoaster, YoYo Ride, Flying Elephants, Giant Astroslide, Space Orbiter, Caucus Race, Indoor Play Area, Herb Garden, Croquet, Go-Karts, Queen's Bouncy Castle, Trampolines and much more besides. At 12 noon and 15.00 everyday the characters present an hilarious panto-style show in the Alice Theatre. The Mad Hatter's Café has an excellent menu for large and small appetites and the Alice Shop has a whole range of themed souvenirs, gifts and clothes.
27 Mar-12 Sept Mon-Sun 10.00-18.00, 18 Sept-17 Oct Sat-Sun 10.00-17.00, 23-31 Oct Mon-Sun 10.00-17.00
A&C(3+)£7.25 C(0-2)Free Family Ticket (4 people) £28.00. Groups (12+): A&C(3+)£5.00 +2 free with every 12 paying

Toy & Childhood Museums

Dorset Teddy Bear Museum

Antelope Walk Dorchester Dorset DT1 1BE
Tel: 01305 263200 Fax: 01305 268885
Visit the home of Mr Edward Bear and his large family of human-sized teddy bears! Join the bears as they relax around the house then descend to the Dorset Teddy Bear Museum in the vaulted cellars. Finally visit the shop containing hundreds of teddy bears of all kinds.
All year Mon-Sat 09.30-17.00, Sun 10.00-16.30. Closed 25-26 Dec
A£2.95 C£1.95 Family Ticket £8.95

Eire

Animal Attractions

Ballylane Visitor Farm

Ballylane New Ross County Wexford Eire
Tel: 00 353 51 425666
Fax: 00 353 51 422898
*[Off N25 (2km Wexford side of New Ross),
County Wexford]*

A working farm available to visitors. 1 hr walk
(self guided with aid of a guide book) to see our
crops, sheep, deer, historical items, nature and
wildlife. Play in the woods en route. All are welcome.
*Week before Easter, special events Easter Sun &
Mon, July-Aug daily 10.00-18.00. At other times
by appointment only*
Prices are in Euros: A5.00 C&Students4.00
Family Ticket 20.00

Arts, Crafts & Textiles

Irish Museum of Modern Art

Royal Hospital Military Road Kilmainham
Dublin 8 Eire
Tel: 00 353 1 612 9900
Fax: 00 353 1 612 9999
*[3.5km from City Centre, just off the N7 opposite
Heuston Station]*

The Irish Museum of Modern Art opened in
1991 in the magnificent Royal Hospital building
and grounds, which include a formal garden,
meadow and medieval burial grounds as well as
a series of other historic buildings. It presents a
wide-ranging programme of Irish and
International 20th century art from its own collections and through temporary exhibitions,
along with talks, seminars and musical events.
*Museum and Formal Gardens: All year Tue-Sat
10.00-17.30, Sun & Bank Hols 12.00-17.30.
Closed Mon. Closed 24-26 Dec & Good Friday*
Admission Free

Festivals & Shows

Cork Jazz Festival

Various venues Cork County Cork Eire
Tel: 00 353 21 427 8979
Cork City, situated on Southern Ireland's scenic
coast, is well used to invasion. For two hundred
years the Vikings made it an important trading
post, then it was the turn of the Anglo
Normans. Now it's the turn of up to 40,000
music fans who travel to Cork each October to
sample great music, atmosphere, food and fun
plus plenty of the Dark Stuff aka Guinness.
Renowned as Europe's friendliest Jazz Festival,
the event has hosted many of the jazz 'greats'
in its 25 year history - Ella Fitzgerald, Oscar
Peterson, Dizzy Gillespie, Lionel Hampton,
Buddy Rich, Mel Torme, Cleo Laine, Dave
Brubeck, Benny Carter, Joe Zawinul, Art Blakey,
Gerry Mulligan, Sonny Rollins, Wynton Marsalis,
Stephane Grappelli, Chick Corea, John
McLaughlin and lots more. The Guinness Cork
Jazz Festival is Ireland's biggest and most pres-
tigious jazz event and is one of the most impor-
tant events on Ireland's arts and cultural calen-
dar.
October 22-25 2004
Prices vary according to event attended

Kilkenny Arts Festival

Kilkenny County Kilkenny Eire
Tel: 00 353 56 52175 Fax: 00 353 56 51704
*[Events held at various venues in Kilkenny. N7
from Dublin]*

The rich heritage of the beautiful medieval city of
Kilkenny, with its narrow streets and historic
venues, lends a special atmosphere to this
unique festival. Experience a warm welcome,
and catch Ireland and the world's finest performers in all artforms at this world renowned
festival. Stroll through the narrow streets and
engage with the fun, colour and atmosphere of
one of Ireland's premier arts events. With a variety of events for all ages and tastes, a visit to
Kilkenny is essential in August.
August 6-15 2004
Prices vary according to event attended

Pan Celtic 2004

Tralee County Kerry Eire
Tel: 00 353 66 7180050
Trá Lí in the Kingdom of Kerry looks forward to the return of the Pan Celtic International Festival in 2004 and to the "Ceol, Caint agus Craic" the Féile will bring to our town when Celts from the six nations, Scotland, Wales, Cornwall, Isle of Man, Brittany and Ireland will gather for the Pan Celtic Festival extravaganza. We also look forward to meeting old friends and new and invite them to join with us in the Pan Celtic celebration. The Pan Celtic Festival is the ideal opportunity to enjoy majestic displays of Celtic dancing, pipe band performances, a colourful street parade and choral performances in all of the Celtic languages.
April 13-18 2004
Prices are in Euros:- Weekly Ticket: 50.00
Weekend Ticket 35.00

Wexford Festival Opera

Theatre Royal High Street Wexford
County Wexford Eire
Tel: 00 353 53 22144 Fax: 00 353 53 24289
[15min from ferry port of Rosslare, Wexford is 2 hr drive from Dublin, 115m from Cork and 130m from Shannon airport. Rail: Wexford 2.5 hrs from Dublin. Bus: Bus Eireann operates regular services]

The Wexford Festival has been hailed as 'one of the world's great parties'. And it's true. For eighteen days each autumn the town becomes the centre of the operatic world, presenting three major productions and over forty other events in a festival programme which has drawn artists and audiences from all over the world for nigh on fifty years. It is, as the New York Times described it, 'unlike any other festival, the enthusiasm is unique; it is the total experience that matters'.
October 14-31 2004
Prices vary, please call for details

Wicklow Gardens Festival

Wicklow County Tourism Ltd St Manntan's House Kilmantin Hill Wicklow Eire
Tel: 00 353 4042 0070 Fax: 00 353 4042 0072
[Throughout the county. 40mins S of Dublin]

The Wicklow Gardens Festival is a great opportunity for visitors to discover the beauty of the gardens throughout County Wicklow. Wicklow has been blessed with an abundance of marvellous gardens ranging from the 17th century to the recently created ones, from the grand scale to the small cottage type. While many of the larger gardens are open throughout the season, most of the smaller ones are only open on certain days during the festival. It is an ideal time to experience these wonderful creations where your guide is invariably the garden owner. You will find each garden to be different- from the grand landscape of the great gardens to the intimate personal detail found in the smaller ones.
May 1- July 31 2004
Admission Free

Wicklow Mountains Autumn Walking Festival

Wicklow County Tourism Ltd St Manntan's House Kilmantin Hill Wicklow County Wicklow Eire
Tel: 00 353 4042 0070 Fax: 00 353 4042 0072
[40 miles from Dublin]

The Wicklow Mountains offer some of the most spectacular views and walks anywhere in the country. The autumn walking festival draws huge crowds as it marks the end of the festival season.
October 22-24 2004

Food & Drink

Guinness Storehouse

St James Gate Dublin 8 Ireland
Tel: 00 353 1 408 4800

Fax: 00 353 1 408 4965

[Entrance on Market Street. Bus: 51B/78A from Aston Quay, 123 from O'Connell Street or Dame Street]

At the Guinness Storehouse, you will discover all there is to know about the world famous beer. The unique Guinness experience at Storehouse has been developed in a 1904 listed building and houses an excellent visitor experience, retail store, gallery and event venue. The journey ends in Gravity with panoramic views of Dublin and the perfect pint of Guinness.

All year daily 09.30-17.00, July & Aug open until 21.00. Closed Good Fri, 24-25 Dec & St Stephen's Day

Prices are in Euros: A13.50 C(6-12)5.00 C(under6)Free OAPs9.00 Students(under18)7.00 Students(over18)9.00 Family Ticket (A2+C4) 30.00

Heritage & Industrial

Cobh Queenstown Story

Cobh Railway Station Cobh County Cork Eire

Tel: 00 353 21 481 3591
Fax: 00 353 21 481 3595

Commanding panoramic views of one of the finest natural harbours in the world, the tiny fishing village of Cobh (the Cove of Cork) was virtually unknown up to the early 1800s. From 1848-1950 over 6 million adults and children emigrated from Ireland - about 2.5 million left Cobh, making it the single most important port of immigration.

All year daily, Nov-Mar 10.00-17.00, May-Oct 10.00-18.00

Prices are in Euros: A5.00 C2.50 Family Ticket 15.50 OAPs&Students4.00

Irish National Heritage Park

Ferrycarrig County Wexford Eire

Tel: 00 353 53 20733 Fax: 00 353 53 20911

[Just off the N11 in Ferrycarrig 2m town N25 to Wexford turn onto the N11]

The Region's showpiece exhibition, on a well developed, 35 acre site overlooking the Slaney River. The National Heritage Park is a series of reconstructions of settlements set within a large wooded area, depicting mans settlement in Ireland from 7000 BC. 14 reconstructed sites, including a ring fort, a crannóg and dolmen. Audio-Visual displays, craft & book shop and restaurant.

Jan-Dec daily 09.30-18.30

Prices are in Euros A7.00 C3.50 Family Ticket (A2+C3)17.50 Student&OAPs5.50

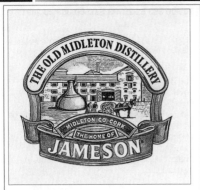

Old Midleton Distillery

Midleton County Cork Eire

Tel: 00 353 21 461 3594
Fax: 00 353 21 461 3704

www.whiskeytours.ie

[Midleton town is off the N25, Cork to Waterford route. Plenty of parking on site]

A tour of the Old Midleton Distillery consists of a 15 minute audio-visual presentation, a 35 minute guided tour of the Old Distillery and then back to the Jameson Bar for a whiskey tasting - minerals are available for children. Visitors can see the largest Pot Still in the world with a capacity of 32,000 gallons and the Old Waterwheel manufactured in 1825 to provide motive power prior to the days of electricity and still turning today. The guided tour and audio-visual aids are available in six languages. After the tour why not relax in the Centre's elegant restaurant specialising in country farmhouse fare or perhaps browse through the gift and craft shop.

All year daily 10.00-18.00. Tours during the day

Prices are in Euros: A7.95 C3.50 OAPs6.25
Family Ticket (A2+C3) 19.50. Group rates 6.25

Skellig Experience

Visitor Centre Valentia Island County Kerry Eire
Tel: 00 353 66 9476 306
Fax: 00 353 66 9476 351
[Off Ring of Kerry]

Once considered the edge of the world, Skellig Islands stand like fairytale castles 8 miles off the coast of County Kerry. Their fascinating story is retold in an exciting multi-media exhibition on the mainland at Valentia Island. Experience the legend of the 7th century Monastic beehive huts, the wild seabird and underwater life and learn about the heroic lives of the lighthouse keepers.
Dec-Feb 09.30-17.00 Mar-Nov 10.00-18.00 daily
Prices are in Euros: A5.00 C2.50
OAPs&Student 4.00 Family Ticket 15.50

Steam Museum

Lodge Park Heritage Yard Straffan County Kildare Eire
Tel: 00 353 1 627 3155
Fax: 00 353 1 627 3477
[N7 to Kill traffic lights turn R and follow signs. N4 to Maynooth, follow signs for Straffan]

The Steam Museum opened by the President of Ireland 1992 displays the Richard Guinness Collection of Historic Prototype Locomotive Models. In the Power Hall you will see full size stationary engines removed from industrial premises in Ireland working under steam. Hands on toys, multimedia channel, memorabilia. Tea-house and shop open on Sundays.
June-Aug Wed-Sun & Bank Hols 14.00-18.00 (from May-Sept open by advance arrangement)
Prices are in Euros A7.50 C&Concessions5.00
Family Ticket 20.00

Historical

Malahide Castle

Malahide Castle Demesne Malahide County Dublin Eire

Tel: 00 353 1 846 2184
Fax: 00 353 1 846 2537

www.visitdublin.com

[8m N of Dublin. Bus: 42. Suburban rail and northbound DART. Plenty of on site parking]

Set on 250 acres of parkland in the pretty sea-side town of Malahide, the Castle has been both a fortress and a family home for nearly eight hundred years. The house, which has been the home of the Talbot family from 1185 till 1973, is an interesting mix of architectural styles. Furnished with beautiful period furniture, it is home to an extensive collection of Irish paintings, mainly from the National Gallery, the family portraits in particular telling their own story of Ireland's turbulent history.

All year Mon-Sat 10.00-17.00, Sun & Public Hol 11.00-17.00

Prices are in Euros: A6.25 C(3-12)3.75 Family Ticket (A2+C2/3) 17.50 Concessions(&12-18s)5.25. Group rates available

Discount Offer: Two For The Price Of One

Shaw Birthplace

33 Synge Street Dublin 8 Eire

Tel: 00 353 1 475 0854/872 2077
Fax: 00 353 1 872 2231

www.visitdublin.com

[On Synge Street, 15min walk from St. Stephen's Green]

Victorian showhouse where George Bernard Shaw, author, dramatist and Nobel Prize winner for literature was born and spent his early years. The neat terraced house is as much a celebration of Victorian Dublin domestic life as of the early years of one of Dublin's Nobel prize-winners for literature. This charming residence is a wonderful insight into the everyday life of Victorian Dublin, and a pleasure to all who visit.

May-Sept Mon-Sat 10.00-13.00 & 14.00-17.00, Sun & Public Hol 11.00-13.00 & 14.00-17.00. Oct-Mar open by arrangement for groups

Prices are in Euros: A6.25 C(3-12)3.75 Family Ticket (A2+C2/3) 17.50 Concessions(&12-18s)5.25. Group rates available

Discount Offer: Two For The Price Of One

Literature & Libraries

Dublin Writers Museum

18 Parnell Square Dublin 1 Eire

Tel: 00 353 1 872 2077
Fax: 00 353 1 872 2231

www.visitdublin.com

[On Parnell Square, 5mins walk from O'Connell Street. Limited on site parking]

Situated in a magnificent eighteenth century mansion in the North city centre, the Dublin Writers Museum celebrates the lives and works of Dublin's literary celebrities over the past three hundred years. Swift and Sheridan, Shaw and Wilde, Yeats, Joyce and Beckett are among those brought to life through their books, letters, portraits and personal items. Special exhibitions and lunchtime theatre, a specialist bookshop and café make this compact and informative Museum all the more appealing to anyone interested in discovering more about Dublin's immense literary heritage. Photography allowed in some areas.

All year Mon-Sat 10.00-17.00, Sun & Public Hol 11.00-17.00. Late opening June-Aug Mon-Fri 10.00-18.00

Prices are in Euros: A6.25 C(3-12)3.95 Family Ticket (A2+C2/3) 17.50 Concessions(&12-18s)5.25. Group rates available

Discount Offer: Two For The Price Of One

Special Events

James Joyce Exhibition
01/04/2004-30/06/2004

Jonathan Barry Exhibition
05/07/2004-30/09/2004
A local artist exhibiting scenes from children's literature

Brian Breathnach, 'Process'
01/11/2004-20/12/2004
Journals, texts, paintings, the work involves the process of evaluating and editing journals, texts and paintings 1980-2003.

James Joyce Museum

Joyce Tower Sandycove County Dublin Eire

Tel: 00 353 1 280 9265/872 2077
Fax: 00 353 1 280 9265/872 2231

www.visitdublin.com

[8m S of Dublin along coast road. DART rail service]

The Joyce Tower is one of a series of Martello Towers build to withstand an invasion by Napoleon, and now holds a museum devoted to the life and works of James Joyce, who made the tower the setting for the first chapter of his masterpiece, Ulysses. This tower is the perfect setting for a museum dedicated to Joyce, a writer of international renown who remains, world-wide, the writer most associated with Dublin. Joyce's brief stay here inspired the opening of his great novel Ulysses, whose first chapter is set in this very tower. The gun platform with its panoramic view, and the living room inside the tower, are much as he described them in his book. Ulysses is a giant work of the imagination, both epic and hilarious, which immortalised Dublin and established Joyce as one of the greatest writers of the age. Joyce's relationship with Ireland and the church and his unrelenting dedication to his art, makes his own life as enthralling as his books.

Feb-Oct Mon-Sat 10.00-17.00, Sun & Public Hol 14.00-18.00. Closed for lunch 13.00-14.00. Other months open by arrangement

Prices are in Euros: A6.25 C(3-12)3.75 Family Ticket (A2+C2/3) 17.50 Concessions(&12-18s)5.25. Group rates available

Discount Offer: Two Admissions For The Price Of One

Special Events

Bloomsday Celebrations
16/06/2004
The Joyce Tower will be open all day from 08.00-18.00 for readings and celebrations

Maritime

Mizen Head Signal Station

Harbour Road Goleen West Cork Eire

Tel: 00 353 28 35115 / 35225

Fax: 00 353 28 35603

www.mizenhead.ie

[Leave N71 at Ballydehob, through Schull and Goleen to Mizen Head or leave N71 at Bantry,

through Durrus on R591 to Goleen and Mizen Head. Plenty of on site parking]

Mizen Head Signal Station is open to the public for the first time since it was completed in 1910. The award winning Mizen Head Visitor Centre in the Keeper's House and the Engine Room, the famous Suspension Bridge, the 99 Steps, the Fastnet Hall Navigational Aids Simulator and the views up the South and West Coasts guarantee a unique and authentic experience. Shop@theMizen and Mizen Cafe. A different experience every time you visit.

Mid-Mar Apr May & Oct daily 10.30-17.00, June-end Sept 10.00-18.00, Nov-mid Mar Sat & Sun 11.00-16.00

Prices are in Euros: A4.50 C(0-4)Free C(5-11)2.50 OAPs&Students3.50 Family Ticket (A2+C3) 14.00. Group rates less 10%

Model Towns & Villages

West Cork Model Railway Village

Inchydoney Road Clonakilty County Cork Eire
Tel: 00 353 2 333224
Follow the route of a miniaturised version of the now defunct West Cork Railway and step back in time to experience the way of life in West Cork during the 1940s. Here you can see exhibitions of the railways and industries which once linked six West Cork towns: Bandon, Clonakilty, Kinsale, Dunmanway, Bantry and Skibbereen. View buildings of architectural and historical interest which are featured within their natural terrain, settings which range from grassy hillsides to inland waterways and coastal inlets.

Feb-Oct daily 11.00-17.00

Prices are in Euros: A6.00 OAPs&Student4.50 C(under5)1.25 C3.50 Family Ticket 19.00

Railways

Fry Model Railway

Malahide Castle Demesne Malahide
County Dublin Eire

Tel: 00 353 1 846 3779 / 2184
Fax: 00 353 1 846 3723/2537

www.visitdublin.com

*[8m N of Dublin. Bus 42 and Suburban rail,
northbound DART. Plenty of parking on site]*

The Fry Model Railway is a unique collection of
handmade models of Irish trains, from the
beginning of rail travel to modern times. One of
the world's largest miniature railway, the exhibition in that it is a working railway covering an
area 2,500 sq.ft. Situated in the beautiful
grounds surrounding Malahide Castle, this
delightful collection is a treat for railway enthusiasts, children and adults alike. The beautifully
engineered models are from a collection originally built up in the 1920s and 1930s by Cyril
Fry, a railway engineer and draughtsman, with
each piece assembled with the finest attention
to detail. Irish and international exhibits from the
earliest railway developments are run on a
Grand Transport Complex which includes stations, bridges, trams, buses, barges and even
the river Liffey… pick out the models of Cork
and Heuston Stations, O'Connell Bridge and
other Dublin landmarks, perfectly constructed in
miniature, definitely a treat for all the family
including adults.

*Apr-Sept Mon-Sat 10.00-17.00, Sun & Public
Hols 14.00-18.00. Closed for lunch 13.00-14.00*

Prices are in Euros: A6.25 C(3-12)3.75 Family
Ticket (A2+C2/3) 17.50 Concessions(&12-
18s)5.25. Group rates available

**Discount Offer: Two For The Price Of
One**

Zoos

Dublin Zoo

Phoenix Park Dublin 8 Ireland

Tel: 00 353 1 474 8900

Fax: 00 353 1 677 1660

www.dublinzoo.ie

*[From Dublin City Centre: Bus: 10/10A, 25/25A,
26, 66/66A/66B, 67/67A, 68, 69. Dart feeder
bus 90 from Connolly and Tara Street DART stations. From rest of Ireland: Zoo easily accessible
by train and bus services]*

Dublin Zoo… Go Wild! Dublin Zoo is Ireland's
No. 1 family visitor attraction. Visitors can
explore the African Plains, which have doubled
the size of the Zoo and is home to giraffes,
zebras, hippos, rhinos, cheetahs, lions and
chimpanzees. Discover World of Cats, World of
Primates, Fringes of the Arctic, and City Farm,
taking in a 'Meet the Keeper' talk along the way,
and be sure to take a trip to the Nakuru Safari
in the African Plains! For a unique, fun, and wild
experience, just a few minutes from the city
centre, visit Dublin Zoo!

*All year, Mar-Sept Mon-Sat 09.30-18.00, Sun
10.30-18.00, Oct-Feb Mon-Sat 09.30-dusk, Sun
10.30-dusk*

Prices are in Euros: A12.50 C(under3)Free
C(under16)8.00 OAPs8.00 Concessions10.00
Family Tickets from 35.00. Special group rates
are also available

Essex

Agriculture / Working Farms

Barleylands Farm Centre

Barleylands Farm Barleylands Road Billericay
Essex CM11 2UD
Tel: 01268 290229 / 532253
Fax: 01268 290222
*[J29 M25 onto A127, then take A176 exit onto
South Wash Road, 2nd left into Barleylands Road
follow signposts]*

Visit Barleylands Farm Centre, where children
can meet and feed our friendly farm animals,
cuddle a rabbit in the bunny barn and feed the
ducks on the pond. Ride our mini tractors
around the farm and let off steam in our
Adventure Play area.
1 Mar-31 Oct daily 10.00-17.00
£2.50 (Adult, Child, Concessions)

**Discount Offer: Two For The Price Of
One.**

Arts, Crafts & Textiles

Blake House Craft Centre and The Original Great Maze

Blake End Rayne Braintree Essex CM7 8SH
Tel: 01376 553146
*[Just off the A120 midway between Braintree and
Great Dunmow AA signed]*

The carefully preserved original farm buildings
are centred around a courtyard, which was previously the farmyard. Wander around the fine
variety of craft shops in a friendly relaxed
atmosphere. The highly acclaimed master of the
maze, David E Partridge, has constructed his
Original Great Maze at Blake House Craft
Centre creating an even bigger and more challenging maze for you to conquer
*Craft Centre: daily 10.00-17.00 and Bank Hol
Mon. Maze: 10 July-12 Sept 10.00 onwards*
Maze: A£4.00 C£2.50 OAPs£2.50

Animal Attractions

Marsh Farm Country Park

Marsh Farm Road South Woodham Ferrers
Chelmsford Essex CM3 5WP

Tel: 01245 321552 Fax: 01245 323163
*[A130 Chelmsford / Southend road, venue is off
this road, follow brown tourist signs saying Open
Farm and Country Park]*

Working farm, family tourist attraction, housing
pigs, sheep, cattle, chickens, goats, ponies and
a pets' barn. Indoor and outdoor play areas, tea
room and gift shop. Daily milking demonstrations. Special events run throughout the season.
*14 Feb-29 Oct daily 10.00-16.00, (31 May-3
Sept 10.00-17.30), 30 Oct-19 Dec weekends
10.00-17.30*
A£5.60 C(under3)£Free C(3-16)£2.90
Concessions£3.90 Family Ticket (A2+C2)
£16.00

Festivals & Shows

8th Annual Leigh Art Trail

Leigh-on-Sea Essex SS9
Tel: 01702 470490
A range of art on display at cafes, shops, gal-
leries and studios in Leigh.
June 5-12 2004
Admission Free

Castle Point Show

Waterside Farm Showground Somnes Avenue
Canvey Island Essex SS8 9RA
*[J30 M25, head E on A13, turn off A130 towards
Canvey Island]*

Show highlights include a full programme of
arena acts, funfair, craft fair, commercial stands,
children's corner, live music, side shows and

much more. Something for all the family to see and do!

June 27 2004, 11.00-18.00
£1.00 C(under5)£Free

Chelmsford Cathedral Festival 2004

Chelmsford Cathedral New Street Chelmsford Essex CM1 1TY
Tel: 01245 359890 Fax: 01245 280456
[A12, then A1016 into Chelmsford. A414 into Chelmsford. Rail: Chelmsford 5mins walk]

Programme includes orchestral concerts, choral music, chamber music, solo recitals and jazz. Also literary events, lectures, films, walks, street performers. Lively festival club. The superb acoustic properties of Chelmsford Cathedral make it a wonderful venue for the main concerts.
May 8-15 2004. Main concerts 20.00, other events vary
Various prices. Tickets available from: Box Office, Civic Theatre: 01245 606505

Concert in the Park

Priory Park Southend-On-Sea Essex SS1
Tel: 01702 431770
Open air concert in the Park featuring the Royal Philharmonic Orchestra and Grand Fireworks Finale.
June 26 2004. Gates open 16.00, Musical entertainment from 18.00
Tickets available from High Street TIC from 1st May

Designfront'04

Cliff Pavilion Station Road Westcliff-on-Sea Essex SS0
Tel: 020 8355 5355
A new major annual cultural event in Southend giving a public platform to over 100 British designer/makers.

June 17-20 2004

Jim Peter's Southend Half Marathon and Fun Run

Southend Tennis and Leisure Centre Eastern Avenue Southend-On-Sea Essex SS2 4FA
Tel: 01702 220350
[Located in the Southend Leisure and Tennis Centre]

This annual event, starting at the Leisure and Tennis Centre, Garon's Park, is in aid of Fairhavens and Little Haven Children's Hospice. Please telephone for entry forms and further information.
June 13 2004
Admission Free

Leigh Folk Festival

Leigh-On-Sea Essex SS9
Tel: 01702 390454
[Leigh Broadway and Old Leigh Town]

One of the largest free festivals of music, song and dance in the County with more than 500 performers including Folk, Cajun, Country and Western and Appalachian Dance companies.
June 25-27 2004 Fri 20.00-23.00, Sat 11.00-23.00, Sun 11.00-21.30
Admission Free

Leukaemia Research Fund Bikeathon

Southend-on-Sea Essex SS1

Tel: 01702 479623

Around 800 people are expected to take part in this 12 mile cycle ride around Southend including the seafront. The mayor will open the event.
September 2004 (day to be confirmed) Set off in small groups from 09.00 and end between 14.00-15.00

London to Southend Classic Car Run

Western Esplanade Southend-On-Sea Essex
Tel: 01268 752548
[Southend Seafront]

One of the biggest classic car shows in the South East. Approx. 200 pre 1970 vehicles will set off from London and follow a route to Southend seafront where they will be on display bringing a touch of nostalgia with them!
July 25 2004 12.00-17.00
Admission Free

Old Leigh Regatta

Old Leigh Town Southend-On-Sea Essex SS2
Tel: 01702 710851

The annual weekend of fun and frivolity held in a traditional old fishing town atmosphere, the unique combination of sailing races and novelty water events, together with the usual sights of cockle and banana eating contests, football on the mud, have made this an eagerly awaited event. Features a variety of famous jazz musicians at both free and ticket venues around the town.
September 11-12 2004 12.00-17.00 daily
Prices vary according to event attended, some free

Southend Bus And Transport Show

Southchurch Park East Southend-on-Sea Essex
Almost 200 vehicles from 1915 to 2002 including Fire Engines, Taxis and Cars.
June 6 2004 10.00-17.30

Southend Carnival Week

Southend-On-Sea Essex SS1
Tel: 01702 431770
[Venue: various places around Southend]

Many carnival events throughout the week and a Carnival Fair all week at Chalkwell Park with rides and games for the whole family.
August 13-21 2004

Southend Cricket Festival

Southchurch Park Southend-On-Sea Essex
Tel: 01245 252420
Putting fun back into Festival cricket!
July 25-31 2004

Southend Free Fireworks Spectaculars

Southend Seafront Southend-on-Sea Essex
Tel: 01702 215120
Please telephone our Tourist Information Centre for more details, including times of displays.
September 18-November 6, Sat nights only. 18 Sept-2 Oct 20.00, 9 Oct-6 Nov 19.00. Times approximate
Admission Free

Southend Garden Show

Garon Park Southend-on-Sea Essex SS1

Tel: 01702 549623

[Garon Park- Southend Leisure & Tennis Centre Showground]

Over 100 stands selling a variety of garden equipment and plants.

May 1-3 2004

Tickets in advance are available by calling 01702 549623 or may be purchased on the day.

Southend Illuminated Carnival Procession

Southend-on-Sea Essex

Tel: 01702 431770

Illuminated carnival procession along the seafront culminating in a Grand Fireworks Spectacular.

August 21 2004

Southend Shakedown - Ace Café

Western Esplanade Southend-On-Sea Essex

Tel: 020 8961 1000

Several thousand motorcyclists will leave Ace Café, London and ride to Southend's Seafront.

April 12 2004 10.00-18.00

Admission Free

Southend's 3rd International Jazz Festival

Southend-On-Sea Essex

Tel: 01702 351135

[To be held at various venues within Southend]

This annual event features a variety of famous jazz musicians at both free and ticket venues around the town.

July 29 - August 3 2004

Prices vary according to event attended, some free

Thaxted Festival

Clarance House Watling Street Thaxted Dunmow Essex CM6 2PJ

Tel: 01371 831421 Fax: 01371 831421

[From J8 M11, take A120 to Dunmow, then B184 to Thaxted]

Concerts, recitals, and a wide variety of classical music and jazz, mainly in Thaxted Church. One concert-goer wrote: 'As someone who works in London, the venue of Thaxted together with the superb music is far above any event I have attended in London.'

June 18-July 11 2004, held on Fri, Sat & Sun only

Dependent on event. Prices range from £5.00 to £33.00

The Oyster Fayre

Lower Castle Park Colchesrer Essex

Tel: 01206 794916

[From A12 follow signs for Colchester Central. Follow temporary signs for History Fayre parking. Rail: Colchester North]

Colchester History Fayre Trust presents the Oyster Fayre. A period re-creation of a country fair and market in Lower Castle Park, Colchester; the market features all the colour and noise of an annual medieval fair with traders

selling everything from a pin to a full suit of armour. Costumed re-enactors offer period entertainment, and there are crafts, strolling players, falconry, hand to hand armed combat, puppetiers and musicians. Also a costumed longbow archery competition. There will be plenty to eat and the real ale tent too. An experience for all the family.
June 13-14 2004, 10.00-17.00
A£4.00 C£2.00. No advance tickets. Half price for those in medieval costume

Westcliff Casino Southend Airshow

Western Esplanade Southend-On-Sea Essex
Tel: 01702 390333
Europe's largest FREE Airshow. An action packed two days-full flying programme plus ground entertainment.
May 30-31 2004 from 10.00 daily
Admission Free

Folk & Local History Museums

Chelmsford Museum and Essex Regiment Museum

Oaklands Park Moulsham Street Chelmsford Essex CM2 9AQ

Tel: 01245 615100 Fax: 01245 262726

www.chelmsfordmuseums.co.uk

[33m from London, near the A1016 & A12. Bus: 14, 15, 32, 42, (43 & 44 to park rear), 351 & 140 (Sun only) from bus and railway stations. Limited parking on site]

Victorian Villa houses: Local and Social history from prehistory to present day; Essex Regiment history; fine and decorative arts (including ceramics, costume and glass); Natural history (including geology, animals and a live beehive). Temporary Exhibitions. Other services: School loans service, Art loan service (fee), Essex Regiment Archive, Family History database, Identifications service. Photography by arrangement, wheelchair and pushchair access to ground floor only.

All year Mon-Sat 10.00-17.00, Sun 14.00-17.00 summer and 13.00-16.00 winter. Closed 25-26 Dec & Good Fri

Admission Free. Parties and Schools by arrangement please. Coach parking outside park (150metres)

Special Events

Mr Punch and Friends
24/01/2004-17/04/2004
Meet Mr Punch and his friends - a rare collection of hand-crafted puppets, some of which once entertained the crowds along the Norfolk and Suffolk coast. Put on your own Punch and Judy show with our special replica puppets, or try giving the ventriloquist's dummy a voice

Ivor's Sculpture Group
24/04/2004-03/07/2004
An exhibition of sculpture in mixed media by members of the Chelmsford Sculpture Group tutored by Ivor Livi

Wildlife Guided Walk: Hylands Park
19/05/2004
A spring walk to look at woodland, meadow and ponds. With Tony Walentowicz, Keeper of Natural Sciences. Time: 18.45 at main Writtle car park. Cost: A£2.00, please call to book

Wildlife Guided Walk: Galleywood Common
26/05/2004
A walk around Chelmsford's first Local Nature Reserve (LNR). Exploring lowland heath habitats and conservation in action. With Tony Walentowicz, Keeper of Natural Sciences. Time:

18.45 at main Writtle car park. Cost: A£2.00, please call to book

Half-term Activity Corner
31/05/2004-04/06/2004
Free drop-in craft activities and quizzes for children of all ages

Wildlife Fun Day
05/06/2004
Hugely popular family fun with snakes, other reptiles, candle making with Essex Beekeepers and fossil rubbing. Time: 10.00-17.00. Free event

Wildlife Guided Walk: Sandford Mill
09/06/2004
A rare opportunity to see the Museum's own wildlife site in the heart of the lower Chelmer Valley. With Tony Walentowicz, Keeper of Natural Sciences. Time: 18.45 at main Writtle car park. Cost: A£2.00, please call to book

Family Sculpture Day
26/06/2004
Have a go at making your own sculpture with help from experienced artists! Suitable for all ages. Time: 10.00-17.00. Free event

Handle with Care
10/07/2004-29/08/2004
An exhibition based around the Museums' history and new science loans boxes, used in schools and reminiscence sessions

National Archaeology Day
17/07/2004
Hands-on discovery for all the family. Activities include finds sorting, mosaic making, candle making. Time: 10.00-17.00. Free event

Holiday Activities for Children at Sandford Mill
17/08/2004-25/08/2004
Held on 17-18 & 24-25 Aug. An exciting variety of art, craft and science activities. At Sandford Mill there is plenty of space so we do things on a really big scale! For children aged 5+ (children under 8 years must be accompanied by an adult). Time: 10.30-12.30 & 14.00-16.00. Cost: C£3.00, call to book

Margery Allingham 1904-1966
04/09/2004-31/10/2004
An exhibition to celebrate the centenary of a great 'Queen' of crime - one of the most distinguished writers of detective fiction's golden age, creator of detective Albert Campion

Essex Regiment Day
25/09/2004

A day of military display and activities. Time: 10.00-17.00. Free event

Half-term Activity Corner
25/10/2004-30/10/2004
Put your own stamp on a book! Free, drop in event for children of all ages

Unnaturally Natural, Derek Frampton Unmasked
06/11/2004-30/01/2005
Derek Frampton makes models and replicas for museums, artists and other clients, works of art for himself and has completed countless professional taxidermy works

Creative Christmas Crafts
18/12/2004
Come and make something special for Christmas! Suitable for children aged 4+ (children under 8 years must be accompanied by an adult). Time: 10.30-12.30 & 14.00-16.00. Cost: C£3.00, call 01245 615100 to book

Gardens & Horticulture

RHS Garden Hyde Hall

Buckhatch Lane Rettendon Chelmsford Essex CM3 8ET
Tel: 01245 400256 Fax: 01245 402100
[A130 follow tourist signs]

The 28 acre Garden, has roses, herbaceous borders, alpine and woodland plantings and two ornamental ponds. The Dry Garden of drought tolerant plants and the Hillside Garden including the Millennium Avenue are areas of new and continuing development.
All year daily, Jan-Mar 10.00-dusk (or 17.00), Apr-Sept 10.00-18.00, Oct-Dec 10.00-dusk (or 17.00). Closed 25 Dec
A£4.50 C(6-16)£1.00 C(0-6)£Free

Wickham Place Farm - Open Garden

Station Road Wickham Bishops Witham Essex
CM8 3JB

Tel: 01621 891282 Fax: 01621 891282

*[Take B1018 from Witham towards Maldon. After
going under the A12 take 3rd L (Station Rd), 1st
property on L]*

A two acre walled garden with a further 12
acres of woodland. Huge climbers, roses and
wisterias cascade down into wide borders filled
with shrubs, perennials and bulbs. Planted for
year round colour. Knot garden and natural
pond. Mixed woodland with plants and bulbs.
Profits to Farleigh Hospice and N.G.S.

*May-Sept (closed Aug) Fri only 11.00-16.00. Also
open Sun 16 May 14.00-17.00 & 5-6 June
11.00-17.00*

A£2.50 C(over5)£0.50

Hedingham Castle

Castle Hedingham Halstead Essex CO9 3DJ

Tel: 01787 460261 Fax: 01787 461473

www.hedinghamcastle.co.uk

*[On B1058 1m off A1017 between Colchester &
Cambridge, close to constable country. Easy
reach of London and M11]*

Hedingham Castle was built in 1140 by Aubrey
de Vere II and was the home of the de Veres,
Earls of Oxford for 550 years. The Castle was
besieged by King John in 1216, and attacked
by the Dauphin of France in 1217. Hedingham
has welcomed many royal visitors including King
Henry VII, King Henry VIII and Queen Elizabeth I.
The Keep stands over 110 feet high with walls
12 feet thick. Most of the Norman architectural
features remain around the Keep - especially
the chevron stone carvings and the splendid
arch, which spans the entire width of the
Banqueting Hall and is the widest Norman arch
in Western Europe. There are beautiful woodland and lakeside walks and areas where visitors can enjoy a picnic. Unfortunately, disabled
access is limited to the grounds. Dogs are
allowed in the grounds if kept on leads. Member
of the Historic Houses Association.

*Apr-Oct Thur, Fri, Sun 11.00-16.00. Also open
during school hols, 4-16 Apr, 30 May-3 June, 26
July-26 Aug & 24-29 Oct*

A£4.00 C(under5)£Free C£3.00
Concessions£3.50 Family Ticket (A2+C3)
£14.00. There may be an extra charge for special events

Historical

Audley End House

Audley End Saffron Walden Essex CB11 4JF

Tel: 01799 522399 (info line)

Fax: 01799 521276

*[1m W of Saffron Walden on B1383, J8 J9 & J10
M11 Northbound only]*

Built by Thomas Howard, Earl of Suffolk to
entertain King James I, Audley End is one of
England's most magnificent stately homes.
Enjoy over 30 lavishly decorated room interiors
by Robert Adam and a wonderful collection of
paintings and furnishings.

*House: by guided tour only, 1-31 Mar Thur-Mon
10.00-16.00, 1 Apr-30 Sept Wed-Mon & Bank
Hols 12.00-17.00, 1-31 Oct Thur-Mon 10.00-
16.00. Gardens: 1-31 Mar Thur-Mon 10.00-
17.00, 1 Apr-30 Sept Wed-Mon & Bank Hols
10.00-18.00, 1-31 Oct Thur-Mon 10.00-17.00*

House & Gardens: A£8.50 C£4.30
Concessions£6.40 Family Ticket £21.30.
Gardens only: A£4.50 C£2.30
Concessions£3.40 Family Ticket £11.30

Discount Offer: Two For The Price Of One

Special Events

Medieval Festival
11/04/2004-12/04/2004

Presented by The Lion Rampart. See history brought to life in this colourful and dramatic re-enactment of medieval life, with music and dancing and knights in armed combat. Also Jim the Potter with his fascinating pottery demonstrations, have-a-go archery and enjoyable displays of Falconry. Cost: A£7.00 C£5.00 Concessions£6.50 Family Ticket £25.00

Jousting Tournament
02/05/2004-03/05/2004

Cheer on the Jousting Knights as they bring to life the excitement and chivalry of the medieval tourney with an action packed day for all the family. Have fun with Taro the Jester, enjoy Gordon's delightful displays of Falconry and try your skill at Archery. Time: 12.30 and 15.30. Cost: A£8.00 C£6.00 Concessions£7.50 Family Ticket (A2+C3) £30.00

Jousting Tournament
29/05/2004-31/05/2004

Presented by The Knights of Royal England who due to the popularity of their joust will be returning for a magnificent medieval jousting tournament. Enjoy Gordon's delightful displays of Falconry and try your skill at ArcheryTime: 12.30 & 15.30. Cost: A£8.00 C£6.00 Concessions£7.50 Family Ticket (A2+C3) £30.00

Jousting Tournament
25/07/2004

Presented by The Knights of Royal England who due to the popularity of their joust will be returning for a magnificent medieval jousting tournament. Enjoy Gordon's delightful displays of Falconry and try your skill at ArcheryTime: 12.30 & 15.30. Cost: A£8.00 C£6.00 Concessions£7.50 Family Ticket (A2+C3) £30.00

Jousting Tournament
24/08/2004-25/08/2004

A final chance to see the Jousting Knights before the children go back to school. Thrilling duels on horseback plus fun with Taro the Jester, Have-a-go Archery and enjoyable Falconry displays. Time: 12.30 and 15.30. Cost: A£8.00 C£6.00 Concessions£7.50 Family Ticket (A2+C3) £30.00

Mountfitchet Castle and Norman Village

Stansted Essex CM24 8SP
Tel: 01279 813237 Fax: 01279 816391
[Off B1383 in centre of village]

Norman motte and bailey castle and village reconstructed as it was in Norman England of 1066, on its historic site. A vivid illustration of village life in Domesday England, complete with houses, church, siege tower and weapons and many types of animals roaming freely
14 Mar-14 Nov daily 10.00-17.00. Open Bank Hols
A£6.00 C(under14)£5.00 OAPs&Students£5.50

Military & Defence Museums

Kelvedon Hatch Secret Nuclear Bunker

Brentwood Essex CM14 5TL

Tel: 01277 364883 Fax: 01277 372562
[J28 M25, take A1023 to Brentwood then A128 to Ongar. M11 take A414 to Ongar then A128 to Brentwood at Kelvedon Hatch]

Step inside the door of this rural bungalow nestling in the Essex countryside and discover the twilight world of the Government Cold War. Behind the blast screens that protect this bungalow is the entrance to an amazing labyrinth of rooms built into a hillside, encased in 10ft thick reinforced concrete and 100ft underground.
Mar-Oct daily 10.00-16.00, Sat, Sun & Bank Hol 10.00-17.00. Nov-Feb Thur-Sun inclusive 10.00-16.00
A£5.00 C(5-16)£3.00 Family Ticket (A2+C2)£12.00

On the Water

Southend Pier

Western Esplanade Southend-On-Sea Essex
SS1 1EE

Tel: 01702 215620 Fax: 01702 611889
www.southendpier.co.uk

[A13 or A127 into Southend-On-Sea follow signs to seafront]

Southend Pier is the longest pleasure pier in the world. At 1.33 miles in length, the pier stretches into the Estuary giving you the chance to enjoy a brisk walk, or ride on the unique pier trains. Watch fishermen reel in a cod and don't forget to save time for a trip on one of the pleasure boats from the pier head. Picnic areas available (outside).

Pier: Easter-Oct daily 08.15-21.00 (22.00 Sat & Sun), Oct-Easter daily 08.15-16.00 (18.00 Sat & Sun). Pier Museum: May-Oct Tues, Wed, Sat & Sun

A£2.50 C£1.20 OAPs£1.20 Family Ticket £6.00. Group rates available

Special Events

Easter Event
14/04/2004
All children will receive a free Easter egg. Normal admission applies, please call for further details. Time: 11.00-16.00

Southend Pier Heritage Festival
26/06/2004-27/06/2004
Normal admission applies. Time: 11.00-17.00

Grand Puppet Festival
06/08/2004-08/08/2004
Normal admission applies.Time: from 11.00

Southend Sailing Barge Match
28/08/2004
Watch the splendour of a bygone era when around 15 of the majestic Thames Sailing Barges race for various trophies, supported with water based activity. Normal Pier admissions apply

Santa on the Pier
27/11/2004-19/12/2004
Held on: 27, 28 Nov, 4, 5, 11, 12, 18 & 19 Dec. Children can visit Santa in his grotto in the RNLI gift shop. There is no charge to see Santa and every child will receive a gift. Normal Pier admissions apply, the free walkway does not apply to those wishing to see Santa

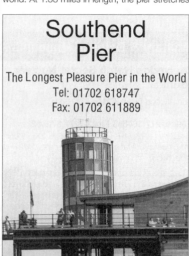

Railways

East Anglian Railway Museum

Chappel and Wakes Station Station Road
Wakes Colne Colchester Essex CO6 2DS

Tel: 01206 242524 Fax: 01787 224473

*[Situated near big brick viaduct across the A1124
formerly A604)]*

The Museum has a wide collection of locomotives and rolling stock, some of which are fully
restored and others are undergoing repair.
Visitors are welcome to look around the restoration shed and ask questions about the ongoing
work.

All year daily 10.00-17.00. Closed 25 Dec
Non-operating days: A£3.00 C£1.50
OAPs£2.00 Family Ticket £8.00. Operating
Days: A£6.00 C£3.00 OAPs£4.50 Family Ticket
£15.00

Sealife Centres & Aquariums

Sealife Adventure

Eastern Esplanade Southend-On-Sea Essex
SS1 2ER

Tel: 01702 442211 Fax: 01702 462444
www.sealifeadventure.co.uk

[On seafront 0.5m E of the pier]

Just along the seafront from Adventure Island.
The Sea Life Adventure is bursting with our
unique mixture of Education and Fun that families love. Journey through the Sea Cavern, hop
aboard H.M.S. Sub Tropical. Mosey on in to the
Seahorse Rodeo and wander around the Ray
Bay, walk under the waves in Deepwater World
then examine the Sea Nursery. Point out the
crabs in the Rock Pool. On your journey you will
enjoy a wealth of marine marvels from Starfish
to Sharks, Piranhas to Stingrays. Everyday there
is a full programme of demonstrations, talks and
presentations.

*All year daily from 10.00 closing between 17.00 &
19.00*

A£5.50 C(4-14)£4.00 C(under 4)£Free
OAPs£4.25

Sport & Recreation

Kursaal

Eastern Esplanade Southend-On-Sea Essex
SS1 2WW
Tel: 01702 322322 Fax: 01702 322387
*[Leave M25 J29 heading for Southend along
A127. Drive for approximately 21m, head for
Seafront]*

Come to the Kursaal, we have something for
everyone, from 30 lanes of Ten Pin Bowling to
an Amusement Arcade. We also have American
Pool tables, a snack bar for your refreshments,
serving hot food and drinks, and if you fancy
something a bit stronger you can enjoy the
great atmosphere of our Sports Bar which has
satellite TV showing the up-to-date sporting
events.
*All year Sun-Wed 10.00-00.00, Thur-Sat 10.00-
02.00. Closed Christmas Day*
Admission Free. Bowling Prices Per Game. Call
for details of current offers & prices

Theme & Adventure Parks

Adventure Island

Sunken Gardens West Western Esplanade
Southend-On-Sea Essex SS1 1EE

Tel: 01702 443400 Fax: 01702 601044

www.adventureisland.co.uk

*[1hr from central London, on both sides of
Southend Pier. M25 J29 then A127 or M25 J30
then A13]*

Adventure Island on Southend seafront is the
number one fun park in the South of England.
With over 40 rides and attractions, there's
something for the whole family to enjoy. From
the Raging River Log Flume to the Green
Scream Roller Coaster, Dragons Claw,
Scorpion, and 4 new rides for 2004. There are
also many rides for the tiny tots, and a themed
Jungle Jive Cafe. Admission to Adventure Island
is free, "you only pay if you play".

*3 Apr-5 Sept & 28-31 Oct daily from 11.00, 11
Sept-Mar Sat & Sun from 11.00*

Super Saver wristband £18.00, TinyTots mini
band £12.00 or £1.20 per ticket (rides require 1
or 2 tickets). Nov & Dec all tickets and wristbands half price. Discounted group rates available on request, saving up to £9.50 per wristband

Toy & Childhood Museums

House on the Hill Toy Museum

Grove Hill Stansted Essex CM24 8SP
Tel: 01279 813567 Fax: 01279 816391
[Off B1383]

One of the largest toy museums in Europe,
housed on two floors. A huge variety of toys,
books and games from the late Victorian period
up to the 1970s.
*All year daily 10.00-16.00. Closed Christmas,
please call for further details*
A£4.00 C(under14)£3.20 OAPs£3.50

Zoos

Colchester Zoo

Maldon Road Stanway Colchester Essex
CO3 0SL
Tel: 01206 331292 Fax: 01206 331392
*[Follow signs along A1124 exit from A12 S of
town]*

Colchester Zoo has over 200 species of animals, with informative daily displays. New enclosures include Kingdom of the Wild for Giraffe,
Rhino and Pygmy Hippos, Elephant Kingdom -
Spirit of Africa, Penguin Shores, the Wilds of
Asia and Chimp World. There is an undercover
soft play complex, road train, four adventure
play areas set in sixty acres of beautiful gardens. Disabled access, although there are some
steep hills. Don't miss Playa Patagonia, the
underwater sealion experience with its 24metre
tunnel under the water.
All year daily from 09.30. Closed 25 Dec
A£11.99 C(Under3)£Free C(3-14)£6.99
OAPs£8.99

Gloucestershire

Animal Attractions

Cotswold Farm Park

Guiting Power Stow on the Wold Cheltenham
Gloucestershire GL54 5UG

Tel: 01451 850307 Fax: 01451 850423

www.cotswoldfarmpark.co.uk

*[J9 M5 off B4077 Tewkesbury / Stow road.
Plenty of free parking available]*

Home to Britain's most comprehensive collection of rare breeds of British farm animals. There are lots of activities for the youngsters; rabbits and guinea pigs to cuddle, lambs and calves to bottle feed, tractor and trailer rides, battery powered tractors, seasonal farming demonstrations, including lambing, shearing and milking, together with great children's play areas both indoors and outside.

20 Mar-12 Sept daily 10.30-17.00, 18 Sept-end Oct Sat-Sun & Autumn Half Term (18-31 Oct) 10.30-16.00

A£4.95 C£3.50 OAPs£4.65 Family Ticket £15.50. Group rates available

Discount Offer: One Child Free With A Full Paying Adult.

<u>Special Events</u>

Lambing Demonstrations
20/03/2004-03/05/2004

Shearing Demonstrations
22/05/2004-27/06/2004

Milking Demonstrations
28/06/2004-31/10/2004

Oldown Country Park

Foxholes Lane Tockington Bristol South
Gloucestershire BS32 4PG

Tel: 01454 413605 Fax: 01454 413955
www.oldown.co.uk

[M48 J1, B4461 or the M5 J16, A38 to Alveston, follow the brown signs. Plenty of on site parking available]

Oldown Country Park is in beautiful countryside just North of Bristol. There is lots for families and groups to enjoy. Get to know the animals in the farmyard, help feed some of them and ride round the farm on a tractor and trailer, play in the ball pool and sand pit and ride the pedal tractors and go-karts. Let the miniature steam train take you on a mile journey through the woods and gardens. Challenge yourself on the adventure equipment in the woods or wander peacefully along the trails through the 80 acres of ancient woodland. Have a picnic or enjoy refreshment in the coffee shop and pick your own strawberries or other fruit in season. There is so much to do at Oldown and we hope you will want to return again and again.

Feb Half Term-Oct Sat-Sun, School Hols, June & July daily, Sept Tue-Sun 10.00-17.00

A£5.00 C(under2)£Free C&OAPs£4.50. Train ride is an additional £1.25 per person. School and group discounts available

Arts, Crafts & Textiles

Cheltenham Art Gallery and Museum

Clarence Street Cheltenham Gloucestershire GL50 3JT
Tel: 01242 237431 Fax: 01242 262334
[M5 J10 then A4019 & J11 then A40, also A435 and A46 meet at Cheltenham]

This museum, close to the town centre of Cheltenham, has a world-famous collection relating to the Arts & Crafts Movement, including fine furniture and exquisite metalwork, made by Cotswold craftsmen - inspired by William Morris. Also Chinese and English pottery; 300 years of painting by Dutch and British artists; the story of Edward Wilson, Cheltenham's Antarctic explorer. Special exhibitions throughout the year.

All year Mon-Sat 10.00-17.20, Sun 14.00-16.20. Closed Bank Hol and Easter Sunday
Admission Free, donations welcome

Nature in Art

Wallsworth Hall Twigworth Gloucester Gloucestershire GL2 9PA

Tel: 0845 450 0233 Fax: 01452 730937

www.nature-in-art.org.uk

[On A38, 2m N of Gloucester. Plenty of free parking on site]

The world's first museum dedicated to art inspired by nature, from Picasso to David Shepherd, ethnic art to Flemish Masters, plus sculpture, tapestries and ceramics. Artists from around the world demonstrate from February to November. Collection includes work by over 600 artists from 60 countries, spanning 1500 years. All housed in fine Georgian Mansion. Twice specially commended in the National Heritage Museum of the Year Awards.

All year Tue-Sun & Bank Hol 10.00-17.00, Mon by arrangement. Closed 24-26 Dec

A£3.60 C&OAPs&Students£3.00 C(0-8)£Free Family Ticket £11.00

Discount Offer: One Child Free With Every Full Paying Adult

<u>Special Events</u>

'The Fabric of Nature' Quilters Guild
16/03/2004-25/04/2004
Nature inspired work by some of the UK's foremost contemporary quilters

Celebration of Ceramics
06/04/2004-02/05/2004
Contemporary work by David Burnham Smith plus selected items from the collection and borrowed exhibits spanning nearly 200 years

The Art of Travel
11/05/2004-20/06/2004
Part of National Museum Month and Gloucestershire Museums Week. Nature inspired work that was completed during or as a direct result of taking part in travel

The Heart of Stone
25/05/2004-05/09/2004
Stunning Zimbabwean Stone Sculpture

English Nature
20/07/2004-05/09/2004
Specially commissioned works celebrating English nature. In association with English Nature. An exciting exhibition embracing work by artists as diverse as Michael Porter, Andrew Dark, Richard Tratt, Anthony Gibbs and Bruce Pearson

Flying High - J C Harrison (1898-1985)
14/09/2004-24/10/2004
A celebration of the work of one of the twentieth century's most influential wildlife artists

Gloucestershire Society for Botanical Illustration
02/11/2004-14/11/2004
Annual exhibition of work. A selection of approximately 100 exhibits by this active and respected group which includes a number of RHS medal winners

British Contemporary Crafts
09/11/2004-06/12/2004
Multi media selling exhibition of nature inspired work by some of the UK's foremost makers in response to the RHS Year of the Garden

Caverns & Caves

Clearwell Caves Ancient Iron Mines

Royal Forest of Dean Coleford Gloucestershire GL16 8JR

Tel: 01594 832535 Fax: 01594 833362

www.clearwellcaves.com

[1.5m S of Coleford town centre on B4228 signposted from Coleford Town Centre. Plenty of on site parking available]

Selected as the 'Best Attraction in Gloucestershire for 2003' by the Good Britain Guide you will see why when you enjoy a journey of discovery to see how ochre and iron ore have been 'won' here for over 5,000 years - from the Neolithic period through to the present day. The mines are famous for their ochre produced to make pigments for artist's and other natural paints; red, yellow, brown and purple ochre is still produced today and sold in the mine shop. There are nine impressive caverns for visitors to discover, with mining and geological displays throughout. Visitors will also see the ochre preparation area and blacksmith's workshop. Excellent gift shop and tempting tearoom to visit afterwards. Picnic area. Ample free parking. For the more adventurous, 'Deep Level' visits can be arranged for small groups.

1 Mar-31 Oct daily 10.00-17.00. Christmas Fantasy; 1-24 Dec 10.00-17.00

A£4.00 C£2.50 Concessions£3.50

Discount Offer: Two For The Price Of One

Festivals & Shows

60th Cheltenham International Festival of Music and Fringe

City Centre Cheltenham GL50 1QA
Tel: 01242 521621 Fax: 01242 256457
[Venues: various throughout Cheltenham. J11 M5, 40m W of Oxford on A40]

The Cheltenham International Festival of Music is bold, bright and bursting with assorted entertainment to suit all. The emphasis is on variety, accessibility and affordability. There is also a host of free outdoor events when Cheltenham's streets and parks become open-air stages for wacky street theatre and all kinds of musical entertainment. The Cheltenham Fringe Festival runs alongside the Music Festival.
July 2-18 2004
From £Free-£30.00

9th Cheltenham International Jazz Festival

Town Hall Imperial Square Cheltenham
Gloucestershire GL50 1QA
Tel: 01242 227979 Fax: 01594 573902
The Cheltenham International Jazz Festival
ranks among the top British festivals of its kind.
Since its inception in 1996 the Festival has
brought some of the biggest names in jazz to
the town.
April 29-May 3 2004

Cheltenham Festival of Science

Town Hall Imperial Square Cheltenham
GL50 1QA
Tel: 01242 227979 Fax: 01242 573902
After the phenomenal success of the first two
Festivals, this year once again offers an exciting
and challenging experience for all ages.
Exploring the theme of perception, lectures,
talks, debates and workshops make up a
packed and varied programme including big
names, interactive events, the Discover Zone -
a free interactive area - and Robot Wars.
June 9-13 2004

Cirencester Early Music Festival

Cirencester Gloucestershire GL7 5TT
Tel: 01285 654180
Now in its fifth successive year, the Cirencester
Early Music Festival provides a full week of con-
certs, recitals and workshops. Plenty for every-
one at affordable prices. Cirencester Church,
Holy Trinity Church, Watermoor & Watermoor
Church Hall this year play host to a feast of
Renaissance, Baroque and Classical delights.
July 19-26 2004

Gloucester Three Choirs Festival

Various venues Gloucester GL1 2LR
Tel: 01452 529819 Fax: 01452 502854
At the heart of the history of the Festival lies the
work of the Cathedral Choirs of Gloucester,
Hereford and Worcester, whose contribution
underpins much of the ethos of what is probably the oldest musical festival of its kind anywhere in the world. This will be a week of splendid music held in one of the most beautiful of
English Cathedrals, especially furnished as a
comfortable concert hall.
August 7-14 2004
Vary, range from £4.00-£29.00

Randwick WAP 2004

Randwick Village Gloucestershire
Tel: 01453 766782
*[Around village lanes and playing field. Rail:
Stroud. Car park on field next to playing field]*

The Randwick Wap is an ancient procession
and festival that dates back to the Middle Ages.
The colourful and musical procession of villagers
in traditional costume winds its way from the
War Memorial to the Mayor's Pool. The procession is lead by the Mop Man who swishes his
wet mop to clear the crowds. During the procession, the Mayor and Queen are carried
shoulder high and escorted by an entourage of
flag boys, ladies in waiting, cheese bearers,
Princesses, a sword bearer and a flag man. The
Mayor is dunked in the Mayor's Pool before
being doused with spring water. The procession
continues to the Well Leaze where two double
Gloucester Cheeses are rolled down the steep
slope. After the procession there are bands
playing all afternoon, country dancing, stalls,
and entertainments for everyone.
May 8 2004
Admission Free

Gardens & Horticulture

Kiftsgate Court Garden

Mickleton Chipping Campden GL55 6LW
Tel: 01386 438777 Fax: 01386 438777
[0.5m S off A46 adjacent Hidcote Garden]

This magnificently situated house has a garden

which is open to the public. The main attraction lies in its collection of old-fashioned roses, including the largest rose in England the R Filipes Kiftsgate.

Apr-May & Aug-Sept Wed, Thur & Sun 14.00-18.00, June-July Mon, Wed, Thur, Sat & Sun 12.00-18.00
A£5.00 C£1.50

Painswick Rococo Garden

Gloucester Road Painswick Stroud GL6 6TH
Tel: 01452 813204 Fax: 01452 814888
[On B4073]

This beautiful Rococo garden is the only one of its period to survive completely and is nearing the end of an ambitious restoration programme.
10 Jan-31 Oct daily 11.00-17.00
A£4.00 C£2.00 OAPs£3.50

Dean Heritage Museum Trust
Royal Forest of Dean

Museum and Galleries
Beam Engine Café
Clock Collection Craft Shops
Art Gallery
Victorian Cottage Woodland Walks
Freemine Adventure Playground
Gage Research Library

Dean
01594 824024
www.deanheritagemuseum.com
Camp Mill, Soudley, Gloucestershire, GL14 2UB

Westonbirt - The National Arboretum

Tetbury Gloucestershire GL8 8QS

Tel: 01666 880220 Fax: 01666 880559
www.westonbirtarboretum.com

[3m S Tetbury on A433. Plenty of on site parking available]

Westonbirt is a wonderful world of trees. There are 18,000 of them dating from 1829, including 96 'champions' (the tallest, oldest etc). Set in 600 acres with 17 miles of paths, it is famous for its autumn colour, but is beautiful at any time of the year.

All year daily 10.00-20.00 or sunset if earlier
A£6.00 C£1.00 Concessions£5.00 except between 4 June-5 Sept A£7.50 C£1.00

Concessions£6.50. Group rates available

Heritage & Industrial

Dean Heritage Centre
Camp Mill Soudley Cinderford GL14 2UB
Tel: 01594 822170 / 824024

Fax: 01594 823711

www.deanheritagemuseum.com

[On B4227 between Blakeney / Cinderford. Plenty of on site parking available]

In the heart of the Forest of Dean, the centre is set around a restored mill and pond. The newly refurbished Museum explores the area from pre-historic times until the present day with hands-on models and activities. Grounds include a Victorian cottage, with pigs, ducks and hens, woodland sculptures and an adventure play-ground, as well as a traditional charcoal burn taking place twice a year. The centre has craft shops and a café, in addition to picnic and bar-beque facilities. Nature trails start from the museum. The centre has an active programme of temporary exhibitions and special events.

Oct-Mar daily 10.00-16.00, Apr-Sept 10.00-17.00

A£4.00 C£2.50 Concessions£3.50 Family Ticket (A2+C2)£12.00. Group Rates: A£3.00 C£1.50 OAPs£2.50. Season Ticket: A£10.00 C£6.00 Family Ticket £24.00 Concessions£8.00

Discount Offer: One Child Free With Every Full Paying Adult

Special Events

Apple Day and Cider Making
19/10/2003-19/10/3003

Berkeley Castle
Berkeley Gloucestershire GL13 9BQ

Tel: 01453 810332 Fax: 01453 512995

www.berkeley-castle.com

[On B4509 1.5m W of A38]

Simon Jenkins, in 'England's Thousand Best Houses' describes Berkeley Castle as 'Britain's rose red city half as old as time'. Visit this gem-stone of England's ancient past for a unique experience of architectural history - a living home reflecting a thousand years of habitation. In an amazing state of preservation and bursting with stories of an eventful past, Berkeley Castle is a treasure not to be missed. The Berkeley family is one of England's best untold stories: powerful players through turbulent centuries who influenced the course of history while man-aging to keep both their property and their lives intact. Their influence can be seen throughout a millennium and across the world, from the founding of Berkeley Square in London to the founding of the American colonies. Visit and you will encounter the murder of a King, a struggle with a Queen, a butcher's daughter who became a Countess... and much, much more.

1 Apr-end Sept Tue-Sat & Bank Hol Mon 11.00-16.00, Sun 14.00-17.00, Oct Sun only 14.00-17.00

Global Ticket (includes Castle, Grounds & Butterfly House): A£7.00 C£4.00 OAPs£5.50 Family Ticket (A2+C2) £18.50. Group rates (25+ people): A£6.50 C£3.50 OAPs£5.00. Season Tickets: A£20.00 C£10.00 Concessions£14.00 Family Ticket £45.00

Special Events

Easter Extravaganza - Family Fun
09/04/2004-12/04/2004

Woodcarving Exhibition
14/04/2004-18/04/2004

Mediaeval Living History Re-enactment
01/05/2004-03/05/2004

Living History: American Civil War
29/05/2004-31/05/2004

Antiques and Classic Car Show
31/05/2004

Month of Roses
01/06/2004-30/06/2004

Bochmann Quartet Evening Concert
06/06/2004

Fancy Dress and 'Make and Take' for Fathers' Day
12/06/2004

Evening Picnic Play
19/06/2004
Shakespeare's A Midsummer Night's Dream, performed by the Chapterhouse Theatre Company

Living History: Mediaeval Berkeley Household
19/06/2004

Evening Outdoor Concert
26/06/2004

Living History: Mediaeval Berkeley Household
03/07/2004

Photography Weeks
06/07/2004-18/07/2004

Children's Make and Take Day
10/07/2004

Cheltenham Festival Concert
12/07/2004

Teddy Bear's Picnic and Puppets, Make and Take
17/07/2004

Joust - Mediaeval Festival
24/07/2004-25/07/2004
Berekeley Castle will once again be the backdrop for the UK's most magnificent recreation of mediaeval history. Joust creates a fun, entertaining, cultural and educational event by making the UK's heritage and history come alive for both adults and children.

Joust - Mediaeval Festival
31/07/2004-01/08/2004

Military Costumes through the Centuries Exhibition
03/08/2004-05/09/2004

Art Exhibition - Landscape Artist Rob Collins
03/08/2004-15/08/2004

Live Crafts Show
13/08/2004-15/08/2004

Jester Day
21/08/2004

Band Music Day
28/08/2004
With the Devonshire and Dorset Regiment, finishing with Beating the Retreat at 17.00

Dinner Dance
28/08/2004
Held in the Castle Courtyard, with live dance band, 1940s style. 1940s fancy dress welcome! Limited tickets so book early for this fantastic one of a kind event

Evening Picnic Play
29/08/2004
Alice's Adventures in Wonderland performed by Chapterhouse Theatre Company

The Berkeley Show
30/08/2004

Homes and Gardens Show
17/09/2004-19/09/2004

Orchestra of the Age of the Enlightenment
17/11/2004
A world premiere performance of recently discovered manuscript at Berkeley

Christmas Concert with the English String Orchestra
05/12/2004

Christmas Open Weekend
10/12/2004-12/12/2004

Holst Birthplace Museum

4 Clarence Road Pittville Cheltenham
Gloucestershire GL52 2AY

Tel: 01242 524846 Fax: 01242 580182

www.holstmuseum.org.uk

[Just off A435 Evesham Road N of town centre]

Regency terrace house, where the composer of
The Planets was born, shows the 'upstairs-
downstairs' way of life of Victorian and
Edwardian times. Includes a working kitchen,
elegant Regency drawing room and children's
nursery, as well as Gustav Holst's original piano
and the story of the man and his music.
Photography allowed with permission.

*All year Feb-mid Dec Tue-Sat 10.00-16.00, Jan
by appointment only. Closed some Bank Hols*

A£2.50 Concessions£2.00 Family Ticket £7.00.
Special school rates available on request

Owlpen Manor

Owlpen Uley Dursley Gloucestershire GL11 5BZ

Tel: 01453 860261 Fax: 01453 860819

[3m E of Dursley off B4066 signposted]

A romantic Tudor manor house dating from
1450 to 1616. Housing unique 17th century
painted cloth wall hangings, furniture, textiles
and pictures. Set in formal terraced gardens
and part of a picturesque Cotswold manorial
group including a watermill, a Victorian church
and medieval tithe barn. Member of the Historic
Houses Association.

*1 Apr-30 Sept Tue-Sun & Bank Hol Mon 14.00-
17.00*

A£4.80 C£2.00 Family Ticket (A2+C4) £13.50

Rodmarton Manor

Rodmarton Cirencester Gloucestershire
GL7 6PF

Tel: 01285 841253 Fax: 01285 841298

[Off A433 6m W of Cirencester]

Rodmarton Manor, near Cirencester in
Gloucestershire, was one of the last country
houses to be built in the old traditional style
when everything was done by hand with local
stone, local timber and local craftsmen. It was
done at a time when mass factory and machine
production had already become the norm.
Ernest Barnsley and the Cotswold group of
Craftsmen, who built and furnished the house
for Claud and Margaret Biddulph, beginning in
1909, were responsible for the revival of many
traditional crafts in the Cotswolds which were in
danger of dying out. The garden was designed
to comprise a series of outdoor rooms, or separate areas each with its own character. Disabled
access limited, please call for details.

*Garden: 8, 12 & 15 Feb from 13.30. House &
Garden: 3 May-30 Aug Wed, Sat & Bank Hol
Mon 14.00-17.00. Garden: June-July Mon
14.00-17.00*

House & Garden: A£7.00 C(5-15)£3.50.
Minimum Group charge £140.00.

Garden only: A£4.00 Accompanied C(5-15)£1.00

Places of Worship

Gloucester Cathedral

2 College Green Gloucester GL1 2LR

Tel: 01452 528095 Fax: 01452 300469

At first, there was a small Anglo-Saxon monastery founded by Prince Osric. Early in the 11th century, Benedictine monks came to live and work here. William the Conqueror ordered the construction of the present building in 1089. It was called St Peter's Abbey and a community of monks lived and worshipped here. Henry VIII dissolved the Abbey, and in 1541 this church became the Cathedral for the new diocese of Gloucester. Highlights include a Norman Nave with massive cylindrical pillars, glorious fan-vaulted cloisters, a magnificent east window with medieval glass and an exhibition telling the story from the founding to the present day.

All year daily. Tower Tours: Apr-early Nov Wed-Sat, usually starting at 14.30 and last about an hour

Admission Free, donations suggested A£3.50. Tower Tours: A£2.50 C£1.00, Certificates £1.00

Railways

Avon Valley Railway

Bitton Station Bath Road Bitton Bristol South Gloucestershire BS30 6HD
Tel: 0117 932 7296 Fax: 0117 932 5935
[On A431, 1m from Keynsham]

The Avon Valley Railway is more than just a train ride, offering a whole new experience for some or a nostalgic memory for others. Take a trip on a steam train into the scenic Avon Valley.

Weekends & school holidays. Steam trains operate Easter-Oct every Sun & Bank Hol, Tue, Wed &

Thurs during Aug, Easter & Christmas
Unlimited travel on day of issue tickets*: A£4.50 C£3.00 OAPs£3.50 Family Ticket (A2+C2) £12.50. *Except some special events

Dean Forest Railway

Norchard Centre Forest Road Lydney Gloucestershire GL15 4ET
Tel: 01594 843423 Fax: 01594 845840
[On B4234 N of Lydney from A48]

Standard gauge steam passenger line from Norchard to Lydney Junction (2 miles).
Trains Run: Apr-May Sun, June-July Wed & Sun, Aug Wed-Thur & Sat-Sun, Sept Wed and Sat-Sun, Oct Sun
Standard Rover Fares: A£5.50 C(5-16)£3.50 OAPs£4.50

Gloucestershire Warwickshire Railway

The Railway Station Toddington Cheltenham Gloucestershire GL54 5DT

Tel: 01242 621405 Fax: 01242 233845

www.gwsr.plc.uk/

[J between B4632 / B4077 on Stow Road (8m from J9 M5)]

The 'Friendly Line in the Cotswolds' offers a 20 mile round trip between Toddington and Cheltenham Racecourse. The views of The Cotswolds, Malverns and The Vale of Evesham are superb, since most of the line runs along embankments. The exciting 693 yard Greet Tunnel is one of the longest on a preserved railway and surely the darkest! Pop along and see the driver and fireman. Break your journey at picturesque Winchcombe Station with its tree lined picnic area or sample the delicious home-made cakes in the 'Flag & Whistle' tearooms at Toddington Station. Refreshments are also available from the buffet car on most trains. A well-stocked station shop sells a variety of 'railway' gifts. Special events are held throughout the year. Visiting locomotives. Wheelchairs can be catered for. Tickets give unlimited travel on the day of purchase. Special group rates available. There is ample free parking.

Mar-Dec Sat Sun & Bank Hol Mon and selected summer weekdays

Return tickets: A£9.00 C(0-4)£Free C(5-15)£5.50 OAPs£7.50 Family Ticket (A2+C3)£24.00. Group rates 20+

Special Events

Day out with Thomas
24/04/2004-25/04/2004
Join us for a fun packed weekend as 'Thomas' and his friends take over the railway. The Fat Controller 'Sir Topham Hatt' will be at Toddington to ensure everyone behaves! Special guests Toby the Tram Engine and City of Truro. Time: 10.00-17.00

Anniversary Steam Gala
07/05/2004-09/05/2004
Featuring special guest engines. Trains from 10.00-18.00

Transport Nostalgia Day
27/06/2004
Travel by steam train to see vehicles and memorabilia on display at Winchcombe Station. Train services from 10.00-18.00

Transport Nostalgia Day
25/07/2004
A variety of historic vehicles are expected to be on display at Winchcombe Station. Train services will operate from 10.00-18.00

Transport Nostalgia Day
05/09/2004
Please see event details above

Day out with Thomas
09/10/2004-10/10/2004
Join us for a fun packed weekend as 'Thomas' and his friends take over the railway. The Fat Controller 'Sir Topham Hatt' will be at Toddington to ensure everyone behaves! Special guest Toby the Tram engine. Time: 10.00-17.00

Autumn Diesel Gala
16/10/2004-17/10/2004
An intensive service of trains hauled by our magnificently restored fleet of heritage diesel locomotives. Time: 10.00-18.00

Winter Diesel Gala
27/11/2004-28/11/2004
An intensive service of trains hauled by our magnificently restored fleet of heritage diesel locomotives. Time: 10.00-18.00

Santa Specials
04/12/2004-24/12/2004
Held on 4, 5, 11, 12, 18, 19, 22, 23, 24 Dec only. Father Christmas comes to GWR every December. Children who travel by train to see him each receive a special present. Advance bookings are essential

Christmas Diesel Day
27/12/2004
An intensive service of trains hauled by our magnificently restored fleet of heritage diesel locomotives. Time: 10.00-18.00

Science - Earth & Planetary

Jenner Museum

Church Lane High Street Berkeley
Gloucestershire GL13 9BN

Tel: 01453 810631 Fax: 01453 811690

*[J13/14 M5, then A38 to Berkeley turn, follow
brown signs from A38. Plenty of on site parking
available]*

Beautiful Georgian home of Edward Jenner, dis-
coverer of vaccination against smallpox. The
displays record Jenner's life as an 18th century
country doctor and his work on vaccination.
Also his study of the cuckoo and hibernation.
Computerised exhibition explaining immunology,
the medical science founded by Jenner.

*Apr-Sept Bank Hol Mon & Tue-Sat 12.30-17.30
Sun 13.00-17.30, Oct Sun only 13.00-17.30*
A£3.50 C£2.00 OAPs£2.80 Family Ticket £9.00

Sport & Recreation

Cotswold Water Park and Keynes Country Park

Spratsgate Lane Shorncote Cirencester
Gloucestershire GL7 6DF

Tel: 01285 861459 Fax: 01285 860186

www.waterpark.org

*[On the Spine Road junction of the A419 the
Cirencester to Swindon Road]*

Britain's largest Water Park. 50% larger than the
Norfolk Broads. Plenty of outdoor activities
including simple country walks to camping and
caravanning, nature and birdwatching, cycling,
sailing, windsurfing, canoeing, kayaking, water-
skiing and fishing. The area's historic towns and
villages such as Crickdale, South Cerney,
Fairford and Lechlade are well worth a visit. You
could even try the Thames Path National Trail.
All the information on the park activities can be
found at Keynes Country Park along with the
visitor eco-centre, the famous bathing beach,
children's play area, lakeside café, wood sculpture trails, boating and cycle hire. Visit the new
Gateway Centre at Lake 6 for a cafe, visitor
information and a gift shop. A great day out for
the whole family. Leisure guide available.

All year daily 09.00-21.00

Parking charges for Keynes Country Park

**Discount Offer: Car Parking Discount
50% Off For Keynes Country Park**

Theme & Adventure Parks

The Cattle Country Adventure Park

Berkeley Heath Farm Berkeley Gloucestershire
GL13 9EW

Tel: 01453 810510 Fax: 01453 811574

*[On outskirts of Berkeley on A38 between J13 &
J14 of M5. Signposted from A38 Berkeley
Junction]*

A good day out for families with children under
15 years. Big indoor and outdoor play areas
where mums and dads can join in too. Drop
slides, mini go carts, trampolines, zipwires,
splash pool, mini golf etc. Separate areas for
toddlers. Farm trail which passes a pets corner,
willow maze and herd of American bison.
Special attractions during summer. Private parties may be booked during evenings or daytime
whenever Cattle Country is closed to the public.

Spring half term-Autumn half term, school holidays and weekends (Sun only during spring and autumn), 10.00-17.00

Please call for price details

Transport Museums

The National Waterways Museum

Llanthony Warehouse Gloucester Docks
Gloucester Gloucestershire GL1 2EH

Tel: 01452 318200 Fax: 01452 318202

[Js 11, 12a & 12 M5, A38 & A40 then follow brown signs for Historic Docks]

Award winning Museum based within the historic Gloucester Docks, on three floors of a listed seven storey Victorian Warehouse. Entry is via a lock Chamber with running water, where a sense of adventure takes you into the secret world of canals. Relive the 200 year story of Britain's first transport system, its tale of pioneers and fortunes gained/lost.

All year daily 10.00-17.00. Closed 25 Dec

A£5.00 C&OAPs£4.00 Family Tickets
(A2+C1)£12.00, (A2+C2)£14.00,
(A2+C3)£16.00

Hampshire

Animal Attractions

Longdown Activity Farm

Longdown Ashurst Southampton Hampshire
SO40 7EH

Tel: 023 8029 3326 Fax: 023 8029 3376

www.longdownfarm.co.uk

*[Off A35 between Lyndhurst & Southampton.
Plenty of on site parking available]*

Meet lots of friendly farm animals, and join in
our range of daily activities - for example, pony
grooming, bottle-feeding goat kids or calves,
small animal handling and goat feeding. Watch
milking every afternoon, enjoy a tractor and trailer ride. Farmer Bryan can arrange a birthday
party with a difference, for a minimum of 10
children. We have indoor and outdoor play
areas where children can let off steam, in safe
surroundings. We also have both outdoor and
under-cover picnic areas.

*14 Feb-31 Oct daily, Nov Sat-Sun, 2-23 Dec
daily 10.00-17.00*

A£5.00 C(3-14)£4.25 Family Ticket (A2+C2)
£17.50 OAPs£4.25. Season tickets and group
discounts available, groups of 15 or more are
given a fully guided tour at no extra charge.
Tours are tailored to suit the age range or par-
icular interest of the group, and must be pre-
booked

**Discount Offer: One Child Free With
Two Full Paying Adults**

Factory Outlets & Tours

Whiteley Village Shopping Outlet

Whiteley Way Whiteley Fareham Hampshire
PO15 7LJ

Tel: 01489 886886

www.whiteleyvillage.co.uk

[J9 M27]

At Whiteley Village, outlet shopping means
famous brands at up to 75% off their high street
price. Thousands of great savings on quality
mechandise which include some current season
ranges alongside end of season bargains.

*All year daily, Mon-Sat 10.00-18.00, Sun 11.00-
17.00*

Admission Free

Festivals & Shows

Basingstoke Kite Festival

Down Grange Sports Complex Pack Lane
Basingstoke Hampshire RG22
Tel: 01256 845455
This will be the 12th Basingstoke Kite Festival.
There will be kites to fly and buy with a free children's kite workshop and refreshments available. The guest flyers will be travelling from as
far afield as Europe. See giant inflatable kites
and displays from top kite teams from around
the country. Come and have a great family day
out!
June 5-6 2004, 10.30-17.00
Admission Free

Fareham and Gosport Easter Folk Festival

Ferneham Hall & Ashcroft Arts Centre Fareham Hampshire PO16 7DB
Tel: 01329 231942 Box Office
[M27, J11 (Fareham/Gosport)]

England's biggest indoor folk and Irish music festival. Over 300 musicians from around the world. Concerts, ceilidhs, workshops, sessions, dance displays and late night festival club. Children under 16 must be accompanied by an adult.
April 8-12 2004, 09.00-02.00 daily
Weekend Season Tickets: A£60.00. Day Tickets: A£7.50-£25.00 C(under16)£Free

Farnborough International Airshow 2004

Farnborough Airfield Farnborough Hampshire
Tel: 020 7227 1043
[M3 J4a then follow AA/Police signs]

The Farnborough International Airshow 2004 takes place at the Farnborough Airbase just outside of London. Farnborough is a biennial event and trade show organised by the Society of British Aerospace Companies. There is a huge range of attractions available for the public over the two days including 5 exhibition halls full of everything you could possibly want to know about aviation and aerospace. Also on display here will be the 'Discovery Stands' with demonstrations and presentations specifically aimed at kids. On the ground, there will be over 200 aircraft on display, as well as rides, flight simulators, and a whole host of children's entertainment including a bungee trampoline and the 'climb the rock' task. Airborne entertainment will take place from 12:30 onwards and will include the opening and closing ceremonies by the famous Red Arrows, as well as military and civilian aircrafts and numerous aerobatic displays. A highlight will be the 'Battle of Britain memorial

flight' which will include such classic planes as the Hurricane, Spitfire, and Lancaster bomber. For anyone remotely interested in aviation, this promises to be a must see and a superb day out for all the family.
July 24-25 2004, 09.30-18.00

Folk & Local History Museums

Breamore House and Countryside Museum

Breamore Fordingbridge Hampshire SP6 2DF
Tel: 01725 512468 Fax: 01725 512858
[On A338]

Life in a typical village like Breamore can be relived in the Breamore Countryside Museum which provides a fascinating insight into the days when a village was self-sufficient. Visitors can see full size replicas of a Farm Worker's cottage before the advent of electricity, a Blacksmith's shop, a Dairy, a Wheelwright's shop, a Brewery, a Saddler's shop and a Cobbler's shop.
House: Easter weekend, Apr Tue & Sun, May-Jun & Sept Tue-Thur & Weekends & all Bank Hol, Aug daily 14.00-17.30. Countryside Museum: As for House 13.00-17.30
A£6.00 C(5-16)£4.00 C(0-4)£Free OAPs£5.00 Family Ticket (A2+C2) £15.00

Gardens & Horticulture

Exbury Gardens and Steam Railway

The Estate Office Exbury Southampton Hampshire SO45 1AZ

Tel: 023 8089 1203 / 8089 9422
Fax: 023 8089 9940

www.exbury.co.uk

[3m from Beaulieu off B3054, 20mins from J2 M27. Plenty of on site parking]

Natural beauty is in abundance at Exbury Gardens, a 200 acre woodland garden on the east bank of the Beaulieu River. Created by Lionel de Rothschild in the 1920s, the Gardens are a stunning vision of his inspiration. The spring displays of rhododendrons, azaleas, camellias and magnolias are world famous. The daffodil meadow, rock garden, rose garden, herbaceous borders, ponds and cascades ensure year round interest, and why not 'let our steam train take the strain' on a 1 1/4 mile journey over a bridge, through a tunnel across a pond in the Summer Lane Garden planted with bulbs, herbaceous perennials and grasses? Then travel along the top of the rock garden and across a viaduct into the American Garden. Fun for all the family and a day out at Exbury that the weather cannot spoil. Dogs allowed on short lead.

28 Feb-31 Oct daily 10.00-17.30. Limited winter opening dates to be confirmed

High Season: Gardens A£6.00 C(under5)£Free C(5-15)£1.50 OAPs£5.50 (£5.00 Tue-Thur) Family Ticket (A2+C3) £15.00. Train A£2.50 C(3+)£2.50 OAPs£2.50. Low Season: Gardens A£4.00 C(under5)£Free C(5-15)£1.00 OAPs£3.50 Family Ticket (A2+C3) £10.00. Train A£2.00 C(3+)£2.00 OAPs£2.00

Special Events

George Forrest Trail
01/03/2004-31/05/2004

'Drawn from Nature' Sculpture Exhibition
01/03/2004-30/06/2004

The 'Forrest Explorer' Easter Trail
10/04/2004-12/04/2004

Marianna Kneller Exhibition - Five Arrows Gallery
24/04/2004-05/05/2004

Hampshire's Beautiful Craft and Garden Show
01/05/2004-03/05/2004

Exbury at its Best - Walks
01/05/2004-31/05/2004

Jazz Picnic
04/05/2004

Society Botanical Artists Exhibition - Five Arrows Gallery
08/05/2004-31/05/2004

The Exbury Festival of Arts, Crafts and Gardens
29/05/2004-31/05/2004

Exbury as HMS Mastodon Exhibition - Five Arrows Gallery
05/06/2004-30/06/2004

Exbury / HMS Mastodon Celebrates D-Day 60th anniversary
05/06/2004-06/06/2004

Narrow Gauge in the Gardens
19/06/2004-20/06/2004

BSO Evening Concert
03/07/2004

Chapterhouse Theare - Alice in Wonderland
28/07/2004

Vintage Exbury Railway Event
07/08/2004-08/08/2004

Chapterhouse Theatre - A Midsummer Night's Dream
28/08/2004

The Exbury Scarecrow Festival
28/08/2004-30/08/2004

Exbury Jewel Lily Exhibition
01/10/2004-31/10/2004

Festival of Early Autumn Colours
01/10/2004-15/10/2004
Please call for specific dates

Steam in the Gardens
02/10/2004-03/10/2004

The Exbury Ghost Train
27/10/2004-31/10/2004

Santa Steam Specials
01/12/2004-31/12/2004
Please call for specific dates

Historical

Broadlands

Romsey Hampshire SO51 9ZD
Tel: 01794 505010 Fax: 01794 505040
[Main entrance on A3090 Romsey bypass]

The home of the late Lord Mountbatten, Broadlands is now lived in by his grandson Lord Romsey. An elegant Palladian mansion in a beautiful landscaped setting on the banks of the River Test.
30 June-2 Sept Mon-Fri, House by guided tour only, first tour 13.05, last one 16.05
A£7.00 C(12-16)£4.00 C(0-12)£Free Concessions£6.00

The Vyne

Vyne Road Sherborne St. John Basingstoke Hampshire RG24 9HL
Tel: 01256 881337 Fax: 01256 881720
[4m N of Basingstoke. Brown heritage signs from major roads]

Built in the early 16th century in beautiful diaper brickwork by William Sandys, Lord Chamberlain to Henry VIII. Passed to the Chute family in the mid-17th century resulting in extensive alterations. Tudor chapel contains extremely fine renaissance glass and majolica floor tiles. A wealth of Tudor panelling and collections of furniture, ceramics and textiles.
House & Grounds: 20 Mar-31 Oct Sat-Sun 11.00-17.00, Mon-Wed House 13.00-17.00, Grounds 11.00-17.00. Open Good Fri. Grounds also open Feb-Mar Sat-Sun 11.00-17.00
House & Grounds: A£7.00 C£3.50 Family Ticket £17.50. Grounds only: A£4.50 C£2.00

Uppark

South Harting Petersfield Hampshire GU31 5QR
Tel: 01730 825415 Fax: 01730 825873
[1.5m S of South Harting, West Sussex, on B2146]

The National Trust's most ambitious restoration project: Georgian interiors, paintings, ceramics, textiles, furniture, dolls house rescued from the 1989 fire. Multi-media exhibition. Interesting servants' rooms. H. G. Wells connections. Garden restored to Repton's design.
28 Mar-28 Oct Sun-Thur Grounds, Garden etc 11.00-17.30. House: from 13.00 (11.00-17.00 Bank Hols)
A£5.50 Family Ticket £13.75

Winchester College

73 Kingsgate Street Winchester Hampshire SO23 9PE

Tel: 01962 621209 Fax: 01962 621166

www.winchestercollege.org

[From the N J9 M3, from the S J10 M3. Limited on site parking]

Founded in 1382, Winchester College is believed to be the oldest continuously running school in the country. Concentrating on the medieval heart of the College, guided tours last approximately 1 hour and include Chamber

Court which takes its name from the Scholars' and Fellows' chambers which surround it, the Gothic Chapel whose 14th century vaulted roof is one of the earliest examples constructed from wood rather than stone, College Hall the original Scholars' dining room, School the 17th century red brick schoolroom built in the style of Christopher Wren, and the original Cloister which contains a memorial to Mallory the mountaineer.

Guided Tours: all year daily except Christmas and New Year. For individuals and small groups - walk in tours Mon, Wed, Fri & Sat 10.45, 12.00, 14.15, 15.30; Tue & Thur 10.45, 12.00; Sun 14.15, 15.30. Group tours for parties of 10+ people can be arranged at times to suit but must be booked in advance

A£3.50 Students/OAPs£3.00

Literature & Libraries

Charles Dickens' Birthplace

393 Old Commercial Road Portsmouth Hampshire PO1 4QL

Tel: 023 9282 7261 Fax: 023 9287 5276

[From M275 turn L at 'The News' roundabout - follow signpost for Charles Dickens Birthplace]

Built in 1805, this is Dickens' birthplace and early home. Restored and furnished to illustrate middle-class taste of the early 19th century, the museum displays items pertaining to Dickens' work and the couch on which he died. There are Dickens' readings at 15.00 on the first Sunday of each month.

Apr-Sept daily 10.00-17.30, Oct daily 10.00-17.00, Charles Dickens Birthday 7 Feb 10.00-17.00

A£2.50 C(0-13)£Free C(13+)&Students£1.50 Family Ticket £6.50 OAPs£1.80

Living History Museums

Milestones Living History Museum

Leisure Park Churchill Way West Basingstoke Hampshire RG21 6YR
Tel: 01256 477766 Fax: 01256 477784
www.milestones-museum.com

[M3 J6, take ringway (W) and follow brown signs for Leisure Park]

Milestones brings Hampshire's recent past to life through stunning period street scenes, shops and buildings all displayed under one roof inside one of the biggest buildings in Basingstoke. Staff in period costumes, mannequins and sounds bring the streets to life and recreate the story of life at work and at home in the Victorian and 1930s periods. Nationally important collections of transport, technology and everyday life are presented in an entertaining and engaging way for visitors of all ages.
All year Tue-Fri 10.00-17.00, Sat & Sun 11.00-17.00, Bank Hol 10.00-17.00. Closed Mon, 25-26 Dec & 1 Jan
A£6.50 C(under5)£Free C(5-16)£3.50 Family Ticket (A2+C2) £16.50 Extra C£2.50 OAPs/Students£5.25. Schools Visit C£3.00. Group rates available for 17+ people. Prices subject to change in April

Discount Offer: One Child Free When Accompanied By One Full Paying Adult

Maritime

Buckler's Hard Village and Maritime Museum

Bucklers Hard Brockenhurst SO42 7XB

Tel: 01590 616203 Fax: 01590 612283

[J2 M27, A326, B3054 then follow signs]

This historic and picturesque village is situated on the banks of the Beaulieu River. The Maritime Museum shows the shipbuilding history of the village and displays of 18th century life.

All year daily 10.30-17.00 (11.00-16.00 Oct-Apr). Closed 25 Dec

A£5.25 C£3.75 OAPs&Students£4.75

follow their fascinating story...

through jungles...

through the Arctic...

through time...

Kids Go Free
(From 1 April 04 - 31 Mar 05)

Open 7 days a week...Tea rooms... Free parking

Tel: 023 9281 9385
E-mail: info@royalmarinesmuseum.co.uk
Royal Marines Museum, Southsea, Hampshire PO4 9PX
www.royalmarinesmuseum.co.uk

Royal Marines Museum

Eastney Esplanade Southsea Hampshire PO4 9PX

Tel: 023 9281 9385 Fax: 023 9283 8420
www.royalmarinesmuseum.co.uk

[3M27, M3, A3M to Portsmouth Southsea front, at Eastney follow brown tourist signs. Plenty of on site parking and dog 'park' available]

At this award winning museum, in what was one of the most stately Officers Messes in England you can discover the exciting 330 year story of the Royal Marines brought to life through dramatic and interactive displays and tour its world famous medal collection. Come and find out for yourself how Hannah Snell posed as a man and served as a marine in India in 1740. Explore the Jungle warfare room but watch out for the live snake and scorpion! Find out how the elite troops of the Royal Marines were closely involved in both World Wars, Battle of Trafalgar, Falklands War - the list goes on. Every year the Royal Marines play a key part in resolving conflicts and keeping peace around the world - here's your chance to see it all under one roof. It's the closest you'll get to experiencing life as a Royal Marine without joining up!

Spring Bank Hol-Aug daily 10.00-17.00, Sept-May daily 10.00-16.30. Closed 24-26 Dec

A£4.75 C&Students£2.25 OAPs£3.50. Army/RAF £2.25. Group rates 10+ 10% discount (organiser and coach driver £Free) Schools rates £Free plus 1 Teacher £Free for each 8 children, Cadets £0.60 per head. Special Offer: Kids go Free (from 1 Apr 2004-31 Mar 2005)

Discount Offer: Two For The Price Of One.

Military & Defence Museums

Aldershot Military Museum and Rushmoor Local History Gallery

Evelyn Woods Road Queen's Avenue Aldershot
Hampshire GU11 2LG

Tel: 01252 314598 Fax: 01252 342942

[Parallel with A325 1m from Aldershot town]

A look behind the scenes at the life of both soldiers and civilians as Aldershot grew up around the military camps to become the home of the British Army. Displays include a Victorian barrack room, training tunnel, the birth of British aviation, and the Canadian Army in Aldershot during World War II.
All year daily 10.00-17.00. Closed over Christmas & New Year
A£2.50 Concessions£1.50

D-Day Museum and Overlord Embroidery

Clarence Esplanade Southsea Hampshire
PO5 3NT

Tel: 023 9282 7261 Fax: 023 9287 5276

www.portsmouthmuseums.co.uk

[M27/M275 into Portsmouth, follow Museum symbol then D-Day Museum on brown signposts. Plenty of parking on site. Rail: Harbour Station. Bus: No. 6 to Palmerston Road (shopping area) then 7min walk]

D-Day 60th Anniversary 6 June 2004 - Visit this year and see the Faces of History (Winston Churchill, Montgomery and Eisenhower) come alive in the magnificent 83 metre 'Overlord Embroidery' depicting scenes of 'Operation Overlord' - 6 June 1944. The Museum's unique and dramatic film show, which includes original, historic footage and archive film bringing this period of the Second World War alive to the visitor. Experience life on the 'Home Front' in an Anderson Shelter and the period front room of the ARP Warden. 'Listen While You Work' in the factory scene; keep vigil with the troops camped in the forest waiting their time to embark; eavesdrop on communications in 'The Map Room', Southwick House. Listen to the story behind the crashed Horda Glider; pass through the German pillbox to the 'Beach Landing' gallery with video / archive film of the landings and interactive touch screens. Tanks, Jeep, Dingo Scout Car, anti-aircraft gun, military equipment, models, photographs, uniforms and Veterans memories, make this museum a necessity for military-history enthusiasts.

All year, Apr-Sept daily 10.00-17.30, Oct-Mar 10.00-17.00. Closed 24-26 Dec. Cafe facilities available Apr-Sept only

A£5.00 C£3.00 OAPs£3.75 Family Ticket £13.00. Group Rates: A£4.25 C£2.50 OAPs£3.20. Educational Groups: Student(18yrs+)£3.00 Student(under 18yrs)£2.30

Discount Offer: 20% Off Single Price Ticket With Voucher

Special Events

D-Day Anniversary Museum
28/05/2004-31/10/2004
The D-Day Museum's exhibition will focus on the important part played by the Portsmouth area in the preparations for D-Day. Launch of 'Walk the Story', a series of information panels around the cities of Portsmouth and Caen, revealing the significance played by various locations at the time of D-Day

Special Events at the D-Day Museum to celebrate the 60th Anniversary of D-Day
04/06/2004-06/06/2004

Crossing of the English Channel
05/06/2004
A Royal Navy warship and a Brittany Ferry will cross the English Channel, echoing the crossing made by the Allied fleet 60 years ago. Events on Southsea Seafront and Common will include the Para Spectacular, a display of historic military

vehicles by the Military Vehicle Trust, a Vera Lynn Tribute at the Bandstand, and in the evening a D-Day themed film show

60th Anniversary of D-Day
06/06/2004

At 11.00, a traditional ceremony at the D-Day Stone, Portsmouth, organised by the Royal British Legion. Free entrance to the D-Day Museum for all visitors (6 June only). Afternoon programme of events on Castle Field, Southsea Seafront, to include the Glenn Miller Sound and tea dance. Display of historic military vehicles by the Military Vehicle Trust on Southsea Common

Explosion! The Museum of Naval Firepower

Priddy's Hard Heritage Way Gosport Hampshire PO12 4LE

Tel: 023 9250 5600 Fax: 023 9250 5605

www.explosion.org.uk

[M27 to J11. Follow A32 to Gosport and blue RAC signs. Explosion! is situated at the end of Heritage Way a brand new road which runs through a new housing development by Barratts Homes. Plenty of on site parking available]

Explosion! The Museum of Naval Firepower voted Small Visitor Attraction of the Year 2003 and Specialist Museum of the Year 2002, is a hands-on, interactive museum set in the historic setting of a former Royal Navy gunpowder and munitions depot at Priddy's Hard, on the Gosport side of Portsmouth Harbour, England. Telling the story of naval warfare from the days of gunpowder to modern missiles. The two-hour tour of the museum includes a stunning multi-media film show set in the original 18th century gunpowder vault, hands-on exhibits and inter-active touch screens which bring presentations to life.

Apr-Oct & School hol daily 10.00-17.30, Nov-Mar Thur, Sat & Sun only 10.00-16.30. Closed 24-26 Dec. Open daily throughout year for pre-booked groups

A£5.50 C(under5)£Free C(5-16)£3.50 OAPs£4.50 Concessions£3.50 Family Ticket (A2+C4) £15.00, (A1+C3) £12.50. Group rates (10+): A£4.40 C(5-16)£2.80 OAPs£3.60

Discount Offer: Two For The Price Of One.

Special Events

Museums Month - Rails to the Yards
09/05/2004

A look at the unique railway system within the Armaments Depot including a short film on the last armaments train from Priddy's Hard. Time: 15.00

The Blunt End - The Build Up to D-Day at Priddy's Hard
22/05/2004-09/01/2005

During the D-Day campaign the preparation could be justifiably claimed to have been one of the greatest invasion armadas the world has ever seen. But how was it prepared? How was it sup-plied? The answers to these questions and more will be the focus of a new exhibition of visual images at Explosion, the Museum of Naval Firepower

An Evening with Lilian Harry
17/06/2004

Best selling author Lilian Harry will be launching her new novel based on the lives of women muni-tions workers during the Second World War.

Limited places, please book in advance. Time: 19.00. Admission Free

Model Warship Weekend
03/07/2004-04/07/2004

With the Surface Warship Association. Displays of old and modern warships on the boating pool. Rum tasting ceremony. Time: 10.00-16.30. Admission Free with valid Museum ticket

Heritage Open Days
10/09/2004-12/09/2004

Go behind the scenes for one weekend only... visit the reserve gun collection and a Victorian explosives vault at The Museum of Naval Firepower. Admission Free - excludes entrance to Explosion! Tours held every 2hrs from 10.15 at the Coffee Shop

The Big Draw at Explosion!
11/10/2004-31/10/2004

Join us to create a giant drawing to record your memories of Explosion! or Priddy's Hard. If you have visited us before, if you remember the Priddy's Hard Armaments Depot, if you have just visited us today... Draw your memory... There will be a prize for the best drawings to be judged on Sat 1 Nov. No experience necessary - alll materials and ages welcome. Admisson Free

Firework Spectacular
06/11/2004

Firework spectacular, family entertainment at Priddy's Hard and early evening preview of Explosion! Fireworks start at 19.30. Under 3s £Free. Tickets can be bought from Explosion!

Christmas Carol Concert in the Grand Magazine
19/12/2004

Carols and mulled wine in the majestic setting of the 18th century gunpowder vault. Book early to avoid disappointment. Time: 19.00. Cost: £5.00 per person

Museum of Army Flying
Middle Wallop Stockbridge Hampshire
SO20 8DY

Tel: 01980 674421 Fax: 01264 781694

www.flying-museum.org.uk

[On A343 between Andover and Salisbury. Plenty of parking on site]

Celebrating over one hundred years of aviation, this award-winning museum is home to one of the country's finest historical collections of military kites, gliders, aircraft and helicopters. There are over 35 fixed wing and rotary aircraft to see at the museum including the largest collection of military gliders in Europe. The Museum's imaginative dioramas and static displays trace the developments of Army flying from pre World War I years through to today's modern Army Air Corps. Explorers World - a Science and Education Centre - features an imaginative range of hands-on activities and experiments for children of all ages. Coffee shop with airfield views, shop and cinema.

All year daily 10.00-16.30. Closed Christmas week

A£5.00 C£3.50 OAPs&Student£4.00 Family Ticket (A2+C2) £15.00. Group Rates: A£4.50 C£2.50 OAPs&Student£3.50. Group Concessions: complimentary meal and admission for coach drivers

Discount Offer: Two For The Price Of One.

Royal Hampshire Regiment Museum and Memorial Garden

Serle's House Southgate Street Winchester Hampshire SO23 9EG

Tel: 01962 863658 Fax: 01962 863658

www.royalhampshireregiment.org.uk

[Between St Thomas's Church and Hotel Du Vin]

This fine 18th century early Georgian House contains an excellent collection of militaria showing the history of the Royal Hampshire Regiment 1702-1992. It includes weapons, medals, uniforms and many individual artefacts, the whole brought to life with pictures and photographs. The gardens in front of the house are maintained by the regiment as is the War Memorial and Garden of Remembrance. Photography is permitted on request. Families and children are welcome. An extensive archive exists from which information about the Regiment and its members can be provided - a telephone call in advance is advised.

Closed for renovation until May 2004. All year Mon-Fri 11.00-15.30, Apr-Oct additionally weekends & Bank Hol 12.00-16.00. Closed for 2 weeks during the Christmas-New Year period

Admission Free

Railways

Watercress Line

The Railway Station Alresford Hampshire SO24 9JG
Tel: 01962 733810 Fax: 01962 735448
www.watercressline.co.uk

[Alresford & Alton stations are signposted off the A31 Guildford to Winchester road, follow the brown tourist signs]

The Watercress Line, a preserved steam railway, runs through ten miles of rolling scenic countryside between Alton and Alresford. All four stations are authentic in period style, with attractive gardens and there is a locomotive yard and picnic area at Ropley.
Mid Jan-Nov weekends, May-Sept selected weekdays
Unlimited travel for the day A£10.00 C(3-16)£5.00 OAPs£9.00 Family Ticket (A2+C2) £25.00

Discount Offer: Two For The Price Of One.

Special Events

Diesel Gala
21/05/2004-23/05/2004
Many visiting diesel locomotives will provide an intensive train service on all three days

Father's Day
13/06/2004
Dad travels FREE if one child ticket is purchased

War on the Line
19/06/2004-20/06/2004
Travel back in time to the 1940s with the Watercress Line. Military vehicles on display plus military and civilian re-enactors

Morris Day
04/07/2004
*See Morris cars on display plus the colourful
Morris Dancers!*

Bus Rally
18/07/2004
*For one day only the Watercress Line teams up
with a variety of bus enthusiasts to provide one of
the largest Bus rallies in the South. Features FREE
bus trips between our stations*

Day Out with Thomas
07/08/2004-15/08/2004
Discount for pre-booking. FREE parking at Ropley

Steam Gala
17/09/2004-19/09/2004
*Visiting large steam engines plus the Watercress
Line's own locos will provide an intensive train service with regular change over of locos on all 3
days*

Wizard Week
23/10/2004-31/10/2004
*Following the success of the 2003 event, the
Wizard Week returns for another magical tour.
Competitions, Fancy Dress, puppet show and
lots more surprises!*

Sealife Centres & Aquariums

Blue Reef Aquarium
Clarence Esplanade Southsea Portsmouth
Hampshire PO5 3PB

Tel: 023 9287 5222 Fax: 023 9229 4443

www.bluereefaquarium.co.uk

*[Situated on seafront road midway between the
two piers. Signposted]*

Portsmouth's Blue Reef Aquarium offers visitors
a dazzling underwater safari through the oceans
of the world. Overlooking the bustling Solent,
the aquarium transports visitors to the spectacular 'underwater gardens' of the Mediterranean
and the stunning beauty of tropical waters -
home to everything from seahorses and puffer
fish to living corals and tropical sharks. At its
heart is a giant tropical ocean tank where an
underwater walkthrough tunnel offers incredibly
close encounters with sharks, stingrays and
hundreds of colourful reef fish. More than 30
naturally-themed displays reveal the variety of
life in the deep from inquisitive rays to amazing
octopus and bizarre shape-shifting cuttlefish!
Don't miss the giant freshwater carp, ferocious
piranhas and the adorable family of otters in
their spacious riverside home. New from
February half term 2004, meet our 'Toxic Frogs'.
Plus, from Easter 2004, visit the Blue Reef
Nursery where you can meet baby seahorses
and miniature sharks in our pioneering breeding
display.

All year daily from 10.00. Closed 25 Dec

A£5.95 C(3-16)£3.95 OAPs£4.95 Family Ticket
(A2+C2/3)£17.99

**Discount Offer: One Child Free With
One Full Paying Adult**

Special Events

Launch of Blue Reef Nursery
09/04/2004-12/04/2004
*The new Blue Reef nursery provides a fascinating
insight into the life cycles of marine creatures from
around the world. Please call for further details*

Shark Awareness Week
29/05/2004-05/06/2004
*Shark Week is a celebration of the oceans' great-
est predator. Learn the facts behind the fiction
and discover why sharks have got lots more to
fear from us than we have from them. Regular
talks, workshops and feeding demonstrations*

Summer Holidays - Family Fun
01/07/2004-31/08/2004

Throughout the summer holidays, Blue Reef is organising a series of fun activities aimed at families. From rockpool encounters to marine themed quiz trails, talks and feeding demonstrations, there's something for visitors of all ages to enjoy

October Half Term Event - Claws
01/10/2004-31/10/2004

From comical hermit crabs and 'fashion conscious' decorator crabs to giant lobsters and the mighty king crab, this exciting feature offers a fascinating insight into the incredible world of crustaceans. Please call for specific dates

Stately Homes

Stansted House

Stansted Park Rowlands Castle Hampshire PO9 6DX

Tel: 023 9241 2265 Fax: 023 9241 3773

[2m E of Rowlands Castle. Follow brown signs from A3 or A27]

One of the South's most beautiful stately homes, set in 1,750 acres of glorious park and woodland. Stansted House is a prime example of The Caroline revival, with elegant staterooms displaying fine period furniture and an important collection of paintings.

House, Below Stairs, Grounds, Chapel & Bessborough Arboretum 11 Apr-27 Sept Sun & Mon 13.00-17.00, Jul & Aug Sun-Wed 13.00-17.00

For all areas, A£5.50 C£3.50 OAPs£4.50 Family Ticket £14.50

Theme & Adventure Parks

Go Ape! High Wire Forest Adventure

Moors Valley Country Park Nr Ringwood Hampshire BH24 2ET

Tel: 0870 420 7876

www.goape.cc

[12m W of New Forest, 20mins N of Bournemouth]

Rural Tourist Attraction of the Year 2003 - NFU Countryside Awards. Designed to appeal to all ages, Go Ape! is an extreme, high wire aerial adventure course of some 35 zip slides, scramble nets and hanging rope bridges - at heights of up to almost 30 feet off the forest floor. Not for the faint hearted, Go Ape! is a thrilling test of agility, courage and determination. Minimum age 10 years, minimum height 1m 40cm/ 4'7". Under 18s must be accompanied by a participating adult. Booking essential.

Apr-Oct daily, Nov-Mar weekends only and by prior arrangement. Please call the bookings and information line or check the website for further details

Standard rates: A(18+)£16.00 C(10-17)£11.00

Paultons Park

Ower Romsey Hampshire SO51 6AL

Tel: 023 8081 4455 24 hour
Fax: 023 8081 3025

www.paultonspark.co.uk

[J2 M27, near junction of A31 & A36. Plenty of on site parking available]

A great day out for all the family with over 50 attractions included in the price. The variety of things to see and do includes big rides and small rides, play areas, entertainment, muse-ums, beautiful bird gardens, horseshoe-shaped lake, dinosaurs and lots more! Great favourites are the Raging River Ride log flume, Pirate Ship swingboat, Dragon roundabout, Viking Boats, Whirly Copter and Tea Cups. Children love Kids Kingdom, Tiny Tots Town, the Magic Forest where nursery rhymes come to life, the Ladybird and Rabbit Rides. Get lost in the hedge maze, see over 100 species of exotic birds and the largest collection of genuine Gypsy wagons in the country. Two thrilling new drop rides for 2004 plus Humboldt penguins.

13 Mar-31 Oct daily 10.00-18.30. Rides and Catering closes 17.30. Earlier closing at certain times in the year. Weekends only Nov-Dec until Christmas

A£13.50 C(under14)&OAPs£12.50 Children under 1 metre £Free. Family Ticket (3 people) £37.00, (4 people) £48.00, (5 people) £60.00, (each family must contain at least 1 paying child and not more than 3 adults)

Transport Museums

Beaulieu

John Montagu Building Beaulieu Brockenhurst Hampshire SO42 7ZN
Tel: 01590 612345 Fax: 01590 612624
[J2 M27, A326, B3054, follow brown tourist signs]

Set in 75 acres of grounds at Beaulieu you can see the world famous National Motor Museum featuring 250 historic vehicles plus motoring memorabilia. Palace House and gardens, set on the banks of the Beaulieu River, Lord Montagu's ancestral home, Abbey Ruins and exhibition of monastic life.

All year May-Sept 10.00-18.00, Oct-Apr 10.00-17.00. Closed 25 Dec

A£14.00 C£6.75 Family Ticket (A2+C3 or A1+C4) £38.50 Student&OAPs£13.00

Zoos

Marwell Zoological Park

Colden Common Winchester Hampshire SO21 1JH

Tel: 01962 777407 Fax: 01962 777511
www.marwell.org.uk

[J5 M27, J11 M3. Rail: Eastleigh/ Winchester. Plenty of on site free parking]

Beautiful Marwell is six miles southeast of Winchester in Hampshire and makes a wonderful day out for all the family. There are over 200 species of rare animals including tigers in a magnificent enclosure. Don't miss the snow leopards, rhino, jaguar and hippo! Marwell has one of Europe's largest collections of rare hoofed animals including zebra and antelope and is dedicated to the conservation of endangered species. There are many popular favourites such as giraffe, meerkats, kangaroos and gibbons. Enjoy the World of Lemurs, Into Africa, Tropical World, Penguin World, the Fossa Exhibit, Aridlands and the Bat House. Road and rail trains, restaurant, gift shops and adventure playgrounds. Special activity days held throughout the year. Marwell offers a day full of fun and interest for all ages.

All year daily, Summer 10.00-18.00, Winter 10.00-16.00. Closed 25 Dec

29 Mar-31 Oct: A£11.50 C(3-14)£8.00 Concessions£9.50 Family Ticket (A2+C2) £37.50; 1 Nov-18 Mar: A£10.50 C£7.50 Concessions£9.00 Family Ticket £34.50. Tuesday Special: OAPs£5.75

Herefordshire

Food & Drink

Cider Museum and King Offa Distillery

21 Ryelands Street Hereford Herefordshire
HR4 0LW
Tel: 01432 354207 Fax: 01432 371641
[Off A438 to Brecon]

Housed in a former cider works, the museum tells the fascinating story of cidermaking through the ages. Displays include advertising material, prints, English and French beam presses, farm cider house, travelling cidermakers' tack, champagne cider cellars, press house and early bottling equipment. A varied programme of temporary exhibitions and events is held throughout the year, for further details please call venue.

All year Apr-Oct daily 10.00-17.00, Nov-Dec daily 12.00-16.00, Jan-Mar Tue-Sun 12.00-16.00
A£3.00 C£2.00 OAPs£2.50

Gardens & Horticulture

Hampton Court Gardens

Hope-Under-Dinmore Leominster Herefordshire
HR6 0PN
Tel: 01568 797777 Fax: 01568 797472
[On the A417 near to J with A49]

Hampton Court's Gardens are extensive new gardens in the historic grounds of the medieval fortified manor house. There is a walled flower garden, herbaceous borders, canals, pavilions, follies, a maze and a secret tunnel, a hermit's grotto, waterfalls and a flooded sunken garden. The Orangery Restaurant serves light lunches, tea and cake from a grand Joseph Paxton designed greenhouse adjoining the castle. The kitchen garden is entirely organic and grows fruit and vegetables for the restaurant.
Please call for opening time details
A£5.00 C£3.00 OAPs£4.50 Family Ticket £14.00

Hergest Croft Gardens

Kington Herefordshire HR5 3EG
Tel: 01544 230160 Fax: 01544 232031
www.hergest.co.uk

[0.25m W of Kington, off A44. Plenty of on site parking available]

From spring bulbs to autumn colour, this is a garden for all seasons. One of the finest collections of trees and shrubs surround the Edwardian house, an old fashioned kitchen garden has spring and summer borders and Park Wood, a hidden valley, has rhododendrons up to 30ft tall. Member of the Historic Houses Association. Limited disabled access.

3 Apr-31 Oct daily 12.30-17.30 (May-June 12.00-18.00). Also opening on Sat & Sun in March, 12.30-17.00, to see the Spring Bulbs

A£4.50 C£Free. Group rates 20+ A£4.00. Pre-booked Guided Tours 20+ A£6.00. Season tickets A£17.00

Discount Offer: Two For The Price Of One.

How Caple Court Gardens

How Caple Hereford Herefordshire HR1 4SX
Tel: 01989 740626 Fax: 01989 740611
[B4224 Ross on Wye 4.5m to Hereford 9m]

11 acres overlooking the River Wye. Formal Edwardian gardens, extensive plantings of mature trees and shrubs, water features and a sunken Florentine garden. Norman church with 16th century Diptych.
15 Mar-17 Oct daily 10.00-17.00

A£2.50 C£Free

Historical

Berrington Hall

Berrington Leominster Herefordshire HR6 0DW
Tel: 01568 615721 Fax: 01568 613263
[3m N of Leominster 7m S of Ludlow on W side of A49]

An elegant neo-classical house of late 18th century set in a park landscaped by Capability Brown. Formal exterior belies the delicate interior with beautifully decorated ceilings and fine furniture. Nursery, Victorian laundry and Georgian dairy. Attractive garden and historic apple orchard.
House: 6 Mar-4 Apr Sat & Sun, 5 Apr-31 Oct Sat-Wed (open Good Fri), Sat & Sun 12.00-17.00, Mon-Wed 13.00-17.00 (16.30 in Oct). Garden: As house plus 1 Nov-14 Dec Sat & Sun
A£4.80 C£2.40 Family Ticket £12.00. Grounds: £3.40

Discount Offer: Two For The Price Of One

Kinnersley Castle

Kinnersley Herefordshire HR3 6QF
Tel: 01544 327507 Fax: 01544 327663
[4m W of Weobley on A4112, Black and White Village Trail. Rail: Hereford / Leominster]

Kinnersley Castle started life as a Norman, Welsh border strong hold, seen today as the predominantly Elizabethan Manor House of the Vaughan family. Housing various fine oak panelled rooms and the original 1588 plaster work ceiling of the solar, it is set in grounds containing yew hedges, a walled kitchen garden and a notable ginko tree.
For Guided Tours: 19 July-20 Aug Mon-Fri 14.30 & 15.30, also 11-14, 17-19 Sept 14.30 only
A£2.50 C£1.50 Concessions£2.00

Stately Homes

Eastnor Castle

Eastnor Ledbury Herefordshire HR8 1RL

Tel: 01531 633160 Fax: 01531 631776

www.eastnorcastle.com

[2m E of Ledbury on A438 Tewkesbury Rd. Alternatively, J2 M50 then A449/A438 to Eastnor. Plenty of on site parking]

A magnificent Georgian castle in a fairytale setting with a deer park, arboretum and lake. Inside tapestries, fine art and armour. The Italianate and Gothic interiors have been restored to a superb standard. There is a children's adventure playground and delightful nature trails and lakeside walks. Homemade teas are available. Member of the Historic Houses Association.

Easter-3 Oct Sun & Bank Hol Mon 11.00-17.00, July-Aug Sun-Fri 11.00-17.00

Castle & Grounds: A£6.50 C£4.00 Family Ticket £17.00. Grounds: A£4.50 C£3.00. Groups 20+ £5.50, guided tours £8.50

Hertfordshire

Animal Attractions

Willows Farm Village

Coursers Road London Colney St Albans
Hertfordshire AL2 1BB

Tel: 01727 822444 Fax: 01727 822365

[J22 M25. Follow brown tourist signs]

Acres of fun can be had at Willows Farm
Village, rediscovering the great outdoors. Meet
all your farmyard favourites, learn the Legend of
the Lake, pan for gold in the Gold Stream,
watch the Daft Duck Trials, sheepdog trials
gone quackers, discover the agility of birds of
prey in the stunning 'Bird-o-batics' falconry displays, take a ride on Tristan the Runaway
Tractor as he takes some unexpected turns.

27 Mar-31 Oct daily 10.00-17.30

Term Time & Weekdays: A£6.95 C£5.95.
School Hols & Weekends: A£8.50 C£7.50

Arts, Crafts & Textiles

Henry Moore Foundation

Dane Tree House Perry Green Much Hadham
Hertfordshire SG10 6EE

Tel: 01279 843333 Fax: 01279 843647

[M11 J8 no signposts]

Major works are displayed in the grounds and in
the studios where Moore worked. Visitors are
guided around the grounds and into the studios.

*By appointment, Apr-mid Oct weekday afternoons
only for Guided Tours at 10.30 or 14.30*

A£7.00 C(0-18)&Students£Free OAPs£3.00

Country Parks & Estates

Knebworth House, Gardens and Park

Knebworth Hertfordshire SG3 6PY
Tel: 01438 812661 Fax: 01438 811908
www.knebworthhouse.com

*[Direct access from J7 A1(M) at Stevenage
South. Plenty of on site parking]*

Home to the Lytton family since 1490, the
romantic Victorian gothic exterior of Knebworth
House does little to prepare the visitor for what
to expect inside. The house, its décor and contents encapsulate 500 years of English history
from early Tudor times to the present day
through 19 generations of one family. British Raj
Display. Guided tours of the house most days.
Member of the Historic Houses Association
Formal gardens, maze, Dinosaur Trail (new for
2004) outdoor adventure playground, miniature
railway and 250-acre country park.

*27-28 Mar Sat-Sun, 3-18 Apr daily, 24 Apr-23
May Sat-Sun & Bank Hol, 29 May-6 June daily,
12-27 June Sat-Sun, 3 July-31 Aug daily, 4-26
Sept Sat-Sun. House & Indian Raj display open
12.00-17.00, Park, Gardens, Dinosaur Trail &
Railway 11.00-17.30*

Including House: A£8.50 Concessions£8.00
Family Ticket £29.00. Excluding House: A£6.50
Concessions£6.50 Family Ticket £22.00.
Special rates available for pre-booked groups of
20+ people

**Discount Offer: Knebworth Park &
Gardens: Two For The Price Of One.**

Special Events

Medieval Jousting
11/04/2004-12/04/2004
By the Knights of Royal England

Knebworth Country Show
02/05/2004-03/05/2004
Sporting and country crafts and trade stands, fly casting, clay pigeon shooting, gun dog and sheep dog demos, archery, ferret racing

Hertfordshire Garden Show
22/05/2004-23/05/2004
Approximately 100 stallholders, craft tent and other attractions

'Rienzi' by Wagner
30/05/2004
Celebrating Edward Bulwer Lytton's 201st birthday, Rienzi, the opera by Richard Wagner was based on Bulwer Lytton's 1835 novel of the same name. Time: 19.30-21.30. Tickets: £20.00

Classic Motorcycle Show
06/06/2004
Classic displays (including BSA, Norton, Triumph, Yamaha, Suzuki, Harley Davidson), motorcycle spares, concours, tools, accessories, books, literature, bikes for sale

Scottish Pipes and Highland Dancing
20/06/2004
Pipe band competition, drum majors contest, highland dancing, Scottish dancing displays, piping contest, themed stalls

Classic Corvetts Rally
27/06/2004
Trade stands, arena, club stand. Approximately 600 cars on display

SALVO Fair
03/07/2004-04/07/2004
Trade stands - dealers in architectural antiques, antique garden ornaments, reclaimed building materials, craftspeople and green building technology

Pre 50s American Auto Club Rally
18/07/2004
Approximately 400-500 cars on show

Alice's Adventures in Wonderland
31/07/2004
Performed in the beautiful formal gardens, by the Chapterhouse Theatre Company. Full of wonder-

ful characters, songs and dance. Time: 18.00-21.00. Tickets: A£11.00 C£8.00 Family Ticket £34.00

Hertfordshire Craft Show
21/08/2004-22/08/2004
Craft stalls, sheepdogs, falconry, ferrets, gun dogs and children's entertainment

Classic Motor Show
29/08/2004-30/08/2004
Approximately 2,000 show cars expected

National Garden Scheme Day
01/09/2004
Special one-day ticket price to the Gardens, all proceeds go to the National Gardens Scheme

Medieval Jousting
12/09/2004
By the Knights of Royal England

Home Design and Interiors Show (Provisional)
01/10/2004-03/10/2004
Approximately 150 stands including furniture, rugs, art, sculpture, glass-ware, ceramics, fabrics and soft furnishings

Christmas Craft Fair
04/12/2004-05/12/2004
A large selection of quality crafts plus demonstration areas, Christmas music, food and drink

Festivals & Shows

Hertford Music Festival

Hertford Hertfordshire
Tel: 01992 503129
[Hertford is situated on the A414, accessible from the M11 or A1(M)]

The Hertford Music Festival runs throughout May 2004 and includes all forms of music 'by the people, for the people'. Over 100 events are planned, ranging from pop, rock and jazz to choral, orchestral, folk and ethnic music.
April 27-June 1 2004 at various times

Folk & Local History Museums

Museum of St Albans

Hatfield Road St Albans Hertfordshire AL1 3RR
Tel: 01727 819340 Fax: 01727 837472
[On A1057 J9 M1 J21A M25 signed to St Albans]

Exhibits include the Salaman collection of craft tools and reconstructed workshops. The history of St Albans is traced from the departure of the Romans up to the present day.
All year daily Mon-Sat 10.00-17.00, Sun 14.00-17.00. Closed over Christmas
Admission Free

Historical

Hatfield House, Park and Gardens

Hatfield Hertfordshire AL9 5NQ

Tel: 01707 287010 Fax: 01707 287033

www.hatfield-house.co.uk

[7m from J23 M25 & 2m from J4 A1(M), opposite Hatfield railway station. Plenty of free on site parking]

Celebrated Jacobean House with magnificent paintings, furniture and tapestries. Within the delightful and extensive formal gardens stands a surviving wing of the Old Tudor Palace, the childhood home of Elizabeth I. 1,000 acres of parkland with nature trails and a children's play area. The national collection of model soldiers is in the Stable Yard near the gift shop and licensed restaurant. Functions, weddings and banquets, call (01707) 262055. Guided tours

only on weekdays. Photography not allowed in the House.
Easter Sat-30 Sept House: daily 12.00-16.00. Park, West Gardens, Restaurant & Shop: daily 11.00-17.30. East Gardens: only open on Fri

House, Park & Gardens: A£7.50 C£4.00. Group rates 20+ (except Fri) £6.50. Park only: A£2.00 C£1.00. Friday £10.50 (£6.50 Park & all gardens only)

Discount Offer: Two For The Price Of One, For Gardens Only.

Special Events

Packard Automobile Club of GB Rally
02/05/2004

Living Crafts 30th Anniversary
06/05/2004-09/05/2004
Tel: 023 9286 3871 for further information

Model Soldiers Day
16/05/2004
Tel: 020 8979 7137

Stewart Linford Furniture Exhibition
22/05/2004-23/05/2004

Flower Festival
11/06/2004-13/06/2004

Shakespeare in the Park
20/06/2004
'Theatre Setup' perform The Merry Wives of Windsor

Bentley Drivers Club National Rally
26/06/2004

Children's Folk Dance Festival
03/07/2004
For further details call 01707 262082

Shakespeare in the Park 'As You Like It'
11/07/2004
Presented by Mad Dogs & Englishmen Theatre Company

The Battle Proms
24/07/2004
Music with Cavalry, Cannons and Fireworks. For advance tickets call 01432 355416

Art in Clay (10th National Pottery and Ceramics Festival)
06/08/2004-08/08/2004
For further details call 0115 987 3966

Shakespeare in the Park 'A Midsummer Night's Dream'
29/08/2004
Presented by Chapter House Theatre Company

Country Homes, Gardens and Rare Breeds Show
03/09/2004-05/09/2004
For further details call 01494 450504

Equestrian Theatre 'Spirit of the Horse'
16/09/2004-19/09/2004
Please call 01260 288681 for details

Rock 'n' Gem Show
02/10/2004-03/10/2004

Book Fair
17/10/2004-28/11/2004
Held on 17 Oct & 28 Nov

Antiques and Fine Art Fair
05/11/2004-07/11/2004

Gifts for Christmas Fair
12/11/2004-14/11/2004
For further information call 01494 450504

A Christmas Market
20/11/2004

Christmas Shopping Weekends
20/11/2004-19/12/2004

Christmas Tree Sales
01/12/2004-23/12/2004

Dolls Houses & Miniatures Fair
05/12/2004

Mills - Water & Wind

Mill Green Museum and Mill

Mill Green Hatfield Hertfordshire AL9 5PD
Tel: 01707 271362 Fax: 01707 272511
www.hertsmuseums.org.uk

[Between Hatfield & Welwyn Garden City at J of A1000 and A414. Limited on site parking]

Enjoy the working watermill, which produces flour every week, as well as a local history museum with a temporary exhibition gallery. There are also various craft demonstrations and special events on summer weekends. A new Jubilee Garden was opened in 2003.
All year Tue-Fri 10.00-17.00, Sat Sun & Bank Hol 14.00-17.00
Admission Free

Discount Offer: 20p Off A Bag Of Mill Green Flour. Any Size

Music & Theatre Museums

St Albans Organ Museum

320 Camp Road St Albans Hertfordshire
AL1 5PE

Tel: 01727 869693/768652

*[The Museum is 2m from St Albans city centre.
Buses: S2 & C2 come from the city centre and
the railway station. Located next to Camp School]*

A permanent playing exhibition of mechanical
musical instruments. Dance Organs by Decap,
Bursens, and Mortier; Mills Violano-Virtuoso self
playing violin and piano; reproducing pianos by
Steinway, Weber and Ampico; musical boxes.
Wurlitzer and Rutt theatre pipe organs. Regular
monthly theatre organ concerts.

*Every Sun 14.00-16.30. Other times by arrange-
ment for groups. Closed 25 Dec*

A£4.00 C£1.50 Concessions£3.00 Family
Ticket £8.50

Natural History Museums

Walter Rothschild Zoological Museum

Akeman Street Tring Hertfordshire HP23 6AP

Tel: 020 7942 6171 Fax: 020 7942 6150

*[Tring is on the A41, 7m SE of Aylesbury and
33m from London]*

This museum was once the private collection of
Lionel Walter, 2nd Baron Rothschild, and is now
part of the Natural History Museum. It houses
more than 4,000 specimens in a unique
Victorian setting. The displays comprise of
mounted specimens of animals from all parts of
the world - from whales to fleas, hummingbirds
to tigers, even a large collection of domestic
dogs.

*All year Mon-Sat 10.00-17.00, Sun 14.00-17.00.
Closed 24-26 Dec*

Admission Free

Places of Worship

St Albans Cathedral

Sumpter Yard Holywell Hill St Albans
Hertfordshire AL1 1BY
**Tel: 01727 860780 Fax: 01727 850944
www.stalbanscathedral.org.uk**

*[Centre of St. Albans, J3 A1(M), M1 from N J7,
from S J6, M25 from E J22, from W J21a]*

St Albans Cathedral is an imposing former
Norman Abbey Church set in the centre of the
City of St Albans overlooking Verulamium Park.
The present church was built from recycled
Roman brick between 1077-1115 on the execution site of Alban (c.250), Britain's first martyr.
A site of Christian worship for over 17 centuries
the cathedral remains an active parish church
and focus for ecumenical worship. There are
many interesting architectural features including
the shrine of Saint Alban (1308), the tomb of
Duke Humphrey of Gloucester (1447), wooden
watching loft (1400), painted vaulted presbytery
ceiling (1280) and a series of 12-13th century
wall paintings unequalled in England. Guided
tours are available by arrangement and there is
a wide screen multi media show describing the
history of the building and life of the cathedral
community today. Bookstall, gift shop and the
'Café at the Abbey'.
All year daily 08.00-17.45
Suggested Donations: £2.50

Special Events

Easter Monday Pilgrimage
12/04/2004

Festival of Saint Alban the Martyr
19/06/2004-20/06/2004

Caribbean Links Festival
17/07/2004

Heritage Open Days
11/09/2004-12/09/2004

Fireworks Spectacular
06/11/2004

Festival of Lessons and Carols
22/12/2004-23/12/2004

Roman Era

Welwyn Roman Baths

Welwyn By Pass Welwyn Hertfordshire AL6 9HT
Tel: 01707 271362 Fax: 01707 272511

*[Under A1M at J with A1000, access off central
roundabout of Welwyn by-pass]*

Third century AD bathing suite, the only visible
remains of a Romano-British villa, ingeniously
preserved within the embankment of the A1(M).

*Jan-Nov Sat, Sun & Bank Hol 14.00-17.00 or
dusk if earlier. Open daily during school half terms
& holidays (except Dec) 14.00-17.00 or dusk if
earlier*

A£1.00 C£Free

**Discount Offer: Two For The Price Of
One (On Adult Admission)**

Wildlife & Safari Parks

Paradise Wildlife Park

White Stubbs Lane Broxbourne Hertfordshire
EN10 7QA
Tel: 01992 470490 Fax: 01992 440525
www.pwpark.com

*[6m from J25 off M25, follow brown signs off A10
at Turnford. Plenty of free on site parking available]*

Paradise Wildlife Park is Britain's Friendliest Zoo!
That applies to both its animals and staff! Enjoy
a great day out for all of the family. It has an
extensive range of animals including tigers,
lions, monkeys, zebras and camels. What
makes it unique is the fact you can get really
close, meeting and feeding many of the animals. New for 2004 are Snow Leopards,
ReptileMania, The Parrot Olympics Training
Camp, the On Safari Crazy Golf and a Gold
Panning and Children's Craft Area. There is a full
programme of daily activities including meet the
animals (literally!), Bird of Paradise Show, feeding of the lions and tigers, DJ Jazzy Jungles
Amazing World of Animals and much more. The
Park offers many other attractions including 3
themed adventure playgrounds, children's rides,
the world's largest inflatable paddling pool,
indoor soft play area, tractor trailer rides and for
a small additional charge woodland railway,
crazy golf and pony rides. Paradise has good
fast food restaurant and catering facilities, picnic
areas, toilets and ample car parking.
*All year daily Mar-Oct 09.30-18.00, Nov-Feb
10.00-dusk*
A£10.00 C(2-15)£7.00 OAPs£7.00

Discount Offer: One Child Free With Two Full Paying Adults

A£1.65 C£0.95 OAPs£1.35. Group rates 15+ 10% discount on the day, 20% if booked and paid for 3 weeks in advance

Discount Offer: One Child Free With Two Full Paying Adults.

Shepreth Wildlife Park

Willersmill Station Road Shepreth Nr Royston Hertfordshire SG8 6PZ
Tel: 09066 800031 25p min
Fax: 01763 260582
www.sheprethwildlifepark.co.uk

[Just off the A10 between Cambridge and Royston, next to the train station. Plenty of on site parking available]

Shepreth Wildlife Park at Willersmill began in 1979 as a refuge for injured birds and mammals. Since then is has become one of East Anglia's major places of interest, with a wide variety of wildlife to see, from tigers to giant fish which feed from your hands. Set in natural surroundings with large lakes, it offers a memorable day out for all the family - even Dad! The exotic creepy-crawlies are all the stars in our major attraction called Waterworld and Bug City where young fans of the digital cartoon characters Flick and Hopper from Disney's insect blockbuster, A Bug's Life, can now come face-to-face with the real thing. Also see the insects from the National Geographic Channel series 'Insects from Hell'.

All year daily 10.00-18.00 (10.00-dusk during winter months). Closed 25 Dec
Park: A£5.50 C£3.95 OAPs£4.50. Bug City: £2.10 C£1.40 OAPs£1.75. Combined Ticket:

Isle of Man

Animal Attractions

Home of Rest for Old Horses

Bulrhenny Richmond Hill Douglas Isle of Man
IM4 1JH
Tel: 01624 674594 Fax: 01624 613278
On A5 Airport Road, half way up Richmond Hill
approximately 3 miles S of Douglas. Home is on
bus route]

The wonderful retirement home for ex-Douglas
tram Horses along with homeless, friendly
horses and donkeys set in 92 acres of glorious
countryside. Come and say hello to our residents who enjoy meeting their old and new
friends, where many an hour can be spent in
the peaceful and tranquil setting of the Home.
Browse around our Museum and Shop and
enjoy our home baking in the Café where afternoon teas are a speciality. Parties are catered
or by arrangement. Adoption of horses and
donkeys are encouraged as we are run entirely
by voluntary contributions.
7 May-17 Sept Mon-Fri 10.00-16.00
Admission Free

Arts, Crafts & Textiles

The Fabric Centre

2 Crown Street Peel Isle of Man IM5 1AJ
Tel: 01624 844991 Fax: 01624 801887
[Next to the Perevil Hotel, just off East Quay and
behind Peel Sailing Club]

The Isle of Man's specialist needlework shop.
Stockist of Stewart Gill Textile Paints, DMC
Anchor, Stef Francis, Rahjmahal Rowan, Jaeger
and also now stocking a wide range of patchwork fabrics.
Winter: Mon-Wed & Fri 10.15-16.00 Sat 10.15-
16.30. Summer: Mon-Wed & Fri-Sat 10.15-
16.30, Thur: closed

Festivals & Shows

Bushy's Big Wheel Blues Festival

Various venues Laxey Isle of Man IM4 7AY
Tel: 07624 422964 (Mobile)
Bushy's Big Wheel Blues Festival, spread over
three days on 6 stages - 4 of which are FREE -
is a showcase of cosmopolitan musical talent. If
you love Gibson and Fender guitars, valve
amplifiers, denim and the Blues, this is the place
to be; the beautiful Isle of Man for three won-
derful days in May. This year's line-up includes
Marcus Malone and his band, Watermelon Slim,
Tim Hain and The Worx, Smokestack, and
Wheatbread Johnson.
May 14-16 2004
Most events are free, please call for details

Mananan International Summer Festival 2004

Erin Arts Centre Victoria Square Port Erin
Isle of Man IM9 6LD
Tel: 01624 832662 Fax: 01624 836658
[Signposted from Promenade]

The Celtic Sea God Mananan presides over this
cornucopia of events in the Isle of Man. Its special blend of the very best of recitals, jazz, lectures, opera, theatre and cabaret promises a
certain delight for those who venture to dip in.
Includes Young Singer of Mann Competition.
June 24-July 4 2004

Vagabonds International Festival of Rugby

Glencrutchery Road Douglas Isle Of Man
IM2 6DA
Tel: 01624 661996 Fax: 01624 673029
[Behind T.T. Grandstand]

From its early beginnings of two teams travelling
to our shores for a couple of friendly games, the
Festival has grown to become the highlight of
the Manx season. Teams from all over the U.K.
and Europe converge on the Island to play the
game of rugby, with the only reward being a
sore head the following day!
April 9-12 2004
Admission Free

Folk & Local History Museums

Leece Museum

The Old Courthouse East Quay Peel IM5 1AR
Tel: 01624 845366
[Located on the Harbourside in Peel alongside the Peveril Hotel]

The Leece Museum was established in 1984 by Mr.T.E. (Eddie) Leece, a retired headmaster of Peel Clothworkers School, and former Town Commissioner and Mr. Frank Quayle who served as the museum's curator for the first 15 years of its existence. In June 2000 the museum was relocated to its new premises in the Old Courthouse building which served as the town's seat of justice until the beginning of the 20th Century. It still retains many original features including the atmospheric 'Black Hole' prison cell in which the town's wrongdoers were incarcerated.
Daily (except Christmas and New Year) Summer 10.00-16.00, Winter 13.00-16.00
Admission free

Living History Museums

Moores Traditional Curers

Mill Road Peel Isle Of Man IM5 1TA
Tel: 01624 843622 Fax: 01624 812155
Since around 1770 Manx Kippers have been smoked in the traditional long red herring houses on the Island. At Peel, the last of these old style curing yards is now a living museum, and you are invited to experience a working display of this almost lost culinary art.
Tours 15.30; Shop 10.00-17.00 Mon-Sat
A£2.00 C£1.00 Family Ticket (A2+C3) £5.00

Performing Arts

Erin Arts Centre

Victoria Square Port Erin Isle of Man IM9 6LD
Tel: 01624 832662 Fax: 01624 836658
Community-based, it provides an essential and unique key to access to, and participation in, arts based activities. It is the only accessibly-local arts venue with appropriate facilities- a dedicated performance space and exhibition gallery space with full access for the disabled - for the presentation of arts whereby performance, participation and enjoyment can be encouraged and advanced.
13.30-16.30 Tue-Fri
Prices vary

Railways

Isle of Man Transport

Banks Circus Douglas Isle of Man IM1 5PT
Tel: 01624 663366 Fax: 01624 663637
The Isle of Man Steam Railway began operations in 1873 and for the last 128 years it has played a part in the life and legends of the Isle of Man. Take the Manx Electric Railway, opened in 1893, to the glens and hills and around rugged coastlines and cliff tops and to Snaefell mountain. Mountain railway from Laxey to Summit of Snaefell. 4 and three quarter mile double track electric railway, rising to 2,000ft above sea level, virtually the Summit.
Apr-Oct
Various fares, please phone for details

Wildlife & Safari Parks

Curraghs Wildlife Park

Ballaugh Isle of Man IM7 5EA
Tel: 01624 897323 Fax: 01624 897327
Developed adjacent to the reserve area of the Ballaugh Curraghs is the wildlife park, which exhibits a large variety of animals and birds in natural settings. Large walk through enclosures let visitors explore the world of wildlife, including local habitats along the Curraghs nature trail. The miniature railway runs on Summer Sundays.
Easter-Oct 10.00-18.00
A£4.50 C£2.25. Group rates A£3.00 C£1.50

Isle of Wight

Animal Attractions

Flamingo Park - Wildlife Encounter

Oakhill Road Seaview Isle of Wight PO34 5AP
Tel: 01983 612153 Fax: 01983 613465
[Situated on the B3330, between Ryde and Seaview (well signposted from Ryde)]

A world of wildlife awaits you at this top 'Award Winning' attraction that offers a unique daily programme of events for all the family. Interactive and educational keeper presentations will introduce you to an exotic array of wildlife - penguins, flamingos, pets' corner, wallabies, beavers, red squirrels, pelicans, meerkats, plus thousands of free roaming birds, tame enough to feed by hand.
27 Mar-30 Sept daily 10.00-17.00, Oct daily 10.00-16.00
A£6.75 C(3-15)£4.75 OAPs£5.75 Family Ticket (A2+C2) £21.00, each additional child £4.50

Arts, Crafts & Textiles

Quay Arts Centre

Sea Street Newport Isle of Wight PO30 5BD
Tel: 01983 528825 Fax: 01983 526606
[On waterfront off Newport High Street (turn left at the Guildhall clock)]

Situated in converted 18th century warehouse, The Quay Arts Centre is the central space for arts activity on the Isle of Wight. The Centre is home to the Anthony Minghella Studio Theatre and is the only place on the IOW to catch regular professional performances of comedy, children's shows, medium-scale touring theatre and cultural cinema, folk, jazz and world music.
All year Mon-Sat 10.00-16.00 and during the evenings for special events. Closed 25 Dec
Admission Free to Galleries. Live events individually ticketed

Birds, Butterflies & Bees

Butterfly World and Fountain World

Staplers Road Wooton Isle of Wight PO33 4RW
Tel: 01983 883430 Fax: 01983 883430
[Mid-way between Wooton and Newport]

Butterfly World is a colourful and enthralling experience as you watch hundreds of exotic butterflies fly freely in the tropical indoor garden. Fountain World introduces the magic of moving water with soothing sounds and glittering colour. Enjoy the Italian and Japanese Water Gardens, then visit the gift shop, restaurant and garden centre.
1 April-31 Oct 10.00-17.00
A£4.75 C£2.90 OAPs£3.80

Festivals & Shows

Isle of Wight Festival

Various venues across the Isle of Wight
Tel: 01983 823352 Fax: 01983 823369
After an absence of 32 years, the Isle of Wight Festival returned with a bang in 2002. The 2004 festival will take place across the Island and will run for two weeks. These dates will incorporate the Isle of Wight 3 day Rock Festival on 11-13 June 2004.
June 4-19 2004
Call 01983 823352 for further details

Isle of Wight Walking Festival

Newport Isle of Wight PO30 1JS
Tel: 01983 813813/813818
The Walking Festival will take visitors on a journey through time as they follow in the footsteps

of one of our greatest poets Alfred Lord Tennyson. So often in fact did Lord Tennyson walk his favourite Island path that the route now bears his name - 'The Tennyson Trail' and whilst we can't promise that Walking the Wight will produce yet another Poet Laureate, discerning walkers of all ages and abilities are still able to enjoy the Island's diverse landscape and rich literary past. The festival programme, featuring 16 days of great walking to help you unwind, has been designed to enable everyone to talk part. There are over 80 walks during the festival fortnight including cliff walks, country walks, garden walks, forest walks, ghost walks and lighthouse walks.
May 8-23 2004
Call 01983 813818 for further details, most walks are £Free

Skandia Life Cowes Week

Regatta Centre: 18 Bath Road Cowes
Isle of Wight PO31 7QN
Tel: 01983 295744 Fax: 01983 295329
[Ferry: Red Jet ferry from Southampton to Cowes, Isle of Wight]

Skandia Life Cowes Week is an eight day international yacht racing regatta, the largest and most prestigious sailing regatta in the world. Approximately 1,000 yachts compete within 36 classes. Racing starts at 10.15 daily and takes place within the confines of The Solent. Public entertainment ashore includes balls and shows at Northwood House, live music and discos, nightclubs, street entertainment for both adults and children, beer tents, fast foods etc. A spectacular fireworks display takes place at the end of the week.
August 7-14 2004
Admission Free, other entertainment may be charged

Folk & Local History Museums

Museum of Island History

Guildhall High Street Newport Isle of Wight
PO30 1TY
Tel: 01983 823366 Fax: 01983 823841

A new museum presenting the story of the Isle of Wight from the time of the dinosaurs to the present day. Discover the Island through interactive displays and touch screen technology.
All year Mon-Sat 10.00-17.00, Sun 11.00-15.30
A£1.80 C£1.00 OAPs£1.00 Family Ticket £4.00

Historical

Nunwell House and Gardens

West Lane Nunwell Sandown Isle of Wight
PO36 0JQ
Tel: 01983 407240
[Signposted off Ryde to Sandown road A3055]

Set in 5 acres of beautiful gardens, an impressive lived-in and much loved house where King Charles I spent his last night of freedom. Partake in a guided tour of the house containing fine furniture, Old Kitchen exhibition and interesting collections of family militaria.
House & Gardens: 30-31 May & 13.00-17.00 then 5 July-8 Sept Mon-Wed 13.00-17.00
A£4.00 (incl Guide Book) Couple£7.50
Accompanied C(under12) £1.00 OAPs£3.50.
Gardens only: £2.50

Mills - Water & Wind

Calbourne Watermill and Rural Museum

Calbourne Newport Isle of Wight PO30 4JN
Tel: 01983 531227 Fax: 01983 531227
[On B3401 between Newport and Freshwater]

There has been a mill here since at least 1299, and the present 17th-century machinery still works when turned by the 20ft water wheel. The millpond and stream have been converted into an attractive water garden. Working mill - grinds flour on sale in the cafe.
Easter-Oct daily 10.00-17.00 & 19.00 peak times. Pre booked guided tours
A£5.00 C(7+)£3.00 OAPs£4.00

Natural History Museums

Dinosaur Farm Museum

Military Road Brighstone Newport Isle of Wight
PO30 4PG
Tel: 01983 740844 / 07970 626456
Fax: 01983 740844
[Military Rd (Coast Road A3055), approx halfway between Blackgang Chine and Isle of Wight Pearl Centre]

Follow the discovery in 1992 of Europe's best brachiosaur, Dinosaur Farm Museum was launched to bring palaeontology to a wider audience. Today, we are still the only British museum where visitors can see experts conserving dinosaur bones, and can also talk freely with them, a combination that makes a truly 'interactive' experience.
1 Apr-31 Oct Sun, Tue, Thur 10.00-17.00, plus daily July-Aug
A£2.50 C£1.50 OAPs£2.00

Dinosaur Isle

Culver Parade Sandown Isle of Wight
PO36 8QA

Tel: 01983 404344 Fax: 01983 407502

www.dinosaurisle.com

[Follow brown signs to Dinosaur Isle in Sandown area. Ample on site parking]

In Britain's first purpose built dinosaur attraction discover, experience, encounter the lost world of dinosaurs. Walk back through fossilised time to the period of the dinosaurs and meet life sized replicas set in prehistoric landscape including an animatronic Neovenator, all this in a unique pterosaur-shaped building.

Open all year, Education room, guided tours and field trips available by appointment.

All year daily, Apr-Sept 10.00-18.00, Oct 10.00-17.00, Nov-Mar 10.00-16.00. Closed 24-26 Dec & 1 Jan. Please call to confirm January opening

A£4.60 C£2.60 Family Ticket £12.00

Discount Offer: One Child Free With Each Full Paying Adult

Nature & Conservation Parks

Shanklin Chine

2 Pomona Road Shanklin Isle of Wight
PO37 6PF

Tel: 01983 866432 Fax: 01983 866145

www.shanklinchine.co.uk

[Venue signposted on A3055. Entrance from Shanklin Esplanade or Shanklin Old Village]

Part of our national heritage, this scenic gorge at Shanklin, Isle of Wight, is a magical world of unique beauty and a rich haven of rare plants, woodland, wildlife, including red squirrels and enchanting waterfalls. A path winds through the ravine with overhanging trees, ferns and other flora covering its steep sides. The exhibition 'The Island - Then and Now' is housed in the Heritage Centre and in 2004 will feature 'D-Day 60 Anniversary Special' together with PLUTO (Pipe Line Under The Ocean) which carried petrol to the Allied troops in Normandy, and local history displays. The Memorial to 40 Royal Marine Commandos, who trained here during the war in preparation for the Dieppe Raid of 1942, can be seen at the lower entrance. After dusk, during the main summer months, subtle illuminations create a different world. Gift Shop and Tea Room. On the beach below, Fisherman's Cottage, built by William Colenutt in 1819, offers a choice of excellent food and real ale, which can be enjoyed on the sun terrace. Excellence in England Special Award.

1 Apr-31 Oct daily, 1 Apr-20 May 10.00-17.00, 21 May-26 Sept 10.00-22.00 (illuminated after dusk), 27 Sept-31 Oct 10.00-17.00. Please be aware that weather conditions may influence period of opening

A£3.50 C(under16)£2.00 OAPs&Students£2.50. Family Ticket (A2+C2) £9.00, (A2+C3) £11.00. Group rates (10+) (excluding schools) 10% discount. Mobility Impaired £1.50 due to restricted access

Discount Offer: Two For The Price Of One

Performing Arts

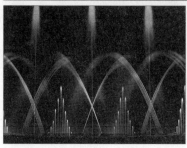

Waltzing Waters

Aqua Theatre Westridge Centre Brading Road Ryde Isle of Wight PO33 1QS

Tel: 01983 811333 Fax: 01983 811333

[Behind the Tesco Superstore on the outskirts of Ryde. Plenty of on site parking]

The world's most elaborate water, light and music production. 'It's like nothing you've ever seen before'... a triumph of artistry and engineering. Visitors are overwhelmed by thousands of dazzling patterns of moving water synchronised with music in spectacular fashion. This indoor production is an entertainment that one never forgets. The very first of its kind in England, this venue will provide a completely different set of musical selections on each day of the week, therefore appealing to all tastes and to all ages. So if you're looking for something entirely new in entertainment... don't miss this unique show.

2 Feb-17 Dec daily from 10.00 on the hour every hour until 4pm & from 3 Apr-29 Oct evening show 19.15 & 20.15

A£4.00 C£2.00 Concessions£3.50. Group rates 15+ available

Discount Offer: One Child Free With Each Full Paying Adult

Sealife Centres & Aquariums

Marine Aquarium

Fort Victoria Yarmouth Isle of Wight PO41 0RR
Tel: 01983 760283
[0.5m W of Yarmouth on A3054. Follow sign posts down to Fort Victoria]

Be amazed by the variety of bizarre creatures found in our local waters. Poisonous Weever fish lurk in the sand, graceful rays swim in our larger tanks, beautiful anemones snare unsuspecting prey while the amazing Cuttlefish change colour before your eyes. Walk over the Conger Pool! In our Tropical Reef section you see some of the extraordinary and stunningly beautiful inhabitants of coral reefs.
Easter-end Oct daily 10.00-18.00.
A£1.90 C£0.95 OAPs£1.50 Family Ticket (A2+C2) £5.00

Theme & Adventure Parks

Blackgang Chine Fantasy Park

Blackgang Ventnor Isle of Wight PO38 2HN
Tel: 01983 730330 Fax: 01983 731267
[Off A3055]

Opened as scenic gardens in 1843 covering some 40 acres, the park has imaginative play areas, water gardens, maze and coastal gardens and a water force high speed boat ride. Set on the steep wooded slopes of the Chine are the themed areas where you will find a magical mix of fantasy, legend and heritage.
22 Mar-31 Oct daily from 10.00
A&C£7.50 C(under4)£Free OAPs£5.50 Disabled Concession£4.00 Family Saver Ticket (4 persons) £27.00. These prices include free return visit within 4 days

The Needles Park

Alum Bay Totland Bay Isle of Wight PO39 0JD

Tel: 0870 458 0022 Fax: 01983 755260

www.theneedles.co.uk

[Signposted on B3322. Plenty of on site parking available]

Set in heritage coastline, offering a range of attractions from the spectacular chairlift to the beach to view the Island's famous landmark and unique coloured sandcliffs to the popular Alum Bay Glass. Full catering and retail facilities including Sand Shop and Sweet Manufactory. New for 2004, 'Junior Driver' - it's fun and exciting for children aged 4-11 as they learn about road safety, whilst driving an electric car and hopefully obeying road signs and working traffic lights!

1 Apr-31 Oct 10.00-17.00, hours extended during High Season

Admission free, all day parking £3.00 plus pay-as-you-go attractions. Supersaver Tickets available. Facilities subject to availability

Special Events

Magic in the Skies
29/07/2004-26/08/2004
Held on 29 July, 5, 12, 19, 26 Aug. A fireworks finale following late night opening on Thursdays

ent

Agriculture / Working Farms

Hop Farm Country Park

Maidstone Road Paddock Wood Tonbridge
Kent TN12 6PY

**Tel: 01622 872068 Fax: 01622 872630
www.thehopfarm.co.uk**

*[On the A228. 20mins from M25 J5 & 15mins
from M20 J4. Plenty of on site parking]*

Based in the Heart of Kent, the Hop Farm
Country Park includes award winning Museums,
Exhibitions, Animal Farm and Shire Horses,
indoor and outdoor play areas and restaurant
providing a great day out for all ages and interests. The Hop Farm also hosts a number of
special events throughout the year, from Motor
Shows, the 'War and Peace Show' the largest
Military Vehicle Extravaganza in the world, to
garden shows, craft shows and Food and Drink
Fairs. Picnic areas indoor and out.

All year daily 10.00-17.00

A£7.50 C£6.50 Family Ticket (A2+C2) £27.00.
Prices vary on event days

**Discount Offer: Half Price Child
Admission With Full Paying Adult.**

Special Events

Boat Jumble
15/02/2004

Half Term Week - Splat and Splodge
16/02/2004-29/02/2004

Easter Holiday Capers
03/04/2004-23/04/2004
Includes Easter Eggstravaganza, 9-12 April

Weald of Kent Garden Show
24/04/2004-25/04/2004

Wild West
01/05/2004-03/05/2004

Craft Fair
15/05/2004-16/05/2004

Half Term Week - Dinosaur Days
29/05/2004-04/06/2004

Invicta FM's Party in the Park
06/06/2004

Garden of England Motor Bike Show
12/06/2004-13/06/2004

British Food and Drink Festival
19/06/2004-20/06/2004

KM Motoring Pageant
03/07/2004-04/07/2004

KM War & Peace Show
21/07/2004-25/07/2004

Holiday Themed Weeks
26/07/2004-05/09/2004

Southern Mini Days
07/08/2004-08/07/2004

European Fast Car Show
14/08/2004-15/08/2004

South of England Garden Show
28/08/2004-30/08/2004

Hop Festival
04/09/2004-05/09/2004

Kent Country Fair
11/09/2004-12/09/2004

KM Wedding Extravaganza
03/10/2004

KM Caring Parent Show
09/10/2004-10/10/2004

Boat Jumble
24/10/2004

Half Term Week - Witches and Wizards
25/10/2004-31/10/2004

Fireworks Party
06/11/2004

Christmas Craft Fair
27/11/2004-28/11/2004

Festive Fun
21/12/2004-05/01/2005

Animal Attractions

South of England Rare Breeds Centre

Woodchurch Ashford Kent TN26 3RJ
Tel: 01233 861493 Fax: 01233 861457
[M20, J10 9m, on B2067 between Hamstreet / Tenterden follow brown tourist signs]

A fun family day out with rare farm animals, many to touch. Children's Barn where children can play with young animals, also regular 'Meet the Animals' sessions. You can see the reconstruction of an historic Georgian farmstead, enjoy farm rides, woodland walks, toddlers sandpit and paddling pool, indoor and outdoor play areas.
All year 1 Apr-30 Sept daily 10.30-17.30, 1 Oct-31 Mar Tue-Sun 10.30-16.30. Closed 24-25 Dec
A&C(3-15)£5.50 C(under3)£Free
Concessions£4.50 Staff Carers £3.00

Birds, Butterflies & Bees

Wingham Wildlife Park

Rusham Road Shatterling Canterbury Kent CT3 1JL

Tel: 01227 722053 / 720836
Fax: 01227 722452
www.winghamwildlifepark.co.uk

[A257 between Canterbury and Sandwich. Plenty of on site parking]

A fascinating day out for the whole family. Wander around the landscaped gardens and walk through aviaries to see our collection of birds and animals including llamas, meerkats, lemurs, otters, prairie dogs, wallabies, parrots, ducks, peafowl, emus and rheas. Then enjoy a snack in the tea-room and a browse through the gift shop. New! Tropical House opening Easter 2004.

All year daily 10.00-18.00, dusk in Winter months

A£4.90 C£3.50 OAPs£4.50 Family Ticket (A2+C2)£15.00

Discount Offer: One Child Free With Two Full Paying Adults

Festivals & Shows

Broadstairs Dickens Festival

Broadstairs Kent CT10 3NH
Tel: 01843 861118 during event
[M2 from London. Rail: London Victoria to Broadstairs]

Charles Dickens visited Broadstairs between 1837 and 1859. He named it 'Our English Watering Place' and enjoyed its sun, sea and air. It is still the quaint town which he encouraged his friends to visit. For nine days every June at the Broadstairs Dickens Festival, you can mix with crinoline ladies and their top hatted escorts. See them promenade in Dickensian splendour and even better, wear costume of the 1837-1859 period and join in the fun. Many events, both Free and Ticketed, during the 9 Day Festival, including: Opening Parade followed by; Opening Ceremony with Entertainment, Victorian Cricket Match, Duels, Melodramas, Festival Play - Nicholas Nickleby, Victorian Bazaar, Victorian Music Hall, Victorian Sea Bathing, Talks, Victoriana Collectors' Fair, Morning Coffee with the Dickensians, Musical Entertainment and a 3 day Victorian Country Fayre with goods ranging from antiquities and collectables to crafts both traditional and new
June 19-27 2004
Many events are Free

Hever 2004

The Lakeside Theatre Hever Castle Hever Edenbridge Kent TN8 7NG
Tel: 01732 866114 Fax: 01732 864824
[3m SE of Edenbridge off B2026 between Sevenoaks and East Grinstead. M25, J5/6]

Since it opened in the early eighties, the Lakeside Theatre has become one of the most popular outdoor venues in the south-east, attracting many thousands every summer, many of whom return year after year. Situated in the beautiful Italian Garden of Hever Castle in Kent, overlooking the lake, it offers the perfect setting for a pre-show picnic with family and friends. The tiered and covered seating make for an unusually intimate auditorium to enjoy the programme of music, opera and drama which comprises the Summer Festival.
June 25-August 29 2004, Tue-Sun, all perfor-

mances commence 20.00. Gates open for Picnics at 18.30, Cafeteria Restaurant and Bar open from 19.00
Tickets from £13.00

Kent County Showground

Kent Event and Exhibition Centre Detling Maidstone Kent ME14 3JF
Tel: 01622 630975 Fax: 01622 630978
[Off A249 Link Rd between M20 and M2]

County showground holding many special events. Kent County Show - an enjoyable, entertaining, educational experience for all the family. See the cattle, sheep, pigs, horses, show jumping, llamas, alpacas, ring displays, farming food & wine, visit the hundreds of trade stands, flower show, cookery demonstrations and forestry area. Schools very welcome too. It's a great day out! Kent Steam and Transport Rally tractor pulling display, kangaroo kid display, undercover craft and model displays, fair, beer tent, refreshments and free parking.
Kent County Show: July 16-18 2004. Kent Steam and Transport Rally: 21-22 Aug 2004

Folk & Local History Museums

Museum of Kent Life

Lock Lane Sandling Maidstone Kent ME14 3AU
Tel: 01622 763936 Fax: 01622 662024
[Museum just off A229 Maidstone-Chatham road, follow signs to Aylesford]

This award-winning 40 acre open air museum reflects changing times and lives in the 'Garden of England' over the last century. The UK's last working oast house plus barn, granary, hoppers huts and cottages.
1 Mar-2 Nov daily 10.00-17.30
A£6.00 C(under4)£Free C(5-15)£4.00
OAPs£4.50 Family Ticket (A2+C2) £18.00

Pines Garden and St Margaret's Museum

Pines Garden Beach Road St. Margaret's Bay Dover Kent CT15 6EF

Tel: 01304 852764 Fax: 01304 853626
[Off A258 Deal to Dover road. Travel through the village of St Margaret's on Station Road, then Sea Street, Bay Hill. The Museum is on Beach Road which runs along the coast line]

The Pines Garden is situated beside the spectacular White Cliffs of Dover. Its 6 acres host a fine collection of trees and shrubs. The outstanding features of this garden are the large ornamental lake and waterfall, the Millennium garden and the impressive bronze statue of Sir Winston Churchill.
The Pines Garden: all year daily 10.00-17.00. St Margaret's Museum: Easter & May Bank Hol, end May-early Sept Wed-Sun 14.00-17.00
Garden: A£3.00 C£0.50 Concessions£2.50
Disabled Visitors (in wheelchair) £1.60.
Museum: A£1.00 C£Free

Food & Drink

Biddenden Vineyards and Cider Works

Little Whatmans Gribble Bridge Lane Biddenden Kent TN27 8DF

Tel: 01580 291726 Fax: 01580 291933
www.biddendenvineyards.com

[Off A262, between Biddenden and Tenterden. 1.5m from old Wealden village. Plenty of on site parking]

Biddenden Vineyards, Kent's oldest commercial vineyard is located just outside the village, the legendary home of the famous Biddenden Maids (Siamese twins). Enjoy a tranquil walk through 22 acres of vines, visit the winery and shop, containing a 17th century cider press and sample our fine English wines, Kentish ciders and Apple juice. Coaches welcome. Tea/coffee available daily.

All year Mar-Dec Mon-Sat 10.00-17.00, Sun & Bank Hol 11.00-17.00, Jan-Feb Mon-Sat 10.00-17.00. Closed Dec 24 from 12.00 -1 Jan incl. Guided tours for pre-booked groups - call for details

Admission and Tastings £Free. Pre-booked Guided Tours £3.40 (minimum of 15 adults)

Discount Offer: 10% Discount On All Shop Purchases.

Gardens & Horticulture

Emmetts Garden

Ide Hill Sevenoaks Kent TN14 6AY

Tel: 01732 868381 / 750367
Fax: 01732 750490

www.nationaltrust.org.uk

[4m from M25, J5. 1.5m S of A25 on Sundridge-Ide Hill road. 1.5m N of Ide Hill off B2042. Rail: Sevenoaks 4.5m, Penshurst 5.5m. Bus: JRS Traveline 404 from Sevenoaks, alight Ide Hill, 1.5m. Plenty of on site parking available]

Influenced by William Robinson, this charming and informal garden - with the highest treetop in Kent - was laid out in the late 19th century, with many exotic and rare trees and shrubs from across the world. There are glorious shows of daffodils and bluebells, azaleas, rhododendrons, acers and cornus in autumn and also a rose garden and rock garden. Volunteer-driven buggy can take visitors and one folded wheelchair from car park to ticket hut. Garden, shop and tea room largely accessible, wheelchairs available. Note: there is a sheer drop at end of shrub garden. Occasional guided tours available.

20 Mar-30 June Wed-Sun & Bank Hol Mon 11.00-17.00, 1 July-31 Oct Wed, Sat-Sun & Bank Hol Mon 11.00-17.00. Stable Tearoom and Shop: As Garden 11.30-16.30

A£4.00 C£1.00 Family Ticket (A2+C3) £9.00. Group rates (15+): £3.50, must be booked in advance

Groombridge Place Gardens and Enchanted Forest

Groombridge Place Groombridge
Tunbridge Wells Kent TN3 9QG

Tel: 01892 863999 Fax: 01892 863996

www.groombridge.co.uk

[Off A264 on B2110. Plenty of on site parking]

Experience magic and mystery, history and romance at these beautiful award winning gardens - such an unusual mix of traditional heritage gardens with the excitement, challenge and contemporary landscaping of the ancient forest - appealing to young and old alike. Set in 200 acres of wooded parkland, the magnificent walled gardens are set against the romantic backdrop of a 17th century moated manor and include herbaceous borders, white rose garden, drunken topiary, secret garden and more. Wonderful colour through the seasons. In ancient woodland there's an 'Enchanted Forest' with quirky and mysterious gardens developed by innovative designer, Ivan Hicks, to excite and challenge the imagination. Children love the Dark Walk, Tree Fern Valley, the Groms Village, Romany Camp and the Giant Swings. Also Birds of Prey flying displays, canal boat cruises and a great programme of special events.

1 Apr-6 Nov daily 09.30-18.00

A£8.50 C(3-12)£7.00 OAPs£7.20 Family Ticket (A2+C2) £28.50. Season tickets and group rates available

Special Events

Easter Eggstravaganza
11/04/2004-12/04/2004
'Eggcentric' outdoor pantomime, circus workshops, free mini Easter egg for every child

The Adventures of Robin Hood
02/05/2004-03/05/2004
Back for the 7th year to popular acclaim. Jugglers, storyteller, dancers and minstrels

Bank Holiday Family Fun
30/05/2004-31/05/2004
A magical inflatable world comes to life at Groombridge - plus cartoon characters and chocolate give-aways!

A Midsummer Garden Celebration - Groombridge in Bloom
12/06/2004-27/06/2004
Blazing June borders and the formal gardens at their best; guided tours, garden workshops, 'meet the gardener' sessions and more

Hot Air Balloons and Ferraris
11/07/2004
Prestigious cars, the romance of hot air balloons parachute team and music from the Caribbean. Gardens open until 20.00

Classic Open Air Picnic Concert
17/07/2004
A magical evening of musical entertainment with firework finale. Tickets: call 01892 761444. Event subject to license

Theatre in the Gardens
27/07/2004-28/07/2004

The Groundling Theatre Company present 'The Taming of the Shrew' and 'As You Like It'. Evening performances at 19.30. Please call the Box Office on 023 9273 7370 for details

Wings, Wheels and Steam
08/08/2004
Over 500 vintage and classical vehicles plus thrilling air display

Scarecrows, Shires and Sheepdogs
29/08/2004-30/08/2004
Scarecrow workshops, sheep dog displays and dray rides. Watch out for the scarecrow statue!

Wars of the Roses Skirmish
18/09/2004-19/09/2004
Medieval battles and demonstrations of archery, longbow and crossbow, man-at-arms and gunnery

Hallowe'en in the Spooky Forest
31/10/2004
Scary witches and wizards with spooky special effects. Time: 16.30-20.00. For tickets please call the Box Office on 01892 861444

Fireworks Spectacular to Music
06/11/2004
Breathtaking pyrotechnics lighting up the night sky over the moated house. One of the best shows in the South East. For tickets please call 01892 861444

Owl House Gardens
Mount Pleasant Lamberhurst Tunbridge Wells Kent TN3 8LY
Tel: 01892 891290 Fax: 01892 891222
[1m NE off A21]

The Owl House is a small, timber-framed 16th-century house, a former haunt of wool smugglers. Surrounding it are 13 acres of gardens with spring flowers, azaleas, rhododendrons, roses, shrubs and ornamental fruit trees.
All year daily 11.00-18.00. Closed 25-26 Dec & 1 Jan
A£4.00 C£1.00

Yalding Organic Gardens
Benover Road Yalding Maidstone Kent ME18 6EX

Tel: 01622 814650 Fax: 01622 814650

www.hdra.org.uk

[6m SW of Maidstone, 0.5m S of Yalding on B2162. Plenty of on site parking available]

Described in the Daily Telegraph as 'among the most inspirational garden acres anywhere, for anyone', the gardens are rapidly gaining a reputation for being amongst the very best in the South East. Nestling against a traditional backdrop of hop gardens and oast houses, the gardens trace garden history through sixteen landscaped displays, including a 13th century apothecary's garden, a Tudor knot, a cottager's garden in the early 19th century and a stunning herbaceous border, inspired by Gertrude Jekyll. Yalding is run by HDRA, Britain's leading organic gardening organisation, so naturally the gardens also demonstrate the best ways of making compost and how to control pests and diseases without using pesticides. Kids will love the children's garden. Home cooking is a speciality, using vegetables and salads fresh from the garden whenever possible - delicious! Garden raised unusual plants for sale. The gardens regularly appear on TV.

May-Sept Wed-Sun plus weekends over Easter, Apr & Oct

A£3.50 C£Free (applies to children under 16 years, must be accompanied by an adult) OAPs£3.00. Group rates: A£2.75

Discount Offer: Two Adults For The Price Of One Full Paying Adult.

Special Events

Composting Workshop
17/04/2004
A practical demonstration of different composting techniques and containers

Organic Pests and Disease Solutions
15/05/2004
A detailed look at how to control pests and diseases without chemicals

Go Forth and Multiply
12/06/2004
An organic gardening weekend special, with a practical workshop on taking cuttings

A Stroll Through Garden History
17/07/2004
A guided tour of the historic themed gardens

Organic Fruit for Small Gardens
07/08/2004
An organic gardening weekend special. A look at trained forms in the fruit cage with practical demonstrations of summer pruning

Seed Saving Day
11/09/2004
A look at the work of HDRA's Heritage Seed Library and an introduction to producing your own home-grown ornamental and vegetable seeds

Composting Workshop
16/10/2004
A second chance to see a practical demonstration of different composting techniques and containers

Pumpkin Weekend
30/10/2004-31/10/2004
A celebration of pumpkins and squashes, to carve and to eat, with recipes to take away. Come and buy

Heritage & Industrial

Chart Gunpowder Mills

Chart Close Faversham Kent ME13 7SE
Tel: 01795 534542 Fax: 01795 533261

[Off the M2 at Faversham exit to A2, turn L along A2, turn R into B2040, 500mtrs on L]

Oldest gunpowder mills in the world, made powder for Nelson at Trafalgar and Wellington at Waterloo.
9 Apr-31 Oct Weekends and Bank Hol 14.00-17.00
Admission Free

Fleur de Lis Heritage Centre

10-13 Preston Street Faversham Kent ME13 8NS
Tel: 01795 534542 Fax: 01795 533261
[Off M2 at Faversham exit to A2]

Housed in a 16th century former coaching inn, and newly extended and upgraded, the Centre traces the history of one of Britain's most historic and attractive towns from prehistoric times to the present day.
All year daily 10.00-16.00, Sun 10.00-13.00. Guided town tours: Apr-Oct Sat 10.30
A£2.00 OAPs&Concessions£1.00. Guided town tour £1.00

Maison Dieu

Ospringe Street Faversham Kent ME13 8TW
Tel: 01795 534542 Fax: 01795 533261

[In Ospringe on A2, 0.5m W of Faversham, 20mins walk]

Dating from 1234, this timber-framed building once formed part of a complex which served as a Royal Lodge, pilgrims' hostel and retirement home for royal retainers. Now serving as Ospringe's museum it features Roman finds from the locality and colourful displays on the village's eventful history.

11 Apr-31 Oct Weekends & Bank Hol 14.00-17.00. For further details contact The Faversham Society on 01795 534542. Keykeeper in Winter
A£1.00 C£0.50 OAPs£0.80

Historical

Charles Dickens Centre

Eastgate House High Street Rochester Kent
ME1 1EW
Tel: 01634 844176 Fax: 01634 8844676
*[Bus: pass along the A2 (Corporation Street) and
stop a few yards from the door. Rail: Rochester
0.5m, Strood 1.5m or Chatham 1.5m]*

The Charles Dickens Centre is housed in a fine
Elizabethan building that Dickens knew well.
Here scenes are created from some of the
author's most well known books, Mr Pickwick
addresses the Pickwick club, Marley's ghost will
come and go and Miss Havisham maintains her
lonely vigil.
*1 Apr-30 Sept Wed-Sun 10.00-18.00, 1 Oct-31
Mar Wed-Sun 10.00-16.00*
A£4.00 C&OAPs&Students£3.00 Family Ticket
£11.00

Cobham Hall

Cobham Gravesend Kent DA12 3BL

Tel: 01474 823371 Fax: 01474 825904

www.cobhamhall.com

*[Adjacent to A2 / M2 between Gravesend /
Rochester. 8m from J2 M25, 27m from London]*

Cobham Hall is an outstandingly beautiful, red
brick mansion in Elizabethan, Jacobean,
Carolian and 18th century styles. This former
home of the Earls of Darnley is set in 150 acres
of parkland and is now an Independent international boarding and day school. The Gothic
Dairy and some of the classical garden buildings

are being renovated. The grounds yield many
delights for the lover of nature, especially in
spring, when the gardens and woods are
resplendent with daffodils, narcissi and myriad
of rare bulbs. The House is open for Guided
Tours each day from 14.00-17.00 with delicious
cream teas available in the dining room.

*Apr Wed, Sun & Easter Weekend 14.00-17.00,
July-Aug Wed & Sun 14.00-17.00*

A£4.50 C&OAPs£3.50

Hever Castle and Gardens

Hever Castle Hever Edenbridge Kent TN8 7NG

**Tel: 01732 865224 Fax: 01732 866796
www.hevercastle.co.uk**

*[Off M25, J5/6, off B2026. 3m from Rail: Victoria
London to Edenbridge Town. Plenty of on site
parking]*

This romantic 13th century moated Castle was
the childhood home of Anne Boleyn. In 1903
William Waldorf Astor acquired the Castle and
created beautiful gardens. He filled the Castle
with wonderful furniture, paintings and tapestries which visitors can see today. Children will
enjoy the costumed figure exhibition of Henry
VIII and his six wives, and the Anne Boleyn
Books of Hours. The spectacular award winning
gardens include topiary, Italian and Tudor
Gardens, a 110 metre herbaceous border and a
lake. Families will enjoy the yew maze (open
Apr-Oct), the splashing water maze (open Apr-
Oct), the 'From Castles to Country Houses'
miniature model houses exhibition and the

Adventure Playground. Pushchair access to gardens only.

1 Mar-30 Nov daily. Castle: 12.00-18.00. Gardens: 11.00-18.00. Winter months 11.00-16.00

Castle & Gardens: A£8.80 C(5-14)£4.80 C(under5)£Free OAPs£7.40 Family Ticket (A2+C2) £22.40. Gardens only: A£7.00 C(5-14)£4.60 C(under5)£Free OAPs£6.00 Family Ticket (A2+C2) £18.60. Group rates (15+): available on request. Guided Tours: for pre-booked groups ONLY

Special Events

Easter Weekend
09/04/2004-12/04/2004
'Easter Egg Trail' around the gardens and local brass bands in front of the castle

May Day Festivities
01/05/2004-03/05/2004
Entertainment by period costumed musicians and dancers

Merrie England
29/05/2004-31/05/2004
A celebration of Tudor and Elizabethan times

Rose Week
18/06/2004-24/06/2004
The Castle will be decked with roses, with tours of the gardens plus talks and demonstrations relating to roses and gardening topics

Jousting Tournaments
17/07/2004-28/08/2004
Held on 17, 24, 31 July and 1, 7, 8, 14, 15, 21, 28 Aug. Performed by the Knights of Royal England

Tudor Archery
18/07/2004-30/08/2004
Held on 18, 25 July and 22, 29, 30 Aug. Demonstrated by the 'Company of 1415'

Patchwork and Quilting Exhibition
10/09/2004-12/09/2004
Magnificent display of patchwork quilts and wall hangings with demonstrations and stalls

Autumn Colour Week
11/10/2004-17/10/2004
Castle gardeners will show visitors the main areas of Autumn colour in the gardens and discuss Autumn gardening topics

Leeds Castle and Gardens

Maidstone Kent ME17 1PL
Tel: 01622 765400 Fax: 01622 735616
[4m at J8 of M20 A20]

The site of a manor of the Saxon royal family in the 9th century, Leeds Castle was described by Lord Conway as 'the loveliest Castle in the world.' Built on two islands in the middle of a lake and set in 500 acres of landscaped parkland.

All year daily, Apr-Oct 10.00-17.00, Nov-Mar 10.00-15.00. Closed 26 June, 3 July, 6 Nov prior to special events

Castle & Grounds: A£12.50/£10.50 C£9.00/£7.00

Lullingstone Castle

Lullingstone Park Eynsford Dartford Kent DA4 0JA
Tel: 01322 862114 Fax: 01322 862115
[M25 sliproad to Brands Hatch, A20 / A225 0.5m South Eynsford station]

In house, Queen Anne State rooms, family portraits, armour. Church of Norman origin, herb garden, flower borders.
May-Aug Sat-Sun & Bank Hol Mon 14.00-18.00
House & Gardens: A£5.00 C£2.00 OAPs£4.00 Family Ticket £10.00

KCC Collaboration
07/08/2004-12/09/2004
An exhibition where local artists are asked to respond to and produce visual art from objects in the Museum's collections

Embroiderers Guild
25/09/2004-28/11/2004
A collection of embroidery from the Embroiderers' Guild

Picasso
15/01/2005-20/03/2005
An exhibition hired from the Hayward Gallery. A collection of prints (about 40) from some of Picasso's earlier works

Maidstone Museum and Bentlif Art Gallery

St. Faiths Street Maidstone Kent ME14 1LH

Tel: 01622 602838 Fax: 01622 685022

[Close to Maidstone East Station in the town centre]

An absolute must-see, this exceptionally fine regional museum houses a number of intriguing collections in an Elizabethan manor house. Collections range from natural history to military memorabilia and the costume gallery. Look out for the life-size dinosaurs and the fossils under your feet in the Earth Heritage Gallery, and don't miss the real Egyptian Mummy! Interactive areas and an exciting programme of temporary exhibitions, workshops and children's activities mean that there is something to capture everybody's imagination. Limited disabled access. Special workshops for children during half term and school holidays.

All year Mon-Sat 10.00-17.15, Sun 11.00-16.00. Closed 25-26 Dec

Admission Free

Special Events

MAAC Summer Festival
05/06/2004-25/07/2004
An exhibition of paintings, sculpture and other media by local artists tied in with the Music and Dance Festival. There will be dance and music evenings also

Penshurst Place and Gardens

Penshurst Tonbridge Kent TN11 8DG

Tel: 01892 870307 Fax: 01892 870866

www.penshurstplace.com

[From M25, J5, follow A21 to Hastings, exit Hildenborough then follow brown tourist signs. From M26, J2a, follow A25 (Sevenoaks) then A21 for Hastings then as above. Ample on site parking available. Rail: Tonbridge]

Ancestral home of the Sidney family since 1552, with a history going back six and a half centuries, Penshurst Place has been described as 'the grandest and most perfectly preserved example of a fortified manor house in all England'. At the heart of this medieval masterpiece is the Barons Hall, built in 1341, and the adjoining Staterooms contain a wonderful collection of tapestries, furniture, portraits and armour. The ten acres of gardens are as old as the original house - the walls and terraces were added in the Elizabethan era - which ensures a continuous display from spring to autumn. There is also a Toy Museum, Venture Playground, Gift Shop, Plant Centre, Garden Tea Room and Family Exhibition.

6 Mar-27 Mar Sat & Sun, 27 Mar-31 Oct daily. Grounds: 10.30-18.00. House: 12.00-17.30 (16.00 Sat). Shop & Plant Centre: Mar-Oct 10.30-18.00 (Shop Nov-Dec also 10.30-16.30)

House & Grounds: A£7.00 C(5-16)£5.00 Family Ticket (A2+C2) £20.00 OAPs&Students£6.50. Groups of 20 + people: A£6.50. Grounds only: A£5.50 C(5-16)£4.50 Family Ticket £17.00 OAPs&Students£5.00. Garden Season Ticket £35.00. Pre-booked guided house tours for groups: A£7.50 C(5-16)£4.50. Garden Tours: A£8.50 C(5-16)£5.00, House & Garden A£11.00

Powell-Cotton Museum, Quex House and Gardens

Quex Park Birchington Kent CT7 0BH

Tel: 01843 842168 Fax: 01843 846661

[In Birchington 0.5m S of Birchington Square, SW of Margate, 13m E of Canterbury. Signposted. Rail: Birchington. Plenty of on site parking]

Quex House was built as a Regency gentleman's Country residence and grew to become the Victorian mansion we see today. Still home to Powell-Cotton family, it has a mellow atmosphere, many of the rooms appearing much as they did during Major Powell-Cotton's lifetime along with 15 acres of Pleasure Gardens and a Victorian Walled Garden, open to the public. There are some splendid pieces of oriental and period furniture, fine rugs and porcelain, as well as family portraits and an extensive collection of silver, clocks and memorabilia. The polished mahogany cases displaying Major Powell-Cotton's treasures give the Museum its authentic quality, so often lacking in modern visitor attractions. There are eight galleries in all - three of them built by the Major himself - containing an amazing variety of items from the animal dioramas to striking tribal art, weapons, carvings and costumes, as well as valuable collections of European and Chinese porcelain and local archaeology. What began as one man's museum has been painstakingly cared for and added to by members of the Powell-Cotton family and now offers visitors an exciting insight into discoveries of a great Victorian Explorer. Member of the Historic Houses Association.

Museum, Gardens & Restaurant: Mar & Nov Sun only 11.00-16.00, Apr-Oct Tue-Thur, Sun & Bank Hol 11.00-17.00, Quex House 14.00-16.30

Summer: A£5.00 C(5-16)&OAPs£4.00 Family Ticket (A2+C3) £14.00, Winter: A£4.00 C(5-16)&OAPs£3.00 Family Ticket (A2+C3) £10.00. Garden only: A£1.50 C(5-16)&OAPs£1.00

Special Events

Easter Egg Hunt
11/04/2004-12/04/2004
Time: 11.00-16.00

Museums and Galleries Month
01/05/2004-31/05/2004

National Garden Scheme
06/06/2004
With Radio Kent Gardening Programme (live broadcast 08.00-11.00), bring your questions and queries. Family Flower Trail within the Victorian Walled Garden. Time: 09.00-17.00

Victorian Day
04/07/2004
Croquet on the lawn, demonstration and participation. Bee Keeping and Skep making demonstration, pony & carriage rides, Thanet Concert Clarinets playing in restaurant and house, ladies in victorian costume, cream teas. For the children; Victorian portrait silhouette making, Regency House quiz and activity table. Time: 11.00-17.00

Poetry Festival
18/07/2004
Time: 11.00-13.00 children, 14.00-16.00 adults

Making Clay Animals
25/07/2004
A family drop in day. Time: 11.00-15.00

National Garden Scheme
04/08/2004
Mini Beasts - insect anatomy and handling, suitable for children and adults. Evening opening, 18.00-21.00

Jungle Tales
04/08/2004-25/08/2004
Held on Wednesdays, 4, 11, 18, 25 Aug. Suitable for children under 7 years, includes art activities. Time: 14.00-15.00

Beekeeping Lecture and Demonstration
11/08/2004
Time: 19.00 prompt in the Seminar Room

Family Drop in Session
15/08/2004-17/08/2004
Held on 15 & 17 Aug only. Help us make a larger than life animal sculpture! Time: 11.00-15.00

Evening Opening
18/08/2004
Time: 18.00-21.00

Evening Opening
25/08/2004
Time: 18.00-21.00 with Curator's guided tour at 18.00 prompt

Heritage Open Day
12/09/2004
Be surprised, come and see something not previously on view!

The Big Draw
17/10/2004
Join in the fun and have your picture displayed as part of the nationwide 'Big Draw' event

Rochester Castle

The Keep Rochester Kent ME1 1SX
Tel: 01634 402276 Fax: 01634 402276
[M2, J1, M25, J2, by Rochester Bridge A2]

No one can miss the great square keep as it towers above the River Medway, a daunting reminder of the history of the City. The castle is well known as one of the best preserved and finest examples of Norman architecture in England.
All year 1 Apr-30 Sept daily 10.00-18.00, 1 Oct-31 Mar daily 10.00-16.00. Closed 24-26 Dec & 1 Jan
Prices vary, please call for details

Upnor Castle

High Street Upper Upnor Rochester Kent

Kent

ME2 4XG

Tel: 01634 718742/338110

[On unclassified road off A228. Parking before Village slight distance from Castle. Rail: Strood 2m]

Upnor Castle, is set in the village of Upper Upnor on the banks of the river Medway. This attractive turreted Castle is backed by rolling wooded hills and fronted by a water battery jutting out into the river Medway.

1 Apr-30 Sept daily 10.00-18.00, 1-31 Oct daily 10.00-16.00

Prices vary, please call for details

Maritime

The Historic Dockyard Chatham

Chatham Kent ME4 4TZ

Tel: 01634 823800 Fax: 01634 823801

[J1 or J3 M2 or from J6 M20 follow signs for Chatham and then Brown Anchor. Rail: Chatham]

The Historic Dockyard Chatham is one of the world's most fascinating and significant maritime heritage locations. Eighty acres containing spectacular architecture and exciting naval and maritime exhibits.

14 Feb-31 Oct daily 10.00-18.00 or dusk if sooner

A£10.00 C(5-15)£6.50 Concessions£7.50 Family Ticket (A2+C2) £26.50, additional child £3.25

Military & Defence Museums

Kent and Sharpshooters Yeomanry Museum

Hever Castle Hever Edenbridge Kent TN8 7NG
Tel: 01732 865224 Fax: 01732 866796
[J5/6 M25. Follow signs to Hever Castle. Plenty of on site parking available]

The Kent and Sharpshooters Yeomanry Museum is housed in the Gate House of Hever

Castle. It is open on days when the castle is open but has to close on busy days due to congestion. It houses many interesting artefacts linked to the regiment.

1 Mar-30 Nov daily (except on busy days) 12.00-18.00

Museum: Admission Free. Castle & Gardens: A£8.80 C(5-14)£4.80 OAPs£7.40 Family Ticket £22.40

Railways

Kent and East Sussex Steam Railway

Tenterden Town Station Tenterden Kent TN30 6HE

Tel: 01580 765155 Fax: 01580 765654

www.kesr.org.uk

[On the A28 main road between Ashford and Hastings]

Join us for a magical ride through 10.5 miles of beautiful countryside. Vintage steam trains and historic diesel trains dating from Victorian times will transport you back in time on your journey between Tenterden and Bodiam where you can visit the beautiful castle. In addition, there are regular special events including Thomas the Tank Engine weekends and Santa Specials. Hot and cold refreshments are available at Tenterden station and on many trains, including cream teas and light lunches. Or, for that extra special occasion we offer luxury Pullman dining for dinners, and Sunday lunches. Advance booking for all on-board dining and special events is essential.

Please call 24hr talking timetable for further details, 01580 762943

A£10.00 C£5.00 OAPs£9.00 Family Ticket (A2+C3) £25.00. 1st class travel available for a supplement

Discount Offer: £1.00 Off Adult & £0.50 Off Child's Fare On Any Full Return Train Ride To Bodiam.

Special Events

Day Out with Thomas
19/06/2004-26/09/2004
Held on 19-20, 26-27 June and 18-19, 25-26 Sept. Come and meet Thomas and some of his friends at Tenterden Town Station for a whole day of fun and entertainment

Hoppers Weekend
11/09/2004-12/09/2004
Revisit the golden era of hopping. Goods trains, special exhibits and real ale make this a memorable weekend

Santa Specials
04/12/2004-24/12/2004
Held on 4, 5, 11, 12, 18, 19, 22, 23, 24 Dec. Bring all the family along for a trip through a Winter Wonderland of delightful countryside to Wittersham Road and back. Santa and his elves travel with you, visiting each child and giving out presents. Special Yuletide entertainment and refreshments are provided at Tenterden Town Station too

Romney Hythe and Dymchurch Railway

New Romney Station Littlestone Road
New Romney Kent TN28 8PL

Tel: 01797 362353 Fax: 01797 363591

www.rhdr.org.uk

[M20, J11 signposted, Hythe station, other stations on A259. Plenty of parking places]

The world's smallest public railway has its headquarters here. The concept of two enthusiasts coincided with Southern Railway's plans for expansion, and so the thirteen-and-a-half mile stretch of 15 inch gauge railway came into being, running from Hythe through New Romney and Dymchurch to Dungeness Lighthouse. Picnic areas available (indoor and outdoor). Visit can be anything from 1 hour to a full day.

Regular services Easter-Sept daily also weekends in Mar & Oct and October half-term daily

Fares depend on length of journey, C£half-price, discount for pre-booked parties of 12+. OAP concessions available

Discount Offer: One Child Travels Free With One Adult Paying Full Rate.

Special Events

Easter Family Fun Days
09/04/2004-12/04/2004

Steam and Diesel Gala
15/05/2004-16/05/2004

Dungeness Fishermen
12/06/2004-25/09/2004
Special trains run on 12, 26 June, 11, 25 Sept only. A first class train takes diners from New Romney to Dungeness for a three course meal. Please call 01797 362353 to book

Fathers Day Family Fun Day
20/06/2004

Hythe Festival Week
02/07/2004-11/07/2004
Including the Romney Jazz Train on Thur 8 July

A Day Out with Thomas
17/07/2004-18/07/2004
Special prices apply

RNLI Dungeness Lifeboat Station Open Day
15/08/2004

Dymchurch Day of Syn celebrations
29/08/2004-30/08/2004

Basil the Bug's Friends and Family Event
04/09/2004-05/09/2004

Autumn Romney Steam and Diesel Spectacular
02/10/2004-03/10/2004

Half-Term Halloween Special Event
23/10/2004-31/10/2004

Santa Specials
01/12/2004-31/12/2004
Held on selected days in December. Details and booking forms will be available from July 2004 at our stations or by calling the Santa hotline on 01797 362353

New Year Steam Event
02/01/2005-03/01/2005

Theme & Adventure Parks

Diggerland

Roman Way Medway Valley Leisure Park Strood Kent ME2 2NU
Tel: 08700 344437 Fax: 09012 010300
www.diggerland.com

[M2 J2, A228 towards Strood. At roundabout turn right. We are on the right. Plenty of on site parking available]

All ages will enjoy the opportunity to ride in and drive different types of machines from Dumpertrucks to JCB Mini Diggers and Large Diggers (all under strict supervision). Taking up challenges like fishing ducks out of a pond using a JCB digger and learning about the machines, makes it a fun and informative attraction. There are over 20 different rides and attractions at Diggerland. Birthday parties are catered for, so you fancy a party with a difference for your young children then contact us for details.

Weekends & Bank Hols and daily during half-term and school holidays 10.00-17.00

A&OAPs£2.50 C(under2)£Free C£2.50 which covers all non-mechanical rides. Group rates (20+): 20% discount. To drive the real diggers costs from £1.00 per ride OR an all day wristband at £18.00

Discount Offer: 1/2 Price Entry For Up To 6 People.

Special Events

Easter Sunday
11/04/2004
Free Easter eggs on arrival for kids

4x4 Off Road Day
17/04/2004
Bring your own 4x4 and tackle the challenge of the custom built Diggerland Off Road course - can you get round it or will you get stuck in the

mud? Please call for entry tickets well in advance, numbers strictly limited

Metal Micky's Birthday Party
25/04/2004
Metal Micky is 4 years old. Come and join him for a day of fun and celebration

Stunt Demonstrations
03/05/2004
Amazing Digger stunts from our Dancing Diggers display performed hourly throughout the afternoon

Bob the Builder Day
22/05/2004
Come along dressed as Bob the Builder and enter Diggerland Free. Also a few other Bob surprises!

Fathers Day
20/06/2004
Free admission to Diggerland for all Dads on this special day. Dads are just big kids anyway!

Stunt Demonstrations
04/07/2004
Amazing Digger stunts from our Dancing Diggers display performed hourly throughout the afternoon

Young Driver Experience
15/07/2004
Personal Tuition on, and a great chance to drive a selection of vehicles including Land Rovers and Diggers, for ages 9-16. Can be purchased as a gift. Ring or email well in advance to book. Cost: £49.00. Numbers strictly limited

Diggerland Summer Fete
25/07/2004
Join in our Summer Fete with an all-day Barbeque, face painting and lots more

Young Driver Experience
12/08/2004
Personal Tuition on, and a great chance to drive a selection of vehicles including Land Rovers and Diggers, for ages 9-16. Can be purchased as a gift. Ring or email well in advance to book. Cost: £49.00. Numbers strictly limited

Bob the Builder Day
04/09/2004
Come along dressed as Bob the Builder and enter Diggerland Free. Also a few other Bob surprises!

4x4 Off Road Day
10/10/2004
Bring your own 4x4 and tackle the challenge of

the custom built Diggerland Off Road course - can you get round it or will you get stuck in the mud? Please call for entry tickets well in advance, numbers strictly limited

Transport Museums

Eurotunnel

Administration Building Cheriton Parc Folkestone Kent CT19 4QS
Tel: 01303 288700 Fax: 01303 288742

Terminal Tour (TTUK) - These services are available ONLY for groups in own coach or minibus. A 45min guided tour of the Eurotunnel terminal at Folkestone. Specialist Site Visit (SSV) - An opportunity to visit the operational heart of Eurotunnel. Restricted to adults and groups of 12 and subject to operational restrictions. Trainspotters Special (TSS) - A unique opportunity to look at Eurotunnel's own rolling stock on the Folkestone and Coquelles terminals.
Variable depending upon booking type
TTUK: £3.00 per person. SVS: £25.00 per person. TTS: details on application

Wildlife & Safari Parks

Port Lympne Wild Animal Park

Aldington Road Lympne Hythe Kent CT21 4PD
Tel: 09068 800605 (info line)
Fax: 01303 264944
[J11 M20. Park is 5mins away signposted from J]

John Aspinall's 400-acre wild animal park houses hundreds of rare animals: Black rhinos, Indian elephants, wolves, bison, snow leopards, Siberian and Indian tigers, gorillas and monkeys.
All year daily 10.00-18.00. Winter closing at dusk. Closed 25 Dec
A£11.95 C(under4)£Free C(4-14)&OAPs£8.95

Lancashire

irfields / Flight Centres

elicentre Blackpool Ltd

lackpool Airport Blackpool Lancashire
Y4 2QY
el: 01253 343082 Fax: 01253 407351
nd of M55, bear L at roundabout, follow signs
r Lytham St Anne's, follow signs]

elicopter Trial Flights - You've seen the top of
lackpool Tower, been in awe of the Pepsi Max
ig One Roller Coaster and walked along the
ylde Coast. Now have the ultimate thrill and
ee them all from a different angle. Take to the
r in a Robinson R22 Helicopter for a thrilling
ands-on helicopter flying experience.
ll year daily 09.00-17.30
0min trial lesson £115.00, 60min trial lesson
210.00

rts, Crafts & Textiles

laworth Art Gallery

lanchester Rd Accrington Lancashire BB5 2JS
el: 01254 233782 Fax: 01254 301954
.5m S of the M65 and 1.5m N of the A56, M66
r the M62]

n Edwardian-Tudor house set in beautiful park-
nd, the Haworth is home to a world-famous
ollection of Tiffany Glass. Also on show are
orks from the Haworth Bequest.
ll year Wed-Fri & Bank Hols 14.00-17.00, Sat &
un 12.00-16.30
dmission Free

lanchester Art Gallery

losley Street Manchester Greater Manchester
2 3JL
el: 0161 235 8888 Fax: 0161 235 8899
Corner of Mosley St and Princess St near
lanchester Town Hall]

lanchester Art Gallery houses one of the UK's
nest art collections in spectacular surround-
gs. The Gallery has recently benefited from a
35m transformation and has superb visitor
acilities and friendly, welcoming staff.

*All year Tue-Sun 10.00-17.00. Open Bank Hol
Mons. Closed 1 Jan, Good Fri, 24-26 & 31 Dec*
Admission Free

Salford Museum and Art Gallery

Peel Park The Crescent Salford
Greater Manchester M5 4WU

Tel: 0161 736 2649 Fax: 0161 745 9490

*[A6 in front of Salford University to end of M602
signposted. Plenty of on site parking available]*

A gallery of Victorian art and a 20th century collection. Temporary exhibitions throughout the
year and home to Lark Hill Place, a reproduction Victorian Street and a local history library. A
new Life Times gallery documents Salford past
and present with audio, interactives and IT
zone.

*All year Mon-Fri 10.00-16.45, Sat & Sun 13.00-
17.00. Closed 25-26 Dec, 1 Jan, Good Fri &
Easter Sat*

Admission Free

Country Parks & Estates

Croxteth Hall and Country Park

Muirhead Avenue Liverpool Lancashire L12 0HB
Tel: 0151 228 5311 Fax: 0151 228 2817
[5m NE of city centre]

The Edwardian rooms are furnished with period pieces and character figures. The grounds contain a Victorian walled garden, a unique collection of rare breed animals, a miniature railway and an adventure playground.
Apr-Sept daily 10.30-17.00. Country Park all year until 20.00 or dusk

Hall: A£2.10 C&OAPs£1.30. Farm: A£2.10 C&OAPs£1.30. Walled Garden: A£1.30 C&OAPs£0.75. All inclusive ticket £4.20 C&OAPs£2.10 Family Ticket (A2+C2) £10.40. Country Park £Free

Haigh Hall and Country Park

Copperas Lane Haigh Wigan Lancashire WN2 1PE

Tel: 01942 832895 Fax: 01942 831081
www.haighhall.net

[Haigh Country Park is within easy reach of M6, J27, and M61, J6. Follow brown and white signs to Haigh Hall and Country Park. Plenty of parking on site]

Free admission to 350 acres of parkland. Large play area and picnic areas. Cafeteria. Pay as you go attractions - miniature railway, bouncy castle, model village, crazy golf. Busy arts and crafts centre offering workshops, formal or drop in classes, or just admire works of art. Warden service provides educational visits and free events throughout the year. Other major events include craft fairs, annual arts festival, gala day, open air theatre productions, children's entertainers, brass band concerts, festive Christmas activities.

All year daily dawn-dusk. Closed Christmas Hol

Admission Free. Car Park: £1.00

Festivals & Shows

Annual Fireworks Spectacular And Beacon Lighting

Castle Hill Lancaster Lancashire
Tel: 01524 32878 Fax: 01524 582663
[M6, J34/J35]

Preceded by a day of events in Lancaster with fireworks launched at 20.00 from Castle Hill. Call 01524 32878 for further information.
November 6 2004
Admission Free

Blackpool Dance Festival

Winter Gardens Church Street Blackpool Lancashire FY1 1HW
Tel: 01253 625252 Fax: 01253 299347
May 28-June 4 2004
Please call for further details

Britannia Coconut Dancers

Travellers Rest Public House Rochdale Road
Bacup Lancashire OL13 9SD
Tel: 01706 874765
[On A671 between Rochdale / Burnley]

Every Easter Saturday, no matter what the
weather, the Britannia Coconutters accompanied by members of Stacksteads Silver Band,
keep up the tradition of dancing boundary to
boundary the town of Bacup. Starting at 09.00
from the Travellers Rest Public House on the
A671, with an exhibition in the festive atmosphere of the town centre at approx. 13.00-
4.00. The festival ends at approx. 19.00 at the
senior citizens bungalows on the boundary to
the Glenn on the A681. The Britannia Coconut
Dancers are the only surviving troupe practising
this kind of dance.
April 10 2004
Admission Free

Chipping Steam Fair

Agricultural Showground Chipping Preston
[M6 (N), J31a (Preston East & Longridge). Follow
the signs for Longridge. M6 (S), J32 leave the
M55 immediately). Head N on A6 towards
Garstang for about 1m. Turn R at traffic lights
signposted Longridge. Follow signs]

Traction Engines, Tractors, Commercials,
Vintage and Classic Cars, Military, Working
Exhibits, Trade, Vintage Collections, Tractor and
Auto Jumble, Barn Engines, Motor Bikes, Pedal
Cycles, Rare Breeds, Crafts, Fashion Show,
Accordion Band. A fun day out for all the family.
The village is beautifully situated in the Forest of
Bowland and the exquisite setting of the
Ground, in the shadow of Parlick Pike and the
Bowland Fells, adds to the wonderful experi-
ence that all show visitors witness. So as we
look forward to the last weekend in May in
eager anticipation we hope that you are able to
join us in what we are sure will be a great show!
May 29-31 2004, 10.00-17.00

Lancashire Food Festival

Accrington Town Hall Blackburn Road

Accrington Lancashire BB5 1LA
Tel: 01254 872595 Fax: 01254 380291
[M6, J29 or M65, J7 or M61, J9]

The Lancashire Food Festival returns once more
to Accrington in 2004, and to cope with the
huge demand, the Festival has now been
extended to cover two days. Hopefully, everyone will get the chance to taste the many foods
on offer and return home with bags 'a' bulging.
There'll be plenty of food to buy and sample,
and alongside the tradional favourites, visitors
can also expect to sample food of a more exotic nature, with Ostrich and Potted Shrimps
proving particular favourites in past years. The
Festival will once again feature a wide range of
food stalls and cooking demonstrations, and
even a few surprises!
March 26-27 2004 10.30-15.30
A£0.50 C(under16)£Free

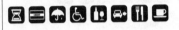

Lancaster Maritime Festival

St. Georges Quay Lancaster LA1 1RD
Tel: 01524 32878 Fax: 01524 582663
[Town Centre/Quay side: M6, J34/J35]

Regarded as the world's biggest and most
prestigious gathering of traditional sea-song and
shanty performers.
April 9-12 2004
Charges apply to Maritime Museum and some
concerts. All other venues: Admission Free

Lancaster's Georgian Festival Fair

Vicarage Fields Castle Hill Lancaster Lancashire
Tel: 01524 32878 Fax: 01524 582663
[Town Centre: M6, J34/J35]

The Georgian Festival Fair includes a recreation
of a Georgian Fair with stalls, sideshows, entertainers and including the National Sedan Chair
Carrying Championships
August 30 2004 11.00
Admission Free, small charge for some of the
booths/sideshows

Morecambe Festival of Light and Water

Morecambe Lancashire LA4 4DB
Tel: 01524 582828
It's the biggest festival of the summer - a week-end of great live music on Morecambe Arena, climaxing with two fantastic firework displays over Morecambe Bay.
July 24-25 2004
Admission Free

RNCM International Cello Festival 2004

Oxford Road Manchester M13 9RD
Tel: 01625 571091 Fax: 01625 571092
[1m S of Manchester City Centre]

The RNCM Manchester International Cello Festival was inaugurated in 1988 with 3 simple aims - to honour the memory of the masterly French cellist Pierre Fournier - to celebrate the cello, its music and musicians, - to give a unique opportunity to students, professionals and enthusiasts to listen to, learn from, and intermingle with some of the greatest artist-teachers in the world.
May 5-9 2004

Saddleworth Folk Festival

In and around Uppermill Saddleworth Oldham Lancashire OL3 7AH
Tel: 07711 214191
[M62, J22, follow signs for Uppermill on A672]

Welcome to the 7th annual Saddleworth Folk Festival at Uppermill near Oldham, the friendly festival on the edge of the Pennines. As ever there's something for everyone, with Concerts, Ceilidhs, Singarounds, Workshops and Sessions and some of the top names in folk music.

July 16-18 2004

Worldbeat Weekend 2004

The Platform Station Buildings
Central Promenade Morecambe LA4 4DB
Tel: 01524 582 828 / 582 803
Fax: 01524 832 745 / 831 704
[M6, J34/J35]

The wildest weekend of the summer and if you like dance then this weekend is for you. Special children's workshops throughout the weekend and don't forget to pay a visit to the popular Global Market not to mention the beer tent!
August 27-29 2004
Admission charges: Call 01524 582 803

Folk & Local History Museums

Clitheroe Castle Museum

Castle Hill Castle Gate Clitheroe Lancashire BB7 1BA

Tel: 01200 424635 Fax: 01200 424568

www.ribblevalley.gov.uk/tourism/index.htm

Signposted off A59 Clitheroe]

The museum in Castle House has a good collection of carboniferous fossils, and items of local interest. It is close to Clitheroe Castle, which ranks among Lancashire's oldest buildings and has one of the smallest Norman keeps in England. Displays include local history and the industrial archaeology of the Ribble Valley, features include the restored Hacking ferry boat, Edwardian kitchen (with hearing loop) and Clogger's Shop both with taped commentary, printer's shop, and a 'Birds of the Ribble Valley' display. The Witches Trail which is featured here and Pendle Heritage Centre and the Judges Chambers at the Museum in Lancaster. The first floor houses an 18th century Lead Mine with sound effects. Our gift shop is well stocked. Wheelchair accessible on ground floor only.

Mar-Easter Sat-Wed 11.00-16.30, Easter-end Oct daily 11.00-16.30, Nov-19 Dec Sat-Sun 11.00-16.30. Reopens 31 Jan, Sat-Sun 11.00-16.30 (open all week during half term)

A£1.70 C£0.25 OAPs£0.85 Family Ticket (A2+C2) £3.60

Historical

Rufford Old Hall

Liverpool Road Rufford Ormskirk Lancashire L40 1SG

Tel: 01704 821254 Fax: 01704 823823

www.nationaltrust.org.uk

[3 Off A59. Bus: Arriva North West 303 Preston-Ormskirk; Stagecoach in Lancashire 758 Liverpool-Blackpool; Blue Bus 347 Southport-Chorley. Rail: Rufford (not Sun) 0.5m, Burscough Bridge 2.5m]

There is a story that William Shakespeare performed here for the owner Sir Thomas Hesketh in the Great Hall of this, one of the finest 16th century buildings in Lancashire. The bard would have delighted in the magnificent hall, built in 1530, with its intricately carved movable wooden screen. The Carolean Wing, altered in 1821 features fine collections of 16th and 17th century oak furniture, arms, armour and tapestries.

Hall: 3 Apr-27 Oct Sat-Wed 13.00-17.00. Garden & Shop: 11.00-17.30

House & Garden: A£4.50 C£2.00 Family Ticket £11.00. Garden only: A£2.50 C£1.00. Group rates available

Living History Museums

People's History Museum

The Pump House Bridge Street Manchester
Greater Manchester M3 3ER

Tel: 0161 839 6061 Fax: 0161 839 6027

www.peopleshistorymuseum.org.uk

[From motorways follow brown signs to Castlefield then signs to Salford Central Station or Gartside St car park. Bus: 8, 9, 10, 11, 12, 21, 25, 26, 28, 29, 30, 31, 32, 34, 35, 36, 37, 38, 39, 64, 67, 68, 100, x61, x62, x64 all stop on Bridge St. Metrolink: St Peter's Square then 10 min walk. Rail: Salford Central is 1min from museum, Manchester Victoria 15 mins walk and Manchester Piccadilly 25 mins. Parking on site available for disabled visitors only]

The People's History Museum is dedicated to the lives of ordinary people over the last 200 years. The displays range from life in the Victorian cotton mills to the growth of football as a leisure activity. They include reconstructed scenes as well as objects in cases and combine text, hands-on exhibits and sound to vividly recreate the day-to-day lives at home, at work and during leisure time. Play Your Part are interactive displays, developed with families in mind, situated throughout the main galleries. Create your own badge, shop at a 1930s Co-op counter, perform your own Punch & Judy show, build an arch, record your opinions, produce a fuzzy felt banner... the list goes on. The museum also has one of the largest collections of historic, labour movement banners in the world. The banners are conserved in the Textile Conservation Studio and a selection are always on display in the museum. Photography allowed with permission only.

All year Tue-Sun & Bank Hol Mon 11.00-16.30. Closed 24-26, 31 Dec, 1 Jan and Good Fri

A£1.00 C&Concessions £Free. £Free to everyone on Fri

Discount Offer: Two For The Price Of One.

Special Events

REDS!: The Communist Party of Great Britain
08/11/2003-25/04/2004
At its peak in the 1940s the Communist Party of Great Britain was the fourth largest political party in the country. This will therefore be the fourth exhibition in a series looking at the major British political parties and the support they gained from working people

Bluffers Guide to the Communist Party of Great Britain
02/04/2004

From Butties to Bhajis- Working People's Food in Great Britain
01/05/2004-30/11/2004

Multicultural Museums

British In India Museum

1 Newtown Street Colne Lancashire BB8 0JJ

**Tel: 01282 613129 / 860174
Fax: 01282 870215**

[M65 J14, Skipton 12m. A56-A6068 from Burnley 6m, to Keighley 12m. Rail: Colne 1m]

Founded in 1972, the museum contains over 2,000 exhibits relating to the British rule of India from the 17th century to the independence of India and the creation of Pakistan in 1947.

Apr-Sept Wed & Sat 14.00-17.00

A£3.00 C(0-16)£0.50

Railways

East Lancashire Railway and The Bury Transport Museum

Bolton Street Station Bolton Street Bury Lancashire BL9 0EY

Tel: 0161 764 7790 Fax: 0161 763 4408

www.east-lancs-rly.co.uk

[M66 J2. The Railway is signposted from all the major roads]

A mainly steam hauled train service between Bury to Ramsbottom, Rawtenstall and Heywood. This popular steam railway offers a day out for all the family with all the trimmings you expect on a railway (tunnels, level crossings etc). You can break your journey at any station to visit the shops at Dickensian Ramsbottom with its Farmers and Sunday markets. A riverside picnic area allows you to view the trains. Then, rejoin the train, and complete your journey with views of the Pennine Moors - an ideal day out for the family whatever the weather. Special events are held throughout the year and include a Day Out with Thomas, Teddy Bears Picnic, 1940s weekend and Santa Specials to name just a few. The Railway also runs Sunday Lunch and Diners trains and Drive a Steam Engine makes an ideal present.

Weekend service & Bank Hol. Santa specials in Dec. Closed 25 Dec

Full Line Return Ticket: A£9.00 C£5.00

Social History Museums

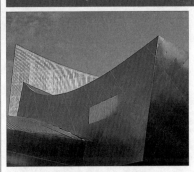

Imperial War Museum North

The Quays Trafford Wharf Road Trafford Park Manchester M17 1TZ

**Tel: 0161 836 4000 Fax: 0161 836 4012
www.iwm.org.uk/north/index.htm**

[Rail: Manchester Piccadilly. Metrolink: Harbour City (15min walk). Bus: 250 from Piccadilly Bus Station to Trafford Centre. Museum is across the pedestrian bridge from The Lowry and 10mins walk from Manchester United Football Club]

Designed by Daniel Libeskind and situated opposite The Lowry, Imperial War Museum North opened on 5 July 2002. It is built to resemble three shards of a shattered globe representing conflict on land, in the air and on water. Inside it houses thousands of objects and engaging exhibitions alongside a huge, dynamic audio-visual presentation - 'The Big Picture' - shown every hour. New dramatic display techniques portray our experience of conflicts from the 20th and 21st century and reflect how people's lives are shaped by war. The Museum also has a café, waterside restaurant, shop, learning studio and facilities for corporate entertainment.

All year daily 10.00-18.00. Closed 24, 25, 26 Dec. Guided tours available for groups

Admission Free

Special Events

Shipbuilding: See for Yourself
07/02/2004-07/06/2004
Every Tue, Fri & Sat, there will be short taster sessions for visitors wanting to find out more about Stanley Spencer, Patricia McKinnon-Day and how artists express ideas through their work. This session is an ideal introduction for first time visitors to art exhibitions. Time: 15.00-15.30

Shipbuilding: Stanley Spencer and Patricia McKinnon-Day
07/02/2004-07/06/2004

This exhibition provides a rare opportunity to see the entire series of Spencer's Shipbuilding paintings, one of the 20th century's greatest series of monumental paintings. Contemporary artist Patricia McKinnon-Day, formerly artist-in-residence at Cammell Laird shipyard, has created a new work to be shown alongside Spencer's paintings. Held in the Special Exhibitions Gallery

21 Countries - Ceramic Plates by Steve Dixon
21/02/2004-30/05/2004

21 Countries is a series of ceramic plates that consider the bombing of 21 countries by the United States since the end of the Second World War. Steve Dixon will be exhibiting his newest work in the Museum's most intimate exhibition space, The Waterway. He has an established reputation for making ceramics with a political edge, and 21 Countries is an openly challenging work examining the complex issues of war and conflict

Evacuee Reunion
23/04/2004

The Evacuee Reunion Association extends an open invitation to a Reunion at the Museum, with other evacuees and members of the Association. There will be a talk about Evacuee experiences, music from the 1940s, performances, artefact handling and showings of the Children and War Big Picture Show at 13.30 & 16.30. Free ticket event but booking essential.

Museums and Galleries Month 2004: Travel and Transport
01/05/2004-31/05/2004

IWM North tells the stories and experiences of the hundreds and thousands of British and Commonwealth soldiers who have travelled abroad in service. The Main Exhibition Space features a variety of land and air vehicles, including the impressive AV8A Harrier Jet, a Russian T40 tank, a motorcycle, and the recent addition of a Leopard Patrol Vehicle

D-Day 60th Anniversary
29/05/2004-06/06/2004

IWM North will be marking the 60th anniversary of D-Day with a wealth of personal stories. Exhibitions and archive film will be joined by the voices of those who were involved in 1944, encouraging young people today to understand their own histories. The anniversary will be marked with a full week's programme of events and exhibitions

Sport and War
03/07/2004-01/10/2004

This will be the first major exhibition to examine the links between sport and war, from football matches in the First World War trenches to recent attempts to bring the Pakistani cricket team to India for the first time since 1989. The exhibition will comprise objects, film, sound, art and photography, with many loans from national sports museums and associations around the country. Exhibition due to end in Oct, please call for specific date

Highlights of IWM North's First World War art and collections
01/11/2004-01/03/2005

This exhibition will show the best of Imperial War Museum's First World War art collection. Many of the works were commissioned under the official war artists scheme, begun in 1916, and led to the creation of a unique record of the Great War. These paintings are by some of the best and most avant-garde British artists of the day, including Percy Wyndham Lewis, Paul Nash, CRW Nevinson, John Singer Sargent, and Stanley Spencer. Exhibition due to run from Nov-Mar, please call for specific dates

Sport & Recreation

Sandcastle Waterworld

outh Promenade Blackpool Lancashire

Y4 1BB

Tel: 01253 343602 Fax: 01253 406490

www.sandcastle-waterworld.co.uk

[M6 J32, M55 to Blackpool, follow brown signs to Sandcastle Waterworld. Once on promenade we are opposite Pleasure Beach and next to South Pier. Rail: Blackpool North Station then No. 2 bus or tram to South Pier. Alternatively catch train to Blackpool South Station and walk 5mins to promenade. Bus: call us on 01253 340709 for more information]

Inside the award winning Sandcastle Waterworld it's a sub-tropical 84°F. There are wave and fun pools, 300ft Giant Waterslides and White Knuckle water chutes. The younger children can play in our Sleepy Lagoon, which is a shallow water area with a tree slide, fountains and bubblers. All our pool areas are manned by R.L.S.S. trained lifeguards. On most days we have a children's entertainer, Tazz, who will delight your children with his zany antics. Other facilities include a sauna (adults only), cafes and amusements. No costume? No problem! You can buy or hire from our swimwear shop. New for Easter 2004 we will be opening our Caribbean Storm Treehouse which is a fabulous interactive water play area set on three levels with over 35 fun features including water cannons, magic jets, water blasters and a fantastic 3 lane multi-slide. Watch out though, every 5 minutes there is a tropical deluge where 300 gallons of water are dropped from a giant coconut into the pool below. Sandcastle Waterworld, the biggest and best Waterworld in the North-West.

Feb-Nov, please telephone for specific opening times

Please call for price information. Discounts available for group bookings

Sporting History Museums

Manchester United Museum and Tour Centre

Sir Matt Busby Way Old Trafford Manchester Greater Manchester M16 0RA

Tel: 0870 442 1994 Fax: 0161 868 8861

www.manutd.com

[2m from city centre off A56. Plenty of on site parking]

Re-live the Clubs triumphs, tragedies and trophies at the Manchester United Museum, including the Hall of Fame and dazzling Trophy Room as well as the new speed ball and reflex wall interactive displays. Delve behind the scenes at the Theatre of Dreams by taking the Stadium Tour. Stand in Sir Alex Ferguson's spot in the dug out, visit the players changing room and emerge from the tunnel to the roar of the crowd.

All year daily 09.30-17.00. Match Day closing before kickoff, tours not available on match days. Closed 25 Dec

Tour & Museum: A£9.00 C&OAPs£6.00 Family Ticket £25.00. Museum only: A£5.50 C&OAPs£3.75 Family Ticket £15.50

Discount Offer: £2.00 Off Admission To Museum And Tour.

Theme & Adventure Parks

Blackpool Pleasure Beach

Ocean Boulevard Blackpool FY4 1EZ
Tel: 0870 444 5566 Fax: 01253 343958
[M6 J32 then take M55]

Blackpool Pleasure Beach - the entertainment
adventure capital.
Mar-Nov daily
Purchase discounted sheets of ride tickets or
wristbands

Blackpool Tower and Circus

Central Promenade Blackpool Lancashire
FY1 4BJ

Tel: 01253 292029 Fax: 01253 297937

www.blackpooltower.co.uk

[M55, J1/J2 A583 to Promenade]

There's entertainment for all ages, night and
day, at the world famous Blackpool Tower and
Circus. See Mooky the Clown at the award winning international Tower Circus voted the 'Best
in the UK' four years in succession. It's non-
stop daily live entertainment from the family
party in the Hornpipe Galley to the Wurlitzer
organ by day, or the sound of the big bands by
night. Jungle Jim's will keep younger ones
entertained for hours and you really haven't

seen the spectacular views of Blackpool until
you've seen it from the top of the Tower and
experienced the glass floored Walk of Faith 380
feet above the promenade. Telephone 01253
292029 for further information.

*3 Apr-7 Nov daily 10.00-18.00 and evenings 3
July-6 Nov 19.00-23.00. For details of winter
opening times and Christmas Circus call 01253
292029*

Daytime 10.00-18.00: A£10.00 C&OAPs£8.00
Family Tickets (A1+C2) £24.00, (A2+C2)
£35.00, (A2+C3) £42.00. Evening 19.00
onwards: (includes Big Band Show, and Circus
and family entertainment in Hornpipe Galley) all
classes £7.00. Peak pricing and trade up ticket
apply

**Discount Offer: Two For The Price Of
One.**

Camelot Theme Park

Park Hall Road Charnock Richard Chorley
Lancashire PR7 5LP
Tel: 01257 452100 Fax: 01257 452320
[J27 N on M6, J28 S on M6, J8 M61]

The magical kingdom of Camelot is filled with
wondrous rides, spectacular shows and spellbinding attractions!
*27 Mar-31 Oct 10.00-17.00. Please call the 24hr
info line on 01257 452100 to check specific day*
A&C£15.00 OAPs£11.00 Family Ticket (4
Guests) £50.00. Children under 1 metre in
height £Free

**Discount Offer: Buy Two Tickets At
Full Price And Get One Ticket Free.**

Transport Museums

British Commercial Vehicle Museum

King Street Leyland Preston Lancashire
PR25 2LE

Tel: 01772 451011 Fax: 01772 623404

[5 mins from J28 M6. Off Towngate in Leyland]

The largest commercial vehicle museum in
Europe is located in a town long associated
with the British motor industry. Over sixty
restored British commercial vehicles are on display ranging from horse-drawn examples to
modern.

*Apr-Sept Sun, Tue-Thur 10.00-17.00, Oct Sun
only*

A£4.00 Concessions£2.00 Family Ticket £10.00

Wax Works

Louis Tussauds Waxworks

87/89 Central Promenade Blackpool Lancashire
FY1 5AA

Tel: 01253 625953 Fax: 01253 621611

www.blackpoollive.com

[At the end of M55 on the Central Promenade]

Blackpool's Biggest All Star Cast! Come face to
face with Hollywood legends, world politicians,
royalty and history's most chilling criminals as
you tour these stunning waxworks with pop
stars and the chilling Chamber of Horrors.

Easter-7 Nov daily from 10.00

A£6.50 C&OAPs£4.50. Various Family Tickets
available

**Discount Offer: Two For The Price Of
One.**

Leicestershire

Agriculture / Working Farms

Gorse Hill City Farm

Anstey Lane Leicester Leicestershire LE4 0FL
Tel: 0116 253 7582 Fax: 0116 253 7582
[B5327 next to English Martyrs School layby]

A community working farm in the City of
Leicester. Voluntary project practising small
scale humane farming and organic horticulture.
See daily working of the farm. Touch and feed
the animals in a relaxed friendly environment.
Adventure playground, picnic area, farm pro-
duce for sale.
*All year daily summer 10.00-16.30, winter 10.00-
16.00*
Admission by donation, requested A£1.50
C£0.75 (as a guide)

Factory Outlets & Tours

Ye Olde Pork Pie Shoppe and The Sausage Shop

8-10 Nottingham Street Melton Mowbray
Leicestershire LE13 1NW
Tel: 01664 482068 Fax: 01664 568052
[Rail: Melton Mowbray 0.25m]

Melton Mowbray's oldest and only remaining
bakery producing truly authentic Melton Pork
Pies. Learn about the fascinating history of the
shoppe and why Melton Mowbray became the
original home of the pork pie industry. Watch
demonstrations of hand raised pork pies and
sample the unique taste and visit our new
Sausage Shop next door.
*All year Mon-Sat 08.00-17.00. Closed most Sun
and some Bank Hols*
Admission Free

Festivals & Shows

Heart Link, Street Organ Festival

Leicester City Centre Leicester Leicestershire
Tel: 01509 880803
[M1, J21/22]

The largest of all British Organ Festival's in
England with around 35 street fair organs coming from all over England and Wales to support
Heart Link, the East Midlands Children's Heart
Care Association for which there is a street collection. The streets of Leicester are filled with
music played on instruments recalling the music
of yesteryear. The organ grinders will be delighted to explain how their instruments work and
allow you to "Have a Grind"!
May 15 2004, 10.00-16.00
Admission Free

Leicester Early Music Festival

Castle Park Leicester Leicestershire LE1 5FQ
Tel: 0116 270 9984 Fax: 0116 270 9984
Now in its 15th year, the Festival presents a
wide range of music from 1200-1750 and associated events for all the family. Two innovations
this year are extra workshops and a Family Day.
Most concerts take place in the historic Church
of Saint Mary de Castro. "I don't like early music
just because it is Early Music, but because it is
such wonderful music." Join us this year and
find out what you have been missing!
May 22-June 12 2004
Concerts range from £8.00-£12.00

Folk & Local History Museums

Harborough Museum

Council Offices Adam & Eve Street Market
Harborough Leicestershire LE16 7AG

Tel: 01858 821085 Fax: 01858 821086
[A6]

The Museum illustrates the history of the town
and its surrounding area, from the medieval
planned town to its role as a market, social, and
hunting area and also as a stagecoach post.

*All year Mon-Sat 10.00-16.30, Sun 14.00-17.00.
Open most Bank Hols 10.00-16.30. Closed
Good Fri, 25-26 Dec, and last full week in Jan*

Admission Free

Melton Carnegie Museum

Thorpe End Melton Mowbray LE13 1RB
Tel: 01664 569946 Fax: 01664 564060
[A607]

This exciting newly refurbished museum contains informative and innovative displays about the rich and varied heritage of Melton Mowbray and the surrounding area, a temporary exhibition space and an area for local groups to put on displays.
All year daily 10.00-16.30. Closed 25-26 Dec & Good Fri
Admission Free

Forests & Woods

Bagworth Heath Woods

Bagworth Coalville Leicestershire LE67
A 75ha reclaimed colliery site owned by Leicestershire County Council between Bagworth and Thornton.
Open during daylight hours
Admission Free

Sence Valley Forest Park

Ravenstone Road Ibstock Leicestershire LE67

Tel: 01889 586593 Fax: 01889 574217
www.forestry.gov.uk

[On the A447 between Ibstock and Ravenstone. Ample parking]

Sence Valley Forest Park is a wonderful example of how a disused opencast colliery can be transformed into a diverse wildlife haven. After being planted with over 98,000 trees this 150 acre site was opened to the public in September 1998 as part of The National Forest. The park contains woodland, lakes linking to the River Sence, grassland and a wildflower meadow. Thanks to the varied habitat 150 bird species have been recorded at the park. This along with the bird hide makes the site an excellent spot for birdwatchers. Opportunities for recreation at the park include fishing on one of the lakes, a bridleway, surfaced trails providing access for walkers, cyclists, and disabled visitors and a varied events programme.

All year daily during daylight hours. Car park open from 08.30-dusk. See notice in the car park for precise times.

Admission Free

Special Events

Easter Extravaganza
11/04/2004
While kids hunt for Easter eggs around the park you can help build a bat box for the park. Then join us on a bat walk in August to see how well the boxes are doing. Kids go free when accompanying adult builds a bat box! Times: Bat Boxing 09.30-13.00, Egg hunt 11.00-12.30. Booking essential

Bank Holiday Weekend Wildlife Walk
02/05/2004
Learn about the wildlife inhabiting the park and how we are managing the site to improve it for both visitors and wildlife now and in the future. Time: 14.00-16.00. Cost: £2.00. Booking essential

Evening Wildflower Walk
15/06/2004
Please call 01455 290429 for further details. Booking essential

Butterfly Walk and Survey
20/06/2004
Ever wanted to know more about butterflies? Well now you can whilst helping us to complete a butterfly survey for the park. All levels of experience can join in - we'll provide identification keys and assistance to help you along. Time: 09.30-13.00. Cost: £2.00 per person. Booking essential

Park Open Day
25/07/2004

Attractions include country crafts demonstrations, environmental activities, arts and crafts stalls, plant sales, guided walks around the site, refreshments and fun and games for all the family. Time: 10.00-16.00

Bat Walk
12/08/2004

Join Forestry Commission rangers on an evening walk to see and hear these elusive nocturnal creatures. Also find out if any have taken residence in a bat box made at our Easter event! Time: 20.30-late. Cost: A£3.00 C£2.00. Booking essential

Moth Night
14/09/2004

David Brown, Warwickshire's County Moth recorder will be discovering just what comes out when the sun goes down at Sence Valley Forest Park. Time: 19.00-22.00. Cost: £2.00 per person. Booking essential

Gardens & Horticulture

Barnsdale Gardens

The Avenue Exton Oakham Rutland LE15 8AH

Tel: 01572 813200 Fax: 01572 813346
[Turn off A606 Oakham / Stamford road at Barnsdale Lodge Hotel, then 1m on the L]

8 acres of Gardens laid out as part of Barnsdale television gardens. All told, there are 37 individual gardens and features in every possible style - each a living stage from which visitors can glean ideas.

Garden and Nursery: All year daily Mar-May 09.00-17.00, June-Aug 09.00-19.00, Sept-Oct 09.00-17.00, Nov-Feb 10.00-16.00. Closed 23 & 25 Dec. Coffee Shop: Mar-Oct daily 10.00-17.00 (stop serving 16.30), Nov-Feb Sat-Sun 10.00-16.00

T.V. Garden & Small Nursery: A&OAPs£5.00 C£Free

Heritage & Industrial

Snibston Discovery Park

Ashby Road Coalville Leicestershire LE67 3LN

Tel: 01530 278444 Fax: 01530 813301

[10 mins from J22 of the M1 or J13 M42 / A42]

Set on a 100 acre site at a former colliery, enjoy a full interactive day out to suit all ages, especially of you have an interest in the arts, history or science.

All year daily, 10.00-17.00. Closed 25-26 Dec and one week in January

A£5.50 C£3.50 Concessions£3.75

Historical

Stanford Hall

Lutterworth Leicestershire LE17 6DH

Tel: 01788 860250 Fax: 01788 860870

www.stanfordhall.co.uk

[M1, J18 and 19 (from N only) M6 exit at A14/M1(N). Signposted off A426, A4304, A5199, A5, A14. 1.5m from Swinford. NB: No exit at M1, J19 northbound to A14 OR Swinford. Plenty of parking on site]

Beautiful William and Mary (1690s) house set in an attractive Park besides Shakespeare's River Avon. The house contains antique furniture, fine pictures (including the Stuart Collection) and family costumes. In the Grounds there is a Motorcycle Museum (extra charge), Craft Centre and Pottery (most Sundays), Walled Rose Garden, Nature Trail and a full-size replica of Percy Pilcher's 1898 Flying Machine, 'The Hawk'. The Tea Room is the perfect place to relax and enjoy a homemade cream tea. On Event Days breakfasts and light lunches are also served here. The Hall and Grounds are both available for Conferences, Company Incentive Days, Wedding Receptions, Dinners and Lunches. All enquiries should be addressed to the Administrator. Member of the Historic Houses Association. Dogs on leads in grounds only. Limited disabled access. For the following special events, gates are normally open by 10.00, please call for further details. Also, for those events marked with an *, there are special admission prices.

Easter Sun (11 Apr)-end Sept Sun & Bank Hol Mons 13.30-17.00. On Bank Hol Mons Grounds open at 12.00, earlier on event days

House & Grounds: A£5.00 C£2.00. Grounds only: A£3.00 C£1.00. Motorcycle Museum: A£1.00 C£0.35

Special Events

Volkswagen Owners Club Rally*
02/05/2004
Warks and Leics Branch

Wartburg/Trabant/IFA Club UK Rally
09/05/2004
and DAF owners club rally

Leicestershire Ford RS Owners Club Rally*
16/05/2004-17/05/2004

The National Classic Bike Clubs Show*
30/05/2004

The Italian Car Concours (including the Maserati & Ferrari Owners Club Concours)
06/06/2004

Ford AVO Owners Club Rally*
20/06/2004

Mini Owners Club National Rally*
27/06/2004

Velocette Motorcycle Owners Club Rally
04/07/2004
and Norton Rotary Enthusiasts' Club Rally

Farina (Austin Westminster) Owners Club Rally
11/07/2004

Sporting Escort Owners Club National Rally*
11/07/2004

The American Civil War Society*
17/07/2004-18/07/2004

RS Escort Mk II Owners Club Rally*
18/07/2004
and Triumph Razoredge Owners Club Rally

Vintage Motorcycle Club Founders Day Rally*
25/07/2004

Jaguar Drivers Club Rally*
01/08/2004

Rugby Amateur Transmitting Society Radio and Computer Fair*
07/08/2004

Triumph Sports 6 Owners Club Rally*
08/08/2004

Zundapp Bella Enthusiasts' Club Rally
15/08/2004

Semi Professional Firework Championships*
21/08/2004
Time: Gates open 18.00

Laverda International Owners Club Rally
22/08/2004

Midlands Austin 7 Car Club Rally
05/09/2004
Scott Motorcycle Owners Club Rally, Standard Vanguard I & II Club Rally and Minx and Hunters Club Rally

L.E Velo Motorcycle Owners Club Rally
19/09/2004

Historic Transport Festival*
26/09/2004

Craft at Stanford Hall*
02/10/2004-03/10/2004
Time: 10.00-17.00

Homes and Interiors Exhibition*
08/10/2004-10/10/2004

Railways

Battlefield Line Railway

Shackerstone Station Shackerstone Nuneaton
CV13 6NW
Tel: 01827 880754 Fax: 01827 881050
www.battlefield-line-railway.co.uk

*[Situated midway between Ashby-de-la-Zouch
and Hinckley in Leicestershire and is sign posted
from both the A444 and A447 trunk roads. Follow
the brown tourist signs from B585 Market
Bosworth road, through the villages of
Congerstone and Shackerstone, to the large free
Shackerstone Station car park. Narrowboats can
be moored nearby at Ashby Canal bridge No. 52.
NB: There is NO access to Market Bosworth
Station]*

Join us for a steam hauled 10 mile round trip
from Shackerstone to Shenton through the
delightful scenery of south west Leicestershire.
Impressive museum of railway memorabilia,
locomotives and rolling stock at Shackerstone.

*Easter-Oct Sunday Service departures from
Shackerstone at 12.30, 13.45, 15.00 & 16.15.
Extra train at 11.15 on Bank Hol, Sat Diesel service May-Sept 12.30, 13.45, 15.00 & 16.15,
also Wed in July and Aug 13.00, 14.00, 15.00 &
16.00. Museum: all year 11.30-17.30 Sat & Sun*

Return Fare: A£7.00 C£4.00 OAPs£5.00 Family
Ticket £20.00. Group rates (15+): 10% discount

**Discount Offer: Two Adults For The
Price Of One**

Great Central Railway

Great Central Road Loughborough
Leicestershire LE11 1RW

Tel: 01509 230726 Fax: 01509 239791

*[3m E of M1 J23. Loughborough Central Station
is SE of town centre, off A6]*

This private steam railway runs over eight miles
from Loughborough Central to Leicester, with all
trains calling at Quorn & Woodhouse, Rothley
and Leicester North. The locomotive depot and
museum are at Loughborough Central.

*Trains run on Sat, Sun & Bank Hol Mon through-
out the year. Also Easter Tue. Trains run on
Weekdays on 17-20 Feb, 5-16 Apr, 2 June-20
Aug & 18-21 Oct*

Return fares: A£11.00 C&OAPs£7.50

Science - Earth & Planetary

National Space Centre

Exploration Drive Leicester Leicestershire

LE4 5NS

Tel: 0116 261 0261 Fax: 0116 258 2100

[Just off A6, 2m N of Leicester City Centre]

The UK's largest attraction dedicated to space
science and astronomy. From the minute you
catch sight of the futuristic Rocket Tower, you'll
be treated to hours of breathtaking discoveries
where the stories, personalities and technology
of the past and present are used to explain our
current understanding of space and how it will
affect our future.

*All year Tue-Sun 10.00-17.00. During
Leicestershire Schools Hols Mon 12.00-16.30*

A£8.95 C£6.95 Concessions£6.95 Family
Ticket (A2+C2) £28.00, (A2+C3) £34.00. All
children under the age of 14 must be accompanied by an adult

Lincolnshire

Animal Attractions

Skegness Natureland Seal Sanctuary

North Parade Skegness Lincolnshire PE25 1DB
Tel: 01754 764345 Fax: 01754 764345
[A52 & A158 signposted]

Natureland houses a specialised collection of animals including seals, penguins, tropical birds, aquarium, reptiles, pets' corner etc. Also free-flight tropical butterflies. Well known for its rescue of abandoned seal pups.
All year daily Summer 10.00-17.00, Winter 10.00-16.00. Closed 25-26 Dec & 1 Jan
A£4.95 C(under3)£Free C£3.25 OAPs£3.95 Family Ticket (A2+C2) £14.70

Discount Offer: One Child Free With Full Paying Adult

Arts, Crafts & Textiles

20-21 Visual Arts Centre

St John's Church Church Square Scunthorpe North Lincolnshire DN15 6TB
Tel: 01724 297070 Fax: 01724 297080

[Exit the M180 at J4 follow the signs to A18 the centre is situated on Brigg Road A1029]

St John's Church has been converted into a visual arts centre that boasts a wide range of facilities including three excellent spaces for a regularly changing programme of art and craft exhibitions.

Tues-Sat 10.00-17.00

Admission Free

Country Parks & Estates

Normanby Hall Country Park

Normanby Park Normanby Scunthorpe North Lincolnshire DN15 9HU

Tel: 01724 720588 Fax: 01724 721248
[5m N off B1430]

Regency Mansion, Farming Museum, Gift Shop, Tea Rooms, 350 acres of Parkland, red and fallow deer, duck ponds, working restored Victorian Walled Garden.
Park: all year daily. Walled Garden: daily 10.30-15.30 in winter, 10.30-17.00 in summer. Hall & Farming Museum: Apr-Sept daily 13.00-17.00
A£4.00 C£2.00 Family Season Ticket £12.00

Gardens & Horticulture

Springfields Outlet Shopping and Festival Gardens

Camelgate Spalding Lincolnshire PE12 6ET

Tel: 020 7287 6620 Fax: 020 7287 6621
www.springfieldsshopping.com

[1m E of Spalding signposted off A16]

Springfields Outlet Shopping and Festival Gardens in Spalding will be open to the public from May 2004. The new Springfields will include 40 factory outlet shops, themed educational gardens, celebrity designed showcase gardens, striking water features and woodland walks. The 40 shops will feature well known brands all retailing at up to 60% off the high street price. Brands include Mexx, Suits You, Caterpillar, Virgin Cosmetics, Pilot, Cotton Traders, XS Music and many more. There will also be a garden centre run by Blue Diamond that will sell most of the plants found within the Festival Gardens. With the involvement of celebrity gardeners such as Charlie Dimmock, Kim Wilde, Chris Beardshaw and Ali Ward, the scheme is set to be one of the best family days out in the country. And don't forget to visit during the famous Spalding Flower Parade on 1 May 2004 from 14.00 and Spalding Country Fair 1-3 May 2004, which draws crowds of over 150,000.

All year Mon-Sat 10.00-18.00, Sun 11.00-17.00

Admission free

Historical

Belton House

Grantham Lincolnshire NG32 2LS

Tel: 01476 566116 Fax: 01476 579071

[40mins from Nottingham, Leicester and Lincoln, Belton House is on A607 Grantham / Lincoln road easily reached and signposted from A1. Rail: Grantham. Plenty of parking on site]

Built 1685-88 for Sir John Brownlow. The rooms contain portraits, furniture, tapestries, oriental porcelain, family silver and Speaker Cust's silver. Formal gardens, an Orangery and a magnificent landscaped park with a lakeside walk and the Bellmount Tower. Adventure playground and miniature train rides. On weekends throughout August the room at the top of Bellmount Tower will be open for visitors to view. Separate admission charges apply. Please call property for further details. Braille, audio guides and Hearing Scheme. Family guide. Children's menu available in restaurant. Front baby slings on loan. Dogs on leads only in parkland.

House: 31 Mar-31 Oct Wed-Sun & Bank Hol Mon 12.30-17.00. Open Good Friday. Garden

and Park 11.00-17.30, shop and restaurant 11.00-17.15. (Park may occasionally be closed for special events)

House & Garden: A£6.50 C(under5)Free C(5-16)£3.00 Family ticket (A2+C3) £15.00. Reductions for pre-booked parties

Special Events

Easter Trail
11/04/2004
Normal admission charges to property apply as well as a £1.50 charge for trail map. Time: 11.00-16.00

The Garden in Spring
21/04/2004
Join our Head Gardener on this Spring walk through Belton's magnificent gardens. Fred will be on hand to answer your garden queries in the Orangery, where you are invited to join him in a glass of wine and nibbles. Time: 18.30. Cost: £8.00

Paint the Garden Day
25/04/2004-19/09/2004
Held on 25 Apr, 28 July, 19 Sept only. Join accomplished local artist, Malcolm Doughty, at the Orangery and capture the beauty of the English garden on paper.

National Gardens Scheme
01/05/2004-04/09/2004
Held on 1 May, 3 July, 4 Sept only. Enjoy and be inspired by the magnificent gardens at Belton. Opened in support of the National Gardens Scheme

Sow a Seed at Belton
09/05/2004
Pot up a plant for summer. Take home your pot and watch your seed grow. Free event aimed at families

Ghost Tour
13/05/2004-28/10/2004
Held on 13 May & 28 Oct. Evening tour of the mansion with the House Manager. Bring a torch. Time: 19.30. Tickets: A£10.00 C(5-16)£5.00 includes glass of wine or soft drink. Booking essential

Backstairs Tour
20/05/2004-21/10/2004
Held on 20 May & 21 Oct. Visit parts of the house not normally seen by visitors. Time: 19.30. Tickets: A£12.50 C(5-16)£6.50 to include glass of wine or soft drink, booking essential

An Evening of Gershwin
22/06/2004

Delight in the sounds of Gershwin on this magical midsummer evening. Enjoy a glass of wine and stroll in the gardens during the interval. Time: 19.30. Tickets: £12.50. Booking essential

Family Day
27/06/2004

Entertain the whole family with a variety of fun activities at this special Family Day to mark "20 Years of Trust".

Pride and Prejudice
04/07/2004

Outdoor performance by Illyria. Time: 18.00. Tickets: A£11.00, C£5.50 booking essential

Longbow and Lionheart
11/07/2004-12/09/2004

Held on 11 July & 12 Sept. Have a go at archery with the Lionheart Company of Bowmen. Time: 11.00-17.00. Cost: £1.50 for six arrows

'The Spitfire Prom'
17/07/2004

Soak up the atmosphere with the English National Orchestra. Time: 17.00 for 20.00. Tickets: £20 advance, £25 on the day

Boredom Busters
01/08/2004-01/09/2004

Bellmount Tower Openings
01/08/2004-29/08/2004

Held on 1, 7-8, 14-15, 21-22 & 28-29 Aug

Dull and Dusty or Fun and Fascinating
06/08/2004-27/08/2004

Held on 6, 20, 27 Aug. Become an art connoisseur and consider the artists and sitters in some of Belton's portraits, as well as learn some portrait techniques of your own. Aimed at 7-10 year olds. Pre-booking is essential

The National Trust Theatre's Entertainment for Families
13/08/2004-14/08/2004

Outdoor theatre with a 'green' theme for families with children aged from 4 years

An Autumn Garden Walk
01/09/2004

Time: 18.30 meet in the stable yard. Cost: £8.00

Open Furniture
20/09/2004-26/09/2004

Admire the craftsmanship of some of Belton's finest pieces of furniture

Halloween Happenings
27/10/2004-29/10/2004

Why not visit Belton this half-term wearing your Halloween costume where you will find extra fun activities throughout the afternoon

Putting the House to Bed
10/11/2004

Help us put the house to bed. Practical skills in how the National Trust put the Mansion and its contents to bed for the winter. Time: 10.00 start. Cost: £12.00 to include coffee and cake

Warden's Winter Walk
05/12/2004

A short guided walk through Belton Park with a National Trust Warden, followed by a mince pie and mulled wine. Time: meet 11.00 in the stable yard. Tickets: A£6.50 book in advance

Christmas Carols in the Marble Hall
11/12/2004

Enjoy preparing for Christmas on this special evening opening. Why not join in the carol singing and round off your evening with a visit to the Housekeepers Room for a glass of mulled wine and mince pies. Children are invited to visit Santa in the Butler's Pantry before departure. Time: 17.30. Cost: £6.00. Pre-booking essential

Boundary Walk
12/12/2004

Guided Walk through the park of approximately 6 miles. Meet in the Stable Yard at 10.00 and return in time for a traditional Christmas Lunch in the Stables Restaurant. Tickets: £22.50 per person. Booking essential

Festive Winter Walk
19/12/2004

Join one of Save the Children's sponsored Stately Walks. An opportunity to involve family and friends, by taking part in a sponsored walk set in magnificent Belton Park. For further information and registration pack, please contact Shirley on 0121 5580111

Gainsborough Old Hall

Parnell Street Gainsborough Lincolnshire
DN21 2NB

Tel: 01427 612669 Fax: 01427 612779

www.lincolnshire.gov.uk

*[In Gainsborough town centre, 20m W of Lincoln,
30m E of Sheffield. Rail: Gainsborough Central
0.5m, Gainsborough Lea Road 1m]*

A complete medieval manor house dating back
to 1460-80 and containing a remarkable Great
Hall and original kitchen with room settings.
Richard III, Henry VIII, the Mayflower Pilgrims
and John Wesley all in their day visited the Old
Hall. Photography allowed on request.

*All year Mon-Sat 10.00-17.00, Easter-Oct Sun
14.00-17.30. Closed 24-26 Dec & 1 Jan*

A£3.20 Concessions£2.40 Family Ticket £8.80.
Please pre-book guided tours

Special Events

Greek Odyssey
30/01/2004-16/04/2004
*Take a trip to ancient Greece and learn about all
the lifestyle of that ancient civilisation. Free admission to the exhibition*

Easter Trail
09/04/2004-16/04/2004
*A fun, family trail highlighting hidden aspects of
the building*

Family Quiz Day
12/04/2004
*A novel way to explore, discover and learn - and
a fun day out*

Living History Weekend
02/05/2004-03/05/2004
*Crime and punishment. Visit the manorial court -
are you guilty or not guilty?*

Museums Month - Behind the Scenes
06/05/2004
*Come along and meet the museum team at the
opening of an exhibition about our work. Please
book in advance. Normal admission. Free refreshments*

People from the Past
02/07/2004-02/09/2004
*An exhibition which examines evidence to high-
light the development of museum detective work.
See how the puzzle fits together to learn about
people from the past. Free admission to the exhibition*

Crafts and Past Times
29/08/2004-30/08/2004
*A unique chance to see items from the
Gainsborough Old Hall collection. Learn how they
were used and watch today's craftspeople work
in traditional methods*

'A Monstrous Crime!'
25/09/2004
*An evening of cryptic clues, red herrings and dev-
ilish dangers as you join the members of Lord
Burgh's household to unravel the mystery and
solve the monstrous crime. Tickets: £10.00 to
include supper*

Family Learning Week and the Big Draw
01/10/2004-31/10/2004
*Workshops and activities to celebrate both these
events*

Crime and Punishment
08/10/2004-01/01/2005
*An exhibition portraying life in Lincolnshire during
less lenient times. Please call for specific end
date*

Christmas Craft Fair
27/11/2004-28/11/2004
*Christmas shopping, carols, punch and mince
pies at our traditional fair. Admission: £1.00*

Medieval Christmas
11/12/2004
*'Deck the Halls' with Lord Burgh's Retinue on their
last visit of the year. Watch as they prepare their
meal and join in their Christmas celebrations.
Normal admission applies*

Gunby Hall

Gunby Spilsby Lincolnshire PE23 5SS
Tel: 01909 486411
[2.5m NW of Burgh le Marsh, 7m W of Skegness on S side of A158, access off roundabout]

A fine red-brick house with stone dressings, built in 1700 and extended in 1870s. Within the house, there is a good early 18th century wainscotting and a fine oak staircase, also English furniture and portraits by Reynolds.

House (only ground floor and basement shown): 31 Mar-29 Sept Wed 14.00-18.00. Garden: 31 Mar-30 Sept Wed & Thur 14.00-18.00. House & Garden also Tue, Thur & Fri by written appointment only

House & Garden: A£3.80 C(under5)£Free C(5-15)£1.90 Family Ticket (A2+C3) £9.50. Garden only: A£2.70 C(5-15)£1.30

Spectator Sports

Market Rasen Racecourse

Legsby Road Market Rasen Lincolnshire LN8 3EA
Tel: 01673 843434 Fax: 01673 844532
www.marketrasenracecourse.co.uk

[Alongside A631 Louth / Gainsborough road signposted on all race days. Plenty of on site parking available]

A picturesque country racecourse nestling at the foot of the Lincolnshire Wolds. Jumping only fixtures throughout the year. Picnic packs to A La Carte, something for everyone. Free crèche at weekend meetings, please call for details.

See special events listings. Group bookings available

Premier Members: A£21.00. Racecard Members: A£17.00. Tattersalls: A£12.00. Silver Ring: A£7.00 C(0-16)£Free

Discount Offer: £2.00 Off Tattersalls

<u>Special Events</u>
Race Fixture
24/04/2004

Macmillan Cancer Relief Day
09/05/2004

June Race Fixtures
09/06/2004-25/06/2004
Held on 9 & 25 June only

Independence Day
04/07/2004

Tote Scoop 6 Summer Plate Day
17/07/2004

Family Funday
01/08/2004

Irish Night
14/08/2004

Ladies Day
21/08/2004

Race Fixture
25/09/2004

Countryside Day
03/10/2004

Race Fixture
17/10/2004

November Race Fixtures
07/11/2004-18/11/2004
Held on 7 & 18 Nov only

Race Fixture
02/12/2004

Boxing Day
26/12/2004

Theme & Adventure Parks

Butlins

Skegness Lincolnshire PE25 1NJ

Tel: 01754 765567 Fax: 01754 767833

www.butlins.com

[On A52 3M N of Skegness town centre heading towards Ingoldmells. Plenty of on site parking available]

Butlins is a fantastic day out! A paradise for every generation, with an amazing range of activities on offer. You can enjoy the fun of the wet 'n' wild sub-tropical Splash Waterworld, burn off that extra energy on the multi-sports court, or challenge the kids to a race round the Go-Kart track. If you fancy taking things at an easier pace relax with a game of crazy golf or enjoy the latest blockbuster in the cinema! Butlins have been entertaining holidaymakers for 60 years so why not find out what makes us so special. We offer you all the best bits of a Butlins holiday in a day for an incredible price! Don't miss the Skyline Pavilion at the heart of each Resort which offers non-stop entertainment whatever the weather and our Traditional Funfairs, Adventure Forts and Playgrounds will keep the kids amused for hours!

20 Apr-31 Oct daily 10.00-23.00 (last admission 16.00). Excludes 8-10 Oct inclusive

Afrom£7.50 Cfrom£5.00

Spalding Fun Farm / Laserstorm

High Road Weston Spalding PE12 6JD
Tel: 01406 373444 / 373111
Fax: 01406 373445
[Just off the A151 next to Baytree Nurseries]

Come and meet Harry the Spider in his Spooky cave. There is a Super Wavey Waterfall Slide, a fun Log Maze and Snakey Tube Slides. Come and see the real waterfall and cross the spectacular rope bridge which extends above it in the Jungle area. The under fives can explore the separate farm area with their own Helter Skelter slide, Biff Bash, stepping stones, rope bridges and soft play animals. New! Play Laserstorm, an all action laser tag game and laser bowl, a compact ten pin bowling game.
All year daily 10.00-18.00
Mon-Fri C£2.99 School Holidays and weekends C£4.49

Transport Museums

The Trolleybus Museum at Sandtoft

Belton Road Sandtoft Doncaster North Lincolnshire DN8 5SX

Tel: 01724 711391 24hr info
Fax: 01724 711846

www.sandtoft.org.uk

[J2 M180 (A161) to Belton, R at roundabout and travel approx. 2.5m. Free bus from Doncaster (South Bus and Rail Stations) most open days (call info line for details)]

The museum boasts the world's largest collection of historic trolleybuses (45) that date from between 1927 and 1985. Many of the exhibits are restored to working order and carry visitors 0.25 miles around the museum, which has adopted a 1950s/1960s feel, with contemporary motorbuses, street scene and shop window displays, prefab 'home' exhibition, cycle and lawnmower museum as well as an exhibition of trolleybus and transport artefacts. Adequate free parking, tours, gardens, play and picnic areas, AV shows, souvenir shop, light refreshments and occasional additional visiting attractions days complete the offerings. Sandtoft Gathering is the museum's major annual event with many added attractions. Disabled access to most areas but wheelchair access to trolleybus rides not always available. The operating company, Sandtoft Transport Centre Ltd is a Registered Charity (no. 514382) run by volunteer members and established to preserve the trolleybus as part of Britain's Transport Heritage.

Trolleydays held on 20-21 Mar (National Science Week), 10-12 Apr, 29-31 May (pre-WWII weekend), 20 June, 21-25 June (combined Trolleydays and Schools Week), 26-27 June, 10 July, 11 July (Vintage Cycle Day), 24-25 July (Sandtoft Gathering 2004), 14-15 Aug, 28-30 Aug (Six Wheel Weekend), 25-26 Sept (European Weekend), 16 Oct, 17 Oct (St Leger Rally), 6-7 Nov (Twilight Running), 11-12 Dec (Santa Days). Trolleydays 11.00-17.00; Sandtoft Gathering 24 July (preview) 11.00-22.00, 25 July 10.00-18.00, Santa Days 11.00-16.00

Trolleydays & Pre-booked parties: A£4.50 Concessions£2.50 C(under5)£Free Family Ticket (A2+C4) £12.00. Group rates, 15% discount available for 12+ people. Sandtoft Gathering: A£6.00 Concessions£4.00 C(under5)£Free, whole weekend ticket available A£7.50 Concessions£5.50. Please call for Santa Days prices

Wildlife & Safari Parks

Butterfly and Wildlife Park

Long Sutton Spalding Lincolnshire PE12 9LE
Tel: 01406 363833 Fax: 01406 363182
[A17 off Long Sutton by-pass]

The Butterfly and Wildlife Park houses so much for the family to see including a huge walk-through tropical butterfly, bird house, and Reptile Land - from crocodiles to chameleons. Ant Room, Insectarium and Furry Friends House.
20 Mar-31 Oct daily from 10.00

A£5.50 C(3-16)£3.80 OAPs£4.80 Family Tickets (A2+C2) £17.00, (A2+C3) £20.00

Elsham Hall Country and Wildlife Park

Elsham Brigg Lincolnshire DN20 0QZ
Tel: 01652 688698 Fax: 01652 688240

[J5 M180 A15 Humber Bridge]

Attractions include; arboretum, garden centre, animal farm, adventure playground, carp and trout lakes with carp feeding jetty, wild butterfly garden and walkway, granary restaurant and tearooms. Falconry Centre opening 2004 with public displays. Special events on Bank Holidays with entertainment in the courtyard. New for 2004 is the exciting new development within the Walled Garden.
Easter Sat-mid Sept Wed-Sun 11.00-17.00. Open Bank Hols plus Mon-Tue during school hols
A£4.50 C(0-3)£Free C£3.50 OAPs£4.00

London

Abbeys

Westminster Abbey

Broad Sanctuary London SW1P 3PA
Tel: 020 7222 5152 Fax: 020 7233 2072
[Tube: St James's Park]

A millennium ago Westminster Abbey was a monastery offering traditional Benedictine hospitality to its visitors. The present building, begun by Henry III in 1245 is one of the most visited churches in the world.
Abbey: All year Mon-Fri 09.30-15.45, Sat 09.30-13.45. Cloisters: All year daily 08.00-18.00
Abbey: A£7.50 C(0-11)£Free Concessions£5.00 Family Ticket £15.00. Cloisters: Admission Free

Agriculture / Working Farms

Freightliners Farm

Sheringham Road Islington London N7 8PF
Tel: 020 7609 0467 Fax: 020 7609 9934
[Holloway Road (A1), off Liverpool Road. Rail: Highbury & Islington. Tube: Highbury & Islington / Caledonian / Holloway Road]

Freightliners Farm is a model of a working farm in the heart of Islington. It is a great place to get away from the bustle of city life and make contacts with the farming world. We produce and sell delicious fresh eggs, honey and vegetables.
All year Tue-Sun 10.00-17.00, winter 14.00-16.00
Admission Free

Animal Attractions

Battersea Dogs Home

4 Battersea Park Road London SW8 4AA
Tel: 020 7622 3626 Fax: 020 7622 6451
[Rail: Battersea Park. Tube: Vauxhall. Bus: 137]

Battersea Dogs Home was founded in 1860, and since then we've cared for over three million canine and feline waifs and strays. Our aims are to rescue lost and abandoned dogs and cats, reunite them with their owners through the Lost Dogs and Cats Line in London, rehabilitate any that need extra help and rehome the ones that are left behind into loving and permanent new homes.
All year Mon-Wed & Fri 10.30-16.15, Sat-Sun & Bank Hols 10.30-15.15
A£1.00 C&OAPs£0.50

London Aquarium

County Hall Westminster Bridge Road London SE1 7PB

Tel: 020 7967 8000 Fax: 020 7967 8029

www.londonaquarium.co.uk

[Tube: Waterloo or Westminster. Across Westminster Bridge from Houses of Parliament, next to London Eye]

Flood your senses at London Aquarium, where you will discover over 350 species of fish and animal life from oceans, lakes, rivers and streams around the world. For the adventurous there are several species you may stroke or touch, including rayes, starfish and crabs.

Throughout the year, the award winning London Aquarium runs themed weeks of activities, displays and presentations. These are free and are available to adults and children.

All year daily 10.00-18.00

A£8.75 C(under3)£Free C(3-14)£5.25 Concessions£6.50 Family Ticket (A2+C2) £25.00

Discount Offer: One Child Free when accompanied by a full paying adult.

Arts, Crafts & Textiles

British Museum

Great Russell Street London WC1B 3DG

Tel: 020 7323 8000 Fax: 020 7323 8616

[Tube: Holborn, Tottenham Court Road, Russell Square, Goodge Street]

Founded in 1753, this is the world's oldest museum. Two and a half miles of galleries display the national collection of antiquities, prints and drawings. The new Great Court is Europe's largest covered courtyard.

Main Museum: Sat-Wed 10.00-17.30, Thur & Fri 10.00-20.30 (only selected galleries open after 17.30). Great Court: Sun-Wed 09.00-18.00, Thur-Sat 09.00-23.00. Closed 24-26 Dec, 1 Jan and Good Friday

Admission Free. A charge may be made for Temporary Exhibitions

Dali Universe

County Hall Gallery Riverside Building London SE1 7PB

Tel: 0870 744 7485 Fax: 020 7620 3120

www.daliuniverse.com

[Tube: Westminster, cross over Westminster Bridge and turn L. Waterloo, follow directions to County Hall attractions. Dali Universe is on the riverside next to the London Eye. Bus: RV1]

On May 11th, the legend of Salvador Dali becomes a century old. Commemorating the 100th anniversary of his birth in May 1904, the Dali Universe celebrates the life of the art world's first living superstar and greatest surreal icon, Salvador Dali. Set in the heart of London's South Bank, the Dali Universe is host to the world's largest and most important exhibit of sculpture by the artist, including the magnificent Profile of Time and Alice in Wonderland. The exhibition also features a multiplicity of gold ornaments and works in crystal, an unrivalled collection of rare graphics, surreal furniture pieces - notably the lush Mae West Lips Sofa - and the monumental Spellbound canvas commissioned for the 1945 Hitchcock film of the same name. In the Dali Universe you find yourself inside the wild and twisted mind of the Catalan master, his enigmatic personality ebbs from every piece.

All year daily 10.00-17.30, late night summer openings

A£8.50 C(8-16)£5.50 C(4-7)£3.50 Concessions£7.00. For group discounts, corporate hire, educational visits or guided group tour enquiries, please call 0870 744 7485

Design Museum

Butler's Wharf 28 Shad Thames London
SE1 2YD

Tel: 0870 833 9955 Fax: 0870 909 1909

www.designmuseum.org

[Tube: London Bridge / Tower Hill]

The Design Museum is the world's leading museum of 20th and 21st century design. A changing programme of exhibitions covers architecture, engineering, fashion, furniture, graphics, interiors and product design.

All year daily 10.00-17.45 (closes at 14.00 on 24 & 31 Dec). Closed 25 & 26 Dec

A£6.00 C&Concessions£4.00 Family Ticket (2A+2C) £16.00 Students £4.00

Special Events

The History of Modern Design - The Home
01/11/2003-31/10/2004

At a time of growing public interest in design and its impact on our daily lives, the Design Museum will trace The History of Modern Design in the home from the late 19th to the early 21st centuries. Combining recreations of iconic modern homes with detailed deconstructions of the development of equally influential objects, this exhibition will bring modern design history to life

Designer of the Year
06/03/2004-13/06/2004

Embracing every area of design from chairs and cars, to graphics and websites, this prestigious award celebrates the UK designer that made the biggest impact on design last year

Archigram - A Retrospective
03/04/2004-04/07/2004

Ask any young architect to cite their influences and one name is almost certain to appear -

Archigram. The exuberant, pop-inspired visions of the Archigram group dominated avant garde architecture throughout the 1960s and has an enduring influence on design today.

Zest for Life - The Designs of Fernando and Humberto Campana
19/06/2004-19/09/2004

At a time when Brazil is enjoying a cultural renaissance, the Design Museum is to present the first UK exhibition of the work of Fernando and Humberto Campana, the Brazilian brothers whose vibrant and ingenious objects and furniture are injecting a new energy and visual drama to contemporary design

Saul Bass - on Film
17/07/2004-10/10/2004

One of the greatest graphic designers of the 20th century, Saul Bass was the undisputed master of film title design. The hauntingly elegant film titles that Bass created for Hitchcock, Preminger, Kubrick and Scorcese are among the most compelling images in design and cinema history

Design Mart - Celebrating Young Design Talent
01/09/2004-30/09/2004

The next generation of international designers will be given an invaluable opportunity to show off their talent to the public, media and industry in Design Mart, an exhibition of work by young product and furniture designers to be presented during 100% Design and the London Design Festival

Marc Newson
23/10/2004-30/01/2005

Ever since he exploded onto the design scene in the late 1980s with his futuristic sculptural furniture which now sells for hundreds of thousands of dollars at auction, Marc Newson has been regarded as one of the world's most influential designers. He has stamped his distinctive retro-futuristic style on everything from bars and bicycles, to a concept car for Ford and the Design Museum's toilets. This exciting exhibition will be specially designed by Marc Newson

Dulwich Picture Gallery

Gallery Road Dulwich London SE21 7AD

Tel: 020 8693 5254 Fax: 020 8299 8700

www.dulwichpicturegallery.org.uk

[Just off A205 South Circular. Rail: Victoria / West Dulwich. Plenty of parking on site]

The oldest public picture gallery in England is also one of the most beautiful. Housed in a building designed by Sir John Soane in 1811, displaying a fine cross-section of Old Masters. The Gallery was recently reopened following a £9m refurbishment and extension. Development project includes facilities such as a lecture hall, practical art room and cafe. The Gallery puts on three critically acclaimed exhibitions each year.

All year Tue-Fri 10.00-17.00, Sat, Sun & Bank Hol 11.00-17.00. Closed Mon except Bank Hols. Guided tours Sat & Sun at 15.00. Closed Good Friday, 24-26 Dec and 1 Jan.

A£4.00 C(0-16)&Disabled&UB40s£Free OAPs£3.00. Free to all on Fridays.

Discount Offer: Two For The Price Of One With This Voucher

Special Events

Crystal Palace at Sydenham
04/02/2004-18/04/2004
Just above Dulwich Picture Gallery, the second
Crystal Palace, Paxton's masterpiece, stood on the horizon for eighty-two years until the spectacular fire of 1936. This exhibition coincides with the 150th Anniversary of the completion of the Crystal Palace at Sydenham, twice the size of the Hyde Park structure, and aims to place the Crystal Palace in the context of social and cultural history of national and local history, of the history of museums, the history of taste, and of public education in architecture, colour, design and the grammar of ornament

Henry Moore
12/05/2004-12/09/2004
Dulwich Picture Gallery is mounting a major show devoted to the work of Henry Moore. The exhibition will explore the astonishing fluidity with which Moore continually developed and enriched such familiar and well-loved themes as the mother and child, the family group, the reclining figure and other, less familiar and more abstract forms. There will also be a fine selection of the artist's remarkable war-time drawings showing figures sheltering in the Tube

Institute of Contemporary Arts

The Mall London SW1Y 5AH

Tel: 020 7930 3647

[Tube: Charing Cross / Piccadilly Circus]

ICA contains two Galleries with changing art exhibitions of contemporary art by both well known and new artists, 2 cinemas, and a theatre, along with a bookshop, licensed bar, café and a blossoming music programme.

All year daily Mon 12.00-23.00, Tue-Sat closes 01.00, Sun closes 22.30. Galleries: daily 12.00-19.30. Closed 24-26 Dec and Public Hol

Mon-Fri Admission: A£1.50 Concessions£1.00. Weekend: A£2.50 Concessions£1.50

Little Holland House

0 Beeches Avenue Carshalton SM5 3LW
el: 020 8770 4781 Fax: 020 8770 4777
*On B278 off A232. Rail: Carshalton Beeches.
us: 154]*

n Arts and Crafts style house built in 1902-04
y artist, designer and craftsman Frank
Dickinson (1874-1961) who created and fur-
ished his home in line with the theories of
William Morris and John Ruskin.
*irst Sun in the month plus Bank Hol Sun & Mon
3.30-17.30*
dmission Free

Mall Galleries

he Mall London SW1
el: 020 7930 6844 Fax: 020 7839 7830
*Tube: Charing Cross / Embankment / Piccadilly
ircus]*

hese galleries are the exhibition venue for eight
rt society's annual exhibitions including the
oyal Society of Portrait Painters. It also hosts a
umber of high profile art competitions, and one
an and small group shows.
ll year daily 10.00-17.00, during exhibitions
£2.50 C&Concessions£1.00

National Gallery

rafalgar Square London WC2N 5DN
el: 020 7747 2885 Fax: 020 7747 2423
*ube/Rail: Charing Cross. Tube: Leicester Sq /
mbankment / Piccadilly Circus]*

neo-classical building opened in 1838. All the
reat periods of European paintings are repre-
ented here although only a selection of British
orks are included. Particular treasures include
an Eyck's Arnolfini Marriage, Van Gogh's
unflowers and Constable's Haywain.
*l year daily 10.00-18.00, Wed 10.00-21.00.
losed 24-26 Dec & 1 Jan*
dmission Free - some exhibitions charged

National Portrait Gallery

St. Martins Place London WC2H 0HE

Tel: 020 7306 0055 / 7312 2463
Fax: 020 7306 0056
www.npg.org.uk

*[Tube: Charing Cross / Leicester Square.
Opposite Church of St Martin-in-the-Fields to the
N of Trafalgar Square. Disabled access found at
the Orange Street entrance and St Martin's Place
entrance]*

From Elizabeth I to Oscar Wilde, William
Shakespeare to Florence Nightingale... With the
largest collection of portraiture in the world, the
National Portrait Gallery has over 10,000 works
of famous British men and women who have
created the history and culture of the nation
from the Middle Ages until the present day. In
addition to the main collection, the Gallery offers
a varied programme of special exhibitions
throughout the year. The Ondaatje Wing offers
new public galleries, a roof-top Restaurant with
views across London and an IT Gallery offering
a touch-screen database of the Gallery's collection. For exhibition details, please see Special
Events section, ** denotes a major exhibition.

*All year daily, Sat-Wed 10.00-18.00, Thur & Fri
10.00-21.00. Closed 24-26 Dec, 1 Jan & Good
Fri. Recorded Information Line: 020 7312 2463*

Admission Free, some special exhibitions are
charged

Special Events

Mario Testino: Portraits
24/01/2004-13/06/2004
Fifteen of Testino's most iconic portraits of British subjects were recently purchased for the Gallery's permanent collection. They include the Prince and Princess of Wales, John Galliano, Naomi Campbell, Stella McCartney, Darcey Bussell and Kate Moss. Held in Room 36, admission free

**Cecil Beaton: Portraits
05/02/2004-31/05/2004
Celebrating the centenary of the birth of Sir Cecil Beaton (1904-1980), this major retrospective exhibition shows him to be one of the most outstanding photographers of the twentieth century. Subjects include Greta Garbo, Audrey Hepburn, Marilyn Monroe, Gertrude Stein, Andre Gide, Jean Paul Sartre, Albert Camus, Edith Sitwell, Picasso, Hockney, Twiggy and Andy Warhol. Held in the Wolfson Gallery. Admission: A£7.00 Concessions£4.50

We are the People: Postcards from the Collection of Tom Phillips
02/03/2004-20/06/2004
In this exhibition, the artist Tom Phillips brings together key images from his vast collection of picture postcards from the first half of the twentieth century. Entertaining, intriguing, humorous, and at times haunting, We are the People presents a fresh and original approach to portraiture

Gaiety Girls: Footlight Favourites from the 1900s to the 1920s
05/04/2004-22/08/2004
This exciting display features highlights from a remarkable collection of over 3,000 negatives donated to the National Portrait Gallery by John Culme and the many actresses of Edwardian London who were life long favourites of Cecil Beaton and inspired his many theatrical designs. Held in the Bookshop Gallery, admission free

BP Portrait Award 2004 & BP Travel Award 2003
17/06/2004-19/09/2004
With a first prize of £25,000 the BP Portrait Award is one of the most prestigious art prizes in the UK. The Portrait Award is a highly successful annual art prize aimed at encouraging young painters to focus upon, and develop, the theme of portraiture within their work. Held in the Wolfson Gallery

Off the Beaten Track: Three Centuries of Women Travellers
07/07/2004-31/10/2004
Women travellers of the past three centuries have amazing and varied tales to tell. Some of them were extreme individuals and broke all the rules, while others travelled as dutiful wives, mothers or daughters. This exhibition combines the women's portraits from the National Portrait Gallery's collections with some of their souvenirs. Held in the Porter Gallery

**George Frederic Watts
14/10/2004-09/01/2005
Timed to coincide with the centenary of his death this is the first exhibition to focus on the portrait painting of the great but often forgotten Victorian portrait painter George Frederic Watts. Watts was a central personality of the Victorian era: a friend of Tennyson, the Pre-Raphaelite artists, photographic pioneer Julia Margaret Cameron and, not least, the husband of the actress and muse Ellen Terry. Held in the Wolfson Gallery. Admission: A£7.00 Concessions£4.75

Royal Academy of Arts

Burlington House Piccadilly London W1J 0BD
Tel: 020 7300 8000 Fax: 020 7300 8001
[Tube: Piccadilly Circus / Green Park. Bus: 9 / 14 / 19 / 22 / 38]

The Royal Academy, in the heart of London's West End, is world famous for its exhibition programme. Founded in 1768, the Royal Academy is the oldest fine arts institution in Britain.

All year daily 10.00-18.00, Fri until 22.00

Royal College of Art

Kensington Gore London SW7 2EU
Tel: 020 7590 4444 Fax: 020 7590 4124
[Tube: South Kensington / High Street Kensington. Next to the Royal Albert Hall]

Founded in 1837 the Royal College of Art started life as the Government School of Design. It an exclusively postgraduate institution that has established and maintained a worldwide reputation for work of the highest quality.

All year daily 10.00-18.00 - but dependant on
individual exhibition - call for fuller details
Most exhibitions are free

Saatchi Gallery

County Hall Southbank London SE1 7PB
Tel: 020 7823 2363
*Tube: Waterloo (Northern, Jubilee, Bakerloo,
Waterloo & City)]*

The Gallery exhibits many key pieces from the
Saatchi collection including pieces by Damien
Hirst, Tracey Emin, Sarah Lucas and Jenny
Saville.
All year Sun-Thur 10.00-20.00, Fri-Sat 10.00-22.00
£8.50 Concessions£6.50 Family Ticket £25.00

Serpentine Gallery

Kensington Gardens Kensington London
W2 3XA
Tel: 020 7298 1515 / 7402 6075
Fax: 020 7402 4103
*Tube: Knightsbridge / South Kensington /
Lancaster Gate]*

The Serpentine Gallery, situated in the heart of
Kensington Gardens in a 1934 tea pavilion, was
founded in 1970 by the Arts Council of England.
*All year daily 10.00-18.00. Closed 24-26 Dec, 1
Jan. Bookshop open daily 10.00-18.00*
Admission Free

Sir John Soane's Museum

13 Lincoln's Inn Fields London WC2A 3BP
Tel: 020 7407 2105 Fax: 020 7831 3957
*Tube: Holborn, Central Line, just a short walk to
Museum]*

The house built in 1812 contains Sir John
Soane's splendid collection of antiquities, sculp-
ture, paintings, drawings and books. Disabled
access is limited please call beforehand.
*All year Tue-Sat 10.00-17.00, First Tue of month
18.00-21.00. Closed Sun, Mon Bank Hols.
Please call for Christmas opening times*
Admission free, donations appreciated

Tate Britain

Millbank London SW1P 4RG
Tel: 020 7887 8008 Fax: 020 7887 8007
[Tube: Pimlico]

Tate Britain holds the greatest collection of
British art in the world. It shows British art from
the sixteenth century to the present day in a
dynamic series of new displays and exhibitions.
All year daily 10.00-17.50. Closed 24-26 Dec
Admission Free (excluding special exhibitions)

Tate Modern

Bankside London SE1 9TG
Tel: 020 7887 8008 Fax: 020 7887 8007
[Tube: Southwark/Blackfriars]

Tate Modern is a symbol of London in the 21st
century. It features major works by the most
influential artists of this century including
Picasso, Matisse, Mondrian, Duchamp, Dali,
Bacon, Giacometti, Pollock, Rothko and
Warhol.

*All year Sun-Thur 10.00-18.00, Fri-Sat 10.00-
22.00. Closed 24-26 Dec*

Admission Free, donations welcome. Special
exhibitions may be charged

The Queen's Gallery at Buckingham Palace

Buckingham Palace Buckingham Palace Road London SW1A 1AA
Tel: 020 7321 2233 Fax: 020 7930 9625
[Tube: Green Park / St James' Park / Victoria]

The Queen's Gallery is a permanent space dedicated to changing exhibitions of items from the Royal Collection, the wide-ranging collection of art and treasures held in trust by The Queen for the Nation.
All year daily 10.00-17.30 on timed ticket. Closed 8-25 Mar, 9 Apr, 25-26 Dec
A£4.50 C£2.00 Concessions£3.50 Family Ticket (A2+C3) £11.00

Victoria and Albert Museum

Cromwell Road South Kensington London SW7 2RL

Tel: 020 7942 2000

www.vam.ac.uk

[Tube: South Kensington. There are two car parks in the area, charges vary, limited meter parking]

The Victoria and Albert Museum holds one of the world's largest and most diverse collections of decorative arts. 146 galleries contain unrivalled collections dating from 3,000 BC to the present day. Furniture, fashion, textiles, paintings, silver, glass, ceramics, sculpture, jeweller books, prints and photographs illustrate the artistic life of many different cultures from around the world. Superb highlights for any vis should include: the V&A's collection of Italian Renaissance sculpture, the largest outside Italy, the superb Photography gallery; the Dress gallery, covering over four hundred years of European fashionable dress from the mid-16th century to the present day; and the British Galleries 1500-1900, telling the story of British design from the Tudor period to the Victorian age. Free family activities on selected days. Guided tours, disabled access, shop, restaurant, Friends society, galleries and rooms available for hire.

All year daily 10.00-17.45, Wed and the last Fri of the month 10.00-22.00. Closed 24-26 Dec

Admission Free. Some exhibitions and events may carry a separate charge

Special Events

Ossie Clark
01/07/2003-02/05/2004
This mini-retrospective will celebrate the work of Ossie Clark, covering the years from 1965 to 1974 when his designs defined the high style of 1960s London and help establish London as the centre of the fashion world. It will trace the designer's influence from the 1960s to today when his influence can still be seen in recent collections by Prada, Gucci and Stella McCartney

Brilliant
12/02/2004-25/04/2004
The first UK exhibition of the best in contemporary lighting, Brilliant will focus on creative and innovative uses of light through a display of domestic lighting, new experiments in light objects and previously unseen prototypes by designers such as Todd Boontje, Sharon Marston and Catellani & Smith

Bill Brandt: A Centenary Retrospective
24/03/2004-25/07/2004
The V&A will celebrate the centenary of the birth of Bill Brandt (1904-83), Britain's best loved photographer of modern times, with a major exhibition and an international conference. The exhibition presents 155 vintage gelatin-silver prints from the Bill Brandt Archive and is the most important Brandt exhibition for over 30 years. Brandt's best

own work documents the vivid social contrasts
Britain during the World Wars

vienne Westwood: A Retrospective
/04/2004-11/07/2004

he first major retrospective of Vivienne
estwood, one of the most influential designers
the last 30 years. The exhibition will feature
ore than 150 ensembles mainly selected from
e V&A's collection and Vivienne Westwood's
ersonal archive. Items on show will range from
arly examples of her work including provocative
unk clothing worn by members of the Sex
stols and outfits that have been inspired by
ritishness

hhh!!...
/05/2004-01/08/2004

hhh!!... is a journey through the V&A, featuring
ew music by an eclectic mix of leading musi-
ans and artists who have created works inspired
the objects and spaces in the museum. Pick
your headphones and follow an invisible trail of
ounds through the galleries of the V&A. Shhh!!...
accompanied by an exhibition of sounds and
ages in the V&A's Contemporary Space

hristopher Dresser
6/09/2004-05/12/2004

hristopher Dresser (1834-1904) is considered
e first independent industrial designer, running a
udio supplying designs to manufacturers includ-
g Wedgwood, Minton and Coalbrookdale. This
xhibition will examine Dresser's career with
xamples of silver, metalwork, furniture, ceramics,
xtiles, wallpaper and watercolours on display.
lease call to confirm dates

xotic Encounters: The Meeting of Asia and
urope 1500-1800
3/09/2004-05/12/2004

xotic will explore three hundred years of artistic,
ultural and technolgical interaction and exchange
etween Asia and Europe. The exhibition will
how how East and West have always been fas-
nated with each other, and that the desire for
e appeal of the exotic has shaped the material
ulture of both

ternational Arts and Crafts
1/03/2005-01/07/2005

xhibition due to run from Mar-July, specific dates
be confirmed. This exhibition sets out the story
the Arts and Crafts Movement which laid the
undation for approaches to design in the 20th
entury. It will be the first exhibition to trace the
ovement's global progress from its origins in
ritain to subsequent widespread international
doption and development

White Cube

48 Hoxton Square London N1 6PB

Tel: 020 7930 5373 Fax: 020 7749 7480

[Tube: Hoxton, Old Street Underground]

White Cube was set up by Jay Jopling in 1993
as a project room in Duke Street St James's for
contemporary art. It was possibly the smallest
exhibition space in Europe, yet arguably one of
the most influential galleries of the past decade.
Tues-Sat 10.00-18.00
Admission free

William Morris Gallery

Lloyd Park Forest Road Walthamstow London E17 4PP

Tel: 020 8527 3782 Fax: 020 8527 7070

[Tube: Walthamstow Central or Blackhorse Road then Bus 123 direct to Lloyd Park]

The world's only museum devoted to William Morris, the great Victorian artist-craftsman, is located in his family home (built 1740s). Newly designed displays show the whole range of Morris's work.
All year Tue-Sat and 1st Sun in each month 10.00-13.00 & 14.00-17.00. Closed Mon & Bank Hol. Phone for details of Christmas & New Year opening

Admission Free

Caverns & Caves

Chislehurst Caves

Old Hill Chislehurst Kent BR7 5NB

Tel: 020 8467 3264 Fax: 020 8295 0407

www.chislehurstcaves.co.uk

[A222 between A20 & A21, at Chislehurst railway bridge, turn into Station Road then R & R again into Caveside Close. Bus: Bromley 269, 726. Rail: Charing Cross to Chislehurst, Caves are around corner from the station and entrance off Caveside Close near the Olde Stationmaster Pub. Plenty of on site parking]

Miles of mystery and history beneath your feet! Grab a lantern and get ready for an amazing underground adventure. At Chislehurst Caves your whole family can travel back in time as you explore the labyrinth of dark mysterious pas-

sageways which have been hewn by hand from the chalk cliff deep beneath Chislehurst. Accompanied by an experienced guide on a 45 minute tour you will learn of the Druids, Roman and Saxons who used the caves, as well as the more recent history of this underground maze. In the 1950s and 60s, a series of concerts were held here and during World War Two they became the largest air raid shelter outside London. Included in the tours, which run on the hour, are visits to the Caves Church, the Druid Altar, the Haunted Pool and much more! The caves should hold the imagination of even the most easily-bored child and if nothing else, there are almost 20 miles of tunnels to wear them out!
All year Wed-Sun, tours run hourly 10.00-16.00. Open daily during school holidays except Christmas and New Year

45 Minute Tour A£4.00 C&OAPs£2.00

Discount Offer: One Free Admission When A Second Admission Of Equal Or Greater Value Is Purchased

Costume & Jewellery Museums

Fan Museum

12 Crooms Hill Greenwich London SE10 8ER

Tel: 020 8305 1441 Fax: 020 8293 1889

www.fan-museum.org

[Rail: Greenwich opposite Greenwich Theatre. DLR: Cutty Sark Maritime Greenwich]

The world's only Fan Museum with its unsurpassed collections of more than 3,000 fans dating from the 11th century is housed in

eautifully restored listed Georgian houses.
:hanging exhibitions, shop, workshop, study
acilities. Orangery and landscaped garden.
:pecial tours and private functions. Fan making
lasses. Refreshments available by prior
rrangement. Exhibitions are listed within the
pecial events section, you can contact the
Museum for further details on the above num-
er.

ll year Tue-Sat 11.00-17.00, Sun 12.00-17.00.
Refreshments available Tue & Sun

£3.50 Concessions£2.50

Special Events

ncient Myths and Legends
6/01/2004-09/05/2004
*n exhibition of very fine early European fans that
how, by subject, the influence of antiquity and
he classical tradition on European fan painters,
makers and collectors of the 17th, 18th and 19th
enturies. The exhibition of over 60 fans and fan
eaves drawn from the Museum's own collections
xamines the survival of classical imagery in this
decorative art. Scenes from the lives of the Gods,
he Trojan War, the Heroes and Women in ancient
mes are all surveyed and explained*

 Garden of Fans
1/05/2004-19/09/2004
*n exhibition celebrating the Year of Gardening.
This exhibition explores the representations of
lowers on fans from the 17th century to the present. The fans in this exhibition will include fans
rom China and Japan as well as those of many
other countries*

Festivals & Shows

Chelsea Flower Show

Royal Hospital Chelsea London SW3
Tel: 0870 906 3781
*[Rail: Victoria then shuttle bus. Tube: Sloane
Square (on the District and Circle lines) 10min
walk from the Showground]*

The Chelsea Flower Show is the world's most
popular and renowned flower show. The best in
gardening and horticulture is brought together in
one place for four days in May. A floral and gardening feast for all, there are over 600 exhibitors
in total and there are 64 gardens in all shapes,
sizes and styles. Children under 5 and babes in

arms are not admitted to the showground for
reasons of safety.
*May 25-28 2004. Show closes at 17.30 on final
day*
Prices vary, please call for details

**City and Guilds of London Art
School 2004**

124 Kennington Park Road London SE11 4DJ
Tel: 020 7735 2306 Fax: 020 7582 5361
[Tube: Kennington]

Graduate Show for painting, sculpture, conser-
vation studies, decorative arts, stone and wood
carving and gilding. MA Fine Art Show for paint-
ing and sculpture. Work for sale.
*Graduate Show: June 23-27 2004 (tbc). MA Fine
Art Show: September 8-12 2004 10.00-19.30
Thur-Fri 10.00-17.00 Sat-Sun*
Admission Free

City of London Festival

Office: Bishopsgate Hall 230 Bishopsgate
London EC2M4HW
Tel: 020 7377 0540 Fax: 020 7377 1972
*[Numerous venues and open spaces in the City,
all of which are within easy walking distance of
London Underground, mainline stations and bus
routes]*

Set against the magnificent architecture of
London's 'Square Mile', using a Trading Places
theme to explore the cultural exchange between
London and Johannesburg. Reflecting the daily
commercial activity throughout history between
the City and its global counterparts, South
African musicians, dancers and visual artists will
join with British and American performers,
appearing throughout the Festival in a combined
celebration of the arts. A programme of world-
class arts events in the City's finest buildings
and green and/or open spaces. The festival features the extraordinary talents of many artists
and offers artistic excellence, diversity and cultural richness. Please call the Festival office and
ask to be added to free mailing list for full details
of this year's festival.

June 21-July 23 2004. Lunchtime, rush-hour, evening and weekend events

Prices vary according to event, some events are £Free. Tickets available from Barbican Box Office (booking fee applies): tel 020 7638 8891, 09.00-20.00 daily (from 12.00 Sun), fax 020 7382 7270

Coin Street Festival

South Bank London SE1
Tel: 020 7928 0960 Fax: 020 7928 2927
[Rail: Blackfriars/ Waterloo East/ Waterloo/ Charing Cross. Tube: Blackfriars/ Waterloo/ Southwark/ Embankme.]

Welcome to the 2004 Coin Street Festival, with summer events and activities to delight and entertain. Each year we raise money and work with different partners to put on the free events that make up the Coin Street Festival. A variety of events will be programmed, including the festival favourite - Celebrating Sanctuary and Community Celebration.
May-July 2004
Admission Free

Flora London Marathon

Greenwich London SE1 8RZ
Tel: 020 7902 0199
[Starting points: Charlton Road, St John's Park, Shooters Hill Road. All competitors join up after 3m]

On Sunday, 18 April, the eyes of the world will be on 26.2 miles of Londons streets to watch around 30,000 people take part in the 2004 Flora London Marathon. The race's international status comes from its success in combining elite sport with human endeavour and spirit - there is something for everyone to enjoy whether running or viewing - it's truly the 'people's race'. The Flora London Marathon is also world renowned for its success as a charity fundraising event - tens of thousands of runners raise sponsorship for charities of their choice, making their efforts count for worthy causes. The Flora London Wheelchair Marathon - is a race organised by the Flora London Marathon in close collaboration with a Flora London

Wheelchair Marathon committee and is open to disabled athletes. Many of the world's best wheelchair athletes travel to London to compete.
April 18 2004
Admission Free

Grosvenor House Art and Antiques Fair

Le Meridien Grosvenor House Park Lane London W1K 7TN
Tel: 020 7399 8100 Fax: 020 7495 8747
[NCP Car Park opposite Grosvenor House. Buses 2 10 16 36 73 74 82 137 137A. Underground Marble Arch, Hyde Park Corner, Green Park. Train, Eurostar from Paris to Waterloo]

Some of the top dealers from all over the world to exhibit £300million of the very finest art and antiques. Anything from antiquities to modern art, pieces are vetted by 140 specialists with prices ranging from a few hundred to over £1million.
June 9-15. June 9 & 11: 11.00-20.00; June 10, 12-15: 11.00-18.00. Charity Gala in aid of Cancer Relief Macmillian Fund: June 10 19.00-21.00.
A£16.00 for 2A£27.00. Each ticket includes or copy of the Fair Handbook

London Bach Festival

London NW1 5HT
Tel: 01883 717372 Fax: 01883 715851
The London Bach Festival was founded in 199 in order to develop the work of the London Bach Society and create a platform for Bach scholars, players and singers, to gather together for an annual autumn series of events. The programmes attempt to convey the life of J S Bach, his antecedents, contemporaries and descendants, with the music performed in period settings and using resources with which Bach himself would have been familiar. Programmes will be available from September.
October 31-November 10 2004
Prices vary according to event

London Comedy Festival

Tel: 08700 119 611 Fax: 08700 111 970

The London Comedy Festival is a city wide celebration of London's stature as the Comedy Capital of the world and is Europe's fastest growing festival! Bringing together many genres of comedy and humour it also encourages new talent and broad community participation. The festival features a diverse programme of events from prestige events in locations such as Trafalgar Square and Covent Garden to stand-up, classic comedy, film and cabaret. There are events for newcomers and young people, and a series of events celebrating London's rich cultural diversity. As well as driving comedy into schools, libraries and the workplace and onto the streets, the festival will be spread over 300 events at theatres, cinemas, parks and comedy clubs as well as some of London's most recognisable landmarks.
May 13-23 2004
Prices vary according to event

London Lesbian and Gay Film Festival

National Film Centre South Bank London SE1 8XT
Tel: 020 7928 3232
[Tube: Waterloo and Embankment]

The National Film Theatre plays host to this key event in the gay calendar. The LLGFF is an annual festival showcasing over 50 features as well as a wide selection of short films.
March 24-April 7 2004

Mayor's Thames Festival

The Barge House Barge House Street South Bank London SE1 9PH
Tel: 020 7928 8998 Fax: 020 7928 2927
[Advisable to park and ride in via the Underground or take the bus]

The Mayor's Thames Festival is a large-scale, free celebration on and around the Thames between Westminster and Blackfriars Bridges. Its programme of high profile, innovative and entertaining events includes a night procession, fireworks display, participatory activities, creative and river orientated events. This programme hopes to challenge and provoke changes to the public's relationship to the river Thames. The festival arranges for Victoria Embankment to be closed for traffic and for the South Bank riverside walkway to be transformed with food and craft stalls, funfair rides, street theatre and other animations.
September 18-19 2004, 12.00-22.00
Admission £Free

Meltdown 2004

Various venues on the South Bank London
Tel: 020 7960 4242
[Royal Festival Hall, Queen Elizabeth Hall, Purcell Room]

Meltdown is the South Bank's highest profile, most popular festival. Each year a guest director is invited to programme two weeks of performances that reflect their diverse cultural interests and tastes.
June 8-30 2004, please call for specific dates

Ricky Week

Bury Grounds Bury Lane Rickmansworth WD3
Tel: 01923 772325
[J18 M25, follow signs to Rickmansworth A412 / A404. Rail: Metropolitan line to Rickmansworth]

Ricky Week started in 1954 and has been celebrated each year since then. It enables societies/clubs to stage events to boost their funds and give to charity. The Canal Festival is very popular.
May 8-15 2004
Various ticket prices dependent on event

Folk & Local History Museums

Bromley Museum and Priory Gardens

The Priory Church Hill Orpington BR6 0HH

Tel: 01689 873826

www.bromley.gov.uk/museums

[J4 M25, A224. Off Orpington High Street. Rail: Orpington. Bus: 51, 61, 208, 353. Limited on site parking]

The museum is housed in an impressive medieval / post medieval building set in attractive gardens. Find out about the archaeology of the London Borough of Bromley. Learn about Sir John Lubbock, 1st Lord Avebury, the eminent Victorian responsible for giving this country its Bank Holidays. Visit 'Your Place', a new, exciting interactive area for families to enjoy. Guided tours by arrangement. Throughout the year there are changing exhibitions by the Museum and local groups. Gardens and ground floor of museum only is suitable for wheelchairs. For details of events and exhibitions, call the venue.

Bromley Museum: All year Mon-Fri 13.00-17.00, Sat 10.00-17.00. 1 Apr-31 Oct Sun 13.00-17.00, Bank Hol 13.00-17.00 Mornings Mon-Fri for educational purposes only. Priory Gardens: All year Mon-Fri 07.30-dusk, Sat Sun & Bank Hol 09.00-dusk

Admission Free

Honeywood Heritage Centre

Honeywood Walk Carshalton Surrey SM5 3NX
Tel: 020 8770 4297 Fax: 020 8770 4777
[By Carshalton Ponds off A232. Rail: Carshalton. Bus: 157, 407, 726]

The history of the borough and its people plus programme of exhibitions, presented in a 17th century listed building. Features include Edwardian Billiard Room, Tudor Gallery and Art Gallery. Pushchair access to Ground Floor only.
All year Wed-Fri 11.00-17.00, Sat Sun & Bank Hol Mon 10.00-17.00
A£1.20 £0.60

Food & Drink

The Clay Café

8-12 Monkville Parade Temple Fortune London NW11 0AL

Tel: 020 8905 5353 Fax: 020 8201 8656

www.theclaycafe.co.uk

[Tube: Golders Green, Finchley Central. Bus: 82, 260]

A combined creative art studio and restaurant under one roof. Come in and choose a piece of blank pottery from our extensive collection starting from £1.00. Now paint it... we fire it in our kiln and you may return to collect it a few days later. We cater for birthday parties and school outings too!

All year Mon-Fri 11.00-22.00, Sat 10.00-23.00, Sun 11.00-22.00. During School Holidays from 10.00

Pottery cost: from £1.00 + studio fee A£4.75 C£3.50. Children's Menu: £3.95 incl desert and drink. Adult Meals: for 2 approx £10.00-£12.00

or 4 approx £20.00-£24.00, for 6 approx
£30.00-£36.00 excl drinks

tive to the usual London visits, the Vinopolis
wine tasting packages offer exceptional value
for money. Boasting an on-site restaurant,
Cantina Vinopolis and Wine Wharf wine bar,
Vinopolis offers the ultimate afternoon or
evening out for individuals or groups daring to
do something a little different. Why not plan a
trip to remember and come to Vinopolis?

*All year Mon 12.00-21.00, Tue-Thur 12.00-
18.00, Fri-Sat 12.00-21.00, Sun 12.00-18.00.
For December and Bank Hol opening times
please call 0870 241 4040*

Tue-Thur A£11.00 C(5-15)£Free OAPs£10.00,
Fri-Mon A£12.50 C£Free OAPs£11.50. Please
note, no person under 18 is allowed to con-
sume alcohol

**Discount Offer: £2.50 Off For Up To
Four Guests.**

Vinopolis, City of Wine

1 Bank End London SE1 9BU

Tel: 0870 780 6782 Fax: 020 7940 8302

www.vinopolis.co.uk

*[On Bankside, between Southwark Cathedral and
Shakespeare's Globe. 5 mins walk from London
Bridge. Rail: London Bridge. Tube: London Bridge
(Northern & Jubilee lines). Bus: 17, 21, 35, 40,
43, 48, 133, 149, 343, 344, 501, 521, P3]*

Located in the vibrant Bankside area of London,
close to Borough Market, Vinopolis is the only
visitor attraction dedicated to good food and
drink. Armed with your audio guide, enjoy a luxurious regional tour of tastes, with five wine
tastings to enjoy along the way. The opening of
the Bombay Sapphire Experience at Vinopolis
means that a fabulous cocktail prepared by our
mixologist is also included in the price. For
groups of 15 or more, Vinopolis offer a selection
of exclusive private wine tastings. Prices start
from £25.00 for an Introduction to Wine, including 6 wines. Offering an interactive, fun alterna-

Gardens & Horticulture

Morden Hall Park

Morden Hall Road Morden London SM4 5JD

Tel: 020 8545 6850 Fax: 020 8687 0094

*[Off A24 and A297 S of Wimbledon, N of Sutton.
Tube: Morden. Tramlink: Phipps Bridge]*

A green oasis in the heart of London suburbia,
this former deer park has an extensive network
of waterways, ancient hay meadows, an
impressive avenue of trees and an interesting
collection of old estate buildings.

*Park only open all year in daylight hours. Please
note, the car park by the cafe/shop and garden
centre closes at 18.00*

Admission Free

Museum of Garden History

St-Mary-at-Lambeth Lambeth Palace Road
Lambeth London SE1 7LB

Tel: 020 7401 8865 Fax: 020 7401 8869

www.museumgardenhistory.org

[Located on the south side of the River Thames, next to Lambeth Palace, almost opposite the Houses of Parliament at the southeast end of Lambeth Bridge. Bus: 3/344/C10 to Lambeth Road & 507/77 to Lambeth Palace Road (507 weekdays only) Rail: Victoria/Waterloo then Bus 507 Mon-Fri. 15 min walk from Waterloo Tube: Lambeth North (Bakerloo)/Westminster (District, Circle & Jubilee)/Vauxhall (Victoria)]

The Museum of Garden History is in the former Parish Church of St Mary at Lambeth, now a listed building. It was the world's first Museum dedicated to garden history. Tombs of the John Tradescants, elder and younger, the royal gardeners to Charles I and II, and Captain Bligh of the Bounty can be found in the grounds, along with a 17th Century-style knot garden which provides a peaceful haven, full of plants that can be traced back to that period. Within the Museum there are displays illustrating the history of the Tradescants and plant hunting, and the development of garden design alongside a fine collection of historic garden tools and curiosities, and seasonal exhibitions. Lectures, concerts, fairs and art exhibitions are regularly held throughout the year. Guided tours by appointment and photography allowed with permission. Café and shop.

Mid Mar-mid Dec daily 10.30-17.00

Voluntary donations requested, A£3.00
Concessions£2.50

Special Events

Annual Spring Plants And Gardens Fair
25/04/2004
The Fair transforms the Museum again into a 'plantaholic's' dreamland, filled with plants displayed and sold by leading specialist nurseries, many offering rare and unusual plants. Time: 10.30-17.00. Cost: A£3.00 C£Free Concessions£2.50

Spring Lecture
05/05/2004
David Howard, head gardener at Highgrove House, will give an insight into the working life of head gardener on a large estate, with a particula focus on maintaining the organic nature of Highgrove. Time: 18.30 for 19.00 Cost: £10.00 (Friends £5.00)

Ashmole And The Ark
19/05/2004
A play by Priscilla Waugh, 'Ashmole and the Ark' centres on the elderly Elias Ashmole, in poor health, preparing a speech for the opening of the Ashmole Museum of Oxford University. Time: 17.30 & 19.30 Cost: £5.00

National Gardens Scheme Opening
05/06/2004
The 2004 date had been selected to coincide with the opening of the neighbouring Lambeth Palace Gardens under the same scheme so visitors can see both venues on one day. Entrance to the Museum garden also includes access to the Museum, café and shop. Time: 10.30-17.00 Cost: A£3.00 C£Free Concessions £2.50

London Squares Weekend
12/06/2004-13/06/2004
The Museum will be open as part of London Squares Weekend. Visitors will be able to purchase a £5.00 pass for all participating gardens from the Museum on the day. Time: 10.30-17.00

Contemporary Art Exhibition: The Head Gardene
01/07/2004-31/08/2004
The fourth annual summer art exhibition organise by Danielle Arnaud. Artists will collaborate with head gardeners, horticulturists and botanists to create new work reflecting the many and varied roles and responsibilities present in the creation and maintenance of British gardens. Time: 10.30 17.00 Cost: Suggested donation £3.00 Concessions £2.50

Head Gardener Symposium
14/07/2004
To be confirmed. The Museum's summer event I a Symposium, led by Chris Beardshaw. This yea it will focus on the historic and contemporary role

...f the head gardener and their team. *Time: 18.00
or 18.30 Cost: £15.00 (Friends £10.00)*

Autumn Lecture
06/10/2004
*A lecture by Mike Nelhams, garden curator at
Tresco Abby Gardens in the Isles of Scilly. Mike
will speak about his work and explain how he bal-
ances the demands of caring for a historic garden
whilst at the same time ensuring it moves forward
into the 21st century. Time: 18.30 for 19.00 Cost:
£10.00 (Friends £5.00)*

Christmas Lecture
01/12/2004
*Steven Crisp is the head gardener of the USA
Ambassador's residence in Regent's Park,
Winfield House. The illustrated lecture will provide
ideas and inspiration for those looking to use
fresh material from the garden in Christmas decorations. Time: 18.30 for 19.00. Tickets: £10.00
(Friends £5.00)*

Royal Botanic Gardens, Kew
Kew Richmond Surrey TW9 3AB

Tel: 020 8332 5655

www.kew.org

[Tube: Kew Gardens. Rail: Kew Bridge]

Kew Gardens is paradise throughout the season. The world famous visitor attraction houses
more than 40,000 different kinds of plants in the
121 riverside hectares. Lose yourself in the
magnificent conservatories, explore the tropics
and sub-tropics and discover plants from the
world's deserts, mountains and oceans. Wide-
open spaces, stunning vistas, listed buildings
and wildlife contribute to the Garden's unique
atmosphere. Children's activities, themed displays and festivals take place throughout the
year. To make your visit even more enjoyable,
there are great places to eat and shop, for
example eating in the delightful surroundings of
the listed Orangery.

*All year daily, Garden: from 09.30 closing times
vary according to season, from 16.00 in Winter
up to 19.30 in Summer. Conservatories close
earlier. Closed 24 & 25 Dec. Open 1 Jan*

A£7.50 C(under16)£Free Concessions£5.50

Discount Offer: 2 Adults For £11.00

Special Events

Being in Place by Judith Cain
20/03/2004-09/05/2004
*Leeds artist Judith Cain presents twenty large
scale paintings inspired by her travels in Europe
and Central Asia. Her contemporary style conveys
the overwhelming beauty of the natural landscape
and wild flora, in sharp contract to the dereliction
and decay left over from the Soviet Era*

Spring to Life at Kew
20/03/2004-09/05/2004
*Against a background of stately trees with their
new fresh leaves, two and a half million bulbs
burst into flower from February through to May*

Easter Activities
03/04/2004-18/04/2004
*The cuddly stars of Miller's Ark Animal Farm return
to Kew this Easter. Miniature donkeys, Shetland
ponies, chicks, baby rabbits and guinea pigs are
waiting to be stroked, groomed, and bottle-fed by
visitors. Storytellers weave magical tales of spring
folklore in daily sessions. On Easter Sun & Mon
the annual Easter Egg hunt takes place. Visitors
can also book a special Easter lunch*

Bluebell Weekends
24/04/2004-09/05/2004
*24 Apr & 8 May - regular walks through some of
the most beautiful bluebells in Sussex and a
chance to see wild spring flowers, ending at the
Parterre beds outside the Wellcome Trust
Millennium Building. 25 Apr & 9 May - minibus
tours of the bluebell areas*

May Bank Holiday - Woodland Wonders
01/05/2004-03/05/2004

A host of traditional woodland skills including willow weaving, basket and broom making, coracle making and charcoal burning are all demonstrated by skilled craftspeople. Morris dancers, storytelling and a 30metre 'zip line' between the trees keep younger visitors entertained. Huge working horses, birds of prey, traditional tools, spinning, weaving and chainsaw sculpture all illustrate the rich diversity of woodland skills that still survive in Britain today

New Views
29/05/2004-26/09/2004

Four month long summer festival with special displays, exhibits and family activities focused on new ways of looking at Kew and the historic landscape. Plus the GWG Garden Photographers are holding a major photographic exhibition of stunning plant and landscape images taken in Kew

Autumn Cornucopia
09/10/2004-31/10/2004

Kew's majestic trees come into their own in October when the leaves change to vivid hues of oranges, reds and yellows. Around the gardens, autumnal fruits and fungi abound, and the season is complemented by colourful displays of harvest produce, identification sessions and autumn walks

Making Spirits Bright
27/11/2004-02/01/2005

Visitors to Kew Gardens at Christmas time step into a magical world of twinkling lights and festive decorations, a million miles away from the frantic hustle and bustle elsewhere. As dusk falls, the Gardens transform into a shimmering scene of coloured illuminations. The willow tree glitters with 30,000 white lights that drip delicately over the water's surface. A carousel, music and Father Christmas provide traditional family entertainment throughout the festivities. Late night openings offer the chance to shop amid the magical setting of the Gardens at night

Guided Tours

BBC TOURS

BBC Television Centre Tours

BBC Television Centre Wood Lane London W12 7RJ

Tel: 0870 60 30 304 Booking
Fax: 020 8576 7466

www.bbc.co.uk/tours

[Tube: White City (Central Line). Bus: 72, 95, 22 all stop opposite Television Centre. There is a public car park for cars and coaches on Ariel Way]

On a tour of London's BBC Television Centre, you will see behind the scenes of the most famous TV centre in the world. Winner of the Group Travel Awards 'Best Guided Tour Experience' 2003, you may experience areas such as the News Centre, Weather Centre, dressing rooms and studios. Television Centre a working building so we plan your exact itinerary around what is happening on the day, therefore no two tours are ever the same. Please note that visitors must be 9 years and over and tours must be pre-booked. Television Centre is a large complex and tours involve a l of walking.

Tours run regularly throughout the week. Please call for further details.

A£7.95 C(over10)&Students£5.95 Concessions£6.95 Family Ticket £21.95. Grou rates (15+): A£6.95 C&Students£4.95 Concessions£5.95 School Group (under 16 years)£3.50. Please note, the maximum numbe on each tour is 22 people. Pre-booking essential, please state Television Centre when booking

Historical

Apsley House, Wellington Museum

Hyde Park Corner 149 Piccadilly London W1J 7NT

Tel: 020 7499 5676 Fax: 020 7493 6576

www.apsleyhouse.org.uk

Tube: Hyde Park Corner]

Apsley House (No. 1 London) was home to the great 'Iron' Duke of Wellington and contains his magnificent art collection. See outstanding paintings by Velazquez, Goya and Rubens as well as porcelain, silver and sculpture.
All year Tue-Sun & Bank Hol Mon 11.00-17.00. Closed Good Fri, May Day, 24-26 Dec & 1 Jan. Current arrangements may be subject to change from 1 April 2004, please contact us on 020 7499 5676 before you visit
A£4.50 Concessions£3.00, price includes sound guide, C(under18)£Free OAPS£Free. Pre-booked Group rates £2.50

Discount Offer: Two For The Price Of One

Carshalton House

St Philomena's School Pound Street Carshalton Surrey SM5 3PN
Tel: 020 8770 4781 Fax: 020 8770 4777
[A232 at J with B278, Carshalton Road Bus: 154, 157, 407, 726]

A mansion built around 1707 with grounds laid out originally by Charles Bridgeman. The principal rooms contain 18th century decoration and garden buildings include a Hermitage and unique Water Tower, with Delft-tiled plunge bath.
Open on limited occasions during Spring & Summer. Please call for details. Water Tower only open Easter-end Sept Sun 14.30-17.00
A£3.50 C£2.00

Dennis Severs House

18 Folgate Street London E1 6BX
Tel: 020 7247 4013
[Tube/Rail: Liverpool Street]

The house is a time capsule - sometimes opened. Its owner, Dennis Severs, was an artist who used his visitor's imagination as his canvas, and who lived in the house in much the same way today as its original occupants might have done in the early 18th century. The Experience, conducted in silence, titled by Mr Severs as 'Still-life Drama' enables the visitor to become lost in another time as they appear to be on their own.
All year, 1st & 3rd Sun of each month 14.00-17.00 & Mons following these days between 12.00-14.00 & Mon evenings, times vary. Booking essential for Mon evening visit, not for others
Sunday tour: A£8.00, Mon Afternoon Tour: £5.00, Mon Evening Tour: £12.00

Eastbury Manor House

Eastbury Square Barking Essex IG11 9SN
Tel: 020 8724 1000 Fax: 020 8724 1003
[In Eastbury Square 10mins walk S from Upney station. Rail: Barking then one stop on Tube: District Line to Upney. Bus: LT 287, 368 Barking-Rainham / Chadwell Heath]

An important example of a medium-sized brick-built Elizabethan manor house. The house is architecturally distinguished and well preserved. Recent restoration has revealed notable wall paintings.
Mar-Dec 1st & 2nd Sat in every month 10.00-16.00, and 2 Feb-21 Dec Mon-Tue 10.00-16.00
A£2.50 C£0.65 Concessions£1.25 Family Ticket £5.00

Fenton House

Windmill Hill Hampstead London NW3 6RT
Tel: 020 7435 3471 Fax: 020 7435 3471
*[Visitors' entrance on W side of Hampstead
Grove. Tube: Hampstead 300yds. Rail:
Hampstead Heath 1m]*

A delightful late 17th century merchant's house,
set on the winding streets of Old Hampstead.
The charming interior contains an outstanding
collection of porcelain, needlework and furniture. Fenton is set in walled gardens, with formal lawn and walks, an orchard and vegetable
garden.
*1-30 Mar Weekends only 14.00-17.00, 3 Apr-31
Oct Wed-Fri 14.00-17.00, Sat-Sun & Bank Hol
Mon 11.00-17.00*
A£4.60 C£2.30 Family Ticket £11.50

Freud Museum

20 Maresfield Gardens Hampstead London
NW3 5SX

**Tel: 020 7435 2002 / 7435 5167
Fax: 020 7431 5452**

www.freud.org.uk

[Tube: Finchley Road]

Sigmund Freud left his home in Vienna (1938)
as a refugee from Nazi occupation and chose
exile in England, transferring his entire domesti
and working environment to this house. He
resumed work until his death a year later.
Bequeathed by his daughter Anna Freud whos
pioneering development of her father's work is
also represented. Freud's collections include:
Egyptian, Greek, Roman, and Oriental antiquities, plus fine Oriental rugs. The household con
tains Biedermeier furniture. Educational visits fo
pre-booked groups.

*All year Wed-Sun 12.00-17.00. Closed Bank Ho
24-26 Dec*

A£5.00 C(0-12)£Free C(12-
18)&Concessions£2.00

Geffrye Museum

Kingsland Road London E2 8EA
Tel: 020 7739 9893 Fax: 020 7729 5647
*[Tube: Liverpool Street then bus 149 or 242 / O
Street (exit 2), then bus 243, situated on A10
Kingsland Road]*

One of London's most friendly and enjoyable
museums, the Geffrye specialises in the dome
tic interiors of the urban middle class. Its displays span from 1600 to 2000, forming a
sequence of period rooms.
*All year Tue-Sat 10.00-17.00, Sun & Bank Hol
Mon 12.00-17.00. Closed Mon, Good Fri, 24-2
31 Dec & 1 Jan*
Admission Free

Horse Guards

Whitehall London SW1
Tel: 0891 505452
[Tube: Westminster]

Once Henry VIII's tiltyard (tournament ground),
the 'Changing of The Queen's Life Guard' still
takes place here every day. The elegant build-

…gs, completed in 1755, were designed by …illiam Kent.
…hanging of The Queen's Life Guard' & …ismounting Ceremonies: All year daily
…dmission Free

…indsay House

…00 Cheyne Walk London SW10 0DQ
el: 020 7447 6605
…V of Battersea Bridge near J with Milman's …treet on Chelsea Embankment. Tube: South …ensington. Rail: Victoria]

…art of Lindsay House was built in 1674 on the …te of Sir Thomas More's garden, overlooking …e River Thames. It has one of the finest 17th …entury exteriors in London. Nearest parking …attersea Park. Inaccessible to wheelchairs.
…round floor entrance hall & garden room, main …aircase to first floor and the front and rear gar-…ens by written appointment only on the following …ates: 12 May, 16 June, 8 Sept & 6 Oct 14.00-…6.00
…dmission Free

…useum of Fulham Palace

…ishops Avenue London SW6 6EA
el: 020 7736 3233 Fax: 020 7736 3233
…ube: Putney Bridge. Bus: 14, 22, 74, 220, 414, …30]

…he former residence of the Bishop of London …udor with Georgian additions and a Victorian …napel). The museum (in part of the Palace) tells …e story of this ancient site. The displays …clude paintings, archaeology, garden history …nd architecture.
…rounds, Botanic Garden and herb collection: …aily during daylight hours. Museum: Mar-Oct …ed-Sun 14.00-17.00, Nov-Feb Thur-Sun …3.00-16.00
…dmission Free. Guided Tours of Palace and …rounds: £4.00

Queen's House

Romney Road Greenwich London SE10 9NF

Tel: 020 8858 4422 Fax: 020 8312 6632

www.nmm.ac.uk

[J2 M25 then A2 and A206, follow signposts into central Greenwich. Rail: Greenwich. DLR: Cutty Sark]

The first Palladian-style villa in England, designed by Inigo Jones for Anne of Denmark and completed for Queen Henrietta Maria, wife of Charles I. Includes a loggia overlooking Greenwich Park. Now the home of the fine art collection of the National Maritime Museum with additional displays on historic Greenwich.

All year daily 10.00-17.00. Closed 13 Apr-4 June 2004, 24-26 Dec

Admission Free

Rainham Hall

The Broadway Rainham Essex RM13 9YN
Tel: 020 7447 6605
[Just S of the church, 5m E of Barking. Rail: Rainham]

An elegant Georgian house, built in 1729 to a symmetrical plan and with fine wrought iron gates, carved porch and interior panelling and plasterwork.
Apr-end Oct Wed & Bank Hol Mons 14.00-18.00. Sat by written appointment with tenant
A£2.20 C£1.10 Family Ticket £5.50

Shakespeare's Globe Theatre Tour and Exhibition

21 New Globe Walk Bankside London SE1 9DT

Tel: 020 7902 1500 Fax: 020 7902 1515

www.shakespeares-globe.org

[Tube: London Bridge / Mansion House / Southwark / St Paul's]

The largest exhibition of its kind devoted to the world of Shakespeare, from Elizabethan times to the present day - situated beneath the Globe Theatre itself. Explore Bankside, the Soho of Elizabethan London, follow Sam Wanamaker's struggle to recreate an authentic Globe for the twentieth century and beyond, and take a fascinating guided tour of today's working theatre. Globe Education provides workshops, lectures and courses for students of all ages and nationalities. For further information please call (020) 7902 1433. GlobeLink is the Globe's association for schools and colleges and provides a range of services including a designated website, examination hotline, regular newsletters and priority booking. Performances in the Globe Theatre: May-September. Box Office (020) 7401 9919. The Globe Cafe offers light refreshments and main dishes. The Globe Restaurant offers full a la carte dining as well as pre and post performance menus.

Shakespeare's Globe Exhibition: Oct-Apr daily 10.00-17.00, May-Sept (theatre season) 09.00-12.00 exhibition and guided tour into the theatre, 12.30-17.00 exhibition and virtual tour. Closed Christmas Eve & Christmas Day

A£8.00 Concessions£6.50 C£5.50 Family Ticket £24.00. Admission includes a guided tour of the Theatre. Group rates (15+) available

Somerset House

Strand London WC2R 1LA

Tel: 020 7845 4600 Fax: 020 7836 7613

www.somerset-house.org.uk

[Entrances on Victoria Embankment, Strand, and Waterloo Bridge. Rail: Charing Cross. Tube: Temple (closed Sun), Covent Garden, and Charing Cross. Bus: 1, 4, 6, 9, 11, 13, 15, 23, 26, 59, 68, 76, 77a, 91, 139, 168, 171, 172, 176, 243, 341, 521 & RV1 to Strand]

After extensive renovation, this magnificent 18th-century building is now a thriving cultural centre for London - a place for enjoyment, refreshment, arts and learning. Somerset House is the inspirational setting for the world famous art collection of the Courtauld Institute of Art Gallery, the gold, silver and decorative arts of the Gilbert Collection, and the Hermitage Rooms which provide London with a unique window on Russian art and history. The Courtyard, featuring the Edmond J. Safra Fountain Court, is at the centre of Somerset House and provides a venue for open-air events, including the annual winter ice rink. Inside, the dramatic Navy Stair, Stamp Office Stair, Seaman's Hall and King's Barge House (complete with a gilded 18th-century navy commissioner's barge) are open to the public. There is an on-going programme of exhibitions, workshops, seminars and events. Visitors to Somerset House can enjoy great art collections, learn more about the role of Somerset House, the history of England, appreciate the fine architecture of Sir William Chambers, architect to King George III, and discover the views and open spaces of its stunning Thames side loca

...on. An award winning restaurant, cafés, and ...ift shops complete the scene and provide a ...ange of refreshments and unusual gifts.

...ll year daily 10.00-18.00. Closed 25 Dec. Art ...ollections may have separate closure dates. ...xtended opening hours apply to the Courtyard ...nd River Terrace

...ntry to Somerset House is free. Separate ...ayable admission applies to all art collections ...n site

Syon House and Gardens

Syon Park Brentford Middlesex TW8 8JF

Tel: 020 8560 0882 Fax: 020 8568 0936

www.syonpark.co.uk

[Approach via A310 Twickenham Road into Park Road. Plenty of on site parking available]

Syon House is the London home of the Duke of Northumberland. The present house is Tudor in origin but famed for its splendid Robert Adam interiors. The Gardens contain the spectacular Great Conservatory. Member of the Historic Houses Association.
House: 24 Mar-31 Oct Wed, Thur, Sun & Bank Hol 11.00-17.00. Gardens: all year daily 10.00-17.30 or dusk, whichever is earlier. Closed 25 & 26 Dec

Gardens: A£3.75 Concessions£2.50 Family Ticket £9.00. Combined ticket for House & Gardens: A£7.25 Concessions£5.95 Family Ticket £16.00

Discount Offer: Two For The Price Of One

Special Events

The Nine Day Queen
11/04/2004-12/04/2004
To commemorate the 450th anniversary of Lady Jane Grey's execution, Baroque 'n' Roll re-enact

Sutton House

& 4 Homerton High Street Hackney London ..9 6JQ

Tel: 020 8986 2264 Fax: 020 8525 9051

[At the corner of Isabella Road & Homerton High Street. Rail: Hackney Central / Hackney Downs]

..National Trust Property. A rare example of a ..udor red-brick house, built in 1535 by Sir Rafe ..adleir, Principal Secretary of State for Henry ..III, with 18th century alterations and later addi-..ons. The recent restoration has revealed many ..6th century details which are displayed. ..round floor only accessible for wheelchairs.

..3 Jan-19 Dec Fri-Sat 13.00-17.30, Sun & Bank ..ol 11.30-17.30. Closed Good Fri

..£2.20 C£0.50 Family Ticket £4.90

her being offered the throne at Syon. Easter Egg
Hunt for children

Study Day - Lady Jane Grey
20/04/2004
*By her biographer Alison Plowden. Tickets:
£10.00. Please contact the Estate Office for further details*

Meet the 3rd Duke and Duchess of Northumberland
02/05/2004-06/06/2004
*Held on 2-3, 30-31 May & 6 June. Costumed
interpreters give visitors an insight into Regency
Syon*

The Mystery of Syon Abbey
16/06/2004-25/07/2004
*Held on 16 June & 25 July only. Following discov-
eries of Channel 4's Time Team investigations,
students from Birkbeck College will continue to
carry out further on site archaeological investiga-
tion during this period. Please call the Estate
Office on 020 8560 0882 for further details*

Syon and its Monastic Origins
29/06/2004
*A study day in association with Art Pursuits.
Please call 01280 813027 or 820307 for further
details*

Meet the 3rd Duke and Duchess of Northumberland
04/07/2004-30/08/2004
*Held on 4 July, 1, 29, 30 Aug. Costumed inter-
preters give visitors an insight into Syon during the
Regency period*

Mistress of the House
01/08/2004-05/09/2004
*Held on 1 Aug & 5 Sept only. An exhibition about
Great Ladies and Grand Houses, 1670-1830,
including Elizabeth, First Duchess of
Northumberland*

Henry Percy, 9th Earl of Northumberland
23/10/2004
*A study day about the extraordinary life of the
'Wizard Earl'. Please call the Estate Office on 020
8560 0882 for further details*

Special Event to celebrate 400 years of the Percy family at Syon
24/10/2004
*Gunpowder, Treason and Plot - displays and re-
enactment about the life and times of Henry
Percy, 'the wizard Earl' in Syon House. Plus,
Autumn Trees at Syon, guided garden tours and
woodland craft demonstration*

The Royal Hospital Chelsea (Museum and Buildings)

Royal Hospital Road Chelsea London SW3 4S
Tel: 020 7881 5244 Fax: 020 7881 5463
www.chelsea-pensioners.org.uk

*[Entrance London Gate. Tube: Sloane Square.
Coach party parking can be arranged if pre-
booked]*

The Royal Hospital Chelsea was built by Sir
Christopher Wren on the instruction of King
Charles II to house war veterans and has been
the home of the Scarlet Coated Chelsea
Pensioners since 1682. Visit the beautiful buildings, museum and gift shop. The public are we
come to visit and pensioner guided tours can
be arranged by calling 020 7881 5244.
Grounds also open to the public except during
the Chelsea Flower Show. For group bookings
please call 020 7881 5204.

*All year Mon-Sat 10.00-12.00 & 14.00-16.00,
Apr-Sept Sun 14.00-16.00*

Admission Free

Special Events

Chelsea Flower Show
24/05/2004-27/05/2004

Tower of London

Tower Hill London EC3N 4AB
Tel: 0870 756 6060 (info line)
www.tower-of-london.org.uk

[Tube: Tower Hill]

Begun by William the Conqueror in 1078, the Tower of London has served as a royal residence, fortress, mint, armoury and more infamously as a place of execution. Nowadays the Tower is the most visited heritage attraction in the country. Since the seventeenth century, the Crown Jewels have been on public display and today visitors can see them in all their glory in the magnificent Jewel House. Take time to explore the White Tower, the original Tower of London, which houses the stunning collections of the Royal Armouries Museum - the national collection of arms and armour. Yeoman Warder 'Beefeaters' give guided tours providing an unrivalled insight into the dark secrets of the Tower's history. Above the notorious Traitor's Gate, costumed guides evoke life at the court of King Edward I in the restored chambers of the Medieval Palace. Visitors can stand on Tower Green where three queens of England lost their heads; enter the Bloody Tower where Sir Walter Raleigh was imprisoned; stroll along the Wall Walk with its panoramic views of the River Thames; see the Salt Tower where not only dogs refuse to enter but Yeoman Warders are also unwilling to visit after nightfall. With 900 years of British history within its walls, the Tower really is London. Disabled access is limited, please call for details. Events are free to Tower ticket holders.

All year, 1 Mar-31 Oct Mon-Sat 09.00-17.00, Sun 10.00-17.00, 1 Nov-28 Feb Tue-Sat 09.00-16.00, Mon & Sun 10.00-16.00. Closed 24-26 Dec & 1 Jan

A£13.50 C£9.00 Concessions£10.50 Family Ticket £37.50. Advance ticket sales tel: 0870 756 7070. Prices subject to change

Whitehall

1 Malden Road Cheam Sutton Surrey SM3 8QD
Tel: 020 8643 1236 Fax: 020 8770 4777
[On A2043 just N of J with A232. Rail: Cheam. Bus: 151, 213, 408, 726]

A unique timber-framed house built 1500. Displays include medieval Cheam pottery; Nonsuch Palace; timber-framed buildings and Cheam School. Pushchair access to Ground Floor only. New for 2004 - Audio Tour.
All year Wed-Fri 14.00-17.00, Sat 10.00-17.00, Sun & Bank Hol Mon 14.00-17.00. Closed Good Friday and 24 Dec-2 Jan
A£1.20 C£0.60

Landmarks

Tower Bridge Exhibition

Tower Bridge Tower Bridge Road London SE1 2UP
Tel: 020 7940 3985 Fax: 020 7357 7935
[In centre of London signposted. Bus: 15 / 25 / 40 / 42 / 27 / 78 / 100 / D1 / P11. Tube: Tower Hill / London Bridge. Car Parking in: Tooley Street & Lower Thames Street]

Over 100 years ago, the Victorians built a bridge that has become one of London's most famous landmarks. At the Tower Bridge exhibition you can enjoy breathtaking views, learn about the history of the Bridge and how it was built from the interactive displays and videos.
All year daily 09.30-18.00. Last ticket sold 17.00. Closed 24-25 Dec.
A£4.50 C&Concessions£3.50 C(under5)£Free

Wellington Arch

Hyde Park Corner London W1J 7JZ
Tel: 020 7930 2726 Fax: 020 7925 1019

[Rail: Victoria 0.75m. Tube: Hyde Park Corner adjacent]

One of the most splendid landmarks in London, Wellington Arch is now open to the public for the first time in history. It offers spectacular views of London skyline and surrounding Royal Parks and houses an exhibition on London's statues and monuments.

1 Apr-30 Sept Wed-Sun 10.00-17.00, 1-31 Oct Wed-Sun 10.00-17.00, 1 Nov-31 Mar pre-booked guided tours only
A£3.00 C£1.50 Concessions£2.30

Literature & Libraries

British Library

96 Euston Road London NW1 2DB
Tel: 020 7412 7332 Fax: 020 7412 7340
www.bl.uk

[Rail: St Pancras. Tube: King's Cross / St Pancras / Euston. Bus: 10 / 30 / 73 / 91 / SL1 & SL2]

The British Library is the national library of the UK and one of the great libraries of the world. The new St Pancras building in London is its headquarters. A spectacular new building designed by Colin St John Wilson, is now open to the public. The large Piazza is a new public space for London, with a bronze statue of Isaac Newton and the Amphitheatre will be used for poetry reading, outdoor performances and other public events. There is a full programme of

talks, seminars, films and musical and dramatic performances. The main venue will be the purpose-built Conference Centre which has a raked (seating arranged so that everyone has an optimum view as in a cinema) 255 seat auditorium. Admission to the Reading Rooms at St Pancras is by Reader's Pass, obtainable from Reader Admissions.

All year daily, Mon, Wed, Thur & Fri 09.30-18.00 Tue 09.30-20.00, Sat 09.30-17.00, Sun and Bank Hols 11.00-17.00. Closed 24-27 Dec and 31 Dec-1 Jan

Admission Free, reader passes can only be issued in person. Admission to events are by ticket from the Box Office. Doors open 15mins before the advertised start time

Special Events

The Silk Road: Trade, Travel, War and Faith
07/05/2004-12/09/2004
Priceless and rarely seen Silk Road treasures from Aurel Stein's collection - considered one of the richest in the world - will go on display alongside key items from around the globe in this major exhibition

The Charles Dickens Museum

48 Doughty Street London WC1N 2LX

Tel: 020 7405 2127 Fax: 020 7831 5175

www.dickensmuseum.com

[Tube: Russell Square]

Charles Dickens lived in Doughty Street in his twenties and it was here that he worked on his first full-length novel, The Pickwick Papers, Oliver Twist and Nicholas Nickleby. Pages of the original manuscript are on view. Dickens' drawing room has been reconstructed. Please note flash photography is not permitted.

All year Mon-Sat 10.00-17.00, Sun 11.00-17.00

A£5.00 C(5-15)£3.00 Family Ticket £14.00 OAPs&Students£4.00

Discount Offer: Two For The Price Of One

Special Events

'These garish lights' - Charles Dickens' public readings
01/12/2003-30/05/2004
December 1853 was the date on which Dickens first gave a public reading of his own works. In later years he peformed with such as obsessive intensity that it hastened his death. This exhibition reveals the amazing popularity of these performances

Living History Museums

Sir Winston Churchill's Britain at War Experience

64-66 Tooley Street London Bridge London SE1 2TF
Tel: 020 7403 3171 Fax: 020 7403 5104
[Close to London Bridge]

Take an unforgettable journey back in time to the dark days of the Second World War and experience the fury and danger of war torn Britain and life on the Home Front.
All year Apr-Sept daily 10.00-17.30, Oct-Mar daily 10.00-16.30. Closed 24-26 Dec
A£7.50 C£4.00 Family Ticket £16.00 Concessions£5.00

Discount Offer: One Child Free When Accompanied By A Full Paying Adult

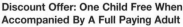

Maritime

National Maritime Museum

Romney Road Greenwich London SE10 9NF

Tel: 020 8858 4422 / 8312 6565
Fax: 020 8312 6522
www.nmm.ac.uk

[J2 M25 then A2 and A206, follow signposts into central Greenwich. Rail: Greenwich. DLR: Cutty Sark]

See how the sea affects our daily lives in this impressive modern museum. Themes include exploration and discovery, Nelson, trade and empire, passenger shipping and luxury liners, maritime London, costume, art and the sea, the future of the sea and making waves. Special 'Tintin's Adventures at Sea' exhibition 2004.

All year daily 10.00-17.00 (18.00 in July & Aug). Closed 24-26 Dec

Admission Free except for special exhibitions

Special Events

Shipshape: James Dodds
25/11/2003-12/04/2004
James Dodds is one of England's leading contemporary marine artists. This exhibition of his work includes dramatic life-size paintings, woodcuts of clinker workboats and coastal panoramas some on display for the first time

Mary Rose

15/12/2003-19/11/2004

The flagship of Henry VIII's navy, the Mary Rose mysteriously sank in 1545. She was raised from the sea-bed in 1982 along with many artefacts, some of which are on display here in the Queen's House

Medical Museums

The Old Operating Theatre, Museum and Herb Garret

9a St Thomas Street Southwark London SE1 9RY

Tel: 020 7955 4791 Fax: 020 7378 8383

[Tube: London Bridge]

Climb up a steep spiral staircase and into the roof of a church, which houses the oldest surviving operating theatre in Britain, dating back to 1821 before the advent of antiseptic surgery or anaesthetic.

All year daily 10.30-17.00. Closed 15 Dec-5 Jan.
A£4.25 C(4-16)£2.50 Family Ticket (A2+C4) £11.00 Concessions£3.25

Military & Defence Museums

Cabinet War Rooms

Clive Steps King Charles Street London SW1A 2AQ

Tel: 020 7930 6961 Fax: 020 7839 5897

[Tube: Westminster or St. James's Park. Buses: 3, 11, 12, 24, 53, 77a, 88, 109, 159, 184, 211]

The secret underground emergency headquarters of Winston Churchill and his cabinet during the Second World War.

All year Apr-Sept daily 09.30-18.00. Oct-Mar 10.00-18.00. Closed 24-26 Dec

A£7.50 C(under 16)£Free OAPs&Students£6.00. Disabled visitors and carers: A£4.00 OAPs&Students£3.50

Firepower! the Royal Artillery Museum

Royal Arsenal Woolwich London SE18 6ST

Tel: 020 8855 7755 Fax: 020 8855 7100

www.firepower.org.uk

[Rail: Charing Cross, Cannon Street, London Bridge and Waterloo to Woolwich Arsenal, the 5min walk. Tube: Jubilee Line to North Greenwich, bus stops from A to B to Plumstead Road (422) or Woolwich Town Centre (161, 472). Bus: 53, 54, 380, 422 stop in Woolwich Town Centre, 472, 161 and 180 stop on Plumstead Road. Plenty of parking on site]

Located in the historic Royal Arsenal, the world's centre for munitions manufacture, Firepower takes you from slingshot to supergun, starting in the Field of Fire, where big screens, dramatic surround sound and moving eye-witness accounts illuminate the conflicts of the 20th century. See and touch artillery from early cannon to modern missile systems. Learn how they work with touch-screen interactives. Get your hands on in the Real Weapon gallery to find out how ammunition reaches its target and what it does when it gets there. From April 2004, the Cold War Gallery will be open to the public where Firepower will be double in size! This brand new part of the museum will display large self-propelled guns, from the Cold War era to the present day.

All year, Winter Nov-Mar Fri-Sun 11.00-17.00 (pre-booked groups welcome on Thursdays), Summer Apr-Oct Wed-Sun 11.00-17.30

A£6.50 C£4.50 Concessions£5.50. Group rates (10+ people): A£5.50 C£3.50 Concessions£4.50

Discount Offer: £1.00 Off A Full Paying Adult Admission

HMS Belfast
(Imperial War Museum)

Morgan's Lane Tooley Street London SE1 2JH

Tel: 020 7940 6300 Fax: 020 7403 0719

www.iwm.org.uk

[Rail/Tube: London Bridge. Tube: Tower Hill / London Bridge. DLR: Tower Gateway]

HMS Belfast - the last of the Royal Navy's big-gun armoured warships from the Second World War. With nine huge decks, you can see for yourself where 850 men lived, worked and fought. Visitors can explore from the Captain's bridge all the way down to the massive six inch gun turrets, boiler rooms, hammock-slung messdecks, galley, sick bay, punishment cells and more. Leave at least two hours for whole visit. Children's Birthday Party facilities available on board for pre-booked groups, please telephone for details. Disabled access available to two decks.

Mar-Oct daily 10.00-18.00, Nov-Feb daily 10.00-17.00. Closed 24-26 Dec

A£7.00 C(0-16)£Free Concessions£5.00. Group bookings A£5.50 C(0-16)£Free Concessions£4.50. Pre-booked School Group up to age 18 £Free, 1 teacher free for 10 children

National Army Museum

Royal Hospital Road Chelsea London SW3 4HT
Tel: 020 7730 0717 Fax: 020 7823 6573
[Rail: Victoria, Tube: Sloane Square, Bus: 11 / 19 / 22 & 211; 137; 239]

Discover the lives, legends and legacies of the men and women who have served in the British Army. Find out about some of the most remarkable episodes in Britain's history.
All year daily 10.00-17.30. Closed Good Fri, May Day, 24-26 Dec & 1 Jan
Admission Free

Mills - Water & Wind

Wimbledon Windmill Museum

Windmill Road Wimbledon Common Wimbledon London SW19 5NR

Tel: 020 8947 2825

www.wimbledonwindmillmuseum.org.uk

[Windmill Road off Parkside (A219). Plenty of on site parking available]

Have you ever visited a windmill and not understood how it worked? This is your opportunity to find out. The Windmill Museum is housed in the historic Wimbledon Windmill, built in 1817. It tells the story of windmills and milling in pictures, working models and the machinery and tools of the trade. Children can grind their own flour using a hand quern, saddle stone or mortar and have the working of the millstones explained. We have a collection of over 400 woodworking tools, donated by a millwright, and there are life size displays showing how the mill was built and what it was like to live in the mill after it stopped working in 1864. There is parking space for 300 cars and the mill is surrounded by Wimbledon Common with its 1,100 acres of heath, lakes and woodland. Our shop sells cut out model windmills, miniature millstones and querns!

Apr-mid Nov Sat 14.00-17.00 Sun and Public Hol 11.00-17.00
A£1.00 C£0.50 Concessions£0.50. Group visits by arrangement

Multicultural Museums

Horniman Museum and Gardens
100 London Road Forest Hill London
SE23 3PQ

Tel: 020 8699 1872 Fax: 020 8291 5506

www.horniman.ac.uk

[Situated on the South Circular Road (A205) Rail: Forest Hill. Bus: 176 / 185 / 312 / 122 / P4 / P13 / 356 / 363]

Set in 16 acres of beautiful gardens, this fascinating, free museum has unique exhibitions, events and activities to delight adults and children alike. Housed in Townsend's stunning 1901 landmark building, the Museum has outstanding collections which illustrate the natural and cultural world. A new Centenary Development opened in 2002 doubling the public space and dramatically transforming the Museum for the future. With a new main entrance linking the Museum and Gardens, the development includes four new galleries, a new cafe and shop, plus a lift to all gallery spaces. Sound out the new Music Gallery with Britain's largest collection of musical instruments from around the world, discover African Worlds featuring the largest African mask, celebrate world cultures in the Centenary Gallery, experience the Natural History gallery with specimens from the Victorian age, observe aquatic life up close in the Aquarium and from February 2004 explore the prehistoric world of Dinomites.

All year daily 10.30-17.30. Closed 24, 25 & 26 Dec. Gardens close at sunset

Admission Free (a charge applies to Dinomites)

Special Events

Dinomites Dinosaur Exhibition
12/02/2004-31/10/2004
Go back 150 million years and come face to face with baby and juvenile dinosaurs in this fantastic new temporary exhibition. Explore these lifelike models, complete with sound and a jungle setting, and learn about their cycle of life, from birth to death. From the fearsome predator, the Tyrannosaurus rex, to the leaf eating Stegosaurus, Dinomites will show off the power and majesty of these formidable creatures. Alongside the exhibits will be dino-facts aplenty to be discovered in interactive displays. Tickets: A£4.00 Concessions£2.00 C(under3)£Free Family Ticket £10.00

Indonesian Textiles Exhibition
01/04/2004-01/11/2004
Exhibition due to run from Apr-Nov, please call for specific dates

Spring Classical Music Concert Series
01/05/2004-31/05/2004

Summer Music Concert Series
01/07/2004-31/07/2004

Autumn World Music Concert Series
01/09/2004-30/09/2004

Black History Month Celebrations
01/10/2004-31/10/2004

Christmas Concert
01/12/2004-31/12/2004
Please call for specific date

Music & Theatre Museums

Handel House Museum
25 Brook Street Mayfair London W1K 4HB

Tel: 020 7495 1685 Fax: 020 7495 1759

www.handelhouse.org

[Tube: Bond St. From Oxford St, walk straight down South Molton St, turn L on Brook St and R down to Lancashire Court. The Museum entrance is here in Lancashire Court]

Located at 25 Brook Street, London, home to George Frideric Handel from 1723 until his death in 1759, the Handel House Museum celebrates Handel's career and times. The refurbished 1720s interiors create the perfect setting for 18th century furniture and fine art, evoking the spirit of Handel's age. It was here that Handel composed Messiah, Zadok the Priest and Fireworks Music. Over 200 years later, live music, educational projects, exhibitions and public events continue to bring this landmark address to life. The adjoining house, number 23, houses displays from the Museum's collection and temporary exhibitions.

Tue-Sat 10.00-18.00 (open until 20.00 on Thur), Sun 12.00-18.00

A£4.50 C£2.00 Concessions£3.50 OAPs£3.50

Theatre Museum
(Public Entrance) Russell Street Covent Garden London WC2E 7PR

Tel: 020 7943 4700 Fax: 020 7943 4777

www.theatremuseum.org

[Tube: Covent Garden]

Discover the magic of the stage past and present - exhibitions on the British stage and its stars from Shakespeare's time to the present. Daily Costume workshops and demonstrations on the art of stage make-up available for all ages.

All year Tue-Sun 10.00-18.00

Admission Free. Groups are advised to book to ensure securing activity and tours. Booked groups 10+ A£4.00

Special Events

The Redgraves - A Family on the Public Stage
09/07/2003-01/09/2004
An interactive exhibition spanning five generations of a unique theatrical family, illuminating through their work the social and political history of the time. The exhibition is based on the Archive of Sir Michael Redgrave (1908-1985), the acquisition of which was made possible by grants from the Heritage Lottery Fund and Friends of the National Libraries. End date has yet to be confirmed

Observe and Show: The Theatre Art of Michael Annals
18/11/2003-01/11/2004
A retrospective of the work of theatre designer Michael Annals (1938-1990) who gave a distinctive visual stamp to many important productions during the formative years of the National Theatre under Laurence Olivier. The exhibition curated by Professor Arnold Wengrow, includes designs for The Royal Hunt of the Sun in 1964 and Noises Off in 1982. Specific end date to be confirmed

Cheap Thrills... Paper, Gloves, Rods and Strings
03/04/2004-25/04/2004
The Theatre Museum will become home to a host of performances in miniature during the Easter holidays. The shows, which will appeal to older children and adults, include Joe Gladwin Paperplay Puppets, the Museum's own Tiller Clowes Marionettes and Garlic Theatre

Natural History Museums

Natural History Museum
Cromwell Road London SW7 5BD

Tel: 020 7942 5000 Fax: 020 7942 5536

www.nhm.ac.uk

[Tube: South Kensington]

A day out for all the family. Highlights include the huge roaring, breathing robotic Tyrannosaurus rex in 'Dinosaurs', an earthquake experience in 'The Power Within' and the beautiful Earth's Treasury, displaying the Museum's famous collections of gems and minerals.

All year Mon-Sat 10.00-17.50, Sun 11.00-17.50. Closed 24-26 Dec

Admission Free to Permanent Galleries, a charge is made for special exhibitions

Nature & Conservation Parks

London Wetland Centre
Queen Elizabeth's Walk Barnes London SW13 9WT

Tel: 020 8409 4400 Fax: 020 8409 4401

www.wwt.org.uk

[S Circular Roehampton exit to Barnes, R at Rocks Lane by Red Lion Pub. Plenty of free on site parking available. Tube: Hammersmith. Bus: from Hammersmith Tube take the 283, our specially branded Duck Bus, which will bring you directly into the centre. Alternatively, buses 33, 72 and 209 stop nearby (alight Red Lion Pub). From Barnes mainline station take bus 33 or 72, or from Barnes Bridge take 209]

The Wetland Centre is a major new attraction for London that brings wildlife and wetlands into the heart of the city. Stretching over 105 acres, a mosaic of wetland habitats has been created on the site of four disused Victorian reservoirs. It is now home to a wealth of wildlife - in particular wildbirds. There are two exhibition areas, World Wetlands and Waterlife and a state of the art visitor centre - the Peter Scott Centre. You will also find a gift shop, restaurant and café. In addition you can take part in special events, courses and workshops.

Winter daily 09.30-17.00, Summer 09.30-18.00

A£6.75 C£4.00 Family Ticket (A2+C2)£17.50 OAPs£5.50. Pre-booked group rates (10+) discounted rates plus season tickets available

Discount Offer: £0.50 Off Child Admission With Full Paying Adult

Special Events

Art Gallery: Brin Edwards
28/02/2004-20/04/2004
Superb watercolours of bird life which delight the eye with their freshness and attention to detail

On the Water

Bateaux London / Catamaran Cruisers

Embankment Pier Victoria Embankment London WC2N 6NU
Tel: 020 7925 2215 Fax: 020 7839 1034
www.bateauxlondon.com

[Tube: Embankment]

Bateaux London: London's premier operator of luxury lunch and dinner cruises on the River Thames. Guests can indulge in a relaxing lunch cruise or experience the excitement of London by night with a dinner cruise onboard one of our elegant restaurant cruisers. A magical blend of fine food, friendly service and world-class entertainment combine to create this unique experience. Also available for private hire. Catamaran Cruisers: Catamaran Cruisers operate daily sightseeing cruises, with full commentary from Westminster, Embankment, Waterloo, Bankside, Tower and Greenwich Piers. See all of London's sights including the London Eye, Shakespeare's Globe and the Tate Modern. Our multi-lingual, non-stop Thames Circular Cruise also offers an insight into London's history and encompasses London's best loved sights.

Catamaran Cruisers: Point-to-Point Service - daily from Embankment, Waterloo, Bankside, Tower and Greenwich Piers every 45mins from 10.00-18.00. Thames Circular Cruise - daily from Westminster or Waterloo Piers from 10.00-18.00. Please call for further timetable information. Bateaux London: Lunch cruises operate all year, 7 days a week, apart from 1 Jan-15 Mar where they will only operate Thur-Sat. Departing Embankment Pier at 12.30 and Waterloo Pier at 13.00. Sunday Lunch Jazz Cruise: all year Sun, departs Embankment Pier at 12.30 and Waterloo Pier at 13.00. Dinner Cruises: all year every night apart from 1 Jan-15 Mar where operation is Tue-Sat, depart Embankment Pier at 20.00

Catamaran Cruises: Point-to-Point start from A£3.00 C£1.50.

Thames Circular Cruise: A£7.50 C£5.50 Family Ticket (A2+C3) £19.50. Bateaux London: Lunch Cruise: £16.00 2 course set menu, £18.50 3 course set menu, £10.00 children's menu. Sunday Lunch Jazz Cruise: £37.50, £20.00 children's menu. Dinner Cruises: Prices start from £63.00 per person

Canal Cruises - Jenny Wren

250 Camden High Street London NW1 8QS
Tel: 020 7485 4433/6210 Fax: 020 7485 9098
www.walkersquay.com

[Tube: Camden Town]

Discover London's fascinating hidden waterways aboard Jenny Wren, a traditionally decorated narrow boat, and enjoy the unique experience of passing through a canal lock. Our regular 90 minute tours take you past London Zoo and through picturesque Regent's Park, then by way of the 'haunted' Maida Hill tunnel to elegant Little Venice with its Regency style houses where you may alight for a short visit. An interesting commentary is provided by our crew. You may complement your cruise with refreshments, available from our restaurant. Jenny Wren is also available for Party Buffet Cruises and Children's Parties.

Mar-Oct daily all day

A£6.80 C£3.50 OAPs&Students£5.00. School Groups each £3.00. Other group rates call for details

Canal Cruises - My Fair Lady Cruising Restaurant

250 Camden High Street London NW1 8QS
Tel: 020 7485 4433 / 6210
Fax: 020 7485 9098
www.walkersquay.com

[Tube: Camden Town]

Enjoy a leisurely dining cruise aboard the luxury Cruising Restaurant, 'My Fair Lady', where you are served an excellent three course a la carte meal freshly prepared in our on-board gallery, whilst cruising London's fascinating hidden waterways. Our cruise takes you through the lock at Camden, past London Zoo and through the picturesque Regent's Park, then by way of the 'haunted' Maida Hill tunnel, to elegant Little Venice with its Regency style houses. 'My Fair Lady' offers evening dinner cruises and a family orientated traditional Sunday lunch cruise throughout the year. It is a unique venue for all occasions, both private and corporate, catering for all sizes of groups, up to 98 in number.

All year, public cruise for lunch on Sunday, public cruise for dinner Tue & Sun

Lunch £22.50, Dinner £37.50. Reduced prices available for children

City Cruises

Cherry Garden Pier Cherry Garden Street
London SE16 4TU

Tel: 020 7740 0400 Fax: 020 7740 0495
www.citycruises.com

*[Tube: Westminster (for Westminster Millennium
Pier, Waterloo (for Waterloo Millennium Pier),
Tower Hill (for Tower Millennium Pier) and Cutty
Sark (DLR) (for Greenwich Pier)]*

City Cruises plc, the largest operator of passenger services on the Thames, carries some
250,000 people annually on its extensive sightseeing, entertainment and charter services. The
company offers a variety of boat services during
the day and evening to suit all tastes. With City
Cruises you can rest assured of a warm welcome and a friendly efficient service.
Westminster/Waterloo/Tower/Greenwich
Sightseeing Service; a hop-on hop-off facility
between the three major destination piers on
the Thames. Passengers are able to travel in
comfort on one of four new state of the art luxury Riverliners which offer on-board catering and
bar services. Pre-booked breakfast, lunch, and
tea also available on board. A joint ticket is also
available with the DLR. London Showboat; a
unique floating entertainment experience with
dinner and cabaret. Imagine your favourite
songs from the world's famous musicals as the
perfect accompaniment to the sights of London.
Add a river trip, welcome drink, cocktails,
superb 4-course dinner, half a bottle of wine
and dancing and you have the perfect combination for an unforgettable evening. Corporate and
Private Charters; City Cruises has years of
experience hosting important and memorable
functions from Christmas and Birthday celebrations to corporate dinners and weddings. Our
menus and staff make every occasion special.
The company has an extensive fleet of 15 vessels catering for all budgets. These include the
newest purpose built boats for the Thames. City
Cruises is the sole company on the Thames to
possess its own catering facilities, including a
dedicated floating kitchen at Cherry Garden
Pier, and to employ a team of experienced
chefs. These factors allow the company to offer
a variety of quality menus to suit all tastes, cultures and religions, and freshly prepared food
that can be loaded directly onto boats, straight
from the kitchen. Baby changing facilities,
pushchair access and shelter available on some
boats, please specify if you require these services when booking.
*Westminster/Waterloo/Tower/Greenwich
Sightseeing Service - operates every 40mins from
10.00. Boarding at either Westminster Millennium
Pier, Waterloo Millennium Pier, Tower Millennium
Pier or Greenwich Pier. London Showboat - Apr-
Oct, Wed-Sun and Nov-Mar Thur-Sat. Corporate
and Private Charters - please call for Charter information pack and further details*
Westminster/Waterloo/Tower/Greenwich
Sightseeing service - A£8.70
C/Concessions£4.35 Family Ticket (A2+C3)
£23.00, these River Red Rover tickets offer
unlimited travel throughout the day. Single and
return tickets also available. London Showboat -
£55.00 inclusive of welcome drink, half bottle of
wine, 4 course meal, cruise, cabaret and dancing. Corporate and Private Charters - please call
for Charter information pack and further details

**Discount Offer: £1.50 Off Full Adult
River Red Rover Ticket And £0.75 Off
Full Child River Red Rover Ticket.**

London Ducktours

County Hall Riverside Building London SE1 7PB

Tel: 020 7928 3132 Fax: 020 7928 2050
www.londonducktours.co.uk

[Pick up point is in Chicheley Street, behind the London Eye on South Bank]

London Ducktours operates unique, year-round tours of London and the river Thames using completely refurbished 30 seater amphibious vehicles called 'Ducks'. London Ducktours is an exciting road and river adventure set against the historic and dramatic background of London and its history. Each complete tour lasts 80 minutes and includes sightseeing through the heart of London followed by 'splashdown' from our newly constructed slipway near Vauxhall Bridge then a 30-minute river cruise - all in the same vehicle! All tours will feature a live commentary by one of our 'character' guides, who will tell the story of London and its sights in a fun and funky fashion! Although new and unique to the UK, London Ducktours is based on similar operations in the USA that have been running safely and very successfully for some years.

Feb-Dec 10.00-dusk

A£16.50 C(under12)£11.00 Concessions£13.00 Family Ticket (A2+C2) £49.00

Palaces

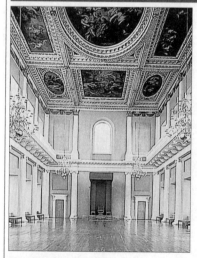

Banqueting House

Whitehall London SW1A2ER
Tel: 0870 7515178 Fax: 020 7930 8268
www.hrp.org.uk

[Tube: Westminster / Embankment / Charing Cross]

This fascinating building offers a haven of tranquility amidst the bustle of Westminster. Designed by Inigo Jones in 1619, the Banqueting House is all that survives of the Palace of Whitehall, that was destroyed by fire in 1698. It has been the scene of many historic events including the execution of Charles I and restoration of Charles II. Features include magnificent ceilings painted by Rubens in 1635 and the Undercroft, where James I used to retreat from the commotion of court life.

All year Mon-Sat 10.00-17.00. Closed Good Fri 24 Dec-2 Jan, Bank Hol & Government Function

A£4.00 C£2.60 Concessions£3.00. Prices subject to change

Buckingham Palace

Buckingham Palace Road London SW1A 1AA
Tel: 020 7321 2233 Fax: 020 7930 9625
[Tube: Victoria / Green Park / Hyde Park Corner / St James Park]

During August and September when The Queen makes her annual visit to Scotland, the Palace's nineteen state rooms are open to visitors. These rooms form the heart of the working palace and are lavishly furnished with some of the finest treasures from the Royal Collection.
31 July-26 Sept, timed ticket system in operation
A£12.50 C£6.50 OAPs/Students£10.50 Family Ticket £31.50

Eltham Palace

Court Yard Eltham London SE9 5QE
Tel: 020 8294 2548 Fax: 020 8294 2621
[J3 M25 then A20 to Eltham]

Visit Eltham Palace, the finest example of domestic Art Deco in the country and the only home of its kind open to visitors. A masterpiece

contemporary design, it dramatically shows
e glamour and allure of the 1930s.
*Apr-31 Oct Wed-Fri, Sat & Bank Hols 10.00-
7.00, 1 Nov-23 Dec Wed-Fri & Sun 10.00-
.00, 2 Feb-31 Mar Wed-Fri & Sun 10.00-
.00. Closed 24 Dec-1 Feb*
ouse & Garden: A£7.00 C£3.50
oncessions£5.30 Family Ticket £17.50.
ardens only: A£4.50 C£2.30
oncessions£3.40

Kensington Palace State Apartments

ensington Gardens London W8 4PX

el: 0870 751 5170 (info line)

ww.kensington-palace.org.uk

ube: High Street Kensington or Queensway]

ensington Palace dates back to 1689, and has
een such momentous events as the death of
eorge II and the birth of Queen Victoria. Today
provides an oasis of tranquility from the hustle
nd bustle of London. Multi language sound
uides lead visitors round the magnificent State
partments, including the lavishly decorated
upola Room, where Queen Victoria was bap-
sed, and the beautifully restored King's Gallery.
he Royal Court and Ceremonial Dress collec-
on dates from the 18th century, and audio
ours allow visitors to participate in the excite-
ent of dressing for court, from invitation to

presentation. There are also selections of dress-
es owned and worn by HM Queen Elizabeth II,
and Diana, Princess of Wales, with other exhibitions throughout the year.

*1 Mar-31 Oct daily 10.00-18.00, 1 Nov-28 Feb
daily 10.00-17.00. Closed 24-26 Dec*

A£10.50 C£7.00 Concessions£8.00 Family
Ticket £31.00. Advance ticket sales tel: 0870
751 5180. Prices subject to change

Special Events

Hats and Handbags: Accessories from the Royal
Wardrobe
23/05/2003-18/04/2004
*This unique exhibition celebrating royal acces-
sories includes over 70 eye catching hats belonging to HM Queen Elizabeth II. Beginning with
headdresses worn by the young Princess
Elizabeth, the exhibition will feature items associated with significant moments in Her Majesty's life
and reign. The display will represent work of The
Queen's chief designers and include accessories
chosen as particularly fine examples of British
craftsmanship*

Performing Arts

National Theatre
South Bank London SE1 9PX
Tel: 020 7452 3000 Box Office

www.nationaltheatre.org.uk

[Rail: Waterloo. Tube: Waterloo or cross the river from Charing Cross, Embankment or Temple. Car Park: Spaces in the car park below the National are £5.70 after 17.00. If you attend a daytime ticketed event, the rate is also £5.70 if you leave before 19.00 and validation must be obtained from the Information Desk. There is free parking for Blue Badge holders - validation required when booking tickets or on the day from the Information Desk. Phone 020 7452 3400 for details]

The National is on the South Bank of the Thames, just minutes from Covent Garden and the West End. It is one of the world's most successful theatres, renowned for its first-class productions and with awards to its credit. On its three stages the National offers a wealth of drama to suit every age and interest ranging from great classics to award-winning new plays; from comedies to shows for young people and spectacular musicals. There are also backstage tours offering the chance for visitors to see one of the most technically advanced theatres in the world, including a well-informed guided journey through all three auditoriums, front-of-house, scenic workshops and backstage areas. In addition, the National offers places to eat and drink, bookshops, early evening events, free foyer exhibitions and live music. Information and Backstage Tours: 020 7452 3400; Mezzanine Restaurant: 020 7452 3600 Terrace Café: 020 7452 3555

All year Foyers Mon-Sat 10.00-23.00 (open from 12.00 Bank Hols). Backstage Tours: Mon-Sat. Main Foyer Bookshop: Mon-Sat 10.00-22.45. Olivier & Cottesloe Bookshops open from 1 hour before performances. Costume Hire Dept: by appointment Mon-Fri 10.00-13.00 & 14.00-18.00 (020 7735 4774 / 020 7587 0404). Mezzanine: 17.00-23.00 and 12.00-14.00 on Olivier and Lyttelton matinee days. Terrace Café: opens 17.30 and from 12.00 on Lyttelton matinee days, to 19.30. Circle Café: open from 17.30-19.30 on Olivier performance days and from 12.00 on Olivier matinee days. Espresso Bar: Mon-Sat 09.00-20.00 (summer), Mon-Fri 09.00-16.00, Sat 09.00-20.00 (winter). Lyttelton Buffet: 12.00-23.00

Prices vary according to performance and seating areas. To book by post: Write enclosing payment, including a £0.50 handling charge for return of tickets. Mailing list members are given priority. By phone: 020 7452 3000 10.00-20.00. No further written confirmation is needed. Minicom for deaf people: 020 7452 3009 Mon-Sat 10.00-17.00. By Cheque: made payable to Royal National Theatre. By Card: Access / American Express / Artscard / Diners Club / Mastercard / Switch or Visa. Overseas payment

by credit card (as above), international money order or bankers draft in £ sterling drawn on a London bank. Ticket Exchange: Tickets may b exchanged for later performances or credit vouchers, provided 5 days notice is given. The handling charge is £1.00 per ticket. Tickets cannot be refunded. Standing tickets are only sold after all seats have been sold. Backstage Tours: £5.00 per person. Groups (10+), Students, OAPs, unemployed, Equity, SOLT & BECTU £4.25

Open Air Theatre

Inner Circle Regent's Park London NW1 4NP
Tel: 08700 601811 Box Office
Fax: 020 7487 4562
[Tube: Baker Street. Bus: 13 / 18 / 27 / 30 / 74 82 / 113 / 139 / 159]

A trip to see a production at the Open Air Theatre along with a cool drink and a picnic ha often been described as the total alfresco exp rience.
Performances from June-Sept
Ticket Prices: £28.00, £24.00, £19.00, £15.00 £10.00

Watermans

40 High Street Brentford London TW8 0DS
Tel: 020 8232 1010 Fax: 020 8232 1030
Watermans is a multipurpose arts centre base in Brentford, West London. Located on the River Thames, overlooking Kew Gardens. The venue comprises a 239 seat theatre, 125 seat cinema, gallery space and two newly built studios
Mon-Fri 12.00-23.00 Sat 10.00-23.00 Sun 12.00-23.00. Box office closes at 21.00 Mon-Sun

laces of Worship

t Paul's Cathedral

e Chapter House St Paul's Churchyard
ondon EC4M 8AD
el: 020 7236 4128 Fax: 020 7248 3104
ube: St Paul's]

r Christopher Wren's architectural master-
ece. Climb to the Whispering Gallery where
ur whisper can be heard on the other side.
*' year Mon-Sat 08.30-16.00 (Galleries from
.00), Sun services only. Please note, Cathedral
ay occasionally close due to special events*
athedral, Crypt & Galleries: A£7.00 C(6-
)£3.00 Concessions£6.00 Family Ticket
2+C2) £17.00

Westminster Cathedral

lergy House Victoria Street London
W1P 1QW

el: 020 7798 9055 Fax: 020 7798 9090

www.westminstercathedral.org.uk

[300 yards from Rail: Victoria Station. Tube: Victoria]

Called 'A Series of Surprises' because of its architecture, mosaics and marble decorations, Westminster Cathedral was begun in 1895. Its origins go back much further, being designed in the early Christian Byzantine style by the Victorian architect, John Francis Bentley. Appointed by the third Archbishop of Westminster, Cardinal Herbert Vaughan, Bentley took much of his inspiration from the Italian churches and cathedrals he visited during the winter of 1894, particularly those in Ravenna, Pisa, Bologna and Venice where he undertook a detailed study of St Mark's Cathedral. His other inspiration was the Emperor Justinian's great church of Santa Sophia in Istanbul. The Cathedral was conceived to be built quickly with inside decorations added, as funds became available. The structure was completed in 1903. Brick built, the vast domed interior has the widest and highest nave in England and is dec-orated with mosaics plus 125 varieties of mar-ble from around the world.

Cathedral: All year Mon-Fri 07.00-19.00, Sat 08.00-19.00, Sun closes 20.00. Tower: Apr-Nov daily 09.00-17.00. Dec-Mar Thur-Sun 09.00-17.00

Admission Free, Tower lift charged

Roman Era

Crofton Roman Villa

Crofton Road Orpington BR6 8AD

Tel: 01689 873826 / 020 8462 4737

www.bromley.gov.uk/museums

[J4 M25, A232 adjacent Orpington Railway station, signs on cover building. Rail: Orpington. Bus: 61, 208, 353]

The only Roman Villa in Greater London which is open to the public. The Crofton Villa house was inhabited from about AD140 to 400 and was the centre of a farming estate of about 200 hectares. Nearby would have been farm buildings, surrounded by fields, meadows and woods. The house was altered several times during its 260 years of occupation and at its largest probably had at least 20 rooms. The remains of 10 rooms can be seen today, with tiled floors and underfloor heating systems, within a modern cover building. Graphic displays, children's activity corner, schools service.

2 Apr-31 Oct Wed & Fri 10.00-13.00 & 14.00-17.00, Sun 14.00-17.00, Bank Hol Mon 10.00-13.00 & 14.00-17.00

A£0.80 C£0.50

Science - Earth & Planetary

Faraday's Laboratory and Museum

The Royal Institution of Great Britain
21 Albemarle Street London W1S 4BS

Tel: 020 7409 2992 Fax: 020 7629 3569

www.rigb.org

[Tube: Green Park & Piccadilly]

The Michael Faraday Museum houses his apparatus, manuscripts, pictures and personal memorabilia which include his medals, watches, microscopes and an inkstand. His Magnetic Laboratory has been restored on its original si Among his many discoveries are the principle of electric motor, the transformer and the dynamo - the basis of electrical power and other electrical engineering industries. The instruments which he made or commissioned are on display, as well as the first sample of Benzene which he discovered, and the appara tus used in his pioneering work on the liquifac tion of gases. Beautiful brass and wooden instruments to study the nature of conductors and insulators, an electric egg to examine elec trical discharges, samples of many substance which he was the first to classify as para or dia magnetic (concepts of great importance to material scientists nowadays), vast electrical machines and early batteries and voltameters his own invention tell a story of this great expe mental scientist and inspired teacher whose legacy has brought about the birth of the moc ern world. Christmas lectures for young peopl which he initiated and which are enjoyed by m lions of people on television. The tradition of research and educational activities thrives at t Royal Institution and many functions constitute a lively programme for members as well as the public at large, adults and children alike.

All year Mon-Fri 09.00-18.00. Groups at other times, by arrangement

A£1.00 Concessions£0.50

Royal Observatory Greenwich
Greenwich Park Greenwich London SE10 9NF

el: 020 8858 4422 / 8312 6565
ax: 020 8312 6652

www.rog.nmm.ac.uk

[ff the A2. Rail: Greenwich. DLR: Cutty Sark]

and on the longitude zero, the Greenwich
eridian, the home of time. Explore the history
time and astronomy in this charming Wren
uilding. See the Astronomer Royal's apart-
ents. Watch the time-ball fall at 1 o'clock.
dmire Harrison's amazing time-keepers and
her historic clocks. Climb to the giant refract-
g telescope. Limited wheelchair access,
ease call for further information.

year daily 10.00-17.00 (until 18.00 July-Aug).
osed 24-26 Dec

dmission Free

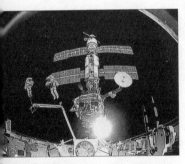

Science Museum

xhibition Road South Kensington London
W7 2DD

Tel: 0870 870 4868

www.sciencemuseum.org.uk

Bus: 9 / 10 / 14 / 345 / 49 / 52 / 70 / 74 / 360
414 / C1. Tube: South Kensington]

See, touch and experience the major scientific
advances of the last 30 years at the largest
Museum of its kind in the world, with over 40
galleries, and 2,000 hands on exhibits. Step into
the future in the Wellcome Wing - change your
sex, age 30 years in 30 seconds and create
your own identity profile to store on your own
Website. With a state-of-the-art IMAX cinema
and virtual reality simulator there really is something to entertain and inspire all!

All year daily 10.00-18.00. Closed 24-26 Dec.
IMAX shows take place daily

Admission Free - charges may apply to special
exhibitions. IMAX entry: A£7.50
Students&Concessions£5.95

Sealife Centres & Aquariums

London Aquarium

County Hall Westminster Bridge Road London
SE1 7PB

Tel: 020 7967 8000 Fax: 020 7967 8029

www.londonaquarium.co.uk

[Tube: Waterloo or Westminster. Across
Westminster Bridge from the Houses of
Parliament and next to the London Eye]

Experience one of Europe's largest displays of
aquatic life. Just across the river Thames, opposite Big Ben, the award winning London
Aquarium has over 350 different species to discover. Visitors are able to touch or stroke several fish such as rays, starfish and even crabs.
The one million litre Pacific tank is home to several varieties of shark, while a myriad of colourful fish can be seen in the tropical tank, including the popular clownfish.

All year daily 10.00-18.00

A£8.75 C(under3)£Free C(3-14)£5.25 Concessions£6.50 Family Ticket (A2+C2) £25.00

Discount Offer: One Child Free When Accompanied By A Full Paying Adult.

Social History Museums

Imperial War Museum

Lambeth Road London SE1 6HZ
Tel: 020 7416 5320 Fax: 020 7416 5374
[Tube: Lambeth North, Waterloo, Elephant & Castle, well signposted]

This award-winning museum covers all aspects of conflict since 1914 and tells the story of life on the home front and in the front line. Permanent exhibitions include First and Second World War Galleries, Conflicts since 1945 and The Holocaust Exhibition.
All year daily 10.00-18.00. Closed 24-26 Dec
Admission Free

Jewish Museum - Camden

Raymond Burton House 129-131 Albert Street London NW1 7NB

Tel: 020 7284 1997 Fax: 020 7267 9008

www.jewishmuseum.org.uk

[Off Camden High Street / Parkway. Tube: Camden Town]

Explores the history and religious life of the Jewish community in Britain and beyond. Its attractive galleries tell the story of the Jewish community from the Norman Conquest until recent times, and illustrate Jewish religious life with outstanding examples of Jewish ceremonial art. The Museum has been awarded Designated Status in recognition of the national importance of its collections. There are constantly changing temporary exhibitions, together with talks and lectures; as well as audio-visual programmes explaining Jewish faith and customs. Educational programmes, group visits and refreshments by prior arrangement.

All year Mon-Thur 10.00-16.00, Sun 10.00-17.00. Closed Jewish Festivals & Bank Hol

A£3.50 C£1.50 OAPs£2.50 Family Ticket £8.00

Museum in Docklands

No. 1 Warehouse West India Quay
Hertsmere Road London E14 4AL
Tel: 0870 444 3855 Fax: 0870 444 3858

[DLR: West India Quay. Tube: Canary Wharf Jubilee Line. Bus: 277, D3, D6, D7, D8, 115. Bookable disabled parking available]

The Museum in Docklands unlocks the history of London's river, port and people in a nine-teenth century warehouse at West India Quay.
All year daily 10.00-18.00. Box Office: Mon-Fri 09.00-18.00, Sat-Sun 10.00-18.00
A£5.00 C£Free Concessions£3.00. All tickets valid for one year

Museum of London

150 London Wall London EC2Y 5HN
Tel: 020 7600 3699 Fax: 020 7600 1058
[Tube: St Paul's, Barbican, Moorgate, Bank. Rail: Moorgate, Liverpool Street, City Thameslink. Bus: Museum 4, 8, 25, 56, 100, 172, 242, 501, 521]

Officially opened in December 1976, the collec

ons of the former London and Guildhall muse-
ms were brought together in one specially
esigned building. The Museum details all
spects of London life, from prehistoric times to
he twentieth century

*Museum and Shop: All year Mon-Sat 10.00-
7.50, Sun 12.00-17.50. Café: All year Mon-Sat
0.00-17.00, Sun 11.30-17.00. Closed 24-26
Dec and 3 Jan*

Admission Free

Sporting History Museums

Lord's Tour and MCC Museum

Lord's Ground St John's Wood London
NW8 8QN

Tel: 020 7616 8595/6 Fax: 020 7266 3825

www.lords.org

[Tube: St John's Wood. Limited parking on site]

Lord's was established in 1787 and is the home
of the MCC and cricket. When you tour this
famous arena you follow in the footsteps of the
'greats' of the game, from W G Grace to Ian
Botham. Daily guided tours take you behind the
scenes at this venue. You will visit the Members'
Pavilion including the hallowed Long Room and
the Players' Dressing Room, the MCC Museum
where the Ashes Urn is on display and many
other places of interest including the newly constructed Grand Stand and futuristic Natwest
Media Centre.

*All year, tours normally 12.00 & 14.00, vary on
cricket days, call to book*

A£7.00 C£4.50 OAPs&Students£5.50 Family
Ticket £20.00

**Discount Offer: Two For The Price Of
One**

Museum of Rugby and
Twickenham Stadium Tours

Rugby Football Union Rugby Road Twickenham
TW1 1DZ

Tel: 020 8892 8877 Fax: 020 8892 2817

www.rfu.com/microsites/museum

*[Follow A316 from Central London and Richmond
then turn R at the Currie Motors roundabout onto
Whitton Road, at mini roundabout turn R into
Rugby Road. Keep stadium to your L, turn L at
gate. Rail: Twickenham 10mins walk from the
ground. Plenty of on site parking available]*

A fascinating behind the scenes Guided Tour.
Includes breathtaking views from the top of the
North Stand, and a visit to the players tunnel
and the famous changing rooms with their 60
year old baths. The multi-media Museum of
Rugby appeals to enthusiasts of all ages and
charts the history and world-wide growth of
rugby, using touchscreens, video clips and film.
See the Webb Ellis Cup (please call in advance
to check availability). Cafe/restaurant available
during week only.

*All year Tue-Sat & Bank Hol 10.00-17.00, Sun
11.00-17.00. Stadium Tours: Tue-Sat & Bank
Hols at 10.30, 12.00, 13.30, 15.00, Sun 13.00,
15.00. It is advisable to pre-book these with the
Tours Officer on 020 8892 8877. Match Days:
stadium accessible to match ticket holders only.
Closed on post match Sun, Mon (excluding Bank
Hols), Easter Sun, 24, 25, 26, 31 Dec and 1 Jan*

Museum & Tour: A£8.00 C&Concessions£5.00 Family Ticket (A2&C3) £25.00. Group rate (15+): 10% discount. For Group Catering Requirements, please pre-book on 020 8891 4565. School Parties Welcome, call for details. Identification is required for Students & Senior Citizens for concession price

Discount Offer: Two For The Price Of One (Highest Price Applies)

Wimbledon Lawn Tennis Museum and Tour

Centre Court All England Lawn Tennis & Croquet Club Church Road Wimbledon London SW19 5AE

Tel: 020 8946 6131 Fax: 020 8944 6497

www.wimbledon.org/museum

[Tube: Southfields. Car: from central London take the A3 Portsmouth Road to Tibbet's Corner, at the underpass turn L towards Wimbledon, down Parkside. Entrance is in Church Road, ample free parking from Aug-May - drive in the Museum gates. Bus: 493 from Wimbledon Station and Southfields Tube]

Wimbledon is synonymous with lawn tennis and the museum in Centre Court at the All England Lawn Tennis Club is the only one of its kind in the world. Trophies, pictures, equipment, displays and memorabilia trace the development of the game over the last century. See the famous

Centre Court and the enjoyable interactive quizzes and data banks for all ages. Exclusive behind the scenes tour of the site, operated throughout the year, please call for times and prices. The Library containing the finest collection in the world of books and periodicals relating to Lawn Tennis is open by appointment.

All year daily 10.30-17.00. Café Centre Court: As Museum but 10.00-17.00. Open to tournament visitors only during Championship 23 June-6 July. Closed middle Sun and Mon after Championship 29 June & 7 July

A£6.00 C£3.75 Concessions£5.00. Group rates available

Discount Offer: £1.00 Off Adult Admission

Theme & Adventure Parks

Namco Station

County Hall Riverside Building Westminster Bridge Road London SE1 7PB

Tel: 020 7967 1066 Fax: 020 7967 1060

[Opposite Big Ben & Houses of Parliament on South Bank of Thames. Tube: Waterloo / Westminster, 5 mins]

It's a dazzling, brilliant, interactive experience on a massive scale. 35,000 square feet of pulsating fun, developed and operated by the global Japanese entertainment corporation, Namco.

All year daily 10.00-24.00

Admission Free but charges on individual games

The London Dungeon

28-34 Tooley Street London SE1 2SZ

Tel: 020 7403 7221 Fax: 020 7378 1529

[Rail/Tube: London Bridge Station]

The London Dungeon is the historic horror experience which dispenses fun and fear in equal doses.

All year daily; Jan-Mar 10.30-17.00, Apr-July 10.00-17.30, July-Aug 10.00-19.30, Sept-Nov 10.00-17.30, Nov-Jan 10.30-17.00. Closed 25 Dec

A£12.95 C(4-9)£8.95 C(10-14)£9.95 Concessions£11.25

Transport Museums

London Canal Museum

12-13 New Wharf Road King's Cross London N1 9RT

Tel: 020 7713 0836 Fax: 020 7689 6679

[Buses: 10 / 17 / 30 / 45 / 46 / 63 / 73 / 91 / 205 / 214 / 259 / A2 / 390 / 476. Tube: Kings Cross 5 min walk]

The museum tells the story of the development of London's Canals. Visitors can learn about the people who strove to make a meagre livelihood by living and working on them, the horses which pulled their boats, and the cargoes they carried. Good access for disabled visitors.

All year Tue-Sun & Bank Hol Mon 10.00-16.30. Closed 24-26 & 31 Dec

A£3.00 C£1.50 Concessions£2.00

London's Transport Museum

Covent Garden Piazza Covent Garden London WC2E 7BB

Tel: 020 7379 6344 Fax: 020 7565 7254

www.ltmuseum.co.uk

[Tube: Covent Garden / Leicester Square / Holborn. Bus: to Strand or Aldwych]

Travel through time and discover the colourful story of London and its famous transport system from 1800 to the present day. Spectacular displays of buses, trams, trains, posters, plus touch-screen displays, videos and working models bring the whole story to life. There's hands-on fun with KidZones - fifteen interactive exhibits, plus a clamber-on fun bus for the under fives. Enjoy our great changing programme of events and activities. There's something for everyone, from special exhibitions, actors and guided tours to film shows, gallery talks and children's craft workshops. A lift and ramp give access throughout the Museum. Facilities include disabled toilet, baby changing shop and café. For details of school visits contact the school booking service on 020 7565 7298.

All year Sat-Thur 10.00-18.00, Fri 11.00-18.00. Closed 24-26 Dec

A£5.95 Concessions£4.50 C(0-15)£Free when accompanied by an adult

Discount Offer: £1.00 Off One Full Paying Adult Or 50p Off One Concession

Special Events

BBC London Photography Exhibition
31/03/2004-06/06/2004

Interactive Streets Exhibition
30/06/2004-31/10/2004

Wax Works

Madame Tussauds

Marylebone Road London NW1 5LR
Tel: 020 7487 0200 Fax: 020 7465 0862
[Tube: Baker Street]

Madame Tussauds invites you to experience what it is like to be famous as you join a host of the world's hottest celebrities. Avoid the queues, book in advance on 0870 400 3000

All year daily 10.00-17.30 (earlier opening throughout the summer)

Madame Tussaud's and London Planetarium: 28 Apr-16 May 09.00-15.00; A£18.95/£16.95/£19.95 C(under16)£14.00/£12.50/£14.50

erseyside

Arts, Crafts & Textiles

Tate Liverpool

Albert Dock Liverpool Merseyside L3 4BB

Tel: 0151 702 7400 Fax: 0151 702 7401

www.tate.org.uk/liverpool/

[Rail: Lime Street. Bus: Smartbus 1 & 4. Ample free parking at King's Dock, 5min walk from Gallery]

Tate Liverpool is one of the largest galleries of modern and contemporary art outside London and is housed in a beautiful converted warehouse in the historic Albert Dock. Tate Liverpool displays work selected from the Tate Collection and special exhibitions which bring together artwork loaned from around the world. The displays and exhibitions show modern and contemporary art from 1900 to the present day which includes photography, video, performance and installation as well as painting and sculpture. There are a wide range of events and family activities which include free introductory tours, exhibition talks and lectures as well as free family events which take place every Sunday afternoon. Tate Shop and Tate Café are open during gallery hours.

All year Tue-Sun & Bank Hol Mon 10.00-17.50. Closed Good Fri, 24-26 Dec & 1 Jan

Admission Free to Tate Collection. Charges for special exhibitions, please call for details

Special Events

International Modern Art
21/06/2003-01/06/2005
A new sequence of display from the Tate Collection - International Modern Art - will focus on international developments in modern art since 1900. The programme will follow a loose chronology, showcasing works from major international movements such as Fauvism, Cubism, Abstract Expressionism, Land art and Arte Povera

The Shape of Ideas - Models and Sculptures from the Tate Collection
13/12/2003-31/05/2004
The Shape of Ideas examines small-scale sculpture, models and maquettes by some of the most important and innovative artists of the twentieth century. It includes work by artists Kurt Schwitters, Henry Moore, Naum Gabo, Jacques Lipchitz, Reg Butler, Barbara Hepworth and Ben Nicholson

Project Space - Michel Majerus Pop Reloaded
24/01/2004-18/04/2004
Michel Majerus was a key figure amongst a new generation of artists emerging from Berlin in the 1990s. Painting was Majerus' preferred medium and this exhibition features a group of large-format works from an ambitious series that he began during time spent in Los Angeles in 2001

Mike Kelley - The Uncanny
20/02/2004-03/05/2004
Mike Kelley, Los Angeles based sculptor, performance and installation artist, is one of the most significant artists working today. In The Uncanny, Kelley's first solo show in the UK since 1992, the artist explores memory and recollection, horror and anxiety through the juxtaposition of uncanny realist figurative sculpture with a highly personal collection of objects (the Harems). Admission: A£4.00 Concessions£3.00

Antony Gormley: Field
10/04/2004-22/08/2004
In 1993, Tate Liverpool showed Antony Gormley Field for the British Isles which was made in St Helens, Merseyside, as part of his major exhibition Testing a World View. Complementing A Secret History of Clay: From Gauguin to Gormley (which opens on 28 May 2004) another version of Field will be on display

Project Space - Kara Walker
01/05/2004-31/10/2004
Born in 1969, Kara Walker is an African-American artist who quickly came to international attention with her room-sized silhouette cut-outs depicting controversial and provocative racial and sexual themes

A Secret History of Clay from Gauguin to Gormley
28/05/2004-30/08/2004
This is a unique opportunity to see works by some of the greatest artists of the twentieth century including Paul Gauguin, Pablo Picasso, Joan Miro, Antony Gormley, Jeff Koons and Turner Prize winner Grayson Perry. Admission: A£4.00 Concessions£3.00

Liverpool Biennial - The International
18/09/2004-28/11/2004

This ten-week festival is the UK's only Biennial of contemporary visual art. Tate Liverpool is a major venue for The International - one of the four core programme strands - and is collaborating with the Biennial's team to realize new commissions by a range of international artists

Exhibition & Visitor Centres

World of Glass

Chalon Way East St Helen's Merseyside
WA10 1BX
Tel: 08700 11 44 66 Fax: 01744 616966
[M62 J7. Rail: St Helen's Central]

Get ready for an incredible journey as you discover the World of Glass. An exciting Visitor Centre in the heart of St Helens. A fascinating experience for all the family.
All year Tues-Sun 10.00-17.00. Open all Bank Hols, except Christmas Day, Boxing Day and New Year's Day
A£5.30 C(5-16)£3.80 C(under5)£Free
OAPs/Students£3.80

Festivals & Shows

Liverpool Comedy Festival

Various venues Liverpool Merseyside
Tel: 07004 729 4433 Fax: 0151 726 2401
[M62 follow signs to City Centre]

Liverpool's annual Comedy Festival returns in July for sixteen days of fun and laughter in venues across Liverpool. Previous years have seen Johnny Vegas, Peter Kay, Jimmy Carr, Des O' Connor, Tom O' Connor and many more. Radio plays, stage plays, stand up and comedy tours have all been staples of the Festival for the past two years and they return. More of the same for 2004 plus a comic short film competition and much more. Disabled access to most venues.
July 2-18 2004

Oye 2004

Various venues Liverpool Merseyside
Tel: 0151 708 6305
The only African Music Festival in the UK live! From our unending journeys to and from Africa, and via very many pirate radio broadcasts came Africa Oye in Liverpool 1992. From that relatively insignificant beginning has emerged one of the very best live music festivals in the UK. Oye is unique. Always pioneering, bringing the best of Africa's new young artists, and the older maestros.
June 19-27 2004

Admission Free

Historical

Speke Hall

The Walk Speke Liverpool Merseyside L24 1XD

Tel: 08457 585702 info line
Fax: 0151 427 9860

[8m SE of Liverpool city centre, S of A561. Signposted]

One of the most famous half-timbered houses in the country set in varied gardens and an attractive woodland estate. The Great Hall, Oak Parlour and priest holes evoke Tudor times while the small rooms, some with original William Morris wallpapers, show the Victorian desire for privacy and comfort. Fine plasterwork and tapestries, plus a fully equipped Victorian Kitchen and Servants' Hall. The restored garden has spring bulbs, rose garden, Summer border and stream garden; bluebell walks in the ancient Clough Woodland, rhododendrons, spectacular views of the grounds and Mersey Basin from a high embankment - the Bund. Peaceful walks in the wildlife oasis of Stocktons Wood. 1998 was the 400th anniversary of Speke Hall and this marks the four hundred years since the date of 1598 was carved over the front door during the time of Edward Norris, the first owner of Speke Hall, to mark the completion of the North Range and the building we see today. Events and activities reflect the different eras of the history of Speke, its estate and the families who lived and worked there, including open air theatre, children's activities, a special musical evening and much more. Picnic area by children's play area. Partial disabled access please call before visit, 0151 427 7231.

Hall: 20 Mar-31 Oct Wed-Sun 13.00-17.00, 6 Nov-5 Dec Sat-Sun 13.00-16.00. Gardens: all year daily 11.00-17.30 (or dusk). Closed 1 Jan, 24, 24, 26, 31 Dec

Hall & Gardens: A£6.00 C£3.50 Family Ticket £17.00. Garden: A£3.00 C£1.50 Family Ticket £9.00. Free Tudor tours with a House ticket, subject to availability. National Trust Members £Free

Maritime

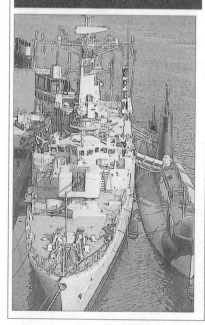

Historic Warships: HMS Plymouth and HMS Onyx

East Float Dock Road Birkenhead Wirral CH41 1DJ

Tel: 0151 650 1573 Fax: 0151 650 1473
www.historicwarships.org

[J1 M53 to All Docks then follow signs to Historic Warships, Wallesey Tunnel 1st Exit off. Plenty of on site parking]

Visit the largest collection of 20th century fighting ships in the UK. Including the frigate HMS Plymouth and submarine HMS Onyx both of which served with distinction during the Falklands conflict. Explore both vessels and experience what life was really like onboard a warship. The most recent addition is HMS Bronington, one of the last wooden hulled mine hunters, which was once commanded by Prince Charles. The German U-boat U-534, raised from the deep after 48 years, can also be explored.

All year, Summer daily 10.00-17.00, Winter Jan-mid Feb Sat & Sun, rest of Winter daily 10.00-16.00

A£6.00 C£4.00 OAPs£5.00 Family Ticket £16.00. Does NOT include U534 tour. Available for adults and accompanied children over the age of 12 on organised tours, bookable in advance. U-boat only tour, £8.50 (no concessions), combined ticket to include other vessels £14.50

Discount Offer: One Child Free With Full Paying Adult

Music & Theatre Museums

Beatles Story

Britannia Vaults Albert Dock Liverpool
Merseyside L3 4AA

Tel: 0151 709 1963 Fax: 0151 708 0039

www.beatlesstory.com

[The Albert Dock is easily accessible from road, rail, and on foot. Road: follow M62 into Liverpool, then follow road signs for Albert Dock. There is a large car park adjacent to the Dock. Rail: James Street Station, follow tourist signs to the Albert Dock, approx. 10min walk. By foot: 10min walk from city centre, follow tourist signs. The Beatles Story can be found between the Holiday Inn Express and Premier Lodge Hotels]

Imagine experiencing the most sensational story the pop world has ever known, in the City where it all began! Relive the Fab Four's meteoric rise to fame with a nostalgic journey through the multi-award winning Beatles Story. The story is told in 18 separate features including the streets of Hamburg, a full-size replica of the Cavern Club (complete with basement smells!), the Merseybeat office, Matthew Street, Abbey Road studios, 'Beatlemania', the Psychedelic Years, a walk-through Yellow Submarine in it's underwater setting, the White Room dedicated to John Lennon and the new 'Solo Years - Paul McCartney' section. Recent acquisitions include George Harrison's first ever guitar, valued at £1 million and on display for the first time in the UK, and the emotional and evocative feature 'Lenses of Lennon' where you can actually peer through his iconic round spectacles. To see it is to live it!

All year daily 10.00-18.00. Closed 25-26 Dec

A£8.45 C£4.95 Concessions£5.75. Group rates available for 10+ people

Discount Offer: Two For The Price Of One

Fingerprints of Elvis

Units 17-19 The Colonnades Albert Dock
Liverpool Merseyside L3 4AA

Tel: 0151 709 1790 Fax: 0151 709 5510

www.fingerprintsofelvis.com

[The Albert Dock is easily accessible from road, rail, and on foot. Road: follow M62 into Liverpool, then follow road signs for Albert Dock. There is a large car park adjacent to the Dock. Rail: James Street Station, follow tourist signs to the Albert Dock, approx. 10min walk. By foot: 10min walk from city centre, follow tourist signs. Fingerprints of Elvis is close to the Tate Gallery]

Ladies & Gentlemen, Elvis has not left the building, he's in Liverpool and he's here to stay! Curated by the makers of the award winning 'Beatles Story', Fingerprints of Elvis provides the ultimate account of Elvis Presley's life - bringing together the world's largest selection of memorabilia outside of the USA, alongside detailed accounts and first hand personal insights from his stepbrother, David Stanley and DJ Fontana in our exclusive Audio Guide. 'Fingerprints of Elvis' takes visitors on a comprehensive, dramatic and moving journey through the life of The King, offering a unique opportunity to discover the real Elvis through a combination of unheard anecdotes and unseen artefacts. These include his favourite Harley Davidson motorcycle and Gold Mercedes, legendary stage suits and instruments, personal jewellery and hand-written notes, and of course, a set of The King's actual fingerprints!

All year daily 10.00-18.00

A£4.95 C£3.95 Concessions£3.95

Discount Offer: £1.00 Off Admission.

Mendips and 20 Forthlin Road

Liverpool Merseyside

Tel: 0151 427 8574/7231 Fax: 0151 427 9860

www.nationaltrust.org.uk

[Scheduled mini-bus tours from the Albert Dock in the morning OR Speke Hall in afternoon. Advance booking recommended. Tickets available on the day subject to availability]

Mendips was the childhood home of John Lennon, he lived there with his Aunt Mimi and Uncle George and composed early songs in the front porch and in his bedroom. 20 Forthlin Road is a 1950s terraced house and the former home of the McCartney family, where the Beatles met, rehearsed and wrote many of their earliest songs. Displays include contemporary photographs by Michael McCartney and early Beatles memorabilia. The audio tour features contributions from both Michael and Sir Paul McCartney. During 2004 we are offering visitors a combined trip to both 20 Forthlin Road and Mendips. Tours depart from Albert Dock in the morning, call 0151 708 8574 to book. Afternoon tours to Speke Hall are also available, call 0151 427 7231 to book. There is partial disabled access to Ground Floors only.

27 Mar-31 Oct Wed-Sun and Bank Hols

A£12.00 C£Free NT Members£6.00. Price includes admission to garden and grounds of Speke Hall. Call 0151 427 7231 for details of combined ticket for Forthlin Road and Mendip.

Nature & Conservation Parks

Formby Point

National Trust Victoria Road Freshfield Formby Liverpool L37 1LJ

Tel: 01704 878591 Fax: 01704 835378

www.nationaltrust.org.uk

[15m N of Liverpool, 2m W of Formby, 2m off A565. Rail: Freshfield]

202ha of dune, foreshore and pinewood between the sea and the town of Formby. Red squirrels can frequently be seen in the pine trees and the shoreline attracts waders such as oystercatchers and sanderlings. Dogs must be kept on leads around the squirrel walk, and under control at all times. Education Officer fax/tel: 01704 874949.

All year from 09.00-18.00, or daylight hours in winter

£3.10 per car. Coaches £15.00 all year (must be pre-booked). School groups must book in advance

National Wildflower Centre

Court Hey Park Roby Road Liverpool
Merseyside L16 3NA

Tel: 0151 738 1913 Fax: 0151 737 1820

www.nwc.org.uk

*0.5m from J5 M62, on the outskirts of Liverpool.
Plenty of on site parking. Rail: Broadgreen
station. Centre approx 10mins walk from the station, take exit marked Bowring Park Road. Follow
the road under the bridge and straight across the
traffic lights. Continue down Bowring Park Road
keeping the M62 motorway on your left) for
approximately half a mile. Bus: The following
buses run from Queens Square, Liverpool city
centre, stop at Broadgreen station and then on to
a bus stop opposite and very close to Court Hey
Park's main entrance, Nos. 6 & 61]*

The Centre provides a national focus for pro-
moting new wildflower landscapes and the creation of new wildlife habitats. Located in a 35
acre park, once the home of the Gladstone
family, a former walled garden now produces
the wildflower seeds and plants that help fund
the charity. Nearby is a stunning and innovative
50 metre long visitor building, it features a café
and shop, outdoor exhibitions, the wildflower
garden centre and a children's area, whilst a
roof top walkway looks out across the complex.
There are seasonal wildflower demonstration
areas.

Apr-Sept daily 10.00-17.00, Oct-Mar closed

£3.00 C&Concessions£1.50 Family Ticket
(A2+C2) £7.50. Season Ticket £5.00, Family
Season Ticket £12.00

Special Events

Events and Activities
01/04/2004-30/09/2004
*Events and activities will follow monthly themes:
Apr - Gardening Month, May - Wildlife Month,
June - Environment Month, July - Wildflower*
Month, Aug - Arts Month, Sept - Food Month

Green Fayre
13/06/2004

Knowsley Flower Show
08/08/2004

Winter Celebration
05/12/2004

On the Water

Mersey Ferries Ltd

Victoria Place Wallasey Merseyside CH44 6QY

Tel: 0151 330 1444 Fax: 0151 639 0578

www.merseyferries.co.uk

*[Pier Head via M62 & Liverpool city centre, Wirral
via M56 / M53 or A41. Parking on site available
at Woodside and Seacombe. Park at Albert Dock
for Pier Head]*

You'll never really know Merseyside until you've
experienced it from the deck of the famous
Mersey Ferry. There's no better way to learn the
area's fascinating history, see its spectacular
sights and discover its unique character. Every

cruise is a great adventure. There's a full commentary, the chance to stop at Seacombe Aquarium or visit Pirates Paradise children's play area. At the historic Woodside Terminal stop off and enjoy lunch or afternoon tea at the Woodside Café as you take in the view of Liverpool's majestic waterfront. Our unmissable River Explorer Cruises leave every day from Pier Head, Liverpool and Seacombe or Woodside on the Wirral. There are themed and special cruises available throughout the year including trips along the Manchester Ship Canal from April until October. Our newly refurbished vessels are also available for private charter. Whether you are looking for a lively birthday celebration, that special wedding reception, a corporate event with a difference or just a fun filled party night, Mersey Ferries can provide the perfect setting with a difference.

All year daily Mon-Fri 07.30-19.30, Sat & Sun 09.00-19.20. Cruise Timetable: See special events guide or call venue

A£5.50 C£3.40 Family Ticket £15.45 Concessions £4.50. Group Rates 10% discount, school parties special discount

The Yellow Duckmarine

Britannia Vaults Albert Dock Liverpool Merseyside L3 4AA

Tel: 0151 708 7799

www.theyellowduckmarine.co.uk

[The Albert Dock is easily accessible from road, rail, and on foot. Road: follow M62 into Liverpool,
then follow road signs for Albert Dock. There is a large car park adjacent to the Dock. Rail: James Street, follow tourist signs to the Albert Dock, approx. 10min walk. By foot: 10min walk from ci centre, follow tourist signs. The Yellow Duckmarine ticket desk can be found within The Beatles Story shop, located between the Holiday Inn Express and Premier Lodge Hotels]

All aboard for this one-hour amphibious sightseeing tour of Liverpool's historic waterfront, City and dockland areas. Travel in comfort on one of our converted WWII DUKW vehicles, which depart from the Albert Dock on a daily basis between mid February and Christmas. From the Albert Dock, the 'Duck's' first port of call is to the magnificent Port of Liverpool building, the Cunard building and the renowned Royal Liver building, before heading up into the City Centre where you will pass the Town Hall, Matthew Street and St George's Hall. The tour then heads north to both the impressive Metropolitan and Anglican cathedrals, the Philharmonic Hall, LIPA and China Town. The third section of the tour takes in Liverpool's dockland waterways with an exciting 'splashdown' into Salthouse Dock, which will be loved by kids of all ages! The Duck then visits Wapping Basin and Dock, Queens and Coburg Dock before concluding the tour in the world-famous Albert Dock. Live commentary throughout. Wa-ter way to see Liverpool!

Tours depart daily from mid Feb-Christmas. Please call 0151 708 7799 for more information

A£9.95 C(2-15)£7.95 Concessions£8.95 Family Ticket (A2+C2) £29.00, extra C£5.00. Groups o 10+ people: 10% discount, must book in advance

Places of Worship

Liverpool Cathedral

St James Mount Liverpool Merseyside L1 7AZ

Tel: 0151 709 6271 Fax: 0151 702 7292

1m from Rail: Lime Street in central Liverpool. Limited on site parking]

The largest Cathedral in Britain and one of the great buildings of the twentieth century. The massive tower stands over the city as a symbol of faith in God amidst the bustle of the modern world. The Cathedral abounds in superlatives: highest gothic arches, largest organ, heaviest ring of bells but the grandeur is balanced by a real sense of welcome and peace. There is a unique collection of Victorian and Edwardian embroidery housed on a triforium gallery which affords breath-taking views down into the Cathedral. The Refectory offers an excellent range of freshly prepared food. Pre-booked educational groups are welcome. SPCK shop available for gifts, souvenirs etc. Photography permitted by permit only.

All year daily 08.00-18.00. Tower: Mar-Oct Mon-Sat 11.00-17.00, Nov-Feb 11.00-16.00 (weather permitting). Refectory: Mon-Sat 10.00-16.00, Sun 12.00-17.00

Admission Free, but voluntary contributions of £3.00 per person invited. Entrance to the Tower and Embroidery Exhibition: A£2.50 Concessions£1.50. (Prices subject to change)

Sporting History Museums

Liverpool Football Club Museum and Tour Centre

Anfield Road Liverpool Merseyside L4 0TH
Tel: 0151 260 6677 Booking
Fax: 0151 264 0149

www.liverpoolfc.tv

[From all major routes into Liverpool. Ground is 3m from city centre, 4m from M62 and 7m from end of M57 and M58. Well signposted from city centre. Weekday - park in Main Stand or Centenary Stand car parks, (except on mid-week match-days). Rail: Lime Street Railway Station 2m from Anfield. Match days use Merseyrail network to link with Soccerbus service from Sandhills Station. Taxis available from Lime Street. Bus: 26 / 27 from Paradise St. bus station or 17B, 17C, 17D, or 217 from Queen Square bus station directly to ground. 68 & 168 operate between Bootle and Aigburth, 14 & 19 stop a short walk away. By Air: Liverpool Airport approx. 10m from Ground. The Soccerbus Service: Leave The Car At Home On Match Day! A direct bus link from anywhere on Merseyrail Network via Sandhills Station]

The L F C Museum and Tour Centre celebrates all things Liverpool, past, present and future. Telling the story of England's most successful football club, including a recreation of the standing Kop. The stadium tour offers a chance to visit the dressing room, walk down the tunnel to the sound of the crowd, touch the famous 'This Is Anfield' sign. The historic 'treble' is on permanent display, and the 'Fab Four' European cups, as well as Michael Owen's 'Ballon d'Or'!

All year daily 10.00-17.00. Match Days: 10.00-1 hr before kick-off. No stadium tours on Match days

Museum Centre: A£5.00 C&OAPs£3.00 Family Ticket £13.00. Museum & Tours: A£9.00 C&OAPs£5.50 Family Ticket £23.00. Special deals for schools and groups

Discount Offer: £1.00 Off All Tickets.

Theme & Adventure Parks

Pleasureland

Marine Drive Southport Merseyside PR8 1RX
Tel: 08702 200204 Fax: 01704 537936
[10min walk from Southport railway station. From N M6 J31 A59 to Preston then A565 to Southport. From S M6 J26 M58 to Ormskirk then A570 to Southport]

At Pleasureland Southport, there's a gold mine of fun to be found. The classic woodie joins its big brother The Cyclone, and complements Pleasureland's three steel coasters,

TRAUMAtizer, The Wild Cat and The Big Apple kiddie coaster.

6 Mar-7 Nov 10.00-21.00 (hours vary call for details)

Free admission then access to rides by wrist-bands: A£16.00 C£11.00

Wildlife & Safari Parks

Knowsley Safari Park

Prescot Merseyside L34 4AN
Tel: 0151 430 9009 Fax: 0151 426 3677
[J6 M62, J2 M57, A57 follow signs. Plenty of on site parking]

A five-mile drive through the reserves enables visitors to see lions, tigers, elephants, rhinos, baboons, and many other animals in spacious natural surroundings. Includes reptile house, children's farm, otters, meerkats, plus a parrot and sealion show. Extra attractions include amusement park and miniature railway. There is also a souvenir centre and fast food restaurant.

All year Mar-Oct daily 10.00-16.00, Nov-Feb daily 10.30-15.00

A£9.00 C(3-16)£6.00 OAPs£6.00 Family Ticket (A2+C2) £25.00

orfolk

Animal Attractions

Redwings Visitor Centre

Caldecott Hall Beccles Road Fritton Great Yarmouth Norfolk NR31 9EY

Tel: 0870 040 0033 Fax: 01493 488531

www.redwings.co.uk

[1m N E of Fritton village on the A143. Plenty of on site parking]

Come to Redwings Visitor Centre and adopt a rescued horse, pony, donkey or mule for yourself or as a gift. There is plenty to keep the whole family occupied. You can meet the horses, visit the information centre, stroll along the farm walks or simply enjoy the tranquillity of the Memorial Garden. The Gift Shop has a wide range of souvenirs to appeal to all ages, and suit all pockets. Lots of special days planned for this year.

Apr-Oct Sun-Wed 10.00-16.00, also daily during main school holidays

A£3.60 C(3-15)£1.60 C(under3)£Free OAPs&Concessions£2.60 Family Ticket (A2+C3) £10.00. Discount available for groups of 6+ people

Country Parks & Estates

Fritton Lake Countryworld

Church Lane Fritton Great Yarmouth Norfolk NR31 9HA

Tel: 01493 488208 Fax: 01493 488355

www.frittonlake.co.uk

[On the A143 near Great Yarmouth. Plenty of on site parking]

Fritton Lake Countryworld provides a great day out for people of all ages in acres of unspoilt countryside beside one of the most beautiful lakes in East Anglia. Attractions include, the large undercover falconry centre where flying displays are scheduled twice daily; the heavy horse stables (home to the magnificent Shires and proud Suffolk Punches); Children's farm (adventure playground, wellie trail, pony rides, miniature tractor rides); lake facilities including rowing boats, pedaloes, fishing and guided boat trips on the lake; a nine hole golf course; 18 hole putting green; miniature tractor railway; beautiful lakeside gardens and woodland walks cyclepaths; gift shop and restaurant and various picnic areas. Great day out for all the family - young and old! New for 2004 is the opening of Decoy Barn which provides a great venue for birthday parties, special occasions, corporate events and wedding receptions.

28 Mar-26 Sept daily 10.00-17.30, Oct Sat-Sun & half term

A£6.50 C(under3)£Free C(3+)£4.50 OAPs£5.50

Festivals & Shows

Downham Market Festival 2004

Various town centre venues Downham Market
Norfolk PE38 9JZ
Tel: 01366 382963 Fax: 01366 382963
[Downham Market is located just off the A10 about 11m S of King's Lynn]

A wide variety of events 'by the people, for the people' suitable for all ages. Festival programme available from early April 2004.
May 30-June 6 2004
Carnival £Free, some other events charged

Norfolk and Norwich Festival

Various venues Norwich Norfolk NR3 1AB
Tel: 01603 766400 Fax: 01603 632303
[M11, A11. Trains from Liverpool Street - London]

THE festival of the East of England. A vibrant, fun-packed experience with literally something for everyone. Alongside this spectacular programme of events, you will find open studios and exhibitions, street performers and special events - the perfect platform from which to explore and enjoy East Anglia.
May 5-15 2004
Range from £3.00-£34.00, please call 01603 766400 for further details.

Royal Norfolk Show and Show Ground

Dereham Road New Costessey Norwich Norfolk NR5 0TT
Tel: 01603 748931 Fax: 01603 748729
[Off A47 southern bypass]

We are looking forward to yet another bumper Royal Norfolk Show for 2004. Major entertainment is planned for the Grand Ring and will be suitable for all age groups. Come along to the showground and enjoy two packed days of entertainment. The showground also hosts many other events throughout the year.
June 30-July 1 2004

Walpole St Peters' Church Flower Festival

Rectory Church Road Walpole St. Peter
Wisbech PE14 7NS
Tel: 01945 780252
[Watch for signs to The Walpoles off the A17 and A47 between Kings Lynn and Wisbech and follow the brown tourist signs]

This exceptional parish church of the Walpole villages is recognised as a masterpiece of 14th century architecture and attracts visitors throughout the years but especially for the famous Annual Flower Festival. One of the oldest and grandest of its kind attracting coach parties and family outings from far and wide, all enjoying the huge displays of choice blooms inside the church and the many stalls and popular catering outside the building. Facilities are available for the disabled.
June 5-9 2004
Admission and Car Park Free

Folk & Local History Museums

Cockley Cley Iceni Village and Museums

Cockley Cley Swaffham Norfolk PE37 8AG
Tel: 01760 721339 / 724588
Fax: 01760 721339
The Reconstructed settlement has been revamped and now boasts a second road house. The East Anglia Museum is now a big 17th-century farmhouse cottage. Nature trail now has bird watching hide and boardwalk.
1 Apr-end Oct daily 11.00-17.30, July & Aug from 10.00
A£4.00 C£2.50 Concessions£3.00

Cromer Museum

East Cottages Tucker Street Cromer Norfolk
NR27 9HB

Tel: 01263 513543 Fax: 01263 511651
[In the centre of Cromer, signposted]

The museum is housed in five 19th-century fish-ermen's cottages, one of which has period fur-nishings. There are pictures and exhibits from Victorian Cromer, with collections illustrating local natural history, archaeology, social history and geology.

*All year Mon-Sat 10.00-17.00, Sun 14.00-17.00.
Closed Mon 13.00-14.00, Good Fri, Christmas
period & 1 Jan, Sun until Easter 2004*
A£1.80 C£0.90 Concessions£1.40

Elizabethan House Museum

4 South Quay Great Yarmouth Norfolk
NR30 2QH
Tel: 01493 855746 Fax: 01493 745459
[On Quayside. Rail: Great Yarmouth 0.5m]

A Tudor merchant's house hidden behind a Georgian street front, with furnished rooms and displays of home life through the ages. Visit the panelled parlour where it is alleged that the death of King Charles I was decided.

*5 Apr-31 Oct Mon-Fri 10.00-17.00, Sat & Sun
13.15-17.00. Pre-booked guided tours available*
A£2.70 C£1.50 Concessions£2.30

Gardens & Horticulture

African Violet Garden Centre

Station Road Terrington St Clement King's Lynn
Norfolk PE34 4PL
Tel: 01553 828374 Fax: 01553 828376
*[Next to A17 at Terrington St Clement / Tilney All
Saints J]*

Having won many gold medals at the Chelsea Flower Show the African Violet Centre can cer-tainly boast the Best in Britain. The centre has been growing African Violets for over 30 years and has been responsible for introducing many new varieties.

*All year Mon-Sat 09.00-17.00, Sun 10.00-17.00.
Closed Dec 25,26 and 31 only*
Admission Free

Mannington Gardens and Countryside

Mannington Hall Norwich Norfolk NR11 7BB
Tel: 01263 584175 Fax: 01263 761214
*[2m N of Saxthorpe near B1149, 18m NW of
Norwich]*

This moated manor house was built in 1460. Gardens to view and lovely countryside.
*Gardens: May-Sept Sun 12.00-17.00, 2 June-27
Aug Wed-Fri 11.00-17.00. Hall: open only by
appointment for special interest groups. Walks &
Car Park: daily 09.00-dusk*
Gardens: A£3.00 Accompanied C(0-16)£Free
Students&OAPs£2.50

Walsingham Abbey Grounds

Estate Office Common Place Walsingham
Norfolk NR22 6BP
Tel: 01328 820259 Fax: 01328 820098
[On B1105 between Wells / Fakenham]

Set in the picturesque medieval village of Little Walsingham, a place of pilgrimage since the eleventh century, the Abbey Grounds contain the remains of the famous Augustinian Priory. Although little now remains of the priory, the great east window is perhaps the most striking feature and along with the refectory walls, remains of the west tower and monks bath, give an impression of the size and scale of the original building. Visitors can enjoy the tranquil gardens and, over the ancient packhorse bridge, the river and woodland walks lead into unspoilt natural woods and parkland. Entrance to the grounds in the summer is through the Shirehall Museum - a former Magistrates court, now a 'hands-on' museum detailing the history of this interesting village. During the snowdrop season the Abbey Grounds are home to one of the most popular and impressive displays of snowdrops in the country. Member of the HHA.

Courthouse & Museum: Easter-end Oct. Grounds: all year - call 01328 820510 or 01328 820259 for more information

Combined Entrance: A£3.00 C&OAPs£1.50

Special Events

Snowdrop Walks
22/01/2005-28/02/2005
Every year during the snowdrop season (around the end of Jan and most of Feb) the historical Walsingham Abbey Grounds are awash with perhaps the most impressive display of naturalized snowdrops in the country. Although they appear nearly everywhere in the 22 acre gardens, they are at their best in the woodland areas where they are so dense they are often mistaken for a layer of snow. Please call for further details

Historical

Blickling Hall
Blickling Norwich Norfolk NR11 6NF

Tel: 01263 738030 Fax: 01263 731660

www.nationaltrust.org.uk/blickling

[1.5m NW of Aylsham on B1354, 15m N of Norwich, signposted off A140 Cromer Road. Plenty of on site parking available]

Flanked by dark yew hedges and topped by pinnacles, the warm red brick front of Blickling makes a memorable sight. The house was built in the early 17th century, but the hedges may be earlier. The centrepiece of the houses is the carved oak staircase which winds up in double flights from the hall. Dogs on a lead are permitted in the park only. Facilities for visually impaired visitors are available. For special events, please call 0870 0104900.

Hall: 20 Mar-3 Oct Wed-Sun & Bank Hol Mon 13.00-17.00, 6-31 Oct Wed-Sun 13.00-16.00. Garden, Second Hand Bookshop, Shop and Restaurant: 20 Mar-31 Oct Wed-Sun & Bank Hol Mon 10.15-17.15, 4 Nov-19 Dec Thur-Sun 11.00-16.00, 6 Jan-end Mar 2005 Sat & Sun 11.00-16.00. Plant Centre same days as Hall 10.15-17.15

Hall & Garden: A£7.00 C£4.00. Gardens: A£4.00 C£2.00. Family and group rates available, (groups must book with s.a.e. to Property Secretary). Free access to South Front, shop, restaurant, second hand bookshop, art exhibitions and plant centre. Coarse fishing in lake, permits from warden, call 01263 734181

Discount Offer: Two Adults For The Price Of One.

Felbrigg Hall
Felbrigg Norwich Norfolk NR11 8PR
Tel: 01263 837444 Fax: 01263 837032
[2m SW of Cromer on B1436 off the A140 & A148]

One of the finest 17th century houses in East Anglia, the Hall contains its original 18th century furniture and Grand Tour paintings, as well as an outstanding library. The walled garden has been restored and features a working dovecote, a small orchard and the National Collection of Colchicum..
House & Garden: 20 Mar-31 Oct. House: Sat-

Wed 13.00-17.00 (closes at 16.00 from 24 Oct). Garden: Sat-Wed 11.00-17.00, 22 July-3 Sept daily 11.00-17.00. Both House and Garden open Bank Hol Mons. Park & Woods: all year daily, dawn-dusk
House & Garden: A£6.30 C£3.00 Family Ticket £15.50. Garden only: A£2.60 C£1.00

Wolterton Park

Erpingham Aylsham Norfolk NR11 7LY
Tel: 01263 584175 Fax: 01263 761214
[Nr Erpingham signposted from A140 Norwich to Cromer road. Rail: Gunton]

Extensive historic park with lake, Orienteering, Adventure Playground, Walks. The 18th century mansion house open on Fridays, is recommended for adults.
Park: all year daily 09.00-17.00 or dusk if sooner. Hall: end Apr-end Oct Fri 14.00-17.00
£2.00 per car. House: £5.00

Music & Theatre Museums

Thursford Collection

Thursford Fakenham Norfolk NR21 OAS

Tel: 01328 878477 Fax: 01328 878415
www.thursfordcollection.co.uk

[1m off A148 between Fakenham and Holt. Ample on site parking available]

The Thursford collection is a glittering Aladdin's cave of majestic old road engines and mechanical organs of magical variety all gleaming with gilt and colour and rich with exuberant carvings. There is a full programme of music from the nine mechanical pipe organs plus Robert Woolfe who stars live in the Wurlitzer Show.

Good Fri-26 Sept Sun-Fri 12.00-17.00

A£5.30C(4-14)£2.80 OAPs£5.00
Students&Group Rates£4.55

Places of Worship

Norwich Cathedral

12 The Close Norwich Norfolk NR1 4EH
Tel: 01603 218321 / 218324
Fax: 01603 766032
[Signposted from A11, A47 & A12]

A beautiful Norman building set in the largest close in England. Originally a Benedictine foundation, it possesses the largest monastic cloisters in England and is of great architectural and artistic interest.
All year daily 07.30-18.00, mid May-mid Sept 07.30-19.00
Admission Free. Donations welcome

Railways

Bure Valley Railway

Aylsham Station Norwich Road Aylsham Norfolk NR11 6BW

Tel: 01263 733858 Fax: 01263 733814

[Aylsham Station is situated mid-way between Norwich and Cromer on the A140]

Travel through the Norfolk countryside on the 9 mile long, 15 inch Bure Valley Steam Railway. The Boat Train connects with cruises on the Broads - inclusive fares available.
4 Apr-26 Sept daily, call for timetable

Sample fares from A£8.50 C(5-15)£5.00
OAPs£8.00

Theme & Adventure Parks

Dinosaur Adventure Park

Weston Park Lenwade Norwich Norfolk
NR9 5JW
Tel: 01603 876310 Fax: 01603 876315
[9m from Norwich off A1067 or A47. Plenty of parking on site]

A unique family attraction set in acres of woodland. Discover one of the world's largest collections of lifesize dinosaurs along the Dinosaur Trail, then meet the animals in the Secret Animal Garden.

19 Mar-1 Apr Fri-Sun, 2 Apr-5 Sept daily, 6 Sept-20 Oct Fri-Sun, 21-31 Oct daily 10.00-17.00
A£6.95 C(3-14)£5.95 OAPs£5.95

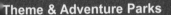

The Village Experience

Burgh St Margaret Fleggburgh Great Yarmouth
Norfolk NR29 3AF

Tel: 01493 369770 Fax: 01493 369318

www.thevillage-experience.com

[The Village Experience is at Fleggburgh on the A1064 between Acle and Caister, 7m from Great Yarmouth. Plenty of free parking on site]

Set in over 35 acres of woodland. Traditional fairground rides, narrow gauge railway, live shows including cinema organ show. Plenty of crafts and shops. Indoor and outdoor play areas. Garden golf, Dancing Waters, Junior Maze, drawing studio and more myths and legends. New Traditional Cake-Walk Ride. All main rides and attractions included in the admission price.

Easter-Sept please call for further details

A£6.50 C(4-15)£5.45 OAPs£5.75 Family Ticket (A2+C2) £20.95. Group rates 10+ A£5.25 C(4-15)£4.20 OAPs£4.50 Schools C£2.85, free teacher ratio 1:6

Great Yarmouth Pleasure Beach

South Beach Parade Great Yarmouth Norfolk
NR30 3EH
Tel: 01493 844585 Fax: 01493 853483

The Pleasure Beach is situated on the seafront at the southern end of Great Yarmouth's Golden Mile and covers 9 acres. Apart from the main ride area, we have a water based ride in the boating lake and the Pleasure Beach Gardens.

Mar-Oct. Opening times and days vary

Admission free: Wristbands £11.00/£13.00 valid till closing time. Ejector seat £25.00 per launch

Zoos

Banham Zoo

The Grove Banham Norwich Norfolk NR16 2HE

Tel: 01953 887771 Fax: 01953 887445

www.banhamzoo.co.uk

*[Between Attleborough and Diss on B1113
Norwich to Bury St Edmunds road, follow brown
tourist signs]*

Banham Zoo - Makes Other Days Out Look
Tame! Enjoy the ultimate fun filled day out at
one of the most exciting wildlife attractions in
the country. Our wildlife spectacular will take
you on a journey around the globe to experience at close quarters some of the world's most
exotic, rare and endangered animals. Set
amongst 35 acres of beautiful Breckland countryside and magnificent landscaped gardens,
you will discover hundreds of animals ranging
from big cats to birds of prey and siamangs to
shire horse. Join the free Safari Roadtrain, all
weather activities centre, exciting daily keeper
feeding talks and displays.

*All year daily from 10.00 Jan-end Mar closes
16.00, Apr-end June closes 17.00, July-7 Sept
closes 17.30, 8 Sept- end Oct closes 17.00,
Nov-end Dec closes 16.00. Closed 25-26 Dec*

Please call for price details

**Discount Offer: One Child Free With
Two Full Paying Adults.**

Northamptonshire

Animal Attractions

West Lodge Rural Centre

Back Lane Desborough Kettering
Northamptonshire NN14 2SH

Tel: 01536 760552 Fax: 01536 764862

*[Signposted off A6 from Desborough and
Market Harborough, access A6 from A14 J3A]*

One of the most spacious open Family Farms
with over 100 acres and 3.5m of walks to
explore. Encompassing rare breeds, cuddle
corner, display barn, tractor rides, fantasy
sculpture trail, nature trails, play areas, play
barn.
*All year, please call for specific times. Closed 25
Dec-3 Jan*
A£3.75 C£2.75 OAPs£3.25

Arts, Crafts & Textiles

78 Derngate

78 Derngate Northampton Northamptonshire
NN1 1UH

Tel: 01604 603407
www.78derngate.org.uk

*[Close to town centre near museum, Gallery &
Northampton Theatres]*

Charles Rennie Mackintosh transformed this
Georgian town house in 1917 for W J Bassett-
Lowke, creating a home of startling modernity
and striking décor. Restoration to its 1917
appearance is underway and the adjoining
property will tell the story of the house, its
owner and architect. For further information
please see our website. Limited disabled
access.

*Mar-Nov Sat-Thur 10.00-16.00 tours last 35
mins and take place every 15 mins, must be
pre-booked*

A£5.00 Concessions£3.50 Family Ticket
£13.50

Northampton Museum and Art
Gallery

Guildhall Road Northampton
Northamptonshire NN1 1DP

Tel: 01604 838111
www.northampton.gov.uk/museums

[M1, J15, signposted town centre]

The Museum reflects Northampton's proud
standing as Britain's shoe capital by housing a
collection considered to be the world's finest.

Following an extensive programme of refurbishment the collection is now displayed in two new galleries. 'Life & Sole' focuses on the industrial, commercial and health aspects of footwear giving visitors the opportunity to try out interactive exhibits and enjoy an audio-visual display. 'Followers of Fashion' is an Aladdin's cave of shoe delights spanning the centuries which looks at shoe fashion and design featuring some of the most influential designers of the last 100 years. Also available is an art gallery featuring permanent and temporary exhibitions of fine art and a stunning display of Oriental and British ceramics as well as two galleries showing the town's history, from Stone Age times right up to the present day.

All year Mon-Sat 10.00-17.00, Sun 14.00-17.00. Closed 25 Dec & 1 Jan

Admission Free

Special Events

Poetic Licence
27/03/2004-24/04/2004

Aspects
01/05/2004-13/06/2004

Northampton Middle Schools
19/06/2004-18/07/2004

Mirror, Bead & Thread
31/07/2004-03/10/2004
Gujerati Textiles from the Kanchan Malde Collection

Paintings by John Bassett
16/10/2004-21/11/2004

Town & County Art Society
04/12/2004-16/01/2005
Dates to be confirmed

Old Dairy Farm Craft Centre

Upper Stowe Nr Weedon Northampton
Northamptonshire NN7 4SH

Tel: 01327 340525 Fax: 01327 349987

www.old-dairy-farm-centre.co.uk

[10mins from J16 of the M1, signposted off A5 between Weedon & Towcester. Ample on site parking available with further facilities nearby]

The Old Dairy Farm Centre is located in beautiful countryside, offering designer clothes, unusual gifts, delicatessen, needlecrafts, antiques, galleries and craft workshops. Licensed restaurant for coffee, lunch and tea.

All year daily 10.00-17.30. Closed 25 Dec and following two weeks

Admission Free with the exception of special events where an admission fee will be charged

Country Parks & Estates

Billing Aquadrome Limited

Crow Lane Great Billing Northampton
Northamptonshire NN3 9DA
Tel: 01604 784948 Fax: 01604 784412
[Follow signs from M1, J15]

The park is renowned for a wide range of leisure facilities, licensed bars offering tempting meals and a variety of amusements.
Mar-Nov
Day Visitor Charges: £10.00 per car, Pedestrians £1.00 at all times, motorcycles £2.00 at all times

Exhibition & Visitor Centres

Stop House Exhibition Centre

The Wharf Braunston Daventry
Northamptonshire NN11 7JQ

Tel: 01788 890666 Fax: 01788 890222

*[Adjacent to Braunston Marina, signposted 'British
Waterways' off the A45 at Braunston, between
Daventry and Rugby]*

Walkers, cyclists, anglers to boaters should visit
the historic Stop House. A good choice of dis-
tinctive and unusual gifts and a monthly display
of crafts and art work by local artists.
*Mon-Thur 09.00-16.30, Fri 9.00-17.00, Sat &
Sun summer only 11.00-17.00 to be confirmed.
Closed 29-31 May*
Admission Free

Festivals & Shows

Cavalcade of Historical Transport and Country Show

Lancaster Farm Nr Higham Ferrers
[E of Higham Ferrers on B645]

Rushden Historical Transport Society proudly
presents the 25th annual Cavalcade. The show
grows larger each year. Tour the displays of
gleaming beautifully restored vehicles. Ride the
Vintage Steam Fairground 'Gallopers'. Watch
the Steam Traction engines. Listen to the
Fairground Organs. See one of the largest dis-
plays of Motorcycles, Lorries, Cars, Buses and
Fire Engines. Some date from 1904. Beer
Festival by Camra Finalist RHTS presents a
wide range of choice of Traditional Beers. Farm
Animal Displays, Model Exhibition, Art & Rural
Craft Marquee, Collectors Fair. Makes this a
Great Day out for all your Family!

May 1-3 2004 09.00-17.00

A£4.50 C&OAPs£2.00 Family Ticket (A2+C2)
£10.00

Northampton Music and Arts Festival

Tel: 01604 238791 Fax: 01604 238796
[Various locations across Northampton]

The 7th Music and Arts Festival continues to
promote a fantastic range of arts performances,
exhibitions, concerts and workshops.
June 2004
Vary according to the event, some free

St Crispin Street Fair

Northampton Town Centre Northampton
Tel: 01604 837837
*[Gold Street, Abington Street, Drapery and the
Market Square]*

Bringing the streets of Northampton Town centre to life during the October half term week.
More than 100 fairground attractions, from
hoop-la stalls to white knuckle rides line the
streets.
October 25-26 2004, 10.30-22.30
Prices vary according to activity

The Northampton Balloon Festival

The Racecourse Kettering Road Northampton
Northamptonshire NN2 7BL
Tel: 01604 238791 Fax: 01604 238796
*[1m N of town on the Kettering Rd. Park and
Ride: Return from Sixfields Stadium, Delapre Park
& Nene College (Boughton Park)]*

Three action-packed days combining a mix of
hot air ballooning, live music, roadshows, entertainment, displays, exhibitions and trade stands
for all the family concluding with the spectacular
balloon glow and fireworks.
*August 20-22 2004; Fri 12.00-22.30, Sat 06.00-
22.30, Sun 06.00-19.00*
Admission Free

Folk & Local History Museums

Abington Museum

Abington Park Park Avenue South Northampton
Northamptonshire NN1 4LW

Tel: 01604 838110

www.northampton.gov.uk/museums

[In Abington Park]

Exhibits in the 15th century manor house include a room with 16th century oak panelling, the history of the people of Northampton and the county's military history, at home and abroad. The museum currently houses the Leathercraft Collection. Please call the Museum for details of Toddler Groups and talks for the over 60s. Disabled access to the ground floor only.

Mar-Oct Tue-Sun & Bank Hol Mon 13.00-17.00, Nov-Feb Tue-Sun 13.00-16.00

Admission Free

Special Events

Art in the Park Exhibition
29/05/2004-04/07/2004

Children's Open Air Art Exhibition
10/07/2004-22/08/2004

Manor House Museum

The Coach House Sheep Street Kettering
Northamptonshire NN16 0AN
Tel: 01536 534219 Fax: 01536 534370
On entering Kettering's Manor House Museum the past is brought to life with refreshingly imaginative displays and reconstructions of everyday life transporting the visitor back in history from recent times to prehistoric Kettering.

All year Mon-Sat 09.30-17.00. Closed Sun & Bank Hol, 25-27 Dec and 1 Jan
Admission Free

Forests & Woods

Fermyn Woods Country Park

Brigstock Northamptonshire NN14 9HA
Tel: 01536 373625
[Access through the Northamptonshire County Council Country Park]

Fermyn Woods Country Park offers excellent opportunities for budding botanists and ecologists to study the natural progression from the open grassland of the park to the ancient woodland site of Fermyn Wood.

All year any reasonable time
Admission free. Parking charged, £0.50-£1.00

Fineshade Woods / Red Kites at Rockingham

Top Lodge Fineshade near Corby
Northamptonshire NN17 3BB
Tel: 01780 444394 Fax: 01780 444561
[OS Grid ref: SP979984, off A43]

An inspirational encounter with the red kites at Rockingham! A small camera mounted in a nest gives live, real time footage of a nesting red kite family, straight to video screens in our information centre.

27 Mar-5 Sept Mon-Fri 10.00-17.00, Sat & Sun 10.00-18.00

Admission free. Guided walks A£1.00
C(under16)£Free

Wakerley Great Wood

Wakerley Village Rockingham Kettering
Northamptonshire
*[OS Grid ref: SP986 962, off A43. Plenty of on
site parking]*

Over 600 acres in extent Wakerley Great Wood
is a legacy of the once vast tract of land that
formed the Royal Forest of Rockingham, which
was kept to provide the King with deer hunting.
All year any reasonable time.
Admission free

Gardens & Horticulture

Coton Manor Garden

Coton Northampton NN6 8RQ
Tel: 01604 740219 Fax: 01604 740838
*[10m N of Northampton, 11m SE of Rugby, follow
tourist signs on A428 and A5199. Rail:
Northampton / Long Buckby]*

Traditional old English garden set in
Northamptonshire countryside, with yew and
holly hedges, extensive herbaceous borders,
rose garden, water garden, herb garden, woodland garden.
*Apr-Sept Tue-Sat & Bank Hols weekends 12.00-
17.30. Also open Sun in Apr/May only*
A£4.00 C(0-16)£2.00 OAPs£3.50

Historical

Althorp

Althorp Northampton NN7 4HQ
Tel: 01604 770107 Fax: 01604 770042
*[M1, J16, A45 to Northampton, A428
Northampton / Rugby Road, approx. 7m NW of
Northampton]*

The history of Althorp is the history of a family.
The Spencers have lived and died here for near-
ly five centuries and twenty generations.
Includes an exhibition celebrating the Life of
Diana, Princess of Wales
*1 July-30 Sept 11.00-17.00 Daily. Closed 31
Aug*
A£11.50 C(5-17)£5.50 OAPs£9.50

Boughton House

The Living Landscape Trust Kettering
Northamptonshire NN14 1BJ
Tel: 01536 515731 Fax: 01536 417255
www.boughtonhouse.org.uk

*[3m N of Kettering on A43 access from A14.
Plenty of on site parking available]*

Northamptonshire home of the Duke of
Buccleuch and his Montagu ancestors since
1528. A Tudor Monastic building, gradually
enlarged until French style addition of 1695 -
'The English Versailles'. Outstanding collection
of fine arts from the Buccleuch Collection: furniture, tapestries, porcelain and paintings.
Incomparable Armoury and Ceremonial Coach.
The Boughton House Insight Programme is an
initiative to give the opportunity to take a closer
look at and participate in discussions focusing
on specific features of Boughton. Grade One
listed parkland with historic avenue of trees,
woodlands, lakes and riverside walks. The Plant
Centre in attractive walled kitchen garden has
quality herbaceous, bedding and indoor plants,
shrubs, garden pots and planters for sale.
Tearooms within the Stable Block, the
Woodland Playarea, (open subject to weather
conditions, parents should supervise children at
all times), and Gift Shop are open weekends
and daily throughout August.
*House & Grounds: 1 Aug-1 Sept 14.00-17.00.
Grounds only: 1 May-1 Sept Sun-Thur 13.00-
17.00. Educational groups by appointment
throughout the year*
House & Grounds: A£6.00 C&OAPs£5.00.
Grounds only: A£1.50 C&OAPs£1.00.
Wheelchair borne visitors admitted free of
charge

Canons Ashby House

Canons Ashby Daventry NN11 3SD
Tel: 01327 860044 Fax: 01327 861909

[M40, J11, A422 exit then L along unclassified road or M1, J16 signposted from A5, 2m S of Weedon crossroads]

The home of the Dryden family since its construction, this Elizabethan manor house has survived more or less unaltered since circa 1710. Intimate and atmospheric interior containing wall paintings and Jacobean plasterwork.

House: 22 Mar-29 Sept Sun-Wed 13.00-17.30, Oct-3 Nov Sun-Wed 12.00-16.30. Gardens open from 11.00

£5.60 C£2.80 Family Ticket £14.00

Cottesbrooke Hall and Gardens

Cottesbrooke Northampton NN6 8PF

Tel: 01604 505808 Fax: 01604 505619

[10m N of Northampton to Creaton on A5199 and signs 1m to Cottesbrooke. N of Northampton to Brixworth on A508 and signs 2m to Cottesbrooke. From E or W A14 J1 Thornby A5199 to Creaton and signs 1m to Cottesbrooke]

Magnificent Queen Anne house, reputed pattern for Jane Austen's 'Mansfield Park,' with fine pictures, furniture and porcelain collections. Celebrated gardens.

House & Gardens: 3 May-30 Sept; May-June Wed-Thur 14.00-17.30, July-Sept Thur 14.00-17.30. Also open Bank Hol Mons May-Sept

House & Gardens: A&OAPs£6.00 C(5-14)£3.00. Gardens only: A&OAPs£4.00 C£2.00

SULGRAVE MANOR

Sulgrave Manor, Near Banbury OX17 2SD

Sulgrave Manor presents a typical wealthy man's house and gardens of the Tudor period. Built in 1539 by Lawrence Washington, seven times Great Grandfather of George Washington. Beautifully presented, making a visit a delight and pleasure. Regular special events, please ring for details. New Herb Society gardens open in 2004.

You can find us: Just off B4525 Banbury to Northampton Road. 7 miles north east of Banbury.
6 miles from Junction 11 of M40 15 miles from Junction 15a of M1.

Tel: 01295 760205 Fax: 01295 768056
email: sulgrave-manor@talk21.com website: www.sulgravemanor.org.uk

Open: Daily (except Mondays & Fridays), 1st April-31st October 2.00pm-5.30pm.
Closed 30th May and 8th August 2004.
Open for pre-booked groups on any day or evening throughout the year (except January).
Access to the house may be restricted during private wedding ceremonies.

Deene Park

Deene Corby Northamptonshire NN17 3EW
Tel: 01780 450223 / 450278
Fax: 01780 450282
[0.5m off A43, between Kettering / Stamford]

Mainly 16th century house of great architectural importance and historical interest. Extensive gardens with old-fashioned roses, rare trees and shrubs.
Easter, May, Spring & Aug Bank Hol Sun & Mon only, June-Aug Sun. House and Garden: 14.00-17.00. Park: 13.00-18.00

House & Garden: A£6.00 C(0-10)£Free C(10-14)£2.50 Concessions£5.50. Garden only: A£3.50 C(0-10)£Free with accompanying Adult C(10-14)£1.50

Kelmarsh Hall

Kelmarsh Northampton Northamptonshire NN6 9LT
Tel: 01604 686543 Fax: 01604 686437
[12m N of Northampton, 5m S of Market Harborough on A508 / A14 J2]

1732 Palladian house designed by James Gibbs and built by Smith of Warwick. Interesting gardens with lake and woodland walks. Herd of British White cattle. Partial disabled access.

House & Garden: 11 Apr-4 Sept Sun, Bank Hol Mon & Thur in July-Aug, 14.30-17.00, guided tours of House. Gardens only: 11 Apr-30 Sept Tue-Thur 14.30-17.00

House & Garden: A£4.50 C(0-4)£Free C(5-16)£2.50 Concessions£4.00. Garden only: A£3.50 C(0-4)£Free C(5-16)£2.50 Concessions£3.00

Lyveden New Bield

nr Oundle Peterborough Northamptonshire PE8 5AT
Tel: 01832 205358
[4m SW of Oundle via A427, 3m E of Brigstock,

leading off A6116. Rail: Kettering 10m]

An incomplete Elizabethan garden house and moated garden. Begun in 1595 by Sir Thomas Tresham to symbolise his Catholic faith, Lyveden remains virtually unaltered since work stopped when Tresham died in 1605.

31 Mar-31 July Wed-Sun 10.30-17.00, 1-31 Aug daily 10.30-17.00, 1 Sept-31 Oct Wed-Sun 10.30-17.00, 6 Nov-27 Mar Sat-Sun 10.30-16.00. Open Bank Hol Mons

A£2.50 C£1.20 Family Ticket £6.20

Prebendal Manor Medieval Centre

Church Street Nassington Peterborough Northamptonshire PE8 6QG
Tel: 01780 782575
[6m N of Oundle A605, 7m S of Stamford A1 to Wansford, 9m W of Peterborough A47]

Dating from the early 13th century and steeped in history the house is the oldest manor in Northamptonshire. Included in the visit are the 15th-century dovecote and tithe barn museum.

Easter Mon-end Sept Wed & Sun & Bank Hol Mons 13.00-17.30

A£4.50 C£2.00. Garden only: A£4.00 C£1.50

Rockingham Castle

Rockingham Market Harborough LE16 8TH
Tel: 01536 770240 Fax: 01536 771692
[2m N of Corby, 9m from Market Harborough]

Set on a hill overlooking five counties, Rockingham Castle was built by William the Conqueror. The Castle was a royal residence for 450 years. Twelve acres of formal and wild garden command splendid views.

Apr, May & Sept Sun & Bank Hol Mons, June-Aug Tue, Sun & Bank Hol Mons 12.00-17.00. Castle opens at 13.00

House & Garden: A£7.00 C(5-16)£4.50 OAPs£6.00 Family Ticket (A2+C2) £18.50.

rounds: All £4.50

stated: A£6.50 C£3.25 Family Ticket £17.50

Discount Offer: Two For The Price Of One.

Sulgrave Manor

Manor Road Sulgrave Banbury OX17 2SD
Tel: 01295 760205 Fax: 01295 768056
www.sulgravemanor.org.uk

*Situated in the village of Sulgrave just off B4525
Banbury to Northampton road. 7m NE of
Banbury. 6m NW of Brackley and the A43. 9m W
of Towcester and the A5. Oxford and Stratford
are approximately 30m distant and London via
either the M1 or M40, 70m. Rail: Banbury. Plenty
of free on site parking]*

Sulgrave Manor was bought in 1539 by
Lawrence Washington, wool merchant and
twice Mayor of Northampton. It was here that
George Washington's ancestors lived until 1656.
Beautiful Tudor House and Gardens. Fine collection of 16th and 18th century furniture and
artefacts, plus Washington memorabilia. School
packs are available for educational visits: A new
Courtyard Range of visitor facilities now open.
George Washington Exhibition and Buttery cafe.
A superb, traditionally timbered and galleried
function hall - an ideal venue for weddings, conferences, society dinners, family celebrations or
other events. Picnic facilities for both in and outdoors available. New herb society garden opens
in 2004.

*1 Apr-31 Oct Tue-Thur Weekends & Bank Hol
14.00-17.30. Open for pre-booked schools and
groups on any day or evening Feb-Dec*

A£5.00 C(5-16)£2.50. Group rates (15+): available. Special events prices unless otherwise

Military & Defence Museums

Harrington Aviation Museums

Sunnyvale Farm and Nursery off Lamport Road
Harrington Northamptonshire NN6 9PF

Tel: 01604 686608
www.harringtonmuseum.org.uk

*[A14 W off J2 on A508 to Kelmarsh. Turn R at
crossroads towards Harrington, follow museum
signs. A14 E off J3, Rothwell, follow signs to
Harrington, go through village, then follow museum signs. Plenty of parking on site]*

The Harrington Aviation Museums comprise the
Carpetbagger Aviation and Secret War Museum
and the Northamptonshire Aviation Society
Museum. These museums offer a rare look at
life on this Top Secret base of the 801st/492nd
American Eighth Air Force Bombardment Group
during World War 2. Photographs and exhibits
vividly present details of Operation
Carpetbagger and the secret war carried out by
the British Special Operations Executive (SOE)

and the American Office of Strategic Services (OSS) in supplying resistance groups in Occupied Europe with weapons, equipment and secret agents from both Harrington and Tempsford airfields during World War 2; The Thor IRBM nuclear armed rockets that were at Harrington during the 1959-63 Cold War Period; The history of the Harrington airfield; The Royal Observer Corps from its inception in 1925 through to its stand down in 1991; air war and the Home Front in Northamptonshire along with other items of similar interest. Disabled access to approximately 80% of exhibits.

3 Apr-end Oct Sat, Sun & Bank Hol Mons 10.00-17.00

A£2.00 C(5-15£1.00. No concessions. School groups by arrangement

HARRINGTON AVIATION MUSEUMS
2 superb museums at one location

**Carpetbagger
Aviation & Secret War Museum
& Northants Aviation Society Museum**

World War 2 SOE & OSS secret operations; 801st/492nd (Carpetbagger) Bombardment Group USAAF; Thor missiles; Royal Observer Corps; Home Defence; Northamptonshire at War

Open: April-October
Weekends and Bank Holidays 10.00 am-5.00 pm

Off Lamport Road, Harrington, Northamptonshire
www.harringtonmuseum.org.uk

Sport & Recreation

Desborough Leisure Centre

The Hawthorns Desborough Kettering Northamptonshire NN14 2TQ
Tel: 01536 761239 Fax: 01536 763363
Desborough Leisure Centre consists of a four court sports hall, two squash courts, a floodlit multi play area, extensive outdoor grass pitches and a lounge and function suite. The Centre caters for a wide range of sporting and social events for all ages and abilities.
Mon-Fri 08.00-23.30, Sat 08.00-18.00 (unless function), Sun 08.00-23.00

Theme & Adventure Parks

Wicksteed Park

Barton Road Kettering Northamptonshire NN15 6NJ
**Tel: 01536 485454 Fax: 01536 518948
www.wicksteedpark.co.uk**

[On the outskirts of Kettering. Follow signs from J10 off A14. Main Gate is on the A6. Plenty of on site parking available]

Wicksteed Park is the oldest leisure park in the country, having opened in 1921. 147 acres of parkland and lakes with rides and attractions suitable for all ages, including Roller Coasters, Dodgems, Laser Tag, Carousel, Rockin Tug, Racing Cars and many more. There are various catering outlets and gift shops around the Park Wicksteed Pavilion is licensed for civil wedding ceremonies and the perfect venue for your party, disco, conference or corporate event.
Mar-Oct, opening patterns vary so please telephone for more details
No entry fee to the Park, car parking charged. Simply buy wristbands / tickets as required. Wristbands: A£9.50 C£13.00 OAPs£5.00. Tickets: Sheet of 12 £8.50, sheet of 30 £13.00, single tickets £1.00 each. Where applicable, children under 0.9m ride free! Buying a wrist-

and entitles the wearer to unlimited rides only
n the day of purchase. This does not include
oin-operated amusements, the Pitch 'n' Putt
admission to certain special events plus only
he use of Laser Tag. In the interests of safety,
ertain rides have passenger height restrictions,
hich are clearly displayed by means of a
olour code

**iscount Offer: Buy Two Wristbands
t Wicksteed Park And Receive
nother Wristband Of An Equal Or
esser Value Absolutely FREE!**

pecial Events

esta Car Rally
6/05/2004

ondeo Car Rally
0/06/2004

obot Wars
7/07/2004-18/07/2004

camps Crossbreed and Mongrels Dog Show
6/09/2004-20/09/2004

ransport Museums

The Canal Museum

Bridge Road Stoke Bruerne Towcester
Northamptonshire NN12 7SE

Tel: 01604 862229 Fax: 01604 864199

www.thewaterwaystrust.co.uk

*[4m S of M1, J15 off the A508 in the village of
Stoke Bruerne, signposted. Plenty of on site parking available]*

The Canal Museum is at the heart of the beautiful canalside village of Stoke Bruerne in
Northamptonshire. The museum has three
floors of exhibits telling the story of our inland
waterways and the people who lived and
worked on them. Children can dress in traditional canal costume, decorate their own ribbon
plates and there are working models for all ages
to enjoy. There is an audio tour included with
the museum admission ticket which will take the
visitor up to the mouth of the famous Blisworth
Tunnel - at 1 3/4 miles one of the longest navi-
gable tunnels on the canal network. You will
hear stories about Stoke Bruerne's past and
how the building of the Grand Junction Canal
split the village in two. Spacious giftshop selling
a wide range of general gifts, canal and waterways books and other souvenirs. Special events
are held throughout the year - please call for
details.
*Easter-Oct daily 10.00-17.00, Oct-Easter Tue-
Sun 10.00-16.00*
A£3.00 Family Ticket£9.00 C/OAPS£2.50

Northern Ireland

Caverns & Caves

Marble Arch Caves and Cuilcagh Mountain Park

Marlbank Scenic Loop Florencecourt
Fermanagh County Fermanagh BT92 1EW
Tel: 028 6634 8855 Fax: 028 6634 8928
[Off A4 Enniskillen to Sligo road]

Marble Arch Caves and Cuilcagh Mountain Park have recently been awarded Geopark status. Marble Arch Caves are one of Europe's finest showcaves and Cuilcagh Mountain Park is a wilderness protected area of mountain blanket bog. Visitors can take a guided tour of the showcave given by lively and informative guides. *Mar-Sept daily 10.00-16.30, July & Aug 10.00-17.00. Tours are weather permitting, please call before setting out if bad weather is predicted* £6.00 C£3.00 OAPs&Students£4.00 Family ticket (A2+C3) £14.00

Armagh City...

A fine City with award winning attractions including Saint Patrick's Trian Visitor Complex, The Palace Stables Heritage Centre, Armagh Ancestry and much more.

Tourist Information Centre
40 English Street, Armagh BT61 7BA
T: 028 3752 1800
F: 028 3752 8329
W: www.visitarmagh.com
E: armagh@nitic.net

Factory Outlets & Tours

Ballydougan Pottery

Bloomvale House, 171 Plantation Road
Portadown Craigavon County Armagh
BT63 5NN
Tel: 028 3834 2201 Fax: 028 3834 2201
[On the B3, 3m from Lurgan and 4m from Gilford. From Dublin: A1 to Banbridge then A50 to Gilford take the B3 to Lurgan. From Belfast: M1 S to J9, first exit at roundabout to Moira then A6 to Lurgan B3 to Gilford. Follow brown tourist signs from Lurgan or Gilford]

Bloomvale House, dating from 1785, is the home to award-winning Ballydougan Pottery, and the historic thatched house built by a local Huguenot family, has been home to generations of skilled craftmen. After visiting the house the courtyard garden, from which visitors can watch the potters at work, is worth discovering. Visitors can buy the full range of Ballydougan pottery and other crafts here.

All year Mon-Sat 09.00-17.00

Admission Free

Festivals & Shows

Ballymena Show and Countryside Festival

Ballymena Showgrounds and Ecos Centre
Ballymena County Antrim BT43
Tel: 028 2565 2666 Fax: 028 2565 2666
www.ballymenaagriculturalshow.com

[A26 - Ballymena by-pass signposted]

For over one hundred years, the Ballymena Show has been one of Ireland's most popular agricultural events attracting significant crowds of town and country dwellers to the showgrounds at Ballymena over the last weekend in May. Sited in new modern purpose built showgrounds, the Ballymena Show has activities and exhibits to interest all age groups and both town and rural dweller. It features one of the largest exhibitions of livestock in the island of Ireland with 100 cattle classes; 69 horse classes; 124 sheep classes; 10 goat classes; 24 rabbit classes and 171 poultry classes and a large pedigree dog show. The Home Industries and Floral Art sections will feature over 100 classes. In addition to the livestock judging there will be horse

and pony jumping and sheep shearing.
Featuring Children's competitions, events and
Country craft displays and country sports trade
stands.
May 28-29 2004
Fri A£5.00, Sat A£7.00. Concessions available
for C/OAPs

Folk & Local History Museums

Armagh County Museum

The Mall East Armagh County Armagh
BT61 9BE
Tel: 028 3752 3070 Fax: 028 3752 2631
Located near the centre of St Patrick's cathedral city, a visit to Armagh County Museum is an
ideal way to experience a flavour of the orchard
country. Discover a rich and varied legacy
revealed in objects ranging from prehistoric artefacts to household items from a bygone age. An
impressive collection of paintings includes
works by many well known Irish artists.
*All year Mon-Fri 10.00-17.00, Sat 10.00.13.00 &
14.00-17.00*
Admission Free

Saint Patrick's Trian Visitor Complex

40 English Street Armagh County Armagh
BT61 7BA
Tel: 028 3752 1801 Fax: 028 3751 0180
www.visit-armagh.com

[City Centre]

An exciting visitor complex located in the heart
of Armagh City, Saint Patrick's Trian, (pro-
nounced Tree-an) derives its name from the
ancient division of Armagh City into three dis-
tinct districts, or 'Trians'. The complex features
three major exhibitions: Armagh Story - Step
back in time and visit historic Armagh - from the
massive stone monuments of pre-history, with
its myths and legends, to the coming of Saint
Patrick and Celtic Christianity. Francis Johnsto
the renowned Armagh architect relates the his
tory of Georgian buildings in the city in a most
unusual manner. A thought provoking audio-
visual presentation portrays 'belief' throughout
the world, with particular emphasis on Armagh
as the Ecclesiastical Capital of Ireland. Saint
Patrick's Testament takes its title from Saint
Patrick's Confession, and examines the life an
work of our patron Saint and his connections
with Armagh as found in the ancient manuscri
- the 'Book of Armagh'. The Land of Lilliput -
Jonathan Swift, author and clergyman spent
time in the district, and his most famous work
'Gullivers Travels' is encapsulated in the fantas
'Land of Lilliput' where the adventures of
Gulliver are narrated with the help of a 20 foot
giant!
All year Mon-Sat 10.00-17.00, Sun 14.00-17.0
A£4.25 C£2.50 OAPs£3.25 Family Ticket
£10.50

**Discount Offer: Two For The Price O
One**

Ulster American Folk Park

Mellon Road Castletown Omagh County Tyror
BT78 5QY

el: 028 8224 3292 Fax: 028 8224 2241
ww.folkpark.com

of Omagh on the A5 Omagh to Strabane road.
enty of on site parking]

n outdoor museum, established in 1976, that
aces the history of Ulster's links with America
nd the emigration of Ulster residents to North
merica during the 18th and 19th centuries.
he 70-acre site is divided into two parts - Old
/orld and New World, illustrating the various
spects of emigrant life on both sides of the
tlantic.

*or-Sept Mon-Sat 10.30-18.00, Sun and Bank
ols 11.00-18.30, Oct-Mar Mon-Fri 10.30-
7.00, (closed weekends and Bank Hols)*

£4.00 C(5-16)£2.50 Concessions£2.50 Family
icket (A2+C4) £10.00. Group discounts avail-
ble

lster Folk and Transport
luseum

angor Road Cultra Holywood County Down
T18 0EU
el: 028 9042 8428 Fax: 028 9042 8728
ww.magni.org.uk

*)n A2 at Cultra, 7m E of Belfast. On the main
elfast to Bangor Road, close to Belfast City
irport and Belfast Harbour]*

The Museum ranks among Ireland's foremost
visitor attractions, recapturing a disappearing
way of life, preserving traditional skills and celebrating transport history. The outdoor Folk
Museum depicts life at the turn of the 19th century. Indoor exhibition galleries include the
award-winning Irish Railway Collection, Road
Transport Galleries, and the Titanic exhibition.
The Museum has a varied programme of major
events and activities from Midsummer Session
to The Spirit of Christmas Past. Skills once
commonly practised such as lace, sampler
making, spinning and weaving, woodturning,
forgework and basket making are among many
demonstrated and taught at the museum.
Guided tours available on request.

*All year Mar-June Mon-Fri 10.00-17.00, Sat
10.00-18.00, Sun 11.00-18.00; July-Sept Mon-
Sat 10.00-18.00, Sun 11.00-18.00; Oct-Feb
Mon-Fri 10.00-16.00, Sat 10.00-17.00, Sun
11.00-17.00. Please call for Christmas opening
times*

A£6.00 C£3.00 Family Ticket £16.00. Group
rates (15+): 10% discount

Special Events

Easter Celebrations
11/04/2004
*Enjoy a wide ranging programme of entertainment
for all the family including egg decorating, Easter
treasure hunt, Easter art activities, magic shows
and many other traditional activities*

North Down Old Vehicles Event
24/04/2004
*Enjoy the spectacle of hundreds of old vehicles
as they travel from Bangor to Cultra to join one of
the largest outdoor displays of cars, buses and
coaches at the Ulster Folk and Transport
Museum. An enthralling day of entertainment for
all the family with model car racing, miniature train
rides, music and barbecues*

May Day Celebrations
03/05/2004
*Traditional May Day Activities for all ages. A re-
creation of the colourful May Day festivities and
entertainment traditionally associated with this
time of year*

Voyaging in Fact and Fiction
09/05/2004
*An illustrated talk by Michael McCaughan, Keeper
of Transport in the Transport Museum*

RSPB Dawn Chorus Walk
15/05/2004

Experience birdsong at its most dramatic. Experts from the Royal Society for the Protection of Birds will lead the early morning walks and identify the birds. There will also be a special scavenger trail and activities for children. Time: 06.00-08.00. A cooked breakfast (£5.00) will be served afterwards. Tickets: Please telephone 028 9042 8428

Titanic, History and Culture
16/05/2004

An illustrated talk by Michael McCaughan, Keeper of Transport in the Transport Museum. Time: 14.30

Horse-Drawn Cavalcade and Drive
22/05/2004

A wide range of magnificent horse drawn, historic vehicles will be displayed and driven in the Transport Museum's great loughside meadow. Visitors will be given the opportunity to have a drive in the Museum's own horse-drawn trap

Old Buses
23/05/2004

An illustrated talk by Mark Kennedy, Railway Curator and Acting Road Curator in the Irish Railway Collection (AV Room). Time: 14.30

Midsummer Session
05/06/2004

An afternoon of enjoyments for all the family. Join dancing and enjoy traditional music, drinks and barbecue in the Museum's own 1900s town of Ballycultra

Wool Day
12/06/2004

See a variety of processes of preparing and using wool, from sheep shearing to spinning, knitting, weaving, embroidery and felt making. Watch the Ulster Spinners and Weavers Guild attempt to spin and knit a jumper within the day

Storytelling Weekend
26/06/2004

The weekend features storytellers and musicians performing a varied programme in the exhibit buildings of the Folk Museum. Includes children's storytelling sessions.

Cultra Hill Climb
03/07/2004

A historic motor car hill climb competition set in the grounds of the museum and organised by the Thoroughbred Sports Car Club

Capri Car Club
25/07/2004

A day when the Ford Capri Club International and the RS Owners Club visit the Transport Museum and stage a display of around 40 vehicles outside the General Transport Galleries

Food for the Table
01/08/2004

See and sample a variety of traditional foods prepared and displayed in a number of the museum's exhibit buildings

Joint Textile Guilds Exhibition
07/08/2004-15/08/2004

An exhibition by the Textile Guilds displaying a selection of contemporary and traditional skills including patchwork, machine knitting, natural dying, spinning, weaving, embroidery and lace work. The exhibition can be viewed in the Museum's 1900s Ballycultra town

Linen Week
07/08/2004-13/08/2004

An opportunity to watch the processes which are used to turn the flax plant into linen. Pull flax, see ripping, scutching and hackling and displays of old and new linen. Also family activities, linen trails, arts and crafts and reminiscence workshop

Rare Breeds Show and Sale
21/08/2004-22/08/2004

Ireland's largest show and only sale devoted to rare, minority and re-established farm animal breeds set in the Market Square of the museum town. The sale (Saturday 21st only) and show are organised in conjunction with the Rare Breeds Survival Trust N.I.

Crafts and Skills Day
28/08/2004

An opportunity to see skills and crafts once commonly practised such as lace work, sampler making, spinning, weaving, woodturning, forge work and basket making. Also meet the tutors and find out more about the Museum's programme of craft courses

Uileann Pipe Tionol Classes and Recital
25/09/2004

Classes for all ages and abilities. Cost: £10.00, to book a place and for further information please call 028 9042 8428

Harvest Festival and Service
10/10/2004

Enjoy traditional Harvest Day activities, see countryside skills and crafts and sample traditional foods. At 16.00 everyone is welcome to join in the Harvest Thanksgiving Service in Kilmore

Church

Murder Mystery Evenings
16/10/2004-27/10/2004

As dusk falls on Ballycultra Town in the year 1903, play detective to solve a murder and meet some roguish characters along the way. Question the suspects and consider the evidence over a hearty meal in Ballycultra's Victorian tea rooms. Please call to book. Time: 19.30. Tickets: £25.00

Halloween Family Festival
31/10/2004

A variety of activities traditionally associated with the festival of Halloween for children and adults, including apple games, cabbage reading (fortune telling), ghost walks, Halloween art, craft activities and performances by the Armagh Rhymers. During the half term break there will be other Halloween activities

Model Railway Day
13/11/2004

Railway layouts galore, in a variety of scales and gauges, to entertain and enthral children and adults alike. Come along to see these model engines in a unique setting alongside their full sized counterparts. Organised by the Friends of Cultra

Tin Whistle and Flute Classes and Recital
27/11/2004

Suitable for players and for all levels and held in Cultra Manor. Please call to book a place and for further information 028 9042 8428. Cost: £10.00

Transport Collectables Day
27/11/2004

Bring along your transport collectables, pictures, postcards, models, machines, memorabilia, in fact anything to do with transport, to this roadshow style event in the Transport Museum. Find out more and share your enthusiasm with curators and other Museum specialists. An enjoyable way for everyone to view and learn

Traditional Music Concert
01/12/2004-31/12/2004

An evening event in the Church of St John the Baptist. Mid December date to be confirmed. Please call for details 028 9042 8428. Tickets: £7.00

The Spirit of Christmas Past
02/12/2004

Enjoy the nostalgia of Christmas past in the Museum's candlelit Ballycultra Town. See how the festive season has transformed over the decades into the Christmas we celebrate today. Join in craft activities, sample traditional food and hot lunch and listen to the Silver Band playing carols

Carols by Candlelight
13/12/2004-22/12/2004
Held on: 15-19 and 22-23 Dec. Time: 19.30

Advent Procession
15/12/2004
Time: 19.30

Nine Lessons and Carols
19/12/2004
Time: 16.00

Gardens & Horticulture

Benvarden Garden

Benvarden Dervock Ballymoney County Antrim
BT53 6NN
Tel: 028 2074 1331 Fax: 028 2074 1955
[On B67 Coleraine / Ballycastle road. 7m E of Coleraine, 10m from Giants Causeway signposted]

Benvarden House is situated on the banks of the River Bush where the river is crossed by the Coleraine to Ballycastle road. The Walled Garden, about 2 acres in area, appears on a map dated 1788 and has been cultivated since then without interruption. The Garden is one of the finest in the North of Ireland and ranges from beautiful rose beds to a well stocked kitchen garden. The extensive pleasure grounds stretch down to the banks of the river which is spanned by a splendid iron bridge 90 feet long.
1 June-31 Aug Tue-Sun & Bank Hol 13.30-17.30
A£3.00 C£0.50

Heritage & Industrial

Lagan Lookout Centre

1 Donegall Quay Belfast County Antrim
BT1 3EA
Tel: 028 9031 5444 Fax: 028 9031 1955
The Lagan Lookout Centre offers a range of informative exhibits allowing visitors to celebrate the engineering achievement of the £14 million Weir and interact with both Belfast's historical

and future developments around the river. Visit the Lagan Lookout, study the working of the Lagan Weir and follow the rise of Belfast into today's modern city.

Apr-Sept Mon-Fri 11.00-17.00, Sat 12.00-17.00, Sun 14.00-17.00, Oct-Mar Tue-Fri 11.00-15.30, Sat 13.00-16.30, Sun 14.00-16.30. Closed Mon
A£1.50 C(under5)£Free C£0.75 OAPs£1.00 Family Ticket (A2+C2) £4.00

North Down Heritage Centre

Town Hall The Castle Bangor County Down BT20 4BT

Tel: 028 9127 1200 Fax: 028 9147 8906

www.northdown.gov.uk/heritage

[Centre of town in Castle Park. Plenty of parking on site]

Local History and works of art reflecting aspects of North Down's historical and cultural past. Audio-visual shows, including the Ballycroghan Swords, dating from 500 BC, and a 9th century handbell found near Bangor. Toys and railway displays. Vintage films. Observation Beehive in summer.

Tue-Sat 10.30-16.30, Sun 14.00-16.30, Jul & Aug 10.30-17.30, Sun 14.00-17.30

Admission Free

Old Bushmills Distillery

Distillery Road Bushmills County Antrim BT57 8XH
Tel: 028 2073 1521 Fax: 028 2073 1339
[A2 and follow signposts]

Old Bushmills was granted its licence in 1608 and is the oldest licenced whiskey distillery in the world. Situated just a mile from the spectacular Giant's Causeway, the distillery lies in an area of outstanding natural beauty and rich in history and folklore. There is a good visitor centre from which guided tours of the distillery start. Pushchair and disabled access for the site only and is NOT available for the Tour.

Tour Times Apr-Oct Mon-Sat 09.30-17.30, Sun 12.00-17.30, Nov-Mar Mon-Fri 10.30, 11.30, 13.30, 14.30, 15.30 Sat-Sun 13.30, 14.30, 15.30. Closed 12 July. Please ring to check opening times at Christmas and New Year
A5.00 C(0-18)£2.50 OAPs&Students £4.50 Family Ticket (A2+C2) £13.00

Palace Stables Heritage Centre

The Palace Demense Armagh County Armagh BT60 4EL

olour Section

BEDFORD BUTTERFLY PARK
and nature centre

Visit our exotic tropical house, enjoy the butterfly garden and wander through the colourful wildflower hay meadows.

Other attractions include:
Adventure Playground
Bugs and Beasties
Animal Farm
Tea Room
Gift Shop
Nature Trail

25% discount on admission charges with Days Out UK voucher *please see back of book*

Opening Times
Open daily from Feb 13th to Oct 31st – 10am to 5pm
Open Thursday to Sunday incl from Nov 1st to Dec 20th – 10am to 4pm
Closed from Dec 21st 2004 to January 7th 2005

Renhold Road, Wilden, Bedfordshire MK44 2PX
Tel: 01234 772 770 www.bedford-butterflies.co.uk

BEDFORD MUSEUM

Embark on a fascinating journey through the human and natural history of North Bedfordshire, pausing briefly to glimpse at wonders from more distant lands.

Castle Lane, Bedford, MK40 3XD
Tel: 01234 353323
www.bedfordmuseum.org

WOODSIDE
Animal Farm & Leisure Park

Amazing alpacas, daft ducks, fabulous flamingoes, gorgeous goats, incredible iguanas, lovely llamas, marvellous monkeys, outrageous owls, perfect pigs, ridiculous raccoons, terrific tortoises, wild wallabies.

★ Animal Encounters ★ Tractor Rides
★ Bouncy Castles ★ Trampolines
★ Indoor & Outdoor Play Areas
★ New "Country Fair" (opening Easter)
★ 18 hole Crazy Golf Course
★ Coffee Shop ★ Farm Shop,
★ Birthday Parties ★ Group Visits
★ Special event days including clowns, magicians, reptile celebrities, teddy bears picnic and many more.

Woodside Animal Farm, Woodside Rd, Slip End, Nr. Luton, Beds.
Telephone: 01582 841044
www.woodsidefarm.co.uk

5 mins from J9/J10 of M1. Just off A5.
Follow brown tourist signs for "Wildfowl Park"

See relevant county pages for listing details

2

Old Warden Park

It's so easy to see the attraction!

Discounted Park Passport Tickets Available

Old Warden Park
Nr Biggleswade
Bedfordshire SG18 9EA
**01767
627288**

Shuttleworth Collection Of Historic Aeroplanes
Play Centre · Swiss Garden · Bird Of Prey Centre
Gift Shop · Restaurant · Ample Parking · Open Daily

BEALE · PARK ·

- All New ROPLAY Playground
- Amazing Rare Birds - Flamingos, Parrots, Peacocks & More
- Huge Owlry, Deer Park
- Traditional Steam Railway Pets Corner, animal handling sessions
- Acres of Picnic Areas
- Splash Pools for Kids
- Farm Animals & Ponies, Piggery
- New Meerkat and Wallaby enclosures
- Full Cafeteria
- Summer River Boat Cruises
- Model Boat & Ship Exhibition
- Hartslock Gift Shop
- Gardens, Trails and Walks
- Statues, Ponds & Fountains
- Day Ticket River & Lake Fishing
- Miniature 'Children's' Golf

Beale Park has masses to do for all ages, especially younger children! Come and enjoy a traditional day out at this unique Thames-side Park. We are dedicated to the conservation of rare birds and this remarkable site; help us just by visiting! There's a great new Education Officer on site too!

2003 Prices: £6 Adults, £4 children, under 3s free, great value and many concessions
(Unemployed, student, family, etc.) incl. excellent party rates.
Beale Park, Lower Basildon, Reading, Berks, RG8 9NH
0118 9845172 (Fax 0118 9845171)
bealepark@bun.com www.bealepark.co.uk

Sign posted from Jn 12 of the M4 (Theale), Beale Park is beside the Thames on the A329 just outside Pangbourne, toward Goring & Streatley.

Beale Park... "The Freedom of the Countryside".

The Child-Beale Trust is a registered charity.

A 42-foot drop, abrupt twists and wild 180-degree turns while riders experience extreme acceleration, breaking and maneuverability.

LEGOLAND® Windsor's new JUNGLE coaster is the fastest ride in the Park, topping speeds of 26mph while zipping along 1,300 feet of steel track. It also has a higher drop than any other attraction in the Park, towering nearly five stories above the ground.

2004 Opening Dates: 20th March - 31st Oct
Information and booking number: 08705 040404
For more information visit: www.legoland.co.uk

LEGO, the LEGO logo and LEGOLAND are trademarks of the LEGO Group. ©2003 The LEGO Group.

See relevant county pages for listing details

3

See relevant county pages for listing details

4

See relevant county pages for listing details

Cheshire

HUGE SHARKS

BLUE PLANET
AQUARIUM

The Ultimate Underwater Adventure!
30 mins from J 20a M6. Open from 10am daily

Uncover the fascinating World of hats

Exciting encounters with all aspects of hatmaking

Fully restored working machinery

Displays of historical and contemporary hats

Special events, workshops and demonstrations

Education and group tours by arrangement

Level 2 Internet Cafe and shop

OPENING TIMES:
Mon-Sat: 10am-5pm Sun: 11am-5pm

0161 3557 770

WELLINGTON MILL, WELLINGTON RD. SOUTH,
STOCKPORT SK3 0EU
www.hatworks.org.uk

The Museum of Hatting
· Stockport ·
Hat Works

STOCKPORT
METROPOLITAN BOROUGH COUNCIL

englandsnorthwest
tourism awards
winner
2002

Safeway
EXCELLENCE
IN ENGLAND
SILVER WINNER

See relevant county pages for listing details

6

See relevant county pages for listing details

blueeef
A Q U A R I U M ®

NEWQUAY | PORTSMOUTH | TYNEMOUTH

T H E U L T I M A T E U N D E R S E A S A F A R I

There's a world of underwater adventure waiting to be discovered at Blue Reef Aquarium. Stroll among the colourful inhabitants of a coral reef in a **spectacular underwater tunnel**. Living displays bring the aquatic world to life. With talks, feeding demonstrations and special events, **it's an unforgettable experience.**

Open every day from **10am** | A great visit whatever the weather
NEWQUAY : Towan Beach, Newquay t **01637 878134**
PORTSMOUTH : Southsea, Portsmouth t **023 9287 5222**
TYNEMOUTH : Grand Parade, Tynemouth t **0191 258 1031**
info@bluereefaquarium.co.uk | www.bluereefaquarium.co.uk

See relevant county pages for listing details

See relevant county pages for listing details

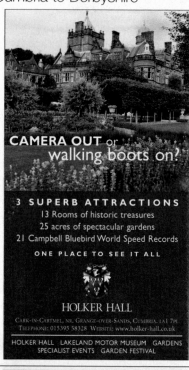

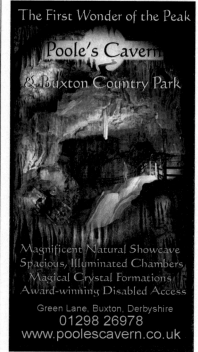
See relevant county pages for listing details

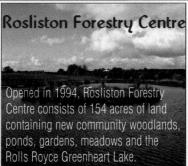

See relevant county pages for listing details

Devon to Dorset

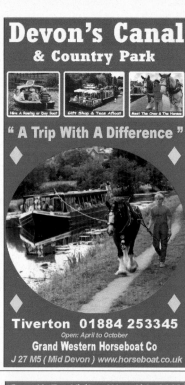

See relevant county pages for listing details

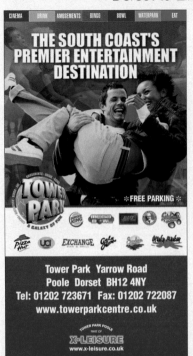

Monkey World

Meet the family ...and the stars of TV's 'Monkey Business'

NOW OPEN The South's Largest Adventure Play Area

Close encounters with over 160 rescued or endangered apes and monkeys in their 65-acre woodland home. Fun and fascination for all!

MONKEY WORLD
APE RESCUE CENTRE
Nr. WAREHAM, DORSET
One mile from Wool on the Bere Regis/Wool road.
OPEN EVERY DAY (except Christmas) FROM 10AM
Information 01929 462537
www.monkeyworld.org

VOTED DORSET'S BEST DAY OUT!

Tower Park

CINEMA | DRINK | AMUSEMENTS | BINGO | BOWL | WATERPARK | EAT

THE SOUTH COAST'S PREMIER ENTERTAINMENT DESTINATION

✳ FREE PARKING ✳

Tower Park Yarrow Road
Poole Dorset BH12 4NY
Tel: 01202 723671 Fax: 01202 722087
www.towerparkcentre.co.uk

TOWER PARK POOLE PART OF
X-LEISURE
www.x-leisure.co.uk

Walford Mill Craft Centre

Walford Mill
CRAFT CENTRE

1/4 mile north of Wimborne

FOR QUALITY CRAFT WORK

A converted mill by the river Allen
with a gallery, craft shop, bistro,
craft school and workshops

OPEN MON-SAT, 10am-5pm. SUN 12 noon-5pm
(closed on Mondays, Jan-Mar)
FREE ENTRY

Walford Mill, Stone Lane, Wimborne Tel: 01202 841400
www.walfordmillcrafts.co.uk

Mizen Head Signal Station

Mizen Head Signal Station
IRELAND'S MOST SOUTHWESTERLY POINT!

In any weather the Mizen is spellbinding.
Keeper's Quarters, The 99 Steps, The famous
Arched Bridge, Navigational Aids Simulator,
Mizen Cafe, Shop@TheMizen.

OPEN DAILY: Mid-march, April, May & Oct Daily 10.30-17.00
June to September Daily 10.00-18.00
OPEN WEEKENDS: November-Mid-March 11.00-16.00

PRICES FOR 2003:

Adult	Euro 4.50
OAP/Student	Euro 3.50
Children Under 12	Euro 2.50
Children Under 5	Free
Family Ticket: 2 Adults/3 Children	£11.00 Euro 14.00
Groups 10+	Less 10%

IF YOU MISS THE MIZEN YOU HAVEN'T DONE IRELAND

Mizen Tourism Co-operative Society Ltd 028-35115 Goleen, West Cork, Ireland
www.mizenhead.net www.mizenhead.ie info@mizenhead.net

See relevant county pages for listing details

See relevant county pages for listing details

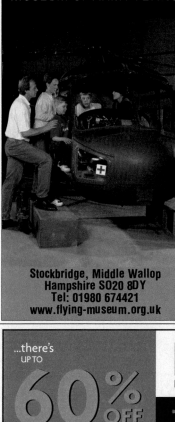

See relevant county pages for listing details

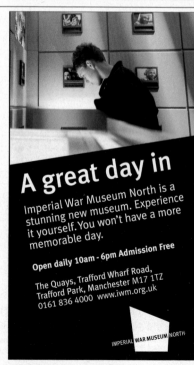
See relevant county pages for listing details

Lancashire

See relevant county pages for listing details

19

BBC Television Centre Tours

Awarded 'Best Sightseeing Tour in London' 2002 by the London Tourist Board.
You must pre-book by calling: **0870 603 0304*** or textphone **0870 903 0304.**

www.bbc.co.uk/tours

* Lines open from 9am to 5pm. Calls are charged at National Rate
and may be monitored or recorded for training.

BBC TOURS

Experience...

breathtaking views of London, fine
dining and world class entertainment
from the best seat on the River Thames.

Try our Thames Circular Cruise or Point-to-Point
service and discover London in style.

FOR FURTHER INFORMATION:

Restaurant Cruises
Tel: 020 7925 2215
www.bateauxlondon.com

Sightseeing Cruises
Tel: 020 7987 1185
www.catamarancruisers.co.uk

CATAMARAN CRUISERS

...Unique

BRITISH LIBRARY

TAKE A LOOK INSIDE

Everyone is welcome

Tour our free galleries
Enjoy a talk or film
Meet friends for a coffee
Browse in our bookshop

**Come in and see
for yourself – we're
open 7 days a week**

96 Euston Rd London NW1
T +44 (0)20 7412 7332

⊖ ⇌ King's Cross & Euston

www.bl.uk

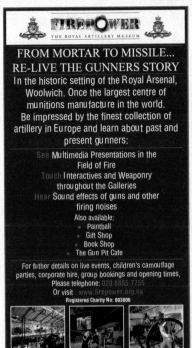

See relevant county pages for listing details

London

MUSEUM OF GARDEN HISTORY

Discover more about the history of gardening and some of the people who have helped shape garden design. Exhibits include a wide variety of artefacts and fascinating displays. Garden, Gift Shop and Cafe.

Lambeth Palace Road
London SE1 7LB
Tel 020 7401 8865
Fax 020 7401 8869
info@museumgardenhistory.org
www.museumgardenhistory.org

ACCESS
ALL AREAS

Experience the heart and soul of England Rugby
on a Twickenham Stadium Tour.
Call 020 8892 8877 or visit www.rfu.com

TWICKENHAM
STADIUM TOURS & MUSEUM OF RUGBY

NATIONAL PORTRAIT GALLERY

Come face to face with Henry VIII,
Beatrix Potter and The Beatles...
all under one roof

ADMISSION FREE OPEN DAILY 10am-6pm
Late Opening Thursday & Friday until 9pm
Portrait Restaurant / Café / Shops ⊖ Leceister Square
www.npg.org.uk   Recorded information: 020 7312 2463

See relevant county pages for listing details

GREAT FUN FOR ALL THE FAMILY

From sharks, stingrays and clownfish to moray eels, lionfish and sideways walking crabs, the London Aquarium is full of surprises with 350 different species to discover.

Located in County Hall, right next to the London Eye, the London Aquarium is just a short walk from Waterloo station.

So, don't plan a day out without visiting London's only Aquarium!

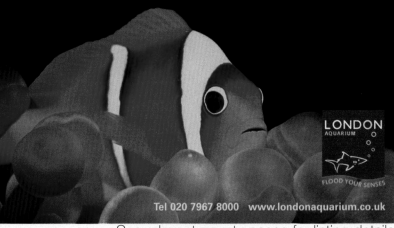

LONDON
AQUARIUM

FLOOD YOUR SENSES

Tel 020 7967 8000   www.londonaquarium.co.uk

See relevant county pages for listing details

London

1 National Maritime Museum

2 Royal Observatory

3 Queen's House

4 FREE*

MARITIME MUSEUM   **O**ROYAL OBSERVATORY GREENWICH

GREENWICH • LONDON

20 minutes from central London
Exhibition and travel details on
www.nmm.ac.uk
or call 0870 780 4564

*Charges may apply to special exhibitions

Kew Gardens
World Heritage Site

ROYAL BOTANIC GARDENS KEW

SHAKESPEARE'S GLOBE THEATRE TOUR AND EXHIBITION
Bankside - London
TEL 020 7902 1500   FAX 020 7902 1515   www.shakespeares-globe.org

See relevant county pages for listing details

26

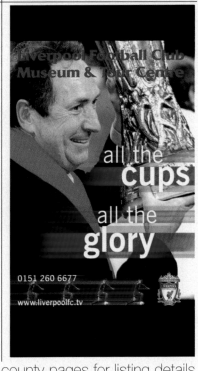
See relevant county pages for listing details

See relevant county pages for listing details

Please turn to p.561 for the Days Out UK discount vouchers. They could help save you money at visitor attractions across the UK

See relevant county pages for listing details

See relevant county pages for listing details

BUCKIE DRIFTER
Maritime Heritage Centre

REGISTERED MUSEUM

Find out about fishing Life

New activities for 2004

Tea Room & Gift Shop

Open from April to October

Families welcome

Catch the spirit of the North East

FREUCHNY RD • BUCKIE
Tel: 01542 834646

KELBURN

The natural place to go

CASTLE & COUNTRY CENTRE

Kelburn is the home of the Earls of Glasgow, famous for its Castle, historic gardens, unique trees and romantic glen.

Waterfalls, deep gorges, attractive woodland and spectacular views over the Firth of Clyde make it a place of great natural beauty. There's a 'History of Kelburn' cartoon exhibition, history trail, family museum, ranger and falconry centre, pony trekking and riding school, stockade, adventure course, pets corner, gift shop and licenced cafe. The 'Secret Forest' is Scotland's most unusual attraction, where you can discover the Giant's Castle, the crocodile swamp, the secret grotto, the gingerbread house, the Chinese garden, the maze of the Green Man, a 40 foot high pagoda and a hundred other surprises.

Centre open 10am - 6pm, 3 April - 31 Oct.
Castle open from 26 June - 5 Sept only.

In winter, only grounds & riding school open - 11am until dusk.

www.kelburncountrycentre.com
Fairlie, near Largs, Ayrshire   Tel: (01475) 568685

The Biggest Family Day Out in Scotland

over 30 MAJOR rides & Attractions

Plus A giant *INDOOR* family **Entertainment Complex • • •** M&D's

**M&D's, Scotland's Theme Park
Strathclyde Park, Motherwell
Call Now on: 01698 333777**

Paxton House,
Gallery & Country Park
Berwick upon Tweed TD15 1SZ

Tel:01289 386291 info@paxtonhouse.com
www.paxtonhouse.com

Magnificent 18th century Palladian Country House, Georgian period rooms, spectacular Picture Gallery, 80acres gardens, woodland and riverside walks. gift shop, tearoom and adventure playground. Special events and exhibitions programme.

For full venue details please see page 367

See relevant county pages for listing details

31

Scotland

From Aviation to Zoology
see it all at the
National Museums of Scotland

Royal Museum
Chambers Street, Edinburgh
Telephone 0131 247 4422

Museum of Scotland
Chambers Street, Edinburgh
Telephone 0131 247 4422

Museum of Scottish Country Life
Kittochside, East Kilbride
Telephone 01355 224 181

Museum of Flight
East Fortune Airfield, East Lothian
Telephone 01620 880 308

National War Museum of Scotland
Edinburgh Castle, Edinburgh
Telephone 0131 225 7534

Shambellie House, Museum of Costume
New Abbey, Dumfries
Telephone 01387 850 375

NM|S National Museums of Scotland

www.nms.ac.uk

See relevant county pages for listing details

32

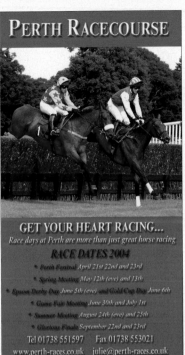
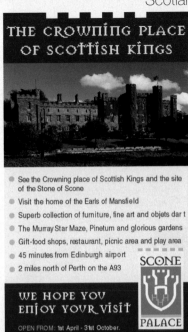
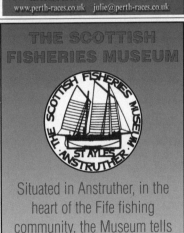

See relevant county pages for listing details

See relevant county pages for listing details

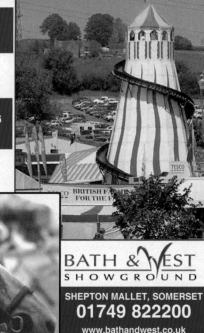

See relevant county pages for listing details

Somerset

Let's go on holiday for the day!

Butlins

BOGNOR REGIS	**01243 822445**
MINEHEAD	**01643 708171**
SKEGNESS	**01754 765567**

Come and experience the best of Butlins with a day crammed with all the best bits of a Butlins holiday. You can enjoy hours of fun with the vast range of entertainment and activities on offer, included in your day pass are:

- SPLASH SUB-TROPICAL WATERWORLD
- OUTDOOR FUN POOL
- TRADITIONAL FUN OF THE FAIR
- NODDY'S TOYLAND RIDES AND SHOWS
- INDOOR ADVENTURE PLAY AREA
- OUTDOOR ADVENTURE PLAY FORT
- SPORTS WORLD
- WEATHERPROOF SKYLINE PAVILION

visit: www.butlins.com

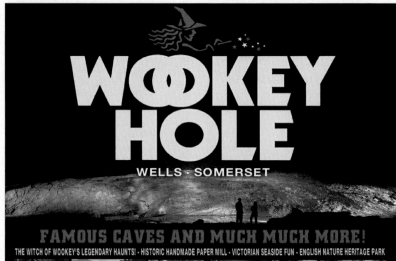

WOOKEY HOLE

WELLS · SOMERSET

FAMOUS CAVES AND MUCH MUCH MORE!

THE WITCH OF WOOKEY'S LEGENDARY HAUNTS! · HISTORIC HANDMADE PAPER MILL · VICTORIAN SEASIDE FUN · ENGLISH NATURE HERITAGE PARK

OPEN ALL YEAR ROUND 7 DAYS A WEEK from 10am. Last admissions: April to October 5pm - November to March 4pm
Phone for details of Late Night Ghost Tours (Wednesdays July 1st to Sept 1st), Special Summer Events & Christmas opening times
Information line 01749 672 243   www.wookey.co.uk

See relevant county pages for listing details

36

www.altontowers.com
please see page 417 for full details

All year Mon-Sat 09.00-17.30,
Sun 11.00-16.00.
Closed 25-26 Dec & 1 Jan

Aynsley China Factory Shop
Longton
Stoke-on-Trent
ST3 1HS
01782 339420

Open 20th March -
31st October 2004

near Tamworth, Staffordshire B78 3TW
Tel: 08708 725252 (24 hour infoline)
draytonmanor.co.uk

Voted Best UK Attraction for Children
(Group Leisure Industry Awards 2003)

GLADSTONE
WORKING POTTERY MUSEUM

The history of the
Potteries all wrapped up in one
amazing museum!

Only at Gladstone can you step back in time,
cross the cobbled yard and explore the sole
surviving Victorian Pottery Factory complete
with bottle ovens

● Skilled pottery demonstrations
● Make & decorate your own pottery
● Special events
● Tearoom, gift shop, free
  parking

Uttoxeter Road Longton Stoke-on-Trent ST3 1PQ
Tel: 01782 319232 www.stoke.gov.uk/gladstone
e-mail: gladstone@stoke.gov.uk

See relevant county pages for listing details

Staffordshire

LICHFIELD HERITAGE CENTRE
Walk through 2000 years of Lichfield's history

See:
- Exciting new exhibition
- Staffordshire Millennium Tapestry gallery
- The City's silver, ancient charters and archives
- Two audio visual presentations covering The Civil War and Lichfield's history
- Plus for the children 'The Mouse Trail' fun & learning at the same time

Relax:
- In our air conditioned Coffee shop
- Select special mementos in our History and Gift Shops

Open Monday to Saturday - 10am-5pm,
Sunday - 10.30am -5pm
(Last admission 4pm)
Adults £3.50, special rates for children, families & concessions
RATES ARE FOR 2003
Market Square,
Lichfield WS13 6LG
Tel: 01543 256611
Fax: 01543 414749
info@lichfieldheritage.org.uk
www.lichfieldheritage.org.uk

Festival Park Stoke-on-Trent
Staffordshire ST1 5PU
Tel: 01782 205747
www.waterworld.co.uk

10% off with Days Out UK
(subject to terms & conditions)

ROYAL DOULTON
VISITOR CENTRE
Home of the Royal Doulton Figure

Nile Street, Burslem, Stoke on Trent Tel - 01782 292434

The home of the Royal Doulton figure
Museum, demonstration area, video, tea room & shop
Open: Mon to Sat 9.30am - 5.00pm; Sun 10.30am - 4.30pm. Factory tours available on weekdays,
Mon-Thurs 1030 & 1400 Fri 1030 & 1330 except during factory holidays
(booking recommended - over 7's only)
Admission: Visitor Centre, Adults £3, Concessions £2.25.
Factory Tour (incl Visitor Centre): Adults £6.50, Conc. £5.
Fully accessible Visitor Centre - Ramps & toilets
(The factory tour is not suitable for disabled visitors)
Group Packages available on request

See relevant county pages for listing details

38

Painshill Park
Portsmouth Road Cobham Surrey KT11 1JE
Tel: 01932 868113 Fax: 01932 868001
www.painshill.co.uk

Painshill Park is a unique award winning restoration of England's Georgian Heritage. Within its 160 acres, its Hamilton landscapes are a work of art that influenced the future of England's countryside and culture.

Rural Life Centre
Reeds Road, Off A287,
Tilford, Farnham, Surrey

Museum of past village life
Café • Playground
Light railway
(Sundays)
Many special events
(send SAE for diary)

Open Wed – Sun 10am to 5pm
(Nov–Mar Wed & Sun only
11am to 4pm)
01252 795571
rural.life@lineone.net
www.rural-life.org.uk

The Old Kiln Museum Trust
is a registered charity

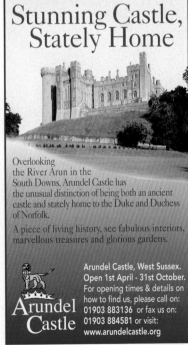

Stunning Castle, Stately Home

Overlooking the River Arun in the South Downs, Arundel Castle has the unusual distinction of being both an ancient castle and stately home to the Duke and Duchess of Norfolk.

A piece of living history, see fabulous interiors, marvellous treasures and glorious gardens.

Arundel Castle

Arundel Castle, West Sussex.
Open 1st April - 31st October.
For opening times & details on how to find us, please call on:
01903 883136 or fax us on:
01903 884581 or visit:
www.arundelcastle.org

See relevant county pages for listing details

Preston Manor

A delightful Manor House, that powerfully evokes the atmosphere of an Edwardian gentry home, both 'Upstairs' and 'Downstairs'. Explore over twenty rooms on four floors, from the superbly renovated servants' quarters in the basement to the attic bedrooms on the top floor. Adjacent to Preston Park, the house also comprises picturesque walled gardens and a pet cemetery.

ADMISSION FEE PAYABLE

PRESTON MANOR, PRESTON DROVE, BRIGHTON, BN1 6SD, TEL: 01273 292770
www.prestonmanor.virtualmuseum.info

The Royal Pavilion, Brighton

If you're amazed by the exterior, just wait until you see the interior…
Universally acclaimed as one of the most exotically beautiful buildings in the British Isles, the Royal Pavilion is the magnificent former seaside residence of King George IV. Decorated in Chinese taste with an Indian exterior, this Regency palace is quite breathtaking. Restored Regency gardens, tearooms, guided tours and giftshop.

ADMISSION FEE PAYABLE

THE ROYAL PAVILION, BRIGHTON, BN1 1EE
GENERAL TEL: 01273 290900
FOR TOURS TELEPHONE: 01273 292820/2
www.royalpavilion.org.uk

Tangmere Military Aviation Museum
Tangmere Chichester W.Sussex PO20 2ES
E-mail: admin@tangmere-museum.org.uk

Don't miss this unique collection of aviation exhibits and poignant stories associated with this famous Battle of Britain airfield.

OPEN FEBRUARY - NOVEMBER

Free Parking Cafeteria Souvenir Shop Picnic Area Memorial Garden Disabled Visitors Welcomed
'The Aviation Museum With More Than Just Aircraft'

For more information telephone
01243 775223

TANGMERE
Charity Commission Reg No 299327 www.tangmere-museum.org.uk

WEST DEAN
GARDENS

Historic Houses Association/ Christie's Garden of the Year 2002

Extensive formal gardens, with stunning 300ft pergola, arboretum and Victorian walled kitchen garden.

Open Daily:
- March, April & October 11am–5pm
- May to Sept 10.30am–5pm

For further details contact:
Gardens Office, West Dean, Chichester, W. Sussex PO18 0QZ
T 01243 818210
E gardens@westdean.org.uk
www.westdean.org.uk

King Arthur's Labyrinth

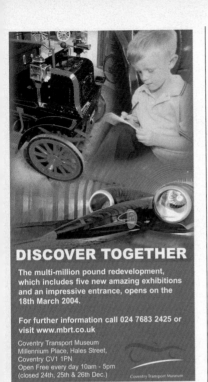

DISCOVER TOGETHER

The multi-million pound redevelopment, which includes five new amazing exhibitions and an impressive entrance, opens on the 18th March 2004.

For further information call 024 7683 2425 or visit www.mbrt.co.uk

Coventry Transport Museum
Millennium Place, Hales Street,
Coventry CV1 1PN
Open Free every day 10am - 5pm
(closed 24th, 25th & 26th Dec.)

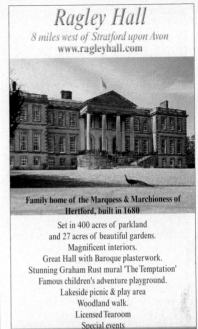

Ragley Hall

8 miles west of Stratford upon Avon
www.ragleyhall.com

Family home of the Marquess & Marchioness of Hertford, built in 1680

Set in 400 acres of parkland
and 27 acres of beautiful gardens.
Magnificent interiors.
Great Hall with Baroque plasterwork.
Stunning Graham Rust mural 'The Temptation'
Famous children's adventure playground.
Lakeside picnic & play area
Woodland walk.
Licensed Tearoom
Special events

Open April to September
Please see our listing on p502 and our website for details

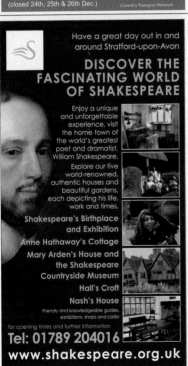

Have a great day out in and around Stratford-upon-Avon

DISCOVER THE FASCINATING WORLD OF SHAKESPEARE

Enjoy a unique and unforgettable experience, visit the home town of the world's greatest poet and dramatist, William Shakespeare.

Explore our five world-renowned, authentic houses and beautiful gardens, each depicting his life, work and times.

Shakespeare's Birthplace and Exhibition

Anne Hathaway's Cottage

Mary Arden's House and the Shakespeare Countryside Museum

Hall's Croft

Nash's House

Friendly and knowledgeable guides, exhibitions, shops and cafés

for opening times and further information

Tel: **01789 204016**

www.shakespeare.org.uk

The Teddy Bear Museum
Stratford upon Avon

Open every day except 25/26 December
19 Greenhill Street
01789 293160
www.theteddybearmuseum.com

See relevant county pages for listing details

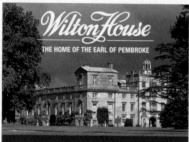

Visit Yorkshire's premier art venue and adjacent Winter Garden

Enjoy Blockbuster exhibitions from national collections including Tate and Victoria and Albert Museum. See the best craft and design, be dazzled by Sheffield's nationally acclaimed collection of metalwork and discover treasures inside the world renowned Ruskin Gallery.

Open Mon - Sat 10am - 5 pm Sun 11am - 5 pm Admission prices vary

Millennium Galleries, Arundel Gate, Sheffield, S1 2PP Telephone: 0114 2782600
Email: info@sheffieldgalleries.org.uk www.sheffieldgalleries.org.uk

BRIDLINGTON LEISURE WORLD

Three pools including a beach effect wave pool

The Promenade
Bridlington
Yorkshire
YO15 2QO
01262 606715
www.bridlington.net/leisureworld

Henry Moore Institute

The Henry Moore Institute is a centre for the study of sculpture, with exhibition galleries, a library and archive, and an active research programme.

74 The Headrow, Leeds
West Yorkshire LS1 3AH
Tel: 0113 246 7467
Recorded Information Line: 0113 234 3158

www.henry-moore-fdn.co.uk

See relevant county pages for listing details

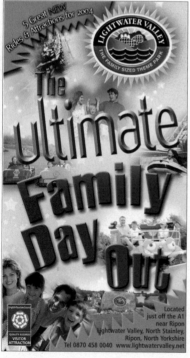
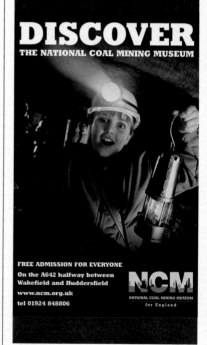
See relevant county pages for listing details

Yorkshire

The World of JAMES HERRIOT

Museum & Visitor Attraction
in THIRSK - North Yorkshire

Fun for all the Family

An 'all-weather'' attraction

Open 7 days
a week

Easter to September
10am to 6pm
(last admission 5pm)

October to Easter
11am to 4pm
(last admission 3pm)

23 Kirkgate, Thirsk, North Yorkshire,
YO7 1PL Tel: 01845 524234
www.worldofjamesherriot.org

Please turn to
p.561 for the
Days Out UK
discount vouchers.
They could help
save you money at
visitor attractions
across the UK

Millennium Galleries

Visit Yorkshire's premier art venue and adjacent Winter Garden

Enjoy Blockbuster exhibitions from national collections including Tate and Victoria and
Albert Museum. See the best craft and design, be dazzled by Sheffield's nationally acclaimed
collection of metalwork and discover treasures inside the world renowned Ruskin Gallery.

Open Mon - Sat 10am - 5 pm Sun 11am - 5 pm Admission prices vary

Millennium Galleries, Arundel Gate, Sheffield, S1 2PP Telephone: 0114 2782600
Email: info@sheffieldgalleries.org.uk www.sheffieldgalleries.org.uk

See relevant county pages for listing details

48

Tel: 028 3752 9629 Fax: 028 3752 9630
www.armagh.gov.uk

[Armagh City]

Leaving Town? Why not leave the 19th century and 20th century too? Visit the Palace Stables Heritage Centre, Armagh where history comes alive. Every day of the week costumed historical interpreters recreate life in the Georgian period in both its grandeur and squalor. Visitors may mingle, speak and ask whatever questions they wish, to obtain a more vivid picture of life in the period. The site includes the Primate's Chapel, Archbishop Robinson's Palace, Period Tack Room and Coachman's Kitchen, Ice House, Children's Adventure Playground, Garden of the Senses and fully licensed Restaurant.
All year Mon-Sat 10.00-17.00, Sun 14.00-17.00
A£4.25 C£2.50 OAPs£3.25 Family Ticket
£10.50

Discount Offer: Two For The Price Of One

Somme Heritage Centre

233 Bangor Road Newtownards County Down
BT23 7PH
Tel: 028 9182 3202 Fax: 028 9182 3214
[Off A21 Bangor to Newtownards road]

The Somme Heritage Centre is a unique visitor attraction of international significance showing the awful reality of the Great War, and its effects on the community at home. The centre commemorates the involvement of the 36th (Ulster) and 16th (Irish) Divisions in the Battle of the Somme, the 10th (Irish) Division in Gallipoli, Salonika and Palestine and provides displays and information on the entire Irish contribution to WWI.
All year; Apr-June & Sept Mon-Thur 10.00-16.00 Sat & Sun 12.00-16.00, July-Aug Mon-Fri 10.00-17.00 Sat & Sun 12.00-17.00. Oct-Mar Mon-Thur 10.00-16.00
A£3.75 C&OAPs£2.75 Family Ticket £10.00

Arthur Ancestral Home

Dreen Cullybackey Ballymena County Antrim
Tel/Fax: 028 2588 0781 (Seasonal)
[NW of the village of Cullybackey]

When you walk up the path you enter a world that has all but disappeared. The cottage is where the forebears of Chester Alan Arthur, 21st President of the USA once lived. It has been carefully restored to let you see how the Arthur family lived there, two centuries ago. Regular demonstrations of traditional cooking and crafts are given by ladies, dressed in period costume, and evenings of music, song and story-telling also take place throughout the summer months.
Easter-Sept Mon-Fri 10.30-17.00, Sat 10.30-16.00. Closed Sun
A£2.10 C(under 5)£Free C(5-15)£1.10 Family Ticket (A2+C2)£4.20

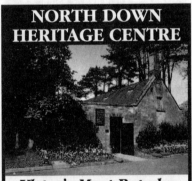

Mount Stewart House, Garden and Temple of the Winds

Mountstewart Portaferry Road Newtownards
County Down BT22 2AD
Tel: 028 4278 8387 Fax: 028 4278 8569
[A20, 5m from Newtownards on Portaferry road]

A fascinating 18th century house with 19th century additions, the childhood home of Lord Castlereagh and famous for its magnificent garden, the creation of Edith, Lady Londonderry. The formal series of outdoor rooms contains an unrivalled collection of plants from all over the world, set in vibrant parterres and lush borders and with superb vistas.

House: 13 Mar-30 Apr Sat-Sun & Bank Hols 12.00-18.00, May-June Mon, Wed-Fri 13.00-18.00, Sat-Sun 12.00-18.00, July-Aug daily 12.00-18.00, Sept Wed-Mon 12.00-18.00, Oct Sat-Sun 12.00-18.00. Formal Gardens: Mar Sat-Sun & Bank Hols 10.00-16.00, Apr 10.00-18.00, May-Sept daily 10.00-18.00. Lakeside Walks: all year daily 10.00-sunset

House & Gardens: A£5.20 C£2.50 Family Ticket (A2+C3) £10.80. Gardens: A£4.20 C£2.20 Family Ticket £9.30. Lakeside Walks (Nov-end Feb): A£3.00 C£1.50 Family Ticket £7.00

Scrabo Tower

Scrabo Country Park Scrabo Road
Newtownards County Down BT23 4SJ
Tel: 028 9181 1491 Fax: 028 9182 0695
[From Belfast take dual carriageway to Newtownards. From roundabout at Newtownards shopping centre turn R and take 2nd L (Blair Mayne Rd) following signs to Scrabo Country Park]

Scrabo Tower is one of Northern Ireland's best known landmarks. Overlooking Strangford Lough and the whole of North Down, the Tower provides the visitor with some of the finest views of the country. There is also an exhibition detailing the history of the Tower and surrounding countryside as well as a twelve minute audio-visual show.

Easter-Sept Sat-Thur 10.30-18.00. Country park open all year daily
Admission Free

Sport & Recreation

Share Holiday Village

Smith's Strand Lisnaskea County Fermanagh
BT92 0EQ
Tel: 028 6772 2122 Fax: 028 6772 1893
[On the Shores of the Upper Lough Erne, 4m from villages of Lisnaskea and Derrylin on B127]

Share is currently the largest activity centre in Ireland, welcoming over 10,000 visitors annually with an unparalelled range of accommodation choices, on-site facilities and activities. Established in 1981, Share works for the inclusion of disabled and non-disabled people. The location and layout of the site provides a fun ye safe environment for all.

Accommodation: All year, call for details.
Inishcruiser: Easter-Sept

Full board accommodation: Week-end & 2 Day courses £75.00 per person, mid-week & 3/5 day courses £140.00 per person, 5/7 day courses: £200.00 per person. Self catering accommodation: weekend £270.00 per chalet, midweek & 7 day reservation £590.00 per chalet. Youth Pavillion £50.00 per day of hire. Inishcruiser: A£7.00 Concessions£6.00

Tourist Information Centres

Armagh Tourist Information Centre

40 English Street The Old Bank Building
Armagh County Armagh BT61 7BA
Tel: 028 3752 1800 Fax: 028 3752 8329
www.visit-armagh.com

[Armagh City]

The staff at Armagh Tourist Information Centre offer the visitor a warm welcome, information o places to visit, events in the area and throughout Northern Ireland. Also offered is an accommodation booking service in first class guesthouses, B&Bs and hotels. Bureau de change and for a small fee photocopying and a fax facility is also available. A nearby car park, restaurant and disabled facilities will enhance the visitor's experience in Armagh.

All year Mon-Sat 09.00-17.00 Sun 14.00-17.00

orthumberland

Abbeys

Hexham Abbey

Beaumont Street Hexham Northumberland
NE46 3NB
Tel: 01434 602031 Fax: 01434 606116
A fine, large church with Saxon Crypt. 15th century paintings. Misericords and Saxon chalice.
7th century Frith stool. Refreshments available
Tue, Sat and Sun May-Sept.
*May-Sept 09.30-19.00, Oct-Apr 09.30-17.00,
closed Good Friday*
Admission Free, £3.00 donation encouraged

Arts, Crafts & Textiles

Pot-A-Doodle-Do

Borewell Scremerston Berwick-Upon-Tweed
Northumberland TD15 2RJ
Tel: 01289 307107 Fax: 01289 331233
*[Leave A1 roundabout signposted Scremerston -
travel 500 yards - turn R signposted Scremerston.
Take sharp L towards Cocklawburn Beach - Pot-
a-Doodle Do is 0.5m on L]*

All our activities are designed for everyone of all
ages and abilities to have a go, no previous
experience is necessary. Also pony trekking and
family fishing.
*Easter-31 Oct daily 10.00-17.00, Nov-Easter 5
days per week Wed-Sun 10.00-16.00*
Admission Free

Country Parks & Estates

Plessey Woods Country Park

Shields Road Hartford Bridge Bedlington
Northumberland NE22 6AN
Tel: 01670 824793 Fax: 01670 825162
[Off the A192 4m S of Morpeth]

Pleasant woodland and riverside walk. Picnic
areas and Visitor Centre with information, shop,
displays and toilets.
All year daily 08.00-dusk
Admission Free. Parking £1.00

Exhibition & Visitor Centres

Otterburn Mill

Otterburn Northumberland NE19 1JT
Tel: 01830 520225 Fax: 01830 520032
*[Near J of A68 (Corbridge-Jedburgh) and A696
(Newcastle-Jedburgh)]*

Otterburn Mill is an ideal day out. Plenty to do
and plenty to see. We offer a large and well-
stocked showroom selling a wide range of outdoor clothing for all ages, a fantastic home baking coffee shop, a 25 acre field where you can
walk and picnic.
All year daily
Admission Free

Festivals & Shows

Northumberland County Show

Tynedale Park Corbridge Northumberland
NE45 5AY
Tel: 01697 747848 Fax: 01697 747847
*[15m W of Newcastle Upon Tyne and 4m E of
Hexham. Tynedale Park is situated on S side of
river at Corrbridge. Event will be AA signposted
from A69 and A68 trunk roads]*

Traditional County Agricultural Show with farm
livestock, show jumping, poultry and dogs.
Hundreds of trade stands, spectacular arena
and air displays. Excellent family day out, entertaining demonstrations, crafts, catering, food
hall and bar.
May 31 2004

Rothbury Traditional Music
Festival

Garleigh House Garleigh Road Rothbury
Morpeth Northumberland NE65 7RB
Tel: 01669 620718
*[Turn off A1 after Morpeth to Coldstream road
(A679). Turn off to Rothbury at Weldon Bridge*

B6344]

The annual gathering of musicians, singers and dancers in Northumberland's Coquet Valley. Dances, ceilidhs, sing-arounds, workshops, pub sessions, outdoor displays (including puppets, dancers, mummers). Concerts, also 19 competitions for fiddle, accordion, ceilidh bands, pipes, traditional singing, flute, recorder, drums, and much more.

July 16-18 2004

Tickets range from £1.00-£4.50

Folk & Local History Museums

Bailiffgate Museum

14 Bailiffgate Alnwick Northumberland NE66 1LU

Tel: 01665 605847 Fax: 01665 605394

www.bailiffgatemuseum.co.uk

[Turn off A1 to Alnwick, far end of town near Castle gatehouse]

Presenting North Northumberland and the old County town of Alnwick in exciting, interactive style, the Museum covers everything from border warfare through local characters to the old shops and trades of Alnwick. Temporary museum based and art exhibitions are staged throughout the year on a variety of themes with complementary workshops and events. The Museum education service caters for all ages, including school groups, further and adult education and informal learning. The Museum has a new outreach service in the form of Reminiscence loan boxes. There is a local history research area, with access to the 1881 census. A programme of varied events is organised in association with our Society of Friends. An area for meetings, functions and presentations is equipped for almost all occasions and available for hire.

Easter-Oct daily 10.00-17.00, Nov-Easter Tue-Sun 10.00-16.00. Closed 21 Dec-10 Jan

A£2.20 C(under5)£Free C(5-16)£1.70 OAPs£2.00 Family Ticket (A2+C2) £5.80, (A2+C1) £5.10 Students/Concessions£1.50. Group rates (10+): A£1.80 C£1.50 OAPs£1.80 Students/Concessions£1.30

Discount Offer: 20% Off With Voucher

Historical

Chillingham Castle and Gardens

Chillingham Alnwick Northumberland NE66 5NJ
Tel: 01668 215359 Fax: 01668 215463

[12m N of Alnwick signposted from A1 & A697]

This remarkable fortress with its alarming dungeons and torture chamber, owned by Earl Grey and his descendants continuously since about 1200, is now undergoing restoration. Lovely woodland walks and a lake.

Easter weekends & 1 May-end Sept Sun-Fri 12.00-17.30. Closed Sat May-Sept

A£6.00 C(under5)£0.50 C(over5)£3.00 OAPs£5.50

Nature & Conservation Parks

Northumberland Wildlife Trust - Hauxley Nature Reserve and Visitor Centre

Low Hauxley Amble-by-the-Sea
Northumberland NE65 0JR
Tel: 01665 711578
[S of Amble directly off the A1068 coast road]

Created following open cast mining on the site, this picturesque lake sprinkled with islands is home to a wide variety of breeding birds, especially terns, and is a popular spot for migrating waders.
All year daily 10.00-dusk (Reception hide has shorter hours)
Admission Free

Places of Worship

St Mary Magdalene Church

The Vicarage Mitford Morpeth Northumberland
NE61 3PZ
Tel: 01670 511468
Consecrated in 1135. Major restoration with tower and steeple in 1874. Contains massive Norman pillars and one of the oldest church bells in Britain.
All year any reasonable time, collect keys from Vicarage. Hosts Tues & Thurs afternoons in summer
Admission Free

Roman Era

Vindolanda

Chesterholm Museum Bardon Mill Hexham
Northumberland NE47 7JN
Tel: 01434 344277 Fax: 01434 344060
[1.25m SE of Twice Brewed, signposted from A69 or B6318]

Visit the fascinating Roman Fort and town excavations and follow the archaeological site trails. Reconstructions of a Roman shop, house and temple, set in charming gardens. Limited dis-

abled access, please call in advance.
Feb-Mar daily 10.00-17.00, Apr-Sept daily 10.00-18.00, Oct-Nov daily 10.00-17.00
A£4.50 C£2.90 OAPs£3.80 Family Ticket (A2+C2) £13.00

Theme & Adventure Parks

Fishwick Mains Amazing Maize Maze

Fishwick Mains Berwick-upon-Tweed
Northumberland TD15 1XQ
Tel: 01289 386111 Fax: 01289 386111
[From Berwick bypass, on N side of River Tweed, take B6461 heading W. Signposted, Paxton House. Travel 5m. (1.5m past Paxton House). Maize Maze is on L near Tweed Hill]

An Adventure Maze with a space age theme puzzle. The actual maze depicts the famous Tweed Swans based at Berwick.
14 July-15 Sept daily 11.00-18.00
A£4.00 C£3.00 Family Ticket (A2+C2)£12.00

Archaeology

Creswell Crags

Crags Road Welbeck Worksop S80 3LH
Tel: 01909 720378 Fax: 01909 724726
[Between A616 / A60, 1m E of Creswell village, 5m SE of J30 M1]

One of Britain's most important archaeology sites! The caves and limestone gorge at Creswell Crags were used by our distant ancestors as seasonal camps during the Ice Age more than 10,000 years ago. Explore the site with its museum displays, audio-visual programme, lakeside trails, site tours (booking advised) and stone tool making demonstrations.
Site: All year Feb-Oct daily 10.30-16.30, Nov-Jan Sun only 10.30-16.30. Public Cave Tours: Weekends and School Hols, booking advised
Cave tour: A£2.75 C£2.00 Family Ticket £8.00. Parking: donation of £1.00 requested

Discount Offer: One Free Adult/Child When One Adult Pays Full Price

Arts, Crafts & Textiles

Lakeside Arts Centre

University Park Nottingham NG7 2RD
Tel: 0115 951 3192 Fax: 0115 951 3192
[Off University Boulevard A6005]

A thriving venue with a year-long programme of events and performances. Lakeside comprises the Djanogly Art Gallery, Djanogly Theatre and Djanogly Recital Hall as well as two informal galleries.
All year Mon-Sat 11.00-17.00, Sun & Bank Hol 14.00-17.00. Closed Christmas
Admission Free

Rufford Craft Centre

Rufford Abbey Rufford Country Park near Ollerton Newark Nottinghamshire NG22 9DF
Tel: 01623 822944 Fax: 01623 824702
[A614, 16m N of Nottingham]

Situated in Rufford country Park an estate built

in the 17th century sited in the Stable block. The Gallery has 6 exhibitions a year.
All year Jan-Feb 11.00-16.00. All other times 10.30-17.00. Closed 25 Dec
Admission Free. Car park £1.50 Easter-Oct

Caverns & Caves

City of Caves

Upper Level Broad Marsh Shopping Centre Nottingham Nottinghamshire NG1 7LS

Tel: 0115 952 0555 Fax: 0115 941 5084
www.cityofcaves.com

[Off M1 J26 from N, off M1 J25 from Derby & W. Situated beneath Broadmarsh Shopping centre. There is plenty of public car parking nearby]

An ancient and mysterious labyrinth of sandstone caves buried deep beneath the modern and vibrant city of Nottingham. Enter and explore a whole new world and descend into the dark depths of the original Anglo Saxon tunnels, meeting real cave dwellers from its dramatic hidden past...

All year daily 10.30-17.00. Please call for details of Christmas opening times

A£4.00 C£3.00 Concessions£3.00 Family Ticket £12.50. Group discounts available, please call for details

Discount Offer: One Child Free With One Full Paying Adult

Country Parks & Estates

Rufford Abbey and Country Park

Ollerton Newark Nottinghamshire NG22 9DF

Tel: 01623 822944 Fax: 01623 824840

www.ruffordcraftcentre.org.uk

[Off A614, 2m S of Ollerton roundabout. 17m N of Nottingham. Plenty of on site parking. For public transport details call Traveline on 0870 608 2 608]

Tour the remains of the 12th century Abbey set in beautiful parklands, including an Exhibition on Cistercian life in the undercroft. Visit our renowned gallery, craft shops and ceramics centre. Enjoy the restored Orangery, formal gardens, Savile Restaurant, Lakeside Garden Shop, Outdoor Living Store and Teddy Bear Shop. Various special events throughout the year, telephone for programme details.

All year, High Season (end Feb-end Oct) 10.00-17.00, Low Season (end Oct-end Feb) 10.00-16.30. Closed afternoon 24 Dec and reopens 26 Dec

Admission £Free. Car Park charge at various times throughout the year

Sherwood Forest Country Park and Visitor Centre

Edwinstowe Mansfield Nottinghamshire NG21 9HN

Tel: 01623 823202 / 824490
Fax: 01623 823202

www.sherwood-forest.org.uk

[On B6034, N of Edwinstowe between A6075 and A616. Plenty of parking on site. For Public transport details to the Park call Traveline on 0870 608 2 608. Minicom 0870 241 2 216]

Visit the legendary home of England's most famous outlaw - Robin Hood. Over 450 acres of ancient oak woodland, including the famous Major Oak. Enjoy the hands on exhibition, video on the history of the former Royal Hunting Forest, heritage and gift shops and restaurant. Explore woodland paths, picnic in forest glades and enjoy a year-round programme of events and activities including the Annual Robin Hood Festival, 2-8 August 2004.

All year, High Season (Easter-Jan) 10.00-17.00, Low Season (Jan-Easter) 10.00-16.30. Closed afternoon 24 Dec and reopens 26 Dec

Admission Free, Car Park charge at various times throughout the year

Wollaton Hall and Park

Wollaton Nottingham Nottinghamshire NG8 2AE
Tel: 0115 915 3900 Fax: 0115 915 3932
[From S J25 M1, from N N26 M1. 3m W off A52

& A6514, off A609 Ilkeston road]

Set in over 500 acres of mature parkland, Wollaton Hall is one of the most spectacular and ornate Tudor buildings in England and today houses Nottingham's Natural History collections. The extensive grounds contain a fishing lake and an adventure playground

Natural History Museum: All year May-end Sept 11.00-17.00, Oct-Apr 11.00-16.00. Industrial Museum: Closed Nov-Mar except for steaming events, open 11.00-17.00. Yard Gallery: daily Apr-Oct 11.00-17.00 Nov-Mar 11.00-16.00. Closed 24-26 Dec & 1 Jan

Hall: Mon-Fri £Free. Weekends & Bank Hol A£1.50 C&Concessions£0.80 Family Ticket(A2+C4)£3.80. Joint Ticket for all at Wollaton Hall and Park: A£2.00 Concessions£1.00 Family Ticket £5.00

Folk & Local History Museums

Brewhouse Yard Museum

Castle Boulevard Nottingham Nottinghamshire NG7 1FB
Tel: 0115 915 3600
17th century cottages on two acre site. Museum depicts everyday life in Nottingham over 300 years. Period rooms with local objects displayed. Recreated shops, including between the wars shopping street. Limited disabled access.
All year daily 10.00-16.30.
Mon-Fri: Free, Weekends & Bank Hol A£1.50 C&Concessions£0.80 Family Ticket (A2+C4) £3.80

Mansfield Museum and Art Gallery

Leeming Street Mansfield Nottinghamshire NG18 1NG
Tel: 01623 463088 Fax: 01623 412922
[Near Town Centre close to A60 to Mansfield Woodhouse]

'Images of Mansfield past and present' uses objects and photographs to illustrate the history of the town, whilst 'Nature of Mansfield' looks at the natural history of the area. The museum's important display of William Bilingsley porcelain and Buxton watercolours show the town and people in the early 19th century.
All year Mon-Sat 10.00-17.00. Closed Sun & Bank Hol
Admission Free

Newark Museum

Appleton Gate Newark Nottinghamshire NG24 1JY
Tel: 01636 655740 Fax: 01636 655745
The museum displays the archaeology and local history of the area. Visitors can see an exhibition of 17th century Civil War items and a collection of militaria of the Sherwood Foresters.
All year Mon-Wed Fri 10.00-13.00 & 14.00-17.00 Sat 10.00-13.00 & 14.00-17.00 Apr-Sept Sun 14.00-17.00 Bank Hol 13.00-17.00
Admission Free

Tales of Robin Hood

30-38 Maid Marian Way Nottingham Nottinghamshire NG1 6GF

Tel: 0115 948 3284 Fax: 0115 950 1536

www.robinhood.uk.com

[J25 M1 Southbound, J26 M1 Northbound, follow signs for the City]

Enter the world's greatest medieval adventure, to a world of mystery and merriment. Be an outlaw for the day and flee through the forest to escape the evil sheriff. Jump on the magical 'Travel back in time' adventure ride and join in the search for Robin. Try your hand at brass rubbing and archery then visit our gift shops.

All year daily 10.00-17.30. Closed Dec 25-26

A£6.95 C£4.95 OAPs£5.95 Family Ticket (A2+C2)£19.95, (A2+C3) £23.50

Discount Offer: Two For The Price Of One

Heritage & Industrial

The Workhouse, Southwell

Upton Road Southwell Nottinghamshire NG25 0PT
Tel: 01636 817250 Fax: 01636 817251
[13m from Nottingham on A612, 8m from Newark on A617 and A612. Rail: Fiskerton 2m, Newark North Gate 7.5m]

The Workhouse at Southwell is a formidable 19th century brick institution with a story to tell about the care of the poor in Britain. The building is the least altered workhouse in existence today, a survivor from the hundreds that once covered the country. Visitors are strongly advised to book for peak times.
29 Mar-31 July Thur-Mon 12.00-17.00, 1-30 Aug Thur-Mon 11.00-17.00, 2 Sept-1 Nov Thur-Mon 12.00-17.00. Open Bank Hol Mons
A£4.40 C£2.20 Family Ticket £11.00

Historical

Clumber Park

Estate Office Clumber Park Worksop Nottinghamshire S80 3AZ
Tel: 01909 544917 (Info Point)
Fax: 01909 500721
[4.5m SE of Worksop, 6.5m SW of Retford, 1m from A1/A57, 11m from M1 J30. Rail: Worksop]

3,800 acres of parkland, farmland and woodlands with a superb serpentine lake at its heart. Clumber was formerly home to the Dukes of Newcastle. The mansion was demolished in 1938, but many fascinating features of the estate remain, including a fine Gothic Revival Chapel, Hardwick village and the walled kitchen garden.
Park: all year daily except 10 July, 21 Aug (concert days) and 25 Dec
Pedestrians and Cyclists Free. Cars and motorbikes £3.80

Mr Straw's House

7 Blyth Grove Worksop Nottinghamshire S81 0JG
Tel: 01909 482380
[House signposted from Blyth Road (B6045)]

This modest semi-detached Edwardian house provides a fascinating insight into everyday life in the early part of the 20th century. The interior has remained unaltered since the 1930s and features contemporary wallpaper, Victorian furniture and household objects.

1 Apr-1 Nov Tue-Sat 11.00-16.30. Admission for all visitors is by timed ticket which must be booked in advance

A£4.40 C£2.20 Family Ticket £11.00

Newark Town Treasures Museum and Art Gallery

Town Hall Market Place Newark Nottinghamshire NG24 1DU

Tel: 01636 680333 Fax: 01636 680350

[Close to A1 and on A46 Lincoln to Leicester road. Rail: Newark Castle and Northgate]

Grade I listed Georgian Town Hall, elegant Ballroom and Mayor's Parlour. Sumptuous civic gifts and paintings from 17th/18th centuries.

All year Mon-Fri 11.00-16.00, Sat 12.00-16.00. Closed Sun & Bank Hol

Admission Free

Newstead Abbey

Newstead Abbey Park Ravenshead
Nottinghamshire NG15 8NA

Tel: 01623 455900 Fax: 01623 455904

[J27 M1 12m N of Nottingham on A60]

Beautiful historic house set in parklands, home
of poet Lord Byron. Byron's own room and
mementoes on display, and rooms from
Medieval to Victorian, splendidly decorated. 300
acres of grounds. Disabled access limited to
ground floor.

*Grounds: all year daily (except last Fri in Nov and
Christmas Day) 09.00-dusk. House: 1 Apr-30
Sept daily 12.00-17.00*

House & Grounds: A£5.00 C£1.50
Concessions£2.50 Family Ticket £12.00.
Grounds only: A£2.00 C£1.50
Concessions£1.50 Family Ticket £7.00

Nottingham Castle

Nottingham Nottinghamshire NG1 6EL

Tel: 0115 915 3700 Fax: 0115 915 3653

Nottingham Castle commands spectacular
views over the city and once rivalled the great
Castles of Windsor and the Tower of London.
The museum contains spectacular fine and dec-
orative arts galleries, and the Sherwood
Foresters Regimental Museum.

*All year daily 10.00-17.00, winter 10.00-16.00.
Closed 24-26 Dec and 1 Jan*

Mon-Fri £Free, Weekends & Bank Hol A£2.00
C&Concessions£1.00 Family Ticket (A2+C4)
£5.00

Living History Museums

Galleries of Justice

Shire Hall High Pavement Lace Market
Nottingham Nottinghamshire NG1 1HN

**Tel: 0115 952 0555 Fax: 0115 993 9828
www.galleriesofjustice.co.uk**

*[City centre, signposted both traffic and pedestri-
an, multi-storey parking signposted, 5-10 mins
walk]*

Journey with us through 300 years of Crime
and Punishment on this unique atmospheric
site. Witness a real trial in the authentic Victorian
courtroom before being sentenced and 'sent
down' to the original cells and medieval caves
of the old county gaol. But beware, you will not
travel through these layers of time alone - prisoners and gaolers will act as your guides. Have
you got what it takes to solve a murder? Will
your powers of deduction crack the case? By
using forensic evidence and hands-on interactives you get to investigate a crime scene in the
Police! exhibition. A series of special events run
throughout the year. Feel the Fear!

*All year Tue-Sun, Bank Hol Mon & Mon through-
out school holidays, Peak Times 10.00-17.00, Off
Peak times 10.00-16.00. Please call to confirm
details*

A£6.95 C£5.25 Family Ticket (A2+C2) £19.95
Concessions£5.95. Tickets are valid for one visit
to each exhibition over 12 months. Group discounts available. Wheelchair access: 85%

**Discount Offer: Two For The Price Of
One**

Military & Defence Museums

Sherwood Foresters Museum (45th/95th Foot)

Nottingham Castle Castle Place Nottingham Nottinghamshire NG1 6EL
Tel: 0115 915 3700 Fax: 0115 913 3653
[M1 J26 - A610 City Centre, M1 J25 - A52 City Centre]

The history of the Regiment from the formation of the 45th Regiment in 1741 to amalgamation with the Worcestershire Regiment in 1970. Many fine exhibits.
Mar-Oct daily 10.00-17.00. Closed Fridays Nov-Feb inclusive
Mon-Fri: Admission Free. Weekends & Bank Hol: A£2.00 C£1.00

Science - Earth & Planetary

Green's Mill and Science Museum

Windmill Lane Sneinton Nottingham Nottinghamshire NG2 4QB
Tel: 0115 915 6878 Fax: 0115 915 6875
[Off A612. Parking available on site for disabled visitors although limited]

Restored to working order, this windmill can be seen in use when conditions allow. The adjacent Science Centre tells the story of George Green, one-time miller here and distinguished mathematician. Flour is on sale. Disabled access limited to Science centre and ground floor of windmill.
All year Wed-Sun 10.00-16.00 & Bank Hol. Closed Dec 24-26, 31 and Jan 1
Admission Free

Theme & Adventure Parks

Go Ape! High Wire Forest Adventure

Sherwood Pines Visitor Centre Sherwood Pines Nottinghamshire NG21 9JL
Tel: 0870 420 7876
www.goape.cc

[Between Ollerton and Old Clipstone off the B6030]

Go Ape! and experience thrilling high wire forest adventure on this spectacular new course. Travel from tree to tree via over 30 hanging rope bridges, scramble nets and zip slides - at 30 feet off the forest floor. Minimum height 1m 40cm / 4'7", minimum age 10. Pre-booking is essential, call 0870 444 5562.
All year Apr-Oct daily 09.00-18.00 (last admittance), Nov-Mar weekends and by prior arrangement only
A(18+)£15.00 C(10-17)£10.00. Under 18s must be accompanied by a participating adult

Oxfordshire

Arts, Crafts & Textiles

Ashmolean Museum of Art and Archaeology

Beaumont Street Oxford Oxfordshire OX1 2PH

Tel: 01865 278000 / 278015
Fax: 01865 278018

[Centre of Oxford opposite The Randolph Hotel. Bus: 5mins. Rail: 10mins]

The Ashmolean is Oxford University's Museum of Art and Archaeology housing world famous collections of fine and applied art from Europe, Japan, India and China, as well as historic coins and medals and artefacts from Ancient Egypt, Greece and Rome.
All year Tue-Sat 10.00-17.00 (Thurs until 19.30 in June, July, Aug), Sun 14.00-17.00. Closed Mon (Cast Gallery Tues-Fri 10.00-16.00, Sat 10.00-13.00, closed Sun-Mon). Please call for details of Christmas and Easter opening times
Admission Free

Festivals & Shows

Henley Festival of Music and the Arts

Regatta Stewards' Enclosure
Henley-On-Thames Oxfordshire RG9 2AQ

Tel: 01491 843404 / 843400
Fax: 01491 410482

[36m W of London, 9m E of Reading, on A4130 Oxford-Maidenhead. From London, M4 J8/9 or M40 J4 via the Marlow bypass. Festival site and car parks on London side of Henley Bridge and clearly signposted. Bus: regular services between Henley and Reading, High Wycombe, Marlow, Maidenhead, London and Heathrow airport]

A ticket to the Festival gains you access to a non-stop feast of music, art and entertainment. There are performance stages, art galleries, sculpture lawns, bars and restaurants. The Festival has a mixed programme of classical, opera, jazz, world music, comedy, poetry, street theatre and the visual arts, with nightly firework events which feature accompanying hi-tech or spectacular performances.

July 7-11 2004

Prices range from £21.00-£85.00

Folk & Local History Museums

Banbury Museum

Spiceball Park Road Banbury Oxfordshire OX16 2PQ
Tel: 01295 259855 Fax: 01295 269461
[Central Banbury]

Museum on the history of Banbury and district. Plus innovative temporary exhibitions.
All year Mon-Sat 09.30-17.00, Sun 10.30-16.30
Admission Free

Oxfordshire Museum

Fletcher's House Park Street Woodstock Oxfordshire OX20 1SN

Tel: 01993 811456 Fax: 01993 813239

[A44 Oxford / Stratford Upon Avon road, J9 M40]

Displayed in Fletcher's House is an exhibition of the story of Oxfordshire and its people, from early times to the present day. The museum, which is situated in an elegant townhouse with pleasant gardens, also has a full programme of temporary exhibitions.

All year Tue-Sat 10.00-17.00, Sun 14.00-17.00. Closed Good Fri & 25-26 Dec & 1 Jan

Admission Free

Gardens & Horticulture

Brook Cottage Garden

Well Lane Alkerton Banbury Oxfordshire OX15 6NL

Tel: 01295 670303 / 670590
Fax: 01295 730362

[6m Banbury, 0.5m off A422 Banbury-Stratford upon Avon Rd]

4 acres of hillside garden, formed since 1964, surrounding 17th century house. Wide variety of trees, shrubs and plants of all kinds; water gardens; alpines; single-colour borders. Over 200 shrub and climbing roses, and many clematis. Plants for sale.

Easter Mon-end Oct Mon-Fri 09.00-18.00
A£4.00 C£Free OAPs£3.00

Cotswold Wildlife Park

Bradwell Grove Burford Oxfordshire OX18 4JW
Tel: 01993 823006 Fax: 01993 823807

Following extensive developments the Park has become an unexpected attraction to gardeners. A firm favourite with animal lovers, garden lovers are surprised at the rich diversity of plants and planting styles encountered throughout the 160 acres of landscaped parkland surrounding a listed Victorian Manor House. Victorians would have been familiar with the formal parterres and the herbaceous borders but not the exuberant and stunning summer displays of hardy and tender exotics now found in the Walled Garden nor the ornamental grasses and perennials which provide a wonderful foil for rhino and zebras. This is the ideal venue for gardeners and their children.

Please see Wildlife & Safari Parks section for full attraction listing

Wallingford Castle Gardens

Castle Street Wallingford Oxfordshire OX10 0DL
[Bear Lane, off Castle Street]

These Gardens are situated on part of the site of Wallingford Castle, which was built by William the Conqueror and demolished by Oliver Cromwell in 1652. The remains of St Nicholas Priory are a feature of the Gardens, which is a haven of beauty and tranquility.

Apr-Oct daily 10.00-17.45, Nov-Mar daily 10.00-15.00, weather permitting
Admission Free

Historical

Broughton Castle

Banbury Oxfordshire OX15 5EB

Tel: 01295 276070 Fax: 01295 276070

www.broughtoncastle.demon.co.uk

[2m W of Banbury on the B4035 Shipston on Stour road. Plenty of on site parking available]

This beautiful house has been the home of the family of Lord and Lady Saye and Sele for 600 years. Surrounded by a moat, it was built in 1300 and greatly enlarged in 1554. It contains its own medieval Chapel, vaulted passages, fine panelling, unique fireplaces, splendid plaster ceilings and good period furniture. Broughton was a centre of resistance to Charles I during the Civil War. It has many Parliamentary connections and mementos of that time, including armour and weapons. It has beautiful walled gardens, with old roses, shrubs, herbaceous borders and many interesting plants. The location for many films and television programmes, including The Madness of King George, Emma, Shakespeare in Love and The Boy Who Would Be King.

1 May-15 Sept Wed & Sun 14.00-17.00, also Thur in July-Aug and all Bank Hol Sun & Mon including Easter. Groups welcome at any time by arrangement

A£5.50 C£2.50 OAPs&Students£4.50

Discount Offer: Two Adults For The Price Of One

Ditchley Park

Ditchley Park Enstone Chipping Norton
Oxfordshire OX7 4ER
Tel: 01608 677346 Fax: 01608 677399
*[1.5m W of A44 at Kiddington 2m from Charlbury
B4437. Rail: Charlbury]*

Third in size and date of the great 18th century
houses of Oxfordshire, Ditchley is famous for its
splendid interior decorations. For three and half
centuries the home of the Lee family, Ditchley
was frequently visited at weekends by Sir
Winston Churchill.
*Group visits by prior arrangement with the Bursar
Mon-Thur pm only*
£5.00 per person, minimum charge £40.00
included guided tour

Great Coxwell Barn

Great Coxwell Faringdon Oxfordshire
Tel: 01793 762209 (Coleshill)
*[2m SW of Farringdon between A420 and
B4019. Rail: Swindon 10m]*

A 13th century monastic barn, stone-built with a
stone-tiled roof and interesting timber structure.
No WC
All year daily, any reasonable time
All £0.50

Multicultural Museums

Pitt Rivers Museum

South Parks Road Oxford Oxfordshire OX1 3PP
Tel: 01865 270927 Fax: 01865 270943
*[M40, A34, join A420. Short walk from the centre
of Oxford (through University Museum on Parks
Rd)]*

World famous museum of anthropology with a
unique Victorian atmosphere. Audio tour provided by Sir David Attenborough. Limited disabled
access, please call for details. Photography permitted.
*All year Mon-Sat 12.00-16.30, Sun 14.00-16.30.
Closed for short periods over Easter & Christmas*
Admission Free

Natural History Museums

Oxford University Museum of Natural History

Parks Road Oxford Oxfordshire OX1 3PW
Tel: 01865 272950 Fax: 01865 272970
[Short walk from the centre of Oxford]

The museum in its high-Victorian Gothic building makes freely available to the public the
University's very extensive natural history collections which include the remains of the Dodo,
fossil dinosaur material and the historic collections.
All year daily 12.00-17.00
Admission Free - donations box

Railways

Cholsey and Wallingford Railway

Hithercroft Road Wallingford Oxfordshire
OX10 9GQ

Tel: 01491 835067 Fax: 01491 651696

www.cholsey-wallingford-railway.com

*[By road: Cholsey is on A329, N from Reading.
Follow roadsigns into Cholsey, then follow railway
station signs to station which has ample parking.
To Wallingford on A4074 from Oxford, or on
A4130 from Didcot. If approaching from Oxford, it
is best to continue to A4130, just S of
Wallingford, from where railway signposted. The
last return journey from Wallingford is 16:10 service. Rail: regular services to Cholsey mainline
station are operated by Thames Trains. For times
of their trains, contact the national railway enquiry
service on 0345 484950. Arrive 20 minutes early
at Cholsey station to see the train arrive from
Wallingford (the sight is worth it!). The last return*

journey from Cholsey station is the 15:35 service]

A ride along a branch line from the days of the Great Western Railway, through the open countryside of Oxfordshire. The line runs for 2.5m (3.75 km) between Cholsey mainline station and the terminus at Hithercroft Road, Wallingford. You can start from either station. Steam trains operate when available. Catering facilities, a shop and the railway's museum are at Wallingford station. All services are provided by volunteers from the Cholsey & Wallingford Railway Preservation Society. The Railway's resident steam locomotive, Andrew Barclay 0-4-OST No. 701 is expected to haul most services together with one of the railway's 08 locomotives.

Mar-Oct & Christmas, special events only 11.00-16.00 for Wallingford departures. Closed Nov, Jan & Feb

A£5.00 C£3.00 Family Ticket £14.00

Discount Offer: One Child Free With Every Full Paying Adult.

Special Events

Ivor the Engine
10/04/2004-12/04/2004

St George's Weekend with afternoon Cream Tea Specials
24/04/2004-25/04/2004

May Bank Holiday Trains and May Day Celebrations
02/05/2004-03/05/2004

Teddy Bears' Picnic
30/05/2004-31/05/2004

Fathers' Day - Vintage Engines and Beer Festival
20/06/2004

Wallingford Fun Day and Cholsey Modelmania
25/07/2004

Ivor the Engine
29/08/2004-30/08/2004

Wallingford BunkFest
03/09/2004-05/09/2004

Operating Day
26/09/2004

Halloween
30/10/2004-31/10/2004

Santa Specials
05/12/2004-19/12/2004
Held on 5, 11, 12, 18, 19 Dec

The Carol Train
11/12/2004
Time: 17.00 & 19.00

Didcot Railway Centre

Didcot Oxfordshire OX11 7NJ

Tel: 01235 817200 Fax: 01235 510621

www.didcotrailwaycentre.org.uk

[On A4130 at Didcot Parkway Station signed from M4, J13 and A34]

Recreating the golden age of the Great Western Railway with a fine collection of over 20 steam locomotives, housed in the original engine shed, together with many passenger coaches and freight wagons. Other locomotives can be seen being overhauled in the Locomotive Works. There is a typical country station and signalbox, and a recreation of Brunel's original broad gauge railway together with an impressive display of smaller items in the Relics Display. On Steamdays some of the locomotives come to life and you can ride the 1930s carriages and see the activities of a typical steam age depot.

All year Sat & Sun plus 3-18 Apr and 29 May-5 Sept daily 10.00-16.00. Steamdays first & last Sun of each month from Mar, Bank Hol, all Sun July-Aug, Wed 14 July-1 Sept, all Sat in Aug, 10.00-17.00

A£4.00-£8.00 C£3.00-£6.50 OAPs£3.50-£6.50 depending on event

Discount Offer: One Adult Or Child Free With A Full Paying Adult

Special Events

Didcot Steamday
04/04/2004

Easter Steamings
09/04/2004-12/04/2004
Special events on Sun & Mon - Easter egg hunt, travelling Post Office demonstration, Radstock signalbox visits. Guided tours at 12.00 & 14.30

New Volunteers' Steamday
24/04/2004
Come along and see if you would like to join us. Meet the restorers

Didcot Tank Engine Steamday
25/04/2004
See the small engines in action

May Bank Holiday Steamings
01/05/2004-03/05/2004
Sat - signalling operating day and freight train in action. Sun & Mon - family activity days including 'Driver for a Fiver'. Lots for younger visitors to do, travelling Post Office in action. Guided tours 12.00 & 14.30

Spring Holiday Steamings
29/05/2004-31/05/2004
Steam trains and diesel railcar operating, Radstock signalbox visits, travelling Post Office in action Sun & Mon. Guided tours 12.00 & 14.30 (Sun/Mon)

Didcot Steam and Railcar Day
06/06/2004
Steam train and diesel railcar operating

Fathers Day Steamday
13/06/2004
Treat Dad to lunch on the steam train

Flower, Fruit and Vegetable Event
26/06/2004-27/06/2004
Local produce competitions and displays

Freight and Passenger Steamday
04/07/2004
Steam freight and passenger trains, signalling operating day

Didcot Steamdays
11/07/2004-02/01/2005
Held on 11, 14, 21 July, 4, 7, 11, 15, 18, 22, 25 Aug, 1 Sept, 31 Oct (with Halloween Craft Fair), 1, 2 Jan

Didcot Steam and Railcar Day
18/07/2004-21/08/2004
Held on 18 & 28 July, 1, 14, 21 Aug, 3 Oct. Steam train and diesel railcar operating

Family Activity Steamday
25/07/2004
Includes 'Driver for a Fiver' and lots more for younger visitors to do. Guided tours at 12.00 & 14.30

Freight and Passenger Steamday
08/08/2004
Freight and passenger trains in action, signalling operating day

Late Summer Holiday Steamings
28/08/2004-30/08/2004
Special events on Sun and Mon, steam trains and diesel railcar, Radstock signalbox visits, guided tours at 12.00 and 14.30

Freight and Passenger Steamday
05/09/2004
Freight and passenger trains in action, signalling operating day

All Steamed Up Weekend
25/09/2004-26/09/2004
Several trains in steam with lots of action, signalling operating day, travelling Post Office in operation

Day Out with Thomas
08/10/2004-10/10/2004
With Thomas the Tank Engine and his friends, rides behind 'Thomas', meet The Fat Controller, children's entertainment

Thomas Santa Special
10/12/2004-19/12/2004
Held on 10, 11, 12, 17, 18, 19 Dec. Rides behind 'Thomas' to Santa's grotto, presents for the children. Advance booking essential

Social History Museums

River and Rowing Museum

Mill Meadows Henley-on-Thames Oxfordshire
RG9 1BF

Tel: 01491 415600 Fax: 01491 415601

www.rrm.co.uk

*[By Car: follow signs for Henley, then Museum
and Mill Meadows, off A4130 Oxford to
Maidenhead road in Henley. Bus: regular bus services from High Wycombe, Marlow, Reading,
Thame, Watlington and Lane End. Hourly X39
service from Oxford to Heathrow via Wallingford,
Henley and Maidenhead. Rail: hourly services
from London (Paddington), Reading and
Maidenhead via Twyford. Henley station is 5mins
walk from museum. By Foot: follow signposts
around town centre. Car Parking - Up to 3 hours:
free to Museum visitors]*

Visit the award winning River & Rowing Museum
with its stunning architecture and unique interpretation of the River Thames, the riverside
town of Henley and the sport of Rowing. History
is brought to life with interactive displays and
fascinating exhibits. Special exhibitions, family
activities and events are held throughout the
year and its Riverside Café offers excellent food
in distinctive surroundings. New for 2004,
Kenneth Grahame's much loved tale is coming
to the Museum in a spectacular permanent
attraction opening in May. Every one of EH
Shepard's famous illustrations will be brought to
life in an enchanting recreation of the classic
English book. You will be able to walk along the
River Bank, through the Wild Wood, into
Badger's house and through all twelve chapters
of this delightful adventure story. Using many
theatrical and audio-visual techniques, models,
lighting, and sound you will be magically transported into the world of Ratty, Mole, Badger
and of course the irrepressible Toad.

*All year 1 May-31 Aug daily 10.00-17.30, 1 Sept-
30 Apr daily 10.00-17.00. Closed 24, 25, 31
Dec & 1 Jan*

Museum Galleries only: A£3.00 C(under3)£Free
C£2.00 Concessions£2.50 Family Ticket (4
people) £10.00, (5 people) £12.00, (6 people)
£14.00. Galleries & Wind in the Willows: A£6.00

C(under3)£Free C£4.00 Concessions£5.00
Family Ticket (4 people) £18.00, (5 people)
£21.00, (6 people) £24.00

Special Events

Battle of the Blues: Boat Race 150
13/03/2004-31/08/2004
*The Battle of the Blues exhibition marks the 150th
University Boat Race since the first was held at
Henley in 1829. The story of the Oxford and
Cambridge boat clubs and their perpetual battle
from Putney to Mortlake, with attendant sinkings,
mutinies and umpiring controversies, will celebrate
a significant rowing institution and a great sporting
occasion*

Story Time
05/04/2004-15/04/2004
*Held on Mon & Thur only. Come and join Teddy
for Story Times. Stories last about 20 mins.
Children must be accompanied by an adult.
Times: Mon 14.30, Thur 11.30. Suitable for children aged 7 and under*

Bags of Fun
05/04/2004-16/04/2004
*Try a Fun Bag while you are on holiday! Activities
are tailored to age groups so there is something
for all from 3-14 year olds. Fairytale Fantasy,
Design a Postcard, Be an Exhibition Designer and
more*

The London Transport posters of E. McKnight Kauffer
17/04/2004
*Edward McKnight Kauffer was London Transport's
most prolific poster artist. Designing more than
100 posters for the company over a 25 year period. Graham Twemlow, University lecturer and
design historian, will give an illustrated talk on
Kauffer. Time: 11.00 for 11.30. Cost: A£6.00 to
include coffee*

Adult Workshop: Jewellery Making
15/05/2004
*Design and make your own individual pieces of
jewellery or accessory with a watery theme. All
abilities welcome, there may be a small extra
charge for materials. Time: 10.00-12.30. Cost:
£15.00*

The Great Thames Read
22/05/2004
*John Jones joins us to read from Three Men in a
Boat. Then join Jane Draycott for a discussion
about your own Great Thames Reads. Time:
11.00-11.30. Cost: A£6.00 to include coffee*

Batty Boaters: Hats for Henley
01/06/2004

Drop into the museum and make a hat for Henley. Get dressed up for Henley's own Regatta. Design your own outrageous headgear for boys and girls. Time: 10.30-16.30. Cost: £1.50 plus Museum admission

Tales from the Riverbank
02/06/2004

Come along to Henley Library and hear stories and join in with craft activities with a river theme. Numbers limited. Time: 13.30-15.45. Suitable for children aged 4-8. Free admission

Chasing Shadows
03/06/2004

Create your own photographs with light by composing a photographic picture. Use the theme of the Boat Race to create shadow boat puppets. Time: 10.30-12.30. Suitable for children aged 7-11. Cost: £5.00

Adult Workshop: Interior Spaces, Drawing, Printing and Creative Writing
26/06/2004

A practical workshop inspired by David Chipperfields's award winning Museum design and his ideas about space. Beginners welcome. Time: 10.00-16.00. Cost: £15.00

Rivers, Reeds and Reflections: Calligraphy by the Oxford Scribes
11/09/2004-05/12/2004

Out of the Woods: Furniture by Phil Koomen
16/09/2004-07/01/2005

Stately Homes

Blenheim Palace

Woodstock Oxfordshire OX20 1PX

Tel: 01993 811325 Fax: 01993 813527

[On A44 Oxford / Evesham road. Rail: Oxford]

Blenheim Palace, home of the 11th Duke of Marlborough and birthplace of Sir Winston Churchill, was built for John Churchill 1st Duke of Marlborough by Vanbrugh, with a magnificent collection of paintings, tapestries and furniture. It is set in a Capability Brown landscaped park, with lake and formal gardens.
Palace: 14 Feb-mid Nov daily 10.30-17.30. Park: All year daily 09.00-17.00

Palace: A£12.50/£11.00 C(5-15)£7.00/£5.50. Park & Gardens: A£7.50/£6.00 C£3.50/£2.00. Private Apartments: A£4.00 Concessions£3.00

Buscot Park

Buscot Park Faringdon Oxfordshire SN7 8BU

Tel: 01367 240786 Fax: 01367 241794

[3m NW of Faringdon on Lechlade-Faringdon road A417]

This 18th-century house contains the Faringdon Collection of paintings and furniture. It includes work by Reynolds, Gainsborough, Rembrandt, Murillo, several of the Pre-Raphaelites, and some 20th century artists. The charming formal water gardens were laid out by Harold Peto in the early 20th century.

House: 1 Apr-30 Sept Wed-Fri & Bank Hols 14.00-18.00. Also 10-11 Apr, 1-2, 8-9, 22-23, 29-30 May, 12-13, 26-27 June, 10-11, 24-25 July, 14-15, 28-29 Aug, 11-12, 25-26 Sept. Tea Room: As house, 14.30-17.30. Grounds: as house plus 1 Apr-30 Sept Mon-Tue 14.00-18.00

House & Grounds: A£6.50 C£3.25. Grounds only: A£4.50 C£2.25

Rousham House

Rousham Bicester Oxfordshire OX25 4QX

Tel: 01869 347110 Fax: 01869 347110

[12m N of Oxford, E of A4260, 0.5m S of B4030]

This attractive mansion was built by Sir Robert Dormer in 1635. During the Civil War it was a

Royalist garrison, and had shooting holes cut into its doors. Rooms were also decorated by William Kent and Roberts of Oxford, during the 18th century. The house contains over 150 portraits and other pictures. Gardens by William Kent include only surviving landscape garden of 1735.

All year Garden: daily 10.00-16.30. House: Apr-Sept Wed Sun & Bank Hol Mon 14.00-16.30

House: £3.00. Garden: £3.00

Victorian Era

Cogges Manor Farm Museum

Church Lane Witney Oxfordshire OX28 3LA

Tel: 01993 772602 Fax: 01993 703056

[0.5m SE of Witney off A40. Plenty of parking on site]

A special place to visit for all the family. Why not visit Cogges Manor Farm Museum and find out what life was like for the Victorians of rural Oxfordshire? Visitors take a step back in time when they enter the beautiful farmstead with its original Cotswold buildings and displays about farming in years gone by. In the Manor House you can talk to the Victorian maids and find out what their lives would have been like. Watch as they cook on the old range and if you are lucky you might be able to sample some of their fresh baking. Upstairs visitors can explore the history of the house and experience the activities room where children can try on Victorian clothes and play with the Victorian toys and games.

Apr-Oct Tue-Fri & Bank Hol Mon 10.30-17.30, Sat & Sun 12.00-17.30. Closed Good Fri

A£4.40 C(3-16)£2.30 Concessions£2.85 Family Ticket (A2+C2)£12.90. Pre-booked groups discounted

Discount Offer: Two For The Price Of One

Wildlife & Safari Parks

Cotswold Wildlife Park

Bradwell Grove Burford Oxfordshire OX18 4JW

Tel: 01993 823006 Fax: 01993 823807

www.cotswoldwildlifepark.co.uk

[2.5m S of A40 on A361. Plenty of free parking on site]

The 160 acre landscaped zoological park, surrounding a Gothic-style Manor House, has a varied collection of animals from around the world. Many of these are endangered in the wild and are part of an international breeding programme, including Asiatic Lions, Amur Leopards and Red Pandas. There is a large

Reptile House, Tropical House, Children's Farmyard and the ever-popular penguins and meerkats. Visitors are surprised and delighted at the beautiful gardens and wide range of planting to be seen as they walk around the Park, from the formal herbaceous borders and parterre by the Manor House to the exotic bananas, Daturas and Canna lilies in the Walled Garden. Other attractions include an adventure playground, animal brass-rubbing centre in the Manor House and the narrow-gauge railway which runs daily during the summer months, limited winter runs. The large self-service cafeteria serves hot and cold meals and snacks. There are also many picnicking areas and a well-stocked Gift Shop.

All year daily from 10.00. Closed Christmas Day

A£8.00 C(3-16)£5.50 OAPs£5.50. Group rates (20+): A£6.50 C£4.00 OAPs£5.00 Disabled with Carer: £4.00. Season Tickets (valid for 12 months): A£40.00 C£27.50 OAPs£27.50 Family Ticket (A2+C2) £125.00, additional child £25.00

Special Events

Birds of Prey Demonstrations
09/04/2004-05/09/2004
Held on 9, 10, 11, 12 Apr, 1, 2, 3, 29, 30, 31 May and all weekends from 17 July-5 Sept

Reptile Awareness Weekends
29/05/2004-30/09/2004
Held on weekends from 29 May through to September, 14.00-17.00, weather permitting - please call for further details

Scotland

Abbeys

Arbroath Abbey

Abbey Street Arbroath Angus DD11 1EG
Tel: 01241 878756 Fax: 01241 878756
In Arbroath town centre, on A92]

The substantial ruins of a Tironensian
monastery, founded by William the Lion in 1178,
who is buried in the Abbey. Parts of the Abbey
church and domestic buildings remain, notably
the gatehouse range and the abbot's house.
*Open all year daily, please call 01241 878756 for
specific details*
A£3.30 C(5-15)£1.00 Concessions£2.50. This
property accepts Euro currency notes

Dryburgh Abbey

Dryburgh Scottish Borders
Tel: 01835 822381
*8m SE of Melrose, near St Boswells. Turn L onto
B6356 from B6404]*

Dryburgh sits by the Tweed River, its remarkably
complete medieval ruins making it easy to
appreciate the attractions of monastic life. The
abbey buildings were destroyed by fire three
times and ravaged by war on four occasions
but fine examples of ecclesiastic architecture
and masonry remain, and its chapter house
reveals plaster and paintwork dating back to its
inception.
All year daily, please call for specific times
A£3.00 C£1.00 Concessions £2.30. This property accepts Euro currency notes

Inchcolm Abbey

Inchcolm Island Fife and Central
Tel: 01383 823332 Fax: 01383 823332
*On Inchcolm in the Firth of Forth. Reached by
ferry from either South Queensferry or North
Queensferry, call 0131 331 4857 for information]*

Situated on a green island on the Firth of Forth,
the Augustinian abbey was founded in about
1123 by Alexander I. The well-preserved
remains include a fine 13th century octagonal
chapter house and a 13th century wall painting.
The island is famed for its seals, wildlife and
coastal defences from two World Wars.
Open during the summer only
A£3.00 C£1.00 Concessions£2.30, ferry charge
is extra. This property accepts Euro currency
notes

Iona Abbey and Nunnery

Island of Iona Scotland
Tel: 01681 700512
*[On the Island of Iona, public ferry from
Fionnphort, Mull]*

One of Scotland's most historic and sacred
sites, Iona Abbey was founded by St Columba
and his Irish followers in AD 563. A celebrated
focus for Christian pilgrimage, Iona retains its
spiritual atmosphere and remains an enduring
symbol of worship.
All year, depending on ferries
A£3.30 C£1.20 Concessions£2.50

Melrose Abbey

Melrose Borders
Tel: 01896 822562
[In Melrose off A7 or A68]

Melrose Abbey is a magnificent ruin on a grand
scale with lavishly decorated masonry. The
Abbey is thought to be the burial place of
Robert the Bruce's heart, marked with a com-
memorative carved stone plaque within the
grounds. Visitors can also visit a small museum
housing a display of artefacts found within the
abbey. Audio guide available.
All year, please call for specific times
A£3.50 C£1.20 Concessions £2.50. This property accepts Euro currency notes

Sweetheart Abbey

New Abbey Dumfriesshire DG2 8BU

Tel: 01387 850397

[In New Abbey village, 7m S of Dumfries on A710]

Splendid ruin of a late 13th century and early 14th century Cistercian abbey founded in 1273 by Lady Devorgilla of Galloway in memory of her husband John Balliot. When she died in 1289 she was buried in front of the altar with her husband's heart resting on her bosom hence the abbey's name. Apart from the abbey church, the principal feature is the well-preserved wall, enclosing the abbey precinct.

All year, please call 01387 850397 for specific times. Closed Thur pm, Fri & Sun am Jan-Mar, plus Thur-Fri Oct-Dec

A£2.00 C£0.75 Concessions £1.50. Joint ticket with New Abbey Corn Mill available: A£4.00 C£1.20 Concessions£3.00. This property accepts Euro currency notes

Museum of Scottish Country Life

Philipshill Road Wester Kittochside East Kilbride G76 9HR

Tel: 01355 224181 Fax: 01355 571290

www.nms.ac.uk/countrylife

[From Glasgow take A749 to East Kilbride. From Edinburgh follow M8 to Glasgow, turn off after J6 on A725 to East Kilbride. Kittochside is clearly signposted. Rail: from Glasgow Central take train to Hairmyres station, 1m from site, catch First Bus 31. Bus: from Glasgow, First Bus 31 from main terminus at St Enoch's Centre to directly opposite Museum entrance, 40 min journey]

Agriculture / Working Farms

Aberdeenshire Farming Museum

Aden Country Park Peterhead Mintlaw Aberdeenshire AB42 5FQ

Tel: 01771 622906 Fax: 01771 622884

[1m W of Mintlaw on A950]

Explore North East farming heritage and estate life at this Museum set in the beautiful surroundings of Aden Country Park. Discover the Aden Estate Story and the award winning Weel Vrocht Grun (Well Worked Ground) exhibitions set in the unique semi-circular Home Farm steading and visit Hareshowe, the working farm where you can step back in time to the 1950s.

Scottish Easter Holidays 3-18 & 24-25 Apr 12.00-16.30, 1 May-30 Sept daily 11.00-16.30, 2-3, 8-24, 30-31 Oct 12.00-16.00

Admission Free

A unique attraction exploring the history of Scottish country life and how it has shaped today's countryside. The 170 acre site comprises an exhibition building, shop, café, historic working farm and Georgian farmhouse. The exhibition building houses the National Museums of Scotland's country life collection, which includes the world's oldest surviving threshing machine amongst other artefacts. A 60-acre Events Area is used to demonstrate the Museum's working collection, contrast traditional farming methods with modern agriculture and hosts a varied programme of special events. The 110-acre historic farm of Wester Kittochside has a history which can be traced back to at least 1567. The farm, complete with cows, is worked to demonstrate traditional methods which illustrate the period of intense change which took place around 1950, allowing visitors to look back to the era of horse power and forward to the tractor and combine harvester. A unique Partnership between the National Museums of Scotland and the National Trust for Scotland.

All year daily 10.00-17.00. Closed 25, 26 Dec, 1 & 2 Jan

A£3.00 C£Free Concessions£1.50. Membership available giving free or reduced admission to all six National Museums of Scotland. Free admis-

sion to NMS and NTS Members (except during some special events). Prices may be subject to increase from April 2004

Special Events

Kittochside in Focus
07/02/2004-16/05/2004
Display of photographs from a competition to capture the Museum of Scottish Country Life on film

Easter Sunday Funday
11/04/2004
The chance to make colourful Easter bonnets, paint eggs and take part in an Easter egg hunt

Classic Car Rally
09/05/2004
A fine selection of classic cars visiting the museum and evoking memories of the more care free days of motoring

Avon Valley Vintage Power Rally
06/06/2004
An opportunity to see many of the most popular tractors and farm vehicles of the past in pristine working condition. Cost: A£5.00 C(under10)£Free Concessions£2.50

Kittochside Heavy Horse Show
11/07/2004
A chance to see working heavy horses in their natural surroundings. Events include a range of show classes and fun drives. Cost: A£5.00 C(under10)£Free Concessions£2.50

Wildlife Photographer of the Year
14/08/2004-07/11/2004
A new collection of magnificent and memorable wildlife photographs, featuring the winners of the annual competition jointly organised by BBC Wildlife Magazine and the Natural History Museum

Country Fair
22/08/2004
An event combing a wide range of country crafts, activities and demonstrations including basket weaving, blacksmithing, chain saw carving, falconry, butter making and much more along with the third Kittochside Sheep Dog Trials. Cost: A£5.00 C(under10)£Free Concessions£2.50

Farriery Competition
18/09/2004-19/09/2004
Our annual competition where many of the
world's best farriers compete against the clock to make and fit shoes. Classes include Hunter and Heavy Horses. The competition allows visitors to see the enormous skill involved whilst helping to promote and maintain the highest standards of craftsmanship. Normal ticket prices apply

Halloween Party
31/10/2004
Apple dooking, games and craft table. Event runs from 17.00-19.00. Admission free

Christmas Event including Foal Show
12/12/2004
A day of activities including The Strathaven Foal Show with a chance to see beautiful Clydesdale Foals on show and take part in Victorian Christmas workshops at the Farmhouse. Booking essential on 0131 247 4377. Santa will also be taking time off from toy making to drive the tractor up to the farmhouse. Normal admission charges apply

Animal Attractions

Scottish Deer Centre

Bow of Fife Cupar Fife KY15 4NQ
Tel: 01337 810391 Fax: 01337 810477
[3m W on A91]

Guided tours take about 40 minutes and allow visitors to meet and stroke the deer. A chance to browse around our Courtyard Shopping Complex, then relax in the Coffee Shop.
Apr-Oct daily 10.00-18.00, Nov-Mar daily 10.00-17.00
A£4.95 C£3.45 OAPs£3.95 Family Ticket (A2&C2) £15.30

Skye Serpentarium

The Old Mill Harrapool Broadford Isle of Skye IV49 9AQ
Tel: 01471 822209 Fax: 01471 822209
[Just before Broadford Bay, beside the main road from Kyleakin to Broadford (leading on to Portree)]

The Skye Serpentarium was opened in 1991 by Catherine and Alex Shearer as an exhibition and educational centre. Catherine is an experienced herpetologist and has helped rescue over 500 abandoned or rescued reptiles and amphibians. There are over 50 animals on display from White's Tree Frogs to Large Green Iguanas.
Easter-Oct Mon-Sat 10.00-17.00 (plus Sun July-Aug). Visits outside these dates may be available
A£2.50 C£1.50 Family Ticket (A2+C4) £7.00

Archaeology

Jarlshof Prehistoric and Norse Settlement

Sumburgh Head Shetland
Tel: 01950 460112
[22m S of Lerwick on the A970]

Jarlshof provides an insight into the way of life of the inhabitants at particularly interesting periods - the late Bronze Age, Iron Age, Pictish era, Norse era and the Middle Ages. It includes oval-shaped Bronze Age houses, Iron Age broch and wheelhouses, Viking long houses, medieval farmstead and 16th century laird's house.
Summer only, please call for specific times
A£3.30 C£1.00 Concessions£2.50. This property accepts Euro currency notes

Arts, Crafts & Textiles

McManus Galleries

Albert Square Dundee Angus DD1 1DA
Tel: 01382 432350 Fax: 01382 432369
[Off A90 in the centre of Dundee. Parking nearby at Wellgate, Bell Street and Overgate]

McManus Galleries, Dundee is a remarkable Gothic building housing one of Scotland's most impressive collections of fine and decorative art and award winning displays of local history, archaeology, wildlife and the environment.
All year Mon-Sat 10.30-17.00, (until 19.00 on Thurs), Sun 12.30-16.00. Closed 25-26 Dec & 1-3 Jan
Admission Free

National Gallery of Scotland

The Mound Edinburgh Midlothian EH2 2EL
Tel: 0131 624 6200 Fax: 0131 220 0917
[5mins walk from Waverley station]

Widely regarded as one of the finest smaller galleries in the world, the Gallery contains an outstanding collection of paintings, drawings, prints and sculpture by the greatest artists from the Renaissance to Post-Impressionism.
All year daily 10.00-17.00, late night Thurs open until 19.00. Closed 25-26 Dec
Admission Free. Some exhibitions charged

Scottish National Gallery of Modern Art

75 Belford Road Edinburgh Midlothian EH4 3DR

Tel: 0131 624 6200 Fax: 0131 623 7126
[15mins from W End of Princes Street and 10mins from Haymarket Station]

Houses Scotland's finest collection of twentieth and twenty-first century paintings, sculpture and graphic art.
All year daily 10.00-17.00, late night Thurs open until 19.00. Closed 25-26 Dec
Admission Free. On occasion some special loan exhibitions have charges

Scottish National Portrait Gallery

1 Queen Street Edinburgh Midlothian EH2 1JD
Tel: 0131 624 6200 Fax: 0131 623 7126
[5mins walk from Waverley station]

The Gallery provides a unique visual history of Scotland, told through portraits of the figures who shaped it: royals and rebels, poets and philosophers, heroes and villains.
All year daily 10.00-17.00, late night Thurs open until 19.00. Closed 25-26 Dec
Admission Free. Some special loan exhibitions have charges

Verdant Works

West Henderson's Wynd Dundee Tayside DD1 5BT
Tel: 01382 225282 Fax: 01382 221612
[Blackness area of Dundee]

A major museum of Dundee's textile industries. The story is told in the authentic and atmospheric setting of an early 19th century flax and jute mill. There are working demonstrations of historic textile machinery together with stunning and imaginative displays, multi-media technology and 'hands on' interactive.

All year Summer 10.00-17.00, Winter 10.30-16.30. Sun open at 11.00. Closed 25-26 Dec, 1 & 2 Jan. Opening times subject to review.

A£5.95 C£3.85 Concessions£4.45 Family

Ticket (A2+C2) £17.00

Birds, Butterflies & Bees

Banff Museum

High Street Banff Banffshire AB45 1AE
Tel: 01771 622906
[A97]

The museum has an exhibition of British birds set out as an aviary. The bird display won the Glenfiddich Living Scotland Award in 1989. Armour and items of local history are also on display. Wheelchair access on ground floor only.
June-Sept Mon-Sat 14.00-16.30
Admission Free

Edinburgh Butterfly and Insect World

at Dobbies Garden World Lasswade Midlothian EH18 1AZ

Tel: 0131 663 4932 Fax: 0131 654 2774

www.edinburgh-butterfly-world.co.uk

[By Car: Located at Dobbies Gardening World off the Edinburgh City Bypass at the Gilmerton exit or from the Sheriffhall Roundabout - just follow the signs. By Bus: Lothian Region Transport 3 from Princes Street (Shops Side) Mon - Sun. Plenty of free on site parking]

352 Scotland

Walk through a tropical paradise and observe stunning exotic butterflies flying around you. Iguanas roam free and quail and a hummingbird can be spotted darting through the jungle flora. There are tarantulas, stick insects, leaf-cutting ants, scorpions and frogs! You can get up close and personal at twice daily 'Meet the Beasties' handling sessions. We can even help cure your phobias! In the Reptile Room you'll find lizards, chameleons, giant pythons and Yellow Anacondas! The nocturnal zone displays bugs and beasties that can be seen going about their night time activities, with the leaf cutter ants nest, and glow in the dark scorpions! Every Friday afternoon you can view the Snake Pit, where our Royal Pythons will be fed! With monthly themes throughout the year, there will always be a new weird and wonderful creature to come and see!

All year, Summer daily 09.30-17.30, Winter daily 10.00-17.00

A£4.70 C£3.60 Family Tickets from £15.00. Group rates 10+ call for details

Caverns & Caves

St Margaret's Cave

Chalmers Street Car Park Dumfermline Fife KY12 8DF

Tel: 01383 314228 Fax: 01383 313837

[2m W of the M90 in Dunfermine town centre]

A cave over 80 steps below ground which was used by Queen Margaret (Saint Margaret) for quiet times and to pray.

1 Apr-30 Sept daily 11.00-16.00. Closed Oct-Mar

Admission Free

Costume & Jewellery Museums

Shambellie House Museum of Costume

New Abbey Dumfries DG2 8HQ

Tel: 01387 850375 Fax: 01387 850461

www.nms.ac.uk/costume

[10 minutes S by car from Dumfries along A710]

Step back in time and experience Victorian and Edwardian grace and refinement at Shambellie House Museum of Costume. Shambellie House, a beautiful Victorian country home set in attractive wooded grounds, offers visitors a chance to see period clothes from the 1850s to the 1950s in appropriate room settings, with accessories, furniture and decorative art. Celebrated Scottish architect David Bryce designed Shambellie House for the Stewart family in 1856. In 1977 Charles Stewart gave the house and his unique collection of costumes to the National Museums of Scotland. The house now displays many of these costumes in appropriate settings, creating a complete picture of the social life of well-off Victorians and Edwardians, with paintings, furnishings, decoration, ceramics and other items common to houses of the time. Shambellie House also has many temporary exhibitions featuring costumes from film and television dramas. Part of the National Museums of Scotland.

Apr-Oct daily 11.00-17.00

A£2.50 C£Free Concessions £1.50.
Membership available giving free or reduced
entry to all six National Museums of Scotland.
Admission charges may be subject to increase
from April 2004

Special Events

Ann Sutton MBE - A Retrospective Exhibition
01/04/2004-15/05/2004
*Featuring work from the early 1970s up to 2004,
this exhibition will comprise works loaned from
major private and public collections in the UK and
overseas, as well as work from Ann Sutton's own
extensive archives. The exhibition will look closely
at the developments Sutton has made in her field,
from cottage industry weaving on a stock
machine, to designing for industry. It will also highlight her use of technology, particularly colour
morphing, only possible with the aid of a computer. The works will be displayed in a variety of ways
including; wall mounted, ceiling hung and plinth
based work. A Crafts Council Touring Exhibition*

Country Parks & Estates

Kelburn Castle and Country Centre

South Offices Fairlie Largs Ayrshire KA29 0BE

Tel: 01475 568685 Fax: 01475 568121

www.kelburncountrycentre.com

[A78 2m S of Largs. Rail: Largs. Plenty of on site parking]

Home of the Earls of Glasgow, Kelburn enjoys
spectacular views over the Firth of Clyde.
Explore its historic gardens and romantic glen,
waterfalls and unique trees. There is also a riding centre, birds of prey, pottery, adventure
playgrounds, craft shop, licensed cafè, exhibitions and Scotland's most unusual attraction -
the 'Secret Forest'.

*Apr-Oct daily 10.00-18.00. Nov-Mar 11.00-
17.00. Castle open July and Aug for afternoon
guided tours, (3 per day)*

A£5.00 Concessions£3.50 Family Ticket
(A2+C3 or A1+C4) £15.00. (Family tickets may
be used again, discounting the next visit to
£10.00)

Discount Offer: For Every Adult, One Child Free

Special Events

Easter Events
09/04/2004-18/04/2004
*Events to include egg painting and rolling, egg
hunt, giant bunnies, egg and spoon challenge
and much more. Time: 12.00-16.00*

Batty Bank Holiday
01/05/2004-03/05/2004
*Build a bat box, play batty games and do batty
arts and crafts. On Sat 1 May there will be an
evening bat walk at 20.30. Cost: £2.00. Join our
bat expert to learn about bats and explore the bat
glen and pick up bat sounds on special detectors*

Weekly Tuesday Evening Walks
04/05/2004-24/08/2004
*Join the rangers to explore Kelburn's walks and
wildlife. Time: 19.00. Cost: £1.00. Walks continue
all summer, please call for further details*

Herbalist Courses
16/05/2004-19/09/2004
*Held on 16 May, 18 July, 19 Sept only. Learn
remedies and techniques from Bill Cleeve, our
local herbal expert. Booking and fee required,
please call for further details*

Highland Rustic Games
28/05/2004-31/05/2004
*Horse shoe throwing, rustic skittles, welly tossing,
tug-o-war, stocks, haggis throwing, mini obstacle
course, barrel rolling and other rustic games.
Time: 12.00-16.00*

Rustic Art Family Days
26/06/2004-27/06/2004
Use your imagination along with natural resources to create environmental sculptures, mosaics and designs. Time: 12.00-16.00

Woodland Folklore and Medicinal Plants
03/07/2004-04/07/2004
Join the Rangers and explore nature's medicine cupboard and taste its magical produce. Be intrigued by our folklore tales from the woodland. Time: 12.00-16.00

Save the Planet Weekend
10/07/2004-11/07/2004
Make recycled paper with the rangers, crush a can, try the 'rubbish' quiz and find out how nature takes care of its rubbish. Time: 12.00-16.00

Dog Show
17/07/2004-18/07/2004
Bring along your furry friends to take part in our fun show. Can your dog win the waggiest tale, an agility test or scruffiest mutt? Time: 12.00-16.00

Nature's Music
24/07/2004-25/07/2004
Work with the Rangers in constructing musical instruments from nature's music store then express yourself in Kelburn's orchestra. Time: 12.00-16.00

Minibeast Weekend
24/07/2004-25/07/2004
Join the Rangers on a minibeast safari and a special pond dip. Meet at 14.30 at the Ranger centre and learn more about the creatures under our feet and in our ponds. Meet the Beekeeper and his bees at work. Time: 12.00-16.00

New Zealand Weekend
07/08/2004-08/08/2004
Maori facepainting, special displays and lots of family Kiwi fun, to celebrate Kelburn's historic links with New Zealand. Time: 12.00-16.00

Green Woodwork Weekend
14/08/2004-15/08/2004
Walking stick making, green woodwork, pole lathe demonstration and other rural crafts. Time: 12.00-16.00

International Rocket Festival
20/08/2004-30/08/2004

Outback Weekend
21/08/2004-22/08/2004
Learn a little more about Australian customs and culture. Make, paint and play a didjeridoo, try dot painting on eucalyptus bark, pebble painting and aboriginal face painting. Time: 12.00-16.00

Viking Day at Kelburn
29/08/2004

Autumn Fungal Foray Day
25/09/2004
Time: 12.00-15.00

Mini Walking Festival
16/10/2004-24/10/2004

Halloween Event
31/10/2004

Family Christmas Events
01/12/2004-31/12/2004
Please call for further information and specific dates

Mugdock Country Park
Craigallian Road Milngavie Glasgow
Lanarkshire G62 8EL

Tel: 0141 956 6100

www.mugdock-country-park.org.uk

[Well signposted from A81 Milngavie / Strathblane road. Rail: Milngavie 3m. Bus: Summer service to Park. Plenty of on site parking available]

Mugdock Country Park - 750 acres of stunning countryside (lochs, rivers, woods, heaths and noors) with lovely views over Glasgow and to he Highlands. Treat yourself to some great walks, something from the tearoom, garden centre or gift shop. Take the kids to the extensive adventure (and under 10s) play areas. It's a great day out for everyone!

All year daily 09.00-dusk. Closed 25 Dec

Admission Free

Festivals & Shows

Aberdeen International Youth Festival

Various venues Aberdeen Aberdeenshire
Tel: 01224 641122

This unique youth festival celebrated its 30th Anniversary in 2002. It annually welcomes some of the world's finest youth orchestras (chamber/symphony), jazz and wind bands, choirs, all forms of dance groups (ballet, contemporary, jazz, folk), world music and theatre companies. Participating groups give performances in the major venues within the City of Aberdeen and throughout a network of smaller towns and villages in the Highlands, enabling them to see more of Scotland. In these troubled times, the Festival continues to actively promote international understanding and tolerance and co-operation between young people around the world.
August 4-14 2004

Border Gathering

Dumfries and Galloway College Heath Hall Dumfries Scotland
Tel: 01387 261261
[2m N of Dumfries on the A701]

During August the hills of Scotland are ablaze with purple heather and the borderland shows the history and heritage of its wild past. The Border Reiver families robbed, stole cattle, murdered and plundered as a lifestyle for hundreds of years. The land is now peaceful, the people welcoming and hospitable. Castles and tower houses, once formidable fortresses have many tales to tell of past battles, but are now at peace. The Border Gathering is now well established and enthusiastically enjoyed by many

people from many parts of the world. The gathering draws thousands to watch the traditional games of tossing the caber and throwing the weight, to see historical re-enactments, hear music and song and visit the border clan tents.
August 5-8 2004
Prices vary according to event

Deveron Festival

Venues in Banff and MacDuff Banff Aberdeenshire AB45 3SX
Tel: 01261 818181 Fax: 01261 818900
[In Banff on A96]

Take a beautiful coastal setting, mix with a generous helping of the world's greatest music and serve on a bed of glorious architecture, et voila! You have the perfect weekend. The main course on the menu is Sona Coated - an innovative pairing of clarinet and percussion premiering a new work with orchestra by Steve King. You can hear them with the Deveron Festival Orchestra under the baton of Gareth John in a seafaring programme which will include Mendelssohn's Fingal's Cave and Handel's Water Music. For an appetiser we can offer the glorious music of Brahms for clarinet and piano (Joanna Nicolson and Graham McNaught) and to round things off, a generous helping of Cabaret from the acclaimed Haddo Youth Theatre. Together with many fringe events throughout the weekend, they make a wonderful feast of performances.
June 10-13 2004
Prices vary according to event, from £Free-£7.50

Dumfries and Galloway Arts Festival 2004 - Silver Festival

Various venues Dumfries Dumfries and Galloway
[M74 from N or S, signposted from A75. Rail: Dumfries from London via Carlisle or Glasgow direct]

To mark the 25th year of the Festival, an exciting two week programme of events ranging from a recital by international opera star Willard

White and a Children's Classic Concert conducted by Christopher Bell with the Scottish Chamber Orchestra, to a Celebrity Conversation and including drama, ballet, folk, jazz, exhibitions, literary and children's events.
May 22-June 5 2004

Edinburgh Festival Fringe 2004

180 High Street (Festival Office) Edinburgh EH1 1QS
Tel: 0131 226 0016 Fax: 0131 226 0016
The Edinburgh Festival Fringe is the world's greatest celebration of live art and performance. With up to 1,000 different shows a day including theatre, music, circus, dance, comedy, children's shows and street entertainment, for just over three weeks in August, the whole of Scotland's most majestic city becomes a stage.
August 8-30 2004

Edinburgh International Festival 2004

The Hub Castle Hill Royal Mile Edinburgh EH1 2NE
Tel: 0131 473 2000 Fax: 0131 473 2003
One of the world's most prestigious arts festival, the Edinburgh International Festival celebrates the drama of live performance in Scotland's capital city. The 2004 Edinburgh International Festival presents great orchestras and cutting edge choreographers, familiar names and world premieres, grand opera and intimate chamber music. The audience is just as mixed: whether you've been coming for years, or are thinking about dipping your toe into water for the first time, you can be sure of a warm welcome and life enhancing experiences.

August 15-September 4 2004

Edinburgh International Science Festival

Edinburgh EH6 8BR
Tel: 0131 220 1882 Fax: 0131 226 1771
[M8 / M9 / M90, M6 / M74, A1(M) all lead to Edinburgh. The EISF takes place at various venues throughout Edinburgh]

The Edinburgh International Science Festival is massive public celebration of science and technology. It is one of the most exciting festivals of its kind in the world, and is made up of around 200 entertaining, fun-filled events
April 2-13 2004
Prices vary, range from £Free-£7.00

Edinburgh Military Tattoo

Tattoo Office 32 Market Street Edinburgh Scotland EH1 1QB
Tel: 08707 555 1188 Box Office
Fax: 0131 225 8627
[Tattoo office is in the city centre. The show is staged on floodlit Edinburgh Castle Esplanade]

For over 50 years it has been one of the finest exhibitions of military pomp and splendour in the world, a masterpiece of showmanship. With music, colour and movement at its foundation it commands attention and admiration across the globe. While foreign bands are set to add an absorbing international flavour to the occasion, the heart-stopping sound of the Massed Pipes and Drums, together with the ever popular Massed Military Bands are expected to enrich the proceedings.
August 6-28 2004
Tickets available by calling 0131 225 1188, or in person at The Tattoo Ticket Sales Office, 33-34 Market Street

Gardening Scotland 2004

Royal Highland Centre Ingliston Edinburgh Midlothian EH28 8NF
Tel: 0131 335 6200/6216 Fax: 0131 333 5236
[Adjacent to Edinburgh Airport. Follow directions to the Airport and then Royal Highland Centre]

Over one hundred of the UK's leading nurseries will be on show battling it out for the prestigious

Royal Caledonian Horticultural Society Gold Medals. The spectacle of such high quality, sensational displays and gardens is truly marvellous. Scotland's largest gathering of award winning growers and experts will be on hand to offer advice and to help visitors make the most of their garden space. Key features of the show will be magnificent show gardens, easy and inspirational ideas to support natural habitats, stunning and imaginative exhibits in the Floral Hall, expert advice from TV broadcasters and plant producers, breathtaking displays by Britain's top growers and award winning displays from the specialist gardening clubs, plus much, much more.
June 4-6 2004

Loch Fyne Oysters Ltd Food Fair 2004

Clachan Cairndow Argyll PA26 8BH
Tel: 01499 600264 Fax: 01499 600234
[A83, 10m S of Inveraray, at the head of Loch Fyne]

Annual Food Fair - feast of West Coast Food along with specially selected wines and beers, live music, cooking demonstrations, children's fair and entertainments.
May 29-30 2004

Loch Shiel Spring Festival

Loch Shiel Scotland PH36 4NB
Tel: 01687 470324 Fax: 01687 470280
[Via A830 and A861]

Classical music with international performers which takes place amongst some of Scotland's most spectacular scenery. Based around the beautiful Loch Shiel, near Fort William, with Glenfinnan in the North and Acharacle at the south end of the Loch, a variety of Chamber concerts, Recitals, Wind and Choral concerts are organised.
May 17-22 2004

Peebles Jazz Festival 2004

Various venues Peebles Peeblesshire
EH45 8HN
Tel: 01721 721207
[20m S of Edinburgh on A703 to Galashiels]

Set in the peaceful Scottish Borders, Peebles offers not only beautiful scenery, relaxing walks and hospitable residents but also one of the friendliest and entertaining Trad/Dixieland Jazz Festivals in the country. Now in its 10th year PJF is growing rapidly! Disabled access to most venues, please call to confirm.
May 7-9 2004
Rover Ticket: £18.00. Session Ticket: £5.00. Fri Evening Ticket: £8.00

Perth Festival of the Arts 2004

3-5 High Street Perth Perthshire PH1 5JS
Tel: 01738 472706 / 621031
Fax: 01738 475295
An eleven day Arts Festival including orchestral concerts, opera, chamber music, jazz, folk, rock, drama, ballet and comedy.
May 20-30 2004, 10.00-18.00

Scottish Traditional Boat Festival

Various venues Portsoy
[Portsoy Harbour lies in the middle of the southern shore of the Moray Firth. It sits N of the A98, about 50m W of Aberdeen and about 60m E of Inverness]

The Scottish Traditional Boat Festival is a family festival that features a cornucopia of off shore and on shore activities. Traditional wooden boats: historic vessels to view, with daily sailing races; Grampian food fayre with celebrity chefs, Ready Steady Cook, cooking demonstrations and tastings. Portsoy Music Festival: live music on the shoreside stage, marching bands, highland dancing and an evening ceilidh. Historic street theatre with costumed actors, directed by Charles Barron. Demonstrations of Maritime and shore side related skills and crafts, including an Iron age settlement. Plus simulated rescues by the coastguard and life boat, side stalls, Kidzone activities, maritime games, 20k marathon, fun run and lots, lots more...

July 3-4 2004

St Magnus Festival 2004

Various venues Orkney Isles KW15
Tel: 01856 871445 Fax: 01856 871170
*[Various venues in and around Kirkwall and
Stromness. Ferry: 01856 872044]*

Celebrities, premieres, community performances
and isles excursions are just some of the ingredients of Orkney's prestigious midsummer celebration of the arts. The 2004 St Magnus Festival
features an array of world class performers
including the BBC Scottish Symphony
Orchestra; Ilya Gringotts - violin; Jean-Philippe
Collard - piano; the Nash Ensemble; Walk-the-
Plank - a ship based theatre company; the
Russian Patriarchate Choir of Moscow; Liz
Lockhead - Festival Poet; Mr McFall's Chamber;
the Two Fiddlers - Maxwell Davies's delightful
children's opera, and more besides.
June 18-23 2004

Black House Complex

Arnol Barvas Isle Of Lewis HS2 9DB
Tel: 01851 710395 Fax: 01851 710395
*[In Arnol Village, Lewis, 11m NW of Stornoway on
A858]*

A traditional, fully furnished, Lewis thatched
house, which provides a unique insight into
island life. There is also an attached barn, byre
and stackyard. Beside the Black House, a furnished 1920s crofthouse can also be seen. The
fascinating complex at Arnol has a visitor centre
with interactive displays.
*All year Mon-Sat, please call 01851 710395 for
specific details*
A£3.00 C£1.00 Concessions£2.30. This property accepts Euro currency notes

Huntly Museum

Huntly Scotland AB54 5AD
Tel: 01779 477778
*[Parking available in local car parks that carry a
charge]*

The museum has local history displays and
there are special exhibitions throughout the year.
All year Tues-Sat 14.00-16.30
Admission Free

Inverurie Museum

Town House The Square Inverurie AB51 3SN
Tel: 01771 622906
This busy shopping and business centre is
ringed by many prehistoric sites. There are the-
matic exhibitions, displays of canal relics and
items on local history and archaeology.
*All year Mon & Wed-Fri 14.00-16.30, Sat 10.00-
13.00 & 14.00-16.00*
Admission Free

Perth Museum and Art Gallery

George Street Perth Perthshire PH1 5LB

Tel: 01738 632488 Fax: 01738 443505

www.pkc.gov.uk/ah

[In City centre]

One of the oldest museums in Britain, found in
the centre of the fair city of Perth. Exhibitions,
both permanent and changing, are drawn from
our fantastic collections of fine and applied art,
archaeology, photography and human and natural history. For details of what will be on show
when you will be visiting please see the website
or telephone the museum. Until Spring 2005,
works from The Fergusson Gallery Collection,
the largest collection of works by the Scottish
colourist J. D. Fergusson, are also on show
while The Fergusson Gallery is renovated.

*All year Mon-Sat 10.00-17.00. Closed Christmas
& New Year*

Admission Free

Special Events

Mirror, Mirror on the wall...
13/12/2003-01/05/2004
Who's the fairest, richest, most famous of them all! The who, what, where, when and why portraits are painted

Rhythm of the Land
13/12/2003-24/04/2004
Bold and colourful landscape paintings chart the changing seasons in the Black Isle. Painted by the 2003 J.D. Fergusson Arts Award winner, Clare Blois

The Bellany Family... uncovered!
13/12/2003-08/05/2004
Seven other paintings are used to explore different elements of self-portraiture, still life and symbolism in the painting 'The Bellany Family'

Heads and Tales
19/12/2003-08/05/2004
Portraits of friends, family and unknown faces by J. D. Fergusson. Paintings, drawings, sculptures, and stories highlighting his life

For the Kirk of Perth
01/04/2004-31/12/2010
Be dazzled by this stunning collection of silver and pewter from St John's Kirk, Perth

Wild and Wonderful
15/05/2004-24/12/2004
Biodiversity means the variety of life on earth. Tayside is a very special place for biodiversity. Protecting this unique habitat is essential to the quality of life; plant, animal and man alike. Discover the wild and wonderful places and species that share this part of the world with you

Chan Ky-Yut
22/05/2004-10/07/2004
Taught calligraphy by his grandfather from the age of 3, Chan Ky-Yut's lively, abstract and vibrant watercolours are inspired by Zen, Spiritualism and poetry. This Chinese artist is a must see in the Perthshire Festival of the Arts

Scottish Photographic Federation Annual Salon
22/05/2004-12/06/2004
Founded in Perth 100 years ago and now making a welcome return, The Salon is a showcase for the best in international photography

Asylum Lost
19/06/2004-16/10/2004
An opportunity to see unique and stunning images of life in a mental hospital. Perth's Murray Royal Hospital is now facing closure after a phenomenal 176 years of service to the community

This Old Tree and its Friend the Sun
19/06/2004-16/10/2004
J. D. Fergusson tackles the natural world of flowers and foliage on oil paint, watercolour and sculpture

Tomintoul Museum

The Square Tomintoul Moray AB37 9ET
Tel: 01309 673701 Fax: 01309 673701
[Either take the A95 off A9 at Aviemore to Grantown on Spey then A939 to Tomintoul or the A939 off the A93 at Ballater]

Situated in one of the highest villages in Britain, the museum features a reconstructed crofters kitchen and smiddy, with displays on local wildlife, the story of Tomintoul and the local skiing industry.
31 Mar-30 May Mon-Fri 09.30-12.00 & 14.00-16.00, 1 June-30 Aug Mon-Sat 09.30-12.00 & 14.00-16.30, 1-27 Sept Mon-Sat 09.30-12.00 & 14.00-16.00, 29 Sept-24 Oct Mon-Fri 09.30-12.00 & 14.00-16.00. Closed Good Fri & 5 May
Admission Free

Vikingar

Greenock Road Largs Ayrshire KA30 8QL
Tel: 01475 689777 Fax: 01475 689444
[Barrfields off A78]

Vikingar is an amazing multi-media experience which takes you from the first Viking raids in Scotland to their defeat at the Battle of Largs.
Apr-Sept 10.30-17.30, Oct-Mar 10.30-15.30, Nov-Feb Weekends only 10.30-15.30. Closed Dec & Jan
A£4.00 C£3.00 OAPs£3.00

West Highland Museum

Cameron Square Fort William Inverness-Shire
PH33 6AJ
Tel: 01397 702169 Fax: 01397 701927
[A82 Glasgow to Inverness road]

The displays illustrate traditional Highland life
and history, with numerous Jacobite relics. One
of them is the 'secret portrait' of 'Bonnie' Prince
Charlie, which looks like meaningless daubs of
paint but reveals a portrait when reflected in a
metal cylinder.

June-Sept Mon-Sat 10.00-17.00, Oct-May Mon-Sat 10.00-16.00, July & Aug Sun 14.00-17.00

A£3.00 C(over12)£0.50 Concessions£2.00

Food & Drink

Cardow Distillery Visitor Centre

Knockando Aberlour Banffshire AB38 7RY
Tel: 01340 872555 Fax: 01340 872556
*[Take the B9102 from Grantown-on-Spay for
approximately 17m. From Elgin take the A941 to
Rothes, continue for 3m then travel W on the
B9102 for approximately 7m]*

Share with us the story of Cardow Distillery,
(previously known as the Cardhu Distillery), the
only malt distillery pioneered by a woman.

*Jan-Easter Mon-Fri 11.00-15.00, Easter-June
Mon-Fri 10.00-17.00; July-Sept Mon-Sat 10.00-17.00, Sun 12.00-16.00, Oct Mon-Fri 11.00-16.00, Nov-Dec Mon-Fri 11.00-15.00*
A£4.00 C£Free

Glen Grant Distillery and Garden

Elgin Road Rothes Aberlour Banffshire
AB38 7BS
Tel: 01340 832118 Fax: 01340 832104
[On A941 in Rothes 10m S of Elgin]

Today the Glen Grant Distillery retains its original
character and the Victorian garden has been
restored to its former glory for all to enjoy. Visitor
can go on a guided tour of the distillery.
1 Apr-31 Oct Mon-Sat 10.00-16.00, Sun 12.30-16.00
Admission Free. C(under8) are not admitted to
production areas but are welcome in the Visitor
Centre and garden

The Glenlivet Distillery

Glenlivet Ballindalloch Banffshire AB37 9DB
Tel: 01340 821720 Fax: 01340 821718
[Off B9009 10m N of Tomintoul]

The Glenlivet Distillery was founded in 1824 by
George Smith and is home to the world famous
12 year old single malt Scotch whisky. Enjoy a
guided tour of the distillery which includes a
viewing of a vast bonded warehouse before
sampling a complimentary dram of whisky.
1 Apr-31 Oct Mon-Sat 10.00-16.00, Sun 12.30-16.00
Admission Free. C(under8) are not admitted to
production areas though welcome in the Visitor
Centre

Gardens & Horticulture

Benmore Botanic Garden

Dunoon Argyll PA23 8QU
Tel: 01369 706261 Fax: 01369 706369
[7m N of Dunoon on A815]

In the wonderful woodland setting of the
Eachaig Valley, lies Benmore, a Garden steeped
in history and surrounded by dramatic scenery.
Benmore boasts a world-famous collection of
magnificent conifers, flowering trees and shrubs
1 Mar-31 Oct daily 10.00-18.00 (17.00 in Mar & Oct)
A£3.50 C£1.00 C£1.00 Concessions£3.00
Family Ticket £8.00

Royal Botanic Garden Edinburgh

20a Inverleith Row Edinburgh Midlothian
EH3 5LR
Tel: 0131 552 7171 Fax: 0131 248 2901
*[Off A902 1m N of City centre. Entrances at
Inverleith Row (East Gate) and Arboretum Place*

(West Gate). Rail: Waverley]

Known locally as the 'Botanics' and established way back in 1670, Scotland's premier garden is one of the UK's favourite attractions.

All year daily, Nov-Feb 10.00-16.00, Mar & Oct 10.00-18.00, Apr-Sept 10.00-19.00. Closed 25 Dec & 1 Jan. Please be aware that Inverleith House Gallery will be closed to the public until midsummer 2004

Admission Free, donations welcome. Admission to the Glasshouses (from June 2004): A£3.50 C£1.00 Concessions£3.00 Family Ticket £8.00

Guided Tours

Blair Athol Distillery

Perth Road Pitlochry Perthshire PH16 5LY
Tel: 01796 482003 Fax: 01796 482001
[0.5m S of Pitlochry, off the A9 to Inverness]

A visit to Blair Athol is a visit to one of the oldest working distilleries in Scotland, established in 1798 in the picturesque town of Pitlochry. Here you can see the distillers utilising the most valuable of local resources, the crystal clear waters of the Allt Dour, the burn of the Otter. The distillery produces a 12 year old Single Malt.
Easter-Sept Mon-Sat 09.30-17.00, Sun 12.00-17.00, last tour 1hr before closing, Oct-Easter Mon-Fri tours at 11.00, 13.00, 15.00
A£4.00 C£Free

Heritage & Industrial

Garlogie Mill Power House Museum

Skene Westhill Scotland AB32 6RX
Tel: 01771 622906 Fax: 01771 622884
[Take Alford road from Aberdeen at the end of Garlogie village turn right into mill grounds]

A restored building housing the power sources for the now demolished mill. Notable for the use of power generating machinery and in particular the only beam engine left in situ in Scotland. Machinery is currently under restoration.
Please call for details of opening times
Admission Free

Motherwell Heritage Centre

High Road Motherwell North Lanarkshire ML1 3HU

Tel: 01698 251000 Fax: 01698 268867

http://motherwellheritage.freeservers.com

[From the S J6 M74 from the N J6 M74. Limited on site parking available]

Motherwell Heritage Centre is situated in High Road, just off the top of the A723 Hamilton Road. It has a Scottish Tourist Board '4 Star' award. The centre's main feature is the multimedia 'Technopolis' interactive facility. This takes the visitor from the arrival of the Romans, through the rise and fall of heavy industry to the present day regeneration of the district. The use of 'hands on' technology with recreated streets and foundry scenes really brings history of the area to life. The centre also has an exhibition gallery, the focus of many fascinating displays and community projects. There is also a family history research room, with staff available to advise on tracing family and local histories. A fifth floor viewing platform gives an outlook over the Clyde Valley and, on the ground floor, a small shop sells books, postcards and gifts with local heritage flavour.

All year Wed-Sat 10.00-17.00, Sun 12.00-17.00. Closed Mon & Tue

Admission Free

New Abbey Corn Mill

New Abbey Dumfrieshire
Tel: 01387 850260
[In New Abbey village, 7m S of Dumfries on A710]

In full working order, the water-powered New Abbey Corn Mill has been carefully restored and is operated regularly in summer months to demonstrate how oatmeal is produced.
All year, please call for specific times. Closed Thur pm and Fri & Sun am Jan-Mar plus Thur-Fri Oct-Dec
A£2.80 C£1.00 Concessions£2.00. Joint ticket with Sweetheart Abbey available: A£4.00 C£1.20 Concessions £3.00. This property accepts Euro currency notes

New Lanark World Heritage Site

New Lanark Mills Lanark Strathclyde ML11 9DB
Tel: 01555 661345 Fax: 01555 665738
[1m S of Lanark. Less than 1 hour by car from Glasgow (M74) and Edinburgh (A70)]

Long famous as a beauty spot and the site of Robert Owen's social and educational reforms, this beautiful 18th century cotton mill village is Scotland's latest UNESCO World Heritage Site, carefully restored as a living community, with an award-winning Visitor Centre and Hotel.
All year daily 11.00-17.00. Closed 25 Dec & 1 Jan
A£5.95 Concessions£3.95 Family Ticket (A2+C2) £16.95

Scotch Whisky Heritage Centre

354 Castlehill The Royal Mile Edinburgh Midlothian EH1 2NE
Tel: 0131 220 0441 Fax: 0131 220 6288
[The Centre is next to Edinburgh Castle]

The Scottish Tourist Board 5* Tourist Attraction - The Scotch Whisky Heritage Centre brings the story of whisky to life in an entertaining and informative way. Experience Scotland's turbulent past and learn the ancient traditions surrounding Scotch Whisky making.
All year daily, summer 09.30-17.30, winter 10.00-17.00. Closed 25 Dec

A£7.95 C(5-17)£3.95 Concessions£5.95 Family Ticket £18.00

Scottish Mining Museum

Lady Victoria Colliery Newtongrange outside Edinburgh Midlothian EH22 4QN
Tel: 0131 663 7519 Fax: 0131 654 1618
[Situated in Newtongrange, 9m S of Edinburgh via A7]

Come and marvel at the sheer size of the Scottish Mining Museum, be astounded by the engineering brilliance behind all the machinery and retrace the footsteps and struggles of thousands of miners and their families before you.
All year daily Mar-Oct 10.00-17.00, Nov-Feb 10.00-16.00. Closed 24-26, 31 Dec, 1-2 Jan
A£4.95 C&Concessions£3.30

Speyside Cooperage Visitor Centre

Dufftown Road Craigellachie Banffshire AB38 9RS
Tel: 01340 871108 Fax: 01340 881437
[1m S of Craigellachie on A941]

Award-winning working cooperage with unique visitor centre, where skilled coopers and their apprentices practise their ancient craft of coopering.
Early Jan-Mid Dec Mon-Fri 09.30-16.30. Closed Christmas and New Year
A£3.10 C&OAPs£2.50 Family Ticket £8.50

Summerlee Heritage Park

Heritage Way Coatbridge North Lanarkshire
ML5 1QD

Tel: 01236 431261 Fax: 01236 440429

[J8 M8 Eastbound A8 Westbound. Just to W of
town centre, by Central Station]

Summerlee Heritage Park is an STB '4 Star' visitor attraction and 'Best Working Attraction'
award-winner. Its 22 acres are based around
the site of the 19th century Summerlee
Ironworks and its branch of Monklands Canal.
Main features of the park are: Scotland's only
electric tramway, offering rides on modern and
Edwardian open-topped trams. A huge undercover exhibition hall with working machinery and
period room settings. Re-created addit mine
and miners cottage. There is also a separate
exhibition gallery, tearoom and gift shop. Free
parking adjacent and free admission. Summer
programme of heritage events. Great new playground for tots to teens!

All year daily 10.00-17.00 (16.00 Nov-Mar).
Closed 25-26 Dec & 1-2 Jan

Admission Free. Tram ride A£0.80 C£0.45

Historical

Aberdour Castle

Aberdour Burntisland Fife KY3 0SL
Tel: 01383 860519 Fax: 01383 860519
[In Aberdour, 5m E of the Forth Bridges on the
A921]

Built by the Douglas family, the 13th century fortified residence, extended in the 15th, 16th and
17th centuries, providing accommodation with a
gallery and fine painted ceiling. It boasts a
delightful walled garden and terraces with bee-
hive-shaped dovecot.

All year, please call 01383 860519 for specific
times. Closed Thur & Fri in winter
A£2.50 C£0.75 Concessions£1.90. This property accepts Euro currency notes

Balmoral Castle Grounds and Exhibition

Balmoral Ballater Aberdeenshire AB35 5TB
Tel: 013397 42534 Fax: 013397 42034
www.balmoralcastle.com

[On A93 between Ballater / Braemar. Parking on
site limited]

Queen Victoria and Prince Albert first rented the
property in 1848 and later commissioned
William Smith to build a new castle which was
completed in 1855 and remains today the Royal
Family's highland residence. A landscape of
woodlands and plantations sweeping up to
grouse moors and distant mountains. Features
pony trekking, exhibitions and waymarked paths
through stunning scenery. Dogs are welcome
except in buildings.

1 Apr-31 July 10.00-17.00 (Exhibitions and
Grounds only open)

A£5.00 C(0-5)£Free C(5-16)£1.00 OAPs£4.00

Bowhill House and Country Park

Bowhill Selkirk Scottish Borders TD7 5ET

Tel: 01750 22204 Fax: 01750 22204

[3m W of Selkirk on A708 Moffat St Marys Loch Road. Plenty of on site parking available]

Scottish Borders home of the Duke and Duchess of Buccleuch. Internationally renowned art collection, including Canaletto's Whitehall works by Guardi, Claude, Gainsborough etc. Superb 17th/18th century French and 19th century British furniture. Meissen and Sevres porcelain, silver and tapestries. Historic relics include Monmouth's saddle and execution shirt, Sir Walter Scott's plaid and some proof editions. Queen Victoria's letter and gifts to successive Duchesses of Buccleuch, her Mistresses of the Robes. Completely restored Victorian Kitchen, 19th century horse-drawn fire engine. Visitors' Centre, picnic areas, gift shop and licensed tearoom. Exciting adventure woodland playground and Victorian treasure trail. Woodland, loch and riverside walks. Ranger-led walks and children's activities throughout the summer. Bowhill Theatre, a lively centre for the performing arts and where, prior to touring the house visitors can see The Quest for Bowhill, a 20 minute audio-visual. The popular visitor attraction featuring the life and work of James Hogg the Ettrick Shepherd is now at Bowhill, cementing Hogg's long connection with the Buccleuch family. Accompanying the story of James Hogg are memorabilia, books, paintings and Anne Carrick's exquisite costume figures.

House: 1-31 July daily 13.00-17.00, limited opening in June & August. Country Park: Easter-end Aug, opening times vary. Please call for further information

House & Park: A£6.00 C£2.00 OAPs£4.50. Wheelchair users £Free. Park only: £2.00 C(under5) and Wheelchair users £Free. Family and group tickets available

Special Events

The Merry Wives of Windsor
04/07/2004
Theatre Set-Up present an outdoors performance of Shakespeare's The Merry Wives of Windsor in the beautiful grounds of Bowhill

Alice in Wonderland
15/08/2004
Chapterhouse Theatre Company presents an outdoors performance of 'Alice in Wonderland' for children and families

Caerlaverock Castle

Caerlaverock Dumfries Dumfriesshire DG1 4RU
Tel: 01387 770244 Fax: 01387 770244
[8m SE of Dumfries on B7253]

One of the finest castles in Scotland. Its most remarkable features are the twin-towered gatehouse and the Nithsdale Lodging, a splendid Renaissance range dating from 1634. Children's adventure park and replica siege engines in front of castle.
All year daily, please call for specific times
A£4.00 C£1.00 Concessions£3.00. This property accepts Euro currency notes

Castle Campbell

Dollar Clackmannanshire FK14 7PP
Tel: 01259 742408
[10m E of Stirling on the A91 at head of Dollar Glen]

In the wooded Dollar Glen stands Castle Campbell. Built in the late 15th century, it was once the home of the chief of Clan Campbell. John Knox is said to have preached here in the 16th century. It stands in the picturesque Ochill Hills and gives wonderful views.

Open all year, please call 01259 742408 for specific details. Closed Thur pm, Fri & Sun am Jan-Mar plus Thur-Fri Oct-Dec

A£3.00 C£1.00 Concessions£2.30. This property accepts Euro currency notes

Cawdor Castle

Nairn Inverness-shire IV12 5RD
Tel: 01667 404401 Fax: 01667 404674
[SW of Nairn on B9090 between Inverness and Nairn]

The 14th century Keep, fortified in the 15th century and impressive additions mainly in the 17th century, form a massive fortress. Gardens, nature trails and splendid grounds. Shakespearian memories of Macbeth. The most romantic castle in the Highlands.
1 May-10 Oct daily 10.00-17.30

A£6.50 C(5-15)£3.70 OAPs£5.50 Family Ticket (A2+C5) £19.20

Craigmillar Castle

Edinburgh
Tel: 0131 661 4445
[2.5m SE of Edinburgh off A7]

A well preserved medieval castle, Craigmillar has a tower house, courtyard and gardens. Craigmillar's story is linked with that of Mary Queen of Scots. Superb views from tower house.
All year, please call 0131 661 4445 for specific times. Closed Thur pm, Fri & Sun am Jan-Mar, Thur & Fri Oct-Dec

A£2.50 C£0.75 Concessions£1.90. This property accepts Euro currency notes

Crichton Castle

Pathhead Lothian
Tel: 01875 320017

[2.5m SSW of Pathhead off A68]

A large and sophisticated castle, of which the most spectacular part is the range erected by the Earl of Bothwell between 1581 and 1591. This has a facade of faceted stonework in an Italian Renaissance style.
Open during the summer months only, please call 01875 320017 for specific details

A£2.20 C£0.75 Concessions£1.60. This property accepts Euro currency notes

Drumlanrig Castle Gardens and Country Park

Thornhill Dumfriesshire DG3 4AQ

Tel: 01848 330248 Fax: 01848 331682

www.buccleuch.com

[18m N of Dumfries, 4m N of Thornhill off A76, 16m from A74 at Elvanfoot, approx 1.5 hrs by road from Edinburgh, Glasgow & Carlisle. Plenty of on site parking available]

Dumfriesshire home of the Duke of Buccleuch and Queensberry, built between 1679 and 1691 by William Douglas, 1st Duke of Queensberry. The Castle and Country Park stand at the centre of the Queensberry Estate, a model of dynamic and enlightened land management. Includes works by Rembrandt and Holbein. Associations with Bonnie Prince Charlie, Robert Bruce and Mary Queen of Scots. French furniture, 300 year old silver chandelier as well as cabinets made for Louis XIV's Versailles. Douglas family exhibition room. Extensive gardens now being restored to original 18th century plans. Woodland walks. Craft Centre. Children's Adventure Woodland Playground. Visitor Centre and Ranger Service. Licensed Restaurant. Cycle Museum and Cycle Hire. Disabled Access.

Castle: 9-12 Apr & 1 May-22 Aug daily, Mon-Sat

11.00-16.00, Sun 12.00-16.00. Gardens & Country Park: 9 Apr-30 Sept daily 11.00-17.00

A£6.00 C£2.00 OAPs£4.00 Family Ticket £14.00 Grounds only: £3.00 Group rates available

Dumbarton Castle

Dumbarton South Strathclyde
Tel: 01389 732167
[In Dumbarton on A82]

Dumbarton was the centre of the ancient kingdom of Strathclyde from the 5th century until 1018. Impressively situated on a volcanic rock overlooking the Firth of Clyde, it was an important royal refuge.
All year, please call 01389 732167 to confirm specific times. Closed Thur pm, Fri & Sun am Jan-Mar plus Thur-Fri Oct-Dec
A£2.50 C£0.75 Concessions£1.90. This property accepts Euro currency notes

Edinburgh Castle

Castle Hill Edinburgh Midlothian EH1 2NG
Tel: 0131 225 9846 Fax: 0131 220 4733
[At the top of the Royal Mile]

This most famous of Scottish castles has a complex building history. There is an audio guide tour available in six languages.
All year daily Apr-Oct 09.30-18.00, Nov-Mar 09.30-17.00. Closed 25-26 Dec
A£9.50 C(5-15)£2.00 Concessions£7.00. This property accepts Euro currency notes

Edzell Castle and Garden

Edzell Tayside
Tel: 01356 648631

[At Edzell 6m N of Brechin, on B966]

The refined beauty of Edzell was a statement of the prestige of its owners, the Lindsays. The stylised walled garden was created around 1604. Resplendent with heraldic sculptures and carved panels, the architectural framework surrounding the garden is unique in Britain.
All year, Jan-Mar closed Thur pm, Fri & Sun am, Oct-Dec closed Thur & Fri
A£3.00 C£1.00 Concessions£2.30. This property accepts Euro currency notes

Fort George

Inverness Inverness-Shire IV1 2TD
Tel: 01667 460232
[6m W of Nairn, 11m NE of Inverness off A96]

Built following the Battle of Culloden as a Highland fortress for the army of George II, it is one of the outstanding artillery fortifications in Europe and still an active army barracks. Reconstructed barracks of the 18th and 19th centuries, Seafield Collection of Arms, Chapel and Regimental Museum of the Queen's Own Highlanders.
All year daily, please call for specific times. Cafe open limited hours in winter
A£6.00 C£1.50 Concessions£4.50. This property accepts Euro currency notes

Glamis Castle

Estates Office Glamis Forfar Angus DD8 1RJ
Tel: 01307 840393 Fax: 01307 840733
[Off A90 / M90 5m W of Forfar on A94. Plenty of on site parking available]

The splendid turreted castle is the family home of the Earls of Strathmore, and was the childhood home of HM The Queen Mother. Legendary setting for Shakespeare's 'Macbeth'.
27 Mar-31 Oct daily 10.00-18.00. Other times by appointment
Castle & Grounds: A£6.80 C(5-16)£3.70. Grounds only: A£3.50 Concessions£2.50

Huntly Castle

Huntly Grampian AB54 5BP
Tel: 01466 793191
[In Huntly signposted from the A96]

Remarkable for its splendid architecture, Huntly Castle served as a baronial residence for five centuries. Many impressive features include a fine heraldic sculpture and inscribed stone friezes.
All year, please call for specific times
A£3.30 C£1.00 Concessions£2.50. This property accepts Euro currency notes

Maes Howe Chambered Cairn

Finstown Orkney
Tel: 01856 761606
[9m W of Kirkwall on A965]

Maes Howe is the finest chambered tomb in north-west Europe and more than 500 years old. It was broken into in the mid-12th century by Viking crusaders who carved graffiti runes on the walls of the main chamber. In 1999, it was designated a World Heritage Site.
All year, please call for specific times
A£3.00 C£1.00 Concessions£2.30. This property accepts Euro currency notes

Newark Castle

Port Glasgow South Strathclyde
Tel: 01475 741858
[A8, turn R at Newark roundabout]

This 15th century castle is most associated with Patrick Maxwell. His achievements in elegantly extending Newark are diminished by his notoriety for murdering two neighbours and beating his wife of 44 years and mother of his 16 children.
Open during the summer only
A£2.50 C£0.75 Concessions£1.90. This property accepts Euro currency notes

Paxton House and Country Park

Northumberland/ Scottish Borders
Berwick Upon Tweed TD15 1SZ

Tel: 01289 386291 Fax: 01289 386660

www.paxtonhouse.com

[5m from Berwick upon Tweed on B6461, signposted from A1. Rail: Berwick upon Tweed 5m]

Scottish Tourist Board 5 star Historic House 2002. Award winning Paxton House is one of the finest 18th century Palladian Country Houses in Britain. Built in 1758 for a dashing young Scottish laird, Patrick Home of Billie to the design of John and James Adam. The House boasts interiors by Robert Adam and the finest collections of furniture by Thomas Chippendale and William Trotter. The restored Regency Picture Gallery is the largest in a Scottish country house and houses over 70 paintings from the National Galleries of Scotland, recently re-hung it now includes masterpieces by Raeburn, Wilkie and Lawrence. With 12 period rooms to explore, over 80 acres of gardens, woodlands, riverside walks and gardens to enjoy, together with gift shop, tearoom, adventure playground, picnic areas, nature trails, changing exhibitions, and more, Paxton is simply not to be missed.

1 Apr-31 Oct. House: daily 11.00-17.00. Grounds: daily 10.00-sunset

House: A£6.00 C£3.00 Family Ticket £16.00. Grounds only: A£3.00 C£1.50 Family Ticket £8.00

Special Events

Britain in Focus III
01/04/2004-05/05/2004
Presenting the combined talents of Duns Camera Club and Berwick Camera Club

Easter Extravaganza
11/04/2004
9th Border Egg Roll and Great 1,000 Egg Hunt, children's games and egg decorating, come and meet Paxton Ted, make an Easter mask. Time: 11.00-16.00

Bird Day
01/05/2004
Dawn chorus walks at 04.00, 05.30, 07.00 and further walks throughout the day with Raju Raman, young ornithologist

The Paxton Painters
08/05/2004-04/06/2004
The Paxton Painters return with another collection of paintings and drawings to delight the eye. Their styles are strongly individualistic and this exhibition ranges in a variety of media, through exquisite 'flower-studies' and 'still-lifes' to both dynamic and gentle landscapes

Wild Flower Walk
16/05/2004
Discover the flora of Paxton estate with Scottish Wildlife Trust expert, Denise Walton. Time: 13.30

Guided tour of the Grounds
06/06/2004
A woodland and riverside expedition with Estate Custodian, Tommy Patterson. Time: 14.00

'East meets West' Exhibition of Botanical Paintings
06/06/2004-01/07/2004
An exhibition of paintings by artists associated with the Royal Botanic Garden Edinburgh, linking in with work they are involved with in China and Asia. The exhibition will feature work, in mixed media, of Asiatic species and also plants from the Herbaceous Border at Paxton House

Open Air Concert with the 'Strangers' plus support band
19/06/2004
Bring a seat or a rug, come and dance and relax to this top Borders '60s and '70s band. Time: 19.00

Paxton House 4th Vintage Rally
20/06/2004
This rally just gets bigger and better! Come and marvel at machines from a bygone era, something to interest all the family. Time: 11.00-16.00

Land, Sea and Sky
02/07/2004-19/07/2004
Patrick Murphy, now based in South West Wales, returns for another of his exhibitions of highly collectable and sort after watercolours. The works will include atmospheric landscapes and coastal scenes from home and abroad, as well as floral subjects

Shakespeare - A Midsummer Night's Dream
03/07/2004
Performed by Chapterhouse Theatre Company. Delightful lovers, enchanting fairies and a wonderful comic cast of misfit mechanicals together with a beautiful music score composed for Shakespeare's glorious choral verse. Bring a picnic and a seat to enjoy Shakespeare's best loved comedy

Teddy Bear's Picnic
04/07/2004
Bring your favourite teddy and a packed lunch for Paxton Ted's summer picnic. Time: 13.00

Summer Music Festival 2004
16/07/2004-25/07/2004
Held on 16-18 & 23-25 July. 8 days of exhilarating chamber music performed by some of Britain's most distinguished musicians in the ideal setting of the Regency Picture Gallery. Please call for full details and supper menus

8th Annual Border Art Show
20/07/2004-31/08/2004
All Judith Currie's paintings together with work by some of her artist friends are for sale. Workshops are held each Mon & Fri, leisure painters and beginners are welcome. Demonstrations, help and encouragement are part of a very enjoyable day in the gallery and grounds of Paxton House

Estate Expedition
29/08/2004
A woodland and riverside expedition in and around Paxton House estate, with Estate Custodian, Tommy Patterson. Time: 14.00

Life and Land
03/09/2004-31/10/2004
A unique opportunity to see landscape close-up, abstract, plant and animal images from international wildlife and landscape photographer, Laurie Campbell

Food for Free
12/09/2004
Feast and forage in nature's larder, a fascinating tour of the Grounds with Denise Walton of the Scottish Wildlife Trust. Time: 13.30

8th Annual Fungus Foray
26/09/2004
Tour the grounds with mycologist Dr Mike

*Richardson and find out about identifying fungi.
Time: 13.30*

Red Squirrel Facts - 'Under Attack'
13/10/2004
*Paxton's colony of Red Squirrels have been pro-
tected and supported by volunteers for many
years. Find out about the work that has been
done here and plans for future Red Squirrel conservation at Paxton. Time: 14.00*

Skara Brae
Stromness Orkney SC1
Tel: 01856 841815
[19m NW of Kirkwall on the B9056]

When a wild storm in Orkney in 1850 exposed
the ruins of ancient dwellings, Skara Brae, the
best preserved prehistoric village in northern
Europe, was discovered. The excavated farming
settlement dates back 5,000 years.
*All year, please call for specific times, closed Sun
am in winter*
Summer A£5.00 C£1.30 Concessions £3.75,
Winter A£4.00 C£1.20 Concessions£3.00. This
property accepts Euro currency notes

Sorn Castle
Sorn Mauchline Ayrshire KA5 6HR
Tel: 0141 942 6460 Fax: 0141 931 9110
[4m E of Mauchline on B743]

Dating from the 14th century in impressive set-
ting on sandstone cliff over the River Ayr with
attractive woodland walks.
*July-Aug daily 14.00-16.00 by apointment.
Grounds: Apr-Oct. Call for details*
A£4.00

St Andrews Castle and Visitor Centre
The Scores St. Andrews Fife KY16 9AR
Tel: 01334 477196 Fax: 01334 475068
*[In St Andrews on the A91, on the sea front just
off North Street]*

The ruins of the castle of the Archbishops of St
Andrews, dating in part from the 13th century.
Notable features include a 'bottle-dungeon' and
mine and counter-mine tunnelled during the
siege that followed the murder of Cardinal
Beaton in 1546.
*All year daily, please call 01334 477196 for spe-
cific times*
Joint ticket with the Cathedral: A£4.00 C£1.25
Concessions£3.00. This property accepts Euro
currency notes

Stirling Castle
Upper Castle Hill Stirling Stirlingshire FK8 1EJ
Tel: 01786 450000
*[At the head of Stirling's historic old town off the
M9]*

Without doubt one of the grandest of all
Scottish castles, both in its situation on a commanding rock outcrop and in its architecture.
The Great Hall and the Gatehouse of James IV,
the marvellous Palace of James V, the Chapel
Royal of James VI and the artillery fortifications
of the 16th to 18th centuries are all of outstanding interest.
*All year daily, Apr-Sept 09.30-18.00, Oct-Mar
09.30-17.00*
A£8.00 C£2.00 Concessions£6.00. This property accepts Euro currency notes

Tantallon Castle
North Berwick East Lothian EH39 5PN
Tel: 01620 892727
[3m E of North Berwick off A198]

A formidable stronghold set atop cliffs on the
Firth of Forth, Tantallon Castle was the seat of

the Douglas Earls of Angus, one of the most powerful baronial families in Scotland. Tantallon served as a noble fortification for more than three centuries and endured frequent sieges.

All year, please call 01620 892727 for further details. Closed Thur pm and Fri & Sun am Jan-Mar, plus Thur-Fri Oct-Dec

A£3.00 C£1.00 Concessions£2.30. This property accepts Euro currency notes

Threave Castle

Castle Douglas Kirkcudbrightshire

Tel: 07711 223101 (mobile)

[3m W of Castle Douglas on A75. Approach is via boat then a 0.25m flat walk to the property]

Archibald the Grim, Lord of Galloway built this lonely castle in the late 14th century. It stands on an islet in the River Dee, and is four storeys high with round towers guarding the outer wall built by 1455 when the castle was besieged by James II. Access to the island is by boat. Not recommended for physically disabled persons.

Open during the summer months only, please call 07711 223101 for specific times

A£2.50 C£0.75 Concessions£1.90. Admission prices include ferry transportation. This property accepts Euro currency notes

Traquair House

Innerleithen Peeblesshire EH44 6PW

Tel: 01896 830323 Fax: 01896 830639

www.traquair.co.uk

[On B709 off A72 at Peebles]

Visit romantic Traquair where Alexander I signed a charter over 800 years ago and where the 'modern wings' were completed in 1680. Once a pleasure ground for Scottish kings in times of peace, then a refuge for Catholic priests in times of terror, the Stuarts of Traquair supported Mary, Queen of Scots and the Jacobite cause without counting the cost. Imprisoned, fined and isolated for their beliefs, their home - untouched by time, reflects the tranquillity of their family life. Enjoy the unique atmosphere and history. See the secret stairs, spooky cellars, books, embroideries and letters from former times. Visit the ancient brewery and inhale the delicious aroma, then sample the potent liquor in the brewery museum. Browse through the gift shop and then enjoy a relaxed lunch in the Old Walled Garden. Finally, search for the centre of the maze, explore the enchanted woods and look out for the Grey Lady... a truly magical day out for all the family.

3 Apr-31 Oct daily. House: 12.00-17.00, June-Aug 10.30-17.30 (last admission 17.00), Oct 11.00-16.00. Guided tours can be arranged outside normal opening hours. These may be conducted by the owners and should be booked in advance

House & Grounds: A£5.75 C£3.20 OAPs£5.30 Family Ticket £16.75. Grounds only: A£2.50 C£1.25. Group rates (for 20+ people): A£5.25 C£2.50 OAPs£5.10. Guide Book: £3.50. Guided Tours (for 20+ people): A£6.25. Personal guided tours by Catherine Maxwell Stuart, 21st Lady of Traquair £10.00 per person

Discount Offer: One Child Free With A Full Paying Adult.

Urquhart Castle

Drumnadrochit Highlands
Tel: 01456 450551
[2m S of Drumnadrochit on A82]

Magnificently sited, overlooking Loch Ness. Urquhart is one of the largest castles in Scotland, with a long and colourful history, built in the 1230s, seized by the English in 1296, sacked by the MacDonald Lord of the Isles in 1545 and left to fall into decay after 1689. Most of the existing buildings date from the 14th century.
Open all year daily, please call for specific times
A£6.00 C£1.20 Concessions£4.50. This property accepts Euro currency notes

Literature & Libraries

Robert Burns House

Burns Street Dumfries Dumfriesshire DG1 2PS
Tel: 01387 255297 Fax: 01387 265081
[Signposted from Dumfries town centre, a 5min walk]

It was in this ordinary sandstone building that Robert Burns, Scotland's national poet, spent the last years of his brilliant life. Now a place of pilgrimage for Burns enthusiasts from around the world, the house retains much of its 18th century character and contains many relics of the poet.
All year Apr-Sept Mon-Sat 10.00-17.00, Sun 14.00-17.00, Oct-Mar Tue-Sat 10.00-13.00 & 14.00-17.00. Closed Sun & Mon Oct-Mar
Admission Free

Living History Museums

Archaeolink Prehistory Park

Oyne Insch Aberdeenshire AB52 6QP

Tel: 01464 851500 Fax: 01464 851544

www.archaeolink.co.uk

[1m off A96 Aberdeen-Inverness road, 8m N of Inverurie. Plenty of parking on site]

The fascinating world of ancient Aberdeenshire is brought vividly to life through a variety of interactive displays, a film presentation spanning 6,000 years, a myths and legends gallery, a working Iron Age farm with costumed guides and plenty of hands on opportunities to ensure a great day out for all the family. Relax in the Coffee shop, enjoy homebaking, flavoured coffees, specials and Sunday roasts or browse through the gift hall. It all amounts to a truly all day, all weather attraction.

1 Feb-31 Mar Sun, Mon & Tue 11.00-16.00, 1 Apr-31 Oct daily 11.00-17.00

A£4.75 C(3-16)£3.25 Concessions£4.25 Family Tickets £11.50-£20.00. Schools: £3.00. Group rates and season tickets available

Discount Offer: Two For The Price Of One

Maritime

Buckie Drifter Maritime Heritage Centre

Freuchny Road Buckie Moray AB56 1TT

Tel: 01542 834646 Fax: 01542 835995

www.moray.org/bdrifter

[Plenty of on site parking available]

At the Buckie Drifter you can discover the fishing folks' way of life in the North East of Scotland. The displays tell the story of the herring fishing in the Moray Firth with plenty of hands-on activities for all the family. You can; watch DVDs of the fishing in the 1920s to the 1940s; find out about life in the fishing communities; dress up as gutting women and boat skippers; have a go at making a herring barrel or a fishing net; pack herring into barrels on the recreated quayside. Younger visitors can play in the water tank and make a fishy creation for the wall collage in the Children's Activity Room. When you've had a go at everything you can relax with a cup of tea or stop for lunch and browse through the gift shop.

27 Mar-31 Oct Mon-Sat 10.00-17.00, Sun 12.00-17.00

A£2.75 C&OAPs£1.75 Family Ticket £8.00

Discount Offer: One Child Free With One Paying Adult.

Scottish Fisheries Museum

St Ayles East Shore Harbour Head Anstruther Fife KY10 3AB

Tel: 01333 310628 Fax: 01333 310628

www.scottish-fisheries-museum.org

[10m S of St Andrews, signposted on A95]

This National Museum is the setting for the displays on Scotland's fishing history. The museum is housed in a range of 16th to 19th century buildings and has recently been extended into an old boatyard alongside. Inside you can see our unique collection of art, paintings, models, actual equipment and personal possessions, and can follow the development of the fishing industry. There's lots to see and do - try your hand at net-making, experience the life of a herring lass following the fleet around the coast to process the catch, and visit our 1900 Fisherman's Cottage. You can also see the museum fleet - historic vessels from around Scotland, some on show in the covered Boatyard, others outside in the Harbour. Fishing is still one of Scotland's major industries. This fascinating museum tells the stories of the people involved in it - their customs and beliefs, their hard work and suffering, and the strong community ties forged through making a living from the sea.

Apr-Sept Mon-Sat 10.00-17.30, Sun 11.00-17.00. Oct-Mar Mon-Sat 10.00-16.30, Sun 14.00-16.30

A£4.50 Concessions£3.50

Discount Offer: Free Guide Book Worth £1.00

Stromness Museum

52 Alfred Street Stromness Orkney KW16 3DF

Tel: 01856 850025

www.orkneyheritage.com

[0.5m walk or drive south from Stromness Pier Head]

If you want a glimpse into Orkney's Natural History and Maritime Past, or to study it in more detail, Stromness Museum is a must. Since 1837 the museum has amassed a unique and fascinating collection which has something for everyone. Learn how to survive in the arctic through displays about Dr John Rae, Sir John Franklin and the Arctic Whalers. Find out about local connections with The Hudson Bay Company and the Canadian Fur Trade. On show are artefacts salvaged from the German fleet which was scuttled in Scapa Flow in 1919, in sight of Stromness. The recently refurbished Victorian Natural History Gallery has a magnificent bird collection complemented by displays of eggs, fossils, sea creatures, mammals, butterflies and moths. Also available are kids activities and a photographic archive. You will enjoy your visit, all you have to do is get here!

Apr-Sept Sun-Sat 10.00-17.00, Oct-Mar Mon-Sat 11.00-15.30. Closed mid Feb-mid Mar

£2.50 C(school age)£0.50 Concessions£2.00 Family Ticket (A2+C2) £5.00

The Tall Ship at Glasgow Harbour

100 Stobcross Road Glasgow G3 8QQ

Tel: 0141 222 2513 Fax: 0141 222 2536

www.thetallship.com

[M8 J19 onto Clydeside Expressway A814. Follow brown tourist signs. Free coach and car parking in front of centre. Rail: Low level train from Glasgow Central to Exhibition Centre]

Come along to The Tall Ship at Glasgow Harbour to experience Glasgow's fascinating maritime history first hand. S. V. Glenlee is one of only five remaining Clydebuilt sailing ships in the world and the only one still in Britain. See the city's shipbuilding past come to life and walk around this beautiful vessel, taking in the sights, sounds and smells depicting what life was like in her sailing days. Seamen's voices ring out around the ship, bringing the real story of the Glenlee to life. Read the ship's log, ring the bell and sample the stark sleeping quarters. See where the ship's cook served up his grim fayre then go down to the cargo hold to touch some of the things that the Glenlee would have carried. A programme of events runs throughout the year, ensuring there is always lots to do to keep children and adults amused.

All year daily Mar-Oct 10.00-17.00, Nov-Feb 10.00-16.00

A(+C1)£4.50 Additional C£2.50 C(under5)£Free Concessions£3.25. Group rates 10+ A£3.95, School Parties 10+ A£2.50 C£2.50 (1 A£Free per 10 children). Call for season tickets

Discount Offer: Two Adults For The Price Of One

Military & Defence Museums

Black Watch Regimental Museum

Balhousie Castle Hay Street Perth Perthshire PH1 5HR

Tel: 0131 310 8530 Fax: 01738 643245

[A9, M90, A85 to Perth]

The treasures of the 42nd/73rd Highland Regiment from 1739 to the present day are on show in this museum, together with paintings, silver, colours and uniforms. Disabled access to first floor only.

All year May-Sept Mon-Sat 10.00-16.30, Oct-Apr Mon-Fri 10.00-15.30. Closed last Sat in June & 23 Dec-6 Jan. Other times & Groups 16+ by appointment

Admission Free, donations welcome

National War Museum of Scotland

Edinburgh Castle Edinburgh Lothian EH1 2NG

Tel: 0131 225 7534 Fax: 0131 225 3848

www.nms.ac.uk/war

[Follow signs for Edinburgh Castle throughout central Edinburgh]

The Museum explores the Scottish experience of war and military service over the last 400 years. The lives of many thousands of Scots have been dominated by this experience - the objects in the Museum, and the individuals and events to which they relate, make this very clear. Scotland's military history is presented in galleries housed in mid-18th century buildings at Edinburgh Castle. Each of the six newly-refurbished galleries focuses on a separate theme. 'A Nation in Arms' takes a wide view of the influence of strategy and military service on the history of Scotland during the last four centuries. 'A Grand Life for a Scotsman' explores the individual's experience of military life from recruitment to retirement. 'Tools of the Trade' moves our attention from the individual to the weapons, equipment and clothing developed to meet the demands of war and military service in all its forms. 'The Highland Soldier' tells the story of this unique figure in military history and its impact on Scottish national identity. 'In Defence' highlights the demands of military service on the civilian population in home defence and total war. 'Active Service' explores aspects of battle through the personal experience of Scots. Part of the National Museums of Scotland.

All year daily, Nov-Mar 09.45-16.45, Apr-Oct 09.45-17.45

Admission Free after paying entrance fee to Edinburgh Castle. Membership available giving free or reduced entry to all six National Museums of Scotland

Scotland's Secret Bunker

Crown Buildings Troywood St. Andrews Fife KY16 8QH

Tel: 01333 310301 Fax: 01333 312040

www.secretbunker.co.uk

[7m from St Andrews, signposted off B9131 and B940. Plenty of on site parking]

Scotland's Secret Bunker has been Scotland's best kept secret for over 40 years. An innocent looking farmhouse conceals the entrance to an amazing labyrinth built 100 feet below ground. Government Command Control Centre, radar rooms, BBC broadcast rooms, operations room, dormitories, two cinemas, a café... a legacy of the Cold War. Take the opportunity to discover how they would have survived and you wouldn't! One of Scotland's deepest and best kept secrets.

27 Mar-31 Oct daily 10.00-18.00
A£7.20 C£4.50 OAPs£5.95 Family Ticket £22.00

Discount Offer: One Child Free With One Full Paying Adult.

Multicultural Museums

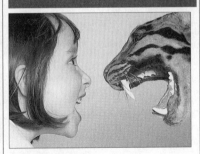

Royal Museum

Chambers Street Edinburgh Midlothian EH1 1JF

Tel: 0131 247 4422 Fax: 0131 220 4819

www.nms.ac.uk

[5 mins walk from Royal Mile and 10 mins walk from main railway station (Waverley). Bus: all buses from Hanover Street, N of Princes Street, bring you to George IV Bridge and Chambers Street where you will find the museum]

This magnificent Museum houses extensive international collections covering the Decorative Arts, Natural History, Science, Social and Technological History, and Geology. A lively programme of special events including temporary exhibitions, films, lectures and concerts take place throughout the year. The Royal Museum stands adjacent to the Museum of Scotland in Chambers Street and together they 'present the World to Scotland and Scotland to the World'. Don't miss the new Communicate! Gallery which combines stunning displays with interactive exhibits, showing the diverse ways in which people have made contact over the centuries. Here you can find out what your name looks like in Morse Code, try out a giant texting game and learn about Alexander Graham Bell's achievements. Part of the National Museums of Scotland.

All year Mon-Sat 10.00-17.00, Tue 10.00-20.00, Sun 12.00-17.00. Closed 25 Dec

Admission Free. There may be a charge for some temporary exhibitions. Membership available giving free or reduced admission to all six National Museums of Scotland and some charging exhibitions

Special Events

Cats... the ultimate predators
13/02/2004-30/05/2004
Cats is a rich and exciting exhibition about the world's cats, great and small. From lions and tigers to domestic moggies, cats have always inspired people as symbols of strength, power and mystery. Discover what it is like to hunt prey, defend a territory and train kittens to be ruthless killers in this stunning exhibition.Cost: A£4.00 C(5-15)£2.50 Concessions£3.00 Family Ticket £12.00

Edinburgh International Science Festival
02/04/2004-16/04/2004
Edinburgh University brings a whole host of experiments and science workshops to the Science Zone

On Your Marks
20/05/2004-20/06/2004
Travelling exhibition from the British Empire and Commonwealth Museum about sport

Treasures from Tuscany
16/07/2004-31/10/2004
A fascinating insight into the Etruscans, an ancient civilisation of highly sophisticated people. This exhibition, shown for the first time in the UK, gathers almost 500 objects from the finest collections in Tuscany, giving visitors a rare opportunity to view a rich and comprehensive display of Etruscan life and death. Admission charged

Claret to Concorde - 100 Years of Entente Cordiale
03/12/2004-16/01/2005
The Entente Cordiale, a diplomatic agreement between Britain and France, was signed on 8 April 1904. This special winter exhibiton marks the 100th anniversary of this event with a display of the exceptional collection of French material acquired by NMS over the last 100 years. Visitors can learn about Scotland's long history with France, from when the Auld Alliance was first established in 1295 to the acquisition of Concorde in 2004. Admission Free

Nature & Conservation Parks

Kylerhea Otter Haven

Strathoich Fort Augustus Inverness PH32 4BT
Tel: 01320 366322 Fax: 01320 366581
www.forestry.gov.uk

[Signposted from the A850]

A hide perched above the shore of Kyle Rhea (Skye) giving an excellent opportunity to watch wide variety of coastal wildlife. C.C.T.V. is operational at the hide for close up viewing. The area around Kyle Rhea/Kintoch is now part of a new initiative to restore the nature woodlands with all their associated flora and fauna. Visitors should expect to see a greater diversity of wildlife from otters to eagles, not just at the Otter Haven but throughout the area. Special disabled access can be arranged by contacting the office.
All year daily Summer 09.00-20.00, Winter 09.00-16.00

Admission Free

Scottish Seabird Centre

The Harbour North Berwick East Lothian
EH39 4SS

Tel: 01620 890202 Fax: 01620 890222

[From Edinburgh follow A1 to North Berwick, follow tourist signs]

Escape to another world at this stunning five star wildlife visitor centre! Exhilarating sea air and breathtaking panoramic views over the sea and beautiful sandy beaches. See wildlife really close up with the amazing live interactive 'Big Brother' cameras.

All year, 1 Apr-31 Oct daily 10.00-18.00, 1 Nov-31 Jan Mon-Fri 10.00-16.00, Sat & Sun 10.00-17.30, 1 Feb-31 Mar Mon-Fri 10.00-17.00, Sat & Sun 10.00-17.30. Closed 25 Dec

A£5.95 C&OAPs£3.95 Family Tickets from £12.50

On the Water

The Falkirk Wheel

Lime Road Tamfourhill Falkirk FK1 4RS
Tel: 08700 500208 / 01324 619888
Fax: 01324 671224

[Take the M9 west for Stirling. From motorway follow Brown and White Tourist signage]

As the world's first and only rotating boat lift, The Falkirk Wheel is quite simply unique. Linking two canals with water levels 115ft apart, it is the innovative and dynamic solution to an age old problem of transferring boats between levels that traditionally required a flight of 11 locks.

Weekdays 09.00-18.00 Apr-Nov, 10.00-16.30 Nov-Mar (visitor centre closes 30 minutes later). Sat 09.00-18.00 Apr-Nov, 10.00-16.30 Nov-Mar (visitor centre closes 30 minutes later) Sun 09.00-18.00 Apr-Nov 10.00-16.30 Nov-Mar (visitor centre closes 30 minutes later).

A£8.00 C(under5)£Free C(under15)£4.00 Concessions£6.00 Family Ticket (A2&C2) £21.00. Booking Line: 08700 500208

Palaces

Bishop's Palace and Earl's Palace

Watergate Kirkwall Orkney KW15 1PD

Tel: 01856 871918 Fax: 01856 871918

[In Kirkwall on the A960 opposite Cathedral]

The Bishop's Palace is a half-house of 12th century date, later much altered, with a round tower built by Bishop Reid in 1541-48. A later addition was made by the notorious Patrick Stewart, Earl of Orkney, who built the adjacent Earl's Palace between 1600 and 1607 in a splendid Renaissance style.

Summer only, please call for specific times

A£2.20 C£0.75 Concessions£1.60. This property accepts Euro currency notes.

Linlithgow Palace

Linlithgow Lothian EH

Tel: 01506 842896

[In Linlithgow off the M9. Exit M9 J3 northbound or J4 southbound]

The magnificent ruin of a great Royal Palace, set in its own park or 'peel'. All the Stewart Kings lived here, and work commissioned by James I, II, IV, V and VI can be seen. The great hall and the chapel are particularly fine. James V (1512) and Mary, Queen of Scots (1542) were born here.

All year, please call 01506 842896 for specific details

A£3.00 C£1.00 Concessions£2.30. This property accepts Euro currency notes

Scone Palace

Scone Perth Perthshire PH2 6BD

Tel: 01738 552300 Fax: 01738 552588

www.scone-palace.co.uk

[2m N of Perth on A93. Plenty of free parking on site]

Family home of the Earl of Mansfield, Scone Palace houses a magnificent and varied collection of works of art. Scone Palace is set in mature and historic grounds, with an adventure playground and the Murray Star Maze. Once the crowning place of the Kings of Scots, Scone offers a fascinating day out for all the family. Also features 'I' Spy for children and a children's Grounds Trail. Exterior photography permitted.

1 Apr-31 Oct daily 09.30-17.30. Grounds close at 18.00. Special groups at other times and Winter by arrangement

Palace & Grounds: A£6.75 C£3.80 Concessions£5.70. Grounds only: A£3.40 C£2.00 Concessions£2.80. Group rates: A£5.50 C£3.40 Concessions£4.75. Guide books: £4.00

Discount Offer: One Free Admission With Every Full Adult Admission.

<u>Special Events</u>

Easter Bunny Hunt
18/04/2004-21/04/2004
Come and hunt for the Easter Bunnies hidden in the Palace State Rooms! Win a prize if you spot them all. Children's entertainment throughout the weekend

A Midsummer Night's Dream
01/07/2004
Delightful lovers, enchanting fairies and a wonder-ful comic cast of misfit mechanicals together with a beautiful music score. Join Chapterhouse Theatre Company in the splendour of the grounds of Scone Palace. Picnic in the summer air and relax in front of Shakespeare's best loved comedy. Please call for further details

Alice's Adventures in Wonderland
12/08/2004
Chapterhouse Theatre perform Alice in Wonderland in the grounds of Scone Palace. Alice in Wonderland is a new departure for the company, but the trusted Chapterhouse formula is still at the heart of this lively rendition of a literary classic. A large cast, a classical picture-book set, traditional costumes and original music performed live in an open air setting. Please call for further details

Farming Yesteryear
12/09/2004
Scotland's largest vintage farming event returns to Scone Palace offering a great day out for all the family. Horse and Plough demonstrations, pipe bands, trade stands and an auto-jumble. Children's entertainment, including bouncy castle and quad bikes

Places of Worship

Elgin Cathedral

North College Street Elgin Morayshire IV30 1EL
Tel: 01343 547171
[In Elgin on the A96]

The superb ruin of what many think was Scotland's most beautiful cathedral. Much of the work is in a rich late 13th century style, much modified after the burning of the church by the Wolf of Badenoch in 1390. The octagonal chapter house is the finest in Scotland.
All year, please call for specific times, Jan-Mar closed Thur pm, Fri & Sun am, Oct-Dec closed Thur & Fri
A£3.00 C£1.00 Concessions£2.30. This property accepts Euro currency notes

Glasgow Cathedral

Cathedral Square Glasgow Lanarkshire G4 0QZ
Tel: 0141 552 6891 / 552 0988
[In central Glasgow. Exit M8 at J15]

Glasgow Cathedral is built on the site where St Kentigern, or Mungo, the first bishop within the ancient British kingdom of Strathclyde, was thought to have been buried in AD 612. The present cathedral was built during the 13th to 15th centuries and is the only medieval cathedral on the Scottish mainland to have survived the 1560 Reformation virtually complete.
All year daily, Apr-Sept 09.30-18.00, Sun 13.00-17.00, Oct-Mar 09.30-16.00, Sun 13.00-16.00. Closed 25-26 Dec & 1-3 Jan
Admission Free

St Andrews Cathedral and St. Rule's Tower

St. Andrews Fife and Central
Tel: 01334 472563
[In St. Andrews on the A91, on the sea front at the head of North Street]

The remains of what was Scotland's largest and most magnificent church still show how impressive St Andrew's Cathedral must have been in its prime. Its museum houses a collection of early and later medieval sculpture and other relics found on the site. St Rule's tower provides access to spectacular views.
Open all year
Joint ticket with St Andrews Castle: A£4.00 C£1.25 Concessions£3.00. This property accepts Euro currency notes

Railways

Bo'ness and Kinneil Railway

Bo'ness Station Union Street Bo'ness West Lothian EH51 9AQ
Tel: 01506 822298 Fax: 01506 828766
[Bo'ness is on the S shore of the River Forth, 8m W of the Forth Road Bridge]

The nostalgia and romance of steam lives on at the Bo'ness and Kinneil Railway. Historic railway buildings have been relocated from sites all over Scotland.
Apr-Oct Weekends, 3 July-30 Aug daily, call for timetable. Closed Nov, Jan-Apr. Open weekends
in Dec for Santa Steam Specials
Railway Return: A£4.50 C(5-15)£2.00

Strathspey Steam Railway

Aviemore Station Dalfaber Road Aviemore Inverness-Shire PH22 1PY

Tel: 01479 810725

www.strathspeyrailway.co.uk

[Off B970, signposted. Plenty of free parking on site]

This steam railway runs the 9.5 miles between Aviemore, Boat of Garten and Broomhill, near the villages of Nethybridge and Dulnain Bridge. Broomhill is also the location for station scenes in 'Monarch of The Glen'. A round trip takes approximately ninety minutes. You can join the train at any of the stations. The railway runs through heather moorland between Aviemore and Boat of Garten. From there onwards the 'strath' opens out into rolling farmland. The Cairngorm Mountains provide a backdrop throughout. Refreshments are available on most trains. Sunday Lunch, served at your seat, booking advisable, also available on Fridays 4 June-24 Sept. Evening Diner trains run

Wednesdays from 2 June-8 Sept, pre-booking required. On most Saturdays the train is made up to resemble a branch line operation and no catering is available on such trains.

Trains run June-Sept daily, Mar, Apr, May & Oct selected days. Call for a timetable

Full 'Round Trip' A£9.00 C£4.50 Family Ticket (A2+C3) £22.50. Day Rover Tickets available

Special Events

Day Out with Thomas
29/05/2004-31/05/2004

Day Out With Thomas
14/08/2004-22/08/2004

Santa Specials
05/12/2004-24/12/2004
Held on 5, 12, 18, 19, 23, 24 Dec only

Science - Earth & Planetary

Glasgow Science Centre

50 Pacific Quay Glasgow G51 1EA
Tel: 0141 420 5010 Fax: 0141 420 5011
[On S bank of Clyde, across from SECC]

The award winning Glasgow Science Centre is one of Scotland's must-see visitor attractions. GSC encapsulates the world of science and technology in new, fun and exciting ways.
Science Mall & IMAX Theatre: daily 10.00-18.00
One Attraction: A£6.95 C&Concessions£4.95.
Two Attractions: A£9.95 C&Concessions£7.95.
ScottishPower Space Theatre: (payable in addition to standard charges): A&C£2.00

Sensation Dundee

Greenmarket Dundee Angus DD1 4QB
Tel: 01382 228800 Fax: 01382 868602
[Greenmarket is between Riverside Drive and Nethergate.]

Sensation is exciting, different and unique - a Science Centre all about the senses. It's hands on fun for everyone - and there are dozens of specially designed interactive exhibits which bring science to life.

All year daily from 10.00. Closed 25-26 Dec and 1 Jan

A£6.50 C(4-15)£4.50 OAPs/Concessions£4.50

Sealife Centres & Aquariums

Deep Sea World, Scotland's Shark Capital

Forthside Terrace North Queensferry Fife

KY11 1JR

Tel: 01383 411880 Fax: 01383 410514

[J1 M90. Plenty of on site parking available]

Scotland's National Aquarium boasts one of Europe's largest collections of Sand Tiger sharks as well as 2,000 other species of marine life. Embark upon a fascinating journey of the underwater world and get a diver's eye view of the creatures of the deep through the world's longest underwater tunnel.

All year Mar-Oct daily 10.00-18.00, Nov-Mar Mon-Fri 10.00-17.00, Sat & Sun and Public Holidays 10.00-18.00

A£7.95 C(under3)£Free C£5.75 Concessions£6.50 Family Ticket (A2+C2) £26.00

Scottish Sea Life Sanctuary

Barcaldine Oban Argyll PA37 1SE

Tel: 01631 720386 Fax: 01631 720529

www.sealsanctuary.co.uk

[10m N of Oban on A828. Plenty of parking on site]

The Sanctuary is Scotland's largest marine mammal rescue centre operating a highly successful 'rear and release' programme for rescued common seal pups. Plus - thousands more sea creatures in natural marine habitats. SOS Seal Rescue allows you to experience what a seal pup rescue is like through the eyes of an abandoned pup. Otter Creek is a purpose built facility in the most stunning of settings which provides a perfect home for a pair of Canadian otters - perfect ambassadors for the conservation cause of otters in the wild. A host more displays provide a fascinating insight into the myriad of marine marvels to be discovered beneath the seas around our own shores, providing close encounters with everything from humble shrimps and starfish to sharks and stingrays.

All year Feb-Nov daily 10.00-17.00, (May-Sept 10.00-18.00). Please call for details of winter opening times.

A£7.50 C£5.50 OAPs£6.00

Discount Offer: £2.00 Off Per Person.

Social History Museums

Museum of Flight

East Fortune Airfield North Berwick East Lothian EH39 5LF

Tel: 01620 880308 Fax: 01620 880355

www.nms.ac.uk/flight

[Signposted off the A1 near Haddington, 20m E of Edinburgh. Bus: Spr-Sept Lowland no. 121 which shuttles between Haddington and North Berwick, calling at museum around 8 times per day. Plus regular services from Edinburgh to North Berwick. Call 0800 232323 for more details. Rail: Edinburgh to North Berwick. Air: Museum has a helicopter landing pad, please call to obtain landing permission]

Concorde is coming to the Museum of Flight! This iconic aircraft will be on public display in summer 2004, topping an aviation collection unsurpassed anywhere in the UK. The Museum of Flight occupies part of a former RAF airfield now scheduled as a historic monument. This was the departure point of the airship R34 which made the first east to west crossing of the Atlantic by air in July 1919; the collection includes a number of R34 relics. The collections comprise around 50 complete aircrafts, ranging from Britain's oldest surviving aeroplane, Percy Pilcher's 'Hawk' glider of 1896 to modern passenger airlines and supersonic jet fighters. The aircraft collection is among the most comprehensive in the UK, as is the collection of around 80 aero engines. There are also over 5,000 items of aircraft related equipment, including radar equipment, weaponry, radios, instruments and propellers as well as large parts of aircraft, including cockpit sections and a full scale interior mock up of a passenger airliner. An exciting programme of events take place each year including the famous Airshow in July. Part of the National Museums of Scotland.

The Museum is closed until 1 April 2004 whilst refurbishment is carried out in preparation for the unveiling of Concorde in Summer 2004. From April open daily 10.00-17.00. Closed 25 & 31 Dec & 1 Jan

A£3.00 C£Free Concessions£1.50. Memberships available giving free or reduced admission to all six National Museums of Scotland. Prices may be subject to increase from April 2004

Special Events

Edinburgh International Science Festival

03/04/2004-13/04/2004

A range of events throughout the fortnight including Hot Air Balloon Shows, Flight Magic workshops and Flyborgs Flying Robots

Car Rally

02/05/2004

The chance to see a wide variety of cars, motorcycles, commercial and military vehicles.

Museum of Flight Airshow

10/07/2004

Scotland's biggest civil airshow, with the chance to see a wide variety of aircraft, from early vintage aeroplaces to modern fast jets

Museum of Scotland

Chambers Street Edinburgh EH1 1JF
Tel: 0131 247 4422 Fax: 0131 220 4819
www.nms.ac.uk

[5 mins walk from Royal Mile and 10 mins walk from main railway station (Waverley). Bus: all buses from Hanover Street, N of Princes Street bring you to George IV Bridge and Chambers Street where you will find the museum]

The Museum presents, for the first time, the history of Scotland - its land, its people and their achievements - through the rich national collections. It houses more than 10,000 of the nation's most precious artefacts, as well as everyday objects which throw light on life in Scotland through the ages. The Museum of Scotland stands adjacent to the Royal Museum in Chambers Street and together they 'present the World to Scotland and Scotland to the World'. There are free family events every Sunday in the Museum. Look out for medieval maids, roman legions, jacobite soldiers and much more! Part of the National Museums of Scotland.

All year Mon-Sat 10.00-17.00, Tue 10.00-20.00 Sun 12.00-17.00. Closed 25 Dec

Admission Free. There may be a charge for special exhibitions. Membership available giving free or reduced admission to all six National Museums of Scotland and some charging exhibitions

Ullapool Museum and Visitor Centre

7 & 8 West Argyle Street Ullapool Wester-Ross
IV26 2TY
Tel: 01854 612987 Fax: 01854 612987
[Approached from N & S by A835]

Ullapool Museum is a multi-award winning
attraction within the Grade A listed former
Thomas Telford Parliamentary Church. The story
of Lochbroom is portrayed through the theme
'The People of the Loch' and an award winning
audio-visual presentation (in six languages) provides a stunningly photographed insight into the
locality and its population.
*Apr-Oct (inclusive) Mon-Sat 09.30-17.30, Nov-
Feb Sat 10.00-16.00, Mar Mon-Sat 11.00-
15.00. Closed Sun*
A£3.00 C(school age)£0.50 Concessions£2.00

Spectator Sports

Perth Racecourse

Scone Palace Park Perth Perthshire PH2 6BB
Tel: 01738 551597 Fax: 01738 553021
www.perth-races.co.uk

[Off A93, 2m A90 on A9]

Perth is one of the most beautiful Racecourses
in the UK. Horses have been racing at Scone
Palace Park since 1908, come and experience
the special atmosphere at Perth and be part of
its future. Superb hospitality packages and a
wide range of restaurant and licensed bar facilities make the Racecourse a perfect venue for
group or family entertainment. Falconry displays
and kids quad bikes feature on major racedays.
Voted 'The Best Small Racecourse in Scotland
and the N.E. 2002'. Children under 16 years get
in free at all meetings.

Race meetings Apr-Sept

Club Enclosure: £15.00 Paddock £10.00
Course £5.00 C(accompanied0-16)£Free
Concessions£5.00 Picnic area on course
£15.00 per car max 4 Adults. Advanced group
bookings rates available

Special Events

Perth Festival
21/04/2004-23/04/2004

Spring Meeting
12/05/2004-13/05/2004
12 May (eve)

Epsom Derby Day and Gold Cup Day
05/06/2004-06/06/2004
5 June (eve)

Game Fair Meeting
30/06/2004-01/07/2004

Summer Meeting
24/08/2004-25/08/2004
24 Aug (eve)

The Glorious Finale
22/09/2004-23/09/2004

Theme & Adventure Parks

Landmark Forest Theme Park

Carrbridge Inverness-Shire PH23 3AJ
Tel: 0800 7313446 Fax: 01479 841384
[Off A9 between Aviemore and Inverness]

Landmark is fun, discovery and adventure for all ages. Don't miss the Watercoaster, a raft ride flume*. Exhibition 'Microworld - a journey into inner space'. The Forestry Heritage Park has a 65 foot viewing tower, demonstrations of timber sawing on a steam powered mill* and log hauling by a Clydesdale Horse*. Try your hand at forestry skills. Have fun in the Giant Adventure.
*All year Apr-Oct daily 10.00-18.00, mid July-late Aug daily 10.00-19.00, Nov-Mar daily 10.00-17.00. * Easter-Oct*
Peak A£7.95 C£5.95

M and D's Scotland's Theme Park

Strathclyde Country Park Motherwell
Lanarkshire ML1 3RT

Tel: 01698 333777
Fax: 01698 303034 / 338733

www.scotlandsthemepark.com

[9m S of Glasgow just off J5 M74. Located in Strathclyde Country Park]

M&D's Scotland's Theme Park has something for everyone. It is bursting with family theme park favourites with the largest collection of spine chilling thrill rides in the country, including 'Tornado', 'Aftershock Bungee Rocket' and 'The Jamming', to name a few. You can enjoy your day out at M&D's whatever the weather. The massive indoor Family Entertainment Complex is packed full of things to occupy the whole family. Enjoy refreshments and a bite to eat in the Wimpy, Bizarre Bar or Guiseppe's Coffee Shop. The Cosmic Bowl boasts a 16 lane state-of-the-art bowling alley, Diamond Lil's American Pool and games parlour.

Indoor complex: All year daily 10.00-midnight. Theme Park Rides: Easter-end Oct peak days 12.00-22.00 Sat, Sun, Bank Hol & School Hol. Off peak times vary so please telephone

Admission Free. Car Park Free. Unlimited Ride Wristband: Under 1.35 metres: £10.00; over 1.35 metres: £14.00 Family Ticket £40.00. Tokens £0.50 (rides start at just 2 tokens). Buy £10.00 of tokens and get £2.50 worth Free. Group discounts available

Discount Offer: Two Wristbands For The Price Of One.

The Edinburgh Dungeon

31 Market Street Edinburgh EH1 1QB
Tel: 0131 240 1000 Fax: 0131 240 1002
[Next to Waverley Bridge]

From Easter you will be invited to board a boat and hunt for 'Vampires' in our new feature for 2004.
All year daily, call for times. Closed 25 Dec
A£8.95 C£4.95-£6.95 OAPs&Students£7.95

Toy & Childhood Museums
Museum of Childhood

42 High Street Edinburgh Lothian EH1 1TG
Tel: 0131 529 4142 Fax: 0131 558 3103
The first museum of its kind, it was reopened in 1986 after major expansion and reorganisation. It has a wonderful collection of toys, games and other belongings of children through the ages.
All year Mon-Sat 10.00-17.00, during July-Aug Sun 12.00-17.00
Admission Free

Transport Museums
Grampian Transport Museum

Main Street Alford Aberdeenshire AB33 8AE
Tel: 01975 562292 Fax: 01975 562180
[Signposted on A944]

There is a strong local theme to this road and
rail museum. Its large collection of vintage vehicles includes cycles and motorcycles, horse-
drawn and steam vehicles, cars and lorries.
1 Apr-31 Oct daily 10.00-17.00 (Oct 16.00)
A£4.80 C£2.30 OAPs£4.40

Victorian Era

Camera Obscura and World of Illusions

Castlehill Royal Mile Edinburgh EH1 2LZ
Tel: 0131 226 3709 Fax: 0131 225 4239

A magical 1850s 'cinema' giving a unique experience of Edinburgh. As the lights go down a
brilliant moving image of the surrounding city
appears. As the panorama unfolds the guide
tells the story of the city's historic past.
*Apr-Sept daily 09.30-18.00. Oct-Mar 10.00-
17.00. Closed 25 Dec*
A£5.95 C£3.80 OAPs/Students£4.75

Wildlife & Safari Parks

Blair Drummond Safari and Adventure Park

Blair Drummond Stirling FK9 4UR
Tel: 01786 841456 / 841396
Fax: 01786 841491
*[J10 M9 4m along A84 towards Callander sign-
posted on M9 & A84]*

Drive through the wild animal reserves and see,
at close range a variety of wonderful animals.
Zebras, rhino, North American bison, antelope,
elephants, giraffes, lions, tigers and camels will
all charm you.
20 Mar-4 Oct daily 10.00-17.30
A£9.00 C(3-14)£5.00 OAPs£5.50

Galloway Wildlife Conservation Park

Wildlife Park Kirkcudbright Lochfergus
Plantation Kirkcudbright Dumfries and Galloway
DG6 4XX

Tel: 01557 331645 Fax: 01557 331645

www.gallowaywildlife.co.uk

*[1m from Kirkcudbright on B727. Turn up the hill
at the Royal Hotel. Signposted from the A75]*

A varied collection of over 200 animals from all
over the world can be seen within the peaceful
and natural settings. Threatened species to be
seen at the park include red pandas, bush
dogs, maned wolves, otters, lemurs and, of
course, our famous Scottish wildcats! New for
2004; South American mixed exhibit, free-flight
aviary and play area.

*Mar-Oct daily 10.00-18.00, Nov-Feb Fri-Sun
10.00-16.00*

A£4.95 C(4-16)£3.50 C(under4)£Free
OAPs£4.50

**Discount Offer: One Child Free With
Two Full Paying Adults**

Special Events

Snake Encounters
10/07/2004-29/08/2004
Held on 10, 24-25 July, 14-15 & 28-29 Aug only

WWF Walk
10/10/2004

Highland Wildlife Park

Kincraig Kingussie Inverness-Shire PH21 1NL
Tel: 01540 651270 Fax: 01540 651236
[7m S of Aviemore on B9152]

Discover Scottish wildlife, past and present at
this unique attraction owned by the Royal
Zoological Society of Scotland.
*All year daily Jan-Mar & Nov-Dec 10.00-16.00,
Apr-May & Sept-Oct 10.00-18.00, June-Aug
10.00-19.00*
A£8.00 C£5.50 OAPs£7.00

Zoos

Edinburgh Zoo

Corstorphine Road Edinburgh Midlothian
EH12 6TS
Tel: 0131 334 9171 Fax: 0131 314 0382
www.edinburghzoo.org.uk

*[3m W of Edinburgh city centre on A8, towards
Glasgow, signposted]*

Scotland's largest and most exciting wildlife
attraction! Discover over 1,000 animals - furry,
feathery and scaly - from all over the world.
Wonder at the amazing variety, from the beautiful and endangered tigers to the ever-popular
penguins, in the world's biggest penguin pool.
Discover one of the rarest animals in the world -
the Asiatic lions - in their wonderful new enclosure, and venture into the African Plains with
high level walkway above the zebras and
antelopes. Don't miss the daily penguin parade,
sealion feeding, hilltop safari and lots of new
'animals in action' presentations every day from
April-September. And there are plenty of cafeterias and snack kiosks, a wonderful gift shop
and two new children's play areas for your very
own little monkeys! Please check our web site
for details of all our events and latest news.

*All year daily. Apr-Sept 09.00-18.00, Oct-Mar
09.00-16.30*

A8.50 C(3-14)£5.50 Family Tickets also available

Special Events

Natural Selection

02/04/2004-02/05/2004

*Fantastic paintings and drawings by Zoo staff and
volunteers, in the main entrance Gallery*

Easter Treasure Trail

11/04/2004-12/04/2004

*Solve the clues around the park and win an
Easter surprise! Usual admission rates apply*

Tigers!

19/04/2004

*Meet our family of Amur tigers, then hear about
tiger conservation in the wild, from Sarah Christie
Conservation Programmes Manager at the
Zoological Society (ZSL) and European breeding
programme coordinator for this critically endangered species. Event part of the Edinburgh
International Science Festival. Cost: A£7.00*

Blooming Lovely!

25/04/2004

*Enjoy an early morning walk around the Zoo,
before it is open to the public, in the company of
our Gardens Manager, who will introduce you to
some of the more unusual plants in the Zoo.
Cost: A£15.00, includes breakfast, booking
essential, please call 0131 314 0324*

The Meaning of Chimpanzee Vocalisations

28/04/2004

*An illustrated talk by Dr Klaus Zuberbuhler and
Katie Slocombe, University of St. Andrews,
revealing their latest research on chimpanzee
communication*

Country Parks & Estates

Hawkstone Park and Follies

Weston-under-Redcastle Near Shrewsbury
Shropshire SY4 5UY
Tel: 01939 200611 Fax: 01939 200311
www.hawkstone.co.uk

[Situated between Whitchurch and Shrewsbury just off A49. Follow brown tourist signs. Plenty of on site parking. Rail: Stafford & Crewe (approx. 45mins taxi ride); Shrewsbury & Telford (30mins drive). Air: Birmingham & Manchester airports approx. 1 hour drive. Helicopter: By prior arrangement]

Hawkstone Historic Park and Follies is a unique place. Created in the 18th century by the Hill family (Sir Rowland and his son Richard), Hawkstone became one of the greatest historic parklands in Europe. Intricate pathways, ravines, arches and bridges, the towering cliffs and follies and King Arthur addressing his troops in the awesome caves combine to create a magical visit that can last around 3.5 exhilarating hours. The park is part of the Hawkstone Park resort, which includes a three star hotel and three golf courses.

Jan-Mar Sat-Sun 10.00-14.00, Apr-May Wed-Sun 10.00-15.30, June-12 Sept daily 10.00-16.00, 13 Sept-31 Oct Wed-Sun 10.00-15.30. Closed Nov-Dec (except for Santa's Grotto trips when pre-booking essential)

A£5.50 C£3.50 Concessions£4.50 Family Ticket (A2+C3) £15.00

Discount Offer: Two For The Price Of One.

Exhibition & Visitor Centres

Secret Hills - The Shropshire Hills Discovery Centre

School Lane Craven Arms Shropshire SY7 9RS

Tel: 01588 676000 Fax: 01588 676030

[On the A49 in Craven Arms. 20m S of Shrewsbury, 7m N of Ludlow]

Unfold the secrets of the Shropshire Hills in an amazing grass roofed building. Enjoyable and informative displays explore the heritage, wildlife and traditions of this special area. Have fun in the simulated hot air balloon ride and see the famous Shropshire Mammoth. Admission to the Centre is free (although there is an admission charge to the exhibition) and visitors have free access to 25 acres of attractive meadows sloping down to the River Onny, together with a Gift Shop, Café and a programme of regular events and craft exhibitions.

All year, Apr-Oct daily 10.00-17.30, Nov-Mar Tue-Sun 10.00-16.30

A£4.25 C£2.75 Family Ticket (A2+C3) £12.20 Concessions£3.75. Group rates: A£3.75 C£2.50 Concessions£3.50. Prices stated are for exhibition only

Discount Offer: One Free Child With One Full Paying Adult

Special Events

Easter Egg Hunt
09/04/2004-12/04/2004
Over the holiday weekend, solve an Easter puzzle and you will be rewarded with chocolate! The Secret Hills exhibition includes a mammoth encounter and a hot air balloon ride across south Shropshire. Time: 10.00-17.30 Cost: £Free with entrance to Exhibition

Guided Meadow Walks
12/04/2004-29/08/2004
Held on 12 Apr, 1, 30 May & 29 Aug. Join our guide who will take you on a trip of revelation around the picturesque Onny Meadows. Discover why the river was made to change its path, how Shropshire once lay under water and the effect of the railway upon the local settlement. Places limited. Time: 13.00 & 15.00. Cost: £Free

'Tails Of The Riverbank'
21/04/2004
Speaker Andy Graham. Join Worcestershire Wildlife Trust's Water for Wildlife Project Officer to discover more about those species that live in or near the River Severn, including the illusive otter and crayfish. Time: 19.30 Cost: A£3.50 C£2.00

Pond Dipping
03/05/2004-17/07/2004
Held on 3 May & 17 July. Pond dipping is like opening presents at Christmas - you never know what you might find in your net! Discover what lies beneath the surface of the pond, learn how to identify pond creatures and find out who eats who. Places limited. Time: 13.00 & 15.00 Cost: C2.00

Dawn Chorus
08/05/2004
Join conservationist, John Tucker, for an early morning stroll (2 miles) into local woodland to experience the sounds of the dawn chorus. Learn to identify woodland and farmland birds by their song. Children must be accompanied by an adult. Places limited. Time: 05.45 for 06.00 prompt. Cost: £4.75 for full English breakfast at 09.00

Riverside Birds
09/05/2004
You may spot farmland, woodland and river birds on this 2 mile walk led by local bird enthusiast, Geoff Hall. Enjoy a ramble along the picturesque River Onny and the tranquillity of the countryside while looking out for kingfishers, dippers and grey wagtails. Places limited. Time: 10.00-13.00 Cost: £Free

'A Highland Fling'
19/05/2004
Local bird watcher, Geoff Hall, talks about his visits to Scotland and his encounters with wildlife from Ardnamurchan to the Outer Hebrides, and across the mainland to Speyside. Time: 19.30. Cost: A£3.50 C£2.00

Minibeast Safari
02/06/2004
Shrink to the size of an ant, learn about the kind of places he likes to hang out and meet a whole new miniature world of friends out in the meadows. Places limited. Time: 13.00 & 15.00. Cost: C£2.00

Natural Art Gallery
05/06/2004
Explore the natural world through games that focus on colour and texture in the environment. Use your imagination to create your own contribution for a natural art collection in the meadows. Places limited. Time: 13.00 & 15.00. Cost C£2.00

'Confessions Of A Wildlife Photographer 2'
16/06/2004
Michael Leach explains the basics of his art in this revealing and humorous insight into the realities of professional wildlife photography. This is definitely not a technical talk and is unlike any you have ever heard before. Time: 19.30. Cost: A£3.50 C£2.00

Hay Meadows
19/06/2004
John Tucker leads this visit to a local wildlife site where you can discover how to identify local flora and fauna, especially the wildflowers that will be at their best by this time. We will also learn about the history of the site from the landowner. Children must be accompainied by an adult. Places limited. Time: 14.00-16.00. Cost: £Free

Bloomin' Wonderful
20/06/2004
Learn to identify wildflowers in the beautiful Onny Meadows and then use what you have observed to be creative with art and craft activities. Places limited. Time: 13.00 & 15.00. Cost: C£2.00

Meadow Mammals
30/08/2004
Beginning with the web life, become a wildlife detective, learning how to track creatures and discover wildlife havens. Places limited. Time: 13.00 & 15.00. Cost: C2.00

Riverside Wildlife
19/09/2004

Young wildlife watchers are invited to come and join Mike Kelly, River Valley's Officer, on a river wildlife safari. Discover the wilder side of the River Onny from the treetops to the river rocks (river levels permitting). Come prepared - wellies essential. Places limited, suitable for ages 8-15. Time: 14.00-15.30. Cost: £Free

Environment Art-Teacher Training Day
29/09/2004

An opportunity to learn more about activities offered at the centre that utilise natural resources and take inspiration from the local environment. Explore a wider variety of responses to the local landscape using different media under the guidance of a professional artist. Book your place through Shirehall on 01743 254522. Time: 13.15-17.15

Maga Mammoth
13/11/2004

Join in our popular prehistory workshop where you will meet the Condover mammoth, examine some fossils and make your own fossil to take home. Places limited. Time 11.00 & 13.30. Cost: C£2.00

Festivals & Shows

Ludlow Festival 2004

Ludlow Shropshire SY8 1AY
Tel: 01584 872150 (Box Office)
Fax: 01584 877673
A programme of wide-ranging events are staged throughout the ancient market town of Ludlow and the surrounding district.
June 19-July 11 2004
Prices vary according to event attended

Ludlow Marches Food and Drink Festival

Outer Bailey Ludlow Castle Ludlow Shropshire SY8 1AY
Tel: 01584 861586 Fax: 01584 861586

[On A49 trunk road. From Birmingham head W on A456 through Kidderminster]

Ludlow, home of beautiful, hilly, unspoilt countryside where England meets Wales. An ideal place for a weekend of sheer pleasure at Britain's foremost Food and Drink Festival! Please come and join us in the amazing events that take place at Ludlow Marches Food and Drink Festival: enjoy the real food and drink that you'll find here, and the wonderful friendly atmosphere that makes this festival so different! Highlights include Ox Roast in the Castle, The Famous Sausage Trail, Real Ale events, Children's Marquee, Pork Pie of the Marches, and much more.
September 10-12 2004 10.00-17.00

Shrewsbury Flower Show

Quarry Park Shrewsbury Shropshire SY1 1RN
Tel: 01743 234050 Fax: 01743 233555
[Follow AA road signs in and around Shrewsbury]

Each August for more than a century the Show has been held in the picturesque setting of Shrewsbury's beautiful 29-acre Quarry Park. Shrewsbury Show is an event for all the family, with eleven hours of non-stop exciting arena entertainment each day, including top grade show jumping. Children get a very warm welcome in their own fun-packed area. More than three million blooms fill the Show's three huge marquees, the culmination of months of effort by the nation's top nurserymen, professional growers and amateur gardeners alike. The Show's musical programme features top class military bands throughout each day. Male voice choirs perform on both days. The Show closes each evening with a spectacular massed bands finale and fireworks display.
August 13-14 2004
Prices vary between A£7.00-£17.00 C£4.00-£9.00 OAPs£6.00-£16.00. Please call for detail

Shrewsbury International Kite and Boomerang Festival

Sundorne Recreation Ground Sundorne Road Shrewsbury Shropshire SY4 4SA

Tel: 01743 358657 Fax: 01743 358681

[From Telford take the A49 towards Newcastle, at 2nd roundabout turn L B5062 towards Shrewsbury. Just past the games hall turn L into Recreation Ground. Plenty of on site parking available]

The 16th British Boomerang competition. Competitors from around Europe will compete in distance, accuracy, trick catch and endurance. Demonstrations and stalls throughout the two days. Kite flyers from around the country will exhibit fun kites of assorted shapes and sizes. Japanese fighting kite competition and competitions for all.
June 19-20 2004 10.00-17.00
Admission Free

Shrewsbury International Music Festival

Shrewsbury Shropshire
The Shrewsbury Festival provides an ideal setting for committed amateur music and dance groups who wish to share and expand their artistic knowledge. Every year hundreds of musicians and dancers join together in this historic capital of Shropshire, beautifully situated on the River Severn near the border of Wales. The participants, of all ages and from many different nationalities and cultures, fill the town with their music and colourful dances. Each group taking part in the full Festival is given a minimum of four performances, including participation in the Gala Finale Concert in the Shrewsbury Music Hall, where the main evening concerts are held. Other individual and joint performances take place in schools, churches and village halls, as well as parks and market squares.
June 25-July 2 2004

West Mid Show

The Showground Berwick Road Shrewsbury Shropshire SY1 2PF

Tel: 01743 289831 Fax: 01743 289920
Follow RAC signs from any approach road into Shrewsbury]

Join us for the West Mid experience! See some of the world's finest and rarest animals at close range, enjoy the magic of cookery, crafts and floral art.

June 26-27 2004, 10.00-20.00

Weston Park International Model Airshow

Weston Park Weston under Lizard Shropshire TF11 8LE

Tel: 01952 587298

[M54, J3, A5 or 8m off M6, J12, A5, then follow signposts. Rail: Stafford or Wolverhampton then shuttle bus]

Don't miss the biggest and best model spectacular plus craft fair this year at the fantastic Weston Park. This year the show will be hosting the biggest swap meet at a weekend show, with over 100 traders all under cover over the two days. The event, now in its 12th year, has something for all ages to enjoy including full-size aircraft displays, large fun fair, craft stalls and model cars. There will also be a free model rocket school for children where they will be able to build a rocket and get to fly it at the end of the show, with prizes for the heights reached.

June 19-20 2004

Folk & Local History Museums

Ludlow Museum

Castle Street Ludlow Shropshire SY8 1AS
Tel: 01584 875384 Fax: 01584 872019
[On the A49]

The Ludlow area is internationally renowned for its geology. Visit the fascinating museum and discover why the rocks of Ludlow gained this reputation and how they contributed to important discoveries in the 1990s.

Apr-Oct Mon-Sat 10.30-13.00 & 14.00-17.00. Also Easter Sun plus Sun in June, July, Aug

Admission Free

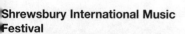

Heritage & Industrial

Ironbridge Gorge Museums

Ironbridge Telford Shropshire TF8 7DQ

Tel: 01952 884391 Fax: 01952 435999

www.ironbridge.org.uk

[J4 M54, signposted. Parking available for visitors with disabilities in marked bays close to the entrance of most sites. Central Ironbridge car parks are 'Pay & Display' but are free to Orange Badge holders. All Museum-owned car parks are free]

It has taken us over 200 years to create the perfect day out. The Iron Bridge Gorge is one of Britain's great World Heritage sites and is home to ten superb attractions set within six square miles of beautiful scenery. These include the world famous Iron Bridge, Blists Hill Victorian Town - where you can change your money into token Victorian coins to spend in the shops, Coalport China Museum - once one of the country's finest porcelain manufacturers, and Jackfield Tile Museum - where you can now see a unique collection from the former world centre of the decorative tile industry. Just opened is Enginuity, a hands on interactive Design & Technology Centre. A great family day out.

Main sites: All year daily 10.00-17.00. Closed 24, 25 Dec & 1 Jan. Some sites close in winter, please call for details 01952 884391

Passport tickets to all attractions: A£13.25 C&Students£8.75 OAPs£11.50 Family Ticket (A2+C5) £42.00. Valid until you have visited all ten attractions. Group rates available. Discounts are not available on individual Passport Tickets

Historical

Ludlow Castle

Castle Square Ludlow Shropshire SY8 1AY

Tel: 01584 873355

www.ludlowcastle.com

[0.75 m from A49, located in centre of Ludlow, road runs out at Castle]

Ludlow Castle dates from about 1086 and was greatly extended as ownership passed through the de Lacy and Mortimer families to the Crown. In 1473 Edward IV sent the Prince of Wales and his brother to Ludlow and Ludlow Castle became a seat of government with the establishment there of the Council for Wales and the Marches. Entry to Shop free of charge. Dogs welcome on leads. Audio guide available.

Apr-July & Sept daily 10.00-17.00, Aug 10.00-19.00, Oct-Dec & Feb-Mar 10.00-16.00, Jan Weekends only 10.00-16.00. Closed 25 Dec

Castle: A£3.50 C(0-6)£Free C(6-16)£1.50 Family Ticket (A2+C)£9.50 OAPs£3.00. School parties by arrangement, 10% discount on parties of 10+. All children must be accompanied by an adult

Special Events

Have a Go Archery, Living History, Castle Tours & Birds of Prey
07/04/2004-14/04/2004
Held on 7 & 14 Apr

Easter Egg Decorating Day
12/04/2004
Time: 10.30-15.00

Marches Transport Festival
09/05/2004

Ludlow Castle Festival of Crafts
29/05/2004-31/05/2004

Ludlow Festival
19/06/2004-11/07/2004
Cymbeline and Twelfth Night. Tickets: Box Office: 01584 872150

Birds of Prey, Have a Go Archery, Living History & Castle Guided Tours
28/07/2004-01/09/2004
Held on Wednesdays, 28 July, 4, 11, 18, 25 Aug & 1 Sept

Castle Green Games Days
27/10/2004

Ludlow Medieval Christmas Fayre
27/11/2004-28/11/2004

Shipton Hall

Shipton Much Wenlock Shropshire TF13 6JZ
Tel: 01746 785225 Fax: 01746 785125
[In Shipton 6m SW of Much Wenlock, J B4376 & B4368]

Delightful Elizabethan stone manor circa 1587 with Georgian additions. Interesting Rococo and Gothic plasterwork by T.F. Pritchard. Family Home. Stone walled garden, medieval dovecot, and Parish Church dating from late

Saxon period.

Easter-end Sept Thur, Bank Hol Sun & Mon, except Christmas and New Year 14.30-17.30 also by appointment for parties of 20+

House and Garden: A£4.00 C£2.00

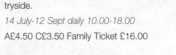

Theme & Adventure Parks

Mickey Miller's Crazy Maize Maze

Oakfield Farm Watling Street Craven Arms Shropshire SY7 8DX
Tel: 01588 640403 / 777612
Fax: 01588 640403
[1 mile W of Craven Arms and just 1.5 miles away from the town's Railway Station]

With a Windmill theme, and based on a completely unique design, Mickey Miller's Crazy Maize Maze covers an area of over 8.5 acres... and is certainly worth a visit during the summer. We invite you to "come and get lost" in the maze which offers over five miles of walking paths, plus four bridges which give superb views over the maze and the surrounding countryside.

14 July-12 Sept daily 10.00-18.00

A£4.50 C£3.50 Family Ticket £16.00

Somerset

Agriculture / Working Farms

Noah's Ark Zoo Farm

Moat House Farm Failand Road Wraxall Bristol
North Somerset BS48 1PG
Tel: 01275 852606 Fax: 01275 857080
[6m from Bristol, clearly signposted on B3128]

Noah's Ark Zoo Farm has 60 different sorts of
animals including llamas, alpacas, camels,
rheas, water buffalo, wallabies, water birds,
calves, goats, meerkats, sheep, monkeys, horses, chicken, pigs, chipmunk, rabbits, reptiles,
deer bison, and guinea pig.
*Feb Half Term-Autumn Half Term Tue-Sat (open
Bank Hols) 10.30-17.00. Closed Mon & Sun*
A£7.00 C(2-16)£5.00 Concessions£6.00

Animal Attractions

Oldown Country Park

Foxholes Lane Tockington Bristol
South Gloucestershire BS32 4PG
Tel: 01454 413605 Fax: 01454 413955
www.oldown.co.uk

Oldown Country Park is in beautiful countryside
just North of Bristol. There is lots for families
and groups to enjoy.
**For full attraction details please see our
main listing in the Gloucestershire section.**

Arts, Crafts & Textiles

Guild Gallery

68 & 70 Park Street Bristol Somerset BS1 5JY

Tel: 0117 926 5548 Fax: 0117 925 5659

*[M32 R at end, follow signs to Clifton and Gallery
is near university tower]*

The Guild Gallery is a well established hiring
gallery in the centre of Bristol. It is located on
the second floor of the Bristol Guild of Applied
Art, a renowned department store in Bristol for
nearly 100 years. The exhibitions change on a
monthly basis showing established and up and
coming artists from around the region. The
exhibits are manned by the artists themselves
for that first hand insight into the work. The
Gallery has recently been refurbished. The
installation of a new and easier hanging system
allows a more flexible use of the wall space.

*All year Mon-Sat 09.30-17.00. Closed Bank Hol,
Christmas and New Year Holidays*
Admission Free

Caverns & Caves

Wookey Hole

Wookey Hole Wells Somerset BA5 1BB

Tel: 01749 672243 Fax: 01749 677749

www.wookey.co.uk

[J22 M5, A39, A38, A371. Plenty of on site parking]

Some of the most spectacular caves in Europe
and imposing home of the legendary Witch of
Wookey, turned to stone, it is said, by an
ancient monk of Glastonbury. Dramatic sound

and lighting effects bring to life the bewitching underground landscape of fantastic rock formations and awesome vaulted caverns. The famous caves are only the start of an entertaining and educational day out for families and all ages - whatever the weather. See paper produced (and have a go if you wish) in Britain's last surviving hand-made papermill, founded in 1610. Enjoy the amusements of our grandparents in the recreated Victorian Pier Pavilion; play the vintage penny slot machines, lose yourself (!) in the mirror maze... Enjoy the natural beauty of exquisite Wookey Gorge where the River Axe cascades into the sunlight from its underground journey, an English Nature heritage sanctuary for rare flora and fauna. Enjoy home-made food in the restaurant - or picnic in sight of the Mendip Hills. New and exciting for 2004; spectacular 'Sound and Light' show that will astound and amaze. No price increases for 2004.

All year daily Apr-Oct 10.00-17.00, Nov-Mar 10.30-16.00

A£8.80 C£5.50

Discount Offer: £24.00 For A Family Group Of 4 People With This Voucher

Costume & Jewellery Museums

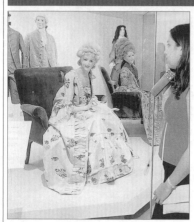

Museum of Costume

Bennett Street Bath Somerset BA1 2QH
Tel: 01225 477785 Fax: 01225 477743
www.museumofcostume.co.uk

[Top of City just off circus. Rail: Bath]

The Museum of Costume is one of the largest and most prestigious collections of original fashionable dress for men, women and children covering the late 16th century to the present day. It is housed in Bath's famous 18th century Assembly Rooms designed by John Wood the Younger in 1771. Audio-guides in seven languages included in price.

All year daily Jan-Feb 11.00-16.00, Mar-Oct 11.00-17.00, Nov-Dec 11.00-16.00. Closed 25-26 Dec. Last exit one hour after closing

A£6.00 C(6-16)£4.00 Family Ticket (A2+C4) £16.50 OAPs£5.00. Groups 20+ call for details (booking essential). Saver Ticket to Museum of Costume & Roman Baths A£12.00 C£7.00 Family Ticket (A2+C4) £31.00 OAPs£10.50

Festivals & Shows

Bath and West Showground

Shepton Mallet Somerset BA4 6QN
Tel: 01749 822200 Fax: 01749 823169
www.bathandwest.co.uk

[By car - follow signs for the Royal Bath & West Showground A371. Rail: train services from Paddington / Penzance / Bristol to Castle Cary Station. Plenty of parking on site]

The Bath & West Showground, also known as Westex, offers visitors a huge range of events all located at the West Country's leading Showground. The year's highlights include The Royal Bath and West Show, the Dairy Show and the National Amateur Gardening Show.
Dates and times are dependent on event, see Special Events for various show details
Admission prices are dependent on event. Book in advance and save money, call 01749 822222 for details

Special Events

Spring Gardening South West
16/04/2004-18/04/2004

The Knit Stitch & Creative Crafts Show
22/04/2004-25/04/2004

Festival of Birds
25/04/2004

Bike Show South West
01/05/2004-02/05/2004

Antique & Collector's Fair
07/05/2004-09/05/2004

Mother, Baby and Child Show
15/05/2004

Toy & Train Collector's Fair
16/05/2004

Stamperama
22/05/2004

Royal Bath & West Show
02/06/2004-05/06/2004

2nd Classic Bike Guide Summer Show
12/06/2004-13/06/2004

The American Show
19/06/2004-20/06/2004

Truckfest SW
03/07/2004-04/07/2004

Antique & Collector's Fair
09/07/2004-11/07/2004

Bristol Arab Show
10/07/2004-11/07/2004

National Adventure Sports Show
16/07/2004-18/07/2004

New Wine Religious Event
31/07/2004-14/08/2004

Soul Survivor Event
15/08/2004-25/08/2004

Flea and Collectors Market
29/08/2004

National Amateur Gardening Show
03/09/2004-05/09/2004

Motor Caravan Show
10/09/2004-12/09/2004

Antique & Collectors Fair
17/09/2004-19/09/2004

Festival of Birds
26/09/2004

City of Bristol Canine Show
02/10/2004

Toy & Train Collectors Fair
03/10/2004

The Dairy Show
06/10/2004

Palmer Snell Vintage Motorcycle Autojumble
Auction
09/10/2004

Vintage Motorcycle Club Autojumble
09/10/2004

Flea & Collectors Market
10/10/2004

Southern Horse and Country Fair
23/10/2004-24/10/2004

Bridgwater and District Canine Show
07/11/2004

Palladwr Historic Road Rally
07/11/2004

FJ Autojumble, Automart and Restoration Show
07/11/2004

West Country Food and Drink Show
13/11/2004-14/11/2004

Antique and Collectors Fair
19/11/2004-21/11/2004

South West Homebuilding and Restoration Show
27/11/2004-28/11/2004

Toy and Train Collectors Fair
05/12/2004

Flea and Collectors Market
12/12/2004

Bath Fringe Festival 2004

103 Walcot Street Bath Somerset BA1 5BW
Tel: 01225 480079 Fax: 01225 480079
Bath Fringe is a collective of local performers
and promoters dedicated to: "Celebrating,
expanding and challenging the arts experience
in our community". Events include drama,
dance, poetry, comedy, cabaret, jazz, folk and
roots music, circus, sculpture, visual arts, children's events and street performance.
May 28-June 13 2004

Bath International Music Festival

2 Church Street (Box Office) Abbey Green Bath
Somerset BA1 1NL
Tel: 01225 463362 Fax: 01225 310377
The Bath International Music Festival presents
some of the finest music from around the world-
classical and early, opera, jazz, world, folk and
contemporary plus visual art.
May 21-June 6 2004

Bristol Balloon Fiesta 2004

Ashton Court Long Ashton Bristol BS41 9JN
Tel: 09068 252262 Fax: 0117 953 5606
[On B3128 4m from J19 M5]

Bristol's biggest event held on the Ashton Court
Estate. An aerial spectacle including 150 hot air
balloons and a wealth of family entertainment.
August 12-15 2004
Admission Free

Bristol Miniday

Bath Racecourse Lansdown Bath Somerset
Tel: 0870 411 2666 Fax: 0870 411 3666
[2m from J18 M4]

Entertainment, Mini motor show, trade stands,
autojumble and demonstrations - something for
everyone. Camping available Sat night.
June 6 2004, 10.00
A£5.00 C(under14)£Free

Bristol Volksfest 2004

Bath Racecourse Lansdown Bath Somerset
Tel: 0870 411 2666 Fax: 0870 411 3666
[2m from J18 M4]

Entertainment, cult fashion, surf wear, VW air-
cooled and water-cooled motor show, trade
stands, autojumble, demonstrations and a car
cruise around Bristol.
June 20 2004 10.00
A£5.00 C(under14)£Free

Glastonbury Festival of Contemporary Performing Arts

Festival Office Worthy Farm Pilton
Shepton Mallet Somerset BA4 4BY
Tel: 01749 890470 Fax: 01749 890285
*[On A361 between Shepton Mallet and
Glastonbury]*

Glastonbury is arguably the best festival in the
world. A beautiful location - 900 acres in the
Vale of Avalon, this is an area steeped in symbolism, mythology and religious traditions. The
scheduled entertainment consists of music, theatre, circus, cabaret (more fringe theatre shows
than any other weekend show in the UK), markets and an enormous menu of food. Please be
aware that you will not be able to attend the
festival without a ticket.

June 25-27 2004 - dates subject to license

North Somerset Show

'The Land at Bathing Pond' Tyntesfield Wraxall
Tel: 0845 634 2464 Fax: 0845 634 2464
[On the B3130]

Agricultural show where country meets town
featuring livestock, power pulling, demonstrations, horticultural displays, British food hall, village green, children's entertainments, trade
stands, modern and vintage agricultural equipment.
May 3 2004, 08.00-18.00
A£6.00 C£2.00

Somerton Summer Arts Festival

Somerton Somerset TA11 6QH
Tel: 01458 273432 Fax: 01458 273432
A colourful and entertaining Summer Festival for
all the family including exhibitions and talks,
markets and fairs, sport and leisure, music and
theatre.
July 9-17 2004

Folk & Local History Museums

Shoe Museum

C & J Clark Ltd 40 High Street Street
Somerset BA16 0YA

Tel: 01458 842169 Fax: 01458 842226

[J23 M5. Bus: services run to High Street]

The museum is in the oldest part of the shoe
factory set up by Cyrus and James Clark in
1825. It contains shoes from Roman times to
the present, buckles, engravings, fashion plates,
machinery, hand tools and advertising material.
One section illustrates the early history of the
shoe firm and its role in the town. Disabled
access available on weekdays only.

*All year Mon-Fri 10.00-16.45, Sat 10.00-17.00,
Sun 11.00-17.00*

Admission Free

The
SHOE MUSEUM
Street, Somerset

opening hours

Monday - Friday
10:00am - 4:45pm

Saturday
10:00am - 5:00pm

Sunday
11:00am - 5:00pm

parties welcome-
please book in advance

Tel: 01458 842169

ADMISSION FREE

Clarks

Gardens & Horticulture

Prior Park Landscape Gardens

Ralph Allen Drive Bath Somerset BA2 5AH
Tel: 01225 833422
[All visitors must use public transport as there are no parking facilities. Bus: Bath Bus Co S1, First Badgerline 2, 4. Rail: Bath Spa 1m]

Beautiful and intimate 18th century landscape garden created by Ralph Allen with advice from the poet Alexander Pope and Lancelot 'Capability' Brown. Sweeping valley with magnificent views of the City of Bath. Palladian Bridge and lakes. Major restoration of the garden continues. Some disabled access, parking available when booked in advance.
All year Feb-Nov Wed-Mon & Bank Hols 11.00-17.30 or dusk if earlier, Dec and Jan Fri-Sun 11.00-17.30 or dusk if earlier. Closed 25-26 Dec and 1 Jan
A£4.00 C£2.00 NT members £Free. Groups must book in advance

Historical

Coleridge Cottage

35 Lime Street Nether Stowey Bridgwater TA5 1NQ
Tel: 01278 732662
[At W end of Nether Stowey, on S side of A39,

8m W of Bridgwater]

Here Coleridge was most inspired as a poet and wrote The Rime of the Ancient Mariner. The family moved here in 1797 and became friendly with the Wordsworths.
1 Apr-26 Sept Thur-Sun & Bank Hol Mons 14.00-17.00
A£3.20 C£1.60

Roman Era

Roman Baths

Pump Room Stall Street Bath Somerset BA1 1LZ
Tel: 01225 477785 Fax: 01225 477743
www.romanbaths.co.uk

[J18 M4 then take A46, in Bath City centre]

This Great Roman Temple and bathing complex is one of Britain's most spectacular ancient monuments, built 2,000 years ago around the country's only hot springs and still flowing with natural hot water. Free personal audio-guided tours, in seven languages, of the Baths and Temple of Sulis Minerva, Goddess of Wisdom and Healing. Disabled access is restricted. Please call for details.
All year daily. Jan-Feb 09.30-16.30, Mar-June 09.00-17.00, July-Aug 09.00-21.00, Sept-Oct 09.00-17.00, Nov-Dec 09.30-16.30. Closed 25-26 Dec. Last exit 60mins after closing time. We recommend you arrive early at peak holiday periods to avoid queues
A£9.00 C£5.00 Concessions£8.00 Family Ticket (A2+C4) £24.00. Group rates for 20+ people: A£6.50 C£3.20/£3.70

Science - Earth & Planetary

At-Bristol

Anchor Road Harbourside Bristol BS1 5DB
Tel: 0845 345 1235 Fax: 0117 915 7200
www.at-bristol.org.uk

[M5 J18 follow A4 (Portway) to The Centre. M4 J19, M32 to city centre where signposted. Plenty of car parking available from 06.30-00.30, entrance located on Canons Way, off Anchor Rd. Rail: GWR, Wales & West or Virgin trains to Bristol Temple Meads - 20 mins walk, 10 mins bus (8, 508, 9, 509), or 5 mins taxi. Bus: all buses stop at The Centre which is a 5 mins walk away]

At-Bristol is a unique destination where the thrill and fascination of nature, science and art are brought together to create the most exciting new attraction complex in Europe. At-Bristol consists of three main attractions: Explore ...an amazing world of hands-on discovery. Experience the everyday and the extraordinary using the very latest hands-on and multimedia techniques, in the UK's most exciting interactive science centre! Wildwalk ...a living rainforest in the heart of the city. Wildwalk's live animals, plants and multimedia exhibits bring you up close with the incredible diversity of the natural world, in a breathtaking journey through the history and variety of life on Earth. IMAX® Theatre ...the biggest cinema screen in the West. Feel the thrill of the world's most immersive movie experience! With a screen that is four storeys high and digital surround sound, the IMAX Theatre draws you into the heart of the action. *Standard opening hours (excluding IMAX) 10.00-18.00 daily. School bookings, in term time, from 09.30.*

Explore: A£7.50 C(under3)£Free C(3-15)£4.95 Concessions£5.95 Family Ticket (A2+C2) or (A1+C3) £21.00. Wildwalk or IMAX Theatre:

A£6.50 C(under3)£Free C(3-15)£4.50 Concessions£5.50 Family Ticket (A2+C2) or (A1+C3) £19.00. Range of discounts available if you book more than one attraction at a time

Special Events

Aardman-At-Bristol
14/02/2004-06/09/2004
Come and find out how Aardman create many of their endearing characters, from the early days of Morph to the more technical times of Wallace, Gromit and the cheeky stars of Chicken Run. Six amazingly intricate original models will take the spotlight. The Studio will be screening a specially created film showing highlights of Aardman's finest films, and behind the scenes footage. Free with a ticket to Explore

Social History Museums

Blake Museum

Blake Street Bridgwater Somerset TA6 3NB

Tel: 01278 456127 Fax: 01278 456127

www.sedgemoor.gov.uk

[Bridgwater town centre, signposted]

Housed in the birthplace of Robert Blake (1598-1657), General at Sea, the museum's displays look at the history and archaeology of Bridgwater and the surrounding area. From the earliest settlements to the colourful excitement of the annual Bridgwater Guy Fawkes Carnival, from the drama of the 1685 Monmouth Rebellion to the humour of John Chubb, 18th Century artist - there is plenty to interest the whole family. There is also a lively programme of temporary exhibitions and events, including holiday activities for children. Wheelchair access limited to ground floor only. Education service, guided tours and research facilities also available.

All year Tue-Sat 10.00-16.00. Closed all Bank Hol Mon, Good Fri, Christmas and New Year

Admission Free

Special Events

The Taunton Stop Line
11/03/2004-29/04/2004
An important local Second World War Defence programme

Museums and Galleries Month
01/05/2004-31/05/2004
Please call for details of activities

Sydenham Camera Club
04/05/2004-29/05/2004

Annual exhibition of members' work

Illuminating!
03/06/2004-31/07/2004
One hundred years of electricity in Bridgwater

Somerfest
03/07/2004-04/07/2004
Activities for Somerfest, Bridgwater's community arts festival

John Chubb and Family
05/08/2004-29/09/2004
Some aspects of the life of a talented 18th century Bridgwater artist

Open Art Exhibition, from Somerset Art Weeks
07/09/2004-02/10/2004
Contact the Museum for details of entry and competition

Carnival!
08/10/2004-27/11/2004
The history of local Guy Fawkes Carnivals

Somerset Museums Week
23/10/2004-30/10/2004

Local Archaeological Discoveries
04/12/2004-29/01/2005

Theme & Adventure Parks

Butlins

The Seafront Minehead Somerset TA24 5SH
Tel: 01643 708171 Fax: 01643 705264
www.butlins.com

[Off the A39 in Minehead, signposted off all major motorways and roads]

Butlins is a fantastic day out! A paradise for every generation, with an amazing range of activities on offer. You can enjoy the fun of the wet 'n' wild sub-tropical Splash Waterworld, burn off that extra energy on the multi-sports Court, or challenge the kids to a race round the Go-Kart track. If you fancy taking things at an easier pace relax with a game of crazy golf or enjoy the latest blockbuster in the cinema! Butlins have been entertaining holidaymakers for 60 years so why not find out what makes us so special. We offer you all the best bits of a Butlins holiday in a day for an incredible price! Don't miss the Skyline Pavilion at the heart of each Resort which offers non-stop entertainment whatever the weather and our Traditional Funfairs, Adventure Forts and Playgrounds will keep the kids amused for hours!

Apr-Oct daily 09.30-18.00

A£9.00 C(under2)£Free C£6.00 Family Ticket (A2+C2) £27.00. Group rates (20+ people): A£6.00 C£5.00. School groups of 20 or more: 1 in every 10 persons £Free

Zoos

Bristol Zoo Gardens
Clifton Bristol Somerset BS8 3HA

Tel: 0117 973 8951 Fax: 0117 973 6814

www.bristolzoo.org.uk

[Follow brown tourist signs from J17 M5 or J18 or the city centre. Rail: from Bristol Temple Meads take the No. 8 or 9 bus to the Zoo gates. Limited on site parking]

Are you ready for a brilliant day out? From the smallest and rarest tortoise in the world, to the largest ape, there are over 300 exotic and endangered species to explore. Enjoy a whole day filled with excitement and discovery at Bristol Zoo Gardens. As well as being a fun place to visit, Bristol Zoo Gardens is dedicated to conservation and involved in international breeding programmes - so watch out for new baby animals throughout the Zoo. As a charity we use any money we receive to uphold our mission to care for and protect animals and plants. Watch out too for our fun programme of events, including family carnival evening, jazz, Shakespeare and salsa nights.

All year summer daily 09.00-17.30, winter daily 09.00-16.30. Closed 25 Dec

A£9.50 C(3-14)£6.00 Concessions£8.50 Family Ticket £28.00

Special Events

Children's Easter Holiday Trail
03/04/2004-18/04/2004
Our fun trail will take place throughout the holiday. Don't miss the bank holiday weekend special, when the Easter Bunny will be visiting the Zoo

Monster Creepy Crawlies
01/04/2004-07/09/2004
A unique exhibition of giant creepy crawlies to enthral, amaze and bemuse!

Redland Wind Band
06/06/2004
A relaxing afternoon at the Zoo with music performed by Redland Wind Band

Toddlers' Weeks
21/06/2004-02/07/2004
Audience participation show aimed at children aged 2-6 years. Weekdays only

As You Like It
01/07/2004
Performed by Mad Dogs and Englishmen. Enjoy classic Shakespeare whilst you picnic in the Zoo grounds

Primary Weeks
05/07/2004-16/07/2004
Audience participation show aimed at children aged 6-10 years. Weekdays only

Comedy of Errors
06/08/2004
Performed by Heartbreak Productions. Enjoy classic Shakespeare whilst you picnic in the Zoo grounds

The Wildlife Art Society National Exhibition
08/09/2004-17/09/2004
A firm favourite with collectors and a must see for anyone interested in the current wildlife art scene

Halloween Festival
21/10/2004-31/10/2004
Enter our pumpkin carving competition and add to the amazing display of lanterns across the Zoo. Pumpkins must be delivered to the Zoo by 14.00 on Thur 28 Oct ready to be lit over the Halloween weekend

taffordshire

Animal Attractions

Ash End House Children's Farm

Middleton Lane Middleton Tamworth
Staffordshire B78 2BL

Tel: 0121 329 3240 Fax: 0121 329 3240

[Travelling along A4091 from either direction]

Small family owned farm with lots of friendly animals to feed and stroke. Three play areas, picnic barns and stables, lots of undercover activities for the children during school holidays and weekends including "Make A Memento" to take home, ie. friendship bands, badges and colouring cards etc.

All year 2nd week Jan-Feb Sat & Sun only, Mar-Dec daily 10.00-17.00, 10.00-16.00 in Winter. Closed 25 Dec-2nd week in Jan

A£2.90 C£4.90 includes feed for the animals, ponyride, farm badge and all activities

Broomey Croft Children's Farm

Bodymoor Heath Lane Bodymoor Heath
Nr Tamworth B76 0EE

Tel: 01827 873844

[10mins from J9 M42. Follow A4091 towards Drayton Manor and pick up the brown tourism signs]

Lots of friendly farm animals, traditional and rare breeds. A place where children and animals come first and the seasons are respected. The farm has been created with children in mind but with something for everyone.

1 Apr-31 Aug daily 10.00-17.00, Mar weekends and half-term 10.00-16.00

A£3.75 C&OAPs£3.25 C(under2)£Free

Arts, Crafts & Textiles

Gladstone Working Pottery Museum

Uttoxeter Road Longton Stoke-On-Trent
Staffordshire ST3 1PQ

**Tel: 01782 319232 Fax: 01782 598640
www.stoke.gov.uk/gladstone**

[On A50 signposted from A500 link with M6. Plenty of free on site parking]

Located at the heart of the Potteries, Gladstone Working Pottery Museum is the last remaining Victorian Pottery factory and perfectly presents the fascinating story of the pottery industry. In original workshops, potters can be found demonstrating traditional pottery skills. There are lots of opportunities for you to have a go at pottery making, throw your own pot on the potters wheel, make china flowers and decorate pottery items to take home. Now open, Flushed with Pride - the story of the toilet - remarkable new interactive galleries dedicated to the development of the humble loo.

All year daily 10.00-17.00. Limited opening Christmas & New Year

A£4.95 C£3.50 Concessions£3.95 Family Ticket (A2+C2) £14.00

Discount Offer: One Child Free With Every Full Paying Adult.

Special Events

Easter Pottery Painting
02/04/2004-19/04/2004
Paint your own special Easter pottery

Great Gladstone Bunny Hunt

02/04/2004-19/04/2004

Find the bunnies that are lost around the site. You could win a prize!

School Holiday Activities

01/07/2004-31/08/2004

Please call for further details

Haunted Evenings

01/10/2004-31/10/2004

Join us - if you dare, on a creepy nighttime walk of the old haunted Victorian pottery factory and hear chilling tales from yesteryear. Fancy dress optional. Gates creak open at 18.30. Please call for further details and to confirm specific dates

Santa Hunts

01/12/2004-24/12/2004

When Santa spotted the huge chimneys at Gladstone, he decided to stop for a visit. He hid pottery Santas around the museum. Join in the hunt, explore the site and see if you can find the Santas and receive your own special gift. Cost: £1.00

Victorian Christmas Festival and Carol Concert

16/12/2004-17/12/2004

Come along and join in with the bands, choirs and great entertainers in the atmospheric cobbled yard at Gladstone. Street entertainers, Punch and Judy, Santa's Grotto, candle-lit pottery demon-strations, storytelling, hand bell ringing, seasonal fayre, mulled wine and lots more. Tickets must be pre-booked. Time: 18.30-21.30

The Potteries Museum and Art Gallery

Bethesda Street Stoke-On-Trent Staffordshire ST1 3DW

Tel: 01782 232323 Fax: 01782 232500

www.stoke.gov.uk/museums

[3m N of Stoke on Trent. A50, A52, A53 all meet at Stoke on Trent]

The home of the World's finest collection of Staffordshire Ceramics. A warm and friendly welcome awaits at one of Britain's leading museums where the unique combination of 'product and place' is celebrated in its out-standing displays. With pottery that will win your heart, galleries that win awards and a Spitfire that won a war. Discover the story of Stoke-on-Trent's people, industry, products and land-scapes through displays of pottery, community history, archaeology, geology and wildlife. Explore rich and diverse collections of paintings, drawings, prints, costume and glass. Relax in the tearoom with a light lunch or Staffordshire Oatcake. Teas, coffee and pastries. Try the Foyer Shop for unique and quality gifts, station-ary and crafts. Ceramic and local history books and souvenirs of the Potteries. Experience our 300 seat Forum Theatre available for hire, for conferences, concerts and talks, not to mention a consistent programme of films for all the fami-ly at great prices. There is also lots to learn for all ages in our wide range of educational activi-ties.

1 Mar-31 Oct Mon-Sat 10.00-17.00, Sun 14.00-17.00, 1 Nov-28 Feb Mon-Sat 10.00-16.00, Sun 13.00-16.00. Closed 25 Dec-1 Jan inclusive

Admission Free

Special Events

Persian Pots
10/01/2004-02/05/2004
A selection of Persian ceramics from the Museum's collections, from the 10th and 18th centuries

Recent Additions to Natural History
17/01/2004-18/04/2004
Everything from beetles to minerals are featured in this fascinating display

Cheap as Chips
28/01/2004-16/05/2004
All about the chip shops of the Potteries, featuring a wonderful scale-model of a fish and chip shop which stood in Bucknall New Road 60 years ago

Travelling Companions Exhibition
14/02/2004-25/04/2004
A wonderful opportunity to see two important paintings of the Thames by Monet and Daubigny. Travelling Companions is an intriguing exhibition which makes all sorts of comparisons between the pictures and places them in a wider context. On tour from the National Gallery, London

English Impressionists Display
14/02/2004-25/04/2004
A display, from the Museum's collections, demonstrating how various artists such as James Holland, Whistler and George Clausen developed their own distinctive forms of Impressionism

Tate Turners Display
28/02/2004-25/04/2004

People and Pets Exhibition
27/03/2004-06/06/2004

The Archaeology of Workers Houses
01/04/2004-29/04/2004
A look at recent excavations in Tunstall, which have unearthed evidence of 19th century housing

Diverse Designs Exhibition
03/04/2004-20/04/2004

Factory Outlets & Tours

Aynsley China Factory Shop

Sutherland Road Longton Stoke-on-Trent
Staffordshire ST3 1HS

Tel: 01782 339420 Fax: 01782 339401

[Signposted from main road. Plenty of on site parking]

Aynsley China Visitor centre has many attractions including a wide selection of giftware and tableware on two floors, with exclusive pieces and extensive collections of Belleek Parian China and Galway Irish Crystal. Factory tours offer a fascinating insight into the creation of th UK's favourite bone China giftware and elegant tableware. From casting to decorating, see for yourself the traditional skills still used today in a working factory. Enjoy a snack in the Pembrok Coffee Shop. Book your place on a factory tou on 01782 339420, please note that tours are only available on weekdays.

*All year Mon-Sat 09.00-17.30, Sun 11.00-16.0(
Closed 25-26 Dec & 1 Jan*

Admission Free. Tours A£3.00
Concessions£2.50 Group rates available

Royal Doulton Visitor Centre

Nile Street Burslem Stoke-On-Trent
Staffordshire ST6 2AJ

Tel: 01782 292434 Fax: 01782 292424

www.royal-
doulton.com/main/level_one/visit-us.htm

*[J15/16 M6, follow A500 to junction with A527.
Royal Doulton is then signposted. Parking on site
is limited]*

Visit the home of the Royal Doulton Figure, featuring live demonstration area showing how figures are made and decorated, museum, tea room and retail shop. Factory tours are available Mon-Fri 10.30 and 14.00 (except factory holidays), prior booking is advised for tours. Photography permitted in Visitor Centre but not on tour.

All year Mon-Sat 09.30-17.00, Sun 10.30-16.30. Factory tours by appointment, Closed Christmas and New Year

Visitor Centre: A£3.00 Concessions£2.25, Visitor Centre & Factory Tour: A£6.50 Concessions£5.00 Group rates (12+): A4.50 Concessions£2.00

Discount Offer: Two For The Price Of One. For The Visitor Centre Only.

Tutbury Crystal Glass

Burton Street Tutbury Burton upon Trent
Staffordshire DE13 9NR
Tel: 01283 813281 Fax: 01283 813228
[Burton on Trent can be reached from the A50]

Tutbury Crystal Glass is one of the last remaining manufacturers of full lead crystal in the UK, manufacturing from their present site in the historic village of Tutbury for over five centuries.
All year, Factory Shop Mon-Sat 09.00-17.00, Sun 10.00-16.00, Visitor Centre Mon-Sat
Visitor Centre: Admission Free

Festivals & Shows

Belvedere Park Club

Belvedere Road Burton-on-Trent

Tel: 01283 540220 Fax: 01283 540220

[Follow signs to the hospital]

These Weekends of Country Music are becoming extremely popular, so please book early to avoid disappointment. We have two large rooms - the Ballroom features bands and acts who play for Line and Western (partner) dancing, whilst the Belvedere Room features artists appearing in concert. We feature the most popular acts in British Country Music. We also offer Line and Partner dance tuition in the mornings. Camping and caravanning is on the sports field adjacent to the club entrance, but there is hard standing available on request, preferably by prior arrangement, particularly for large motor homes.

Easter Weekend of Country Music: April 8-12 2004. Summer Weekend of Country Music: July 2-4 2004. September Weekend of Country Music: September 17-19 2004

Prices vary according to event attended

Inland Waterways National Festival and Boat Show

Shobnall Fields Burton upon Trent Staffordshire

Tel: 0870 240 2438

We expect to be able to accommodate 250 to 300 boats and hope to attract a similar number of tents and caravans. Wide beam boats can cruise as close as Horninglow, 15 minutes along the towpath. An event for all the family includes Theatre groups, Trade show, Children's activities, Music, Craft Stalls, Holiday hire-boats, Food stalls & Real Ales.
August 28-30 2004
A£7.50 Accompanied C(under16)£Free
OAPs&Members£4.00. In advance: A£6.50

Lichfield Folk Festival

HQ: Netherstowe School St. Chads Road Lichfield Staffordshire WS13 7NB

Tel: 01889 582908

The atmosphere of this friendly festival attracts folk dance and song enthusiasts from all over the country. The programme includes morris, clog, and folk dance displays, different styles of dances and workshops. There are sessions for children, singarounds and concerts for song lovers. For those who are new to folk dancing, we offer the Ceilidh on Saturday night. Furthermore, on Sat, there will also be outdoor displays from visiting teams culminating in a mass display.
June 18-20 2004. Commences 19.00 on Fri. Various event times.
Outdoor displays Free, charges vary for other activities

Lichfield International Arts Festival

Lichfield Cathedral, the Garrick Theatre and other venues Lichfield Staffordshire

Tel: 01543 306543 (Box Office)
Fax: 01543 306274

[From S, M1 N, M6 J4 then follow signs on A446. From N, M1 J28, A38 where signposted just after Fradley Junction. From M6 N, J14 then A513 to Rugeley where A51 to Lichfield]

In early July, the majestic cathedral city of Lichfield plays host to one of the UK's most diverse Arts festivals. A varied programme of classical, jazz and music concerts forms the backbone of a fortnight that also includes theatre, film, dance, talks and exhibitions and a range of free family events - from the popular Medieval Market to last night fireworks.

July 8-18 2004

Prices range from £Free-£31.00

Food & Drink

Coors Visitor Centre and The Museum of Brewing

Horninglow Street Burton-On-Trent Staffordshire DE14 1YQ

Tel: 0845 600 0598 Fax: 01283 513613

[A511 from Stoke-on-Trent to Leicester. Car parking is free]

Formerly the Bass Museum, the Coors Visitor Centre houses the UK's premier museum dedicated to brewing, 'The Museum of Brewing', and offers a unique blend of historic galleries and living heritage, including Shire Horse Stables, authentic Cooperage, vintage vehicle collection and working stationary steam engine

All year daily, Museum from 10.00-17.00, Visitor Centre from 08.00. Closed 25-26 Dec & 1 Jan

A£5.50 C(under5)£Free C£3.00
Concessions£4.00 Family Ticket (A2+C3)
£16.50

Heritage & Industrial

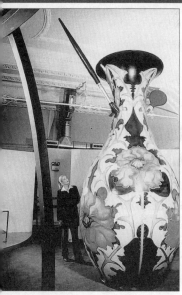

Ceramica

Old Town Hall Market Place Burslem
Stoke-on-Trent Staffordshire ST6 3DS

Tel: 01782 832001 Fax: 01782 823300

www.ceramicauk.com

*In centre of Burslem alongside A50 / B5051.
Use M6 J15/16 and A500]*

There has never been a visitor attraction quite
like Ceramica. It is a new visitor attraction for
the whole family, located in the 'Mothertown of
the Potteries', where they will have the chance
to see, listen and touch as they explore our
interactive displays and activities in which we
will show them how clay is transformed into
ceramic masterpieces. Find out how boatmen
had to 'leg' their narrowboats through canal
tunnels and have a go yourself; dig for evidence
of the past with the Time Team; try your hand at
throwing a pot on a real Potter's wheel; have a
go at painting your own ceramic gift to take
home and take a flying carpet ride over the
Potteries. Specially-created video presentations
and interactive displays combine to make a
highly involving experience. Many of the famous
names associated with Burslem, such as Royal
Doulton, Wade and Moorcroft are represented,
and some very special pieces are on display.
You can even become a newsreader for the day
in the Ceramica TV studio.

All year Mon-Fri 09.30-17.00, Sun 10.30-16.30

A£3.50 Concessions£2.50 Family Ticket
(A2+C2) £9.00

**Discount Offer: One Child Free With A
Full Paying Adult**

Etruria Industrial Museum

Lower Bedford Street Etruria Stoke-On-Trent
Staffordshire ST4 7AF

Tel: 01782 233144 Fax: 01782 233145

www.stoke.gov.uk/museums/etruria/

*[J15 M6 onto A500 then B5045. Free parking off
Etruria Vale Road]*

The Industrial Museum includes the Etruscan
Bone and Flint Mill which was built in 1857 to
grind materials for the agricultural and pottery
industries. It's Britain's sole surviving, steam-
powered potters' mill and contains an 1820s

steam-driven beam engine, 1903 coal fired boiler and original grinding machinery. Tearoom and shop, children's activities every school holiday.

All year Jan-Mar Mon-Wed 12.00-16.30, Apr-Dec Sat-Wed 12.00-16.30

A£2.35 Concessions£1.20

Discount Offer: Two For The Price Of One

A.V. presentations, a fine Treasury plus a Family Trail and for younger children a Mousehole Trail complete the exhibition. Magnificent views from the Spire Viewing Platform (please check as limited opening times).

All year daily Mon-Sat 10.00-17.00, Sun 10.30-17.00. Closed 25-26 Dec & Jan 1

A£3.50 C(under5)£Free C(5-14)£1.00 C&Concessions£2.50 Family Ticket (A2+C2) £8.00. Prices subject to increase

Historical

Lichfield Heritage Centre

Market Square Lichfield Staffordshire
WS13 6LG

Tel: 01543 256611 Fax: 01543 414749

www.lichfieldheritage.org.uk

[J11 M6, A51- A38]

'The Lichfield Story' exhibition gives a vivid account of 2,000 years of Lichfield's rich and varied history. It is home to the unique, important Staffordshire Millenium Embroideries. Two

Ancient High House

Greengate Street Stafford Staffordshire
ST16 2JA

Tel: 01785 619131 Fax: 01785 619132

www.staffordbc.gov.uk/heritage

[J14 M6]

Built in 1595 the Ancient High House is the largest timber framed town house in England.

Room settings reflect the various periods in the history of the House; Tudor Bedroom, Civil War Room, Georgian Room and Edwardian Shop, and each has its own story to tell. With educational displays, art gallery with exhibition programme, gift shop and children's activities in each room - there's something for all the members of the family. The top floor houses the museum of the Staffordshire Yeomanry Regiment. Conveniently situated in the centre of Stafford, ideal for shopping, restaurants, theatre and other local attractions, the High House is a 'must visit' destination.

All year Tue-Sat 10.00-16.00

Admission Free. Events may be charged, please call for details

Special Events

Easter Eggcitement
10/04/2004

Mayor's Parade
08/05/2004

Renaissance Ensemble - Stafford Music Festival
13/05/2004

Palmer the Poisoner: Trial by Media
12/06/2004-31/07/2004

Antiques at the Ancient High House
05/09/2004

Heritage Open Day
11/09/2004

Festival of Fortune
16/10/2004

House of Horror - Halloween
29/10/2004-30/10/2004

A Christmas Cracker
11/12/2004

Erasmus Darwin House

Beacon Street Lichfield Staffordshire WS13 7AD

Tel: 01543 306260

www.erasmusdarwin.org

[Off the M42, follow signs for Lichfield on A446. Park in the city centre and follow pedestrian signs]

Located within the idyllic surroundings of Lichfield's Cathedral Close, this beautiful Georgian house was the home of Erasmus Darwin, grandfather of Charles Darwin, and leading doctor, scientist, botanist, inventor and poet. The house tells the story of Erasmus Darwin's life and discoveries, complete with interactive displays of his theories and inventions.

All year Apr-Sept Tue-Sun & Bank Hol Mon 12.00-17.00, Oct-Mar Sat-Sun 12.00-17.00. Closed Christmas-New Year

A£2.50 Concessions£2.00

Discount Offer: Two For The Price Of One

Ford Green Hall

Ford Green Road Smallthorne Stoke-on-Trent
Staffordshire ST6 1NG

Tel: 01782 233195 Fax: 01782 233194

www.stoke.gov.uk/fordgreenhall

*[NE of Stoke-on-Trent on B551 between Burslem
/ Endon. Signposted from the A500. Situated
next to a Nature Reserve. Plenty of on site park-
ing]*

Ford Green Hall is a 17th century house, home
of the Ford family for almost two centuries.
Designated a museum with an outstanding collection the rooms are richly furnished with original and reproduction pieces according to inven-
tories of the 17th century. Outside a garden has
been reconstructed with Tudor and Stuart features including a knot garden, raised herb beds
and a viewing mount. The museum has an
award winning education service. Shop and tearoom serving light refreshments. Children's
activities held every holiday. Wheelchair access
limited to ground floor only.

*All year Sun-Thur 13.00-17.00. Please call to
confirm Christmas opening times*

A£1.75 Concessions£1.20. Wheelchair users &
C(0-4)£Free. Groups & coaches by appointment

**Discount Offer: Two For The Price Of
One.**

<u>Special Events</u>

Easter Hunt
04/04/2004-18/04/2004

Children's Hands-on Activities
05/04/2004-08/04/2004
Time: 13.00-16.00

Environmental Display
01/05/2004-31/05/2004

Cookery Demonstration - Friends' Event
09/05/2004

Children's Hands-on Activities
31/05/2004-03/06/2004
Time: 13.00-16.00

Goblin and Fairy Hunt
01/07/2004-31/08/2004
Held throughout July and August

Elizabethan Wedding
11/07/2004
*Costumed event with demonstrations. Time:
13.00-16.00*

Teddy Bear's Picnic
29/07/2004
*Bring a teddy for free admission to the Hall. Time
13.30-15.30*

Children's Holiday Activities
02/08/2004-26/08/2004
Held on 2-5, 9-12, 16-19, 23-26 Aug

A Midsummer Night's Dream
15/08/2004

Izaak Walton's Cottage

Worston Lane Shallowford Stafford
Staffordshire ST15 0PA

Tel: 01785 760278 Fax: 01785 760278

www.staffordbc.gov.uk/heritage

[Shallowford off the A5013 5m N of Stafford]

Thatched timber-framed 16th century cottage bequeathed to the people of Stafford by Izaak Walton, the celebrated church biographer and author of the 'Compleat Angler'. The cottage is decorated in period style and is home to a small angling museum. An entertaining events programme is available throughout the opening period and staff are on hand to give an insight into both this unique property and the great man himself. Wander around the rose and herb garden or linger over a pot of tea or refreshments from the tea-room. A gift shop is available to purchase souvenirs to remind you of your visit.

May-Aug Sat-Sun 13.00-17.00

Admission Free. Events may be charged, please call for details

Special Events

Prior to your visit, please call to confirm specific dates for the following events

30th Anniversary of the IWC Trust
01/05/2004-31/05/2004

Cottage in Bloom
01/06/2004-30/06/2004

Fishing Festival
01/07/2004-31/07/2004

Classic Car Show
01/08/2004-31/08/2004

Shugborough

Shugborough Milford Stafford
Staffordshire ST17 0XB

Tel: 01889 881388 Fax: 01889 881323

www.staffordshire.gov.uk/shugborough

[6m E of Stafford off A513. J13 M6 on A513 Stafford / Lichfield Road]

Ancestral home of Lord Lichfield set in 900 acres. Grade I historic garden. Eight neo-classical monuments. 18th century Mansion House. Georgian Park Farm with Rare Breeds Centre. County Museum houses the original Victorian servants' quarters.

House, Servants' Quarters & Farm: 28 Mar-27 Sept Tue-Sun 11.00-17.00, also open first four Sun in Oct. 1 Oct-28 Mar open to pre-booked parties only

House & Museum: A£6.00 Concessions£4.00 Family Ticket £18.00. Farm only: A£2.00 C(under5)£Free Concessions£1.00 Family Ticket £5.00. All sites: Family Voyager £20.00. Site admission £2.00 per vehicle, includes entry to gardens, parkland and picnic area. Season tickets available

Stafford Castle

off Newport Road Stafford Staffordshire
ST16 1DJ

Tel: 01785 257698 Fax: 01785 257698

www.staffordbc.gov.uk/heritage

*[Off the A518 Newport Road, SW of Stafford.
Plenty of on site parking]*

Crowning an important Norman archaeological
site, Stafford Castle's ruined Gothic Revival
Keep is built on the remains of an earlier
medieval structure. The castle site consists of:
Keep, motte and inner and outer baileys. The
site also boasts commanding panoramic views
over the surrounding countryside. The visitor
centre, created to represent a Norman guard-
house, has an audio-visual display, museum
exhibits and a souvenir gift shop. Reproduction
period arms and armour is available to try out -
a fun hands-on experience for all the family.
Limited wheelchair access is available to the visitor centre. A full events programme is planned
and coaches and group tours are welcome.

*Apr-Oct Tue-Sun & Bank Hol Mon 10.00-17.00,
Nov-Mar Sat-Sun 10.00-16.00*

Admission Free. Events may be charged, please
call for details

Special Events

Easter Escapades
11/04/2004

An English Village Fair
01/05/2004-03/05/2004

We'll Meet Again: D-Day Celebrations
05/06/2004-06/06/2004

A Comedy of Errors - Shakespeare at Stafford
Castle
26/06/2004-10/07/2004

Folk and Blues
11/07/2004

The Golden Arrow - Medieval Archery
Tournament
21/08/2004-22/08/2004

Heritage Open Day
11/09/2004

A Gothic Ghost Quest - Halloween at Stafford
Castle
30/10/2004-31/10/2004

A Christmas Chorus
11/12/2004

Railways

Churnet Valley Railway

Cheddleton Station Station Road Cheddleton
Leek Staffordshire ST13 7EE

Tel: 01538 360522 Fax: 01538 361848

www.churnetvalleyrailway.co.uk

*[Access from Cheddleton station. 3m S from
Leek, or 3m N from Cellarhead along the A520.
Follow brown tourist signs]*

The Churnet Valley line was opened in 1846 as
a secondary main line linking Manchester with
Derby and London. During the 1950s and early
1960s the route was used for express freight
and excursion traffic. The train journey, now
behind a traditional steam locomotive, travels
through one of the longest tunnels on Britain's
preserved railways. The 10.5 mile return journey
incorporates Cheddleton, with its splendidly
restored Grade II listed Victorian Station.

Mid March-Oct please call for a timetable

Please telephone for price details

Theme & Adventure Parks

Alton Towers

Alton Stoke-On-Trent Staffordshire ST10 4DB

Tel: 08705 204060 24hr Fax: 01538 704097

www.altontowers.com

[Travelling N J23A M1 or J15 M6 travelling S J28 M1 or J16 M6 clearly signposted. Plenty of on site parking available]

Get ready, hold on tight and prepare yourself for Britain's Number One theme park - Alton Towers, set in 500 acres of beautiful Staffordshire countryside. Enter a world of excitement, thrills and surprises. Enjoy the enchantment of a Park that's filled with sensational rides and attractions. Make it a thrilling break for all the family by 'soaking it up' at Europe's first waterpark hotel, Splash Landings featuring Cariba Creek, an integrated 'waterainment' zone. New for 2004 is Spinball Whizzer - you'll be flippin' crazy to miss this! This new spinning coaster is certain to get plenty of hits! Riders will get to feel like a ball being catapaulted along the 470-metre track at speeds of up to 60km per hour! Each car will spin through 360 degrees whilst hurtling along the track, creating a unique ride experience.

[27 Mar-31 Oct daily, rides open from 10.00 please note the park may be closed for special events)

A from £20.00, C from £17.00. Prices vary according to whether you visit at off peak, standard or peak. Please call 08705 20 40 60 for enquiries

Drayton Manor Family Theme Park

Tamworth Staffordshire B78 3TW

Tel: 08708 725252 (24hr info)
Fax: 01827 288916

www.draytonmanor.co.uk

[M42, J9 or J10 on A4091 near Tamworth. Plenty of parking on site]

Everyone's favourite theme park, packed with over 100 great rides and attractions set in 250 acres of magnificent lakes and parkland. Drayton Manor features some of the biggest, wettest and scariest rides around - 'Apocalypse' is Britain's scariest ride!, 'Stormforce 10' is the best water ride in the country and 'Shockwave' is Europe's only stand-up rollercoaster. NEW for 2004 is 'Pandemonium' - it will turn your world upside down! There's fantastic family adventure in Excalibur - a Dragon's Tale, the Jubilee Circus and the Pirate Adventure. Robinsons Land is packed with fun for youngsters - plus Drayton Manor Zoo, Dinosaurland, museums, a farm and a host of catering and retail outlets. Voted 'Best UK Attraction for Children 2003' (Group Leisure).

From 20 Mar, please call for further details

Prices vary according to time of year, please call infoline on 0870 240 6950 for details

Discount Offer: Buy 2 - Get 1 Free.

Special Events

Halloween Fireworks
30/10/2004-31/10/2004

Waterworld's fantastic new white knuckle ride i 6 seconds of thrills and spills that takes riders through a breathtaking flume of twists and turns, three times faster than the other flume rides. The Twister puts the emphasis on the 'WOW' factor.

All year Peak: daily from 10.00. Off Peak: Mon/Tue closed Wed-Fri from 13.00 Sat & Sun from 10.00

Peak (includes weekends): A£5.75 C(5-14)£5.25 C(under5)£3.00 Concessions£5.25 Spectators£3.50 Family Ticket (4 people) £20.00. Off Peak: A£5.25 C(5-14)£4.75 C(under5)£2.50 Concessions£4.75 Family Ticket (4 people) £18.00. Group rates available

Discount Offer: 10% Discount With Days Out UK Voucher

Waterworld

Festival Park Stoke-on-Trent Staffordshire ST1 5PU

Tel: 01782 205747 Fax: 01782 201815

www.waterworld.co.uk

[On the Festival Park Site at Etruria. 10mins from M6 J15 & 16. Plenty of free on site parking]

Waterworld is home to the UK's first indoor water roller coaster, Nucleus a 375 foot water roller coaster in which you can jet around in special rafts for a thrilling ride, dare you ride it? Waterworld also houses a further 17 water attractions which thrill and entertain everyone in a safe, constantly maintained 86 degrees tropical environment. New - The Twister:

uffolk

Animal Attractions

Easton Farm Park

Pound Corner Easton Farm Woodbridge Suffolk
IP13 0EQ

**Tel: 01728 746475 Fax: 01728 747861
www.eastonfarmpark.co.uk**

*[Signposted off the A12 at Wickham
Market/Framlingham turn off. Plenty of on site
parking available]*

Set in 35 acres of idyllic Suffolk countryside,
Easton Farm Park offers an opportunity for the
whole family to learn about farming and its
development. Each day children can enjoy
FREE pony rides and pat-a-pet. You can feed
and make friends with all the farm animals,
ranging from big Suffolk Punch horses,
Shetland ponies, piglets, lambs, goats, calves,
rabbits, guinea pigs to the tiniest newborn
chicks. Children's indoor soft playbarn and
adventure play area. New for 2004 - New
adventure play area. Come and meet Mildred,
our new milking cow - interactive dairy exhibit.
Enjoy a peaceful walk down by the River Deben
- there are a choice of trails through the meadows and woods. If your legs are tired, stop off
at our Stables Tearoom for a bite to eat or a
refreshing cup of tea... or glass of wine! The
original Victorian buildings at Easton Farm Park
include our octagonal Victorian Dairy, working
Blacksmith Forge and Traditional Woodwright.

Converted holiday cottages are available to rent
all year and are decorated to the highest Tourist
Board standards. Caravan site with electricity,
Gift Shop (open daily). Farmers' Markets held
on the 4th Saturday of each month. Suffolk
Family Attraction of the Year 2001. Highly
Commended Visitor Attraction of the Year 2001
- East of England Tourist Board. We hope you
have a great day!

*20 Mar-26 Sept daily 10.30-18.00. Also open
daily during Feb & Oct half terms, 14-22 Feb, 23-
31 Oct 10.30-16.00*

A£5.50 C£4.00 OAPs£5.00 Family Ticket
£17.00. Disabled: A£5.50 with 1 carer £Free,
C£4.00 with 1 carer £Free. Season tickets and
group discounts available

**Discount Offer: Two For The Price Of
One.**

Redwings Rescue Centre

Stonham Barns Pettaugh Road Stonham Aspal
Stowmarket Suffolk IP14 6AT

Tel: 0870 040 0033

www.redwings.co.uk

[On the A1120 tourist route]

Home to rescued horses, ponies and donkeys including Harry Potter the Shetland pony, Finnegan the coloured cob, Katy the pretty pony and Choccy the donkey. A great family day out!

1 Apr-30 Sept daily 10.00-16.00

A£3.60 C(3-15)£1.60 C(under3)£Free OAPs&Concessions£2.60 Family Ticket (A2+C3) £10.00. Discount available for groups of 6+ people

Archaeology

Sutton Hoo

Woodbridge Suffolk IP12 3DJ
Tel: 01394 389700 Fax: 01394 389702
[Follow signs from A12, located off B1083 Woodbridge-Bawdsey road]

The Anglo-Saxon royal burial site where the priceless Sutton Hoo treasure was discovered in a huge ship grave. New facilities and exhibition hall recently opened. The exhibition tells the story of the site - which has been described as 'page one of English history' - and displays some original objects as well as replicas of the treasure.
Shop, Restaurant & Exhibition Hall: 20 Mar-30 Sept daily 10.00-17.00, 1-31 Oct Wed-Sun 10.00-17.00, 1 Nov-31 Dec Fri-Sun 10.00-16.00, 1 Jan-13 Mar Sat & Sun 10.00-16.00. Closed 25-26 Dec, 1 Jan
A£4.00 C£2.00

West Stow Anglo-Saxon Village

West Stow Country Park Icklingham Road West Stow Bury St Edmunds Suffolk IP28 6HG
Tel: 01284 728718 Fax: 01284 728277
[7m NW of Bury St Edmunds, off the A1101]

West Stow is a reconstructed Anglo-Saxon village built on the site of an original settlement.

Finds from the site are displayed in a specially built interpretation centre. Throughout the year this unique village is brought to life when authentic costume groups host special events.
All year daily 10.00-17.00. Closed Christmas
A£5.00 Concessions£4.00 Family Ticket £15.00. Events A£6.00 Concessions£5.00 Family Ticket £17.50

Discount Offer: Two For The Price Of One.

Festivals & Shows

Aldeburgh Easter Festival 2004

Snape Maltings Concert Hall Snape Saxmundham Aldeburgh Suffolk IP17 1SP
Tel: 01728 687100 Fax: 01728 687120
[Snape signposted from A12, take the A1094 Aldeburgh Road, right at Snape Church]

Aldeburgh Productions presents its annual Easter Weekend Festival.
April 9-12 2004

Aldeburgh Festival of Music and the Arts

Snape Maltings Snape Saxmundham Suffolk IP17 1SR
Tel: 01728 687110 Fax: 01728 687120
[Held in Snape Maltings Concert Hall, Snape is signposted from the A12, take the A1094 Aldeburgh road, turn R at Snape church]

Aldeburgh Festival of Music and the Arts is held at Snape Maltings Concert Hall and other venues in and around Aldeburgh. Founded in 1948 by Benjamin Britten, Peter Pears and Eric Crozier, the festival combines international performers, living composers, new commissions, operas and exhibitions.
June 11-27 2004

Bury St Edmunds Festival

Bury St. Edmunds Suffolk IP33 1LS
Tel: 01284 769505 / 757099
[Bury St Edmunds has excellent access, situated just off A14]

The Bury St Edmunds Festival is one of East Anglia's premier arts events attracting thousands of people to the historic market town at the heart of Heritage Suffolk. Enjoy 17 days of music, dance, drama, comedy, walks, talks and exhibitions.
May 14-30 2004
Prices vary according to event attended, from £Free-£25.00

Gardens & Horticulture

Abbey Gardens

Bury St Edmunds Suffolk IP33 XL
Tel: 01284 757490 Fax: 01284 757091
[A14 to Bury St Edmunds, follow Historic Town Centre signs, E end of town centre]

Beautiful formal gardens surrounding the ruins of the Abbey of Bury St Edmunds. Prize winning bedding displays, plus rose garden, children's play area, putting, tennis and tea rooms.
All year Mon-Sat 07.30-30mins before dusk, Sun & Bank Hol 09.00-30mins before dusk
Admission Free

Guided Tours

Newmarket Equine Tours

99 High Street Newmarket Suffolk CB8 8JL
Tel: 01638 667333 Fax: 01638 665600
[Centre of Newmarket off A14]

Minibus tours of historic Newmarket, visiting people and places that you would never find on your own. Our tour guides are steeped in racing, and will introduce you to stable staff and their horses. View the equine swimming pool and the majestic sight of horses working out on the gallops and entry to the Museum.
Stud & Yard Minibus Tours: Apr-end Oct Tues-Sat when the museum is open. Depart 09.25.
Booking is strongly advised
Regular tours A£20.00 C&OAPs£18.50, includes entry to the National Horseracing Museum

Heritage & Industrial

Long Shop Museum

Main Street Leiston Suffolk IP16 4ES
Tel: 01728 832189 Fax: 01728 832189
[A12 towards Saxmundham A1094 towards Aldeburgh then B1069 towards Leiston]

Come and discover Leiston's unique history and visit the home of the Garrett collection. First production line to first woman doctor. See how Garrett's developed from making hand tools in a forge to a world famous company producing steam engines, electric vehicles, diesel tractors, munitions, radio, radar equipment and plastics.
Apr-Oct Mon-Sat 10.00-17.00, Sun 11.00-17.00
A£3.50 C£1.00 Concessions£3.00

Historical

Ickworth House Park and Gardens

The Rotunda Ickworth Bury St Edmunds Suffolk IP29 5QE

Tel: 01284 735270 Fax: 01284 735175

www.nationaltrust.org.uk/places/ickworth

[2m SW of Bury St Edmunds on the A143, signposted from the A14]

Much to interest visitors with a wonderful collection of paintings including works by Titian, Gainsborough and Velasquez. Set in magnificent Italianate garden and parklands created by Capability Brown with many rare species of plants and trees. Deer enclosure, waymarked walks and an adventure playground. Now includes 'House Opening' and 'Putting to Bed' tours; vineyard open days; family and special needs activity trail and exploration packs; handling collection and replica costumes for children. Dogs on leads and only in park.

House & Garden: 19 Mar-31 Oct Mon-Tue, Fri-Sun, Bank Hol Mon & Good Fri 13.00-17.00. Gardens only: all year, 19 Mar-31 Oct daily 10.00-17.00, 31 Oct-end Mar Mon-Fri 10.00-16.00. Park: daily 07.00-19.00. Shop & Restaurant: same as House but 12.00-17.00. Garden & Park closed 25 Dec. Please call for special events and winter openings

House, Park & Garden: A£6.40 C&Concessions£2.90. Park & Garden only (incl access to shop and restaurant): A£2.95 C£0.85

Kentwell Hall

Long Melford Sudbury Suffolk CO10 9BA

Tel: 01787 310207 Fax: 01787 379318

www.kentwell.co.uk

[Kentwell Hall is in the picturesque village of Long Melford, with many period buildings, good shopping (especially antiques) and one of the finest parish churches in the country. It is just off the A134 between Bury St. Edmunds and Sudbury on the Suffolk/Essex border. Plenty of on site parking available]

Kentwell Hall is a mellow red brick Tudor Manor house, surrounded by a broad, fish filled moat, extensive gardens, woodland walks and Rare Breeds Farm. The house and grounds are open to the public at various times throughout the year. See what one family has done to make a 16th century house and its gardens come alive again. Re-creations of Tudor domestic life, or the house during WWII, take place each Bank Holiday weekend and other selected weekends. Open air concert, opera and theatre season during summer months. Heritage Building of the Year Award 2001, member of Historic Houses Association.

mid Feb-end Mar Sun & Half Term 11.00-16.00 for Spring Bulbs and lambing, Apr-Oct Sun-Wed 12.00-17.00 & Bank Hol events / half term, mid July-early Sept daily 12.00-17.00. (Please call for details on non-event Saturdays as private functions may limit access)

A£6.95 C(5-15)£4.45 OAPs£5.95. Special prices on re-creation days

Discount Offer: One Child Free With Two Or More Full Paying Adults.

Special Events

Great Easter Egg Quiz and Tudor Life at Eastertide
09/04/2004-12/04/2004
Quiz for all the family, Tudor cooking, baking, dairy work and Easter celebrations. Time: 11.00-17.00. Tickets: A£9.50 C£7.00 OAPs£8.50

Tudor May Day Celebrations
01/05/2004-03/05/2004
With May Queen, Jack O'Green, Tudor Maypole and other May Day celebrations. Time: 11.00-18.00. Tickets: A£9.50 C£7.00 OAPs£8.50

WWII Land Girls, Home Guard, Civil Defence and 1940s Fete
29/05/2004-31/05/2004
Life at Kentwell during WWII. Traditional Fete with games and wartime prizes! Time: 11.00-18.00. Tickets: A£8.25 C£6.00 OAPs£7.25

Great Annual Re-creation of Tudor Life
20/06/2004-11/07/2004
Life on the Manor in Tudor times. Held on Sat-Sun & 9 July (weekdays for pre-booked school parties only, please call for details). Time: 11.00-17.00. Tickets: A£12.95 C£9.70 OAPs£11.50

Summer Open Air Theatre and Concerts
16/07/2004-13/08/2004
To be held from late July through to early August. To include Shakespeare's Merry Wives of Windsor, Carmen and Glen Miller Evening

WWII The Home Front
07/08/2004-08/08/2004
Life at Kentwell during WWII, with civilians and Home Front. Time: 11.00-17.00. Tickets: A£8.25 C£6.00 OAPs£7.25

High Summer Re-creation of Tudor Life
27/08/2004-30/08/2004
Tudor life at Kentwell. Time: 11.00-18.00. Tickets: A£9.50 C£7.00 OAPs£8.50

Re-creation of Tudor Life at Michaelmas
25/09/2004-28/09/2004
Kentwell at Michaelmas. Open to the general public Sat-Sun. Time: 11.00-17.00. Tickets: A£8.25 C£6.00

WWII The House Requisitioned
23/10/2004-24/10/2004
Life at Kentwell in October 1941. Civilians, Army and Home Front. Time: 11.00-17.00. Tickets: A£8.25 C£6.00 OAPs£7.25

Christmas Opera Evenings
09/12/2004-10/12/2004

Christmas Concerts
11/12/2004-12/12/2004

Somerleyton Hall and Gardens

Somerleyton Hall Somerleyton Lowestoft
Suffolk NR32 5QQ

Tel: 01502 730224 Fax: 01502 732143

www.somerleyton.co.uk

[5m NW Lowestoft on B1074, 7m from Great Yarmouth off A143. Rail: Somerleyton 1.5m. Plenty of on site parking available]

Somerleyton Hall is a perfect example of a House built to show off the wealth of the early Victorian aristocracy. The house was lavishly remodelled from a modest 17th century Manor House and boasts lavish architectural features and magnificent carved stonework together with fine state rooms, painting and wood carvings. Famous 1846 Yew Hedge Maze, one of the finest in Britain and set in 12 acres of gardens, there is plenty to see and keep the children amused. Other features include the Paxton glasshouses, vegetable garden, walled and sunken gardens, 70 metre iron pergola and 'bygones' collection of garden equipment. Details of our private tours and function facilities (including venue for wedding ceremonies / receptions, hire of our rooms for corporate or private parties) are available upon request.

House, Maze & Gardens: 28 Mar-31 Oct Thur, Sun & Bank Hol also Tue-Wed in July & Aug 11.00-17.30. Gardens & Maze: 11.00-17.30. Hall: 13.00-17.00. Member of the Historic Houses Association. No photography allowed in House

A£6.20 C(5-16)£3.20 OAPs£5.80 Family Ticket (A2+C2) £18.00. Group rates 20+: Schools&C£3.70 A&OAPs£5.30

Discount Offer: One Child Free With Two Full Paying Adults.

Music & Theatre Museums

Mechanical Music Museum and Bygones

Blacksmith Road Cotton Stowmarket Suffolk
IP14 4QN

Tel: 01449 613876

The Mechanical Music Museum & Bygones
houses a unique collection of musical boxes,
polyphons, street pianos, fair organs, the
Wurlitzer Theatre Pipe Organ, plus many unusual items, all played. There is also a large collection of memorabilia.

*June-Sept Sun 14.30-17.30. Private tours by
arrangement during the week*

A£4.00 C£1.00. Parking Free

Spectator Sports

Newmarket Racecourses

Westfield House The Links Newmarket Suffolk
CB8 0TG

Tel: 01638 675500 Fax: 01638 663044

*[The Rowley Mile Racecourse, Newmarket CB8
0TF. The July Racecourse, Newmarket CB8 0XE.
M11, J9, A1304, from E & W A14, from N
A1/A14. Rail: Newmarket, limited service]*

Newmarket has been recognised as the
Headquarters of Racing for over 300 years.
Some 3,000 horses are in training in the immediate vicinity of this unique racing town. Home
of two historic racecourses, The Rowley Mile
and The July Course.

Call for meeting times

Prices vary, please call for details. Racecards:
£2.00. Minimum single bet: £2.00

Theme & Adventure Parks

Go Ape! High Wire Forest Adventure

Thetford Forest High Lodge Forest Centre
Thetford Suffolk IP27 OTJ

Tel: 0870 420 7876

www.goape.cc

*[On the Norfolk / Suffolk border, just off B1107
between Thetford and Brandon]*

Rural Tourist Attraction of the Year 2003 - NFU
Countryside Awards. Designed to appeal to all
ages, Go Ape is a spectacular aerial adventure
course of some 40 zip slides, scramble nets
and rope bridges - at heights of up to 35 feet
off the forest floor. Not for the faint hearted, Go
Ape! is an exhilarating test of agility, courage
and determination. Minimum height 4ft 7ins.
Minimum age 10 years. Under 18s must be
accompanied by an adult. Booking essential.

*All year daily, please call the bookings and infor-
mation line or check the website for details*

Standard rates: A(18+)£17.00 C(10-17)£12.00

New Pleasurewood Hills Leisure Park

Leisure Way Corton Lowestoft Suffolk
NR32 5DZ

Tel: 01502 586000 Fax: 01502 567393

www.pleasurewoodhills.com

[Off A12 between Lowestoft and Great Yarmouth. Plenty of on site parking available]

New Pleasurewood Hills has over 40 rides, shows and attractions set in 50 acres of lovely parkland. You'll have all the space you need for a really good day out. Old favourites and exciting new rides and shows are an unbeatable combination. Families with children of all ages are catered for, as are young teens and adults. Change the pace through the day, mix thrills with shows, take a train ride or enjoy a break with a choice of drinks and delicious food.

3 Apr-31 Oct, please call for specific opening times

Visitors over 1.3 metres in height £13.50, Visitors between 1-1.3 metres £11.50, Visitors under 1 metre £Free

Discount Offer: £1.00 Off Per Person.

Wildlife & Safari Parks

Suffolk Wildlife Park - The African Adventure

Whites Lane Kessingland Lowestoft Suffolk
NR33 7TF

Tel: 01502 740291 Fax: 01502 741104

www.suffolkwildlifepark.co.uk

[5mins S of Lowestoft off A12 at Kessingland, 25mins S of Great Yarmouth]

Voted Suffolk Family Attraction in 2003 by The Good Britain Guide. One of UK's largest and most exciting wildlife attractions - experience the thrill of your very own walking safari, set in 100 acres of dramatic parkland. Follow one of three explorer trails to discover rhino, lions, giraffe, zebra and an abundance of animals and birds from the African continent. Free safari roadtrain, daily feeding talks and displays, indoor soft play and much more.

All year daily from 10.00, Jan-end Mar closes 16.00, Apr-end June closes 17.00, July-7 Sept closes 17.30, 8 Sept-end Oct closes 17.00, Nov-end Dec closes 16.00. Closed 25 & 26 Dec Please call for price details

Discount Offer: One Child Free With Two Full Paying Adults

urrey

Animal Attractions

Godstone Farm

Tilburstow Hill Road Godstone Surrey RH9 8LX

Tel: 01883 742546 Fax: 01883 740380

www.godstonefarm.co.uk

[J6 M25, follow signs to Godstone Village. Plenty of on site parking]

The most popular children's farm in the south east. The animals are very friendly and the children are encouraged to stroke and cuddle the smaller ones. The play areas and sandpits are ENORMOUS and great fun. The mini car run is really popular with the toddlers while the older ones love the dry toboggan run. New for this year is a system of bridges and island (no water!). For wet weather there is an undercover ride-on area and a large indoor play-barn (£0.80 per child extra) which now makes a visit to the farm worthwhile in winter as well as summer. And for the adults? - it's wonderful value, the views are superb and the cakes are legendary!

All year daily, Summer 10.00-18.00, Winter 10.00-17.00

£4.80 per person aged 2+. One adult free with each paying child. OAPs£3.30

Horton Park Children's Farm

Horton Lane Epsom Surrey KT19 8PT

Tel: 01372 743984 Fax: 01372 749069

www.hortonpark.co.uk

[J9 M25 between Epsom and Chessington. Plenty of on site parking available]

A delightfully friendly and informal farm aimed at the under 9s. There are plenty of farm animals and pets (undercover in most areas) for children to watch, talk to and even climb in with some of them. There are lots of chicks and rabbits to cuddle - not to mention Rosy the snake who comes out occasionally to be stroked. And when the children tire of the animals then there's Fort Horton, bridges, slides, an outdoor 'maze-in', an aerial runway, a sand pit and a spider net - all designed to give them fun, fresh air and exercise. And if it is wet then the indoor play-barn (£0.80 per child extra) is great for this age group. The tearoom serves hot and cold lunches with special children's meals and delicious homemade cakes.

All year daily, Summer 10.00-18.00, Winter 10.00-17.00

C(over2)£4.80 includes 1 Free Adult per paying child. OAPs£3.30

Arts, Crafts & Textiles

Toilet Gallery

151 Clarence Street Kingston upon Thames
Surrey KT1 1QP
Tel: 07881 832291
[Located in Central Kingston. Rail: Kingston from Waterloo, 20mins]

The converted public convenience in Clarence Street is set to become an important showcase for young artists across Britain. "For most of the last century, the toilet in Clarence Street provided a vital public service for many people in Kingston," says the gallery's founder Paul Stafford. "We hope the unique setting for this new art space will keep an historic civic building in business well into the 21st century."
Wed-Fri 13.00-19.00, Sat 10.00-19.00, Sun 12.00-19.00
Admission Free

Birds, Butterflies & Bees

Birdworld, Underwater World and Jenny Wren Farm

Farnham Road Holt Pound Farnham Surrey
GU10 4LD

Tel: 01420 22140 Fax: 01420 23715

www.birdworld.co.uk

[By road: follow the brown and white cockatoo sign boards. 3m S of Farnham on the A325. Well signposted from the M3. Easily accessible from the M25. Rail: train service runs from Waterloo through to Aldershot and Farnham. Buses run from Farnham Station. Aldershot to Birdworld: 6m using bus service. Farnham to Birdworld: 3m using a taxi or bus]

28 acres of garden and parkland are home to a wide variety of birds, from penguins to parrots, pelicans to peacocks. Meet some of the birds with their keepers at the Heron Theatre shows and learn more about them. Children will enjoy the special penguin feeding times and animal encounter sessions at the Jenny Wren children's farm. Shop and self-service restaurant. There are play areas and snack bars in the park. Underwater World contains a beautiful collection of marine and freshwater tropical fish, plus the alligators. There is also a link path to award winning Forest Lodge Garden Centre.

14 Feb-end Oct daily, Nov-mid Dec Sat-Sun, mid Dec-early Jan daily, early Jan-mid Feb Sat-Sun. Summer 10.00-18.00, Winter 10.00-16.30. Please call to confirm specific dates

A£9.95 C(3-14)£7.25 Family Ticket (A2+C2) £31.00 Concessions£7.95. Group rates available

Discount Offer: One Child Free Valid With One Full Paying Adult.

Special Events

Easter Egg Hunt
06/04/2004

Farm Fun Week
01/06/2004-04/06/2004

Teddy Bears Picnic
27/07/2004

Life on the Ocean Waves Week
02/08/2004-06/08/2004

Wild West Fun Day
17/08/2004

Get Wild Activity Week
23/08/2004-27/08/2004

Country Parks & Estates

Leith Hill

nr Coldharbour Dorking Surrey RH5 6LX
Tel: 01306 711777 Fax: 01306 712153
*[On summit of Leith Hill, 1m SW of Coldharbour
on A29 / B2126]*

The highest point in south-east England,
crowned by an 18th-century Gothic tower, from
which there are magnificent views.
*Tower: 27 Mar-31 Oct Wed, Fri, Sat-Sun, Bank
Hols 10.00-17.00, 1 Nov-31 Mar Sat-Sun &
Bank Hols 10.00-15.30. Closed 25 Dec.
Rhododendron wood and estate: all year daily*
Tower: A£1.00 C£0.50. Rhododendron Wood:
£1.50 per car

The National Trust, Runnymede

North Lodge Windsor Road Old Windsor
Berkshire SL4 2JL
Tel: 01784 432891 Fax: 01784 479007
*[J13 M25. On the Thames 2m W of Runnymede
Bridge on S side of A308. 6m E of Windsor]*

An attractive area of riverside meadows, grassland and broadleaf woodland, rich in diversity of
flora and fauna, and part-designated a Site of
Special Scientific Interest. It was on this site, in
1215, that King John sealed Magna Carta, an
event commemorated by the American Bar
Association Memorial and John F. Kennedy
Memorial.
*All year. Riverside grass car park: Apr-30 Sept
daily when ground conditions allow 09.00-19.00*
Admission Free. Parking charge

Festivals & Shows

Guilfest 2004

Stoke Park Guildford Surrey
Tel: 01483 454159 Fax: 01483 306551
This will be the 13th Guildford Live Music
Festival and promises a unique atmosphere and
incredible line up. The festival has always been
about covering a wide selection of different
musical genres, to be enjoyed by people of all
ages, but the entertainment doesn't stop at just
music. Stoke Park will house a craft village and

numerous food and drink stalls with the city
centre and further entertainment never far away.
There is plenty of entertainment available for
children in their own special area including jugglers, circus acts, rides and workshops. A
Comedy Tent with an excellent line-up and a
Buskers Marquee. Plus the Unsung Heroes
stage, a chance for up and coming bands to
get up on stage for their 15 mins of fame.
Camping facilities available and don't forget
your swimming cossies as there is a fantastic
outdoor pool, perfect for cooling off between
acts!
July 16-18 2004
Prices vary, contact 01483 536270 for details

Surrey County Show

Stoke Park Guildford Surrey
Tel: 01483 890810 Fax: 01483 890820
*[Next to Guildford College of Technology
entrance on Nightingale Rd - signposted]*

The Golden Jubilee Surrey County Show is
Britain's biggest one-day agricultural event with
fun and activities for all the family! The Show
has been running for over fifty years and has
grown to include a huge range of attractions to
suit every taste, including a Food Hall where visitors can see, sample and buy the best of farm
produce. A Flower Show and a wide variety of
horticultural trade stands make the Show very
popular with amateur gardeners. The Show
attracts livestock entries from all over England
and just about every type of horse and pony is
catered for. The Main Ring programme is varied
and up to date to hold the visitors' interest
throughout the day. Countless other trade
stands and shopping, displays (including rare
breeds and unusual animals) and attractions
including a children's village combine to make
the Surrey County Show a wonderful day out.
This year's Show features a special Golden
Jubilee display with stunt motorbikes, tigers,
freefall parachutes, the Minder Band, Scurry
plus plenty more attractions.
May 31 2004, 09.00-18.00
A£10.00 C(8-16)£4.00 OAPs£5.50

Tilford Bach Festival

Tilford Farnham Surrey GU10 2DA
Tel: 01252 721605
*[Farnham Castle & All Saint's Parish Church.
Tilford can be reached from the M3 via Farnham,
or from the A3 exit at Godalming or Hindhead]*

A festival largely based around and celebrating
the works of JS Bach and his contemporaries.
May 28 and June 4-5 2004
May 28: A£15.00 June 4-5: £10.00-17.50.
£5.00 discount available if you buy tickets for all
three nights. Tickets available from the
Secretary on 01252 782167

Gardens & Horticulture

Claremont Landscape Garden

Portsmouth Road Esher Surrey KT10 9JG
Tel: 01372 467806 Fax: 01372 464394
[S edge of Esher, E side of A307]

One of the earliest surviving English landscape
gardens, restored to its former glory. Features
include a lake, island with pavilion, grotto and
turf amphitheatre.
*All year, Jan-end Mar Tue-Sun 10.00-17.00 or
sunset if sooner, Apr-end Oct Mon-Fri 10.00-
18.00, Sat Sun & Bank Hol Mon 10.00-19.00,
Nov-end Mar Tue-Sun 10.00-17.00 or sunset if
sooner. Closed 25 & 28 July & 25 Dec*
A£4.00 C£2.00 Family Ticket £10.00. £0.50

Painshill Park

Portsmouth Road Cobham Surrey KT11 1JE

Tel: 01932 868113 Fax: 01932 868001

www.painshill.co.uk

*[By road: via M25 J10 and A3. Exit at junction
with A245 (towards Cobham). Entrance between
Streets, 200 metres E of A245/A307 roundabout.
Plenty of on site parking. Rail: from Waterloo to
Cobham or Weybridge. Bus: 515 Tellings
Kingston-Cobham and 408 Epsom buses
Epsom-Cobham]*

Painshill Park is a unique award winning restoration of England's Georgian Heritage. Within its
160 acres, its Hamilton landscapes are a work
of art that influenced the future of England's
countryside and culture. Between 1738 and
1773 the Hon. Charles Hamilton created a parkland setting enriched by the buildings and
waters, trees and shrubberies that help define
the subtle and surprising vistas. Following years
of dereliction The Hamilton landscapes have
been authentically restored to their original pre-
eminence winning the Europa Nostra Medal for
exemplary restoration. Painshill Park is a jewel
of English culture, a source of peace and inspiration, the work of an English gentlemen in all its
quiet charm. Painshill is open throughout the
year. A visit is enhanced by Cafe Hamilton,
Painshill's licensed restaurant, which offers dishes ranging from sandwiches to the hot meal
accompanied by either hot or cold drinks and
Painshill's delicious wines. The gift shop is full of
unique and interesting gifts for adults and children alike.

*Mar-Oct Tue-Sun & Bank Hol 10.30-18.00, Nov-
Feb Wed-Sun & Bank Hol 11.00-16.00 or dusk if
sooner. Closed 25 Dec*

A£6.00 C(under5)£Free C(5-16)£3.50
Concessions£5.25. Group rates 10+ £5.00 with
optional guided tour. Special arrangements for
school parties contact Education Department
on 01932 868113

Special Events

Easter Eggstravaganza!
02/04/2004-19/04/2004
*Follow our special trail around the park to help
you win an Easter egg*

Hamilton's Day
04/04/2004-03/10/2004
*On the first Sunday of every month, 4 Apr, 2 May,
6 June, 4 July, 1 Aug, 5 Sept, 3 Oct, we will be
celebrating Hamilton's extraordinary vision by running short tours where you will be able to meet*

characters from the 18th century

The Hidden Hermit Trail
17/04/2004-18/04/2004
Painhill's infamous hermit has returned! Again you will have the chance to solve the riddles and fulfil the tasks he has set you

Bluebells in Bloom
25/04/2004
The Bluebells on Wood Hill at Painshill should be at their very best around this time

Horse Drawn Carriage Day
03/05/2004
Come and enjoy a horse drawn carriage ride around the lake

Homes and Gardens Fair
07/05/2004-09/05/2004

Dogs on a Lead Day
16/05/2004-15/08/2004
Held on 16 May & 15 Aug only

Cowboys and Cowgirls Day
23/05/2004
Pretend you're in the 'Way out West' and join in the fun of learning how to use a Bow and Arrow

Moon Carrot Puppet Show - Rabbits Magic Adventure
30/05/2004
The story of a rabbit with a fondness for carrots whose present is stolen by a fox. Times: 11.30, 13.30, 15.00

Battle on the Lake
31/05/2004
See the Portsmouth Model Boat Display Team on the lake operating hand built radio controlled vessels and staging two dramatic sea battles

Cyril the Squirrel Day and Dogs on Leads Day
13/06/2004
Come and see Cyril the Squirrel and his racing terriers run riot in the ring as they perform their hilarious display. There will be two displays at 11.30 & 14.30

Fathers Day and Family Trails Day
20/06/2004
Bring your father to Painshill to enjoy a day of special 'treats'

Picnic by the Lake
27/06/2004
Come and sit by the lake and enjoy your picnic while exquisite 18th century music wafts down from the Gothic Temple

Battle of Painshill
10/07/2004-11/07/2004
Following the huge success last year, Napolean and his Army are coming again to Painshill for the weekend!

Kite Making / Flying Day
18/07/2004
Take to the skies at Painshill with this fun activity

Mad Hatters Tea Party
25/07/2004
Come and join Alice, Mad Hatter, Humpty Dumpty and friends at our Mad Hatters Tea Party

Super Summer Fun Trails
01/08/2004-31/08/2004

Moon Carrot Teddy Bear Puppet Show
08/08/2004
When you come for your teddy bear's day out, why not watch the Moon Carrot's famous Teddy Bear Puppet Show, with performances at 11.30, 13.30 and 15.00

Teddy Bears Picnic
08/08/2004
Pack a hamper and come and enjoy a special day out for you and your bear

Surrey Sculpture Society Exhibition
20/08/2004-19/09/2004
Following Surrey Sculpture Society's wonderful exhibition in the Park last year, we invited them back and are increasing their stay to a month

David Seamark Sheepdog Demonstration
22/08/2004
David comes again to Painshill to present two entertaining and skilful shows at 11.30 & 14.30

Noddy and Friends Day
29/08/2004
A fun filled day of entertainment and games

Extra Fun Day for Children
12/09/2004

Hawk Experience
19/09/2004
There will be a static display all day, with two flying displays, one at 11.30 and one at 14.30

Technology Day
26/09/2004
See the 19th century Waterwheel and Horse Pump in action

Poetry Day
10/10/2004
Come and listen to and take part in poetry readings at the idyllic Gothic Temple

Children's Tree Trail
17/10/2004

Gothic Tower Sunday
24/10/2004
The Gothic Tower will be manned all day. You will be greeted by a costumed guide, who will take you through the extraordinary history of the Gothic Tower

Halloween Trail and Pumpkin Carving Workshop
31/10/2004
Children can enjoy autumn's mellow fruitfulness with a harvest Halloween trail around the park

Festival of Fireworks!
05/11/2004-06/11/2004
This year it is being held to celebrate Charles Hamilton's 300th birthday

Santa in the Grotto!
27/11/2004-24/12/2004
Held on 27-28 Nov, 4, 5, 11-24 Dec only. Father Christmas will be back in residence in our beautiful crystal Grotto. Please be sure to book a slot with Santa as this event is guaranteed to sell out

RHS Garden Wisley, Woking, Surrey, GU23 6QB
Tel: 01483 224234 www.rhs.org.uk

Celebrating 200 years of great gardening

RHS Garden Wisley

RHS Garden Wisley Woking Surrey GU23 6QB

Tel: 01483 224234 Fax: 01483 211750

www.rhs.org.uk

[J10 M25 on A3, London 22m, Guildford 7m. Plenty of on site parking available]

Stretching over 240 acres, Wisley is the flagship of the Royal Horticultural Society demonstrating the very best in gardening practices. Highlights include the magnificent Rock Garden, rock pools and Alpine Houses, glories of the Mixed Borders and Rose Garden, the splendid array of Glasshouses and 16 acre Fruit Field containing over 760 apple cultivars. Model Gardens demonstrate design ideas on a realisable scale reflecting changing styles and new techniques. Whatever the season, the Garden serves as a working encyclopedia for gardeners of all levels. Special events and activities take place throughout the year.

All year daily, Mon-Fri 10.00-18.00 (Nov-Feb 16.30), Sat & Sun 09.00-18.00 (Nov-Feb 16.30)

A£7.00 C(0-6)£Free C(6-16)£2.00. Group rates (10+): £5.50

Discount Offer: Two For The Price Of One.

Special Events

RHS Late Daffodil Competition
27/04/2004-28/04/2004

Wisley Music Festival
10/06/2004-12/06/2004

Clematis Weekend in the Plant Centre
12/06/2004-13/06/2004

Wisley Flower Show
22/06/2004-24/06/2004

Summer Fruit and Vegetable Competition
07/07/2004

Wisley Flower Show
17/08/2004-19/08/2004

Wisley Apple Festival
01/10/2004-31/10/2004

Tree Weekend in the Plant Centre
02/10/2004-03/10/2004

Winkworth Arboretum

Hascombe Road Nr Godalming GU8 4AD
Tel: 01483 208477 Fax: 01483 208252
[Near Hascombe, 2m SE of Godalming on E side of B2130]

A hillside woodland, created in the 20th century and now containing over 1,000 different shrubs and trees, many of them rare. The most impressive displays are in spring with magnolias, bluebells and azaleas, and in autumn for stunning colours.
All year daily during daylight hours, may close during bad weather (especially in high winds)
A£4.00 C£2.00 Family Ticket £10.00

Historical

Clandon Park

West Clandon Guildford Surrey GU4 7RQ

Tel: 01483 222482 Fax: 01483 223479

www.nationaltrust.org.uk/clandonpark

[At West Clandon on A247, 3m E of Guildford, if using A3 follow signposts to Ripley to join A247 via B2215. Plenty of on site parking available. Rail: Clandon 1m. Bus: Countryliner 463 Guildford-Woking, Arriva Surrey 478/9 Guildford-Leatherhead]

A grand Palladian mansion built circa 1730 by the Venetian architect Giacomo Leoni. The house is filled with the superb collection of 18th century furniture, porcelain, textiles and carpets acquired in the 1920s by the connoisseur Mrs David Gubbay, and also contains the Ivo Forde Meissen collection of Italian comedy figures and a series of Mortlake tapestries. Attractive gardens contain parterre, sunken Dutch garden and a Maori house. The Queen's Royal Surrey Regiment Museum is also based at Clandon Park. Wheelchair access to ground floor, gardens, shop and restaurant.

House & Grounds: 28 Mar-31 Oct Tue, Wed, Thur & Sun, Good Fri, Easter Sat & all Bank Hols 11.00-17.00. Museum: as house, but 12.00-17.00

House & Garden: A£6.00 C£3.00 Family Ticket £15.00. Museum: £Free. Combined ticket with Hatchlands Park: A£9.00 C£4.50 Family Ticket £22.50. Special group rate; weekdays only

A£5.00. Coach parties welcome, please call to book

Hatchlands Park

East Clandon Guildford Surrey GU4 7RT

Tel: 01483 222482 Fax: 01483 223176

www.nationaltrust.org.uk/hatchlands

[E of E Clandon, N of A246 Guildford to Leatherhead Road, 5m E of Guildford. On site parking available. Rail: Clandon 2.5m, Horsley 3m. Bus: Arriva Surrey 478/9 Guildford-Leatherhead]

A handsome House built in 1758 by Stiff Leadbetter for Admiral Boscawen, and set in a beautiful Repton park offering a variety of park and woodland walks. Hatchlands contains splendid interiors by Robert Adam. It houses the Cobbe Collection, the world's largest group of early keyboard instruments associated with famous composers such as Purcell, J.C. Bach, Chopin, Mahler and Elgar, as well as Marie Antoinette. There is also a small garden by Gertrude Jekyll, flowering from late May to early July.

House & Grounds: 1 Apr-31 Oct Tue, Wed, Thur, Sun (plus Fridays in Aug & Bank Hols) 14.00-17.30. Park walks: Apr-Oct daily 11.00-18.00

House & Grounds: A£6.00 C(5-16)£3.00 Family Ticket £15.00. Park Walks: A£2.50 C£1.25. Special group rate weekdays only: £5.00 Combined Ticket with Clandon Park: A£9.00 C£4.50 Family Ticket £22.50. Coach parties welcome, please call to book

Loseley Park

Estate Offices Loseley Park Guildford GU3 1HS
Tel: 01483 304440 Fax: 01483 302036
[Leave A3 at Compton on B3000 signposted]

Loseley Park has been the home of the More-Molyneux family for over 400 years. The Elizabethan Mansion is set amid 1,400 acres of glorious parkland and rolling pastures grazed by the famous Jersey herd.
Garden, Gift Shop, Courtyard Tea Room & Restaurant: 5 May-30 Sept Wed-Sun & Bank Hol 11.00-17.00 (Restaurant 12.00-15.00). House: 2 June-29 Aug Wed-Sun & Bank Hol 13.00-17.00
House & Gardens: A£6.00 C£3.00. Gardens only: A&Concession£3.00 C£1.50

On the Water

Busbridge Lakes, Waterfowl and Gardens

Hambledon Road Busbridge Godalming Surrey GU8 4AY

Tel: 01483 421955 Fax: 01483 421955

www.busbridgelakes.co.uk

[1.5 miles from Goldalming off the B2130 Bus: To Home Farm Road 6 mins walk. Rail: Milford 2m Godalming 1.5m]

Busbridge Lakes is situated in a valley of some forty acres, with three spring fed lakes, home to over 150 species of wild waterfowl, pheasants, cranes, peafowl and fancy bantams, from all over the world, many endangered. It is a Heritage 2* Garden with follies and grottos; outstanding old specimen trees; nature trails. Much flora and fauna around the lakes and over the hills. Wander amongst the birds in the stunning landscaped gardens, many with their young babies. An ideal place for photography due to the wealth of colour and variety of scenery. A place of outstanding beauty.

9-18 Apr, 2, 3, 30, 31 May & 22-30 Aug 10.30-17.30

A£4.50 C(5-13)£3.00 OAPs£3.00

Palaces

Hampton Court Palace and Gardens

Hampton Court Palace East Molesey Surrey KT8 9AU

Tel: 0870 752 7777 (info line)

www.hampton-court-palace.org.uk

[M25 exit J12 M3 towards central London exit at J1 Sunbury signposts follow for 4m. A308 towards Kingston. From Central London take A4 W towards Hammersmith then A316 / M3 then exit at J1 Sunbury as above. Tube: Richmond, then R68 bus. Rail: Hampton Court Station. Limited parking on site]

Hampton Court Palace was built by Cardinal Wolsey and has been a favoured home to royalty from Henry VIII to George II. Today it promises a magical journey back through 500 years of royal history. Explore the palace's vast Tudor kitchens and magnificent State Apartments, see works of art from the Royal Collection, and look out for the ghost of Catherine Howard in the Haunted Gallery. Complimentary costumed guided tours and audio guides reveal the realities of life under the reigns of Henry VIII and William III, and there is also an exciting programme of special events throughout the year. Step outside, and discover courtyards, cloisters, 60 acres of immaculately restored riverside gardens, the largest and oldest grapevine in Europe and William III's Privy Garden, or lose yourself in the world famous maze.

30 Mar-25 Oct Mon 10.15-17.15, Tue-Sun 09.30-17.15, 26 Oct-29 Mar Mon 10.15-15.45, Tue-Sun 09.30-15.45. Last admission to Gardens is at the time of closing, Palace closed 45 mins after last admission

A£11.50 C£7.50 Concessions£8.50 Family Ticket £34.00. Advance ticket sales tel: 0870 753 7777. Prices subject to change

Social History Museums

Rural Life Centre

The Reeds Tilford Farnham Surrey GU10 2DL

Tel: 01252 795571 Fax: 01252 795571

www.rural-life.org.uk

Off A287 halfway between Frensham / Tilford follow brown signposts. Ample on site parking available]

The Rural Life Centre is a museum of past village life covering the years from 1750 to 1960. It is set in over ten acres of garden and woodland and housed in purpose-built and reconstructed buildings including a chapel, village hall and cricket pavilion. Displays show village crafts and trades such as wheelwrighting of which the centre's collection is probably the finest in the country. An historic village playground provides entertainment for children as does a preserved narrow gauge light railway which operates on Sundays. There is also an arboretum with over 100 species of tree from around the world. Indoor and outdoor picnic areas.

21 Mar-3 Oct Wed-Sun & Bank Hol Mons 10.00-17.00, Winter Wed & Sun only 11.00-16.00

A£5.00 C(5-16)£3.00 OAPs£4.00 Family Ticket (A2+C2) £14.00

Discount Offer: Two For The Price Of One.

Special Events

Wrecclesham's Hidden History
21/03/2004-30/04/2004

Car Boot Sale & Craft Demonstrations
04/04/2004-03/10/2004
Held on 4 Apr, 2 May, 6 June, 4 July, 1 Aug, 5 Sept, 3 Oct

Steam Toy Rally
10/04/2004
Over 250 working miniature steam engines and machines will be on show

Easter Sunday and Monday
11/04/2004-12/04/2004
Easter Chick Hunt around the museum and a service in the chapel (Sunday)

Working with Wood
25/04/2004
From the tree to the shed or ornament. Come and see wood and the people that work with it

Model Railway Exhibition
01/05/2004
The Old Kiln Light Railway hosts a variety of layouts in the museum

Pet Services in the Chapel
02/05/2004
Bring your well behaved pets along to celebrate National Pet Week

Prelude to D-Day
15/05/2004-16/05/2004
To commemorate the 60th anniversary of the largest invasion fleet ever assembled, our living history weekend will take you back to May 1944 to experience the sights, sound and smells of wartime in our village 'somewhere in England'

A Rural Mini Adventure
30/05/2004
Celebrate with us 45 years of the classic British legend - the 'Mini'

The Mower the Merrier
06/06/2004
Members of the Old Lawn Mower Club will display push and motor mowers from the 1880s to the 1960s

Morris Minor Rally
13/06/2004
All owners of Morris Minors are invited to enter the Surrey Hants Border Branch Rally of the Morris Minor Owners Club

Countryside & Farming Day
20/06/2004
Our very popular celebration of the British countryside returns

The Classic & Modern Honda Bike Show
18/07/2004
Members of the owners club will have many gleaming motorcycles on show

Rustic Sunday - A Traditional Celebration of Country Life
25/07/2004
Many rural crafts demonstrated and something for all the family to enjoy. Cost: A£6.00 C£3.00 OAPs£5.00 Family Ticket £15.00

CSVAC Stationary Engine Rally
07/08/2004-08/08/2004
See the different types of engine being cranked up and at work

American Theme Weekend
14/08/2004-15/08/2004
The Guild of Frontiersmen return for their annual living history camp and this year they will be joined (on Sunday) by American classic cars and period frontier music

Going Back in Time
22/08/2004
From industrial archaeology to the Stone Age to celebrate the 150th anniversary of Surrey Archaeological Society

Donkey Day Out
12/09/2004
Members of the Donkey Breed Society will be at the museum for their annual get-together

Classic Vehicle Gathering
19/09/2004
Surrey Classic Vehicle Club will be returning for their very popular event

Steam & Vintage Weekend
25/09/2004-26/09/2004
Steam, great and small, tractors, commericals, motorcycles and more

Harvest Home
03/10/2004
Traditional services in the chapel will mark the end of another busy museum summer programme

Christmas Craft Fair
27/11/2004
A chance to buy some unusual Christmas gifts from our craftspeople

Santa Specials
04/12/2004-12/12/2004
Held on 4, 5, 11, 12 Dec. Be sure to book early for this ever popular event

Spectator Sports

Lingfield Park Racecourse

Racecourse Road Lingfield Surrey RH7 6PQ
Tel: 0870 220 0022 Fax: 01342 835874
[M25 J6, S on A22 signposted]

The busiest racecourse in the country. 92 meetings on turf and all weather tracks. Major races run: Derby Trial; Oaks Trial; Silver Trophy; Summit Junior Hurdle. There is a 18 hole golf course, training permitted on All-Weather Track
All year for 92 publicised race meetings
Members: A£16.00 Accompanied
C(under16)£Free. Grandstand £13.00

Theme & Adventure Parks

Sport & Recreation

Campaign Paintball Park

Old Lane Cobham Surrey KT11 1NH

Tel: 01932 865999 Fax: 01932 865744

www.campaignpaintball.com

[By Car: Turn off the M25 or A3 at J10. At the roundabout, take the exit signposted to Effingham. Before you reach the southbound carriageway of the A3 turn L into Old Lane (also signposted to Effingham). Campaign is 2m down this road on the R hand side. By Train: To 'Effingham Junction' on the Waterloo to Guildford line (passing through Clapham Junction, Wimbledon and Surbiton). A 5min walk from the station up Old Lane. For times of trains call Railtrack information on 0345 484950]

Campaign is situated within a beautiful 200 acre woodland park, near Cobham, Surrey, two minutes from J10 of the M25 & A3 and just 20 minutes from London. Often seen on television and frequently used for film location, Campaign's award-winning venue comes highly recommended for company fun days and team building exercises, with groups from 2 to 250 made very welcome. Opened in 1989, Campaign also specialises in stag, hen and birthday parties and holds regular days solely for junior paintballers. Facilities are of such high quality that they even host the paintball World Championships! With more than a decade's experience and expertise in arranging corporate events, Campaign guarantees all clients a first class service, with park facilities that are unrivalled.

All year daily

From £17.50 per person

**Discount Offer: £2.50 Off Per Person
With This Voucher**

Chessington World of Adventures

Leatherhead Road Chessington Surrey
KT9 2NE

Tel: 0870 444 77 77 Fax: 01372 725050

www.chessington.com

[Situated 12 miles from London on the A243, just 2 miles from the A3 and M25 (J9/J10). Plenty of on site parking available. Rail: Regular South West Train services from Waterloo station, Clapham Junction and Wimbledon to Chessington South station - a 10min walk from the main entrance]

Explore a whole new family adventure land at Chessington World of Adventures in 2004 - the amazing Land of the Dragons for children aged 2-8, plus new Dragon's Fury the family spinning roller coaster. Feel the fantasy of Hocus Pocus Hall - the magical 4-D experience, plus don't miss the fang-tastic Vampire, quick fire challenge of Tomb Blaster or fun-filled Dennis's Madhouse in Beanoland. Take a safari trip down Trail of the Kings, then journey into Toytown with Toadie's Crazy Cars, Berry Bouncers and Tiny Truckers. Or for the more daring find Rameses waiting to seek his Revenge - there's a whole world waiting to feed the imagination!

27 Mar-31 Oct (with some closed days during the mid-week off-peak season). Opening times vary throughout the season and Guests are advised to check online or call the information line on 0870 444 7777 in advance of their visit

For prices and to book in advance visit the website or call the booking and information line on 0870 444 77 77

Thorpe Park

Staines Road Chertsey Surrey KT16 8PN

Tel: 0870 444 44 66 Fax: 01932 566367

www.thorpepark.com

[Situated on the A320. From the M25 take J11/J13 and follow signs to Thorpe Park. Access from J12 is not possible. Plenty of parking on site. Rail: South West Trains run from Waterloo direct to Staines Station where a shuttle bus operates to the Park]

Get ready for thrill overload as the mighty Samurai joins the adrenaline-charged line-up at Thorpe Park in 2004. Feel the heat of Nemesis Inferno, the legendary feet-free coaster, and experience the world's first 10-looping coaster, Colossus. Also on the list of 'must-ride' thrill sensations are the gut-wrenching Quantum, explosive Detonator, awesome Vortex and spinning Zodiac. There's Tidal Wave, one of Europe's highest water drop rides, the white water thrills of Ribena Rumba Rapids and Logger's Leap, plus Eclipse, X:/No Way Out, Pirate's-4D, Neptune's Beach, Thorpe Farm and lots more besides - it's the season to thrill your senses!

20 Mar-31 Oct (with some closed days during the mid-week off-peak season). Opening times vary throughout the season and Guests are advised to check online or call the information line on 0870 444 4466 in advance of their visit

A£17.00-£27.00 C(4-11)£15.50-£20.00. Advance booking adds value, visit the website or call 0870 444 4466 for more information

Transport Museums

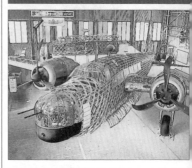

Brooklands Museum

Brooklands Road Weybridge Surrey KT13 0QN

Tel: 01932 857381 Fax: 01932 855465

www.brooklandsmuseum.com

[J10/11 A3 & M25. Plenty of on site parking available]

Brooklands was the birthplace of British motorsport and aviation. From 1907 when it opened, to 1987 when the British aerospace factory closed, it was a world-renowned centre of engineering excellence. The museum opened in 1991 on 30 acres of the original 1907 motor racing circuit and features Brooklands racing cars and historic aircraft which include Sopwith Camel, Wellington bomber and harrier jump-jet as well as related historic buildings. Home also the John Cobb's 24 litre Napier-Railton. The 'Grand Prix' and 'Fastest on Earth' exhibition in the restored motoring village tell the story of racing and record-breaking activities at the Brooklands Track from 1907.

All year Tue-Sun, Summer 10.00-17.00, Winter 10.00-16.00. Closed Good Fri & Christmas week.

A£7.00 OAPs&Students£6.00 C(5-16)£5.00 Family Ticket (A2+C3 £18.00). Credit Cards accepted in shop only

Special Events

Auto Italia Spring Meeting
02/05/2004

Mayday Emergency Vehicles
03/05/2004

The Brooklands Society Annual Reunion. Napier
Railton Run
20/06/2004

Brooklands at Home. Napier Railton Run
29/08/2004

CAAC (American) Meet
03/10/2004

Auto Italia Autumn Meet
03/10/2004

Sussex

Animal Attractions

Fishers Farm Park

Newpound Lane Wisborough Green
Billingshurst West Sussex RH14 0EG
Tel: 01403 700063 Fax: 01403 700823
[Off A272. Signposted from all main roads approaching Wisborough Green]

Fishers Farm Park is a unique place to visit, mixing rural activities with up front fun and gives the whole family a wonderful day out. The farmyard and barns give children and adults the opportunity to see animals well cared for in a happy environment, close enough to touch - you can even enter some of the pens to say hello to the goats and lambs.
All year daily 10.00-17.00. Closed 25 & 26 Dec
Summer holidays A£8.25 C(3-16)£7.75 C£(age2)£4.50 OAPs£6.75. Prices are £1.00 less for the rest of the year

Holmbush Farm World

Crawley Road Faygate Horsham West Sussex RH12 4SE
Tel: 01293 851110 Fax: 01293 851704
Located on A264 between Horsham & Crawley. Off J11 of M23. Signposted on A264]

We offer an exciting, fun day out for the whole family with plenty to see and do. Children are encouraged to experience the farming way of life for themselves with our experienced staff always on hand to supervise the regular animal handling sessions.
Mar-end Oct daily 10.00-17.30.
A£4.25 C£3.75 Family Ticket (A2+C2) £15.00. Prices are subject to alteration

Seven Sisters Sheep Centre

The Fridays East Dean Eastbourne Sussex BN20 0DG

Tel: 01323 423207 Fax: 01323 423302
[4m W of Eastbourne off A259]

A family run farm for animal lovers of all ages, with over 45 British breeds of sheep and all the other farm favourites, tame enough to touch and feed. Daily bottle feeding sessions. Tractor trailer rides, tea room, gift shop and picnic area.
6 Mar-3 May (Lambing) & 3 July-5 Sept (Shearing) Mon-Fri 14.00-17.00, Sat & Sun and East Sussex school hols 11.00-17.00
A£3.50 C(2-15)£2.50 Concessions£3.00 Family Ticket £11.00

Arts, Crafts & Textiles

Brighton Museum & Art Gallery

Royal Pavilion Gardens Brighton East Sussex BN1 1EE

Tel: 01273 290900 Fax: 01273 292841

www.brighton.virtualmuseum.info

[M23 / A23: London A27: Lewes & Worthing. Rail: Brighton Station 15mins walk]

Brighton Museum & Art Gallery reopened on 4 May 2002 after undergoing major restoration. The new look Brighton Museum & Art Gallery features state of the art visitor facilities including a gift shop and cafe, a series of innovative redesigned galleries and wide-ranging collections brought to life using the latest interpretative techniques. Highlights include the nationally important collections of 20th century Art and Design, Fashion, Paintings, Ceramics and World Art. Wheelchair accessible with accessible toilet, baby changing facilities, passenger lift, gift shop and cafe.

Open Tues 10.00-19.00, Wed-Sat 10.00-17.00, Sun 14.00-17.00. Closed Mon, except Public Holidays when open 10.00-17.00. Closed 24-26 Dec, 1 Jan

Admission Free

Hastings Museum and Art Gallery

Johns Place Bohemia Road Hastings Sussex TN34 1ET
Tel: 01424 781155 Fax: 01424 781165
[Off A21 beside sports complex]

A wide variety of displays, including new dinosaur, local wildlife, and North American Indian galleries, also local industry and ironwork as well as painting and ceramics.
All year Mon-Fri 10.00-17.00, Sat 10.00-13.00 & 14.00-17.00, Sun 15.00-17.00
Admission Free

Hove Museum & Art Gallery

19 New Church Road Hove Sussex BN3 4AB

Tel: 01273 290200 Fax: 01273 292827

www.hove.virtualmuseum.info

[Rail: Hove 15-20mins walk. Bus: 1 / 1A / 6 / 6 / 49 all stop near entrance]

Following major redevelopment, Hove Museum & Art Gallery has been transformed into a centre of learning and enjoyment for people of all ages. Permanent displays include toys, film, local history, paintings and contemporary craft. There is also a continuous programme of temporary exhibitions.

All year Tue-Sat 10.00-17.00, Sun 14.00-17.00. Closed every Mon including Bank Hols, Good F 25-26 Dec, 1 Jan

Admission Free

Sculpture at Goodwood

Hat Hill Copse Goodwood Chichester
West Sussex PO18 0QP
Tel: 01243 538449 Fax: 01243 531853
[4m N of Chichester follow signs to Goodwood House from A285 located on Goodwood-East Dean Lane]

Contemporary British sculpture with changing displays. Works commissioned from major and emerging British artists.
25 Mar-31 Oct Thur-Sat & Bank Hol Mon 10.30-16.30
£10.00 C(under10)£Free

Festivals & Shows

Airbourne: Eastbourne International Airshow

Western Lawns and Seafront
King Edwards Parade Eastbourne BN21
Tel: 01323 411400 Fax: 01323 649574
[A22 from London, A259 from Hastings, A27 from Brighton]

Over 80 flying displays featuring Red Arrows, RAF, international aircraft and free fall parachutists. Also includes RAF ground display, vintage vehicles, children's entertainment, helicopter rides, trade stands and Grand Firework

...nale.
...ugust 12-15 2004, 10.00-18.00
...dmission Free

...oxgrove Minerva Series

...inerva Theatre Oaklands Park Chichester
...ussex PO19 6AP
...el: 01243 781312 Box Office
...his highly acclaimed annual series of interna-
...onal concerts has moved to a new venue - the
...inerva Theatre in Chichester, West Sussex. A
...elebratory opening season includes a Gala
...oncert with the Philharmonia Orchestra,
...elebrity Recital with Britain's best-known
...anist, John Lill, and concerts by Configure8,
...ungsbacka Piano Trio, Allegri String Quartet
...nd the Guildhall Strings. Please call 0118 981
...190 for further information.
...ctober 4-9 2004, 19.30
...rices vary from £11.00-£32.00

...righton Festival 2004

...righton East Sussex BN1 1EE
...el: 01273 700747 Fax: 01273 707505
...ngland's biggest arts festival takes place every
...lay in Brighton. Families will enjoy our opening
...hildren's Parade, circus, funfair and special
...hildren's theatre shows. With some 800 events
...ver 3 weeks, there is plenty to see and do in
...righton at Festival time.
...lay 1-23 2004

...righton Kite Festival

...tanmer Park Brighton East Sussex BN1 6JG
...el: 01273 582309
*...On A27 near Uni of Sussex, signposted on the
...ay from A23 & A27. Free parking available in the
...niversity]*

...his is a unique opportunity to experience and
...ke part in one of the country's premier kite
...stivals. In its 26th year Brighton Kite Flyers are
...roud to host one of the oldest, possibly even

'the' oldest, remaining kite festivals in the country and it still remains completely FREE (including car parking)! Enjoy an event in which everyone can participate regardless of age, physical
ability or experience - from children to 'world
class' fliers. An excellent weekend of fun with
something for all the family...
July 10-11 2004, 11.00-17.00
Admission Free

Corpus Christi Carpet of Flowers 2004

Cathedral of Our Lady and St. Philip Howard
Arundel Sussex BN18 9AY
Tel: 01903 882297 Fax: 01903 885335
*[A27 midway between Worthing / Chichester. Car
& coach parking in Mill Road by main Castle
entrance]*

Corpus Christi is celebrated each year 60 days
after Easter and has become a very special
event for the people of Arundel and its many
visitors. A unique event in this country, a carpet
of fresh flowers 93ft long is lain down the centre
aisle of the Cathedral which was first established by the Duke of Norfolk in 1877.
Photographs of the Carpet of Flowers are on
sale in the Cathedral.
*June 9-10 2004, 9th 09.30-21.00, 10th 10.30-
17.30*
Admission Free

Crawley Folk Festival

The Hawth Hawth Avenue Crawley Sussex
RH10 6YZ
Tel: 01293 553636 Box Office
Fax: 01293 533362
[M23 J10, follow signs Hawth Theatre]

A weekend of traditional and contemporary folk
and roots music from Britain, Ireland and
America. Stalls, Real Ale, Singaround,
Workshops.
June 25-27 2004 Fri pm only
Access to Dance and Foyer Stages, Bars &
Stalls £Free

East Preston Festival Week 2004

East Preston Littlehampton Sussex BN16 1HT
Tel: 01903 771161
[Various venues throughout East Preston which is off A259 from A27]

A village festival with over 65 events to suit all ages including sporting events, hobbies, Grand Festival Fete, Carnival Procession, Art and Flowers Exhibition, Antiques and Collectors Market, Open Gardens Day, Quizzes, Craft Fair, Musical Concerts and much more.
June 5-13 2004
Small admission fees charged, many events free

Hastings International Poetry Festival 'First of All'

Yelton Hotel The Byron Room White Rock Hastings East Sussex TN34 1JU
Tel: 01424 428855 / 201370
Fax: 01424 201370
[On the seafront. A21 from London to Hastings]

Arguably the finest poetry festival venue on the South Coast. Fully staffed restaurant and bars. Meet the Editors, enjoy the displayed poetry magazines, meet with your peers and perform your work to probably the most appreciative audience you will be among. Easy parking and literally on the beach. Festival laid out Cabaret Style. Seating for 200 plus.
November 6-7 2004
A£3.00, 2-Day Ticket £5.00

Herstmonceux Castle Medieval Festival

Herstmonceux Castle Herstmonceux Hailsham East Sussex BN27 1RN
Tel: 020 8416 0398 Fax: 020 8416 0398
[Off A271 signposted]

Herstmonceux Castle Medieval Festival is Britain's largest three-day celebration of the colourful Middle Ages. In this magical setting, history will come to life. Hundreds of combatants with cannon support will siege the castle walls. Mounted Knights will joust and Europe's finest archers will compete. Activities and entertainment for the whole family including fire-eaters, falconry, puppeteers, strolling minstrels, period craft stalls, living history village and kid's kingdom. 24hr recorded information available 09068 172902.
August 28-30 2004 10.00-18.00

Hickstead Showground (All England Jumping Course)

London Road Hickstead Haywards Heath Sussex RH17 5NU
Tel: 01273 834315 Fax: 01273 834452
[10m N of Brighton off A23]

The Royal International Horse Show and Hickstead hosts The British Jumping Derby. The complete family day out. 150 Trade Stands, Children's Fun Fair, bars and restaurants.
Royal Int'l Horse Show: July 21-25 2004. Derby Meeting: June 3-6 2004

International Championships (Hastings Direct)

International Lawn Tennis Centre Devonshire Park College Road Eastbourne BN21 4JJ
Tel: 01323 412000 / 411555
Fax: 01323 736373
[Close to seafront, theatres, hotels and town centre. A22 from London, A259 from Hastings, A27 from Brighton]

Pre-Wimbledon ladies tennis tournament in a garden party setting, featuring top tennis stars from the WTA tour.
June 12-19 2004. Gates open 10.00

LTA Tennis Tournaments

International Lawn Tennis Centre
Devonshire Park Eastbourne BN21 4JJ
Tel: 01323 411400 Fax: 01323 649574
Close to seafront & town centre. A22 from London, A259 from Hastings, A27 from Brighton]

A series of tournaments.
July 19-August 28 2004

Skate 2004

Eastbourne Seafront Prince William Parade
Eastbourne East Sussex BN21 4JJ
Tel: 01323 411400 Fax: 01323 736373
A22 from London, A259 from Hastings, A27 from Brighton]

One of the largest FREE In-line and Roller Skating festivals in the UK, open to all ages from artistic to extreme which anyone can join in. Features live music, demonstrations and competitions. Also features 'Saturday Night Skate' around the town and seafront.
July 24-25 2004, 10.00-18.00
Admission Free

South of England Centre

Selsfield Road Ardingly Haywards Heath Sussex
RH17 6TL
Tel: 01444 892700 Fax: 01444 892888
On B2028]

158 acres of parkland with lots of hard roads and permanent toilets. Includes a large pavilion or conferences.
Opens for various events throughout the year

Special Events

Spring Garden & Leisure Show
02/05/2004-03/05/2004

South of England Show
10/06/2004-12/06/2004
Experience everything the countryside has to offer from the magnificent dairy cattle to the world-beating equestrian attractions. The three-day event is also a showcase for hundreds of trade and craft exhibitors.

South of England Autumn Show
02/10/2004-30/10/2004

Festive Food and Drink Fayre
04/12/2004-05/12/2004

visions - The Festival of Visual Performance

Brighton Sussex
Tel: 01273 643194 Fax: 01273 643038
October 2004 sees Brighton get animated with visions 2004, Britain's largest festival of visual performance. visions 2004 shows off extraordinary contemporary theatre which uses puppetry and props in innovative ways, as well as performances for adults and children, there are exhibitions and film. Dramatic, daring and downright entertaining.
October 2004

Folk & Local History Museums

Ditchling Museum

Church Lane Ditchling Hassocks Sussex
BN6 8TB
Tel: 01273 844744 Fax: 01273 844744
[On B2116 off High St in old village school]

The Sussex Village of Ditchling, beneath the South Downs, has long been the home and workplace of many famous artists including Eric Gill - sculptor and engraver and Edward Johnston - calligrapher. Their work and that of other Ditchling craftsmen is on permanent display in the museum..
14 Feb-19 Dec Tue-Sat & Bank Hol Mon 10.30-17.00, Sun 14.00-17.00.
A£3.50 C(0-16)£Free OAPs£2.00

Henfield Museum

Henfield Hall Cooper's Way Henfield Sussex
BN5 9DB
Tel: 01273 492507
[On A281 Horsham to Brighton Road]

Local history including domestic objects, cos-
tume, agricultural tools, archaeology and geolo-
gy. Local paintings and photographs.
*All year Mon, Tue, Thur, Fri & Sat 10.00-12.00,
Wed & Sat 14.30-16.30*
Admission Free

Horsham Museum

9 The Causeway Horsham Sussex RH12 1HE
Tel: 01403 254959
*[In Horsham town centre, 3 min walk from Carfax.
Access from A24, A281, A264 and 9m from
M23]*

Set in a timber-framed Tudor house, Horsham
Museum is like no other in the country. With its
unique collection of prehistoric life including the
Rudgwick polacanthus dinosaur and dragon-
flies, the Museum will delight children and adults
alike. With over 100 years of collecting, the
Museum has a wealth of objects on display
*All year Mon-Sat 10.00-17.00. Closed public hol-
idays*
Admission Free

The Priest House

North Lane West Hoathly near East Grinstead
Sussex RH19 4PP
Tel: 01342 810479
[Off B2028]

The 15th-century house has been converted
into a small folk museum with a variety of interesting exhibits including needlework, furniture,
kitchen and agricultural implements. The house
is set in a traditional English cottage garden.
*2 Mar-31 Oct Tue-Sat (& Bank Hol Mons) 10.30-
17.30, Sun 12.00-17.30. Also open Mon during*

Aug 10.30-17.30
A£2.70 C(5-15)£1.35 Concessions£2.40

Weald and Downland Open Air Museum

Singleton Chichester West Sussex PO18 0EU
Tel: 01243 811348 Fax: 01243 811475

www.wealddown.co.uk

*[On A286 between Midhurst & Chichester.
Discounted combined ticket on Stagecoach
Coastline Bus. Plenty of free parking on site]*

Situated in a beautiful downland setting, this
museum displays more than 45 rescued historic
buildings from south-east England. The buildings range from medieval houses to a 19th century schoolhouse and Victorian labourers cottages. There is a medieval farmstead complete
with animals, seven period gardens, a lakeside
cafe, indoor and outdoor picnic areas, a working watermill, rural crafts, trade demonstrations
and a working Tudor kitchen in an original Tudor
service building. The first major timber gridshell
building in Britain houses a conservation workshop and the museum's collection of rural artefacts.

*All year Mar-Oct daily 10.30-18.00, Nov-Feb Sat
& Sun 10.30-16.00, 26 Dec-2 Jan & Feb half
term daily 10.30-16.00*

A£7.50 C(5+)£4.00 OAPs£6.50 Family Ticket
(A2+C3) £20.00

Special Events

Celebrate the Taste
11/04/2004-12/04/2004

uality fare to sample and buy from the local pro-
ucers of the south east, plus tastings, cookery
lasses and demonstrations

ustainable Building Event
6/05/2004
iscover low impact, sustainable building prod-
cts and techniques for the 21st century, includ-
g presentations, demonstrations and a wide
ariety of exhibits

alf Term Activities
1/05/2004-04/06/2004
reative activities for accompanied children

eavy Horse Spectacular
6/06/2004
n unforgettable day for lovers of heavy horses,
ith horse drawn vehicles, magnificent displays
nd a grand parade, all with continuous ringside
ommentary

arly Music Afternoon
4/07/2004
ongs and dance from medieval Tudor and Stuart
mes. Time: from 14.00

are and Traditional Breeds Show
5/07/2004
ver 500 cattle, sheep, pigs, goats and poultry
ke part in this delightful agricultural show for rare
nd traditional breeds of farm animals

hildren's Activity Wednesdays
8/07/2004-25/08/2004
eally different hands-on activities for accompa-
ed children including countryside arts and crafts,
udor cooking, plus meeting the Shire horses and
rm animals

**he Roses of Eyam Open Air Theatre (evening
erformance)**
1/08/2004-14/08/2004

t Roche at the Trundle
6/08/2004
n open air service on the site of the chapel of St
oche, patron saint of healing. Meet at the
rundle, transport up the hill provided if required

utumn Countryside Celebration
2/10/2004-03/10/2004
ome and experience the sights, sounds and
mells of a traditional harvest: enjoy heavy horses
loughing, vintage tractors and a steam threshing
emonstration

alf Term Activities
5/10/2004-29/10/2004

Creative activities for accompanied children, also
incorporating the Rural History Re-enactment
workshop which runs from 28-30 Oct

Tree Dressing
05/12/2004
*A wonderful celebration, for all the family, of the
life giving properties of trees. Make a lantern
(bring a jam jar!) and join the procession to dress
the tree as darkness falls. Time: from 12.30*

Tastes of a Tudor Christmas
26/12/2004-02/01/2005
*See Bayleaf farmhouse decorated for Christmas
as it would have been 400 years ago and enjoy
festive sweetmeats and warming drinks from the
Tudor kitchen*

Gardens & Horticulture

Borde Hill Garden

Balcombe Road Haywards Heath Sussex
RH16 1XP

Tel: 01444 450326 Fax: 01444 440427

www.bordehill.co.uk

*[1.5m N of Haywards Heath, 3m from M23, sign-
posted from Cuckfield / Haywards Heath. Plenty
of on site parking available]*

Glorious heritage garden offers beauty for all
seasons. Spring is heralded by magnificent
magnolias, rhododendron and azaleas, blending
into summer with fragrant roses and herbaceous plants, developing into rich autumn borders before winter's architectural splendour.
Distinctive formal 'garden rooms', such as the
Rose and Italian Garden, combine with informal
areas like the Azalea Ring, Garden of Allah and
Round Dell. It is a plantsman's paradise, with

rare trees and shrubs introduced in the 1900s from around the world. Victorian greenhouses. 200 acres of parkland affords panoramic views; woodland and lakeside walks to explore and picnic. Wheelchair access. Dogs on leads welcome. Extensive special events programme. Jeremy's Restaurant, Lavender Tea Rooms and Millbrook Garden Centre.

All year daily 10.00-18.00 (or dusk if earlier.) Borde Hill House: open during Rose Celebration Week, 22-27 June

A£6.00 C£3.50 OAPs£5.00. Reduced charges available mid-Oct-mid Mar. Pre booked (20+) guided tours available

Special Events

Easter Eggcitement
03/04/2004-16/04/2004
A free Easter egg on completion of the Easter Bunny Trail and try your hand at egg painting

Camellia, Magnolia and Rhododendron Festival
18/04/2004
Magnificent exhibits of rhododendrons, camellias and magnolias. Nurseries selling a wide variety of plants

Sotheby's Valuation Day
28/04/2004
The RHS and Sotheby's invite you to a valuation day (2 items). Time: 10.00-16.00 with a garden tour by the Head Gardener at 11.00 and 14.30. Cost: A£5.00 plus £1.00 for garden tour

Sculpture in the Garden
01/05/2004-31/05/2004
Surrey Sculpture Society bring the Garden alive with over 60 sculptures

Fun, Fur and Feathers for Kids
16/05/2004
Learn, touch and enjoy a variety of animals and come and bounce for free

Forrest Trail
29/05/2004-06/06/2004
Uncover clues to discover trees and plants collected by the great plant hunter, George Forrest. Enter our drawing competition, 14.00-17.00 each day

Rolls-Royce and Bentley Show
06/06/2004
Cars from pre-war to present day

Painting Workshop with Professional Artist
17/06/2004
Watercolour painting with artist and tutor Julie King. Cost: £30.00, please call 01892 544695 book

Rose Celebration Week
22/06/2004-27/06/2004
Visit Borde Hill House decked with roses (weekdays 14.00-16.00, weekends 11.00-16.00). Cost: A£8.00 OAPs£7.00. Enjoy a guided tour of the Rose Garden at 14.00

Borde Hill Collector's Plant Fair
04/07/2004
Specialist growers and experts selling a wide range of plants

Groundlings Theatre Company
22/07/2004-25/07/2004
A series of plays performed by the nationally acclaimed Groundlings Theatre Company. 22 & 24 July - As You Like It, 19.30, A£9.50 Concessions£7.50. 23 & 25 July - Taming of the Shrew, 19.30, A£9.50 Concessions£7.50, 24 July - Wind in the Willows, 14.30, A£7.50 Concessions£5.50, 25 July - The Wizard of Oz, 14.30, A£7.50 Concessions£5.50. Please call 023 9273 7370 to book

Summer Fun for Kids
01/08/2004-31/08/2004
Different activity each weekday afternoon. New for 2004, Tractor rides Mon-Fri afternoons to allow you to explore the Parkland

Brass Bands
01/08/2004-29/08/2004
Held on 1, 8, 15, 22, 29 Aug only. Relax and enjoy the sounds of Sussex bands

Fuchsia Show
01/08/2004
Displays of fuchsias, plant sales and guided tours

A Night at the Proms
07/08/2004
Full-blooded Proms programme of music played by British Concert Orchestra with solo Spitfire and Hurricane fly pass, finishing with grand Fireworks Finale. Time: 19.30-22.30. Cost: A£18.00 C£7.00

Country Fair
21/08/2004-22/08/2004
Spectacular show by leading Carriage Drivers alongside country fare. Cost: A£6.00 C£3.50 Family Ticket (A2+C2) £15.00

Halloween Week
25/10/2004-29/10/2004
Ghostly magic, scary rides and spooky trails. Find where the ghosts lurk on a tractor ride. Time: 13.00-16.00

Christmas Craft Fair
04/12/2004-05/12/2004
Crafts and gifts for all your presents, plus Santa's Grotto

Santa's Grotto
05/12/2004-24/12/2004
Come and leave your wish list with Santa

Denmans Garden

Clock House Denmans Lane Fontwell Arundel Sussex BN18 0SU

Tel: 01243 542808 Fax: 01243 544064

www.denmans-garden.co.uk

[5m E of Chichester on A27]

A beautiful garden designed for year round interest - through use of forms, colour and texture. Although nearly 4 acres in size, its layout is such that the visitor enjoys lots of quiet sitting areas, for it is punctuated with little incidents of statuary, a nice pot or a warm sitting corner. The home of John Brookes, renowned garden designer and writer it is a garden full of ideas to be interpreted within smaller home spaces. Gravel is used extensively in the garden both to walk on and as a growing medium so that you walk through the plantings rather than past them. A dry gravel 'stream' meanders down to a large natural looking pond. There is a walled

garden and a conservatory - now alive with the chatter of budgerigars - and a larger glass area for tender plants.

1 Mar-31 Oct daily 09.00-17.00

A£3.50 C(4+)£1.95 C(0-4)Free OAPs£3.00. Groups (15+ people) £2.80

Discount Offer: Two Full Paying Adults For The Price Of One.

Holly Gate Cactus Garden and Nursery

Billingshurst Road Ashington West Sussex RH20 3BB
Tel: 01903 892930
[10m equidistant between Horsham and Worthing on A24 0.5m off B2133]

A mecca for the cactus enthusiast, with more than 30,000 succulents and cactus plants, including many rare types.
All year daily 09.00-17.00. Closed 25-26 Dec
A£2.00 C&OAPs£1.50

Pashley Manor Gardens

Pashley Road Ticehurst Wadhurst Sussex TN5 7HE

Tel: 01580 200888 Fax: 01580 200102

www.pashleymanorgardens.com

[On B2099 off A21 follow brown signposts. Plenty of parking on site]

A Winner of the HHA/Christies Garden of the Year Award. Pashley Manor Gardens offer a sumptuous blend of romantic landscaping, imaginative plantings and fine old trees, fountains, springs and large ponds. This is a quintessentially English Garden of a very individual character with exceptional views to the surrounding valleyed fields. Many eras of English history are reflected here, typifying the tradition of the English Country House and its garden. Member of the Historic Houses Association.

Garden & Tea Rooms: 6 Apr-30 Sept Tue, Wed, Thur, Sat & Bank Hol Mon 11.00-17.00. Gardens also open Oct Mon-Fri 10.00-16.00

A£6.00 C(under6)£Free OAPs&C(6-16)£5.50. Season Tickets: A£20.00 OAPs£18.00. Admission for Tulip Festival and Summer Flower Festival A£6.50

Special Events

Sculpture at Pashley
06/04/2004-30/09/2004
Pashley's Gardens make an ideal setting for Sculpture. The work of eminent sculptors will be on display and for sale

Tulip Festival with Bloms Bulbs
29/04/2004-03/05/2004
Spectacular display of massed tulips from Chelsea Gold Medal winning growers, Bloms fill the gardens

Plant Fairs
16/05/2004-15/08/2004
Spring Plant Fair - 16 May and Summer Plant Fair 15 Aug. These fairs offer the chance to buy from approximately 30 first class Nurseries specialising in unusual, rare, herbaceous and alpine plants and shrubs

Summer Flower Festival
17/06/2004-20/06/2004
Stunning flower arrangements by members of the Wadhurst & District Flower Club will be displayed in the beautiful Great Hall of the Manor, complemented by an exhibition in the Garden Room of botanical paintings and drawings by leading artists. In the Garden there will be magnificent displays of roses; there are over 50 different varieties planted in the garden. The renowned firm of rose growers, Peter Beales Roses, will be leading walks around the Garden on 19 June

Two Evenings of Open Air Opera at Pashley
23/07/2004-24/07/2004
23 July - La Boheme, 24 July - The Marriage of Figaro. Experience open-air performances of two popular operas

Sussex Guild Craft Show
04/09/2004-05/09/2004
Works on show and for sale will include; glass, ceramics, jewellery, furniture, textile arts, metal work, quilting, bookbinding, letter cutting and carving. Time: 10.00-17.00

Charity Open Day
24/09/2004
Macmillan coffee morning, 10.30-13.00

West Dean Gardens

West Dean Chichester West Sussex PO18 8Q

Tel: 01243 818210 / 811301

Fax: 01243 811342

www.westdean.org.uk

Signposted off A286. Plenty of on site parking available]

An historic garden of 35 acres in a tranquil downland setting. Noted for its 300ft long pergola, mixed and herbaceous borders, rustic summerhouses and specimen trees. The recently restored walled garden contains a fruit collection, Victorian glasshouses, an apple store and a large working kitchen garden, restaurant and shop. Member of the Historic Houses Association. Photography of the gardens only is permitted. Awarded the Historic Houses Association/Christie's Garden of the Year Award 2002.

Mar, Apr & Oct daily 11.00-17.00, May-Sept daily 10.30-17.00

A£5.50 C£2.50 OAPs£5.00 Family Ticket (A2+C2) £13.00

Discount Offer: One Child Free When One Adult or OAP Ticket Purchased.

Special Events

The Garden Event
19/06/2004-20/06/2004
The Garden Event captures all things horticultural in one venue. Specialist nurseries, garden tools, planters and sundries. Partake of local food and wines. A rare opportunity to glimpse behind the facade of West Dean House. Small supplementary charge applies

Pergola Open Air Theatre
28/06/2004-10/07/2004
Two plays are performed on alternative nights. No Sunday performance. Time: 20.00. Tickets: Please call 01243 780192 from 1 May to reserve your tickets

Chilli Fiesta
07/08/2004-08/08/2004
Not to be missed is the wonderful and vast collection of chillies (170 chilli and 40 sweet peppers) grown in the magnificently restored Victorian Glasshouses and displayed in pristine rows in every shape and size ranging from serene green through to red hot!

Totally Tomato Show
11/09/2004-12/09/2004
The Tomato Happening! Skin them, squeeze them, juice them, reduce them, even eat them as they are - tomatoes - so versatile - no kitchen or

garden should be without them! Over 100 varieties of tomatoes grown in the traditional manner. Cookery demonstrations and tours of the Glasshouses and Gardens make this the really Totally Tomato Show

Apple Affair
16/10/2004-17/10/2004
Apple Affair is one of the many events taking place around the country during this time to celebrate our wonder heritage of over 6,000 varieties of apple and traditional orchards. West Dean's collection contains over 100 varieties of apple. A range of 'appley' events are planned

Heritage & Industrial

Story of Rye

Rye Heritage Centre Strand Quay Rye Sussex TN31 7AY
Tel: 01797 226696 Fax: 01797 223460
[At Strand Quay in Rye, follow TIC signposts]

A complete sound and light show bringing the history of Rye alive! Follow the smugglers' footsteps and experience the medieval life and times of Rye as it was in bygone ages.
Apr-Oct Mon-Sat 09.30-17.00, Sun 10.00-17.00, Nov-Mar Mon-Sat 10.00-16.00, Sun closed
Centre or Personal Stereo Tour: A£2.50 C£1.00 Concessions£1.50

Discount Offer: Two For The Price Of One.

Historical

Anne of Cleves House Museum

52 Southover High Street Lewes Sussex BN7 1JA
Tel: 01273 474610
This 16th century town house was given to Anne of Cleves by Henry VIII as part of her divorce settlement.
1 Jan-29 Feb Tue-Sat 10.00-17.00, 1 Mar-31 Oct Tue-Sat 10.00-17.00, Sun-Mon & Bank Hols 11.00-17.00, 1 Nov-31 Dec Tue-Sat 10.00-

17.00. Closed 24-28 Dec
A£2.90 C£1.45 Concessions£2.60 Family Ticket
(A2+C2) £7.35, (A1+C4) £5.90

Arundel Castle

Arundel Sussex BN18 9AB

Tel: 01903 882173 Fax: 01903 884581

www.arundelcastle.org

*[A27 signposted. Free coach park opposite
Castle entrance. Ample FREE car parking on site.
Rail: Arundel Station 10mins walk from Castle.
Hourly service to Arundel from London Victoria]*

The private home and fortified castle of the
Dukes of Norfolk since 1067, Arundel Castle is a
treasure trove. Its location is awe-inspiring; dom-
inating the town of Arundel and with fantastic
views to the South Coast from the Medieval
Keep. Fine collections of furniture, paintings,
tapestries, armour, all fitting comfortably within
the walls of what is obviously a beloved family
home. Some of the castle rooms have recently
been renovated to echo their Victorian past and
there is an ongoing plan of refurbishment under
the guidance of The Duchess. The gardens continue to evolve having been restored to their former Victorian glory together with two
Glasshouses, reconstructed following the original plans discovered in the Castle Archives. The
charming Fitzalan Chapel in the grounds of the
Castle, burial place of many of The Dukes of
Norfolk, is a restful haven for quiet contemplation and has a small but beautiful white-planted
garden. Limited disabled access, please call for
details. Photography allowed outside only.

Special events throughout the season.

*1 Apr-31 Oct Sun-Fri (closed Sat), Castle Rooms
12.00-17.00, Grounds, Gardens, Shop,
Restaurant, Fitzalan Chapel Keep 11.00-17.00*

A£9.50 C£6.00 Concessions£7.50 Family Ticket
(A2+ up to C5) £26.50. Group rates (for 20+
people): A£8.00 C£5.00 Concessions£6.50

**Discount Offer: Two for the Price of
One.**

Special Events

Antiques and Audacity Fair
13/05/2004-16/05/2004

Medieval Festival
30/05/2004-31/05/2004

Fanfare for Food
01/09/2004-30/09/2004
*Event to be held in Sept but specific dates to be
confirmed*

Hallowe'en Fireworks Spooktacular
31/10/2004

Bodiam Castle

Bodiam Robertsbridge East Sussex TN32 5UA
Tel: 01580 830436 Fax: 01580 830398
[3m S of Hawkhurst, 2m E of A21 Hurst Green]

One of the most famous and evocative castles
in Britain, Bodiam was built in 1385, both as a
defence and a comfortable home. The exterior
virtually complete and the ramparts rise dramatically above the moat below.
*All year 1 Jan-15 Feb Sat & Sun 10.00-16.00, 16
Feb-31 Oct daily 10.00-18.00, 1 Nov-6 Feb Sat-
Sun 10.00-16.00. Bodiam Castle is often used by
education groups during mornings in term time*
A£4.20 C£2.10 Family Ticket £10.50

Glynde Place

The Street Glynde Lewes Sussex BN8 6SX

Tel: 01273 858224 Fax: 01273 858224

www.glyndeplace.com

[Off A27 between Lewes & Eastbourne. Plenty of on site parking]

Glynde Place is a magnificent Elizabethan manor house with fine views of the South Downs. It was built in 1569 from local flint and stone from Normandy but was extensively added on to in the 18th century, with the building of a new stable block, a new village church and the erection of the distinctive lead wyverns. Inside the house there is a collection of Old Masters, family portraits, furniture, embroidery and silver all belonging to the family who lived there for over 400 years. The house is surrounded by a garden giving spectacular views across the park towards the Pevensey Marshes.

June-Sept Sun, Wed & Bank Hol Mon 14.00-17.00

A£5.50 C£2.75. Group rates available

Hammerwood Park

Hammerwood East Grinstead Sussex RH19 3QE
Tel: 01342 850594 Fax: 01342 850864

Gardens and Grounds of Herstmonceux Castle

Herstmonceux Hailsham East Sussex BN27 1RN

Tel: 01323 833816 Fax: 01323 834499

www.herstmonceux-castle.com

[Located just outside the village of Herstmonceux on A271, entrance on Wartling Road. Plenty of free on site parking]

Experience the peace and tranquillity of 550 acres of glorious woodland and Elizabethan gardens surrounding a 15th century moated castle. Visitors Centre, Children's Woodland play area, Tearoom, Nature trail and Gift Shop.

Gardens & Grounds: 9 Apr-24 Oct daily 10.00-8.00. Castle: not open to the public, however guided tours are conducted Sun-Fri subject to availability, and at an additional cost, please call for further details

Gardens & Grounds: A£4.50 C(under15)£3.00 C(under5)£Free Concessions£3.50 Family Ticket (A2+C3 or A1+C4) £12.00. Joint ticket available with the Herstmonceux Science Centre. Castle Tours: A£2.50 C(under15)£1.00 C(under5)£Free. Group booking rates for 15+ call 01323 834457

[3.5m E of East Grinstead on A264 Tunbridge Wells 1m W of Holtye]

Said by visitors to be the most interesting house in Sussex. Built in 1792 as a temple of Apollo, the house was the first work of Latrobex, the architect of the White House and The Capitol Building in Washington DC, USA.

1June-end Sept Wed, Sat & Bank Hol Mon 14.00-17.30. Guided tour starts 14.05

A£5.00 C£1.50

Lewes Castle and Barbican House Museum

169 High Street Lewes Sussex BN7 1YE
Tel: 01273 486290 Fax: 01273 486990
[Lewes is accessed from A27, A26 and A275]

Lewes Castle, built shortly after the Norman Conquest of 1066, dominates the county town. Climb to the top and you'll see outstanding views of the local region.

All year Tue-Sat 10.00-17.30, Sun-Mon & Bank Hols 11.00-17.30. Closed Mon in Jan & 24-28 Dec. Castle closes at dusk during winter

A£4.30 C(5-15)£2.15 Concessions£3.80 Family Ticket (A2+C2) £11.00, (A1+C4) £8.75

Newtimber Place

Newtimber Place Newtimber Hassocks Sussex BN6 9BU
Tel: 01273 833104 Fax: 01273 835099
[A23 towards Brighton, Pyecombe Exit (Signposted Hassocks)]

Newtimber Place is a Sussex moated house, built of flint and brick with a roof of Horsham Stone. The manor is mentioned in the Domesday Book. The current house is mainly late 17th century.

May-Aug Thur 14.00-17.00 by appointment only
A£3.50 C£0.50

Preston Manor

Preston Drove Brighton Sussex BN1 6SD

Tel: 01273 292770 Fax: 01273 292771

www.prestonmanor.virtualmuseum.info

[M23 / A23. Rail: Brighton. Bus: 5 / 5a from Old Steine & 52a from station]

A delightful Manor House which powerfully evokes the atmosphere of an Edwardian gentry home both 'Upstairs' and 'Downstairs'. Explore over twenty rooms on four floors, from the superbly renovated servants' quarters in the basement, to the attic bedrooms on the top floor. Adjacent to Preston Park, the house also comprises picturesque walled gardens and a pet cemetery. Wheelchair accessible (garden only), gift shop.

All year Tue-Sat 10.00-17.00, Sun 14.00-17.00 Mon 13.00-17.00, Bank Hol Mon 10.00-17.00. Closed Good Fri & 25-26 Dec

A£3.70 C(under16)£2.15 Concessions£3.00 Family Ticket (A2+C4) £9.55, (A1+C4) £5.85. Joint ticket to the Royal Pavilion: A£8.20. Group of 20+ A£3.15. Guided Tours: up to 20 people £30.00, thereafter £1.50 per person. School Groups C(under16)£2.15, Students (with ID) £3.00. Winter Concessions (Oct-Feb) £1.85. Prices valid until 31 March 2004

Royal Pavilion

Brighton Sussex BN1 1EE

Tel: 01273 290900 Fax: 01273 292871

www.royalpavilion.org.uk

[A23, M23 central Brighton. Rail: Brighton 10mins)]

Eccentric, Extravagant, Extraordinary... Universally acclaimed as one of the most exotically beautiful buildings in the British Isles, the Royal Pavilion is the magnificent former seaside residence of King George IV. Decorated in Chinese taste with an Indian exterior, this Regency palace is quite breathtaking. Restored Regency gardens, tearooms, guided tours (telephone 01273 292820 / 292822) and giftshop. Wheelchair accessible (ground floor only), accessible toilet, baby changing facilities, tactile tours for visually impaired, Sennheiser system for hard-of-hearing. Events for children and families throughout the year, please call 01273 290900 for more details.

All year daily Apr-Sept 09.30-17.45, Oct-Mar 10.00-17.15. Closed 25-26 Dec

A£5.80 C(under16)£3.40 Concessions£4.00 Family Tickets (A2+C4) £15.00 (A1+C4) £9.20. Joint ticket to Preston Manor £8.20. Group rates 20+ A£4.90. Winter Concession rates: School parties 20+ Oct-Feb only £2.50. Guided tours: up to 20 people £25.00, thereafter £1.25 per person, UK School Parties £15.00, thereafter £0.75 per person. Prices subject to change in April 2004

Discount Offer: One Free Admission with One Full Paying Adult.

Rye Castle Museum

East Street Rye Sussex TN31 7JY
Tel: 01797 226728
[Signposted as either Ypres Tower or East Street Museum]

Housed in stone tower built as a fortification in 1249 later used for three hundred years as the town prison - the cells remain. The Museum is now on two sites, at East Street is Rye's Fire Engine and exhibitions about Rye's past.
Easter-31 Oct Thur-Mon 10.30-17.00 (closed 13.00-14.00), Winter Sat & Sun only 10.30-15.30
Single Site: A£1.90 C£1.00 Concessions£1.50. Both sites: A£2.90 C£1.50
OAPs&Students£2.00

Standen

West Hoathly Road East Grinstead
West Sussex RH19 4NE
Tel: 01342 323029 Fax: 01342 316424
[2m S of East Grinstead, signposted from B2110]

A family house built in the 1890s, designed by Philip Webb, friend of William Morris, and a showpiece of the Arts and Crafts Movement. It is decorated throughout with Morris carpets, fabrics and wallpapers, complemented by contemporary paintings, tapestries and furniture.

27 Mar-31 Oct Wed-Sun & Bank Hol Mon 11.00-17.00. Garden: 27 Mar-31 Oct Wed-Sun 11.00-18.00, 5 Nov-19 Dec 11.00-15.00

House & Garden: A£6.00 C£3.00 Family Ticket £15.00. Garden: A£3.20 C£1.60

Military & Defence Museums

Newhaven Fort

Fort Road Newhaven East Sussex BN9 9DS
Tel: 01273 517622 Fax: 01273 512059
[Follow signs from A259 at Newhaven]

A Victorian coastal fortress built by order of Lord
Palmerston in the 1860s. Covering 10 acres,
overlooking Seaford Bay, this restored fort has
barrack rooms now housing WWI and WWII military and wartime interactive and audio-visual
displays and dioramas.
*1 Mar-31 Oct daily 10.30-18.00, Nov Sat & Sun
10.30-16.00. Closed Dec-Feb*
A£5.00 C£3.50 Family Ticket (A2+C2) £14.90
OAPs£4.55

Tangmere Military Aviation Museum Trust

Tangmere Chichester West Sussex PO20 2ES

Tel: 01243 775223 Fax: 01243 789490

www.tangmere-museum.org.uk

[3m E of Chichester on A27 well signposted.
Limited parking on site]

Established in 1982, the museum tells the story
of military flying from the earliest days to the
present time, with emphasis on the RAF at
Tangmere. Among several aircraft on display are
the actual world speed record-breaking Meteor
and Hunter jets. There is now a special tribute
to Spitfire designer, R.J Mitchell. For the
younger visitor there are many butons to push,
and the chance to 'fly' a Spitfire simulator.

Essentially the Museum is about people, their
bravery, endurance and sacrifice. A unique feature is the Memorial Garden, where visitors can
spend time in quiet and thoughtful reflection.
You will find an intimate and friendly atmosphere
so often lacking in other museums of this kind.

*Mar-Oct daily 10.00-17.30, Feb & Nov daily
10.00-16.30*

A£5.00 C£1.50 OAPs£4.00 Family Ticket
£11.00

Mills - Water & Wind

West Blatchington Windmill

97 Holmes Avenue Hove Sussex BN3 7LE

Tel: 01273 776017

www.blatchington.virtualmuseum.info

[Easily accessible from A27 Brighton Bypass.
Bus: 5B / 27]

Dating from the 1820s, this grade II listed building still has the original mill workings in place
over 5 floors. Discover how grain is turned into
flour in a traditional windmill, and explore a fascinating display of historical milling and agriculture exhibits. Wheelchair accessible (ground
floor only), accessible toilet, cafe.

May-Sept Sun & Bank Hol only 14.30-17.00. Groups by prior arrangement other days

A£1.00 C£0.50. Prices valid until 31 March 2004

Natural History Museums

Booth Museum of Natural History

194 Dyke Road Brighton Sussex BN1 5AA

Tel: 01273 292777 Fax: 01273 292778

www.booth.virtualmuseum.info

[M23 & A23. 1.5m NW of town centre on Dyke Road, opposite Dyke Road Park. Bus: 27 / 27A]

Over half a million specimens and natural history literature and data extending back over three centuries are housed in this fascinating museum, including hundreds of British birds displayed in recreated natural settings. Plus butterfly skeletons, whale and dinosaur bones. Exhibitions and events. Gift kiosk. The Discovery Laboratory offers interactive displays exploring the Booth's collections. Wheelchair accessible via rear door, shop.

All year Mon-Wed & Fri-Sat 10.00-17.00, Sun 14.00-17.00. Closed Thur, Good Fri, 25-26 Dec & 1 Jan

Admission Free

Places of Worship

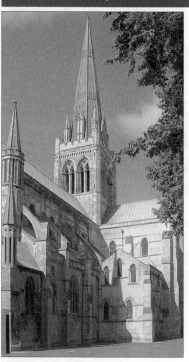

Chichester Cathedral

West Street Chichester Sussex PO19 1PX

Tel: 01243 782595 Fax: 01243 812499

www.chichestercathedral.org.uk

[City centre]

In the heart of the city, this fine Cathedral has been a centre of Christian worship and community life for 900 years and is the site of the Shrine of St Richard. Its treasures range from Romanesque stone carvings to 20th century works of art by Feibusch, Benker-Schirmer, Chagall, Piper, Procktor, Skelton, Sutherland and Jackson. A delightful restaurant on site offering a selection of homemade food, snacks and drinks. Shop situated adjacent to Cathedral. Guided tours are available; general or specialist. Loop system during Cathedral services; touch and hearing centre and Braille guide for the blind. Assistance dogs only.

End Mar-end Sept daily 07.15-19.00, end Sept-end Mar 09.15-18.00

Admission Free - Donations invited

Special Events

Flower Festival
03/06/2004-05/06/2004

Southern Cathedrals Music Festival
15/07/2004-18/07/2004

St Mary's Church

Lion Street Rye Sussex TN31 7LB
Tel: 01797 224935
For 900 years the Parish Church has dominated the hill on which Rye stands. Climb the tower for a wonderful all round view and see the inner workings of the oldest functioning church tower clock in the country.
All year daily 09.00-18.00 or dusk if earlier
Tower: A£2.00 C£1.00

Railways

Lavender Line

Isfield Uckfield East Sussex TN22 5XB
Tel: 01825 750515 / 09068 800645
Fax: 01825 750515
www.lavender-line.co.uk

[A26 Lewes-Uckfield, signposted. Rail: Uckfield & Lewes Tel: National Rail Enquiries 08457 484950

(24 hours, 7 days a week). By bus: Service 729 runs Brighton-Tun Wells, calls at Isfield Station 7 days a week. Please call 01424 433711 for timetable details]

The Lavender Line operates a 1 mile restored section of the Lewes-Uckfield Line closed in 1969. Steam and diesel hauled trains run every 20 minutes during open days. On site are 'Cinders Buffet', gift shop, signal box, family area, museum and model railway, picnic area. Ticket valid all day for unlimited rides.

All year Sun, Summer 11.00-17.00, Winter 11.00-16.00, plus June-Aug Sat 11.00-17.00, Aug Wed-Thur 11.00-16.30. Open Bank Hols. Santa Specials run in Nov & Dec, please call for further details. Closed Christmas & New Year

A£5.00 C(under3)£Free C£3.00 OAPs£4.00 Family Ticket (A2+C3) £14.00. Pay once and ride all day. Prices may change on special event days. Site entrance only £1.50

Special Events

Bank Holiday Trains
09/04/2004-12/04/2004

Bank Holiday Trains
01/05/2004-31/05/2004
To run on 1, 2, 3, 29, 30, 31 May only

Fathers Day
20/06/2004

Goods Train Weekend
10/07/2004-11/07/2004

Vintage Weekend
07/08/2004-08/08/2004

Bank Holiday Trains
28/08/2004-30/08/2004

Goods Train Weekend
11/09/2004-12/09/2004

Santa Trains
28/11/2004-22/12/2004
Held on 28 Nov, 4, 5, 11, 12, 18, 19, 20, 21, 22 Dec only

Roman Era

Bignor Roman Villa and Museum

Bignor Lane Bignor Pulborough West Sussex RH20 1PH

Tel: 01798 869259 Fax: 01798 869259

[Approx 6m N of Arundel, signposted from both A29 (Bognor-Billinghurst) and A285 (Chichester-Petworth). Plenty of parking on site]

Discovered in 1811, this Roman house was built on a grand scale. It is one of the largest known, and has spectacular mosaics. The heating system can also be seen, and various finds from excavations are on show. The longest mosaic in Britain (82ft) is on display here in its original position. Other mosaics in situ include Ganynede, Venus & Cupid Gladiators and Medusa. No dogs permitted.

Mar & Apr Tue-Sun & Bank Hol 10.00-17.00, May & Oct daily 10.00-17.00, June-Sept daily 10.00-18.00

A£4.00 C£1.70 OAPs£2.85. Groups of 10+ people: A£3.20 C£1.35 OAPs£2.30. Guided Tours: (max. of 30 per tour) £18.50

Discount Offer: 20% Discount On Production Of Voucher.

Fishbourne Roman Palace

Salthill Road Fishbourne Chichester Sussex PO19 3QR
Tel: 01243 785859 Fax: 01243 539266
[N of A259 in Fishbourne]

Built in AD43 and discovered by accident in 1960, Fishbourne Roman Palace was probably Roman Britain's largest domestic building; the sumptuous home of King Tiberius Claudius Togidubnus. Today visitors can view Britain's largest collection of in-situ mosaics

Jan Sat & Sun 10.00-16.00, Feb daily 10.00-16.00, Mar-July daily 10.00-17.00, Aug daily 10.00-18.00, Sept-Oct daily 10.00-17.00, Nov-15 Dec & 18-19 Dec daily 10.00-16.00
A£5.20 C(5-15)£2.70 Concessions£4.50

Science - Earth & Planetary

Foredown Tower Countryside Centre

Foredown Road Portslade Brighton Sussex BN41 2EW

Tel: 01273 292092

www.foredown.virtualmuseum.info

[Bus: 6. Limited parking on site]

Foredown Tower Countryside Centre is a learning resource available throughout the year for visits from special interest groups, youth organisations and schools. There are a wide range of exhibits and displays, a viewing gallery, the largest camera obscura in south east England, and a study room for groups. Professional staff and knowledgeable volunteers are available to share their expertise, talking to individuals and making group presentations. Foredown Tower hosts a continuing programme of events and activities, for children and adults, and is also open to the public at weekends between February and October each year. For more information telephone 01273 292092.

Feb-Oct Sat-Sun & Bank Hols 10.00-17.00, mid July-end Aug Thur-Sun & Bank Hols 10.00-17.00. Available for group and school visits by appointment, Mon-Fri all year

Viewing Tower & Camera Obscura: A£2.50 C(under16)£1.60 Family Ticket £6.40. Viewing Tower only: A£1.60 C£1.00 Family Ticket £4.20. Concessions£1.85. Group rates available for 20+ people, A£1.85. Prices valid until 31 Mar 2004

Observatory Science Centre

Herstmonceux Hailsham East Sussex BN27 1RN

Tel: 01323 832731 Fax: 01323 832741

[2m E of Herstmonceux village, on the Boreham Street to Pevensey Road]

The Royal Greenwich Observatory (RGO) was founded at Greenwich in London in 1675 by King Charles II but was moved just after the second world war in order to escape the lights and pollution of the city. The site at Herstmonceux was chosen as the most suitable in the UK.

10 Jan-12 Dec; 10-31 Jan Sat-Sun 10.00-16.00, 1 Feb-30 Nov daily 10.00-16.00 (Apr-Sept 10.00-18.00, Mar & Oct 10.00-17.00), 1-12 Dec Sat-Sun 10.00-16.00

A£5.80 C(under3)£Free C(4-15)£4.20 Concessions£4.50 Family Ticket (A2+C3 or A1+C4) £17.50

Sealife Centres & Aquariums

Brighton Sea Life Centre

Marine Parade Brighton Sussex BN2 1TB

Tel: 01273 604233 / 604234
Fax: 01273 681840

www.sealifeeurope.com

[A23, M23]

For a fun and educational day out, visit Brighton Sea Life Centre and be amazed by our fantastic Ocean Tunnel Display complete with sharks, rays and two giant turtles! Also see our six metre high statue of Medusa complete with golden serpents. Water canons also send shooting water through the air. Walk through our underwater tunnel and see the wonderful shoals of tropical fish and get really close up to the menagerie of sea life. New for 2004 is 'Octopus Challenge', come and marvel at our awesome giant Pacific octopus, a colossus of the sea and able to grow 15 feet across! Also test your own abilities against the skills of the octopus in a series of set tasks. Enjoy holding crabs and learning about the shoreline at our rockpool display. Feeding the juvenile rays and sharks is also a big treat but watch out for the lively Sea Bass! A showpiece of Victorian splendour and considered to be the most amazing, most wonderful aquarium anywhere in the world.

All year daily 10.00-18.00. Additionally later in summer & school hol. Closed 25 Dec

A£7.95 C(0-2)£Free C(3-14)£4.95 OAPs£6.95. Family tickets and group rates available

Discount Offer: One Child Free with One Full Paying Adult

Social History Museums

Buckleys Yesterday's World

80-90 High Street Battle Sussex TN33 0AQ
Tel: 01424 775378 Fax: 01424 775174
[6m N of Hastings on A2100, off A21 (J5 M25)]

Step into the world of yesteryear and discover a magical journey through 100 years of British history.
All year daily from 09.30. Closed 25-26 Dec
A£5.25 C£3.75 OAPs£4.75

Discount Offer: £0.50 Off Each Admission.

Spectator Sports

Fontwell Park Racecourse

Fontwell Park Arundel Sussex BN18 0SX

Tel: 01243 543335 Fax: 01243 543904

[Next to A27 between Chichester & Arundel. Rail: Barnham. Plenty on free on site parking]

Beautifully located within the grounds of Fontwell Park, racing has taken place at this venue since 1924.

Race meetings Aug-May 11.30-18.00

Premier £16.00 Grandstand & Paddock £11.00 C(0-16)£Free when accompanied by an adult

Theme & Adventure Parks

Butlins

Bognor Regis Sussex PO21 1ND

Tel: 01243 822445 Fax: 01243 860591

www.butlins.com

[Rail: Bognor Regis]

Butlins is a fantastic day out! A paradise for every generation, with an amazing range of activities on offer. You can enjoy the fun of the wet 'n' wild sub-tropical Splash Waterworld, burn off that extra energy on the multi-sports ourt, or challenge the kids to a race round the Go-Kart track. If you fancy taking things at an easier pace relax with a game of crazy golf or

enjoy the latest blockbuster in the cinema! Butlins have been entertaining holidaymakers for 60 years so why not find out what makes us so special. We offer you all the best bits of a Butlins holiday in a day for an incredible price! Don't miss the Skyline Pavilion at the heart of each Resort which offers non-stop entertainment whatever the weather and our Traditional Funfairs, Adventure Forts and Playgrounds will keep the kids amused for hours!

Opening times vary, please call Day Visitors Hotline on 01243 822445 for details

A£10.00 C(under2)£Free C£9.00 OAPs£9.00 Family Ticket (A2+C2) £30.00

Knockhatch Adventure Park

Hempstead Lane Hailsham Sussex BN27 3PR

Tel: 01323 442051 Fax: 01323 843878

www.knockhatch.com

[A22, to W of Hailsham. 8m N of Eastbourne, 30mins from Brighton, Hastings & Tunbridge Wells, 60mins from London. Plenty of on site parking]

Exciting, yet relaxing - the most varied day out around. Bird of prey centre, Treetops indoor soft play, adventure playgrounds, trampolines, crazy golf, small childrens' area, sandpit, giant sky leap slide, bouncy castle play barn, reptile centre, boating lake, toboggan slide, ball games, giant astro slide, plus for additional cost, burger bars, coffee corner, karting for children aged 3 years and over, laser adventure game, rodeo bull and corporate hospitality.

1 Apr-31 Oct Apr, June, July & Aug daily 10.00-17.30, May weekends & school holidays, Sept 1-3 & weekends 10.00-17.00, Oct 26-29 & weekends 10.00-17.00

A£6.99 C(under3)£Free C(3-14)&Students£6.99 OAPs£4.99 Family Ticket (4 people) £24.00, additional C£4.99. Season Tickets £20.00 per person. Group rates (16+): 25% discount. Free pre-school visit for teachers, pre-booked C£4.50 during term time through school

Discount Offer: £0.50 Off Park Entry Per Person.

Paradise Park

Avis Road Newhaven East Sussex BN9 0DH

Tel: 01273 512123 Fax: 01273 616000

www.paradisepark.co.uk

[A27 Brighton-Lewes bypass & A26 give easy access to Paradise Park. Rail: regular services to Newhaven. Bus: regular services to Denton Corner. Plenty of on site parking available]

A unique blend of exotic planthouses, museum of natural history, dinosaurs, Sussex History Trail, vast garden and gift centre and a terrace cafe overlooking the gardens. 'Treasures of Planet Earth' follows the extraordinary life story of Planet Earth from its earliest beginnings. The exhibition is home to unique collections of fossils, minerals and crystals. Life size moving dinosaurs provide an unforgettable experience. Enter the Botanical Planthouses and experience a spectacular collection of the world's flora. The gardens are a mixture of formal and informal with a gentle path meandering through hundreds of flowering shrubs and trees that form a backdrop to waterfalls, fountains and small lakes. Follow the history of Sussex through the gardens with handcrafted models of famous landmarks. Enter the new dinosaur Park and relive prehistoric times with life size dinosaurs towering overhead and hear the sounds of the Jurassic Age. Enjoy children's activities including amusements, miniature railway, fantasy golf and much more.

All year daily 09.00-18.00. Closed 25-26 Dec. Alternative tel no: 01273 616006

Combined Ticket to all 3 attractions: A£5.99 C£4.99 Family Ticket (A2+C3) £19.99. Any ParkPass purchased after 16.00 is valid the following day (subject to authorisation upon entry). Group and school rates available

Discount Offer: Two For The Price Of One.

Zoos

Drusillas Park

Alfriston East Sussex BN26 5QS

Tel: 01323 874100 Fax: 01323 874101

www.drusillas.co.uk

[Off A27 between Brighton / Eastbourne, 7m from Seaford beach. Plenty of on site parking]

Situated amidst the stunning scenery of the Cuckmere Valley at Alfriston in East Sussex, Drusillas is widely regarded as the best small zoo in England and is fast becoming recognised as one of the best organised places for children in the entire country. Animals include the famous meerkats, a walk through bat enclosure, Penguin Bay, a splendid range of monkeys, reptiles and creepy crawlies, plus keeper talks. The excellent play areas include masses of climbing, jumping, sliding and swinging fun and there are separate areas set aside for toddlers. Don't miss the Zoolympics Trail, Panning for Gold, the Train Ride through the Llama paddock, paint'n' make activities in the Wacky Workshop, Jungle Adventure Golf and New for 2004 - Tarzan's Tree House and Blue and Gold Macaws.

All year Summer: daily 10.00-18.00, Winter: daily 10.00-17.00. Closed 24-26 Dec. Penguin feeding takes place daily at 11.30 and 16.00

A£9.99 C(under2)£Free C(2-12)£9.49 Family Tickets (3 people) £27.45, (4 people) £36.45, (5 people) £44.95

Special Events

Birds of Prey
05/04/2004-01/09/2004
Held on 5, 7, 8, 14, 15, 16 Apr, 2-4 June, 26, 28-30 July, 2, 4-6, 9, 11-13, 16, 18-20, 23, 25-27 Aug, 1 Sept only. The birds of prey will be on display throughout the day

Charlie the Clown
06/04/2004-31/08/2004
Held on 6, 13 Apr & 10, 31 Aug only. The South's zaniest clown is back to entertain visitors of all ages with his jokes, juggling and just plain silliness

Easter Egg Challenge
09/04/2004-12/04/2004
Come to Drusillas over the Easter Weekend and take up the Easter Egg Challenge

Sheep Dog Display and Sheep Shearing
18/04/2004
Watch an educational and fun demonstration into the art of sheep shearing

Creepy Crawlies Day
02/05/2004-19/09/2004
Held on 2 May & 19 Sept only. Creep down to Drusillas and meet some very unusual 'mini monsters'

Reptile Weekend
29/05/2004-05/09/2004
Held on 29-30 May & 4-5 Sept only. Reptile Experts will take up residence in our Discovery Centre displaying their collection of exotic animals

Clowns Day
01/06/2004-03/08/2004
Held on 1 June & 3 Aug only. Drusillas regular funny man, Charlie the Clown will be here with his merry mates

Guest Appearance of Postman Pat
06/06/2004
Postmas Pat and his helper, Jess the black and white cat, will take a break from delivering the post in Greendale

Fluffy Bunnies
27/06/2004
Drusillas resident rabbit population will multiply on this day. The picnic area will be jumping with bouncy bunnies for visitors to stroke

Costume Character Convention
04/07/2004
All your favourite Costume Characters will be convening at Drusillas for a mad day of fun and competitions

Uniform Group Jamboree
10/07/2004
An evening event, open to all uniform groups

The Merits of Ferrets
11/07/2004
The Sussex Ferret Welfare Society will be on hand to give advice and information about these beautiful creatures

Guest Appearance of Spiderman
27/07/2004
Peter Parker's alter ego will be spinning his stuff at Drusillas with an amazing display of his Special Spider Powers

Zoolympics Challenge Day
08/08/2004
Test your prowess against the animals

Animals at Work
15/08/2004
This day is centred around working animals with experts on hand to discuss how animals help us in our daily lives

Phobias Day
17/08/2004
Experts will be displaying some of their most commonly feared animals in the Discovery Centre. The aim of the day is to be fun and informative for our visitors and to try and overcome some of their phobias

Duck Racing and Field Dogs
24/08/2004
There will be duck racing, together with field dog displays

Adopters Day
02/10/2004
Current Animal Adopters are invited to Drusillas to attend special Zoo Keeper's Question and Answer sessions

Boo's Haunted Cottage

23/10/2004-31/10/2004

Boo, Drusillas' friendly ghost, opens the doors once again to his haunted cottage. Creepy corridors lead visitors to all sorts of supernatural surprises

Santa's Christmas Cottage

27/11/2004-23/12/2004

Held on 27-28 Nov, 4-5 Dec and then daily from 11-23 Dec. Visit Santa and his elves hard at work making all the presents. His cosy cottage is crammed full of the toys that the elves have built

Tyne and Wear

Arts, Crafts & Textiles

Baltic The Centre for Contemporary Art

South Shore Road Gateshead NE8 3BA
Tel: 0191 478 1810 Fax: 0191 478 1922
[Take the A1 N. Follow signs for Angel of North, then Gateshead, then Gateshead Quayside]

This converted Rank Hovis grain warehouse is one of the largest centres for contemporary visual art in Europe. It does not house a permanent collection but shows temporary exhibitions and commissions new work.
Mon-Wed and Fri-Sat 10.00-19.00, Thurs 10.00-22.00, Sun 10.00-17.00
Admission Free

Hatton Gallery

The Quadrangle University of Newcastle
Newcastle Upon Tyne Tyne & Wear NE1 7RU
Tel: 0191 222 6059 Fax: 0191 222 3454
www.ncl.ac.uk/hatton
[Situated in the Quadrangle of the University, just 5 mins walk from Haymarket Metro Station on the Great North Road]

Described by The Times as one of the most impressive exhibition spaces in Britain, the Hatton Gallery shows a changing programme of exciting exhibitions, which include both historic and modern art and innovative contemporary practice. Paintings, prints and sculpture from the 15th century to the present day including works by Bacon, Whistler and Goya are housed in the gallery alongside a collection of West African sculpture. You will also find Kurt Schwitters Merzbarn, originally built in a Lake District barn, which is now acknowledged as one of the most important works of 20th century art. A range of events and activities are held

in the gallery including workshops and talks and can be arranged to suit the needs of your group.
All year Mon-Fri 10.00-17.30, Sat 10.00-16.30. Closed Sun, Bank Hol & 24-31 Dec
Admission Free

Special Events

William Roberts
20/03/2004-29/05/2004
One of Britain's leading twentieth century artists, Roberts' career spanned 70 years from 1910-1980. Throughout his career, Roberts explored the human condition and many of his works relate to aspects of everyday life, rendered in his distinctive style. Curated by the Hatton Gallery in collaboration with Sheffield Galleries and Museum Trust, this will be the first major retrospective of Roberts' work in almost 40 years

University of Newcastle,
Newcastle Upon Tyne,
Tyne & Wear NE1 7RU
www.ncl.ac.uk/hatton

ADMISSION FREE
Open 10am-5pm Monday to Saturday
Closed Sundays and Bank Holidays
Tel: 0191 222 6059

Laing Art Gallery

New Bridge Street Newcastle Upon Tyne
Tyne & Wear NE1 8AG
Tel: 0191 232 7734 Fax: 0191 222 0952
[Metro: Monument & Northumberland Street]

The North of England's premier art gallery displays a stunning array of watercolours, costume, silver, glass, pottery and sculpture alongside a striking programme of historical and contemporary exhibitions.
All year Mon-Sat 10.00-17.00, Sun 14.00-17.00. Closed 25-26 Dec & 1 Jan. New galleries and facilities will open mid 2004
Admission Free

Northern Gallery for Contemporary Art

City Library and Arts Centre Fawcett Street
Sunderland Tyne & Wear SR1 1RE
Tel: 0191 514 1235 Fax: 0191 514 8444
The NGCA is a gallery space housed in the award winning City Library and Arts Centre. It is a venue which is committed to showing the very best of contemporary visual art and craft of regional, national and international significance.
All year Mon & Wed 09.30-19.30, Tue Thur-Fri 09.30-17.00, Sat 09.30-16.00
Admission Free

Shipley Art Gallery

Prince Consort Road Gateshead Tyne & Wear
NE8 4JB
Tel: 0191 477 1495 Fax: 0191 478 7917
[Off the main A167 road into Newcastle.]

The Shipley Art Gallery combines a dazzling display of the latest glass, jewellery, ceramics, textiles and furniture alongside stunning historical artworks.
All year Mon-Sat 10.00-17.00, Sun & Bank Hol 14.00-17.00. Closed Good Fri, 25-26 Dec & 1

Jan
Admission Free

Exhibition & Visitor Centres

Life Science Centre

Times Square Newcastle Upon Tyne
Tyne & Wear NE1 4EP
Tel: 0191 243 8223 Fax: 0191 243 8201
[Next to Newcastle Central Station and metro station, from A1, A69, A184, A1058, A167]

Discover how truly amazing LIFE is. Meet your four billion year old family, explore what makes us all different, test your brainpower and enjoy the thrill of the crazy motion ride.
All year Mon-Sat 10.00-18.00, Sun 11.00-18.00
A£6.95 C£4.50 Family Ticket £19.95
Concessions£5.50

National Glass Centre

Liberty Way Sunderland Tyne & Wear SR6 0GL
Tel: 0191 515 5555 Fax: 0191 515 5556
[From A194, off A1231]

Once inside visitors of all ages and interests can take in some amazing experiences such as the Kaleidoscope Gallery where every aspect is explored. Also witness spectacular glass-making demonstrations.

All year 10.00-17.00

Glass Tour: A£5.00 C£3.00

Discount Offer: One Person Free With Every Full Paying Adult

Festivals & Shows

Cookson Festival 2004

Various venues South Shields Tyne & Wear
Tel: 0191 424 7985 Fax: 0191 427 0469
From A1(M) take A194(M), A194 / A183]

The festival promises three months of free family
fun and entertainment. Past performers include
Rolf Harris, the Bootleg Beatles, Tony Hadley,
10CC, ABC. With Amphitheatre Live Music
every Monday, Wednesday and Saturday
throughout June, Big Name Sunday Shows during July, and children/family events throughout
August, there's something for everyone!
June 1-August 29 2004
Admission Free

Folk & Local History Museums

Sunderland Museum and Winter Gardens

Burdon Road Sunderland Tyne & Wear
SR1 1PP
Tel: 0191 553 2323 Fax: 0191 553 7828
*A1018 from Newcastle and Teeside, A690 from
Durham]*

Exciting hands-on exhibits and interactive displays tell the story of Sunderland from its prehistoric past through to the present day.
*All year daily Mon-Sat 10.00-17.00, Sun 14.00-
17.00. Closed Good Fri, 25-26 Dec & 1 Jan.
Open Bank Hol Mons*
Admission Free

Heritage & Industrial

Ryhope Engines Museum

Ryhope Pumping Station Ryhope Sunderland
Tyne & Wear SR2 0ND
Tel: 0191 521 0235
Just off A1018 signposted]

Ryhope Engines Museum is based upon the
Ryhope Pumping Station and is a distinctive
example of the industrial architecture of mid
Victorian times. Its engines show the high standards of mechanical engineering, design, and
construction of that age.

*Sun 14.00-17.00. In steam Easter-Christmas
11.00-16.30, most Bank Hols Sat-Mon*
Admission Free

Historical

Castle Keep

Castle Garth Newcastle Upon Tyne
Tyne & Wear NE1 1RQ
Tel: 0191 232 7938
One of the country's finest surviving examples of
a Norman Keep. Panoramic views of the city
from the roof. Disabled access by appointment.
*All year daily Apr-Sept 09.30-17.30, Oct-Mar
09.30-16.30. Closed Good Fri, 25-26 Dec & 1
Jan*
A£1.50 Concessions£0.50

Washington Old Hall

The Avenue Washington Village Washington
Tyne & Wear NE38 7LE
Tel: 0191 416 6879 Fax: 0191 419 2065
*[2m from A1 in Washington on E side of Ave, 5m
W of Sunderland, S of Tyne Tunnel follow A1231
to Washington then Washington village, next to
church on hill]*

The home of George Washington's ancestors
and from where the family took their surname
'Washington'. The Old Hall was originally an
early medieval manor, but was partly rebuilt in
the 17th century.
Apr-Oct Sun-Wed & Good Fri 11.00-17.00
A£3.50 Family Ticket (A2+C3) £9.00

Military & Defence Museums

Military Vehicle Museum

Exhibition Park Pavilion Newcastle Upon Tyne
Tyne & Wear NE2 4PZ
Tel: 0191 281 7222
Over 50 vehicles, 60 cabinets mostly from
World War II including guns and artefacts relat-

ing to the war years. Tells story of military life in the last century.

All year daily summer 1 Mar-31 Oct 10.00-16.00, winter 1 Nov-end Feb Sat, Sun & School Hols 10.00-dusk. Closed 25-26 Dec, 1 Jan & Aug Bank Hols

A£2.00 Concessions£1.00

Natural History Museums

Hancock Museum

Barras Bridge Newcastle Upon Tyne
Tyne & Wear NE2 4PT
Tel: 0191 222 7418 (info line)
Fax: 0191 222 6753
[Follow exit signs for City Centre A167 off the A1(M)]

The North of England's premier Natural History Museum unravels the secrets of the natural world through sensational galleries and close encounters with reptiles and insects.
All year Mon-Sat 10.00-17.00 Sun 14.00-17.00
Prices vary according to current exhibition

Nature & Conservation Parks

Washington Wetlands Centre

Pattinson Washington Tyne & Wear NE38 8LE
Tel: 0191 416 5454 Fax: 0191 416 5801
[E of Washington 4m from A1(M), 1m from A19 signposted off A195 & A1231]

Glaxo Wellcome Wetland Discovery Centre; packed full of things to do for all ages; Spring Gill Wood, delightful walk carefully designed to provide access for people with disabilities; James Steel Waterfowl Nursery, watch fluffy ducklings and goslings take their first wobbly steps and the American exhibit - Hunters' Creek.
All year daily 09.30-17.00, winter 09.30-16.30. Closed 25 Dec
A£5.75 C(0-4)£Free C(4-16)£3.75
Concessions£4.75 Family Ticket (A2+C2)
£15.00, any additional C£2.75

Performing Arts

Arts Centre, Washington

Biddick Lane Fatfield Washington Tyne & Wear
NE38 8AB

Tel: 0191 219 3455 Fax: 0191 219 3466

[Easy access from A1 Washinton Services junction on to A195; signposted A19 leading to A1231 to A195]

The Arts Centre is an attractive, award-winning converted 19th century farm offering performance spaces, art gallery & function rooms with licensed bars. A varied programme of arts and craft classes are run throughout the year.

All year Mon 09.00-17.00, Tue-Sat 09.00-19.30 open later if programme running

Admission Free

Roman Era

Segedunum Roman Fort, Baths and Museum

Buddle Street Wallsend Tyne & Wear NE28 6H

Tel: 0191 295 5757 (info line)
Fax: 0191 295 5858

[1min walk from Wallsend Metro and Bus Station]

In AD122 the Emperor Hadrian ordered a mighty frontier system to be built across Britain to defend the Roman Empire from the barbarians to the north. Segedunum Roman Fort stood on the banks of the River Tyne and was the last outpost of Hadrian's Wall.

All year daily 1 Apr-31 Oct 10.00-17.00, 1 Nov-31 Mar 10.00-15.30

A£3.50 C(under4)£Free C£1.95

Science - Earth & Planetary

Planetarium and Observatory

St. Georges Avenue South Tyneside College
South Shields Tyne & Wear NE34 6ET

Tel: 0191 427 3589 Fax: 0191 427 3646

*[2m from Newcastle International Airport, 8m
from Newcastle Central railway station, with a
direct Metro - Train connection to both]*

Planetarium Shows; 'Space Junk' The first
adventure of a little green man called Splunk.
'Whats That Star?' A guide to the heavens for
beginners. 'The Heavenly Host' The Christmas
story told in stars. 'Children of the Universe' The
story of life, the universe. 'The Constellation
Makers' An astronomical detective story.

Please call for specific opening times

Planetarium A£3.00 C£1.50. Admission for
Observatory £1.00 and can be used on any
year Mon or Tue

Sealife Centres & Aquariums

Blue Reef Aquarium

Grand Parade Tynemouth Tyne & Wear
NE30 4JF

Tel: 0191 258 1031 Fax: 0191 257 2116

www.bluereefaquarium.co.uk

[Signposted from A19 & A1058]

Tynemouth's Blue Reef Aquarium offers visitors
a dazzling undersea safari through the oceans
of the world. Overlooking the dramatic North
Sea, the aquarium uses the latest marine technology and innovative new display techniques to
showcase sea creatures from around the globe
in naturally-themed habitats. Blue Reef takes
visitors on an underwater journey from the mysteries of the Newcastle coastline to the colourful
underwater gardens of the Mediterranean and
the exotic tropical waters of the Sea of Cortez
off the coast of Mexico. At its heart is a 200,000
litre tropical ocean tank where an underwater
walkthrough tunnel offers incredibly close
encounters with sharks and thousands of beau-
tifully-coloured reef fish. More than 30 naturally-
themed displays reveal the sheer variety of life in
the deep. New from February half term 2004,
meet our 'Toxic Frogs'.

All year daily 10.00. Closed 25 Dec

A£4.95 C£3.50 Students&OAPs£4.25 Family
Ticket (A2+C2/3) £15.95

**Discount Offer: One Child Free With
One Full Paying Adult**

Special Events

Launch of Blue Reef Nursery
09/04/2004-12/04/2004
*The new Blue Reef nursery provides a fascinating
insight into the life cycles of marine creatures from
around the world. Please call for further details*

Shark Awareness Week
29/05/2004-05/06/2004
*Shark Week is a celebration of the oceans' great-
est predator. Learn the facts behind the fiction
and discover why sharks have got more to fear
from us than we have from them. Regular talks,
workshops and feeding demonstrations*

Summer Holidays - Family Fun
01/07/2004-31/08/2004
*Throughout the summer holidays, Blue Reef is
organising a series of fun activities aimed at families. From rockpool encounters to marine themed
quiz trails, talks and feeding demonstrations,
there's something for visitors of all ages to enjoy*

October Half Term Event - Claws
01/10/2004-31/10/2004
*From comical hermit crabs and 'fashion con-
scious' decorator crabs to giant lobsters and the
mighty king crab, this exciting feature offers a fascinating insight into the incredible world of crustaceans. Please call for specific dates*

Social History Museums

Discovery Museum

Blandford House Blandford Square
Newcastle Upon Tyne NE1 4JA

Tel: 0191 232 6789 Fax: 0191 230 2614

[Off A6115 A6125]

Science and technology are explored through huge working engines, exciting interactives, free internet access and Tyneside inventions that changed the world.

All year Mon-Sat 10.00-17.00, Sun 14.00-17.00. Closed 25-26 Dec & 1 Jan & Good Fri

Admission Free

Theme & Adventure Parks

New Metroland

39 Garden Walk Metrocentre Gateshead
Tyne & Wear NE11 9XY

Tel: 0191 493 2048 Fax: 0191 493 2904

www.metroland.uk.com

[Signposted for MetroCentre from A1/M. Plenty on site parking & indoor picnic areas]

Europe's largest indoor funfair theme park offers 12 major attractions. You can experience the thrills and spills of the New Rollercoaster, test your driving skills on the Disco Dodgems, sail the high seas on the Swashbuckling Pirate Ship, Fly high on the Wonderful Waveswinger, Spin on the Whiling Waltzer, or take a leisurely journey round the park on the Terrific Train. The Children's Adventure Play Area is a great place for children to burn off all their energy while parents can sit and watch. There are four food outlets, MrB's Amusements and Prize Bingo and much more. Parties are a speciality, for any occasion.

School holidays: Mon-Wed, Fri & Sat 10.00-20.00, Thur 10.00-21.00, Sun 11.00-18.00. Term Time: Mon-Fri from 12.00

Standard All Day Pass: A&C£9.20. Gold All Day Pass: A&C£11.10. Evening passes available

Discount Offer: Buy One Get One for £1.50 on a Gold All Day Pass

Transport Museums

Monkwearmouth Station Museum

North Bridge Street Sunderland Tyne & Wear
SR5 1AP
Tel: 0191 567 7075 Fax: 0191 510 9415
[Situated on North Bridge Street (A1018). St Peter's Metro Station is close to the Museum. Limited, free car and coach parking outside the Museum]

This splendid Victorian railway station recreates a sense of rail travel in times past. Explore the ticket office as it would have looked in Victorian times, see the guard's van and goods wagon in the railway sidings and watch today's trains zoom past the Platform Gallery.
All year Mon-Sat 10.00-17.00, Sun 14.00-17.00. Closed Good Friday, 25-26 Dec & 1 Jan
Admission Free

Wales

Abbeys

Tintern Abbey

Tintern Chepstow Gwent NP6 6SE
Tel: 01291 689251
[From Cardiff, M4, J23, M48, J2, A466. From London M4, J21 to M48]

Travellers have been flocking to this riverbank in the wooded Wye Valley for hundreds of years to admire Tintern's grace and sublime beauty. Founded for Cistercian monks in 1131 and largely rebuilt by Roger Bigod, Lord of nearby Chepstow Castle, in the late 13th century, it encompasses grand design and architectural detail of great finesse.

1 Apr-31 May daily 09.30-17.00, 1 June-30 Sept daily 09.30-18.00, 1-31 Oct daily 09.30-17.00, 1 Nov-31 Mar Mon-Sat 09.30-16.00, Sun 11.00-16.00. Closed 24-26 Dec & 1 Jan

A£3.00 C(under5)£Free C(5-15)&Concessions£2.50 Family Ticket (A2+C3) £8.50. Children under 12 years must be accompanied by an adult

Agriculture / Working Farms

Greenmeadow Community Farm

Greenforge Way Cwmbran Gwent NP44 5AJ

Tel: 01633 862202 Fax: 01633 489332

www.farmvisit.co.uk

[1m W of Cwmbran town centre. Bus: No 5 or No 6]

Just four miles from the M4, this is one of Wales' leading farm attractions - milking demonstrations, tractor and trailer rides, dragon adventure play area, farm trail, nature trail and lots more. Phone for details of lambing weekends, shearing, country fair and agricultural shows, Halloween and Christmas events.

All year daily, summer 10.00-18.00, winter 10.00-16.30. Closed 25 Dec

A£3.50 C&Concessions£2.50 Family Ticket (A2+C3) £13.00. Group rates available

Discount Offer: One Child Free With A Full Paying Adult.

Arts, Crafts & Textiles

Andrew Logan Museum of Sculpture

Aquaduct Road Berriew Nr Welshpool Powys SY21 8PJ

Tel: 01686 640689 Fax: 01686 640764

[M54 to Shrewsbury, A488 to Welshpool, Berriew off A483 Welshpool/Newtown Road]

Enter the glittering world of internationally renowned sculptor Andrew Logan, who creates adventures in wonderland. The only museum in Europe dedicated to a living artist. His magical world includes flowers, animals, planets and gods.

Easter: 9-12 Apr inclusive 12.00-18.00, May-Oct Wed-Sun 12.00-18.00, Nov-Dec Sat & Sun 12.00-16.00. Bank Hol Mons 12.00-18.00. Closed Jan-Apr (except Easter)

A£2.00 C£1.00 Concessions£1.00 Family Ticket (A2+C3) £6.00

Newport Museum and Art Gallery

John Frost Square Newport Gwent NP9 1PA

Tel: 01633 840064

[Town Centre of Newport]

Natural science displays including geology; fine and applied art, specialising in early English watercolours, teapots and contemporary crafts; prehistoric finds from Gwent and Romano-British remains from Caerwent; local history including the Chartist movement. Regular exhibitions and associated activities.

All year Mon-Thur 09.30-17.00, Fri 09.30-16.30, Sat 09.30-16.00

Admission Free

Norwegian Church Arts Centre

Harbour Drive Cardiff Bay Cardiff CF10 4PA
Tel: 029 2045 4899
[M4 J33 or from Cardiff city centre follow signs to Cardiff Bay]

The arts centre is a peaceful haven which reflects the warm and friendly ambience of its days as a religious meeting place. Sitting in the cafe you can look out over the boats in Cardiff Bay.
All year daily 09.00-17.00

Admission Free

Rhiannon Welsh Gold Centre

Main Square Tregaron Ceredigion SY25 6JL
Tel: 01974 298415 Fax: 01974 298690
[M4 via Carmarthen or Llandeilo, or more scenic route over the mountains along A44]

Established since 1971, the Centre has an international reputation as the premier Welsh and Celtic Craft Shop. Here, Celtic Art is a living tradition, not just images from a distant past. Mail Order Catalogue available.
All year, Summer daily, Oct-May Mon-Sat 09.30-17.30
Admission Free

Birds, Butterflies & Bees

Felinwynt Rainforest and Butterfly Centre

Felinwynt Cardigan Ceredigion SA43 1RT

Tel: 01239 810250 / 810882

Fax: 01239 810465

www.butterflycentre.co.uk

[From A487 turn onto B4333 at Airfield, follow Rainforest signposts. Plenty of on site parking]

Experience a rainforest atmosphere full of exotic plants and tropical butterflies with the sounds of the Peruvian Amazon. Relax in our new café where hot and cold drinks, lunches, snacks and home-made cakes are served all day. Study the rainforest exhibition and watch a video about butterflies or rainforests and browse in our gift shop. There is something for everyone including colouring for the children's gallery. Personal Guide available. Don't forget that butterflies are more active on sunny days. Picnic areas: both in and outdoor facilities.

Easter-31 Oct daily 10.30-17.00

A£4.00 C(4-14)£1.50 OAPs£3.75

Discount Offer: Two For The Price Of One

National Wetland Centre of Wales

Llanelli Centre Llwynhendy Llanelli Carmarthenshire SA14 9SH

Tel: 01554 741087 Fax: 01554 744101

www.wwt.org.uk

[Off A484 10mins from J47 or J48 - M4 follow brown-duck signs]

A day of discovery all year round, whatever the weather, at this stunning internationally important wetland site. Spectacular views of estuary and wildlife; Discovery Centre with hands-on activities; Visitor Centre with shop and restaurant; landscaped grounds with thousands of tame ducks, geese and swans; play areas.

Summer 09.30-17.00, Winter 09.30-16.30. Closed 24-25 Dec

A£5.50 C£3.50 Family Ticket £14.50 OAPs £4.50. Group rates (10+): A£4.50 C£2.75 OAPs£4.00

Discount Offer: One Child Free With Full Paying Adult

Caverns & Caves

King Arthur's Labyrinth

Corris Craft Centre Corris Machynlleth Powys
SY20 9RF

Tel: 01654 761584 Fax: 01654 761575

www.kingarthurslabyrinth.com

[Off the A487, plenty of on site parking]

King Arthur's Labyrinth is an underground visitor attraction in Mid Wales with a unique presentation which has captured the public imagination. An underground boat takes visitors deep into the spectacular caverns under the Braichgoch mountain at Corris near Machynlleth. As visitors walk through the caverns, Welsh tales of King Arthur are told with tableaux and stunning sound and light effects. The journey ends with a return trip along the beautiful subterranean river into the grounds of the Corris Craft Centre.

7 Mar-7 Nov daily 10.00-17.00. Closed 8 Nov-1 Mar

£5.00 C£3.50 OAPs£4.45

Country Parks & Estates

Pembrey Country Park - Parc Gweldig Pen-bre

Pembrey Carmarthenshire SA16 0EJ
Tel: 01554 833913 Fax: 01554 835498
[Signposted from the A484 Carmarthen to Llanelli Road]

People visit Pembrey Country Park for many different reasons. Some to enjoy the freedom to wander around 202 hectares of glorious parkland, some to take advantage of one of the cleanest beaches in Wales. Whilst others use the host of excellent family attractions to be found in the Park.
Park: all year daily dawn-dusk. Visitor Centre: Apr-6 Sept daily 10.00-17.00, 6 Sept-Mar daily 10.00-15.45. All attractions are subject to seasonal opening, please call for details
Parking charges applicable

Portmeirion

Portmeirion Penrhyndeudraeth Gwynedd
LL48 6ET
Tel: 01766 770000 Fax: 01766 771331
[Portmeirion is 1.5m beyond Penrhyndeudraeth]

Welsh architect Sir Clough Williams Ellis built his fairy-tale, Italiante village on a rocky, tree-clad peninsula on the shores of Cardigan Bay. The nucleus of the estate is a sumptuous waterfront hotel, rebuilt from the original house and containing a fine 18th-century fireplace and a library moved here from the Great Exhibition of 1851.
All year daily 09.30-17.30
A£5.70 C£2.80 OAPs£4.60

Exhibition & Visitor Centres

Dylan Thomas Centre

Somerset Place Swansea Wales SA1 1RR
Tel: 01792 463980 Fax: 01792 463993
[M4, A483. Rail: High Street Station]

The Dylan Thomas Centre is now the main focal point for a celebration of Dylan Marlais Thomas (Swansea's world famous son). Refurbished in 1995 to host the British Year of Literature, this splendid building has a permanent exhibition on Dylan and his life, as well as excellent restaurant, function and conference facilities.
All year Tues-Sun & Bank Hols 10.00-16.30
Admission Free

Gower Heritage Centre

Parkmill Gower Swansea SA3 2EH
Tel: 01792 371206 Fax: 01792 371471
[M4(W), J42 then brown tourist signs to south Gower and A4067. M4(E), J47 then A483 into Swansea and A4118 to Swansea airport]

The Gower Heritage centre is based around a water powered cornmill originally built over 800 years ago by William de Breos, a Knight from Normandy in France. The Mill is one of the oldest 'Toll Mills' in Wales, so called because local farmers were compelled by law to bring their crops here for grinding. Over the last 15 years, since we took over a dilapidated semi derelict group of buildings, we have renovated the 12th Century corn mill into an award winning Educational and Tourism location.
Nov-Mar 10.00-16.00, Apr-Oct 10.00-17.30
A£3.70 OAPs&C£2.60 C(under5)£Free

Festivals & Shows

Cardiff Festival 2004

Tel: 029 2087 3690 after hours
Fax: 029 2087 2087

A truly international summer festival, featuring the very best in street theatre, live music, family, youth and children's entertainment, funfairs and theatre. Most of these events are completely free and take place throughout the open spaces and landmark buildings in the city and on the waterfront. Staged by Cardiff Council, the Cardiff Festival, now in its 18th year, has developed a reputation for being one of the UK's largest FREE open air festivals.
June 28-August 8 2004

Dylan Thomas Festival

Dylan Thomas Centre Somerset Place Swansea SA2 1RR
Tel: 01792 463980 Fax: 01792 463993
[M4, A483. Rail: High Street Station]

The Dylan Thomas Centre runs a year round programme of events, culminating in the annual Dylan Thomas celebration. It is also home to a standing Dylan Thomas Exhibition.
October 27-November 9 2004 Tue-Sun 10.00-16.30

Fishguard Folk Festival/Gwyl Werin y Gwaun

Various venues Fishguard Pembrokeshire
Tel: 01348 875183
Make a date in your diary for this friendly festival during the late spring bank holiday weekend 2004. Begins with a Showcase Concert in Theatr Gwaun, Fishguard - featuring all the major artists who will play over the weekend. Live music at its best, all over town, with a base in the Club Marquee at the Royal Oak, Fishguard. Sessions in the Royal Oak, Market Square, Fishguard over all the weekend, plus other pubs in town. Workshops Sat morning with a chance to demonstrate what you've learnt on the Sun. A riot over the whole weekend until the 'Putting the Horse to Bed' ceremony Sun lunchtime.
May 28-30 2004
Concert: A£6.00 C(under15)£2.00
Concessions£4.00

Fishguard International Music Festival

Festival Office Fishguard Pembrokeshire SA65 9BJ
Tel: 01348 873612 Fax: 01348 873612
This year sees the 35th Anniversary of this highly successful International Festival. Choral,

Orchestral, Recital and Jazz music. Poetry, children's events and 'Live Music Now' will also feature.
July 24-31 2004

Gower Festival 2004

Various Churches in the Gower Swansea
[M4, J47, W of Swansea]

The Gower Festival is a very special blend of beautiful churches, wonderful music and summer evenings. The Gower Peninsula is an area of outstanding natural beauty with sea, cliffs and beaches; great stretches of common land and well-kept farms. Since 1976 the festival has brought good music to churches all over Gower where the excellent acoustics and often breathtaking settings by the sea or in the country make for unforgettable experiences.
July 17-31 2004

Gwyl Gregynog Festival 2004

Gregynog Hall Nr Newtown Powys SY16 3PW
Tel: 01686 625007 (Box Office)
[5m outside Newtown]

From 1924-1964 Gregynog House was home to Gwendoline and Margaret Davies whose aim was to create a national centre for the arts in Wales. They acquired an outstanding collection of Impressionist paintings and fine sculptures which were later bequeathed to the Nation. They also established the Gregynog Music Festival, attracting the leading musical figures of the 1930s, including Vaughan Williams, Edward Elgar, Sir Adrian Boult and Gustav Holst. In 1960 the house was entrusted to the University of Wales. In 1988 the Festival was revived and since that time it has attracted many of the leading musicians of the time.
June 12-26 2004

Prices vary according to event attended. Ticket sales via The Box Office at Theatr Hafren, Newtown. Bookings can be made in person or by telephone, Mon-Sat 10.00-17.30.

Gwyl Machynlleth Festival

Y Tabernacl Heol Penrallt Machynlleth Powys SY20 8AJ
Tel: 01654 703355 Fax: 01654 702160
The Machynlleth Festival is an enjoyable mixture of classical music, jazz, lectures and art exhibitions. All events take place in and around a beautiful old chapel. The Dyfi Valley is a first class tourist destination.
August 21-29 2004

Llangollen International Musical Eisteddfod

Royal International Pavillion Abbey Road Llangollen Denbighshire LL20 8SW
Tel: 01978 862000 Fax: 01978 862005
[Situated on the banks of the River Dee. From Shrewsbury follow A5 signs from Chester A483 onto A529]

Six magical days of music, song and dance from around the world, catering for all ages and tastes. Competitors representing over 45 Nations in colourful National costumes compete in daily competitions. Gala evening concerts with world renowned artists. The festival not only attracts over 6,500 competitors but an enthusiastic audience of nearly 100,000.
July 6-11 2004

Llantilio Crossenny Festival

St Teilos Church Llantilio Crossenny Abergavenny Monmouthshire NP7 8AG
Tel: 01873 856928 Box Office
[Between Abergavenny and Monmouth on B4233]

The Llantilio Crossenny Festival of Music and Drama is comprised of a concert on Thursday, normally of a lighter nature, an Opera on Friday and Saturday and an Orchestral Concert on Sunday. The Sunday concert is followed by afternoon tea and Festival Evensong. The festival has been in existence for over forty years and is held in the beautiful St Teilo's Church which dates from the 12th century. Llantilio Crossenny lies between Abergavenny, the

"Gateway to Wales", and Monmouth. The Festival Orchestra is comprised of leading London professionals and is led by Rolf Wilson.
May 19-23 2004

Royal Welsh Agricultural Show

Llanelwedd Builth Wells Powys LD2 3SY
Tel: 01982 553683 Fax: 01982 553563
[Rail: Builth Road or Llandrindod station]

The Royal Welsh Agricultural Show on the permanent Showground at Llanelwedd, Builth Wells provides a prime shop window for farming in Wales. The show, which runs for four days, attracts more than 200,000 visitors, up to 7,000 entries of livestock and over 1,000 trade stands together with sections covering the whole of farming and rural life in Wales.
July 19-22 2004
A£12.00-14.00 C(under16)£2.00 OAPs£10.00 - proof required C(under4)£Free

Folk & Local History Museums

Cyfarthfa Castle Museum and Art Gallery

Cyfarthfa Park Brecon Road Merthyr Tydfil Mid Glamorgan CF47 8RE
Tel: 01685 723112 Fax: 01685 723112
[Signposted off the A470 from Cardiff, M4 and Brecon A465 from Swansea, Abergavenny and M50]

Georgian castellated mansion, built by William Crawshay II, covering one acre. Varied museum includes fine art, porcelain, local history, family portraits and more.
All year Apr-Sept daily 10.00-17.30, Oct-Mar Tue-Fri 10.00-16.00, Sat & Sun 12.00-16.00. Closed Mon
Admission Free

Powysland Museum and Montgomery Canal Centre

The Canal Wharf Welshpool Powys SY21 7AQ

Tel: 01938 554656 Fax: 01938 554656
[A483, A458 to Welshpool]

The Powysland Museum and Montgomery Canal Centre illustrates the history and development of life in Montgomeryshire from the earliest prehistoric settlers to the 20th century population. It is housed in a carefully restored and renovated 19th century warehouse by the Montgomery Canal.
All year Mon & Tue, Thur & Fri 11.00-13.00 then 14.00-17.00, May-Sept also Sat & Sun 10.00-13.00 then 14.00-17.00, Oct-Apr Sat 11.00-14.00. Closed Wed all year
A£1.00 C(under16)£Free Concessions£0.50

Tenby Museum and Art Gallery

Castle Hill Tenby Pembrokeshire SA70 7BP
Tel: 01834 842809 Fax: 01834 842809
[On the A478]

This museum covers the local heritage from prehistory to the present in galleries devoted to archaeology, geology, maritime history, natural history, militaria and bygones. The art gallery concentrates on local associations.
5 Apr-7 Dec daily 10.00-17.00, 8-19 Dec Mon-Fri 10.00-17.00
A£2.00 C£1.00 Concessions£1.50

Forests & Woods

Llyn Brenig Visitor Centre

Cerrigydrudion Corwen Conwy LL21 9TT

Tel: 01490 420463 Fax: 01490 420694

[Off A5 on B4501 between Cerrigydrudion /

Denbigh]

The Visitor Centre contains a free orbital exhibition and a video on life at Brenig. Visitors can browse for souvenirs or relax with a Welsh Tea in the lakeside café. Outside there is a new adventure playground and a variety of walks from the 11 mile Lake Walk to the shorter archaeological and nature trails.

All year mid Mar-Oct daily, cafe 10.00-17.00, fishing 08.00-30mins after sunset

Admission Free. Car parking £1.00 water sports & fly fishing also charged

Gardens & Horticulture

Bodnant Garden

Tal-y-Cafn Colwyn Bay Conwy LL28 5RE
Tel: 01492 650460 Fax: 01492 650448
[8m S of Llandudno & Colwyn Bay off A470]

Covering nearly 100 acres, Bodnant is one of the finest gardens in Britain with magnificent rhododendrons, camellias and magnolias in the spring followed by herbaceous borders, roses and water lilies in the summer and good colour in the autumn.

13 Mar-31 Oct daily 10.00-17.00
A£5.50 C£2.75

Glansevern Hall Gardens

Berriew Welshpool Powys SY21 8AH
Tel: 01686 640200 Fax: 01686 640829
[4m SW of Powis Castle on the left hand side of A483 travelling towards Newtown]

Glansevern Hall was built in the Greek Revival style for Arthur Davies Owen Esq. The house, faced with Cefn stone, was the seat of the Owen family from 1800 until after the Second World War. Eighteen years ago Neville and Jenny Thomas acquired the property and started to develop the gardens, respecting the plantings and features of the past, but adding a vast collection of new and interesting species.

May-Sept Fri, Sat & Bank Hol Mon 12.00-18.00
A£3.50 C(0-16)£Free OAPs£3.00

Discount Offer: Three For The Price Of Two.

Upton Castle Gardens

Pembrokeshire Coast National Park Cosheston Pembroke Pembrokeshire

Tel: 01646 651782 Fax: 01646 651782

[N of A477 Pembroke Dock to Carmarthen rd via Cosheston, about 4m E of Pembroke Dock. The approach roads are narrow - please drive carefully! Plenty of on site parking available]

Delightful gardens set among thickly wooded slopes overlooking the Milford Haven waterway, in a tranquil, corner of the Pembrokeshire Coast National Park. The gardens surround a fine medieval castle, which is still a private residence. The castle's extensive grounds are open to the public, and include: Footpaths through 35 acres of mature woodland, with more than 250 different species of trees and shrubs; Formal terraces with rose gardens and herbaceous borders; "Lovers' Lane" leading to a tidal creek and the shores of the Carew River; Medieval chapel with family memorials from the 13th to 20th centuries and a picnic site with tables and benches.

29 Mar-31 Oct Sun-Fri 10.00-17.00. Guided tours by arrangement

Gardens: A£2.00 C£1.00 Family Ticket: £5.00

Heritage & Industrial

Blaenavon Ironworks

North Street Blaenavon Pontypool Gwent
NP4 9RN
Tel: 01495 792615
[Via A4043, follow signs]

One of Europe's best preserved 18th century ironworks. The works date from 1788 and soon become the second largest in Wales. Remains of a row of blast furnaces survive, dominated by the tall shell of an ingenious water balance-tower which transported materials. Alongside this place of hard labour are the cottages of Stack Square, built for key workers between 1789-1792.
1 Apr-31 Oct daily, Mon-Fri 09.30-16.30, Sat 10.00-17.00, Sun 10.00-16.30
A£2.00 C(under5)£Free C&Concessions£1.50 Family Ticket (A2+C3) £5.50. Children under 12 years must be accompanied by an adult

Electric Mountain

Llanberis Caernarfon Gwynedd LL55 4UR
Tel: 01286 870636 Fax: 01286 873002
[On A4086 Llanberis by-pass]

Between 1976 and 1982 a remarkable feat was accomplished just outside the Snowdonia National Park in Llanberis. The heart of a mountain, which was once the second largest open cast slate quarry in the world, was tunnelled away and a pumped storage power station - the largest in Europe - built inside.
Feb-Mar & Nov-Dec Wed-Sun 10.30-16.30, Apr-May & Sept-Oct daily 10.30-16.30, June-Aug daily 09.30-17.30. Bank Hols 09.30-17.30. Closed throughout Jan
A£6.00 C£3.00 OAPs/Students£4.50

Ffestiniog Powerstation and Hydro Centre

Tan-y-Grisiau Blaenau Ffestiniog Gwynedd
LL41 3TP
Tel: 01766 830310 / 830465
Fax: 01766 833472
[From N, leave A55 at Llandudno, follow A470, by-passing Betws-y-Coed. The A496 will take you to Hydro Centre. From E use A487]

Take an exclusive guided tour of the UK's first major Hydro-electric power station - discover how your electricity is produced.
Easter week & May Bank Hols, June-Aug daily 10.30-16.30
A£4.00 C£2.00 Concessions£2.50 Family Ticket £10.00

Inigo Jones and Co. Ltd.

Y Groeslon Caernarfon Gwynedd LL54 7ST
Tel: 01286 830242 Fax: 01286 831247
[On A487, 5m from Caernarfon outside little village called Y Groeslon]

Inigo Jones was established in 1861 primarily t prefabricate school writing slates. Today the company prefabricates architectural monumen-tal and craft items from natural Welsh slate. Th slate works are open to the public for self guid-ed tours.
All year daily 09.00-17.00. Closed 25-26 Dec & 1 Jan
A£4.00 C&Concessions£3.50 Family Ticket (A2+C2) £13.50

Historical

Abergavenny Museum and Castle

Castle Street Abergavenny Monmouthshire
NP7 5EE
Tel: 01873 854282 Fax: 01873 736004
[Off A40 / A465 Abergavenny roundabout]

A Welsh kitchen, a saddler's shop and local exhibits are displayed at the museum, and the remains of the castle's walls, towers and gate-way can be seen.
All year. Museum: Mar-Oct Mon-Sat 11.00-13.0(& 14.00-17.00, Sun 14.00-17.00, Nov-Feb Mor Sat 11.00-13.00 & 14.00-16.00. Castle: daily 08.00-dusk
Admission free for all visitors, charge applies fo special events

Caldicot Castle and Country Park

Church Road Caldicot Monmouthshire
NP26 4HU

Tel: 01291 420241 Fax: 01291 435094

*[M4 J23a. B4245 between Chepstow and
Newport. Plenty of parking on site]*

Visit Caldicot's magnificent medieval castle set
in fifty-five acres of beautiful parkland. Founded
by the Normans and developed in royal hands,
discover its romantic and colourful history.

Mar-Oct daily 11.00-17.00

A£3.00 C£1.50

Cardiff Castle

Castle Street Cardiff CF10 3RB

Tel: 029 2087 8100 Fax: 029 2023 1417

*[From J29, 32, 33 of M4 follow signs to City
Centre where signposted]*

The Norman castle was built on the site of a
Roman fort, and Roman walls some 10ft thick
can still be seen. There is also a Norman keep.
Apartments in the Mansion House were started
in the 15th century, but the present-day character of the castle comes from its transformation
in the 19th century, by eccentric architect
William Burges for the Third Marquess of Bute.

*All year Mar-Oct daily 09.30-18.00, Nov-Feb daily
09.30-17.00*

Grounds only: A£3.00 C&OAPs£1.90. Tour of
House & Grounds: A£6.00 C&OAPs£3.70

Carew Castle and Tidal Mill

Carew Tenby Pembrokeshire SA70 8SL

Tel: 01646 651657 / 651782

Fax: 01646 651782

www.carewcastle.com

*[On A4705 5m E of Pembroke. Plenty of on site
parking]*

Carew is one of the few castles to display the
development from Norman fortification to
Elizabethan country house. Archaeological
excavation has revealed a much earlier settlement dating back perhaps some 2,000 years. A
mile long round walk, with delightful views,
takes in the castle, the Celtic cross, the mill, the
causeway, the 23 acre millpond and a medieval
bridge. Also part of the historic site is the only
restored tidal mill in Wales, with all its original
machinery. An introductory slide-tape programme is complemented by automatic 'talking
points' explaining the milling process and a special exhibition on milling through the ages. A
wide range of events are held every year at
Carew, including theatre interpretation, holiday
activities, battle re-enactments, country fairs
and concerts. A special schools programme
enables children to dress in period costume and
experience life in the castle in times past.

April-end Oct daily 10.00-17.00

Castle & Mill: A£2.80 C&OAPs£1.90 Family
Ticket £7.50. Single ticket Castle or Mill A£1.90
C£1.50. Please be aware that prices are cur-
rently under review

Castell Henllys Iron Age Fort

Meline Felindre Farchoc nr Newport
Pembrokeshire SA41 3UT
Tel: 01239 891319 Fax: 01239 891319
[Off A487 between Cardigan / Newport]

This Iron Age hill fort is set in the beautiful
Pembrokeshire Coast National Park.
Excavations began in 1981 and three round-
houses have been reconstructed. A smithy, and
looms can be seen
*25 Mar-3 Nov daily 10.00-17.00. Guided tours
daily 11.30-14.30*
A£2.80 Concessions£1.90 Family Ticket £7.50.
Price increase possible

Chepstow Castle

Bridge Street Chepstow Gwent NP6 5EZ
Tel: 01291 624065
*[From Cardiff M4, J23, M48, J2, A466. From
London M4, J21, M48]*

Chepstow Castle stands guard over a strategic
crossing point into Wales. In a land of castles,
Chepstow can rightly claim special status. It
was started not long after the Battle of Hastings
in 1066 by William Fitz Osbern, a companion of
William the Conqueror. It was amongst the first
of Britain's stone-built strongholds.
*1 Apr-31 May daily 09.30-17.00, 1 June-30 Sept
daily 09.30-18.00, 1-31 Oct daily 09.30-17.00, 1
Nov-31 Mar Mon-Sat 09.30-16.00, Sun 11.00-
16.00. Closed 24-26 Dec & 1 Jan*
A£3.00 C&Concessions£2.50 Children under 12
must be accompanied by an adult

Erddig Hall

Erddig Wrexham Clwyd LL13 0YT
Tel: 01978 355314 / 315151 (info)
Fax: 01978 313333
*[2m S of Wrexham, signposted off the A483 and
A525]*

Described as the most evocative upstairs-
downstairs house in Britain, Erddig is famous for
the way in which it tells the story of a bustling
household community. There are a number of
outbuildings and the state rooms contain most
of the original 18th and 19th century furniture
and furnishings.
*House: 20 Mar-31 Oct Sat-Wed 12.00-17.00,
(30 Sept-31 Oct 12.00-16.00). Garden: 20 Mar-
31 Oct, 20 Mar-30 June Sat-Wed 11.00-18.00,
July-Aug Sat-Wed 10.00-18.00, Sept-Oct Sat-
Wed 11.00-17.00, Nov-Dec Sat & Sun 11.00-
16.00*
House & Garden: A£7.00 C£3.00 Family Ticket
£17.50. Garden only: A£3.50 C£1.80 Family
Ticket £8.80

Joseph Parry's Cottage

Chapel Row George Town Merthyr Tydfil Mid
Glamorgan CF48 1BN
Tel: 01685 721858 / 723112
Fax: 01685 723112
[Just off A460 Cardiff to Brecon, signposted]

The cottage was the birthplace of the musician
and composer, Dr Joseph Parry, and contains
an exhibition devoted to his life and works. The
ground floor is a recreation of the cottage as it
would have appeared in the 1860s. Brand new
displays.
Apr-Sept Thur-Sun 14.00-17.00. Closed Oct-Mar
Admission Free

Kidwelly Castle

Kidwelly Carmarthenshire SA17 5BQ
Tel: 01554 890104
[Kidwelly via A484]

This is an outstanding example of late 13th-cen-
tury castle design, with its walls within walls
defensive system. There were later additions
made to the building, with the chapel dating
from about 1300. Of particular interest are two
vast circular ovens and the massive gatehouse
*1 Apr-1 June daily 09.30-17.00, 2 June-28 Sep
daily 09.30-18.00, 29 Sept-26 Oct daily 09.30-
17.00, 27 Oct-31 Mar Mon-Sat 09.30-16.00
Sun 11.00-16.00. Closed 24-26 Dec & 1 Jan*
A£2.50 C(0-4)£Free C(5-15)&Concessions£2.0
Children under 12 years must be accompanied
by an adult

Penrhos Cottage

Llanycefn Clunderwen Pembrokeshire
SA66 7XT
Tel: 01437 731328 Fax: 01437 760460
[6m N of Haverfordwest via B4329 road to Maenclochog then off B4313 near Llanycefn]

Local tradition has it that cottages built overnight on common land could be claimed by the builders, together with the ground a stone's throw away from the door. Penrhos Cottage is such a dwelling and has survived almost unchanged since the 19th century.
By appointment only
Entry charges vary according to season call for details

Penrhyn Castle

Bangor Gwynedd LL57 4HN
Tel: 01248 353084 / 371337
Fax: 01248 371281
[1m E of Bangor at Llandegai on A5122]

The splendid castle with its towers and battlements was commissioned in 1827 as a sumptuous family home. The architect was Thomas Hopper, who also was responsible for the panelling, plasterwork and furniture, still mostly in the 'Norman' style of the mid-19th century.
Castle: 27 Mar-31 Oct Wed-Mon 12.00-17.00 (July-Aug 11.00-17.00). Grounds: 27 Mar-31 Oct Wed-Mon 11.00-17.00 (July-Aug 10.00-17.00)
Castle & Grounds: A£7.00 Concessions£3.50 Family Ticket £17.50. Grounds & Stableblock: A£5.00 C£2.50

Plas Newydd

Llanfairpwll Anglesey LL61 6DQ
Tel: 01248 714795 Fax: 01248 713673
[2m S of Llanfairpwll and A55]

Cradled in a landscape garden on the banks of the Menai Strait, this elegant 18th century country house by James Wyatt commands magnificent views of the Strait and the mountains of Snowdonia.
27 Mar-2 Nov Sat-Wed. House: 12.00-17.00. Garden: 11.00-17.30. Open Good Fri. Rhododendron garden open 27 Mar-early June 11.00-17.30
A£5.00 C£2.50 Family Ticket (A2+C3) £12.00. Garden only: A£3.00 C£1.50

Raglan Castle

Raglan Gwent NP5 2BT
Tel: 01291 690228
[Signposted off A40]

This magnificent 15th century castle noted for its 'Yellow Tower of Gwent' was built by Sir William ap Thomas and slighted during the Civil War, after a long siege. The ruins are still impressive and the castle's history is illustrated in an exhibition.
1 Apr-31 May daily 09.30-17.00, 1 June-30 Sept daily 09.30-18.00, 1-31 Oct daily 09.30-17.00, 1 Nov-31 Mar Mon-Sat 09.30-16.00m Sun 11.00-16.00. Closed 24-26 Dec & 1 Jan
A£2.75 C(under5)£Free C(5-15)&Concessions£2.25 Children under 12 years must be accompanied by an adult

Scolton Manor House

Spittal Haverfordwest Pembrokeshire SA62 5QL
Tel: 01437 731328
[5m N of Haverfordwest on B4329]

The early Victorian mansion and stables illustrate some of the social history of Pembrokeshire. Within the mansion are period rooms on three floors.
1 Apr-end Oct Tue-Sun 10.30-17.30 (open Bank Hol Mons & Mon during July-Aug). Park: winter 10.00-16.30, summer 10.00-18.00. Closed 25-26 Dec
A£2.00 C£1.00 Concessions£1.50

Mining

Big Pit National Mining Museum of Wales

Blaenafon Torfaen NP4 9XP
Tel: 01495 790311 Fax: 01495 792618
[Off B4246 follow brown tourist signs. J25 or 26 from M4. Follow A4042 and A4043 to Pontypool and Blaenafon; look for brown tourist signs]

'Big Pit' closed as a working coalmine in 1980, but today visitors can don safety helmets and lamps, and go 300ft underground to a different world to find out what life was like for generations of miners in South Wales.
Mar-Nov daily 09.30-17.00. Tours run from 10.00-15.30. Closed in winter
Admission Free

Dolaucothi Gold Mines

Pumsaint Llanwrda Carmarthenshire SA19 8US
Tel: 01558 650177 Fax: 01558 650707
[On A482 Lampeter - Llanwrda]

These unique gold mines are set amid wooded hillsides overlooking the beautiful Cothi Valley. The Romans who exploited the site almost 2,000 years ago left behind a complex of pits, channels, adits and tanks. Mining resumed in the 19th century and continued through the 20th century, reaching a peak in 1938. Guided tours take visitors through the Roman and the more recent underground workings.

2 Apr-2 Nov daily 10.00-17.00

Site: A£3.00 C£1.50 Family Ticket £7.50. Underground Tour: A£3.70 C£1.90 Family Ticket £9.30

Tredegar House and Park

Coedkernew Newport Gwent NP10 8YW

Tel: 01633 815880 Fax: 01633 815895

[2m W signposted from A48/M4 J28. Rail: Newport. Bus: local services 15 & 30 stop nearby. Plenty of parking on site]

Set in ninety acres of award winning Gardens and Parkland, Tredegar House is one of the finest examples of Restoration Architecture in Wales, and was the ancestral home of the Morgans for over five hundred years. Visitors today can discover what life was like for those who lived 'above and below' stairs. A stunning sequence of Staterooms, elaborately decorated with carvings, gilding, and fine paintings contrast with the fascinating and extensive domestic quarters. Lakeside walks, beautiful walled gardens, orangery and spectacular stable block complete the 'Country House' picture. Gift shop, tea room, craft workshops together with special events in the House and Park throughout the year.

Good Fri-end Sept Wed-Sun & Bank Hol 11.30-16.00. Special Christmas & Halloween opening. Group visits at other times

House Tours: A£5.10 C£Free (when accompanied by a full paying adult) Concessions£3.75. Discounts available for Newport Residents. Group rates (20+): (daytime) A£4.50 Concessions£3.60. Evening tours available. Car Park: £1.00 per day or £5.00 season ticket. Please call for price details for wedding ceremonies and Victorian school tours

Elliot Colliery

White Rose Way New Tredegar Caerphilly
NP2 6DF
Tel: 01443 822666 Fax: 01443 838609
Located off the A465 (Heads of the Valleys Road) on A469, signposted Rhymney]

Visit the Winding House and discover the story of Elliot Colliery, the local coal industry, and experience the massive winding engine in action.
All year Wed-Fri 11.00-16.00, Easter-end Sept Sat, Sun and Bank Hol 14.00-17.00
Admission Free

Rhondda Heritage Park

Lewis Merthyr Colliery Coed Cae Road Trehafod Rhondda Cynon Taff CF37 7NP
Tel: 01443 682036 Fax: 01443 687420
Off the A470, between Pontypridd and Porth]

Make a 'Pit Stop' at the award winning Rhondda Heritage Park - a fun day out for all the family, whatever the weather.
All year daily 10.00-18.00. Closed Mon Oct-Easter. Closed 25 Dec-1 Jan
A£5.60 C£4.30 Family Ticket (A2+C2) £16.50 Concessions£4.95

Discount Offer: Two Admitted For The Price Of One.

Places of Worship

Goleulong 2000 Lightship

Waterfront Park Harbour Drive Cardiff Bay Cardiff CF10 4PA
Tel: 029 4028 7609
M4 J33 via A4232 following signs for Cardiff Bay]

In 1988 the churches in Cardiff were called together by the Cardiff Bay Development Corporation to discuss the role of Christianity in the bay area. Helwick LV14 was purchased and restoration begun to create a floating Christian Centre. The Chapel is open daily and is used for worship and quiet meditation. Visitors can view the Chapel, engine room, wheel house, tower room, Heli deck, Mess room, cabins, galley and lounge.
All year Mon-Sat 11.00-17.00, Sun 14.00-17.00
Admission Free

Llandaff Cathedral

The Cathedral Green Cardiff CF5 2LA
Tel: 029 2056 4554 Fax: 029 2056 3897
[Cathedral Road (A4119) and follow tourist signs]

A medieval cathedral built from 12th century on the site of an early Christian place of worship. The cathedral was severely damaged during the bombing raids on Cardiff during World War II. The interior is dominated by a modernistic post-war 'Christ in Majesty' sculpture. Photography permitted for a nominal fee.
All year, call for details
Donations welcomed

St Davids Cathedral

The Close St Davids Pembrokeshire SA62 6RH

Tel: 01437 720199 Fax: 01437 721885

www.stdavidscathedral.org.uk

[A487]

Begun in 1181 on the site reputed to be where St David founded a monastic settlement in the

6th century. The present building was altered during the 12th to the 14th centuries and again in the 16th. It also has an extension added in 1993, so the architecture is varied. The ceilings - oak, painted wood and stone vaulting - are of considerable interest. The floor of the nave slopes a metre over its length while over the entire length of the cathedral the difference is four metres. In addition to services there are organ recitals on Wednesdays from late July through to early September. The Cathedral Music Festival runs from 29 May-6 June.

All year daily 08.30-18.00

Suggested donation of £2.00

Police, Prisons & Dungeons

Beaumaris Gaol and Courthouse

Bunkers Hill Beaumaris Gwynedd LL58 8EW
Tel: 01248 810921 Fax: 01248 750282
[A545 from the Bridges]

With its treadmill and grim cells, the gaol is a vivid reminder of the tough penalties exacted by 19th century law. One particularly gruesome feature is the route that condemned prisoners took to the scaffold.
Easter-Sept daily 10.30-17.00, Court 10.30-17.00 except when in session
Gaol: A£2.50 C&OAPs£1.50. Courthouse: A£1.50 C&OAPs£1.00 Family Ticket £7.00. Joint Ticket: A£3.25 C&OAPs£2.20 Family Ticket £10.00. Prices subject to change

Railways

Bala Lake Railway

Llanuwchllyn Bala Gwynedd LL23 7DD

Tel: 01678 540666 Fax: 01678 540535
[Off A494]

For a perfect day out, why not ride a narrow-gauge train on the Bala Lake Railway, along Wales' largest natural lake. Llanuwchllyn (the village above the lake) is the headquarters of the Railway and regular trains link the village with the delightful market town of Bala.

Easter-end Sept daily except some Mon & Fri
Return Tickets: A£6.70 C(5-15)Unaccompanied £3.00 Family and single tickets available

Brecon Mountain Railway

Pant Station Merthyr Tydfil CF48 2UP

Tel: 01685 722988 Fax: 01685 384854

[Just off Heads of the Valleys trunk road - about 3m N of Merthyr Tydfil]

Whatever the weather visit one of Wales' most popular narrow gauge steam railways. Travel in one of our all-weather observation coaches behind a vintage steam locomotive through beautiful scenery into the Brecon Beacons National Park

End Mar-31 Oct daily. Trains run every 75mins from 11.00. Closed some Mon & Fri in Mar, Apr, May, Sept & Oct

Basic return: A£7.50 C£3.75 OAPs£6.80

Gwili Steam Railway

Bronwydd Arms Station Bronwydd Carmarthen Dyfed SA33 6HT

Tel: 01267 230666

[Follow the brown 'steam railway' signs off the A40 or A484, 3m N of Carmarthen]

Join the train at Bronwydd Arms Station, and take a trip into the past, on a living and growing full size steam railway. Enjoy the beautiful Gwili Valley, relax alongside the river for a picnic, walk the woodland walk, ride the miniature railway, and absorb the nostalgia of bygone days.

Trains run on the following dates: 9-13 Apr (Days

Out with Thomas), 2-3, 9, 16, 23, 30, 31 May, 1-3, 6, 9, 13, 16, 20, 23, 27 June, 4, 11, 14, 18, 21, 25, 28, 31 July, 1-31 Aug, 5, 12, 19, 26 Sept, 28-30 Oct (Days Out with Thomas), 11-12, 18-19, 22-24 Dec (Santa's Special), 25-29 Mar 2005

A£5.00 C(2-15)/Concessions£3.00 Family Ticket (A2+C2) £13.00

Discount Offer: One Child Free With A Full Paying Adult

Llanberis Lake Railway

Padarn Country Park Gilfach Ddu Llanberis Caernarfon Gwynedd LL55 4TY

Tel: 01286 870549 Fax: 01286 870549

[Off A4086 at Llanberis follow Padarn Country Park signs]

Steam locomotives dating from 1889 to 1948 carry passengers on a four-mile return journey along the shore of Padarn Lake.

Easter-late Oct, trains run frequently Sun-Fri 11.00-16.30 in peak season, not Sat. July & Aug daily

A£6.00 C£4.00 Family ticket available

Pontypool and Blaenaven Railway

13a Broad Street Blaenavon Pontypool Gwent NP4 9ND

Tel: 01495 792263

[Off B4248 between Blaenavon and Brynmawr, and well signposted]

Originally the railway extended from Brynmawr to Pontypool. The line closed to passengers in 1941, though the section from Blaenavon to Pontypool was in use for coal from Big Pit and other local mines until 1980. The line northwards is the steepest standard gauge preserved passenger-carrying line in Britain.

Trains run on: Apr 10, 11, 12, 18, 25, May 1, 2, 3, 9, 16, 23, 30, 31, June 5, 6, 12, 13, 19, 20, 26, 27, July 3, 4, 10, 11, 17, 18, 24, 25, 31, Aug 1, 7, 8, 14, 15, 21, 22, 23, 28, 29, 30, Sept 4, 5, 12, 19, 26. Also Dec 4, 5, 11, 12, 18, 19 for Santa Specials (2004). Return journey time is 17mins. Trains run every 30mins 11.00-15.30 from Furnace Sidings

Furnace Sidings to Whistle Inn: A£2.40 C(under14)£1.20 C(under3)£Free Family Ticket (A2+C2) £6.00. Single journey tickets available

Roman Era

Caerleon Roman Baths and Amphitheatre

High Street Caerleon Newport Gwent NP18 1AE

Tel: 01633 422518

[M4(W), J25, (E), J26 on B4236]

Caerleon is one of Europe's most fascinating and revealing Roman sites. To the Romans the town was known as Isca. At Caerleon, the Romans created not just a military camp but an entire township, complete with amphitheatre and bath house.

1 Apr-26 Oct daily 09.30-17.00, 27 Oct-31 Mar Mon-Sat 09.30-17.00, Sun 13.00-17.00. Closed 24, 25, 26 Dec & 1 Jan

A£2.50 C(0-5)£Free C&Concessions£2.00 Family Ticket (A2+C3) £7.00. Children under 12 must be accompanied by an adult

Science - Earth & Planetary

Techniquest

Stuart Street Cardiff CF10 5BW

Tel: 029 2047 5475 Fax: 029 2048 2517

www.techniquest.org

[M4, J33, follow A4232 until signposted. There is limited parking on site (reserved for disabled visitors) but plenty of parking nearby]

Located in the heart of the Cardiff Bay redevelopment area, here you will find science and technology made accessible - and fun - at the UK's most visited interactive science discovery centre. Visitors of all ages can participate in the activities and experiment with the exhibits. A fun filled day for visitors of all ages.

All year Mon-Fri 09.30-16.30, Sat-Sun & Bank Hol 10.30-17.00. Closed 24, 25, 26, 27 Dec, 1 Jan.

A£6.75 C(under3)£Free C&Concessions£4.75 Family Ticket £18.50.

Events in the Planetarium and Laboratory are chargeable in addition to main admission, call for details

Discount Offer: One Child Free With One Or More Full Paying Adult/s.

Sealife Centres & Aquariums

Anglesey Sea Zoo

Brynsiencyn Llanfairpwllgwyngyll Anglesey LL61 6TQ

Tel: 01248 430411 Fax: 01248 430213

[Follow lobster signs from Britannia Bridge, then just off A4080]

A unique collection of marine life found around Anglesey housed in natural seascapes. Shipwrecks, wave tanks, lobster and seahorse nursery.

14 Feb-2 Apr daily 11.00-16.00, 3 Apr-31 Oct daily 10.00-18.00

A£5.95 C£4.95 OAPs£5.50 Family tickets available

Discount Offer: One Child Free For Every Two Full Paying Adults

Theme & Adventure Parks

Oakwood Leisure Park

Canaston Bridge Narberth Pembrokeshire
SA67 8DE

Tel: 01834 891373 Fax: 01834 891380
www.oakwood-leisure.com

[Signposted from the end of the M4 approx 2hrs from Bristol. Plenty of free parking on site]

Oakwood Leisure Park is Wales' top paid for visitor attraction. It features over 40 rides and attractions set in 80 acres of the beautiful Pembrokeshire countryside. Rides include Hydro - Europe's tallest water ride, Megafobia - the UK's largest wooden roller coaster, Vertigo - a 50m sky coaster, The Bounce - 160ft shot and drop tower coaster, Pirate Ship, Bobsleigh, Snake River Falls water ride and many more. Kidzworld for younger children includes under-cover play areas and Brer Rabbit's Burrow. With rides for all the family you can be sure of a great day out.

3 Apr-3 Oct daily 10.00-17.00. Late night open-ing with live entertainment and fireworks 24 July-30 Aug 10.00-22.00

A£13.75 C(3-9)£12.75 Family Ticket (4 persons) £49.00 OAPs/Disabled£9.50. Supplementary Charge for Vertigo. Group rate & School Parties on application

Special Events

Easter Eggstravaganza
03/04/2004-18/04/2004
Extended opening until 19.00, plus a prize give-away!

After Dark
24/07/2004-30/08/2004
Extended opening until 22.00 plus live shows and fireworks

Eerie Evenings Halloween Party
25/10/2004-31/10/2004
Time: 17.00-21.00. Also includes live shows and spooky suppers

Tourist Information Centres

Cardiff Bay Visitor Centre

Harbour Drive Britannia Quay Cardiff Bay Cardiff CF10 4PA

Tel: 029 2046 3833 Fax: 029 2048 6650

The Cardiff Bay Visitor Centre, known locally as 'The Tube', was designed by avant-garde archi-tect William Alsop. Since it opened its doors in 1991, the Centre become a major tourist attrac-tion in its own right.

All year daily, Summer (May-Sept) Mon-Fri 09.30-18.00, Sat-Sun 10.30-18.00, Winter (Oct-Apr) Mon-Fri 09.30-17.00, Sat-Sun 10.30-17.00. Closed 24-26, 31 Dec & 1 Jan
Admission Free

Transport Museums

National Coracle Centre

Cenarth Falls Newcastle Emlyn Carmarthenshire SA38 9JL

Tel: 01239 710980 / 710507

[A484 between Cardigan and Carmarthen]

The National Coracle Centre is situated beside the beautiful Cenarth Falls and Salmon Leap, housing a unique collection of coracles from all over Wales and many parts of the World.

Easter-31 Oct Sun-Fri 10.30-17.30

A£3.00 C(0-5)£Free C(5+)£1.00 Concessions£2.50

Victorian Era

Judge's Lodging

Broad Street Presteigne Powys LD8 2AD

Tel: 01544 260650 Fax: 01544 260652

www.judgeslodging.org.uk

[In the town centre, off the B4362. Presteigne is located on the Wales / England border, within easy access from the A49, A44, A456 and A483]

Explore the fascinating world of the Victorian judges, their servants, and felonious guests at this award-winning historic house. From the stunningly restored judge's apartments to the dingy servants' quarters below, you can wander through their gaslit world, aided by an eaves-dropping audiotour of voices from the past, featuring the voice of actor, Robert Hardy. Damp cells and vast courtroom echo to the 1860s trial of a local duck thief. Totally hands-on, with special activities for children during holidays. Shop, tourist information, local history exhibitions, group tours and interactive school sessions. Britain's Local Museum of the Year 1999 and Interpret Britain 1998. Recently featured in BBC2's series 'Simon Schama's History of Britain'. Partial disabled access, please call for further information.

1 Mar-31 Oct daily 10.00-18.00, 1 Nov-22 Dec Wed-Sun 10.00-16.00. Closed Jan & Feb. Open all year for groups

A£4.50 C£3.50 OAPs£3.95 Family Ticket £13.50. Free admission for disabled visitors

Discount Offer: Two For The Price Of One.

Zoos

The Animalarium

Borth Ceredigion SY24 5NA

Tel: 01970 871224

[In Borth a short walk from the Cardigan Bay beach]

One of the Star Attractions of Mid Wales with a Wales Tourist Board seal of approval, the Animalarium is a collection of small exotic and domestic animals, birds and reptiles. Visitors can see all the animals at close quarters, breeding colonies of monkeys, marmosets, lemurs, Geoffroy's cats, wallabies, rheas and other birds in large aviaries. There is also a petting barn with domestic, pet and farm animals, including miniature pigs and goats, rabbits, guinea pigs and more. Then there is the fruit bat cave, the exotic insects and reptiles such as crocodiles, large Iguana and many species and sizes of snake. A snake handling demonstration takes place daily, when you may touch and handle a snake. Crocodile feeding is a daily attraction. Many exhibits are under cover and the Animalarium, which is close to the beach, also has a picnic area, free car park, outdoor playground and indoor ball pool, an education room, toilets, souvenir shop and café. It is wheelchair friendly, with concrete paths to all exhibits, and a toilet for the disabled.

All year daily Easter-Oct daily 10.00-18.00, Nov-Easter daily 11.00-16.00

A£6.00 C£4.00 Concessions£5.00 Family Ticket (A2+C3) £18.00

Welsh Mountain Zoo

Colwyn Bay North Wales LL28 5UY
Tel: 01492 532938 Fax: 01492 530498
[3min drive from A55 expressway - signposted]

One of Britain's best holiday experiences - a friendly and caring conservation Zoo set in lovely garden surroundings with spectacular scenery. Hundreds of animals from bears to alligators.
All year daily 09.30-17.00 main season, 09.30-16.00 winter
A£6.95 C(under4)£free C£4.95 Students£4.95
OAPs£5.95 Family Ticket (A2+C2) £20.95

Warwickshire

Animal Attractions

Umberslade Children's Farm

Butts Lane Tanworth-In-Arden Nr Solihull
Warwickshire B94 5AE
Tel: 01564 742251
*[3m S of J3/4 M42 & signposted off B4101
Hockley Heath to Redditch Road]*

A working farm that has so much to offer.
Feeding, holding animals, milking, harnessing
up, ferret racing and much much more.
Bottlefeed and cuddle the baby lambs and kids.
Give your pony-mad children a pony or donkey
ride around the farm or why not try a tractor
ride to rest those weary legs.
*22 Mar-2 Nov Sat & Sun 10.00-17.00. Easter,
Summer School hols, Summer & Autumn half
terms daily 10.00-17.00*
A£5.00 C(under2)£Free C(2-16)£4.00
OAPs£3.50 Family Ticket (A2+C2) £16.50,
(A2+C3) £20.00

Archaeology

Warwickshire Museum

Market Place Warwick Warwickshire CV34 4SA
Tel: 01926 412500 Fax: 01926 419840
[Town location in main square]

Wildlife geology, archaeology and history of
Warwickshire including the famous Sheldon
tapestry map and giant fossil plesiosaur.
*All year Tue-Sat & Bank Hol Mon daily 10.00-
17.00, May-Sept Sun 11.00-17.00*
Admission Free

Arts, Crafts & Textiles

Rugby Art Gallery and Museum

Little Elborow Street Rugby Warwickshire
CV21 3BZ
Tel: 01788 533201 Fax: 01788 533204
The Art Gallery has a changing programme of
exhibitions of contemporary visual art and craft
including shows from the Rugby Collection of
20th century British art. The Museum is home
to the Tripontium Collection of Roman artefacts
and a growing Social History Collection.
All year Tue & Thu 10.00-20.00, Wed & Fri

*10.00-17.00, Sat 10.00-16.00, Sun & Bank Hols
13.00-17.00*
Admission Free

Birds, Butterflies & Bees

Stratford-Upon-Avon Butterfly Farm

Tramway Walk Swan's Nest Lane
Stratford-Upon-Avon Warwickshire CV37 7LS

Tel: 01789 299288 Fax: 01789 415878

www.butterflyfarm.co.uk

[South bank of River Avon opposite RSC]

Europe's largest live Butterfly and Insect Exhibit.
Hundreds of the world's most spectacular and
colourful butterflies. Insect City has a huge collection of strange and fascinating animals.
Arachnoland features the 'dealers in death'.
There is also an outdoor British butterfly garden
in the summer.

*Summer daily 10.00-18.00. Winter 10.00-dusk.
Closed 25 Dec*

A£4.45 C£3.45 OAPs/Students£3.95 Family
Ticket (A2+C2) £12.95 + £1.75 for additional
Child. Special school tours can be arranged

Exhibition & Visitor Centres

Royal Pump Rooms Art Gallery and Museum

The Parade Royal Leamington Spa
Warwickshire CV32 4AA
Tel: 01926 742700 Fax: 01926 742705
A new cultural and tourism complex has been
created in Leamington Spa's historic Royal
Pump Rooms. Now housing the town's Art
Gallery and Museum, Library and Tourist
Information Centre in the restored building,
alongside the existing Assembly Rooms and a
new Café.
*All year Tue, Wed, Fri & Sat 10.30-17.00, Thur
13.30-20.00, Sun 11.00-16.00. Closed Mon*
Admission Free

Festivals & Shows

Leamington Festival

Royal Pump Rooms Royal Spa Centre
Leamington Spa Warwickshire
Tel: 01926 496277 Fax: 01926 409050
*[Leave M40 at J13 & follow signs to Leamington
town centre]*

Incorporates the traditional themed May Bank
Holiday Weekend. World music events lead into
a final weekend of jazz and new music. A
potent mixture and new look for Leamington!
April 30-May 9 2004

Sandwell Community Show

Salters Lane West Bromwich B71 4BG
Tel: 0121 569 8276 Fax: 0121 569 4704
*[J1 M5, follow signs for Sandwell Valley Country
Park. Car Park £2.00 per car]*

The Sandwell Community Show attracts over
100,000 visitors each August Bank Holiday. It is
the ideal family show with plenty of entertainment including a fun fair, craft fayre, horticultural
marquee, arena events and much more.

August 29-30 2004
Admission free

Stratford-upon-Avon Poetry Festival

Shakespeare Birthplace Trust
Shakespeare Centre Henley Street
Stratford-upon-Avon Warwickshire CV37 6QW
Tel: 01789 204106 Fax: 01789 296083
[J15, M40. A46 to Stratford]

The 51st Stratford-upon-Avon Festival will
encompass a wide range of poetry and offer
something for everyone interested in verse.
Programme is not yet confirmed, please contact
venue for details.
July 4-August 29 2004 on Sunday evenings

Town and Country Festival 2004

Stoneleigh Park Kenilworth Warwickshire
CV8 2LZ
Tel: 024 7669 6969 Fax: 024 7669 6900
*[Well signposted & approx. half way between
Coventry & Warwick off A46, with the main
motorway network easily accessible]*

The Town and Country Festival will entertain the
whole family over the August Bank Holiday
weekend. There are thousands of things to see
with four worlds rolled into one - Leisure and
Shopping World, Motor World, Countryside
World and Live World. Whatever you do, take
part in, or watch you will not be disappointed!
With all this and much more on offer you can
save money by booking your tickets in advance
on 024 7685 8291, there is also a group rate
available, for every 10 tickets you buy of the
same category you get one free. For more information about the biggest family fun day out in
the Midlands call 024 7685 8278.
August 28-30 2004
Advance Tickets: A£8.50 C(5-15)£3.50
C(under5)£Free OAPs£5.50 Family Ticket
(A2+C2) £23.50. On the Gate: A£9.50 C(5-
15)£4.50 C(under5)£Free OAPs£6.50 Family
Ticket (A2+C2) £26.00

Gardens & Horticulture

Ryton Organic Gardens

Coventry Warwickshire CV8 3LG

Tel: 024 7630 3517 Fax: 024 7663 9229

www.hdra.org.uk

[Situated on rd to Wolston, off A45, 5m SE of Coventry, follow brown 'Ryton Gardens' signboards. NB: NO access to or from the M1 N J17. Travellers from M1 N should take M69 & A46 via Coventry. Plenty of on site parking available]

The UK's national centre for organic gardening has a major new attraction. The £2 million Vegetable Kingdom run by HDRA - the organic organisation - tells the story of Britain's vegetables. Wonderful interactive displays are guaranteed to inform and entrance young and old alike. Outside, enjoy over eight acres of gardens including stunning flower borders, herbs, shrubs, a delightful children's garden and, of course lots of fruit and vegetables. Also learn the best way of making compost and how to control pests and diseases without using pesticides. Our visitor centre, which has a first class restaurant, has been extended, with a new coffee shop. And if you enjoy shopping we have lots to tempt you in our enlarged shop! Ryton regularly appears on TV.

All year daily 09.00-17.00. Closed Christmas week

A£3.95 C(accompanied)£1.50. HDRA/RHS members free

Discount Offer: Two For The Price Of One Full Paying Adult.

Historical

Anne Hathaway's Cottage

Shottery Stratford-Upon-Avon Warwickshire CV37 9HH

Tel: 01789 292100 Fax: 01789 205014

www.shakespeare.org.uk

[Off A422, 1m from the town centre. Plenty of on site parking available]

Before her marriage to William Shakespeare, Anne Hathaway lived in this substantial thatched Tudor farmhouse with her family. Home to descendants of the Hathaway family until 19th century. Includes famous Hathaway bed, courting settle and other furniture owned by her family. Traditional English cottage garden. Enjoy the tree garden, maze and sculpture park. Shop and garden centre. Computer based 'virtual reality' tour of cottage for those with restricted mobility.

All year daily Apr-May Mon-Sat 09.30-17.00, Sun 10.00-17.00, June-Aug Mon-Sat 09.00-17.00, Sun 09.30-17.00, Sept-Oct Mon-Sat 09.30-

17.00, Sun 10.00-17.00, Nov-Mar daily 10.00-16.00. Times listed are opening time to last entry. Closed 23-26 Dec

A£5.20 C£2.00 Concession£4.00 Family Ticket £12.00. Multiple House Tickets: 3 in town houses A£10.00 C£5.00 Concessions£8.00 Family Ticket £20.00, all 5 houses A£13.00 C£6.50 Concessions£12.00 Family Ticket £29.00. Group rates available, please call 01789 210806 for details

Charlecote Park

The National Trust Charlecote Warwick Warwickshire CV35 9ER
Tel: 01789 470277 Fax: 01789 470544
[5m E of Stratford-upon-Avon on N side of B4086]

Elizabeth I and Shakespeare knew Charlecote well. Now you can follow in their footsteps when you visit this stunning house, 'Capability' Brown landscaped deer park and glorious gardens.
House: 6 Mar-2 Nov Fri-Tue plus Wed in July-Aug & Bank Hol weeks, 12.00-17.00 (16.30 Oct).
Park, Gardens, Grounds: 6 Mar-2 Nov Fri-Tue plus Wed in July-Aug & Bank Hol weeks 10.30-17.30, 8-28 Nov Sat & Sun 11.00-16.00, 4-20 Dec Sat & Sun 11.00-16.00
House, Park, Gardens & Grounds: A£6.40 C£3.20 Family Ticket £16.00. Park, Gardens & Grounds only: A£3.00 C£1.50

Coughton Court

Coughton Alcester Warwickshire B49 5JA
Tel: 01789 762435 Fax: 01789 765544
[2m N of Alcester, on A435. 8m NW of Stratford-upon-Avon, 18m S of Birmingham]

An impressive central gatehouse dating from 1530. During the Civil War this formerly moated and mainly Elizabethan house was attacked by both sides. Also has strong connections with the Gun Powder Plot.
House & Gardens: 6-31 Mar Sat & Sun, 1 Apr-30

June Wed-Sun, 1 July-31 Aug Tue-Sun, 1-30 Sept Wed-Sun, 1-31 Oct Sat & Sun. Open Bank Hol Mons and also Tue Apr, May, Aug. Closed Good Fri & 26 June
House & Gardens: A£8.25 C(under5)£Free C(under16)£4.15. Gardens only: A£5.50 C£2.7

Hall's Croft

Old Town Stratford-Upon-Avon Warwickshire CV37

Tel: 01789 292107 Fax: 01789 266209

www.shakespeare.org.uk

[Town centre location]

This impressive 16th-century house, with Jacobean additions, was named after Dr John Hall, who married Shakespeare's daughter Susanna in 1607. It is likely they lived here until moving to New Place after Shakespeare died, 1616. Hall's Croft is near Holy Trinity Church, where Shakespeare is buried. Admire the outstanding 16th and 17th century furniture and paintings. View Dr Hall's 'consulting room' and exhibition about medicine in Shakespeare's time. Walk round the lovely old walled garden and see the herbal bed. Take tea in the shade of a 200-year-old mulberry tree. Disabled access limited to the ground floor and the garden.

All year Apr-May daily 11.00-17.00, June-Aug Mon-Sat 09.30-17.00, Sun 10.00-17.00, Sept-Oct daily 11.00-17.00, Nov-Mar daily 11.00-16.00. Times listed are opening times to last entry. Closed 23-26 Dec

£3.50 C£1.70 Concessions£3.00 Family
Ticket £9.00. Multiple House Tickets: 3 in town
houses A£10.00 C£5.00 Concessions£8.00
Family Ticket £20.00, all 5 houses A£13.00
C£6.50 Concessions£12.00 Family Ticket
£29.00. Group rates available, please call
01789 210806 for details

A£5.70 C£2.50 Concessions£5.00 Family
Ticket £13.50. Multiple House Tickets: 3 in
town houses A£10.00 C£5.00
Concessions£8.00 Family Ticket £20.00, all 5
houses A£13.00 C£6.50 Concessions£12.00
Family Ticket £29.00. Group rates available,
please call 01789 210806 for details

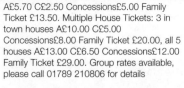

Mary Arden's House and the Shakespeare Countryside Museum

Featherbed Lane Wilmcote
Stratford-Upon-Avon Warwickshire CV37 9UN

Tel: 01789 293455 Fax: 01789 415404

www.shakespeare.org.uk

[3m NW off A34 just 3.5m from the town centre. Plenty of on site parking]

This early Tudor house belonged to Robert
Arden, Shakespeare's Grandfather, and was the
childhood home of Mary Arden, the dramatist's
mother. The site today, with its many farm buildings, activities and rare breeds of farm animals,
brings to life for visitors and families the work
and traditions of the countryside around
Stratford-upon-Avon from Shakespeare's time
to the early 20th century. Daily falconry displays
and regular events for all the family.

*All year daily, Apr-May Mon-Sat 10.00-17.00, Sun
10.30-17.00, June-Aug Mon-Sat 09.30-17.00,
Sun 10.00-17.00, Sept-Oct Mon-Sat 10.00-
17.00, Sun 10.30-17.00, Nov-Mar Mon-Sat
10.00-16.00, Sun 10.30-16.00. Times listed are
opening time to last entry. Closed 23-26 Dec*

Nash's House and New Place

Chapel Street Stratford-Upon-Avon
Warwickshire CV37 6EP

Tel: 01789 292325 Fax: 01789 266228

www.shakespeare.org.uk

*[Located in the town cente next door to
Shakespeare Hotel and opposite Falcon Hotel]*

Step aside from the bustle of Chapel Street into
the tranquility of Nash's House which dates
from the 16th-century. It was owned by Thomas
Nash who married Shakespeare's grand-daugh-
ter Elizabeth Hall in 1626. As well as exceptional
furnishings of Shakespeare's time it has displays
on the history of Stratford. From Nash's House
go outside to explore the site of New Place, the
house where Shakespeare lived from 1597 until
he died in 1616. The house was pulled down in
1759 but its foundations and grounds can be
seen. Visit the colourful Elizabethan style Knott
Garden.

*All year Apr-May daily 11.00-17.00, June-Aug
Mon-Sat 09.30-17.00, Sun 10.00-17.00, Sept-
Oct daily 11.00-17.00, Nov-Mar daily 11.00-
16.00. Times listed are opening times to last
entry. Closed 23-26 Dec*

A£3.50 C£1.70 Concessions£3.00 Family Ticket £9.00. Multiple House Tickets: 3 in town houses A£10.00 C£5.00 Concessions£8.00 Family Ticket £20.00, all 5 houses A£13.00 C£6.50 Concessions£12.00 Family Ticket £29.00. Group rates available, please call 01789 210806 for details

Ragley Hall

Alcester Warwickshire B49 5NJ

**Tel: 01789 762090 Fax: 01789 764791
www.ragleyhall.com**

[2m SW off A435/A46 near Alcester. Plenty of free on site parking available]

The family home of the Marquess and Marchioness of Hertford is one of the earliest and loveliest of England's great Palladian Houses. The perfect symmetry of the architecture of Ragley remains unchanged save for the spectacular portico by Wyatt added in 1780. The majestic Great Hall, two storeys high, is adorned with some of England's finest Baroque plasterwork by James Gibbs, dated 1750. A most striking feature of Ragley is the breathtaking mural 'The Temptation' by Graham Rust in the south staircase hall. Ragley houses a superb collection of 18th century and earlier paintings, china and furniture. Ragley is set in 400 acres of picturesque parkland landscaped by 'Capability' Brown and 27 acres of fascinating gardens including the enchanting rose garden, richly planted borders and mature woodland. For children there is an exciting woodland adventure playground, 3D maze and an extensive lakeside play and picnic area, and for walkers the delightful woodland walk.

Garden, Park, Adventure Playground: 3 Apr-26 Sept Thur-Sun & Bank Hol Mons 10.00-18.00, also open 3-18 Apr, 29 May-6 June & 17 July-5 Sept daily. House: 3 Apr-26 Sept Thur-Sun & Bank Hol Mons 12.00-17.30. Oct-Mar House and Gardens open by special arrangement with the General Manager

House, Garden, Park & Adventure Playground: A£7.50 C£4.50 Concessions£6.50 Family Ticket £25.00. Garden, Park, Adventure Playground: A£6.00 C£4.50 Concessions£5.50 Family Ticket £22.00. Group rates and season tickets available

Special Events

The Importance of Being Earnest
05/05/2004-08/05/2004
Theatre in the Great Hall

Classic Car and Transport Show
30/05/2004-31/05/2004

Ever Changing Light (Glass Sculpture - Garden Exhibition)
05/06/2004-04/07/2004

Jools Holland Outdoor Concert
26/06/2004

Status Quo Outdoor Concert
27/06/2004

Alcester Singers Summer Concert
02/07/2004

Rover Sports Register National Rally
11/07/2004

Alice Through the Looking Glass
14/07/2004

Meet Noddy and Friends
24/07/2004-25/07/2004

Newfoundland Dog Trials
31/07/2004

Queen Extravaganza Tribute Band
06/08/2004

Proms Spectacular Concert
07/08/2004

Warwickshire and West Midlands Game Fair
21/08/2004-22/08/2004

National Gardens Scheme Open Day
1/09/2004

lower Festival/Horticultural Show (tbc)
4/09/2004-05/09/2004

VLA Number Plate Auction
4/09/2004-15/09/2004

ive Craft Show
4/09/2004-26/09/2004

M102 The Bear Radio Wedding Fair
0/10/2004

Christmas Craft Fair - MGA
7/11/2004-28/11/2004

Icester Singers Christmas Concert
0/12/2004-11/12/2004

agley by Candlelight
5/12/2004-17/12/2004

Shakespeare's Birthplace

The Shakespeare Centre Henley Street
Stratford-Upon-Avon Warwickshire CV37 6QW

Tel: 01789 201823 Fax: 01789 299132

www.shakespeare.org.uk

J15 M40, A46 to Stratford upon Avon, located in he town centre]

The half-timbered house where William Shakespeare was born in 1564 continued as a family home until the 19th century. It has welcomed visitors for well over 250 years, and has many fascinating architectural features and 16th and 17th century furniture. Come in through the Visitors' Centre and see the highly-acclaimed Shakespeare exhibition: His Life and Background. Enjoy the traditional English garden. Stand in the rooms where Shakespeare grew up. Read the signatures of famous visitors cut in the window panes. See how the walls were made of wattle and daub. Choose from the selection of gifts in the Birthplace Shop. Browse in the Shakespeare Bookshop (opposite the Birthplace). Disabled access limited to the ground floor and gardens. Computer based 'virtual reality' tour of first floor for those with limited mobility.

All year daily, Apr-May Mon-Sat 10.00-17.00, Sun 10.30-17.00, June-Aug Mon-Sat 09.00-17.00, Sun 09.30-17.00, Sept-Oct Mon-Sat 10.00-17.00, Sun 10.30-17.00, Nov-Mar Mon-Sat 10.00-16.00, Sun 10.30-16.00. Times listed are opening times to last entry. Closed 23-26 Dec

A£6.70 C£2.50 Concessions£5.50 Family Ticket £15.00. Multiple House Tickets: 3 in town houses A£10.00 C£5.00 Concessions£8.00 Family Ticket £20.00, all 5 houses A£13.00 C£6.50 Concessions£12.00 Family Ticket £29.00. Group rates available, please call 01789 210806 for details

Warwick Castle

Warwick Warwickshire CV34 4QU
Tel: 0870 442 2000 Fax: 01926 401692
[J15 M40 then A429 into Warwick]

Over a thousand years of secrets hide in the shadows of Warwick Castle. Murder, mystery, intrigue and scandal: the Castle has witnessed it all, and now you can discover the secret life of England.

All year daily 10.00-18.00, Aug 10.00-19.00, Oct-Mar 10.00-17.00. Closed 25 Dec

Prices vary, A£11.25/£12.95/£14.50/£11.50 C£6.95/£7.95/£8.75/£7.25

Military & Defence Museums

Warwickshire Yeomanry Museum

The Court House Jury Street Warwick
Warwickshire CV34 4EW

Tel: 01926 492212 Fax: 01926 494837

[In centre of Warwick off J15 M40]

After a great fire in 1694, the court house was rebuilt between 1725 and 1728 in a style that befitted the wealthy merchants of the town. In the vaults there is now a museum displaying militaria from the county Yeomanry.

Good Fri-End Sept. Most Fri Sat & Sun & Bank Hol Mon 10.00-13.00 & 14.00-16.00

Admission Free

Places of Worship

Coventry Cathedral and Treasury

Priory Street Coventry Warwickshire CV1 5EP

Tel: 024 7652 1200 Fax: 024 7652 1220

www.coventrycathedral.org.uk

[Signposted from M6 M69 A45 & A46]

Coventry's former Cathedral was bombed during an air raid in November 1940 which devastated the city. Its remains have been carefully preserved. The new Cathedral was designed by Sir Basil Spence and consecrated in May 1962. It contains many pieces of artwork. A continuous loop video tells the story of the city and Cathedral.

All year daily Easter-Sept 08.30-18.00, Oct-Easter 09.30-17.30. Treasury opening times vary

Cathedral: Admission free, requested donation of £3.00. Camera charge £2.00, Video charge £5.00, Guided Tour A£4.00

Discount Offer: 10% Discount in Cathedral Shop

<u>Special Events</u>

Consecration Concert with the Bach Choir
22/05/2004
Time: 19.30. Please call for further details

Moving Forward III
29/05/2004
A fun afternoon for all ages with bands, stalls and games. Time: 13.00-16.00. Admission free to Cathedral Ruins

International Church Music Festival
24/06/2004-26/06/2004

Henley College Graduation Ceremony
09/09/2004
Cathedral closed from 13.00-15.00

Coventry University Degree Week
15/11/2004-19/11/2004
Cathedral will be closed all week

Carols for All
11/12/2004
Time: 19.30. Please call for further details

Family Carols
11/12/2004
Time: 15.00. Admission free

Cathedral Carols
22/12/2004
Time: 19.00. Admission free

Spectator Sports

& Coaches £Free

Special Events

Racing Fixture
18/04/2004

May Fixtures
21/05/2004-22/05/2004
Evening fixtures held on 21 & 22 May only

June Fixtures
06/06/2004-13/06/2004
Race fixtures on 6 & 13 June only

July Fixtures
11/07/2004-29/07/2004
Race fixtures held on 11, 18, 29 July only

Racing Fixture
15/08/2004

September Fixtures
04/09/2004-12/09/2004
Race fixtures on 4 & 12 Sept only

October Fixtures
05/10/2004-28/10/2004
Race fixtures held on 5, 16, 28 Oct only

Stratford-on-Avon Racecourse

Luddington Road Stratford-upon-Avon
Warwickshire CV37 9SE

Tel: 01789 267949 Fax: 01789 415850

www.stratfordracecourse.net

[J15 M40, J7 M5, on B439. Plenty of on site parking available]

Steeplechasing has taken place at Stratford Racecourse since 1755. Today, we have fifteen meetings a year, most of which take place within the summer months. Equipped with a new grandstand (opened in 1997) and having won a major award for the care of the racetrack, we're proud to be in the top flight of Britain's smaller courses. Our goal is to give everyone who comes to Stratford a wonderful day out. We will be very pleased to discuss our facilities with you, either for bringing groups, large or small, to the races, or for using the racecourse buildings for non-raceday events and functions. The flexibility of our restaurant facilities and the attractive rates that we are able to offer for their use have made Stratford Racecourse the place to hold a party.

Race meetings all year

Club £16.00 Tattersalls £12.00 Course £6.00.
Pre-booked group rates 15+: Club £12.80
Tattersalls £9.60 Course £4.80. Parking: Centre Course & Main Car Park £2.00, Public Car Park

Warwick Racecourse

Hampton Street Warwick Warwickshire
CV34 6HN

Tel: 01926 491553 Fax: 01926 403223
[J15 M40, A429 Stratford Road into town centre. Plenty of on site parking]

Warwick has race meetings throughout the year, both over jumps and on the flat.
26 race meetings a year
£12.00 feature days (midweek), £15.00 premier days (Sat, Sun, Bank Hol)

Toy & Childhood Museums

Teddy Bear Museum

19 Greenhill Street Stratford-Upon-Avon
Warwickshire CV37 6LF

Tel: 01789 293160

www.theteddybearmuseum.com

[M40, J15, off the A46, in the centre of Stratford]

Ten settings, in a house which dates from
Shakespeare's time, are devoted to bears of all
shapes and sizes. Many very old bears are displayed and there are also mechanical and musical bears. Some of the bears belong to famous
people, for example, Jeffrey Archer and Barbara
Cartland. Pushchairs are required to be left at
reception. Air conditioned.
All year daily 09.30-17.30. Closed 25-26 Dec

A£2.50 C£1.50 Family Ticket (A2+C3)£7.50
Concessions£1.95. Groups rates (20+): A£2.20
C£1.00

**Discount Offer: One Child Free With
One Full Paying Adult**

Transport Museums

Coventry Transport Museum

Millennium Place Hales Street Coventry
Warwickshire CV1 1PN

Tel: 024 7683 2425 Fax: 024 7683 2465

www.transport-museum.com

*[A45, A423, M6 meet at Coventry, Museum has
a City centre location]*

Coventry is the birthplace of British road transport and the Museum displays the largest collection of British cars, buses, cycles, and motor
cycles in the world, designated as a collection
of national importance. Exciting and interactive
displays are being created all the time.
Landmarques tells the story of the City's pioneering cycles and motorcars, depicts the
heady days of motoring in the twenties and thir-
ties, and emotionally recreates Coventry's darkest hour in the 'Blitz Experience'. Visitors can
share in the City's spirit of optimism as it was
rebuilt after the war, before moving on to the
City's 'boomtime' in the fifties, sixties and sev-
enties. In Icons visitors can explore car design
over the last 70 years, see visions of the future
and even design a dream car! Today's technology is reflected in the Spirit of Speed Gallery featuring the current 763mph Land Speed Record
holder ThrustSSC, together with its predeces-
sor, Thrust2. The Museum is currently undergoing a multi-million pound redevelopment which
includes a new Introductory Gallery,
Technocentre, Eighties and Nineties display,

Futures' Gallery and a dedicated area for temporary exhibitions. These new attractions will open on March 18 2004.

All year daily 10.00-17.00. Closed 24-26 Dec

Admission Free. Groups pre-booking preferred

Heritage Motor Centre

Banbury Road Gaydon Warwickshire CV35 0BJ

Tel: 01926 641188 Fax: 01926 645103

www.heritage-motor-centre.co.uk

[J12 M40, 2-3mins away on the B4100, follow signs. Plenty of on site parking available]

Visit the Heritage Motor Centre and you'll discover much more than just our amazing collection of classic cars - the largest of its kind in the world. There's the all-new Time Road, a fascinating journey through Britain's motoring and social history, and features such as our motoring cinema and 'get behind the wheel' section. Outside, the Land Rover 4x4 off-road experience is fun for all the family, there's go-karting for adults and children aged 8 and over (minimum height 1.35metres) and a great children's miniature roadway, complete with traffic lights and roundabouts! Add to this our licensed cafe, 65 acres of grounds with picnic areas and a mini nature trail and you'll enjoy a great day out for all the family.

All year daily 10.00-17.00. Closed 24-26 Dec

A£8.00 C(0-4)£Free C(5-16)£6.00 OAPs£7.00 Family Ticket (A2+C3) £25.00

Discount Offer: Two For The Price Of One

Zoos

Twycross Zoo Park

Atherstone Warwickshire CV9 3PX
Tel: 01827 880250 / 880440
Fax: 01827 880700
www.twycrosszoo.com

[A444 near Market Bosworth on Burton to Nuneaton Road, J11 M42]

Specialises in primates, and also includes gibbons, gorillas, orang-utangs and chimpanzees. There is a huge range of monkeys from the tiny tamarins and spider monkeys to the large howler monkeys. Also various other animals such as lions, elephants and giraffes, with a pets' corner for younger children.

All year daily 10.00-18.00. Winter closing 16.00. Closed 25 Dec

A£7.00 C(3-14)£4.50 OAPs£5.00. Group rates 25+ A£5.00 C(3-14)£4.00 C(1-3)£0.50. Special rates for school, college, university parties and physically handicapped/special needs. Car Park: £1.00

Discount Offer: One Child Free With Two Adults Paying Full Price.

West Midlands

Arts, Crafts & Textiles

Birmingham Museum And Art Gallery

Chamberlain Square Birmingham B3 3DH
Tel: 0121 303 2834 Fax: 0121 303 1394
Housed in a spectacular Victorian building,
Birmingham Museum and Art Gallery has some
of the finest collections including the largest
Pre-Raphaelite collection in the world as well as
collections of silver, sculpture, ceramics and
ancient and social history.
*All year Mon-Thur 10.00-17.00, Fri 10.30-17.00,
Sat 10.00-17.00, Sun 12.30-17.00*

Admission Free, visitors are kindly requested to
make a donation

Broadfield House Glass Museum

Compton Drive Kingswinford West Midlands
DY6 9NS

Tel: 01384 812745 Fax: 01384 812746

www.glassmuseum.org.uk

*[M5 J4 or J2 A491 Stourbridge / Wolverhampton
Rd or A4101 Dudley / Kingswinford Rd]*

Situated in the historic Stourbridge Glass
Quarter, Broadfield House Glass Museum has
established a reputation as one of the major
glass museums in the world. The Museum has
a magnificent collection of British glass, much of
which was made locally, from 18th century
tableware to Victorian cameo vases, historic
paperweights to modern studio glass.
Permanent displays and temporary exhibitions
reveal the magical art of glassmaking. There is
also a glassmaking studio where visitors can
watch and wonder at the glassblowers' skills.

All year Tue-Sun 12.00-16.00

Admission Free

**Discount Offer: 10% Discount Off
Shop Purchases.**

Special Events

The Art of Fire
10/04/2004-04/07/2004
A hint of Eastern influence is revealed in this exhibition showing contemporary glassmakers alongside masters of raku pottery

Okra: 25 Years of Glass
24/04/2004-15/08/2004
This retrospective exhibition celebrates the history of Okra Glass, founded 25 years ago

Paperweight Collectors' Day
25/04/2004-07/08/2004
Held on 25 Apr and 7 Aug only. Paperweight-making demonstrations by William Manson and trade stands by specialist dealers

The Art of Fire - Raku Day
15/05/2004
Expert potter Geoff Townsend will be demonstrating the dramatic process of raku firing. You can glaze your own pot and watch it being fired for only £5.00

General Collectors' Day
12/06/2004
A range of collecting societies and specialist dealers will be at Broadfield to answer your questions, buy and sell, recruit members and give advice

Heroes of the Wheel
10/07/2004-03/10/2004
This exhibition explores the recent history of wheel engraving and its future as an art form

International Festival of Glass
25/08/2004-30/08/2004
The new look Glass Festival will have a packed programme of events throughout various venues

Bead Collectors' Day
25/09/2004
Demonstrations of bead-making, trade stands by bead makers and bead societies

WaldegraveSweet
09/10/2004-09/01/2005

Samantha Sweet and Tim Waldegrave have occupied the Broadfield House Scholarship Studio since January 2003. This exhibition marks the end of their tenancy and reveals the full range of their glassmaking skills

Family Fun Christmas Weekend
20/11/2004-21/11/2004

Come and meet Father Christmas and join in the activities for all the family! Cost: A£Free C£2.00

Costume & Jewellery Museums

Museum of the Jewellery Quarter

75-79 Vyse Street Hockley Birmingham
B18 6HA
Tel: 0121 554 3598 Fax: 0121 554 9700
[J6 M6 onto A38(M) or J1 M5 situated off A41, follow signs for Hockley & AA signs for Discovery Centre]

Discover the skills of the jeweller's craft and enjoy a unique tour of an original jewellery factory frozen in time. For over eighty years the family run firm and Smith and Pepper produced jewellery from the factory that is now the award-winning Museum of the Jewellery Quarter.
Apr-Oct Tue-Sun & Bank Hol Mons 11.30-16.00
Admission Free

Festivals & Shows

ArtsFest 2004

Birmingham City Centre Birmingham B1 2EA
Tel: 0121 685 2600 Fax: 0121 685 2606
ArtsFest is a free weekend celebrating the finest arts and entertainment from the West Midlands region. ArtsFest takes place in theatres, bars, concert halls and stages throughout Broad Street, Centenary Square and Brindleyplace in Birmingham City Centre showing a truly diverse range of arts. Music, drama, dance, film and visual arts are some of the arts on offer in a wide range of live performances and workshops.

September 11-12 2004

BBC Gardeners' World Live

NEC Birmingham West Midlands
Tel: 0870 902 0555
[Follow the signs from the M42 J6 or the M6 J4,

Show gardens at BBC Gardeners' World Live always have 'wow' factor, with plenty of inspiration and planting ideas for the gardener. There will be over 20 gardens featuring every possible style, ranging from urban chic to gentler more pastoral garden solutions. Look out for the Dai Telegraph Chelsea garden as well as the winning design from our BBC Garden Design Competition. The Design Area offers inspirational ideas and practical advice. In the Let's Talk Design Theatre BBC gardening experts wi be passing on their advice whilst 8 show gardens will showcase the work of professionals, students and amateurs. BBC Gardeners' Worl Live is all about inspiration and ideas. No othe show offers so many opportunities to pick up expert advice. Designated Wheelchair space w be available.
June 16-20 2004, 09.00-18.00
A£14.00-£16.00 C(5-15)£7.00-£7.50
OAPs£13.00-£15.00

Birmingham Eid Mela

Cannon Hill Park Birmingham B13 8RD
Tel: 0121 767 4141
[Situated in Edgbaston on Russell and Pershore roads. Follow signs for Birmingham Nature Cent or Mac (Midlands Arts Centre)]

The annual Birmingham Eid Mela returns to Cannon Hill Park on the 27th June. A celebration of the arts and traditions of the Muslim culture. There will be traditional music and dance provided by local and national musicians. There will also be games, a craft bazaar and food.
June 27 2004
Admission Free

Erdington Carnival

Brookery Park Erdington Birmingham B23
This event is organised by Erdington Carnival
Committee. The Carnival will see an on-stage
programme of music and dance, plus exhibition
displays (Fire Service & Police) with charity
stalls/art crafts stalls, funfair and inflatable, football competition for local schools.
June 19 2004 13.00-17.00
Admission Free

HMV Birmingham International Jazz Festival

PO Box 944 Birmingham West Midlands
B16 8UT
Tel: 0121 454 7020 Fax: 0121 454 9996
Birmingham becomes Jazz City UK with 200
shows in 70 city venues, 90% of which are free.
The emphasis is on accessible and entertaining
music to suit all tastes. From morning to night
jazz is heard in city streets, squares, restaurants, clubs, pubs, hotels and many other informal and unusual locations.
July 2-11 2004

Latin American Festival

Canon Hill Park Birmingham West Midlands
Tel: 0121 449 3090 Fax: 0121 449 3090
The Latin American Festival in Birmingham,
(12th year), has been organised by 'ABS Latin
Promotions' together with Birmingham City
Council in celebration of the Lord Mayor Show.
Join in the carnival atmosphere by taking part in
salsa dancing workshops lead by a team of
over 20 Salsa teachers. Sample the foods and
explore the arts of the American continent by
visiting the various stalls on the day. Enjoy the
very best of Latin American music performed by
salsa, Mexican and Samba bands, local and
international including dancers throughout the
day.
July 3-4 2004
Admission Free

Motor Show Live

The NEC Birmingham B40 1NT
Tel: 0800 378985
*[NEC at hub of UK motorway network, enabling
visitors to travel directly from M6, M1, M40 and
M42]*

Motor Show Live 2004, sponsored by The
Sunday Times, has moved from the traditional
October time to May. Live, Action and Arena -
The 'Live' is real cars, real people in real time.
The 'Action' is the sight, sound and smell of
cars performing to the limit. The 'Arena' is a
purpose-built, 4,000 seater outdoor stadium -
the stage for the Live Action, which will be held
four times each day. 4x4 experience: The
world's largest dedicated 4x4 course ever built
at a motor show will provide you with a driving
experience to remember. Too young to drive a
car? Not any more! Visitors, 14 years and older,
will be able to drive a car even if they are too
young to pass their test!
*May 27-June 6 2004 09.30-19.00 (17.30 on 6
June) May 27 Public preview day*
General Admission only: A£16.00 C(5-15)£9.00,
Live Action Arena only: A&C£7.50, General
Admission & Live Action Arena: A£23.50 C(5-
15)£16.50. Public preview day, General
Admission only: £40.00, Action Arena only:
£7.50, General Admission & Live Action Arena:
£47.50

Walsall Illuminations

Walsall Arboretum off Lichfield Street Broadway
North Walsall West Midlands
Tel: 01922 653148 Fax: 01922 721682
[M1, M6, J10, follow signs]

Visit the fantastic Walsall lights this autumn and
experience the magic of Britain's biggest in-
shore illuminations. For six weeks every year,
Walsall's beautiful Arboretum is transformed into
a magical wonderland of lights and lasers. As
you stroll along tree lined paths, you'll see lakeside lights, state-of-the-art laser shows, floodlit
gardens and over 50 animated light scenes -
many of top children's TV and cartoon characters.
September 18-October 31 2004
In Advance: A£4.00 Concessions £3.00. On
the Gates: A£5.00 Concessions£4.00

Folk & Local History Museums

Blakesley Hall

Blakesley Road Yardley Birmingham B25 8RN
Tel: 0121 783 2193 Fax: 0121 464 0400
[On the A4040 off the A45]

A timber framed house, it was originally built for a local wealthy yeoman, Richard Smalbroke in 1590. Displays include fine 17th century furnishings and architectural aspects of the building.
Mar-Oct Tue-Sun & Bank Hol Mons 11.30-16.00
Admission Free

Food & Drink

Cadbury World

Linden Road Bournville Birmingham B30 2LD
Tel: 0121 451 4159 Fax: 0121 451 1366
[1m S of A38 Bristol Road on A4040]

Cadbury World offers a truly melt-in-the-mouth experience for all the family! Indulge all your senses at this unique chocolate experience.
Opening times vary, please call 0121 451 4159, reservations are essential to gain admission
A£9.00 C(4-15)£6.80 Concessions£7.20 Family Ticket (A2+C2) £27.60, (A2+C3) £33.00

Gardens & Horticulture

Birmingham Botanical Gardens and Glasshouses

Westbourne Road Edgbaston Birmingham B15 3TR

Tel: 0121 454 1860 Fax: 0121 454 7835

www.birminghambotanicalgardens.org.uk

[2m W of City Centre. Plenty of on site parking available]

The lush rainforest vegetation in the Tropical House includes many economic plants. Palms tree ferns, orchids and insectivorous plants are displayed in the Subtropical House. The Mediterranean House features a wide variety of citrus plants, a pelargonium collection and seasonal displays of conservatory plants. A desert scene, with its giant agaves and opuntias, fills the Arid House. Outside there is colourful bedding on the Terrace and a tour of the 15 acres of Gardens includes rhododendrons and azaleas, herbaceous borders, an impressive Rock Garden and a collection of over 200 trees. There are Herb and Cottage Gardens, a Water Garden, Alpine Yard, Historic Gardens, Organic Garden and the National Bonsai Collection. Ferns, grasses and sensory plants all have their own areas. There is a children's adventure playground, Discovery Garden, aviaries, Gallery and Sculpture Trail. Shop at the Gardens and Plant Sales.

All year daily Mon-Sat 09.00-19.00 or dusk if sooner, Sun 10.00-19.00 or dusk if sooner. Closed 25 Dec

A£5.70 Summer Sundays £6.00 Concessions£3.30

Discount Offer: Admission At Group Rate With Voucher

Special Events

Rainbow Easter Egg Hunt
11/04/2004
Children can follow the trail to win an egg

Birmingham and Midland Orchid Society Show, Advice and Sales
18/04/2004

Bonsai Demonstration
16/05/2004-19/09/2004
Held on 16 May, 18 July, 15 Aug, 19 Sept only

Friends' Spring Plant Market
23/05/2004

British Cactus and Succulent Society Show -
Advice, Exhibition, Sales
06/06/2004

Midsummer Big Band Music Evening
13/06/2004
*Bring a picnic and enjoy yourself. Gardens close
at 18.00. Please book tickets in advance*

Midland Bonsai Society Show - Advice, Sales
and Demonstrations
20/06/2004

Much Ado About Nothing by William Shakespeare
23/06/2004-25/06/2004
*Performed by Crescent Open Air Theatre. Tickets
must be booked in advance. Time: 19.15*

Birmingham Geranium Society Show - Advice
and Sales
27/06/2004

A Midsummer Night's Dream by William
Shakespeare
14/07/2004-22/07/2004
*Open air theatre held on 14-15, 21-22 July only.
Tickets must be booked in advance*

Behind the Scenes of the Botanical Gardens with
James Wheeler
14/08/2004
Tickets must be booked in advance

Friends' Teddy Bears' Picnic
15/08/2004

Rotary Club Country Music Festival
05/09/2004

Birmingham Dahlia Society Show plus Friends'
Autumn Plant Market
12/09/2004

British Cactus and Succulent Society Autumn
Show - Advice and Sales
03/10/2004

Family Funday
17/10/2004

Friends' Christmas Market
24/10/2004

Birmingham and Midland Orchid Society Show -
Advice and Sales
31/10/2004

The Secret Garden
26/11/2004-12/12/2004
*Illuminated trail with discreet and sophisticated
lighting effects. Held over three weekends, please
call to confirm dates*

Friends' Craft Fair
28/11/2004

Christmas Gift Shop open daily
01/12/2004-31/12/2004

Castle Bromwich Hall Gardens

Chester Road Castle Bromwich Birmingham
West Midlands B36 9BT

Tel: 0121 749 4100 Fax: 0121 749 4100

www.cbhgt.colebridge.net

[1m from J5 M6 northbound, J6 M6 southbound follow A38 / A452. 4m E of Birmingham City centre, well signposted locally. Limited parking on site]

This rare and enchanting late 17th and early 18th century garden is set within 10 acres and is one of the finest formal walled gardens still in existence. It is an oasis of tranquility that contains many period plants. The parterre vegetable garden has unusual and forgotten varieties of vegetables and is bordered with culinary and medicinal herbs. A vast spectrum of fruits are grown in the orchards and along the pathways, all of which were in existence during the 17th century. The holly maze continues to test the skills of all ages! Refreshments, plants and gifts are available from the visitor centre.

Mar-Oct; Apr-Sept Tue-Thur 13.30-16.30, Sat-Sun & Bank Hol Mon 14.00-18.00, Mar & Oct Sat-Sun 13.30-16.30. Closed Mon & Fri (incl. Good Friday)

A£3.50 C£1.50 OAPs&Concessions£2.50. School Groups £Free

Discount Offer: Two For The Price Of One.

Heritage & Industrial

Soho House

Soho Avenue off Soho Road Birmingham B18 5LB

Tel: 0121 554 9122 Fax: 0121 554 5929
[On Soho road towards M5 J1. Bus: 70 / 74 / 78 & 79]

The elegant home of industrial pioneer Matthew Boulton, who lived at Soho House from 1766 to 1809. Possibly the first centrally heated English house since Roman times, Soho House has been carefully restored to its 18th Century appearance and contains some of Boulton's own furniture.
Apr-Oct Tue-Sun & Bank Hol Mons 11.30-16.00
Admission Free

Historical

Moseley Old Hall

Moseley Old Hall Lane Fordhouses Wolverhampton WV10 7HY
Tel: 01902 782808
[4m N of Wolverhampton, S of M54 between A449 / A460]

An Elizabethan House, altered in the 19th century and famous for its association with Charles II, who hid here after the Battle of Worcester (1651).
20 Mar-31 Oct Wed, Sat-Sun 13.00-17.00, Ba Hol Mon 11.00-17.00 and following Tues 13.00-17.00, 7 Nov-19 Dec Sun only for guided tours 13.00-16.00
A£4.60 C£2.30 Family Ticket £11.50

Packwood House

Packwood Lane Lapworth Solihull B94 6AT
Tel: 01564 783294
[2m E of Hockley Heath on A3400, 11m SE of central Birmingham]

The house, originally 16th century, is a fascinating 20th century evocation of domestic Tudor architecture. Created by Graham Baron Ash, interiors reflect the period between the world wars and contain a fine collection of 16th century textiles and furniture.
House: 3 Mar-7 Nov Wed-Sun 12.00-16.30. Garden: 3 Mar-30 Apr Wed-Sun 11.00-16.30, May-30 Sept Wed-Sun 11.00-17.30, 1 Oct-7 Nov Wed-Sun 11.00-16.30. Open Bank Hols in Good Fri
A£5.60 C£2.80 Family Ticket (A2+C3) £14.00 Garden only: A£2.80 C£1.40

Wightwick Manor

Wightwick Bank Wolverhampton WV6 8EE
Tel: 01902 761400 Fax: 01902 764663
[3m W of Wolverhampton, up Wightwick Bank, off A454 beside Mermaid Inn]

One of only a few surviving examples of a house built and furnished under the influence the Arts & Crafts Movement. The many original William Morris wallpapers and fabrics, Pre-Raphaelite paintings, Kempe glass and de

Morgan ware help conjure up the spirit of the me.

House: 1 Mar-23 Dec Thur & Sat 13.30-17.00, also Bank Hol Sun, Mon for ground floor only).
Garden: Wed, Thur, Sat & Bank Hols 11.00-8.00

A£6.00 C£3.00 Students£3.00 Family Ticket £14.00. Gardens only: A£3.00 C£Free

Mills - Water & Wind

Sarehole Mill

Cole Bank Road Moseley Birmingham B13 0BD
Tel: 0121 777 6612 Fax: 0121 303 2891
On the A34 Stratford Road. Bus: 11]

Home to one of Birmingham's only two working watermills, Sarehole Mill was built in the 1760s. Used for both flour production and metal rolling up to the last century, the Mill can still be seen in action during the summer months. Restored with financial assistance from JRR Tolkien, who grew up in the area.
Apr-Oct Tue-Sat & Bank Hols 11.30-16.00
Admission Free

Sealife Centres & Aquariums

National Sea Life Centre

The Waters Edge Brindleyplace Birmingham B1 2HL

Tel: 0121 633 4700 Fax: 0121 633 4787

www.sealifeeurope.com

[M6 J6, follow signs to Birmingham City Centre & The National Indoor Arena. Follow NIA signs all the way through centre and park in their car park in the allocated Sea-Life level. 3min walk over canal bridge. Rail: New Street Station. Bus: 9, 109, 139, 126 from Stephensons St to Brindleyplace]

Birmingham's unique flagship National Sea Life Centre takes visitors on a unique undersea voyage with over 60 displays of freshwater and marine life, creating a wonderland for visitors of all ages. Its centrepiece is an enormous one million litre ocean tank complete with the world's first 360 degree transparent tubular underwater walk through tunnel. Here visitors can experience the unique sensation of floating in mid ocean while sharks, colourful tropical reef fish and giant green sea turtles swim overhead, alongside and even beneath their feet. A trio of Asian short clawed otters reside in a luxurious, spacious five-star enclosure opening onto a viewing balcony high above the Grand Union Canal. A host more displays provide a fascinating insight into the myriad of marine marvels to be discovered beneath the seas around our own shores, providing close encounters with everything from humble shrimps and starfish to sharks and seahorses. An exciting new feature is planned for Spring 2004, 'The Seahorse Breeding and Conservation Centre'. Voted Aquarium of the Year and Warwickshire Family Attraction of the Year, Good Britain Guide 2004.

All year daily from 10.00 including weekends and bank holidays. Closed Christmas Day

A£8.95 C(0-2)£Free C(3-14)£6.95 OAPs£7.50 Students£7.95. School and group rates available for 15+ people

Discount Offer: Two Children Free With One Full Paying Adult.

Wiltshire

Animal Attractions

Bush Farm Bison Centre

West Knoyle Mere Wiltshire BA12 6AE
Tel: 01747 830263 phone/fax
Follow brown signs from A350. 0.5m from A303]

Bush Farm is tucked away in a great Oak
Wood. Visitors will see herds of Bison, Elk and
Red Deer as they follow the trail through 100
acres of meadows, lakes and woodlands.
*Apr-26 Sept Wed-Sun 10.00-17.00. Winter
months: Shop & Gallery Thur & Fri only
Farmyard & Woodland Walks: A£5.00
C(under4)£Free C£2.00*

Cholderton Rare Breeds Farm

Amesbury Road Cholderton Salisbury Wiltshire
SP4 0EW
Tel: 01980 629438 Fax: 01980 629594
*Just off the A338, signposted from the A303, 9m
W of Andover & 9m N of Salisbury]*

Set in beautiful countryside and winner of The
Best Family Attraction Award 1998, this superb
collection of rare farm animals delights everyone. Touch and feed the friendly creatures.
Rabbit World is probably the world's largest collection with over 50 breeds.
*20 Mar-31 Oct daily 10.00-18.00, weekends
11.00-16.00 low season
A£5.50 C(2-16)£3.95 OAPs£4.50*

Longleat

The Estate Office Longleat Warminster Wiltshire
BA12 7NW
Tel: 01985 844400 Fax: 01985 844885
www.longleat.co.uk

Experience incredibly close encounters with the
world's most magnificent animals

**Please see Wildlife & Safari Parks section
for full attraction listing**

Roves Farm Visitor Centre

Sevenhampton Nr Highworth Swindon Wiltshire
SN6 7QG
Tel: 01793 763939 Fax: 01793 766846
*[2m E of Swindon, off B4000 Highworth /
Shrivenham road in Sevenhampton, or A361]*

Meet and feed the animals, and take tractor and
trailer rides around this working farm. New two
acre living willow maze and a smaller toddler
version for the less adventurous. Indoor big
straw bale 'rabbit warren', bouncy castle and
ball pond.

*mid Mar-end Oct Wed-Sun & Bank Hol 10.30-
17.00, June-Aug daily 10.30-17.00*

A£5.00 C(0-2)£Free C£4.00 Concessions£4.50

Archaeology

Wiltshire Heritage Museum

41 Long Street Devizes Wiltshire SN10 1NS
Tel: 01380 727369 Fax: 01380 722150
[In Devizes, signposted in town]

World-famous collections from Wiltshire, includ-
ing unique finds from barrows around
Stonehenge, are on display. There is a Recent
History gallery, an art gallery with a John Piper
window, displays of natural history, and a
Wiltshire research library.

*All year Mon-Sat 10.00-17.00, Sun 12.00-16.00.
Closed some Bank Hols*

Admission £Free on Mon & Sun, at other times
A£1.00 C(under16)£Free

Country Parks & Estates

Lackham Country Park

Wiltshire College Lackham Lacock Chippenham
Wiltshire SN15 2NY

Tel: 01249 466800 Fax: 01249 444474
[3m S of Chippenham, on A350]

Rural Life Museum and Gardens. Historic
thatched barn and granaries house an intriguing
range of displays depicting aspects of Wiltshire
rural life; attractive walled garden and formal

gardens featuring Wartime kitchen gardens, Rupert Bear's house, a children's laurel maze.
Easter-Aug Sun & Bank Hol Mon 10.00-17.00, plus Tue-Thur during Aug
A£2.00 C&Concessions£1.50

Discount Offer: Two Children Free With Each Full Paying Accompanying Adult.

Festivals & Shows

Corsham Festival

Corsham Town Hall Corsham SN13 9EU
Tel: 01249 712628 Fax: 01249 712628
[8m E of Bath and 4m W of Chippenham. J17 of M4 8m away, head S along A350, W along A4]

Staged in the beautiful Cotswold town of Corsham, the Corsham Festival celebrates the arts with a varied and innovative programme of events featuring music, theatre, visual arts, dance and street theatre.
June 19-26 2004
Some events £Free, otherwise £5.00-£12.00

Folk & Local History Museums

Bedwyn Stone Museum

91 Church Street Great Bedwyn SN8 3PF
Tel: 01672 870234 Fax: 01672 871211
[Near Marlborough]

External display of stone / masonry artefacts many of which are humorous. Working stone-masons yard.
All year 08.00-dusk
Admission Free

Market Lavington Village Museum

Church Street Market Lavington Devizes Wiltshire SN10 4DP
Tel: 01380 818736
[A360 from Devizes, L at West Lavington cross-roads on to B3098, 1m to Market Lavington]

The home of the museum is the old schoolmaster's House which has a pre-detergent kitchen,

fine needlework and the oldest pot plant in the village - 90 and still going strong. The museum illustrates the life and work of the village from christening robe to coffin plate.
May-end Oct Wed, Sat, Sun & Bank Hol 14.30-16.30
Admission Free. Donations welcome

Mere Library and Museum and Tourist Information Centre

Barton Lane Mere Warminster BA12 6JA
Tel: 01747 860546
[Off A303 follow signposts]

Principally a local history collection with a good photographic archive. Displays are changed every 3 months and include travelling exhibition on a variety of subjects from time to time.
All year Mon 10.00-19.00, Tue-Fri 09.00-17.00, Sat 09.00-13.00
Admission Free

Forests & Woods

Brokerswood Country Park

Brokerswood Westbury Wiltshire BA13 4EH
Tel: 01373 822238 Fax: 01373 858474
[Off A36 at Bell Inn, Standerwick, follow signs]

Brokerswood Country Park walks lead through 80 acres of woodlands, with a lake and wild-fowl. Facilities include 2 children's adventure playgrounds, a play trail, guided walks and Woodland railway.
All year; Park daily from 10.00, 10.30 in Winter months. Museum opening times vary
A£3.00 Accompanied C£1.50 OAPs£2.50

Heritage & Industrial

Crofton Beam Engines

Crofton Pumping Station Crofton Marlborough Wiltshire SN8 3DW
Tel: 01672 870300
[6m SE of Marlborough]

Crofton Pumping Station houses two Cornish Beam Engines, the 1812 Boulton and Watt and he 1845 Harvey of Hayle. These engines have been restored and the 1812 engine is the oldest beam engine in the world, still in its original building and still doing its original job of pumping water to the summit level of the Kennet and Avon Canal.

9 Apr-26 Sept daily 10.30-17.00. In Steam: 10-12 Apr, 1-3, 29-31 May, 26-27 June, 24-25 July, 28-30 Aug, 25-26 Sept

Not in Steam: A£3.00 C£1.00. In Steam: A£4.50 C£1.00

Historical

Longleat

The Estate Office Longleat Warminster Wiltshire BA12 7NW

Tel: 01985 844400 Fax: 01985 844885
www.longleat.co.uk

Discover the treasures and heirlooms within Longleat House and experience incredibly close encounters with the world's most magnificent animals

Please see Wildlife & Safari Parks section for full attraction listing

Wilton House

Wilton Salisbury Wiltshire SP2 0BJ

Tel: 01722 746729 Fax: 01722 744447

www.wiltonhouse.com

3m W of Salisbury along A36. 10 miles from Stonehenge. Plenty of on site parking available, including coach park]

Wilton House is the 460 year old home of the Earl of Pembroke. The house contains a superb art collection including works by Van Dyck, Reynolds, Brueghel and Rembrandt. The double cube room was in fact designed to house the family portraits by Sir Anthony Van Dyke and is the greatest collection by the artist still to be seen in its 17th century setting. There are also a large number of classical marble sculptures and antique busts from the Arundel and Mazarine collections, which were purchased by the eighth Earl of Pembroke in 1720. Created within the atmospheric setting of the Old Riding School, is the award winning introductory film, recreated Tudor Kitchen, Victorian laundry and Times Past, Times Present exhibition. Extensive parkland bordered by the river Nadder provides a perfect backdrop for the Palladian bridge, Millennium Water Feature, Whispering Seat, Rose and Water Gardens. For the younger visitor there is a wonderful adventure playground.

2 Apr-31 Oct; House Tue-Sun (open Bank Hol Mon) 10.30-17.30, Grounds daily 10.30-17.30
House & Grounds: A£9.75 C(5-15)£5.50 C(2-5)£1.00 C(0-2)£Free Family Ticket (A2+C2) £24.00 Students&OAPs£8.00. Grounds only: A£4.50 C(5-15)£3.50 C(2-5)£1.00 C(0-2)£Free

Discount Offer: Two For The Price Of One.

Special Events

Wessex Flower Show
16/04/2004-18/04/2004

60th Anniversary of D-Day
05/06/2004-06/06/2004

Wilton Horse Trials
11/06/2004-13/06/2004

10th Anniversary Classical Concert
17/07/2004

Landmarks

Stonehenge

Amesbury Salisbury Wiltshire SP4 7DE
Tel: 01722 624715 Fax: 01722 623465
[2m W of Amesbury at J of A303 & A344/A360]

Stonehenge is a prehistoric monument of unique importance, known throughout the world, which has been designated a World Heritage Site.

All year, please call for specific opening times and prices

Places of Worship

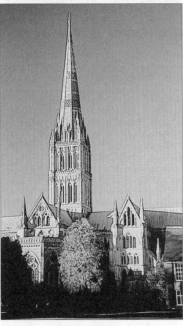

Salisbury Cathedral

33 The Close Salisbury Wiltshire SP1 2EJ

Tel: 01722 555120 Fax: 01722 555116

www.salisburycathedral.org.uk

[A30, M3, M27 signposted locally]

Salisbury is probably the finest medieval Cathedral in Britain - with the highest spire (123 metres/404 ft), the best preserved original Magna Carta (1215 AD), a unique 13th century frieze of bible stories in the octagonal Chapter House and Europe's oldest working clock (1386 AD). Boy and girl choristers sing daily services, continuing a tradition of worship that dates back nearly 800 years. Set within the Cathedral Close, surrounded by eight acres of lawns and eight centuries of beautiful houses, Salisbury Cathedral has been the source of inspiration to generations of artists and writers. The Cathedral is open every day of the year. Volunteers provide guided tours highlighting the Cathedral's many treasures, including tours of the roof and tower. The city of Salisbury, Stonehenge and Old Sarum are all within easy reach.

All year, 1 Jan-6 June 07.15-18.15, 7 June-28 Aug 07.15-19.15, 29 Aug-31 Dec 07.15-18.15

Guidelines for donations: A£3.80 C£2.00 OAPs&Students £3.30 Family Ticket £8.50

Special Events

Holy Week and Easter Events
05/04/2004-11/04/2004

Salisbury Festival
21/05/2004-05/06/2004

D-Day 60th Anniversary Remembered
06/06/2004

RSCM Celebration Day Service
12/06/2004

Organ Recital
23/06/2004-20/10/2004
Held on 23 June, 21 July, 8 & 11 Sept & 20 Oct

Concert: SSAFA
11/09/2004

Concert: Salisbury Community Choir
13/11/2004

City Lights
25/11/2004

Advent Procession 'From Darkness to Light'
27/11/2004-28/11/2004

Carol Services
22/12/2004-23/12/2004

Midnight Mass
24/12/2004

Christmas Services
25/12/2004

Social History Museums

Salisbury and South Wiltshire Museum

The King's House 65 The Close Salisbury Wiltshire SP1 2EN

Tel: 01722 332151 Fax: 01722 325611

[Close to Salisbury Cathedral follow signposts]

Award winning Museum, Designated for its archaeology collections. Museum houses a re-designed Stonehenge Gallery and displays of pre-history, Romans, Saxons, the medieval history of Old Sarum and Salisbury, the Pitt Rivers collection, ceramics and costume, prints and drawings, including Turner watercolours.

All year Mon-Sat 10.00-17.00. Also Sun July & Aug 14.00-17.00. Closed Christmas

A£4.00 C£1.50 C(0-5)£Free Concessions£3.00

Castle Combe Circuit

Chippenham Wiltshire SN14 7EY

Tel: 01249 782417 Fax: 01249 782392

[6m W of Chippenham on the B4039]

One of the fastest circuits in the county with fine viewing areas from each corner. Free parking, easy access and a concentrated race programme make for a great day out.
Opening times and prices vary, please call

Transport Museums

STEAM - Museum of the Great Western Railway

Kemble Drive Swindon Wiltshire SN2 2TA

Tel: 01793 466646 Fax: 01793 466615

[From M4 & other major routes, follow brown tourist signs to 'Outlet Centre' plus M for Museum]

The award winning STEAM - Museum of the Great Western Railway tells the story of the men and women who built, operated and travelled on the Great Western Railway. Hands on displays, world famous locomotives, archive film footage and the testimonies of ex-railway workers bring the story to life.

All year daily Mon-Sat 10.00-17.00, Sun 11.00-17.00. Closed 25-26 Dec & 1 Jan

A£5.95 C(under5)£Free C£3.80 OAPs£3.90. Prices subject to change

Wildlife & Safari Parks

Longleat

The Estate Office Longleat Warminster
Wiltshire BA12 7NW

Tel: 01985 844400 Fax: 01985 844885

www.longleat.co.uk

[A36 between Bath & Salisbury, A362 Warminster to Frome. Plenty of on site parking]

Voted 'UK Family Attraction of the Year 2002' by the Good Britain Guide, Longleat offers a great day out for all the family. Experience incredibly close encounters with the world's most magnificent animals including lions, tigers, and giraffe in the UK's original Safari Park. Get lost in the World's Longest Hedge Maze, voyage on the Safari Boats, journey on the Longleat Railway, let the kids explore the turrets and bridges of the Adventure Castle (including the Blue Peter Maze), discover the treasures and heirlooms within Longleat House and much much more! The Longleat Passport Ticket offers access into all 12 of the Longleat attractions.

Longleat House: 1 Jan-26 Mar weekends and state school holidays 11.00-15.00, 27 Mar-31 Dec daily, Easter-Sept 10.00-17.30, Oct-Dec guided tours at set times between 11.00-15.00. Closed Christmas Day. Longleat Safari Park: 27 Mar-31 Oct weekdays 10.00-16.00, weekends, Bank Hols and State School Hols 10.00-17.00. Longleat Attractions: 27 Mar-31 Oct daily 11.00-17.30

Make huge savings by purchasing the 'Great Value' Passport and seeing all 12 of the Longleat attractions! Visit Longleat in a day or come back at any time before the end of the season to see those attractions previously missed... the choice is yours! Each attraction may be visited only once. A£16.00 C(3-14)£13.00 OAPs£13.00

Special Events

Cadbury Easter Eggstravaganza
09/04/2004-12/04/2004
Free for children aged 3-14 with a valid Longleat Passport. Please call for further details

Pawtrek
23/05/2004
A sponsored Dog Walk and Dog Show in aid of Guide Dogs for the Blind Association. Please call 01725 552437 for sponsorship forms and further information

Longleat Horse Trials
04/06/2004-06/06/2004
Please call 01404 841331 for further information

'Super Beasts' Show
17/07/2004-05/09/2004
Free entry with a valid Longleat Passport

Dog Agility Weekend c/o Chippenham Club
11/09/2004-12/09/2004
Entry free with a valid Longleat Passport. Please call 01225 700743 for further details and entry forms

Tipadel Speed Hill Climb
25/09/2004-26/09/2004
Please call 01258 880778 for more information

Santa Special Trains - Book Early!
28/11/2004-21/12/2004
Held on 28 Nov, 4, 5, 11, 12, 15, 18, 19, 21 Dec only. Pre-booking essential, please call 01985 845408 or 01985 844400

Arts, Crafts & Textiles

Worcester City Museum and Art Gallery

Foregate Street Worcester Worcestershire
WR1 1DT

Tel: 01905 25371 Fax: 01905 616979

[Worcester City Centre J6 or J7 M5]

The gallery has temporary art exhibitions from both local and national sources; while the museum exhibits cover geology, local and natural history. Of particular interest is a complete 19th-century chemists shop.

All year Mon, Tue, Wed & Fri 09.30-17.30, Sat 09.30-17.00. Closed Good Friday

Admission Free

Factory Outlets & Tours

Royal Worcester Visitor Centre

Severn Street Worcester Worcestershire
WR1 2NE

Tel: 01905 746000 Fax: 01905 617807

[M5 J7 follow sign for City Centre, turn left at 7th set of traffic lights near the Cathedral]

Royal Worcester's Porcelain works were established in 1751 and today's Visitor Centre nestles amongst atmospheric Victorian factory buildings and offers a vast array of Best ware, Seconds and Clearance goods at bargain prices.

All year Mon-Sat 09.00-17.30, Sun 11.00-17.00. Closed 25-26 Dec, Easter Sun

Guided Factory Tour: All £5.50 Family Ticket £17.00. Other tours and rates available

Discount Offer: Two For The Price Of One (Admission to Visitor Attractions, pre-booking advised for tours)

Folk & Local History Museums

Avoncroft Museum of Historic Buildings

Redditch Road Stoke Heath Bromsgrove
Worcestershire B60 4JR
Tel: 01527 831363 Fax: 01527 876934
www.avoncroft.org.uk

[2m S of Bromsgrove off A38 Bromsgrove by-pass 400 yards N of its junction with B4091 3m N of J5 M5. 3.5m S of J1 M42. Plenty of on site parking available]

Avoncroft is a fascinating world of historic buildings covering seven centuries, rescued and rebuilt on a beautiful open-air site in the heart of the Worcestershire countryside. Explore a working windmill, fully-furnished 1946 Prefab and 15th century Merchant's House, plus many others. Full programme of events throughout the season and at intervals, demonstrations of brick, nail and chainmaking, milling, breadmaking and woodturning, as well as rides on Model Stream trains! With a tearoom, shop and children's play-area, Avoncroft is a great day out for all the family!

Mar-Nov; Mar Tue-Thur, Sat-Sun 10.30-16.00, Apr-June Tue-Sun 10.30-16.30 (17.00 weekends), July-Aug daily 10.30-17.00 (17.30 weekends), Sept-Oct Tue-Sun 10.30-16.30 (17.00 weekends), Nov Sat-Sun 10.30-16.30

A£6.00 C£3.00 Family Ticket £15.00

Discount Offer: One Child Free With Full Paying Adult, OR £2.00 Off A 2nd Full Paying Adult.

Special Events

Victorian Christmas Event
04/12/2004-05/12/2004

Bewdley Museum

The Shambles Load Street Bewdley
Worcestershire DY12 2AE

Tel: 01299 403573 Fax: 01299 404740

http://bewdleymuseum.tripod.com

[4M W of Kidderminster off A456 on B4190]

Housed in an historic and unusual 18th century
Butchers Shambles, the museum's main exhibitions and galleries provide a fascinating insight
into the trades and crafts of the town and the
surrounding Wyre Forest area. The displays feature the work of basket and besom broom makers, charcoal burning, coracles, fire fighting,
horn working, pewtering and brass founding.
There are daily demonstrations of rope making
in the unique rope walk and clay pipe making.
The site also houses resident craftspeople and
has an attractive herb garden and picnic area.
The special exhibitions gallery has a programme
of changing exhibitions and the museum has a
varied special events programme throughout
the year. Educational programmes are available
for schools and groups.
Apr-31 Oct daily 10.00-16.30 (11.00-16.00 Oct)
Admission Free

Special Events

Exhibition - 'Scholars and Stitches'
01/04/2004-23/05/2004

Feature Showcase Exhibition - 'Severn Steamers'
01/05/2004-28/05/2004

The Wizard of Oz by Storytellers Theatre
Company
03/05/2004

Rock and Fossil Roadshow
31/05/2004

Exhibition - From Teacups to Mini Bikes
01/06/2004-25/07/2004

Feature Showcase Exhibition - 'The Homefront'
05/06/2004-27/06/2004

Brass Rubbing
20/07/2004-24/08/2004
Held on 20 & 27 July, 3, 17, 24 Aug

Exhibition - 'Crafts in Practice'
02/08/2004-05/09/2004

Music in the Park
08/08/2004-29/08/2004
Held on 8, 15, 22, 29 Aug

Woodlands Week
09/08/2004-15/08/2004

Dyeing with Nature
09/08/2004
Children's workshop. Time: 13.30-16.00

Woodland Faces
10/08/2004
Children's Workshop. Time: 14.00-16.00

Natural Print
11/08/2004
Children's workshop. Time: 11.00-16.00

Wild Work with Woodlands
12/08/2004
Children's workshop. Time: 10.00-13.00

Crafts Alive!
30/08/2004

Heritage Open Day
12/09/2004

Exhibition - 'People and Places'
13/09/2004-31/10/2004

Bewdley Festival Open Day
09/10/2004

Festive Wicks, Wax and Bees
27/10/2004
Children's workshop. Time: 13.30-16.00

Bromsgrove Museum

26 Birmingham Road Bromsgrove B61 ODD
Tel: 01527 831809
Take a journey back in time at Bromsgrove Museum. Window shop in our Victorian and Edwardian arcade, including drapers, chemist, radio shop, photographer and cobbler. Find out about local history and craft industries.
Mon-Sat 10.30-12.30 & 13.00-16.30. Closed 25-26 Dec & 1 Jan
Admission Free

THE COMMANDERY

This delightful 15th century timber-framed building was the headquarters of Charles II's army during the Battle of Worcester in 1651. It has an impressive Great Hall with fine examples of 15th century stained glass. The building contains fascinating Civil War displays including audio-visuals.

The Commandery
Sidbury, Worcester
Worcestershire WR1 2HU
01905 361821

Gardens & Horticulture

Bodenham Aboretum and Earth Centre

Wolverley Kidderminster Worcestershire DY11 5SY
Tel: 01562 852444 Fax: 01562 852777
[J4/6 M5 to Wolverley Kidderminster follow brown signs from Wolverley Church Island B4189]

Award winning arboretum, with over 2,500 rare and ornamental trees, shrubs planted around beautifully landscaped pools, set within 134 acres and incorporating a working farm.
All year daily 11.00-17.00. Jan-Feb Mon-Fri, no restaurant facilities available
A£4.00 C£1.50 OAPs£4.00 Family Ticket (A2+C4) £10.00 Wheelchair Bound £1.50

Burford House Gardens

Burford Garden Company Tenbury Wells Worcestershire WR15 8HQ

Tel: 01584 810777 Fax: 01584 810673
www.burford.co.uk

[Off A456, 1m W of Tenbury Wells, 8m from Ludlow]

Burford Garden Company's store at Burford House Gardens has been designed to inspire and delight all garden lovers. Our Garden Centre here is complemented by our superb shop inside Burford House, which sells inspirational home furnishings and accessories. Together with everything imaginable for the English garden, we also specialise in clematis, the 'Queen of Climbers', which in popularity, is second only to the rose in Britain. We have hundreds of varieties for sale, many of which were ored and are grown on site in our own Treasure's Clematis Nursery. Uniquely situated where three counties meet, the 7 acres of lawn and stunning borders of Burford House Gardens sweep along the banks of the picturesque River Teme. Originally designed by the late John Treasure in 1952 around an early Georgian house, the gardens contain the National Clematis Collection, along with around 2,000 other kinds of plants. During the summer there may be as many as 80 clematis in flower in the gardens at any one time, but some of these you might have to look a little hard to find, as they entwine with other plants or trail along the ground. Please linger in the very special place that is Burford House Gardens and sense the 'genus loci' - the spirit of the place. Take in the scene, have a coffee in our riverside cafebar, then let us help you develop your beautiful garden.

All year daily 09.00-18.00, gardens close at dusk if earlier

A£3.95 C£1.00. Group rates (20+): £3.00

Discount Offer: Two For The Price Of One.

Croome Park

National Trust Estate Office The Estate Yard High Green Severn Stoke WR8 9JA
Tel: 01905 371006 Fax: 01905 371090
[8m S of Worcester & E of A38 & M5, 6m W of Pershore B4084]

Croome Park was 'Capability' Brown's first complete landscape, making his reputation and establishing a new style of parkland design that was copied throughout the western world. Now, in its most ambitious garden restoration to date, the National Trust is restoring the elegant buildings, atmospheric shrubberies and spectacular vistas of this epoch-making garden to its former glory.
Gardens & Church: 5 Mar-31 Oct Wed-Sun & Bank Hol Mons 10.00-17.30, 3 Nov-19 Dec Wed-Sun 10.00-16.00. Parkland: open all year
Pleasure Ground: A£3.50 C£1.70 Family Ticket £8.50

Spetchley Park Gardens

Spetchley Worcester Worcestershire WR5 1RS
Tel: 01905 345213 / 345224
Fax: 01453 511915
[3m E of Worcester off A44]

The 110-acre deer park and the 30-acre gardens surround an early 19th-century mansion (not open), with sweeping lawns and herbaceous borders, a rose lawn and enclosed gardens with low box and yew hedges.
Apr-Sept Tue-Fri 11.00-17.00, Sun 14.00-17.00, Bank Hol Mon 11.00-17.00
A£4.00 C£2.00

Heritage & Industrial

Droitwich Heritage Centre

Victoria Square Droitwich Spa Worcestershire WR9 8DS
Tel: 01905 774312 Fax: 01905 794226
Originally the St Andrew's Brine Baths, the building has been carefully converted into a local history museum, exhibition hall and tourist information centre. The town's history display depicts the fascinating development of Droitwich from Iron Age salt settlement to present day luxury spa resort.
All year Mon-Sat 10.00-16.00
Admission Free

Historical

The Commandery

Sidbury Worcester Worcestershire WR1 2HU

Tel: 01905 361821 Fax: 01905 361822

www.worcestercitymuseums.org.uk

[Worcester city centre 3mins walk from the Cathedral. A44 from J7 M5]

This delightful 15th century timber-framed building was the headquarters of Charles II's army during the Battle of Worcester in 1651. It has an impressive Great Hall with fine examples of 15th century stained glass. The building contains fascinating Civil War displays including audio-visuals. A varied events programme all year.

All year Mon-Sat 10.00-17.00, Sun 13.30-17.00. Closed 24-28 Dec & 1 Jan

A£3.95 Concessions£2.95 Family Ticket £10.25

Discount Offer: One Child Free With Every Full Paying Adult

Harvington Hall

Harvington Hall Lane Harvington Kidderminster Worcestershire DY10 4LR
Tel: 01562 777846 Fax: 01562 777190
[3m SE of Kidderminster, 0.5m from J of A448 & A450 at Mustow Green]

Moated medieval and Elizabethan manor-house containing secret hiding places and rare wall-paintings. Georgian Chapel in garden with 18th century altar, rails and organ.
Mar-Oct, Mar Sat & Sun, Apr-Sept Wed-Sun, Oct Sat & Sun, all 11.30-17.00
A£4.20 C£3.00 OAPs£3.50

Little Malvern Court and Gardens

Little Malvern Malvern Worcestershire WR14 4JN
Tel: 01684 892988 Fax: 01684 893057
[3m S of Great Malvern on Upton-on-Severn Rd (A4104)]

14th century Prior's Hall once attached to 12th-century Benedictine Priory, with Victorian addition by Hansom. Family and European paintings and furniture. Collection of 18th and 19th century needlework. Home of the Berington family by descent since the Dissolution.
Mid Apr-Mid July Wed & Thur 14.15-17.00
A£5.00 C£2.50. House or Garden only: A£4.00 C£1.50

Snowshill Manor

Snowshill Broadway Worcestershire WR12 7JU
Tel: 01386 852410 Fax: 01386 842822
[2.5m SW of Broadway approach only from turning off A44 by Broadway Green]

The terraces and ponds of this Arts and Crafts garden were laid out by Charles Paget Wade as a series of outdoor rooms to complement his Cotswold Manor House. The garden is a lively mix of architectural features, bright colours and delightful scents.
Gardens: 19 Mar-31 Oct Wed-Sun and Bank Ho Mons 11.00-17.30. Manor House closed for 2004
A£3.80 C£1.90 Family Ticket £9.50

Worcestershire County Museum and Hartlebury Castle State Rooms

Stourport Road Hartlebury Nr Kidderminster Worcestershire DY11 7XZ
Tel: 01299 250416 Fax: 01299 251890
[4m S of Kidderminster on A449 rd to Worcester]

The elegant interior of this castle, the seat of the Bishops of Worcester since 850, reveals little of its long and sometimes troubled history. Its present Gothic appearance dates from the 18th century. Housed in the North wing of Hartlebury Castle, the County Museum contains a delightful display of crafts and industries.
Museum: Feb-Sept Mon-Thur 10.00-17.00, Fri & Sun 14.00-17.00, Bank Hols 11.00-17.00. Castle State Rooms: Tue-Thur 10.00-17.00. Closed Good Fri
A£3.00 C&OAPs£1.50 Family Ticket (A2+C3) £8.00

Places of Worship

Worcester Cathedral

10a College Green Worcester Worcestershire
WR1 2LH

Tel: 01905 28854 / 21004 / 611002
Fax: 01905 611139
www.cofe-worcester.org.uk

[M5 J6/J7, then follow signs to city centre]

Worcester Cathedral is England's loveliest
cathedral, with Royal tombs, medieval cloisters,
an ancient crypt and Chapter House, and magnificent Victorian stained glass. The Tower is
open in the summer from 10.30-16.00 on
Saturdays and school holidays. We welcome
families, groups and individuals, with refreshments, a gift shop, and disabled access to all
facilities and gardens. We also offer exciting
new Conference facilities, with rooms catering
for 6-60. There is nearby parking, bus and train
stations. Services three times daily.

All year daily 07.30-18.00

Admission Free: Invite donation of A£3.00.
Groups; essential to book in advance

Special Events

May Day Celebration
01/05/2004

Exhibition 'Bizzarte' 5 artists from University
College Worcester
03/05/2004-23/05/2004

Exhibition by Brian Turner
04/05/2004-01/06/2004

Royal Chapel Choir
19/05/2004
Copenhagen Concert

Exhibition
28/05/2004-01/07/2004
Voices and Visions. Schools in Worcestershire

English Symphony Orchestra Concert
05/06/2004
Elgar - The Dream of Gerontius. Time: 19.30

Exhibition
09/06/2004-23/06/2004
Kings School GCSE work

Worcestershire Symphony Orchestra Concert
19/06/2004
Time: 19.30

Cathedral Chamber Choir and St Patrick's
Cathedral Chamber Choir
03/07/2004
Concert. Time: 19.30

Pavilion Opera
08/07/2004

Exhibition by Cathedral Artists in Residence
16/07/2004-09/08/2004

Heart of England Fine Food Fair
30/07/2004-31/07/2004

Bell Ringing Day to Open Worcester Festival
14/08/2004

National Association of Flower Arrangement
Societies
19/08/2004-21/08/2004
Flower Festival

Exhibition 'Summerfield Icons'
06/09/2004-29/10/2004

Midland Festival Chorus Concert
09/10/2004
Time: 19.30

'The Big Event'
28/10/2004

Exhibition
11/11/2004-06/12/2004
Kings School A' Level work

WFCS Concert: Handel Messiah
04/12/2004
Time: 19.30

Son et Lumiere Cathedral Arts and WCFS
17/12/2004-18/12/2004

Three Choirs' Festival
06/08/2005-12/08/2005

Railways

Severn Valley Railway

The Railway Station Bewdley Worcestershire
DY12 1BG
Tel: 01299 403816 Fax: 01299 400839
www.svr.co.uk

[Rail: Kidderminster. Town station is adjacent to railway station. On Comberton Hill on the A448. Plenty of on site parking available]

The leading standard gauge steam railway, with one of the largest collections of locomotives and rolling stock in the country. Services operate from Kidderminster and Bewdley to Bridgnorth through 16 miles of picturesque scenery along the River Severn. 'Day Out With Thomas' events take place during the year.

Weekends throughout year, 8 May-26 Sept daily

plus school holidays

Prices depend on journey undertaken, call for details

Special Events

Easter Egg Hunt
09/04/2004-12/04/2004

Day Out with Thomas events
08/05/2004-16/05/2004
Held on 8-9 & 15-16 May

Heavy Horse Power Weekend
05/06/2004-06/06/2004
Displays of heavy horses showing the various tasks these animals used to do

1940s Weekends
26/06/2004-04/07/2004
Held on 26-27 June and 3-4 July. A nostalgic look at Britain during World War II with period vehicles, costumes and re-enactments

Hampton Loade Station Gala
25/07/2004
A special day for this lovely country station

Severn Valley in Bloom
31/07/2004-01/08/2004
Highlighting the beautiful station gardens

Day Out with Thomas events
04/09/2004-12/09/2004
Held on 4-5 & 11-12 Sept. Further visits from the cheeky little engine with The Fat Controller keeping everyone in order

Beer Festival at Bridgnorth
16/09/2004-19/09/2004
A wide range of Real Ales from across the country

Autumn Steam Gala
24/09/2004-26/09/2004
The UK's premier steam railway event including a night train services

Diesel Gala
01/10/2004-03/10/2004
An intensive service of trains using some of our historic diesel locomotives

Classic Car and Bike Day
10/10/2004

A comprehensive display of classic motorcycles and cars

Railcar 50
15/10/2004-17/10/2004
A celebration of 50 years of BR's first generation of Diesel Multiple Units

Remembrance Day Service
14/11/2004
At Kidderminster Station

Santa Specials
04/12/2004-24/12/2004
Held on 4-5, 11-12, 18-19, 24 Dec. A chance for everyone to visit Santa

Festive Season Service
26/12/2004-03/01/2005
A regular service of trains to help you relax after Christmas

Wildlife & Safari Parks

West Midlands Safari and Leisure Park

Spring Grove Bewdley Worcestershire
DY12 1LF
Tel: 01299 402114 Fax: 01299 404519
[On the A456 between Kidderminster and Bewdley]

A 200 acre site incorporating drive through safari park, pets corner, reptile house, hippo lakes, tiger world, goat walk, live shows and train ride to amusement area with over 25 rides and amusements including the Black Fly, Twister coaster and the Flying Lion Kings ride.
Mar-end Oct daily Peak: Reserve 10.00-17.00, Amusements 11.00-18.00. Off Peak (Mon-Fri during school term time): Reserve 10.00-16.00, Amusements 11.00-17.00.
A&C£7.25 C(0-3)£Free, Wristband: under 1.2metres £7.00, over 1.2metres £8.50. Ride tickets: 2 for £3.00

Yorkshire

Animal Attractions

Cruckley Animal Farm

Foston on the Wolds Driffield Yorkshire
YO25 8BS

Tel: 01262 488337

*[M62, J37 off B1249 between Driffield and
Beeford]*

A working family farm with rare and modern
farm animals. Visitors can stroll around the
farmyard and watch the day to day farming
activities.

Apr-26 Sept daily 10.30-17.30

A£3.25 C(under2)£Free C£2.50 OAPs£2.75

Archaeology

ARC (Archaeological Resource Centre)

St Saviour's Church St. Saviourgate York
Yorkshire YO1 8NN

Tel: 01904 643211 (24hr) Fax: 01904 627097

www.vikingjorvik.com

[M62 / A1041 / A19 to the City Centre]

The ARC is the perfect place to visit if you are
looking for a really unusual way to discover the
story of the City of York and the secrets of
uncovering the past - literally! Housed in the fifteenth century Church of St. Saviour, this
hands-on archaeology centre gives visitors a
fascinating insight into the lives of some of
York's past residents, and the opportunity to
handle the genuine 1,000 or even 2,000 year

old items they left behind. You can also explore
the interactive Sensory Garden. The ARC is
JORVIK's sister attraction, and is run by York
Archaeological Trust.

*2nd week in Jan-2nd week in Dec Mon-Fri
10.00-15.30 (term time) and Mon-Sat 11.00-
15.00 (school hols). Please call 01904 543403 to
check opening and availability and to pre-book
your visit*

A£4.50 C(5-15)£4.00 Family Ticket (A2+C2)
£15.00

Arts, Crafts & Textiles

Graves Art Gallery

Surrey Street Sheffield Yorkshire S1 1XZ

Tel: 0114 278 2600 Fax: 0114 278 2604
www.sheffieldgalleries.org.uk

*[Follow signs to the City Centre and Theatres.
Gallery is above the Central Library and around
the corner from the Lyceum Theatre]*

Home to Sheffield's impressive collection of
British and European late 19th and 20th century
art. The main trends and movements are traced
through key works by notable artists of the period, from Pablo Picasso and Pierre Bonnard to
Sir Stanley Spencer and Helen Chadwick.
Visitors can also enjoy a superb range of major
retrospective exhibitions, chosen to complement the permanent collection.

Mon-Sat 10.00-17.00

Admission Free

Henry Moore Institute

74 The Headrow Leeds West Yorkshire
LS1 3AH

Tel: 0113 246 7467 Fax: 0113 246 1481

www.henry-moore-fdn.co.uk

[The Institute is situated in centre of Leeds, adjacent to Leeds City Art Gallery. Approximately 10mins walk from Leeds railway station. Leeds is equidistant from London and Edinburgh and just 2hrs by train from London King's Cross Station]

The Henry Moore Institute, an award winning, architecturally designed gallery, is a centre for the study of sculpture, with exhibition galleries, a reference library and archive, and an active research programme. The four gallery spaces on the ground floor show temporary sculpture exhibitions of all periods and nationalities. It is advisable to ring the recorded information line (0113 234 3158) prior to a visit for up-to-date information. Wheelchair access from Cookridge Street and a lift serves all floors. Induction loops are sited at ground floor, library and slide library reception areas. Information is available in Braille and large print.

All year daily 10.00-17.30, Wed 10.00-21.00. Closed Bank Hols. Free guided tours require pre-booking (0113 246 7467). Library / Collection enquiries, 0113 246 9469

Admission Free

Leeds City Art Gallery

The Headrow Leeds Yorkshire LS1 3AA
Tel: 0113 247 8248 Fax: 0113 244 9689
[Next to Town Hall and Central Library, 5 min walk from Leeds station]

One of the premier venues for the visual arts in the north. Its nationally designated fine art collections range from the early 19th to the late 20th centuries.
All year Mon-Sat 10.00-17.00, Wed 10.00-20.00, Sun 13.00-17.00. Closed Bank Hols
Admission Free

Millennium Galleries

Arundel Gate Sheffield S1 2PP
Tel: 0114 278 2600 Fax: 0114 278 2604
www.sheffieldgalleries.org.uk

[M1, J33 and follow signs to city centre, close to theatres and main shopping area. Rail: 5mins walk from Sheffield station. Nearest parking is NCP at Crucible Theatre]

Visit Yorkshire's premier art venue and adjacent Winter Garden. Enjoy blockbuster exhibitions from national collections including Tate and Victoria and Albert Museum. See the best craft and design, be dazzled by Sheffield's nationally acclaimed collection of metalwork, discover treasures inside the world renowned Ruskin gallery.
All year Mon-Sat 10.00-17.00, Sun 11.00-17.00
Millennium Galleries: Admission Free. Special Exhibition Gallery exhibitions: prices vary, please call for details

Caverns & Caves

Mother Shipton's Cave and the Petrifying Well

Prophecy House High Bridge Knaresborough
North Yorkshire HG5 8DD
Tel: 01423 864600 Fax: 01423 868888
[On A59 4m W of A1(M)]

Admission includes all day parking, enabling visitors to visit Mother Shipton's Cave, the Petrifying Well (England's oldest visitor attraction), Wishing Well, Museum, Woodland Walk.
1 Mar-31 Oct daily 10.00-16.30
A£4.95 C£3.75 OAPs£4.25 Family Ticket
(A2+C2 or A1+C3) £14.95

Blue-John Cavern and Mine

Buxton Road Castleton Sheffield Yorkshire
S30 2WP

Tel: 01433 620638 Fax: 01433 621586

www.bluejohn-cavern.co.uk

[On A625 at foot of Mam-Tor. Follow brown signs for Blue John Cavern, not Castleton Caverns]

The cavern is a remarkable example of a water-worn cave, and measures over a third of a mile long, with chambers 200ft high. It contains 8 of the 14 veins of Blue John stone and has been the major source of this unique form of fluorspar for nearly 300 years.

All year daily 09.30-18.00 or dusk if sooner. Winter, weather permitting

A£6.50 C(5-15)£3.50 Family Ticket (A2+C2)
£18.00 Students&OAPs£4.50. Group rates on application

Discount Offer: One Child Free With Every Full Paying Adult

White Scar Cave

Ingleton North Yorkshire LA6 3AW

Tel: 015242 41244 Fax: 015242 41700

www.whitescarcave.co.uk

[1.5m from Ingleton on B6255 road to Hawes. Plenty of parking on site]

Britain's longest show cave. Explore the massive ice-age cavern, 200,000 years old. See underground waterfalls and streams, and thousands of stalactites. The one mile guided tour takes about 80 minutes. New for 2004, eco-friendly Visitor Centre with living grass roof. Spectacular location in the Yorkshire Dales National Park. Unspoilt nature.

All year daily from 10.00, weather permitting. Closed 25 and 26 Dec

A£6.75 C£3.75 Family Ticket (A2+C2) £19.50. Group rates (12+): A£5.50 C£3.00

Communication Museums

National Museum of Photography, Film & Television

Bradford Yorkshire BD1 1NQ

Tel: 0870 701 0200 Fax: 01274 394540

www.nmpft.org.uk

[M62, J26, joining M606 follow into Bradford city centre, follow city centre / museum signs]

Take a voyage of discovery at the National Museum of Photography, Film & Television. Explore the ten free interactive galleries where you can ride a magic carpet, read the news or look back at your TV favourites from yesteryear. Don't forget to take in an IMAX film on a screen so huge you actually become part of the action. Insight: Collections and Research Centre, opens up the treasures of the Museum's Collection like never before. Exhibitions, tours and talks allow visitors to discover some of the wonderful arte-facts, from the earliest photography and cam-eras to Hughie Green's clapometer! There's something for everyone at the NMPFT, we guar-antee a great day out!

All year Tue-Sun & Bank Hol 10.00-18.00

Admission Free. IMAX Cinema: A£5.95 C&Concessions£4.20

Factory Outlets & Tours

Freeport Hornsea Retail and Leisure Outlet Village

Rolston Road Hornsea HU18 1UT
Tel: 01964 534211 Fax: 01964 536363
[M62, J38, follow signs to Beverley, then A1035]

The UK's original factory outlet village - fun fille pain free shopping. Leisure attractions, include Pottery, World of Wings, Birds of Prey Display, Model Village, Butterfly World, Adventureland, Outdoor Play Area and Soft Ball Pool.
All year daily 09.30-18.00

Festivals & Shows

10th Leeds Shakespeare Festival

Kirkstall Abbey Cloisters Kirkstall Road Leeds
Tel: 0113 224 3801/3802
Following last year's outstanding success Britain's largest and best-loved open air Shakespeare Company are proud to present the 10th Leeds Shakespeare Festival. The Kirkstall Abbey Cloisters provide an idyllic set-ting for two of Shakespeare's most popular comedies 'Much Ado About Nothing' and 'Twelfth Night'. A magical open-air festival com-bining love, laughter and amorous adventure performed by a professional company that con-tinues to delight audiences and critics alike. These fast-moving productions are suitable for all age groups.
August 17-September 12 2004

Beverley and East Riding Early Music Festival 2004

The National Centre for Early Music Walmgate York Yorkshire YO1 9TL
Tel: 01904 645738 Fax: 01904 612631
A festival which traditionally celebrates the extraordinary architectural heritage of the East Riding of Yorkshire and the Wolds
July 2-10 2004

Beverley and East Riding Folk Festival 2004

Various venues Beverley Yorkshire HU17 0DP
Tel: 01377 217662 / 217569
Fax: 01377 217754
[M62 - A63 - A164, or A1079 from York/Hull]

An international festival of folk, roots and world music with concerts, dances, workshops, informal sessions and children's events. Venues include: Beverley Leisure Centre: The campsite is adjacent to the leisure centre and campers are welcome to use the shower facilities during opening hours; Picture Playhouse: one of the country's oldest working cinemas; Beverley Minster: founded in the 8th century and provides the venue for a major concert on Saturday night. The atmosphere in these concerts has been described as 'Magical'; The Friary: founded in the 13th century with oak beamed rooms adding a traditional atmosphere to the workshops and informal concerts held there. Local public houses provide additional, more informal music and song sessions and small concerts.
June 17-20 2004, 20.00-00.00

British Open Show Jumping Championships

Hallam FM Arena Broughton Lane Sheffield Yorkshire S9 2DF
Tel: 0114 256 5656
[From N: M1, J34 A6109 follow signs for Sheffield Centre then Ring Road A6102. From S: M1, J33 A630 (Sheffield) follow signs for Ring Road/Meadowhall (A6178)]

The first major indoor equestrian event to be launched in England for over 30 years. The British Open Show Jumping Championships will contain world-class show jumping as well as the very best in equestrian entertainment during every performance making it an enjoyable visit for the whole family. A revolutionary competition structure will produce an overall British Open Champion at the end of the final class.
April 15-18 2004

Reserved Seating: A£25.00 C(under16)/OAPs£12.50. Unreserved Seating: £17.50 C(under16)/OAPs£8.75

Cleckheaton Folk Festival 2004

Listerdale Littletown Liversedge West Yorkshire WF15 6EN
Tel: 01924 404346 Fax: 01924 404346
[M62, J26 then A628 Dewsbury turn off into Cleckheaton. Festival office in Town Hall on L of main road]

A small, friendly festival of folk music and street entertainment with something for everyone. Concerts, ceilidh, workshops, street parade, morris dancers, street entertainment, singarounds, music sessions, craft fair etc.
July 2-4 2004

Dales Festival of Food and Drink- "A Taste of the Dales"

Leyburn Wensleydale Yorkshire
Tel: 01969 623069 Fax: 01969 622833
[Various venues around Leyburn town centre]

The Dales Festival of Food and Drink at Leyburn in Wensleydale is a showcase for all that is best in food and drink from the region. Pubs, restaurants and tea shops will be offering Yorkshire dishes traditional and new made from local ingredients. Music and colour, "bands and bunting" will ensure a festive atmosphere and LIVE on 104.3FM BBC North Yorkshire. Also featuring children's entertainment, hog roast, WI market, farming displays and much more.
May 1-3 2004, 10.00-17.00
£2.50 per day £4.00 for 3 days
C(under16)£Free

Gawthorpe World Coal Carrying Championships

Various Venues Gawthorpe Yorkshire
Tel: 01924 272163
Starting around noon at the Royal Oak public house on Owl Lane, Gawthorpe and finishing at The Maypole on the village green. No event in

the Olympic Games could stimulate more enthusiasm than this annual contest of stamina and muscle. The Coal Carrying Championships are recognised by The Guinness Book of Records.
April 12 2004 from 12.00
Admission Free

Great Yorkshire Show 2004

Great Yorkshire Showground Harrogate Yorkshire HG2 8PW
Tel: 01423 541000 Fax: 01423 541414
[Off A661 follow AA signs]

The largest agricultural show in the region. Hundreds of stands for shopping, everything from handbags to tractors. Military bands, hundreds of things to see and do, including a flower show and ferrets!
July 13-15 2004

Harrogate International Festival 2004

(Festival Office) 1 Victoria Avenue Harrogate Yorkshire HG1 1EQ
Tel: 01423 537230 Fax: 01423 521264
[M1 via A61 from Leeds, or from A1 via A661]

Come and celebrate the 39th Harrogate International Festival. Visit Yorkshire's floral resort, set in some of Britain's most breath-taking countryside, and enjoy a feast of international performers in a world class line-up. We promise to inspire, provoke, delight and entertain you with an unrivalled programme of classical music, dance, comedy, jazz, world music and street theatre. Family events include our free outdoor Fiesta of World Music, street theatre and children's activities. Why not join us?
July 22-August 7 2004

Jorvik Viking Festival 2005

York Yorkshire YO1 9WT
Tel: 01904 643211
See the past come alive during the annual Jorvik Viking Festival! Organised by York Archaeological Trust, the Festival sees York invaded by hundreds of fearsome warriors, traders, craftspeople, and even whole Viking families. Events will include 'living history' battle re-enactments, longship races, markets and a spectacular finale. The Festival also has a vibrant fringe involving partners across the City Fringe events include drama, arts, and themed walks.
February 4-13 2005
Call 01904 543403 for full programme of event

Moor and Coast Festival

9 Windsor Terrace Whitby Yorkshire YO21 1ET
Tel: 01947 820408 Fax: 01947 821873
Festival of traditional music, song, dance, and arts. Situated in the historic, picturesque town of Whitby. Singarounds, children's events, gho walks, street entertainment - many events are FREE.
April 30, May 1 & 2 2004
Weekend Tickets A£35.00 C(10-14)£17.50. Da Tickets A£20.00 C(10-14)£10.00

Nidderdale Festival 2004

Various venues Pateley Bridge Nr Harrogate North Yorkshire
Tel: 01423 712580
A rich and varied programme of events celebrates the heritage and culture of this end of this beautiful part of Yorkshire. From Ripley at the eastern end of upper Nidderdale to Middlesmoor at the head of the dale, from 'walks and talks' to rock-climbing, from folk to classical concerts, drama, exhibitions, craft demonstrations, the Festival offers something for everyone - local and visitor, young and not so young alike.
July 9-18 2004

heffield Music in the Round

rucible Studio Theatre Norfolk Street Sheffield
orkshire S1 1DA
el: 0114 249 6000 Box Office
*n the heart of the city, The Crucible Theatre is 3
ins walk from the rail and coach stations]*

1st Festival featuring works by Haydn. At the
eart of all Music in the Round's activities is our
esire to make chamber music accessible and
 break down the barriers between audience
nd musician.
ay 8-15 2004
rices range from £5.00-£12.00

waledale Festival 2004

ichmond North Yorkshire DL11 6TB
el: 01748 880019 (Box Office)
ax: 01748 880028
he villages of Swaledale, Wensleydale and
rkengarthdale will ring to the sounds of sound-
g brass as the 2004 festival features brass
usic of all kinds. The opening concert will be
ne of the highlights as the Reeth and Muker
ands combine to give the first performance of
 new Festival commission by Swedish com-
oser Fredrik Hogberg for Double Brass Band.
n early trumpet recital by Crispian Steele
erkins, who will also be playing with Yorkshire
ach Choir in a programme of choral music
ith brass accompaniment. From Minnesota we
elcome the Bethel College Wind Ensemble -
ver 50 musicians with a repertoire ranging from
opland to Faure to Sousa. And there'll be
ore brass music from a range of soloists and
nsembles. In true Swaledale tradition there's
ways the chance to hear something rare and
nusual alongside well known favourites.
ay 28 - June 13 2004

he York Early Music Christmas
estival 2004

he National Centre for Early Music Walmgate
ork Yorkshire YO1 9TL
el: 01904 658338 Fax: 01904 612631
he York Early Music Christmas Festival, pro-
noted by the National Centre for Early Music
akes place in December each year and is a
opular way in which to start the Christmas
eason. Guest artists attending the Early Music
estival include the European Union Baroque

Orchestra directed by Andrew Manze, the
Classic Buskers and Emma Kirkby sporano with
voices, recorders and continuo.
December 10-13 2004

York Early Music Festival 2004

(Box Office) The National Centre for Early Music
St Margaret's Church Walmgate York Yorkshire
YO1 9TL
Tel: 01904 658338 Fax: 01904 612631
York Early Music Festival is Britain's premier festival of early music. Established in 1977, the
Festival takes place within the myriad of
medieval churches, guildhalls and historic houses that make up the ancient city of York. Guest
artists over the past few years have included
the Gabrieli Consort of Music, the Tallis
Scholars, the Consort of Musicke, the King's
Consort and a whole host of internationally
acclaimed artists. The Festival takes place in
early July each summer and makes a particular
feature of the architecture of the city as well as
offering early music concerts of the highest possible quality. Fortunately for us - we welcome
members of the audience from all over the
world and we have the great benefit of working
alongside BBC Radio 3 who record many of the
Festival concerts each year for broadcast
throughout Europe and via the World Service.
July 2-10 2004

Yorkshire Trucking Spectacular

Driffield Showground Kellythorpe Driffield
Yorkshire YO25 9DN
Tel: 0870 1211223 / 01775 768661
[M62, J38, B1230 Newport Road. Off A164]

Truckfest is the ultimate trucking event in
Europe and a fantastic show piece for thou-
sands of dedicated operators and drivers within
the UK haulage industry.
June 5-6 2004
In advance: A£9.00 C£4.50 Family Ticket
£22.50. On the gate: A£10.00 C£5.00 Family
Ticket £25.00

Folk & Local History Museums

Abbey House Museum

Kirkstall Road Leeds Yorkshire LS5 3EH
Tel: 0113 230 5492
[3m W of Leeds City centre on A65, signposted]

A Museum dedicated to recreating Victorian life in Leeds. Displays include an interactive child-hood gallery; displays devoted to Kirkstall Abbey and a gallery exploring life in Victorian Leeds.
All year Tue-Fri 10.00-17.00, Sat 12.00-17.00, Sun 10.00-17.00
A£3.00 C(accompanied)£1.00
Concessions£3.00 Family Ticket (A2+C3) £5.00

World of James Herriot

23 Kirkgate Thirsk Yorkshire YO7 1PL

Tel: 01845 524234 Fax: 01845 525333

www.worldofjamesherriot.org

[In Thirsk town centre]

The World of James Herriot combines history, humour, nostalgia, science and education in a unique tribute to the author James Herriot. Situated in the real Skeldale House where James Herriot lived and worked, the rooms appear as they would in the 1940s and 1950s. Visitors can watch a short film about James in the atmospheric, recreated Yorkshire foldyard and take a seat in the 1930s Austin 7 car from the 'All Creatures Great and Small' TV series. New for 2004, Children's Interactive Gallery.

All year daily, Apr-Sept 10.00-18.00, Oct-Apr 11.00-16.00. Closed 24-26 Dec

A£4.85 C(under5)£Free C(5-16)£3.30 OAPs£3.70 Family Ticket (A2+C2) £13.00, (A2+C3) £15.00, (A1+C3) £10.00, Students£4.00 Students(16-18)£3.00. Group rates (10+): A£4.00 Organiser/Coach Driver £Free, School: £2.50 1A £Free, OAPs£3.00

Discount Offer: Two For The Price Of One Adult Admission

Special Events

Easter Activity Workshop
07/04/2004-14/04/2004
Held on 7 & 14 Apr. Time: 10.00-12.00. To book call 01845 522447

Lets Look at 1940s Flowers and Gardens
11/05/2004
Time: 16.00-18.00. To book call 01845 524234

Half Term Activity Workshop
02/06/2004
Time: 10.00-12.00. To book call 01845 522447

Weekly Activity Workshops
28/07/2004-25/08/2004
Held on Wed. Time: 10.00-12.00. To book call 01845 522447

Halloween Activity Workshop
27/10/2004
Time: 10.00-12.00. To book call 01845 522447

Halloween Family Fun Day
29/10/2004
Time: 11.00-16.00. No booking required

Forests & Woods

Hardcastle Crags

Hebden Bridge Yorkshire HX7 7AP

Tel: 01422 844518 Fax: 01422 841026

[At end of Midgehole Road, 1.5m NE of Hebden Bridge off A6033 Keighley road]

A popular beauty spot, the Crags rise above a steeply wooded valley. Riverside walks meander through beautiful woodland past a 19th century cotton mill, a reminder of Yorkshire's industrial past.

All year daily, dawn-dusk
Admission Free. Car park charge

Gardens & Horticulture

Bramham Park Gardens

Bramham Park Bramham Wetherby West Yorkshire LS23 6ND

Tel: 01937 846000 Fax: 01937 846007

Bramham Park is situated on the A1 Great North Road, approximately 5m S of Wetherby in West Yorkshire, 10m from Leeds and 15m from York]

18th century French-style park and gardens designed in the style of André Le Notre, now almost unique in England. Fabulous ornamental ponds, cascades, temples and almost 2 miles of monumental Beech avenues. One of the best wildflower gardens in the country.

Apr-30 Sept daily 11.30-16.30. Closed 7-13 June & 16 Aug-4 Sept
£4.00 C(0-5)£Free C&OAPs£2.00

RHS Garden Harlow Carr

Crag Lane Beckwithshaw Harrogate HG3 1QB

Tel: 01423 565418 Fax: 01423 530663

[Off B6162]

Wonderful family attraction with events, courses and activities all year. Beautiful 58-acre gardens, streamside, scented, grasses and foliage gardens, woodland and arboretum, vegetable and flower trials.

All year daily 09.30-18.00, or dusk if earlier
£5.00 C(0-6)£Free C(6-16)£1.00 OAPs£4.50 Students£2.00

Heritage & Industrial

Elsecar Heritage Centre

Wath Road Elsecar Barnsley South Yorkshire S74 8HJ

Tel: 01226 740203 Fax: 01226 350239

Elsecar is located in the beautiful South Yorkshire countryside. It is an historic site with craft workshops, antique centre, history exhibition, conference venue and steam railway; an exciting day out for everyone.

All year Tue-Sun 10.00-17.00. Closed 25 Dec-1 Jan. Open Bank Hol Mons

Site and Craft Shops: £Free except on some event days. Railway: A£2.50 C&Concessions£1.00. Living History Exhibition: A£1.50 C&Concessions£1.00

Leeds Industrial Museum

Armley Mills Canal Road Armley Leeds Yorkshire LS12 2QF

Tel: 0113 263 7861

[2m W of city centre off A65]

Formerly the largest woollen mill in the world, Armley Mills now houses the Leeds Industrial Museum. Located beside the River Aire, the museum explores the city's rich industrial past.

All year Tue-Sat 10.00-17.00, Sun 13.00-17.00. Closed 25, 26 Dec & 1 Jan

A£2.00 C(accompanied)£0.50 Concessions£1.00

Historical

Bishops' House

Meersbrook Park Norton Lees Lane Sheffield
Yorkshire S8 9BE

Tel: 0114 278 2600

www.sheffieldgalleries.org.uk

*[S of Sheffield on A61 Chesterfield road. Bus: 39
from city centre. On street parking nearby]*

Bishops' House is the best surviving example of
a timber-framed house in Sheffield. It was built
around the year 1500 and is tucked away at the
top of Meersbrook Park from where visitors can
enjoy panoramic views of the city. The house
retains many of its original features and looks
much as it would have done in the 17th century,
giving a tantalising flavour of Stuart England.
The Great Parlour is restored as a typical dining
room and the first floor chamber contains the
original bedroom furniture and fittings. Disabled
access restricted to ground floor.

All year Sat 10.00-16.30, Sun 11.30-16.30

Admission Free

Brontë Parsonage Museum

Church Street Haworth Keighley West Yorkshire
BD22 8DR
Tel: 01535 642323 Fax: 01535 647131
[On A6033 from A629 extensively signposted]

Charlotte, Emily and Anne Brontë were the
authors of some of the greatest books in the
English language. Haworth Parsonage was their
much loved home, and Jane Eyre, Wuthering
Heights and The Tenant of Wildfell Hall were all
written here. Gain an insight into the place and

objects that inspired their work.
*All year daily Apr-Sept 10.00-17.30, Oct-Mar
11.00-17.00. Closed 24-27 Dec & 2 Jan-31 Ja*
A£4.80 C£1.50 Concessions£3.50 Family
Ticket (A2+C3) £10.50

Burton Agnes Hall

Burton Agnes Driffield Yorkshire YO25 4NB

Tel: 01262 490324 Fax: 01262 490513

*[On A614 between Driffield / Bridlington. Plenty
on site parking available]*

A lovely Elizabethan Hall with fascinating origin
carving and plasterwork, also a large collectio
of Impressionist and contemporary paintings.
The walled garden contains a maze, giant boa
games in coloured gardens and a large collec
tion of plants and herbs.

1 Apr-31 Oct daily 11.00-17.00

A£5.20 C£2.60 OAPs£4.70

Special Events

Gardeners Fair
12/06/2004-13/06/2004

Michaelmas Fair
30/10/2004-31/10/2004

Castle Howard

York Yorkshire YO60 7DA

Tel: 01653 648333 Fax: 01653 648529

www.castlehoward.co.uk

[15m from York, off A64. Plenty of on site parking available]

Magnificent 18th century house, extensive collections and sweeping parklands with temples, lakes, fountains and famous Rose Garden. Historical character guides, outdoor daily tours, the archaeological dig and special event programme. Gift shops, plant centre and cafeterias, adventure playground and boat trips all combine to ensure a great day out for the family.

4 Feb-31 Oct, Grounds open at 10.00, House opens at 11.00

£9.50 C£6.50 Students&OAPs£8.50. Family ticket and Group rates available

Discount Offer: Two Children Free When Accompanied By Two Full Paying Adults.

Special Events

Dancing Daffodils
01/03/2004-30/04/2004
Subject to weather conditions, see the stunning displays of daffodils in the gardens

More 4 Kids - School Holiday Activities
02/04/2004-18/04/2004
Historical and natural activities for children seasonally themed around the House and Grounds

Maids and Mistresses
03/04/2004-31/10/2004
Come and see the historical ladies of Castle Howard. Mothers, wives, daughters, mingle with cooks, maids and governesses. Find out who really had the power and influence at Castle Howard and celebrate the lives and achievements of all these remarkable women

Easter Eggstravaganza
11/04/2004-12/04/2004
Meet the Easter Bunny and join in the chocolate hunt. Also decorated egg competition, quizzes and bouncy castles

Spring Festival of Colour
01/05/2004-31/05/2004
Subject to weather conditions, see the colourful displays of Rhododendrons in Ray Wood and tulips in the gardens

York Guild Weaving, Spinning and Dyeing
08/05/2004-09/05/2004
As part of the National Weaving, Spinning and Dyeing Week, The York Guild will be showcasing these rural and traditional crafts

Domestic Goddess
15/05/2004-16/05/2004
Go back through history to examine the life of the 18th century woman - part of the Maids and Mistresses celebration

More 4 Kids - School Holiday Activities
29/05/2004-06/06/2004
Historical and natural activities for children seasonally themed around the House and Grounds

Summer Festival of Colour
01/06/2004-31/07/2004
Subject to weather conditions, see the famous Castle Howard Roses and Delphiniums at their best

The Jowett Car Club Rally
05/06/2004
One of the largest gatherings of this classic car in the country

Festival of Roses and Horticultural History
26/06/2004-27/06/2004
Castle Howard will be celebrating their stunning displays of roses with horticultural history displays, rose garden tours, and much more. There will also be a jazz band entertaining visitors in gardens

Ryedale School Swing Band
04/07/2004
Local school swing band will be entertaining visitors in the gardens

Summertime Strings
11/07/2004
Pavilion Music String Quartet will be entertaining the visitors in the gardens of Castle Howard. There will also be workshops by the North Yorkshire Music Therapy Centre

National Archaeology Day
18/07/2004
As part of the national celebration of archaeology there will be a series of activities and events around Castle Howard's own archaeological dig

More 4 Kids - School Holiday Activities
22/07/2004-01/09/2004
Historical and natural activities for children seasonally themed around the House and Grounds

Jazz and Jive
01/08/2004
Non stop toe tapping live entertainment in the gardens at Castle Howard. Featuring; Al Woods Quartet, Finesse Jazz Trio, Some Like It Hot and the John Taylor Band

Castle Howard Proms Spectacular - Outdoor Evening Concert
21/08/2004
Featuring the English National Orchestra. Conducted by Jae Alexander, this concert will bring you an evening of sheer classical brilliance. The concert will feature an aerial display by an original World War II Spitfire

Best of the West End
22/08/2004
This concert will feature all the greatest hits from the musical stages of the West End in London. These will include favourites from Phantom of the Opera, Miss Saigon, Cats, Mamma Mia and many more

Children's Weekend
28/08/2004-30/08/2004
Fun-packed bank holiday weekend for children including bouncy castles, giant garden games, face painting, puppet shows, garden trails and much more

Sunday Stroll - Save the Children Sponsored Walk
26/09/2004
Sponsored walk around the Castle Howard Estate in aid of Save The Children

More 4 Kids - School Holiday Activities
23/10/2004-31/10/2004
Historical and natural activities for children seasonally themed around the House and Grounds

NSPCC Christmas Shopping Fair
04/11/2004
Annual Christmas fair in the House in aid of the NSPCC

Conisbrough Castle

Castle Hill Conisbrough Doncaster Yorkshire DN12 3BU
Tel: 01709 863329 Fax: 01709 866773
[NE off A630. 4.5m SW of Doncaster]

A splendid circular 12th-century keep, with six buttresses, surrounded by a curtain wall. The best preserved in England, refurbished with a roof, two floors and sound and light effects.
1 Apr-30 Sept daily 10.00-17.00, Oct-31 Mar daily 10.00-16.00. Closed 24-26 Dec & 1 Jan
A£3.75 C(6-16)£2.00 Family Ticket (A2+C2) £9.50 Concessions£2.50

Harewood House and Bird Garden

Harewood Leeds West Yorkshire LS17 9LQ
Tel: 0113 218 1010 Fax: 0113 218 1002

www.harewood.org

[The village of Harewood is centrally placed in Yorkshire at the junction of the A61 / A659 on the Leeds to Harrogate road. The M1 begins just the other side of Leeds and feeds into the Trans

ennine M62 which in turn feeds into the M6/M5
o the W and the M18/A1 to the E. Bus: A regular
us service is available to Harewood village from
oth Leeds and Harrogate (no.36) and runs every
'0mins during our opening hours. Plenty of on
ite parking available]

ward winning Harewood is renowned for its
tunning architecture and exquisite Adam interi-
rs, containing a rich collection of Chippendale
urniture, fine porcelain, outstanding art collec-
ons and Royal family memorabilia from HRH
'rincess Mary Princess Royal, Lord Harewood's
nother. Following the popularity of the restored
)ld Kitchen, 'Below Stairs: Harewood's Hidden
Collections' will open in 2004, providing a fur-
ner glimpse into the servants' domain. The
nspiring Grounds, enfold a restored parterre
errace, oriental Rock Garden, lakeside and
voodland walks, a popular Lakeside Bird
arden and thrilling Adventure Playground.
hroughout the season Harewood hosts an
xciting variety of special events.

rounds: 11 Feb-14 Nov daily 10.00-18.00.
errace Gallery: 10.00-17.00. Bird Garden:
0.00-17.00 (or dusk if earlier); 20 Nov-12 Dec
eekends only 10.00-16.00. House: 17 Mar-14
'ov 11.00-16.00

ll attractions: Mon-Sat A£10.00 C£5.50
)APs£8.25 Family Ticket £30.50, Sun A£11.00
:£6.00 OAPs£9.25 Family Ticket £33.50.
rounds: Mon-Sat A£7.25 C£4.50 OAPs£6.25
amily Ticket £23.00, Sun A£8.25 C£5.00
)APs£7.25 Family Ticket £26.00. £Free for
nder 5s and Harewood Card Holders. Group
ates available

**)iscount Offer: One Child Free With A
'ull Paying Adult.**

special Events

Valking With Dinosaurs
1/02/2004-06/06/2004
'sing modern technology this exhibition will bring
ossils to life, allowing you to literally walk with the
inosaurs while you make your on-screen debut
vith these amazing creatures

usan Derges
1/02/2004-27/06/2004
his exhibition explores themes of above and
elow, where we appear at once to be looking up
ough the water, yet we see stars or the moon
ay on its surface and look down from above
rough water

Maids And Mistresses
17/03/2004-01/09/2004
Discover the 'secret lives' through a new trail,
audio guide, and special exhibition of previously
unseen diaries, paintings and correspondence

Below Stairs: Harewood's Hidden Collections
17/03/2004-14/11/2004
For the first time ever the Servants' Hall,
Housekeeper's Room, and corridors of 'Below
Stairs' Harewood, displaying over 1,000 objects
with fascinating tales to tell, will be open to the
public. Time: 11.00-16.30

Noddy's Here... Again!
01/05/2004-03/05/2004
Noddy and his Friends - PC Plod, Big Ears, Sly,
Mr Sparks, Tessie Bear & Bumpy Dog will meet
and greet Harewood visitors

Spirit Of The Horse
20/05/2004-23/05/2004
An international cast of riders, dancers and physical artistes bring out the extraordinary talents of
30 horses in a unique spectacle of Equestrian
Theatre. Time: 3 shows 2 hours long between
14.00-20.00. Cost A£16.00-£32.00

Gardeners' Weekend
22/05/2004-23/05/2004
A brilliant day out for any gardening enthusiasts.
Time: 10.00-17.00. Cost: (Event Only) A£5.00
OAPs £4.00 C£3.00 Family £15.00

Porsche Clun Yorkshire Concours
13/06/2004
Up to 400 examples of this racy sports car that
you can admire and aspire to

Wizard Of Oz
16/06/2004-18/06/2004
Follow the Yellow Brick Road (or rather the lakeside path) in a promenade performance of this
fantastic story with colourful characters and lively
music with a contemporary twist. Time: 19.00-
21.30. Cost: (Event Only) A£9.50 OAPs £7.50
C&Students £5.50 Family £31.00

Harewood Vintage and Classic Vehicle Rally
20/06/2004
Incorporating the Yorkshire Post Motor Show. This
event attracts up to 20 major motor dealers from
the region with their latest models. You can also
see around 700 Classic and Vintage exhibits
along with a variety of trade stands, a children's
fun fair and arena events

Live Crafts
25/06/2004-27/06/2004
A wonderful opportunity to purchase essentials

and gifts from some of the specialist craftspeople exhibiting. Time: 10.00-17.00 Cost: Event Only A£5.00 OAPs £4.50 C£1.00 Family £11.00

Sound Of The 70s-Open Air Concert
03/07/2004
A groovy night of toe tapping music as you are taken to a boogie wonderland. Time: 20.00-22.30. Cost: Event Only Advance A£21.50 C£13.00 On The Day A£25.00 C£16.00

Teddy Bears Picnic with the National Kidney Research Fund
04/07/2004
National Kidney Research fund return with their very popular sponsored Teddy Toddle in the park

Ian Hamilton Finlay
05/07/2004-14/11/2004
Ian Hamilton Finlay is a poet and Modernist artist who has consistently exploited nature, literature and the potency of words in his art

A Midsummer Night's Dream
08/07/2004
An enchanting outdoor production of one of Shakespeare's best loved comedies performed by Chapterhouse Theatre. Time: 13.00-19.30. Cost: Event Only A£10.50 Concessions £7.50

Jaguar Rally
11/07/2004
One of our biggest rallies on the North Front attracting over 500 of these magnificent cars

Alice Through The Looking Glass
18/07/2004
Illyria Theatre Company return with an outdoor production of Lewis Caroll's sequel to Alice in Wonderland. Time: 15.00-19.00. Cost: Event Only A£9.50 OAPs £7.50 C£5.50 Family £31.00

Cycle For Life
18/07/2004
Harewood is delighted to host its own Cycle for Life event, raising money in aid of Cancer Research UK

Leeds Championship Dog Show
24/07/2004-26/07/2004
One of the largest outdoor Dog Shows in the North

Rolls Royce Rally
01/08/2004
This is the event's 25th year at Harewood and the 100th anniversary of Rolls Royce. It is one of the biggest and best of the car rallies at Harewood

Pride & Prejudice
12/08/2004
An enchanting outdoor production of Jane Austin's classic novel by Illyria in the grounds of Harewood House. Time: 19.30. Cost: Event Only A£10.50 Concessions £7.50

Last Night Of The Harewood Proms-Open Air Concert
04/09/2004
A variety of popular classics, beautiful arias and course all the traditional proms favourites. Time: 19.30-22.00. Cost: Event Only Advance A£19. C£13.00, on the day A£23.00 C£16.00

Tournament Of Kings
11/09/2004-12/09/2004
Family fun day themed around spectacular moments, images and characters from history

Alvis Rally With Aston Martin Owner's Club
12/09/2004
These cars were built with nothing but quality in mind so come and admire the appearance and finish that is well above that of your average car

The 54th Northern Antiques Fair
23/09/2004-26/09/2004
An excellent opportunity to buy some of the bes quality antiques in the breathtaking surrounds o Harewood House

'Bob The Roman': Heroic Antiquity & The Architecture Of Robert Adam
08/10/2004-14/11/2004
A major new exhibition from Sir John Soane's Museum explores the work of Robert Adam, (1728-1792), one of the most influential figures British architecture and the architect of Harewoo House

Autumn glory
17/10/2004
Guided walks through some of Harewood's woodland areas collecting seeds and learning more about Harewood's flora!

Live Crafts
26/11/2004-28/11/2004
Live Crafts for Christmas make a welcome retur Time: Fri 12.00-21.00, Sat-Sun 10.00-17.00. Cost: Event Only A£5.00 OAPs£4.50 C£1.00 Family £11.00

Alice Coote
16/12/2004

Alfred Brendel With Pierre Laurent Aimard
06/01/2005

faithfully recreated following twenty years of archaeological and historical research. A programme of special events runs throughout the year, including the Jorvik Viking Festival every February - check the website for further details.

All year Apr-Oct daily 10.00-17.00, Nov-Mar daily 10.00-16.00. Closed 25 Dec. Opening hours may vary over Christmas and New Year, please call to confirm

A£7.20 C(under5)£Free C(5-15)£5.10 Family Ticket (A2+C2) £21.95, (A2+C3) £26.50 Student&OAPs£6.10. Call 01904 543403 for pre-booked tickets

JORVIK

Coppergate York Yorkshire YO1 9WT
Tel: 01904 543403 / 643211 (24hr)
Fax: 01904 627097

www.vikingjorvik.com

In the centre of York. Can be reached from the A1 via A64 or A19 or A1079 Park and Ride service, call 01904 613161]

Explore York's Viking history on the very site where archaeologists uncovered remains of the Viking-Age City of 'Jorvik'. Get face-to-face with our expert Viking residents, see over 800 of the items discovered on site, and learn what life was really like in our Special Exhibitions. 'Fearsome Craftsmen' reveals the skills and artistry of the Vikings and includes live craft demonstrations, and 'Unearthed' tells how the people of York lived - and died - as revealed by real bone material. JORVIK also takes visitors through a reconstruction of the actual Viking-Age streets which stood here 1,000 years ago,

Lotherton Hall

Lotherton Lane Aberford Leeds Yorkshire
LS25 3EB

Tel: 0113 281 3259

[Off the A1 0.75m E of junction with B1217]

Lotherton is an Edwardian gentleman's country residence which retains the character of a charming family home. It houses the Gasgoigne Gift of paintings, furniture, sculpture, silver, jewellery, pottery and porcelain, together with special collections of Oriental and Victorian art, and costume.

Mar Tue-Sat 10.00-16.00, Sun 13.00-16.00, Apr-Oct Tue-Sat 10.00-17.00, Sun 13.00-17.00, Nov-Dec Tue-Sat 10.00-16.00, Sun 12.00-16.00. Closed Jan-Feb. Lotherton Bird Garden: Good Fri-31 Oct 10.00-17.00, 1 Nov-Thur prior to Easter 10.00-15.30. Closed 25, 26 Dec & 1 Jan. Lotherton Park: all year daily dawn-dusk

House: A£2.00 C(accompanied)£0.50 Concessions£1.00. Bird Garden & Park: £Free

Newby Hall and Gardens

Newby Hall Ripon Yorkshire HG4 5AE

Tel: 01423 322583 Fax: 01423 324452

www.newbyhall.com

[2m off A1(M) at Ripon exit (signposted). 40mins (23m) from York. 45mins (27m) NE of Leeds/Bradford Airport. 30mins (15m) from Harrogate. Plenty of on site parking available]

Designed under the guidance of Sir Christopher Wren, this graceful country house epitomizes the Georgian 'Age of Elegance'. Its beautifully restored interior presents Robert Adam at his very best. The contents of the house include a rare set of Gobelins tapestries, a renowned gallery of classical statuary and some of Chippendale's finest furniture. The 25 acres of award winning gardens are a haven for both the specialist and amateur gardener alike. They include a miniature railway, an adventure garden for children, a woodland discovery walk and a new contemporary sculpture park. Newby also has an irresistible shop and well stocked plant centre.

1 Apr-26 Sept Tue-Sun & Bank Hol 12.00-17.00 (Gardens: 11.00-17.30)

House & Garden: A£7.80 C(under4)£Free C£5.30 OAPs£6.80. Gardens only: A£6.30 C(under4)£Free C£4.80 OAPs£5.30

Discount Offer: One Child Free When Accompanied By A Full Paying Adult

Special Events

Jazz Brunch
04/04/2004-05/09/2004
Held on the first Sunday of each month; 4 Apr, 2 May, 6 June, 4 July, 1 Aug & 5 Sept

Easter Fun Day
11/04/2004

Spring Plant Fair
09/05/2004

Craft Fair
04/06/2004-06/06/2004

Historic Vehicle Rally
18/07/2004

Harrogate MG Club Rally
09/08/2004

Autumn Craft Fair
10/09/2004-12/09/2004

Nunnington Hall

Nunnington nr Helmsley York Yorkshire YO62 5UY
Tel: 01439 748283 Fax: 01439 748284
[4.5m SE of Helmsley (A170) Helmsley - Pickering road, 1.5m N of B1257 Malton - Helmsley road, 21m N of York B1363]

Sheltered in a lovely walled garden on a quiet riverbank is this delightful 17th century manor house. It is easy to see why it has remained a much loved family home for over 400 years. A magnificent oak panelled hall leads to cosy family living rooms, the nursery and maid's room.

20 Mar-31 Oct; Apr Wed-Sun 13.30-16.30, May Wed-Sun 13.30-17.00, June-Aug Tue-Sun 13.30-17.00, Sept Wed-Sun 13.30-17.00, Oct Wed-Sun 13.30-16.30. Open Bank Hol Mons. Tea-room and tea-garden opens 12.30 until house closes

A£5.00 C(under5)£Free C(5-16)£2.50 Family Ticket (A2+C3) £12.50. Garden only: A£2.50 C£Free

Rievaulx Terrace and Temples

Rievaulx Helmsley York Yorkshire YO62 5LJ
Tel: 01439 798340 / 748283
Fax: 01439 748284
[2.5m NW of Helmsley on B1257]

A 0.5m long grass-covered terrace and adjoining woodland, with vistas over Rievaulx Abbey (no access) and Rye valley to Ryedale and the Hambleton Hills. There are two mid-18th century temples: the Ionic Temple has elaborate ceiling paintings and fine 18th century furniture.

20 Mar-31 Oct daily 10.30-18.00 (17.00 in Oct). Ionic Temple closed 13.00-14.00

A£3.80 C(under5)£Free C(5-16)£2.00

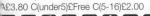

Ripley Castle

Ripley Harrogate North Yorkshire HG3 3AY
Tel: 01423 770152 Fax: 01423 771745
www.ripleycastle.co.uk

[Off A61 3.5m N of Harrogate. Ample parking on site]

Ripley Castle has been home to the Ingilby family since 1320. You will enjoy the informative and amusing guided tours which bring history to life. Set in acres of deer park with delightful walled gardens and hothouses, this is a great place for a family day out.

Castle: Jan-June & Sept-Dec Tue, Thur, Sat & Sun, July-Aug daily 10.30-15.00. Gardens: all year daily 10.00-17.00

Castle & Gardens: A£6.00 C(5-16)£3.50 OAPs&Groups£5.00. Gardens only: A£3.50 C£2.00 OAPs&Groups£3.00

Skipton Castle

Skipton Yorkshire BD23 1AQ
Tel: 01756 792442 Fax: 01756 796100
www.skiptoncastle.co.uk

[Located in Skipton centre]

Skipton Castle is one of the best preserved, most complete medieval castles in England. Dating from Norman times with a charming Tudor Courtyard it withstood a three year siege in the Civil War. Explore this exciting castle and relax in the peaceful grounds. Guided tours for pre-booked groups only.

All year daily Mar-Sept Mon-Sat 10.00-18.00, Sun 12.00-18.00, Oct-Feb Mon-Sat 10.00-16.00, Sun 12.00-16.00. Closed 25 Dec

A£5.00* C(0-5)£Free C(5+)£2.50 OAPs£4.40 Family Ticket (A2+C3) £13.90 Students£4.40 (must show ID). Group rates (15+): £4.00. *Cost includes illustrated tour sheet in choice of 8 languages (English, French, German, Dutch, Italian, Spanish, Japanese or Esperanto)

Special Events

Red Wyvern Society Re-enactment
29/05/2004-31/05/2004
The War of the Roses in the 15th Century

Life and Times Re-enactment
24/07/2004-25/07/2004
The English Civil War in the 17th Century

Feudal Archers Re-enactment
14/08/2004-15/08/2004
A demonstration of arms, armour and domestic life (1135-1216)

Treasurer's House

Minster Yard York Yorkshire YO1 7JL
Tel: 01904 624247 Fax: 01904 647372
[In Minster Yard on N side of Minster. Rail: York]

York's 'hidden treasure', this elegant house stands within the tranquil surroundings of the Minster Close. Medieval in origin (and with even earlier Roman links), the house was rescued from neglect by the wealthy local industrialist Frank Green, who carefully restored it and made it his home.
27 Mar-31 Oct Sat-Thur 11.00-16.30
House: A£4.50 C£2.20 Family Ticket (A2+C3) £11.00

Medical Museums

Thackray Museum

Beckett Street Leeds Yorkshire LS9 7LN

Tel: 0113 244 4343 Fax: 0113 247 0219

www.thackraymuseum.org

[From M621 follow signs for York, then follow the brown signs. From the North, take A58. Next to St James Hospital. Plenty of on site parking]

An award winning interactive museum offering a great day out for all. From a Victorian operating theatre to the wonders of modern surgery, the museum's galleries, collections and interactive displays bring to life the history of medicine. Experience the sights and sounds of a Victorian slum, discover the incredible lotions and potions offered as treatments. Experience pregnancy by trying on an empathy belly and have fun exploring the workings of the human body in the interactive 'Bodyworks' gallery. Please call the information line on 0113 245 7084 for further details on school holiday activities.

All year daily 10.00-17.00. Closed 24-26, 31 Dec & 1 Jan

A£4.90 C£3.50 OAPs&Concessions£3.90 Family Ticket £16.00. Group rates available

Discount Offer: Buy One Full Price Adult Ticket and Receive Another Free

Military & Defence Museums

Green Howards Museum

Trinity Church Square Market Place Richmond Yorkshire DL10 4QN

Tel: 01748 826561 Fax: 01748 821924

[Any turning from A1 signposted to Richmond between Scotch Corner and Catterick]

This award-winning museum traces the military history of the Green Howards from the late 17th century onwards.

Feb-Nov; Feb, Mar & Nov Mon-Fri 10.00-16.30; Apr-mid May Mon-Sat 09.30-16.30; Mid May-Sept Mon-Sat 09.30-16.30, Sun 14.00-16.30; Oct Mon-Sat 09.30-16.30. Closed Dec-Jan

A£2.50 C£Free OAPs£2.00 Family Ticket £5.00

Royal Armouries Museum

Armouries Drive Leeds Yorkshire LS10 1LT

Tel: 0113 220 1999 Fax: 0113 220 1934

www.armouries.org.uk

[Off A61 close to city centre follow brown tourist signs. On site parking available with an overflow car park nearby]

3,000 years of history covered by over 8,000 spectacular exhibits in stunning surroundings make this world famous collection of arms and armour a must-see attraction. Be swept away to another time in history by one of our powerful live interpretations and discover for yourself what it is like to hold a 15th century pollaxe or a black, powder-firing musket. Experience an exciting combination of breathtaking displays, costumed demonstrations, live action events, entertaining films, interactive technology and thrilling exhibitions. Be amazed at the thousands of exquisite objects which are housed in our five magnificent themed galleries: War, Tournament, Oriental, Hunting and Self Defence. You'll marvel at our priceless displays including Henry VIII's magnificent tournament armour. From April to October our interpreters authentically recreate the spectacle of the joust which will leave you clutching the edge of your seat as heart-pounding excitement overtakes you. You will also have the opportunity of seeing our resident falconer fly his beautiful birds of prey and to learn about their predatory traits. Later, visit the Menagerie and get closer to the birds and horses who love to meet our visitors!

All in all, there really is something for the whole family and we guarantee that you will have a truly memorable, fun packed day at the Royal Armouries Museum.

All year daily 10.00-17.00 except 24 & 25 Dec

Admission Free

Special Events

Easter Tournament
03/04/2004-18/04/2004
This really is a jousting event not to be missed. A spectacular medieval sporting feud bursting with nail biting, adrenaline surging action and thrilling live events. The Tiltyard takes centre-stage for this major event and will bring teams together from all over the world including Holland, Belfast, America and of course our very own home grown Royal Armouries troupe. Watch as the teams battle it out in a four day jousting tournament

Sikh Heritage Trail
29/05/2004-06/06/2004
A colourful Eastern delight which will unearth some treasures within our collection

Mills - Water & Wind

Thwaite Mills Watermill

Thwaite Lane Stourton Leeds Yorkshire
LS10 1RP

Tel: 0113 249 6453 Fax: 0113 277 6737
[2m S of City centre off A61]

Lying between river and canal this island-based water-powered mill once sustained a small self-sufficient community. A tour of the early 19th century mill with its two giant turning water-wheels is a journey back in time.
All year Sat & Leeds School holidays 10.00-17.00, Sun 13.00-17.00
A£2.00 C(accompanied)£0.50
Concessions£1.00

Mining

National Coal Mining Museum For England

Caphouse Colliery New Road Overton Wakefield Yorkshire WF4 4RH
Tel: 01924 848806 Fax: 01924 844567
www.ncm.org.uk

[On A642 between Wakefield / Huddersfield. Plenty of free parking on site]

A great day out for all the family. Don't miss the unique opportunity to travel 140 metres underground down one of Britain's oldest working mines, where models and machinery depict methods and conditions of mining from the early 1800s to the present. An experienced local miner will guide your party around the underground workings. Above ground, find out more about the development of mining in the exhibitions around the site. Visit the pit ponies and the Shire horse. Take a train ride right across the site. See the steam winder and the pithead baths. Visit the Museum's well-stocked shop where you can get your very own mining memorabilia. Children under 5 years are not allowed underground. Disabled facilities include level parking, ramp and disabled toilets. Underground tours are also available with prior arrangement. The temperature underground is 12 degrees centigrade. We strongly recommend warm, practical clothing and sensible, flat shoes. Photography permitted above ground only.

*All year daily 10.00-17.00. Closed 24-26 Dec &
1 Jan. During Bank Hols we recommend you
arrive early to ensure a place on an underground
tour*

Admission Free

Special Events

Easter Activities, Arts & Crafts
05/04/2004-16/04/2004

Impressions - Prints inspired by Mining
05/04/2004-04/07/2004

Easter Activities / Interpreters
09/04/2004-12/04/2004

Emergency Services Day
15/05/2004

Balloon Release
22/05/2004

Half Term Activities, Arts and Crafts
31/05/2004-06/06/2004

MG Rally
05/06/2004-06/06/2004

Watercolour Workshop
09/06/2004

Traction Engine Rally
12/06/2004-13/06/2004

Exhibition: Routes/Roots - Mapping Your Mining
Past
19/07/2004-17/10/2004

Summer Activities
26/07/2004-27/08/2004

Watercolour Workshop
08/09/2004

Heritage Open Weekend
10/09/2004-12/09/2004

Family Learning Week
11/10/2004-17/10/2004

Half Term Activities
25/10/2004-29/10/2004

Wakefield Victorian Weekend
20/11/2004-21/11/2004

Santa's Underground Grotto
27/11/2004-19/12/2004
Held on 27-28 Nov, 4-5, 11-12, 18-19 Dec

Places of Worship

St Mary's Church

Studley Royal Ripon Yorkshire
Tel: 01765 608888 Fax: 01765 601002
[2.5m W of Ripon off B6265]

A magnificent church, designed by William
Burges in the 1870s, with a highly decorated
interior.
1 Apr-30 Sept daily 13.00-17.00
Admission Free

York Minster

Deangate York Yorkshire YO1 2JN
Tel: 01904 557216 Fax: 01904 557218
It is believed Edwin King of Northumbria built
the first church on this site in 627: since then
both Saxons and Normans built cathedrals
here, and parts of the latter survive in many
places in the present structure.
Mon-Sat daily 09.00-18.30, Sun after 12.00
A£4.50 C£Free Concessions£3.00. Undercroft
charges: A£3.00 C£1.50 Concessions£2.00.
Tower charges: A£2.50 C£1.00

Railways

Kirklees Light Railway

Park Mill Way Clayton West Huddersfield
Yorkshire HD8 9XJ
Tel: 01484 865727
[From north J39 M1& from south J38 M1 then on

A636 Wakefield-Denby Dale road]

Scenic ride on narrow gauge 15inch steam railway in enclosed carriages on old country branch line. Children's playground and miniature fairground rides.

29 May-5 Sept daily, hourly from 11.00, and most scheduled holidays. Every weekend Sept-May
A£5.50 C(3-15)£3.50 Family Ticket (A2+C2) £16.00

Discount Offer: One Free Child With One Full Paying Adult.

Middleton Railway Leeds

Moor Road Hunslet Leeds Yorkshire LS10 2JQ

Tel: 0113 271 0320

www.middletonrailway.org.uk

[M621, J5 or follow signs from A61]

The first railway authorised by an Act of Parliament (1758) and the first to succeed with steam locomotives (1812). Steam trains run each weekend in season into Middleton Park. A nature trail and playgrounds for children are among the other attractions. A large collection of steam engines is displayed.

Viewing all year. Trains run Apr-Dec Sat-Sun & Bank Hols. Times and prices may vary please call for details

Station Free. Return Fare: A£2.50 C(3-15)£1.50 Family Ticket (A2+C2) £7.00. Tickets valid for unlimited rides on day of purchase

Discount Offer: Two Adults For The Price Of One.

<u>Special Events</u>

Bluebell Walk
09/05/2004

Mischievious Engines Weekend
22/05/2004-23/05/2004

School Trains
15/06/2004-24/06/2004
Available on 15 & 24 June only

Happy Engines Weekend
10/07/2004-11/07/2004

Diesel Weekend
14/08/2004-15/08/2004

Heritage Weekend
11/09/2004-12/09/2004

Enthusiasts Weekend
25/09/2004-26/09/2004
A selection of our Leeds built locos in use

Halloween
31/10/2004

Santa Special
04/12/2004-24/12/2004
Held on 4, 5, 11, 12, 18, 19, 24 Dec only

School Santa
10/12/2004

North Yorkshire Moors Railway

Pickering Station Pickering Yorkshire YO18 7AJ

Tel: 01751 472508 Fax: 01751 476970

www.northyorkshiremoorsrailway.com

[In Pickering off A170]

Operating through the heart of the North York Moors National Park between Pickering and Grosmont, steam trains cover a distance of 18 miles. Beautiful Newtondale Halt gives walkers easy access to forest and moorland. The locomotive sheds at Grosmont are open to the public. Special events throughout the year.

Mar-Nov daily plus some further winter dates, please call for details

All line return A£12.00 C£6.00 OAPs£10.50, please telephone for further details. Group discounts available

Sealife Centres & Aquariums

The Deep - World's only Submarium

Hull East Yorkshire HU1 4DP

Tel: 01482 381000 Fax: 01482 381018

www.thedeep.co.uk

[From N take A1/M, M62/A63. From S take A1/M, A15/A63. From P&O North Sea Ferry Terminal take A1033/A63 for 2m. Rail: Hull, 4 direct trains from London daily, regular services from Manchester, Sheffield, York and East Coast. 15min walk or taxi ride from station. Regular local buses run to The Deep]

As the story of the oceans unfolds, take a journey deeper and deeper until you reach the inky depths of the great ocean floor. Come eye to eye with 13 species of shark and get a close encounter with magical seahorses, arctic starfish and fascinating octopus. Feel the heat of a tropical coral reef and the real ice walls of the far Polar regions. Travel to the future in the underwater research station, Deep Blue One, before you take a trip back to the surface in the breathtaking glass lift. The Deep - Oceans of discovery for all the family!

All year daily 10.00-18.00, closed 24-25 Dec

A£6.50 C£4.50 OAPs£5.00. Family tickets available. Group rates available for 10+ people and school groups

Spectator Sports

COUNTRY RACING AT ITS BEST

Thirsk Racecourse

Station Road Thirsk Yorkshire YO7 1QL

Tel: 01845 522276 Fax: 01845 525353

www.thirskracecourse.net

[A61 Thirsk/Ripon Road, 0.5m W of Thirsk Rail: Thirsk. Helicopter landing by prior arrangement. Plenty of on site parking available]

Thirsk is one of Yorkshire's most beautiful country courses, set between the North Yorkshire Moors and the Dales with easy access from road or rail. Thirsk is a friendly racecourse with compact, well maintained enclosures. Facilities for entertainment have continuously been improved and upgraded in recent years. Hospitality options are available for all sizes of party in either viewing boxes overlooking the winning post or private banqueting suites seating up to 120 guests. Marquees are also an option. Entertainment facilities available on non racedays for private functions.

Race meetings Apr-Sept

Club Day Badge: £15.00 Tattersalls: £10.00 Family Ring: £3.00 C(0-16)£Free OAPs (on production of Pension Book) Tattersalls: £5.00, OAPs Family Ring: £1.50. Group rates available

Special Events

April Race Fixtures
16/04/2004-17/04/2004

May Race Fixtures
01/05/2004-24/05/2004
To be held on 1, 8 (evening), 15 & 24 (evening) May

June Race Fixtures
16/06/2004-24/06/2004
To be held on 16 & 24 June only

July Race Fixtures
23/07/2004-31/07/2004
To be held on 23, 30, 31 July

August Race Fixtures
09/08/2004-27/08/2004
To be held on 9 (evening) & 27 Aug only

September Race Fixtures
04/09/2004-14/09/2004
To be held on 4 & 14 Sept only

York Racecourse

York Race Committee The Racecourse York Yorkshire YO23 1EX

Tel: 01904 620911 Fax: 01904 611071

www.yorkracecourse.co.uk

[1m from City Centre off A64 Leeds / Tadcaster road. Rail: York. Plenty of on site parking]

We at York aim to provide our customers with great sporting events bringing many of the world's top riders and thoroughbreds together to compete for some of racing's most famous and cherished prizes. Visitors to the County Stand and Grandstand enclosures in particular can enjoy the finest facilities, unsurpassed anywhere. Add to this a comprehensive range of bars, restaurants and catering outlets (with sensible prices), together with a magnificent setting and that unique atmosphere of a York Raceday and we promise you and your racing companions an occasion to savour. For further details on the following fixtures, please call.

Race meetings May-Oct

A£4.00-£45.00 dependant on Enclosure C(0-16)£Free. Group rates available

Special Events

May Fixtures
11/05/2004-13/05/2004
Racing on 11, 12 and 13 May

June Fixtures
11/06/2004-12/06/2004

July Fixtures
09/07/2004-24/07/2004
Racing on 9, 11 and 24 May

ugust Fixtures
7/08/2004-19/08/2004
Racing on 17, 18 and 19 Aug

September Fixture
1/09/2004-05/09/2004
Racing on 1 and 5 Sept only

October Fixtures
08/10/2004-09/10/2004

Sport & Recreation

Bridlington Leisure World

The Promenade Bridlington Yorkshire
YO15 2QO

Tel: 01262 606715 Fax: 01262 673458

www.bridlington.net/leisureworld

[M62 - follow A163 for 40m to Bridlington]

Bridlington Leisure World is one of the East
Riding's premier leisure attractions. The main
swimmimg pool, 25metres in length is ideal for
those wanting a traditional swim. The children's
swimming pool is popular with families and
young children, whereas the wave pool is the
main attraction for fun and enjoyment. Designed
with a beach effect for easy access and with a
maximum depth of 1metre, the wave pool is
ideal for everyone. The popular wave machine
and exciting flumes make your visit all the more
pleasurable! The complex also includes the 3B's
Entertainment Centre, which hosts a variety of
different events for all ages throughout the year.
The Multi Purpose Hall offers indoor bowls in
the winter months and hosts various activities
during the summer months. We have a recently
refurbished state of the art fitness suite, which is
fully air-conditioned and is adjacent to a health
suite, which includes a sauna and steam bath.
Both have fantastic panoramic sea views of the

heritage coastline of the local area.

*Daily, opening times vary, call to check. Term
time: 07.30-21.00, Waves & Slides Fri 17.00-
20.00, Sat & Sun 11.00-17.00. Half Term &
Easter: 07.30-21.00, Waves & Slides Mon-Thur
11.00-16.00, Fri 11.00-20.00, Sat & Sun 11.00-
17.00. Summer Hols: 07.30-21.00, Waves &
Slides Mon-Thur 11.00-17.00, Fri 11.00-20.00,
Sat & Sun 11.00-17.00. Please call for details of
specific sessions held during the day*

Our peak prices operate whenever the waves
and slides are in operation

Metrodome Leisure Complex

Queens Ground Queens Road Barnsley
South Yorkshire S71 1AN

Tel: 01226 730060 Fax: 01226 207544

www.themetrodome.co.uk

*[Off J37 of the M1, follow brown signs. Plenty of
on site parking available]*

The Metrodome has plenty to offer and 'It's out
of this World!' With Space Adventure water
rides and 5 swimming pools to 10 badminton

courts and 4 squash courts. Try the Health and Fitness club, Steam room, sauna and sun shower or what about the 5-a-side soccer, trampolining, roller skating, gymnastics and flat green bowling. With the new refurbished Rigby Bar and Restaurant bookable for all types of celebrations.

All year Mon-Fri 07.15-23.30, Sat & Sun 08.00-22.30. Activities subject to availability please call for further details

A£4.40 C(under3)£Free C£2.80 Family Ticket £13.50

Discount Offer: Two For One Swim.

Theme & Adventure Parks

Flamingo Land Theme Park and Zoo

The Rectory Kirby Misperton Malton
North Yorkshire YO17 6UX
Tel: 01653 668287 Fax: 01653 668280

[Off A64 bypass running between York and Scarborough off A169 Malton / Pickering road from N A19 then A170, then A16]

For all round family entertainment there's no better place to visit. With 12 white knuckle thrillers including Europe's only triple looping rollercoaster and the free falling Cliff Hanger, there's no shortage of thrills and spills. There are also many family attractions for those of you who prefer to have their two feet on the ground.

Daily from 10.00 until Nov 2

A&C£15.50 C(0-3)£Free OAPs£7.75 Family Ticket (4 people) £58.00

Lightwater Valley Theme Park

North Stainley Ripon Yorkshire HG4 3HT

Tel: 0870 458 0040 Fax: 01765 635359

www.lightwatervalley.net

[A61 off A1 then A6108 to Masham. Plenty of on site parking available]

The Ultimate day out... experience the fun and thrills of this Family Sized Theme Park. You pay once and enjoy the fun all day long! Five new rides and attractions for 2004, coupled with The Ultimate, Europe's longest roller coaster, make for a fun filled day out for all. For budding Grand Prix drivers who want to experience real excitement try our Go-Karts. There's also a traditional Carousel, a soft play area, Spinning Teacups, Ferris Wheel and much more for younger children. Or why not retreat to the calm of the Swan Lake or perhaps visit Lightwater Country Shopping Village where you can relax and unwind, and even bag a bargain or two. There's also the Bird of Prey Centre where you can handle and feed some of the large selection of birds. Watch chicks hatching, fantastic flying demonstrations and meet Claudia, possibly the largest Golden Eagle in England.

3-18, 24-25 Apr, 1-3, 8-9, 15-16, 22-23 May, 29 May-13 June, 16-20, 23 June-5 Sept, 11-12 18-19, 25-26 Sept, 2-3, 9-10, 16-17, 23-31 Oct. Gates open at 10.00, rides and attractions open at 10.30

Pay once and ride all day: Over 1.2metres £14.50, under 1.2metres £13.00, under 1metre £Free. OAPs£6.95 Family ticket (4 people)

52.00, (5 people) £65.00, (6 people) £78.00. A family ticket admits two adults and up to 4 children under 16, or 1 adult and up to 5 children under 16. Single season ticket £45.00, family season ticket for 4 people £148.00. Group discounts and school rates available

Discount Offer: One Guest Admitted Free When Accompanied By Two Full Paying Guests.

Magna Science Adventure Centre

Sheffield Road Templeborough Rotherham South Yorkshire S60 1DX

Tel: 01709 720002 Fax: 01709 820092

www.visitmagna.co.uk

M1, J33/ J34, close to Meadowhall shopping centre. Plenty of on site parking]

Come to Magna, the UK's first Science Adventure Centre, and you will be amazed, entertained and in awe of the immense surroundings. Set in the old Templeborough Steelworks, you can explore the elements fire, air, earth and water and have fun firing giant water canon, launch rockets, board an airship and spin in a gyroscopic chair. The original steelworks provide a dramatic backdrop where you can experience the spectacular arc furnace sound and light show and step into the personal world of steel in the UK's biggest multimedia show that leads you 30ft up in the air.

All year daily 10.00-17.00. Closed 24-26 Dec & 1 Jan

Individual Prices: A£9.00 C£7.00 Family Ticket

(A2+C2) £28.00, (A2+C3) £30.00 Concessions£7.00. Schools: £4.00. Group rates: A£7.00 C&Concessions£5.50. Annual Pass: A£19.00 C&Concessions£14.00 Family Ticket (A2+C2) £58.00, (A2+C3) £63.00. Tour Organisers & Teachers £Free

Transport Museums

National Railway Museum

Leeman Road York North Yorkshire YO26 4XJ

Tel: 01904 621261 Fax: 01904 611112

www.nrm.org.uk

[A64 from Scarborough, Malton & Pickering. A64 from Tadcaster, Leeds, M62, M1 & A1. A19 from Selby. A19 from Teesside & Thirsk. A59 from Harrogate. A1079 from Hull. Outer ring road A1237. On Leeman Road, just outside the City Centre, behind the Railway Station. Limited parking on site]

Nowhere tells the story of the train better than the National Railway Museum, European Museum of the Year 2001. From Stephenson's Rocket and giant steam engines to Eurostar, the Bullet Train and miniature railway rides, rail travel is brought dramatically to life with interactive displays and lavish exhibitions. Discover it all in one fun-packed family day out where everyone gets in free (excludes Day out with Thomas events). Picnic facilities available both in and outdoors.

All year daily 10.00-18.00. Pre-booked Guided Tours (prices on application)

Admission Free (excludes Day Out with Thomas events)

Special Events

Railfest-Celebrating Rail's Bicentenary
29/05/2004-06/06/2004

A unique 200th anniversary festival of rail, from the first steam locomotive to the latest tilting train. The National Railway Museum is bringing together a once in a lifetime collection of locos along with a carnival of classic funfair attractions, historic train rides and a Great Railway Bazaar. Charges apply, early booking essential call 0870 701 0208

Bedford Butterfly Park

Renhold Road Wilden Bedford Bedfordshire MK44 2PX

25% Discount On Admission Charges

Not to be used in conjunction with any other offer. One voucher per party. Not valid on Bank Hols or special events

Valid until end Feb 2005

DISCOUNT VOUCHER

Please see page 12 for full attraction details

Bedford Museum

Castle Lane Bedford Bedfordshire MK40 3XD

Two For The Price Of One

Valid On Standard Museum Admission

Not to be used in conjunction with any other offer. One voucher per party. Not valid on Bank Hols or special events

Valid until end Feb 2005

DISCOUNT VOUCHER

Please see page 13 for full attraction details

Leighton Buzzard Railway

Page's Park Station Billington Road Leighton Buzzard Bedfordshire LU7 4TN

One Child Travels Free With Fare Paying Adult

Not Valid On Christmas Trains

Not to be used in conjunction with any other offer. One voucher per party. Not valid on Bank Hols or special events

Valid until end Feb 2005

DISCOUNT VOUCHER

Please see page 16 for full attraction details

Woodside Animal Farm and Leisure Park

Woodside Road Slip End Luton Bedfordshire LU1 4DG

One Child Free

With Every Full Paying Adult

Not to be used in conjunction with any other offer. One voucher per party. Not valid on Bank Hols or special events

Valid until end Feb 2005

DISCOUNT VOUCHER

Please see page 10 for full attraction details

Beale Park

Lower Basildon Reading Berkshire RG8 9NH

One Child Free

With One Adult Paying Full Admission Price

Not to be used in conjunction with any other offer. One voucher per party. Not valid on Bank Hols or special events

Valid until end Feb 2005

DISCOUNT VOUCHER

Please see page 27 for full attraction details

Stanley Spencer Gallery

High Street Cookham-On-Thames Berkshire SL6 9SJ

Two For The Price Of One

Not to be used in conjunction with any other offer. One voucher per party. Not valid on Bank Hols or special events

Valid until end Feb 2005

DISCOUNT VOUCHER

Please see page 20 for full attraction details

1. Each voucher entitles the holder to the discount specified by the selected attraction.
2. Valid for use until 28/02/05 (unless otherwise specified or if attraction season finishes prior to this). Vouchers are subject to the terms, conditions and restrictions of the selected attraction.
3. One voucher per party will be accepted, cannot be used in conjunction with any other offer, photocopies will not be accepted.
4. All attractions offering a discount have confirmed their willingness to participate. All information is subject to change without notice and should any attraction close or decline to accept a voucher for any reason, Days Out UK are not liable and cannot be held responsible.
5. Days Out UK shall not accept liability for any loss, accident or injury that may occur at a participating attraction and any dispute arising must be settled direct with the attraction concerned.
6. Cash redemption value of each voucher is 0.001p.
7. You are advised to check all relevant information with your chosen attraction before commencing your journey.

Days Out UK, PO Box 427, Northampton NN1 3YN. Tel: 01604 622445

1. Each voucher entitles the holder to the discount specified by the selected attraction.
2. Valid for use until 28/02/05 (unless otherwise specified. or if attraction season finishes prior to this). Vouchers are subject to the terms, conditions and restrictions of the selected attraction.
3. One voucher per party will be accepted, cannot be used in conjunction with any other offer, photocopies will not be accepted.
4. All attractions offering a discount have confirmed their willingness to participate. All information is subject to change without notice and should any attraction close or decline to accept a voucher for any reason, Days Out UK are not liable and cannot be held responsible.
5. Days Out UK shall not accept liability for any loss, accident or injury that may occur at a participating attraction and any dispute arising must be settled direct with the attraction concerned.
6. Cash redemption value of each voucher is 0.001p.
7. You are advised to check all relevant information with your chosen attraction before commencing your journey.

Days Out UK, PO Box 427, Northampton NN1 3YN. Tel: 01604 622445

1. Each voucher entitles the holder to the discount specified by the selected attraction.
2. Valid for use until 28/02/05 (unless otherwise specified, or if attraction season finishes prior to this). Vouchers are subject to the terms, conditions and restrictions of the selected attraction.
3. One voucher per party will be accepted, cannot be used in conjunction with any other offer, photocopies will not be accepted.
4. All attractions offering a discount have confirmed their willingness to participate. All information is subject to change without notice and should any attraction close or decline to accept a voucher for any reason, Days Out UK are not liable and cannot be held responsible.
5. Days Out UK shall not accept liability for any loss, accident or injury that may occur at a participating attraction and any dispute arising must be settled direct with the attraction concerned.
6. Cash redemption value of each voucher is 0.001p.
7. You are advised to check all relevant information with your chosen attraction before commencing your journey.

Days Out UK, PO Box 427, Northampton NN1 3YN. Tel: 01604 622445

1. Each voucher entitles the holder to the discount specified by the selected attraction.
2. Valid for use until 28/02/05 (unless otherwise specified, or if attraction season finishes prior to this). Vouchers are subject to the terms, conditions and restrictions of the selected attraction.
3. One voucher per party will be accepted, cannot be used in conjunction with any other offer, photocopies will not be accepted.
4. All attractions offering a discount have confirmed their willingness to participate. All information is subject to change without notice and should any attraction close or decline to accept a voucher for any reason, Days Out UK are not liable and cannot be held responsible.
5. Days Out UK shall not accept liability for any loss, accident or injury that may occur at a participating attraction and any dispute arising must be settled direct with the attraction concerned.
6. Cash redemption value of each voucher is 0.001p.
7. You are advised to check all relevant information with your chosen attraction before commencing your journey.

Days Out UK, PO Box 427, Northampton NN1 3YN. Tel: 01604 622445

1. Each voucher entitles the holder to the discount specified by the selected attraction.
2. Valid for use until 28/02/05 (unless otherwise specified, or if attraction season finishes prior to this). Vouchers are subject to the terms, conditions and restrictions of the selected attraction.
3. One voucher per party will be accepted, cannot be used in conjunction with any other offer, photocopies will not be accepted.
4. All attractions offering a discount have confirmed their willingness to participate. All information is subject to change without notice and should any attraction close or decline to accept a voucher for any reason, Days Out UK are not liable and cannot be held responsible.
5. Days Out UK shall not accept liability for any loss, accident or injury that may occur at a participating attraction and any dispute arising must be settled direct with the attraction concerned.
6. Cash redemption value of each voucher is 0.001p.
7. You are advised to check all relevant information with your chosen attraction before commencing your journey.

Days Out UK, PO Box 427, Northampton NN1 3YN. Tel: 01604 622445

Oliver Cromwell's House
29 St. Mary's Street Ely Cambridgeshire CB7 4HF
One Child Free
With A Full Paying Adult
Not to be used in conjunction with any other offer. One voucher per party. Not valid on Bank Hols or special events
Valid until end Feb 2005

Raptor Foundation
The Heath St. Ives Road Woodhurst Cambridgeshire
One Child Free
With Two Adults
Not to be used in conjunction with any other offer. One voucher per party. Not valid on Bank Hols or special events
Valid until end Feb 2005

Sacrewell Farm and Country Centre
Thornhaugh Peterborough Cambridgeshire PE8 6HJ
One Child Free
With Every Full Paying Adult
Not to be used in conjunction with any other offer. One voucher per party. Not valid on Bank Hols or special events
Valid until end Feb 2005

Sausmarez Manor
St. Martin Guernsey Channel Islands GY4 6SG
Two For The Price Of One
In Sculpture Park And Woodland Garden
Not to be used in conjunction with any other offer. One voucher per party. Not valid on Bank Hols or special events
Valid until end Feb 2005

Adlington Hall
Mill Lane Adlington Macclesfield Cheshire SK10 4LF
One Child Free
With Two Full Paying Adults
Not to be used in conjunction with any other offer. One voucher per party. Not valid on Bank Hols or special events
Valid until end Feb 2005

Bramall Hall
Bramall Park Bramall Cheshire SK7 3NX
One Free Adult Or Child
With A Full Paying Adult
Not Valid For Special Events
Not to be used in conjunction with any other offer. One voucher per party. Not valid on Bank Hols or special events
Valid until end Feb 2005

1. Each voucher entitles the holder to the discount specified by the selected attraction.
2. Valid for use until 28/02/05 (unless otherwise specified, or if attraction season finishes prior to this). Vouchers are subject to the terms, conditions and restrictions of the selected attraction.
3. One voucher per party will be accepted, cannot be used in conjunction with any other offer, photocopies will not be accepted.
4. All attractions offering a discount have confirmed their willingness to participate. All information is subject to change without notice and should any attraction close or decline to accept a voucher for any reason, Days Out UK are not liable and cannot be held responsible.
5. Days Out UK shall not accept liability for any loss, accident or injury that may occur at a participating attraction and any dispute arising must be settled direct with the attraction concerned.
6. Cash redemption value of each voucher is 0.001p.
7. You are advised to check all relevant information with your chosen attraction before commencing your journey.

Days Out UK, PO Box 427, Northampton NN1 3YN. Tel: 01604 622445

1. Each voucher entitles the holder to the discount specified by the selected attraction.
2. Valid for use until 28/02/05 (unless otherwise specified, or if attraction season finishes prior to this). Vouchers are subject to the terms, conditions and restrictions of the selected attraction.
3. One voucher per party will be accepted, cannot be used in conjunction with any other offer, photocopies will not be accepted.
4. All attractions offering a discount have confirmed their willingness to participate. All information is subject to change without notice and should any attraction close or decline to accept a voucher for any reason, Days Out UK are not liable and cannot be held responsible.
5. Days Out UK shall not accept liability for any loss, accident or injury that may occur at a participating attraction and any dispute arising must be settled direct with the attraction concerned.
6. Cash redemption value of each voucher is 0.001p.
7. You are advised to check all relevant information with your chosen attraction before commencing your journey.

Days Out UK, PO Box 427, Northampton NN1 3YN. Tel: 01604 622445

1. Each voucher entitles the holder to the discount specified by the selected attraction.
2. Valid for use until 28/02/05 (unless otherwise specified, or if attraction season finishes prior to this). Vouchers are subject to the terms, conditions and restrictions of the selected attraction.
3. One voucher per party will be accepted, cannot be used in conjunction with any other offer, photocopies will not be accepted.
4. All attractions offering a discount have confirmed their willingness to participate. All information is subject to change without notice and should any attraction close or decline to accept a voucher for any reason, Days Out UK are not liable and cannot be held responsible.
5. Days Out UK shall not accept liability for any loss, accident or injury that may occur at a participating attraction and any dispute arising must be settled direct with the attraction concerned.
6. Cash redemption value of each voucher is 0.001p.
7. You are advised to check all relevant information with your chosen attraction before commencing your journey.

Days Out UK, PO Box 427, Northampton NN1 3YN. Tel: 01604 622445

1. Each voucher entitles the holder to the discount specified by the selected attraction.
2. Valid for use until 28/02/05 (unless otherwise specified, or if attraction season finishes prior to this). Vouchers are subject to the terms, conditions and restrictions of the selected attraction.
3. One voucher per party will be accepted, cannot be used in conjunction with any other offer, photocopies will not be accepted.
4. All attractions offering a discount have confirmed their willingness to participate. All information is subject to change without notice and should any attraction close or decline to accept a voucher for any reason, Days Out UK are not liable and cannot be held responsible.
5. Days Out UK shall not accept liability for any loss, accident or injury that may occur at a participating attraction and any dispute arising must be settled direct with the attraction concerned.
6. Cash redemption value of each voucher is 0.001p.
7. You are advised to check all relevant information with your chosen attraction before commencing your journey.

Days Out UK, PO Box 427, Northampton NN1 3YN. Tel: 01604 622445

1. Each voucher entitles the holder to the discount specified by the selected attraction.
2. Valid for use until 28/02/05 (unless otherwise specified, or if attraction season finishes prior to this). Vouchers are subject to the terms, conditions and restrictions of the selected attraction.
3. One voucher per party will be accepted, cannot be used in conjunction with any other offer, photocopies will not be accepted.
4. All attractions offering a discount have confirmed their willingness to participate. All information is subject to change without notice and should any attraction close or decline to accept a voucher for any reason, Days Out UK are not liable and cannot be held responsible.
5. Days Out UK shall not accept liability for any loss, accident or injury that may occur at a participating attraction and any dispute arising must be settled direct with the attraction concerned.
6. Cash redemption value of each voucher is 0.001p.
7. You are advised to check all relevant information with your chosen attraction before commencing your journey.

Days Out UK, PO Box 427, Northampton NN1 3YN. Tel: 01604 622445

1. Each voucher entitles the holder to the discount specified by the selected attraction.
2. Valid for use until 28/02/05 (unless otherwise specified, or if attraction season finishes prior to this). Vouchers are subject to the terms, conditions and restrictions of the selected attraction.
3. One voucher per party will be accepted, cannot be used in conjunction with any other offer, photocopies will not be accepted.
4. All attractions offering a discount have confirmed their willingness to participate. All information is subject to change without notice and should any attraction close or decline to accept a voucher for any reason, Days Out UK are not liable and cannot be held responsible.
5. Days Out UK shall not accept liability for any loss, accident or injury that may occur at a participating attraction and any dispute arising must be settled direct with the attraction concerned.
6. Cash redemption value of each voucher is 0.001p.
7. You are advised to check all relevant information with your chosen attraction before commencing your journey.

Days Out UK, PO Box 427, Northampton NN1 3YN. Tel: 01604 622445

Brookside Miniature Railway

DAYSOUTUK
The place to look for places to go

Brookside Garden Centre Macclesfield Road Poynton Cheshire

Two For One

Two People Can Ride For The Price Of One

Not to be used in conjunction with any other offer. One voucher per party. Not valid on Bank Hols or special events

Valid until end Feb 2005

Please see page 61 for full attraction details

DISCOUNT VOUCHER

Catalyst: Science Discovery Centre

DAYSOUTUK
The place to look for places to go

Mersey Road Widnes Cheshire WA8 0DF

One Child Free

With A Full Paying Adult

Not to be used in conjunction with any other offer. One voucher per party. Not valid on Bank Hols or special events

Valid until end Feb 2005

Please see page 62 for full attraction details

DISCOUNT VOUCHER

Dunham Massey Hall, Garden and Park

DAYSOUTUK
The place to look for places to go

Dunham Massey Hall Altrincham Cheshire

Up To Three Children Free

When Accompanied By Two Full Paying Adults
(To House & Garden). Car Entry Free

Not to be used in conjunction with any other offer. One voucher per party. Not valid on Bank Hols or special events

Valid 27 Mar-3 Nov 2004

Please see page 64 for full attraction details

DISCOUNT VOUCHER

Hat Works - The Museum of Hatting, Stockport

DAYSOUTUK
The place to look for places to go

Wellington Mill Wellington Road South Cheshire

Two For the Price of One

Not Valid For Special Events

Not to be used in conjunction with any other offer. One voucher per party. Not valid on Bank Hols or special events

Valid until end Feb 2005

Please see page 56 for full attraction details

DISCOUNT VOUCHER

Norton Priory Museum and Gardens

DAYSOUTUK
The place to look for places to go

Tudor Road Manor Park Runcorn Cheshire WA7 1SX

Two For The Price Of One

Full Paying Adult
Not Valid On Public Holidays

Not to be used in conjunction with any other offer. One voucher per party. Not valid on Bank Hols or special events

Valid until end Feb 2005

Please see page 59 for full attraction details

DISCOUNT VOUCHER

Stockport Air Raid Shelters

DAYSOUTUK
The place to look for places to go

61 Chestergate Stockport Cheshire SK1 1NE

Two For The Price Of One

Not Valid For Special Events

Not to be used in conjunction with any other offer. One voucher per party. Not valid on Bank Hols or special events

Valid until end Feb 2005

Please see page 63 for full attraction details

DISCOUNT VOUCHER

1. Each voucher entitles the holder to the discount specified by the selected attraction.
2. Valid for use until 28/02/05 (unless otherwise specified, or if attraction season finishes prior to this). Vouchers are subject to the terms, conditions and restrictions of the selected attraction.
3. One voucher per party will be accepted, cannot be used in conjunction with any other offer, photocopies will not be accepted.
4. All attractions offering a discount have confirmed their willingness to participate. All information is subject to change without notice and should any attraction close or decline to accept a voucher for any reason, Days Out UK are not liable and cannot be held responsible.
5. Days Out UK shall not accept liability for any loss, accident or injury that may occur at a participating attraction and any dispute arising must be settled direct with the attraction concerned.
6. Cash redemption value of each voucher is 0.001p.
7. You are advised to check all relevant information with your chosen attraction before commencing your journey.

Days Out UK, PO Box 427, Northampton NN1 3YN. Tel: 01604 622445

1. Each voucher entitles the holder to the discount specified by the selected attraction.
2. Valid for use until 28/02/05 (unless otherwise specified, or if attraction season finishes prior to this). Vouchers are subject to the terms, conditions and restrictions of the selected attraction.
3. One voucher per party will be accepted, cannot be used in conjunction with any other offer, photocopies will not be accepted.
4. All attractions offering a discount have confirmed their willingness to participate. All information is subject to change without notice and should any attraction close or decline to accept a voucher for any reason, Days Out UK are not liable and cannot be held responsible.
5. Days Out UK shall not accept liability for any loss, accident or injury that may occur at a participating attraction and any dispute arising must be settled direct with the attraction concerned.
6. Cash redemption value of each voucher is 0.001p.
7. You are advised to check all relevant information with your chosen attraction before commencing your journey.

Days Out UK, PO Box 427, Northampton NN1 3YN. Tel: 01604 622445

1. Each voucher entitles the holder to the discount specified by the selected attraction.
2. Valid for use until 28/02/05 (unless otherwise specified. or if attraction season finishes prior to this). Vouchers are subject to the terms, conditions and restrictions of the selected attraction.
3. One voucher per party will be accepted, cannot be used in conjunction with any other offer, photocopies will not be accepted.
4. All attractions offering a discount have confirmed their willingness to participate. All information is subject to change without notice and should any attraction close or decline to accept a voucher for any reason, Days Out UK are not liable and cannot be held responsible.
5. Days Out UK shall not accept liability for any loss, accident or injury that may occur at a participating attraction and any dispute arising must be settled direct with the attraction concerned.
6. Cash redemption value of each voucher is 0.001p.
7. You are advised to check all relevant information with your chosen attraction before commencing your journey.

Days Out UK, PO Box 427, Northampton NN1 3YN. Tel: 01604 622445

1. Each voucher entitles the holder to the discount specified by the selected attraction.
2. Valid for use until 28/02/05 (unless otherwise specified, or if attraction season finishes prior to this). Vouchers are subject to the terms, conditions and restrictions of the selected attraction.
3. One voucher per party will be accepted, cannot be used in conjunction with any other offer, photocopies will not be accepted.
4. All attractions offering a discount have confirmed their willingness to participate. All information is subject to change without notice and should any attraction close or decline to accept a voucher for any reason, Days Out UK are not liable and cannot be held responsible.
5. Days Out UK shall not accept liability for any loss, accident or injury that may occur at a participating attraction and any dispute arising must be settled direct with the attraction concerned.
6. Cash redemption value of each voucher is 0.001p.
7. You are advised to check all relevant information with your chosen attraction before commencing your journey.

Days Out UK, PO Box 427, Northampton NN1 3YN. Tel: 01604 622445

1. Each voucher entitles the holder to the discount specified by the selected attraction.
2. Valid for use until 28/02/05 (unless otherwise specified, or if attraction season finishes prior to this). Vouchers are subject to the terms, conditions and restrictions of the selected attraction.
3. One voucher per party will be accepted, cannot be used in conjunction with any other offer, photocopies will not be accepted.
4. All attractions offering a discount have confirmed their willingness to participate. All information is subject to change without notice and should any attraction close or decline to accept a voucher for any reason, Days Out UK are not liable and cannot be held responsible.
5. Days Out UK shall not accept liability for any loss, accident or injury that may occur at a participating attraction and any dispute arising must be settled direct with the attraction concerned.
6. Cash redemption value of each voucher is 0.001p.
7. You are advised to check all relevant information with your chosen attraction before commencing your journey.

Days Out UK, PO Box 427, Northampton NN1 3YN. Tel: 01604 622445

1. Each voucher entitles the holder to the discount specified by the selected attraction.
2. Valid for use until 28/02/05 (unless otherwise specified, or if attraction season finishes prior to this). Vouchers are subject to the terms, conditions and restrictions of the selected attraction.
3. One voucher per party will be accepted, cannot be used in conjunction with any other offer, photocopies will not be accepted.
4. All attractions offering a discount have confirmed their willingness to participate. All information is subject to change without notice and should any attraction close or decline to accept a voucher for any reason, Days Out UK are not liable and cannot be held responsible.
5. Days Out UK shall not accept liability for any loss, accident or injury that may occur at a participating attraction and any dispute arising must be settled direct with the attraction concerned.
6. Cash redemption value of each voucher is 0.001p.
7. You are advised to check all relevant information with your chosen attraction before commencing your journey.

Days Out UK, PO Box 427, Northampton NN1 3YN. Tel: 01604 622445

DAYSOUTUK
The place to look for places to go

Please see page 70 for full attraction details

Nature's World
Ladgate Lane Acklam Middlesbrough Cleveland
One Child Free
When Accompanied By A Full Paying Adult
Not to be used in conjunction with any other offer. One voucher per party. Not valid on Bank Hols or special events
Valid until end Feb 2005

DISCOUNT VOUCHER

DAYSOUTUK
The place to look for places to go

Please see page 67 for full attraction details

Newham Grange Leisure Farm
Wykeham Way Coulby Newham Middlesbrough Cleveland
One Child Free
When Accompanied By A Full Paying Adult. (Not OAP)
Not to be used in conjunction with any other offer. One voucher per party. Not valid on Bank Hols or special events
Valid until end Feb 2005

DISCOUNT VOUCHER

DAYSOUTUK
The place to look for places to go

Please see page 82 for full attraction details

Blue Reef Aquarium
Towan Promenade Newquay Cornwall TR7 1DU
One Child Free
With One Full Paying Adult
Not to be used in conjunction with any other offer. One voucher per party. Not valid on Bank Hols or special events
Valid until end Feb 2005

DISCOUNT VOUCHER

DAYSOUTUK
The place to look for places to go

Please see page 80 for full attraction details

Mount Edgcumbe House and Country Park
Cremyll Torpoint Cornwall PL10 1HZ
Two Adults For The Price Of One
Not to be used in conjunction with any other offer. One voucher per party. Not valid on Bank Hols or special events
Valid until end Sept 2004

DISCOUNT VOUCHER

DAYSOUTUK
The place to look for places to go

Please see page 77 for full attraction details

Royal Cornwall Museum
River Street Truro Cornwall TR1 2SJ
Two Adults For The Price Of One
Not to be used in conjunction with any other offer. One voucher per party. Not valid on Bank Hols or special events
Valid until end Feb 2005

DISCOUNT VOUCHER

DAYSOUTUK
The place to look for places to go

Please see page 75 for full attraction details

Screech Owl Sanctuary
Trewin Farm Nr Indian Queens Goss Moor St Columb Cornwall
One Half Price Entry
With This Voucher
Not to be used in conjunction with any other offer. One voucher per party. Not valid on Bank Hols or special events
Valid until end Feb 2005

DISCOUNT VOUCHER

1. Each voucher entitles the holder to the discount specified by the selected attraction.
2. Valid for use until 28/02/05 (unless otherwise specified, or if attraction season finishes prior to this). Vouchers are subject to the terms, conditions and restrictions of the selected attraction.
3. One voucher per party will be accepted, cannot be used in conjunction with any other offer, photocopies will not be accepted.
4. All attractions offering a discount have confirmed their willingness to participate. All information is subject to change without notice and should any attraction close or decline to accept a voucher for any reason, Days Out UK are not liable and cannot be held responsible.
5. Days Out UK shall not accept liability for any loss, accident or injury that may occur at a participating attraction and any dispute arising must be settled direct with the attraction concerned.
6. Cash redemption value of each voucher is 0.001p.
7. You are advised to check all relevant information with your chosen attraction before commencing your journey.

Days Out UK, PO Box 427, Northampton NN1 3YN. Tel: 01604 622445

1. Each voucher entitles the holder to the discount specified by the selected attraction.
2. Valid for use until 28/02/05 (unless otherwise specified, or if attraction season finishes prior to this). Vouchers are subject to the terms, conditions and restrictions of the selected attraction.
3. One voucher per party will be accepted, cannot be used in conjunction with any other offer, photocopies will not be accepted.
4. All attractions offering a discount have confirmed their willingness to participate. All information is subject to change without notice and should any attraction close or decline to accept a voucher for any reason, Days Out UK are not liable and cannot be held responsible.
5. Days Out UK shall not accept liability for any loss, accident or injury that may occur at a participating attraction and any dispute arising must be settled direct with the attraction concerned.
6. Cash redemption value of each voucher is 0.001p.
7. You are advised to check all relevant information with your chosen attraction before commencing your journey.

Days Out UK, PO Box 427, Northampton NN1 3YN. Tel: 01604 622445

1. Each voucher entitles the holder to the discount specified by the selected attraction.
2. Valid for use until 28/02/05 (unless otherwise specified, or if attraction season finishes prior to this). Vouchers are subject to the terms, conditions and restrictions of the selected attraction.
3. One voucher per party will be accepted, cannot be used in conjunction with any other offer, photocopies will not be accepted.
4. All attractions offering a discount have confirmed their willingness to participate. All information is subject to change without notice and should any attraction close or decline to accept a voucher for any reason, Days Out UK are not liable and cannot be held responsible.
5. Days Out UK shall not accept liability for any loss, accident or injury that may occur at a participating attraction and any dispute arising must be settled direct with the attraction concerned.
6. Cash redemption value of each voucher is 0.001p.
7. You are advised to check all relevant information with your chosen attraction before commencing your journey.

Days Out UK, PO Box 427, Northampton NN1 3YN. Tel: 01604 622445

1. Each voucher entitles the holder to the discount specified by the selected attraction.
2. Valid for use until 28/02/05 (unless otherwise specified, or if attraction season finishes prior to this). Vouchers are subject to the terms, conditions and restrictions of the selected attraction.
3. One voucher per party will be accepted, cannot be used in conjunction with any other offer, photocopies will not be accepted.
4. All attractions offering a discount have confirmed their willingness to participate. All information is subject to change without notice and should any attraction close or decline to accept a voucher for any reason, Days Out UK are not liable and cannot be held responsible.
5. Days Out UK shall not accept liability for any loss, accident or injury that may occur at a participating attraction and any dispute arising must be settled direct with the attraction concerned.
6. Cash redemption value of each voucher is 0.001p.
7. You are advised to check all relevant information with your chosen attraction before commencing your journey.

Days Out UK, PO Box 427, Northampton NN1 3YN. Tel: 01604 622445

1. Each voucher entitles the holder to the discount specified by the selected attraction.
2. Valid for use until 28/02/05 (unless otherwise specified, or if attraction season finishes prior to this). Vouchers are subject to the terms, conditions and restrictions of the selected attraction.
3. One voucher per party will be accepted, cannot be used in conjunction with any other offer, photocopies will not be accepted.
4. All attractions offering a discount have confirmed their willingness to participate. All information is subject to change without notice and should any attraction close or decline to accept a voucher for any reason, Days Out UK are not liable and cannot be held responsible.
5. Days Out UK shall not accept liability for any loss, accident or injury that may occur at a participating attraction and any dispute arising must be settled direct with the attraction concerned.
6. Cash redemption value of each voucher is 0.001p.
7. You are advised to check all relevant information with your chosen attraction before commencing your journey.

Days Out UK, PO Box 427, Northampton NN1 3YN. Tel: 01604 622445

DISCOUNT VOUCHER

American Adventure
Ilkeston Derbyshire DE7 5SX
Two For One On Full Adult Entry Price.

1st Person Pays £16.50 And 2nd Person Free (Adult Or Child). Voucher to be presented at time of transaction. American Adventure reserves the right to change without notice the information and prices stated. Visitors should note that for technical, electrical, operational, weather or other reasons any show, ride or facility may be closed, removed, under repair or unavailable at any time. No refunds are available for any reason.

Valid until 31 Oct 2004

DISCOUNT VOUCHER

Crich Tramway Village
Crich Matlock Derbyshire DE4 5DP
One Child Free
With Every Full Paying Adult

Not to be used in conjunction with any other offer. One voucher per party. Not valid on Bank Hols or special events

Valid until end Feb 2005

DISCOUNT VOUCHER

Heights of Abraham
Cable Cars, Caverns and Hilltop Park
Matlock Bath Matlock Derbyshire DE4 3PD
**One Child Free With Full Paying Adult
For The Cable Car & Caverns**

Not to be used in conjunction with any other offer. One voucher per party. Not valid on Bank Hols or special events

Valid until end Feb 2005

DISCOUNT VOUCHER

Poole's Cavern and Buxton Country Park
Green Lane Buxton Derbyshire SK17 9DH
20% Off Admission Price
With This voucher

Not to be used in conjunction with any other offer. One voucher per party. Not valid on Bank Hols or special events

Valid until end Feb 2005

DISCOUNT VOUCHER

Sir Richard Arkwright's Masson Mills
Working Textile Museum Derby Road Matlock Bath
Derbyshire
Two For The Price Of One

Not to be used in conjunction with any other offer. One voucher per party. Not valid on Bank Hols or special events

Valid until end Feb 2005

DISCOUNT VOUCHER

Combe Martin Wildlife and Dinosaur Park
Combe Martin Ilfracombe Devon EX34 0NG
One Child Free
With Every Two Paying Adults

Not to be used in conjunction with any other offer. One voucher per party. Not valid on Bank Hols or special events

Valid until end Feb 2005

1. Each voucher entitles the holder to the discount specified by the selected attraction.
2. Valid for use until 28/02/05 (unless otherwise specified, or if attraction season finishes prior to this). Vouchers are subject to the terms, conditions and restrictions of the selected attraction.
3. One voucher per party will be accepted, cannot be used in conjunction with any other offer, photocopies will not be accepted.
4. All attractions offering a discount have confirmed their willingness to participate. All information is subject to change without notice and should any attraction close or decline to accept a voucher for any reason, Days Out UK are not liable and cannot be held responsible.
5. Days Out UK shall not accept liability for any loss, accident or injury that may occur at a participating attraction and any dispute arising must be settled direct with the attraction concerned.
6. Cash redemption value of each voucher is 0.001p.
7. You are advised to check all relevant information with your chosen attraction before commencing your journey.

Days Out UK, PO Box 427, Northampton NN1 3YN. Tel: 01604 622445

1. Each voucher entitles the holder to the discount specified by the selected attraction.
2. Valid for use until 28/02/05 (unless otherwise specified. or if attraction season finishes prior to this). Vouchers are subject to the terms, conditions and restrictions of the selected attraction.
3. One voucher per party will be accepted, cannot be used in conjunction with any other offer, photocopies will not be accepted.
4. All attractions offering a discount have confirmed their willingness to participate. All information is subject to change without notice and should any attraction close or decline to accept a voucher for any reason, Days Out UK are not liable and cannot be held responsible.
5. Days Out UK shall not accept liability for any loss, accident or injury that may occur at a participating attraction and any dispute arising must be settled direct with the attraction concerned.
6. Cash redemption value of each voucher is 0.001p.
7. You are advised to check all relevant information with your chosen attraction before commencing your journey.

Days Out UK, PO Box 427, Northampton NN1 3YN. Tel: 01604 622445

1. Each voucher entitles the holder to the discount specified by the selected attraction.
2. Valid for use until 28/02/05 (unless otherwise specified, or if attraction season finishes prior to this). Vouchers are subject to the terms, conditions and restrictions of the selected attraction.
3. One voucher per party will be accepted, cannot be used in conjunction with any other offer, photocopies will not be accepted.
4. All attractions offering a discount have confirmed their willingness to participate. All information is subject to change without notice and should any attraction close or decline to accept a voucher for any reason, Days Out UK are not liable and cannot be held responsible.
5. Days Out UK shall not accept liability for any loss, accident or injury that may occur at a participating attraction and any dispute arising must be settled direct with the attraction concerned.
6. Cash redemption value of each voucher is 0.001p.
7. You are advised to check all relevant information with your chosen attraction before commencing your journey.

Days Out UK, PO Box 427, Northampton NN1 3YN. Tel: 01604 622445

1. Each voucher entitles the holder to the discount specified by the selected attraction.
2. Valid for use until 28/02/05 (unless otherwise specified, or if attraction season finishes prior to this). Vouchers are subject to the terms, conditions and restrictions of the selected attraction.
3. One voucher per party will be accepted, cannot be used in conjunction with any other offer, photocopies will not be accepted.
4. All attractions offering a discount have confirmed their willingness to participate. All information is subject to change without notice and should any attraction close or decline to accept a voucher for any reason, Days Out UK are not liable and cannot be held responsible.
5. Days Out UK shall not accept liability for any loss, accident or injury that may occur at a participating attraction and any dispute arising must be settled direct with the attraction concerned.
6. Cash redemption value of each voucher is 0.001p.
7. You are advised to check all relevant information with your chosen attraction before commencing your journey.

Days Out UK, PO Box 427, Northampton NN1 3YN. Tel: 01604 622445

1. Each voucher entitles the holder to the discount specified by the selected attraction.
2. Valid for use until 28/02/05 (unless otherwise specified, or if attraction season finishes prior to this). Vouchers are subject to the terms, conditions and restrictions of the selected attraction.
3. One voucher per party will be accepted, cannot be used in conjunction with any other offer, photocopies will not be accepted.
4. All attractions offering a discount have confirmed their willingness to participate. All information is subject to change without notice and should any attraction close or decline to accept a voucher for any reason, Days Out UK are not liable and cannot be held responsible.
5. Days Out UK shall not accept liability for any loss, accident or injury that may occur at a participating attraction and any dispute arising must be settled direct with the attraction concerned.
6. Cash redemption value of each voucher is 0.001p.
7. You are advised to check all relevant information with your chosen attraction before commencing your journey.

Days Out UK, PO Box 427, Northampton NN1 3YN. Tel: 01604 622445

Dartington Crystal

Linden Close Torrington Devon EX38 7AN

One Adult Free

With Each Full Paying Adult

Not to be used in conjunction with any other offer. One voucher per party. Not valid on Bank Hols or special events

Valid until end Feb 2005

Please see page 112 for full attraction details

Diggerland

Verbeer Manor Cullompton Devon EX5 2PE

1/2 Price Entry For Up To 6 People

(Voucher Applies To Entry Charge Only)

Not to be used in conjunction with any other offer. One voucher per party. Not valid on Bank Hols or special events

Valid until end Feb 2005

Please see page 118 for full attraction details

National Marine Aquarium

Rope Walk Coxside Plymouth Devon PL4 0LF

£1.00 Off A Souvenir Guide

(Present This Voucher In Order To Receive Discount)

Not to be used in conjunction with any other offer. One voucher per party. Not valid on Bank Hols or special events

Valid until end Feb 2005

Please see page 116 for full attraction details

Torre Abbey Historic House and Gallery

Torre Abbey The Kings Drive Torquay TQ2 5JE

One Child Free

With Every Full Paying Adult

Not to be used in conjunction with any other offer. One voucher per party. Not valid on Bank Hols or special events

Valid until end Feb 2005

Please see page 114 for full attraction details

Athelhampton House and Gardens

Athelhampton Dorchester Dorset DT2 7LG

£1.00 Off Adult & OAPs

Admission To House & Garden

Not to be used in conjunction with any other offer. One voucher per party. Not valid on Bank Hols or special events

Valid until end Feb 2005

Please see page 125 for full attraction details

Monkey World Ape Rescue Centre

Wareham Dorset BH20 6HH

One Child Free

With Two Full Paying Adults

Not Valid On Bank Holidays Or Special Events

Not to be used in conjunction with any other offer. One voucher per party. Not valid on Bank Hols or special events

Valid until end Feb 2005

Please see page 121 for full attraction details

1. Each voucher entitles the holder to the discount specified by the selected attraction.
2. Valid for use until 28/02/05 (unless otherwise specified, or if attraction season finishes prior to this). Vouchers are subject to the terms, conditions and restrictions of the selected attraction.
3. One voucher per party will be accepted, cannot be used in conjunction with any other offer, photocopies will not be accepted.
4. All attractions offering a discount have confirmed their willingness to participate. All information is subject to change without notice and should any attraction close or decline to accept a voucher for any reason, Days Out UK are not liable and cannot be held responsible.
5. Days Out UK shall not accept liability for any loss, accident or injury that may occur at a participating attraction and any dispute arising must be settled direct with the attraction concerned.
6. Cash redemption value of each voucher is 0.001p.
7. You are advised to check all relevant information with your chosen attraction before commencing your journey.

Days Out UK, PO Box 427, Northampton NN1 3YN. Tel: 01604 622445

1. Each voucher entitles the holder to the discount specified by the selected attraction.
2. Valid for use until 28/02/05 (unless otherwise specified. or if attraction season finishes prior to this). Vouchers are subject to the terms, conditions and restrictions of the selected attraction.
3. One voucher per party will be accepted, cannot be used in conjunction with any other offer, photocopies will not be accepted.
4. All attractions offering a discount have confirmed their willingness to participate. All information is subject to change without notice and should any attraction close or decline to accept a voucher for any reason, Days Out UK are not liable and cannot be held responsible.
5. Days Out UK shall not accept liability for any loss, accident or injury that may occur at a participating attraction and any dispute arising must be settled direct with the attraction concerned.
6. Cash redemption value of each voucher is 0.001p.
7. You are advised to check all relevant information with your chosen attraction before commencing your journey.

Days Out UK, PO Box 427, Northampton NN1 3YN. Tel: 01604 622445

1. Each voucher entitles the holder to the discount specified by the selected attraction.
2. Valid for use until 28/02/05 (unless otherwise specified, or if attraction season finishes prior to this). Vouchers are subject to the terms, conditions and restrictions of the selected attraction.
3. One voucher per party will be accepted, cannot be used in conjunction with any other offer, photocopies will not be accepted.
4. All attractions offering a discount have confirmed their willingness to participate. All information is subject to change without notice and should any attraction close or decline to accept a voucher for any reason, Days Out UK are not liable and cannot be held responsible.
5. Days Out UK shall not accept liability for any loss, accident or injury that may occur at a participating attraction and any dispute arising must be settled direct with the attraction concerned.
6. Cash redemption value of each voucher is 0.001p.
7. You are advised to check all relevant information with your chosen attraction before commencing your journey.

Days Out UK, PO Box 427, Northampton NN1 3YN. Tel: 01604 622445

1. Each voucher entitles the holder to the discount specified by the selected attraction.
2. Valid for use until 28/02/05 (unless otherwise specified, or if attraction season finishes prior to this). Vouchers are subject to the terms, conditions and restrictions of the selected attraction.
3. One voucher per party will be accepted, cannot be used in conjunction with any other offer, photocopies will not be accepted.
4. All attractions offering a discount have confirmed their willingness to participate. All information is subject to change without notice and should any attraction close or decline to accept a voucher for any reason, Days Out UK are not liable and cannot be held responsible.
5. Days Out UK shall not accept liability for any loss, accident or injury that may occur at a participating attraction and any dispute arising must be settled direct with the attraction concerned.
6. Cash redemption value of each voucher is 0.001p.
7. You are advised to check all relevant information with your chosen attraction before commencing your journey.

Days Out UK, PO Box 427, Northampton NN1 3YN. Tel: 01604 622445

1. Each voucher entitles the holder to the discount specified by the selected attraction.
2. Valid for use until 28/02/05 (unless otherwise specified, or if attraction season finishes prior to this). Vouchers are subject to the terms, conditions and restrictions of the selected attraction.
3. One voucher per party will be accepted, cannot be used in conjunction with any other offer, photocopies will not be accepted.
4. All attractions offering a discount have confirmed their willingness to participate. All information is subject to change without notice and should any attraction close or decline to accept a voucher for any reason, Days Out UK are not liable and cannot be held responsible.
5. Days Out UK shall not accept liability for any loss, accident or injury that may occur at a participating attraction and any dispute arising must be settled direct with the attraction concerned.
6. Cash redemption value of each voucher is 0.001p.
7. You are advised to check all relevant information with your chosen attraction before commencing your journey.

Days Out UK, PO Box 427, Northampton NN1 3YN. Tel: 01604 622445

Weymouth Sea Life Park and Marine Sanctuary
Lodmoor Country Park Greenhill Weymouth Dorset
£2.00 Off Per Person
Valid for up to 6 people. Ref: DOUK1

Please see page 126 for full attraction details

Not to be used in conjunction with any other offer. One voucher per party. Not valid on Bank Hols or special events

Valid until end Feb 2005

Dublin Writers Museum
18 Parnell Square Dublin 1 Eire
Two For The Price Of One

Please see page 134 for full attraction details

Not to be used in conjunction with any other offer. One voucher per party. Not valid on Bank Hols or special events

Valid until end Feb 2005

Fry Model Rail
Malahide Castle Demesne Malahide
County Dublin Eire
Two For The Price Of One

Please see page 136 for full attraction details

Not to be used in conjunction with any other offer. One voucher per party. Not valid on Bank Hols or special events

Valid until end Feb 2005

James Joyce Museum
Joyce Tower Sandycove County Dublin Eire
Two For The Price Of One

Please see page 134 for full attraction details

Not to be used in conjunction with any other offer. One voucher per party. Not valid on Bank Hols or special events

Valid until end Feb 2005

Malahide Castle
Demesne Malahide County Dublin Eire
Two For The Price Of One

Please see page 133 for full attraction details

Not to be used in conjunction with any other offer. One voucher per party. Not valid on Bank Hols or special events

Valid until end Feb 2005

Shaw Birthplace
33 Synge Street Dublin 8 Eire
Two For The Price Of One

Please see page 133 for full attraction details

Not to be used in conjunction with any other offer. One voucher per party. Not valid on Bank Hols or special events

Valid until end Feb 2005

1. Each voucher entitles the holder to the discount specified by the selected attraction.
2. Valid for use until 28/02/05 (unless otherwise specified, or if attraction season finishes prior to this). Vouchers are subject to the terms, conditions and restrictions of the selected attraction.
3. One voucher per party will be accepted, cannot be used in conjunction with any other offer, photocopies will not be accepted.
4. All attractions offering a discount have confirmed their willingness to participate. All information is subject to change without notice and should any attraction close or decline to accept a voucher for any reason, Days Out UK are not liable and cannot be held responsible.
5. Days Out UK shall not accept liability for any loss, accident or injury that may occur at a participating attraction and any dispute arising must be settled direct with the attraction concerned.
6. Cash redemption value of each voucher is 0.001p.
7. You are advised to check all relevant information with your chosen attraction before commencing your journey.

Days Out UK, PO Box 427, Northampton NN1 3YN. Tel: 01604 622445

1. Each voucher entitles the holder to the discount specified by the selected attraction.
2. Valid for use until 28/02/05 (unless otherwise specified, or if attraction season finishes prior to this). Vouchers are subject to the terms, conditions and restrictions of the selected attraction.
3. One voucher per party will be accepted, cannot be used in conjunction with any other offer, photocopies will not be accepted.
4. All attractions offering a discount have confirmed their willingness to participate. All information is subject to change without notice and should any attraction close or decline to accept a voucher for any reason, Days Out UK are not liable and cannot be held responsible.
5. Days Out UK shall not accept liability for any loss, accident or injury that may occur at a participating attraction and any dispute arising must be settled direct with the attraction concerned.
6. Cash redemption value of each voucher is 0.001p.
7. You are advised to check all relevant information with your chosen attraction before commencing your journey.

Days Out UK, PO Box 427, Northampton NN1 3YN. Tel: 01604 622445

1. Each voucher entitles the holder to the discount specified by the selected attraction.
2. Valid for use until 28/02/05 (unless otherwise specified, or if attraction season finishes prior to this). Vouchers are subject to the terms, conditions and restrictions of the selected attraction.
3. One voucher per party will be accepted, cannot be used in conjunction with any other offer, photocopies will not be accepted.
4. All attractions offering a discount have confirmed their willingness to participate. All information is subject to change without notice and should any attraction close or decline to accept a voucher for any reason, Days Out UK are not liable and cannot be held responsible.
5. Days Out UK shall not accept liability for any loss, accident or injury that may occur at a participating attraction and any dispute arising must be settled direct with the attraction concerned.
6. Cash redemption value of each voucher is 0.001p.
7. You are advised to check all relevant information with your chosen attraction before commencing your journey.

Days Out UK, PO Box 427, Northampton NN1 3YN. Tel: 01604 622445

1. Each voucher entitles the holder to the discount specified by the selected attraction.
2. Valid for use until 28/02/05 (unless otherwise specified, or if attraction season finishes prior to this). Vouchers are subject to the terms, conditions and restrictions of the selected attraction.
3. One voucher per party will be accepted, cannot be used in conjunction with any other offer, photocopies will not be accepted.
4. All attractions offering a discount have confirmed their willingness to participate. All information is subject to change without notice and should any attraction close or decline to accept a voucher for any reason, Days Out UK are not liable and cannot be held responsible.
5. Days Out UK shall not accept liability for any loss, accident or injury that may occur at a participating attraction and any dispute arising must be settled direct with the attraction concerned.
6. Cash redemption value of each voucher is 0.001p.
7. You are advised to check all relevant information with your chosen attraction before commencing your journey.

Days Out UK, PO Box 427, Northampton NN1 3YN. Tel: 01604 622445

1. Each voucher entitles the holder to the discount specified by the selected attraction.
2. Valid for use until 28/02/05 (unless otherwise specified, or if attraction season finishes prior to this). Vouchers are subject to the terms, conditions and restrictions of the selected attraction.
3. One voucher per party will be accepted, cannot be used in conjunction with any other offer, photocopies will not be accepted.
4. All attractions offering a discount have confirmed their willingness to participate. All information is subject to change without notice and should any attraction close or decline to accept a voucher for any reason, Days Out UK are not liable and cannot be held responsible.
5. Days Out UK shall not accept liability for any loss, accident or injury that may occur at a participating attraction and any dispute arising must be settled direct with the attraction concerned.
6. Cash redemption value of each voucher is 0.001p.
7. You are advised to check all relevant information with your chosen attraction before commencing your journey.

Days Out UK, PO Box 427, Northampton NN1 3YN. Tel: 01604 622445

1. Each voucher entitles the holder to the discount specified by the selected attraction.
2. Valid for use until 28/02/05 (unless otherwise specified, or if attraction season finishes prior to this). Vouchers are subject to the terms, conditions and restrictions of the selected attraction.
3. One voucher per party will be accepted, cannot be used in conjunction with any other offer, photocopies will not be accepted.
4. All attractions offering a discount have confirmed their willingness to participate. All information is subject to change without notice and should any attraction close or decline to accept a voucher for any reason, Days Out UK are not liable and cannot be held responsible.
5. Days Out UK shall not accept liability for any loss, accident or injury that may occur at a participating attraction and any dispute arising must be settled direct with the attraction concerned.
6. Cash redemption value of each voucher is 0.001p.
7. You are advised to check all relevant information with your chosen attraction before commencing your journey.

Days Out UK, PO Box 427, Northampton NN1 3YN. Tel: 01604 622445

Barleylands Farm Centre
Barleylands Road Billericay Essex CM11 2UD
Two For The Price Of One
Not to be used in conjunction with any other offer. One voucher per party. Not valid on Bank Hols or special events
Valid until end Oct 2004

Hedingham Castle
Castle Hedingham Halstead Essex CO9 3DJ
Two For The Price Of One
Not to be used in conjunction with any other offer. One voucher per party. Not valid on Bank Hols or special events
Valid until end Feb 2005

Clearwell Caves Ancient Iron Mines
Royal Forest of Dean Coleford Gloucestershire
Two For The Price Of One
Not to be used in conjunction with any other offer. One voucher per party. Not valid on Bank Hols or special events
Valid until end Feb 2005

Cotswold Farm Park
Guiting Power Stow on the Wold Gloucestershire
One Child Free
With A Full Paying Adult
Not to be used in conjunction with any other offer. One voucher per party. Not valid on Bank Hols or special events
Valid 20 Mar- 31 Oct 2004

Cotswold Water Park and Keynes Country Park
Spratsgate Lane Shorncote Gloucestershire
Car Parking Discount 50% Off
For Keynes Country Park
Not to be used in conjunction with any other offer. One voucher per party. Not valid on Bank Hols or special events
Valid until end Feb 2005

Dean Heritage Centre
Camp Mill Soudley Cinderford Gloucestershire
One Child Free
With Every Full Paying Adult
Not to be used in conjunction with any other offer. One voucher per party. Not valid on Bank Hols or special events
Valid until end Feb 2005

1. Each voucher entitles the holder to the discount specified by the selected attraction.
2. Valid for use until 28/02/05 (unless otherwise specified, or if attraction season finishes prior to this). Vouchers are subject to the terms, conditions and restrictions of the selected attraction.
3. One voucher per party will be accepted, cannot be used in conjunction with any other offer, photocopies will not be accepted.
4. All attractions offering a discount have confirmed their willingness to participate. All information is subject to change without notice and should any attraction close or decline to accept a voucher for any reason, Days Out UK are not liable and cannot be held responsible.
5. Days Out UK shall not accept liability for any loss, accident or injury that may occur at a participating attraction and any dispute arising must be settled direct with the attraction concerned.
6. Cash redemption value of each voucher is 0.001p.
7. You are advised to check all relevant information with your chosen attraction before commencing your journey.

Days Out UK, PO Box 427, Northampton NN1 3YN. Tel: 01604 622445

1. Each voucher entitles the holder to the discount specified by the selected attraction.
2. Valid for use until 28/02/05 (unless otherwise specified, or if attraction season finishes prior to this). Vouchers are subject to the terms, conditions and restrictions of the selected attraction.
3. One voucher per party will be accepted, cannot be used in conjunction with any other offer, photocopies will not be accepted.
4. All attractions offering a discount have confirmed their willingness to participate. All information is subject to change without notice and should any attraction close or decline to accept a voucher for any reason, Days Out UK are not liable and cannot be held responsible.
5. Days Out UK shall not accept liability for any loss, accident or injury that may occur at a participating attraction and any dispute arising must be settled direct with the attraction concerned.
6. Cash redemption value of each voucher is 0.001p.
7. You are advised to check all relevant information with your chosen attraction before commencing your journey.

Days Out UK, PO Box 427, Northampton NN1 3YN. Tel: 01604 622445

1. Each voucher entitles the holder to the discount specified by the selected attraction.
2. Valid for use until 28/02/05 (unless otherwise specified, or if attraction season finishes prior to this). Vouchers are subject to the terms, conditions and restrictions of the selected attraction.
3. One voucher per party will be accepted, cannot be used in conjunction with any other offer, photocopies will not be accepted.
4. All attractions offering a discount have confirmed their willingness to participate. All information is subject to change without notice and should any attraction close or decline to accept a voucher for any reason, Days Out UK are not liable and cannot be held responsible.
5. Days Out UK shall not accept liability for any loss, accident or injury that may occur at a participating attraction and any dispute arising must be settled direct with the attraction concerned.
6. Cash redemption value of each voucher is 0.001p.
7. You are advised to check all relevant information with your chosen attraction before commencing your journey.

Days Out UK, PO Box 427, Northampton NN1 3YN. Tel: 01604 622445

1. Each voucher entitles the holder to the discount specified by the selected attraction.
2. Valid for use until 28/02/05 (unless otherwise specified, or if attraction season finishes prior to this). Vouchers are subject to the terms, conditions and restrictions of the selected attraction.
3. One voucher per party will be accepted, cannot be used in conjunction with any other offer, photocopies will not be accepted.
4. All attractions offering a discount have confirmed their willingness to participate. All information is subject to change without notice and should any attraction close or decline to accept a voucher for any reason, Days Out UK are not liable and cannot be held responsible.
5. Days Out UK shall not accept liability for any loss, accident or injury that may occur at a participating attraction and any dispute arising must be settled direct with the attraction concerned.
6. Cash redemption value of each voucher is 0.001p.
7. You are advised to check all relevant information with your chosen attraction before commencing your journey.

Days Out UK, PO Box 427, Northampton NN1 3YN. Tel: 01604 622445

1. Each voucher entitles the holder to the discount specified by the selected attraction.
2. Valid for use until 28/02/05 (unless otherwise specified, or if attraction season finishes prior to this). Vouchers are subject to the terms, conditions and restrictions of the selected attraction.
3. One voucher per party will be accepted, cannot be used in conjunction with any other offer, photocopies will not be accepted.
4. All attractions offering a discount have confirmed their willingness to participate. All information is subject to change without notice and should any attraction close or decline to accept a voucher for any reason, Days Out UK are not liable and cannot be held responsible.
5. Days Out UK shall not accept liability for any loss, accident or injury that may occur at a participating attraction and any dispute arising must be settled direct with the attraction concerned.
6. Cash redemption value of each voucher is 0.001p.
7. You are advised to check all relevant information with your chosen attraction before commencing your journey.

Days Out UK, PO Box 427, Northampton NN1 3YN. Tel: 01604 622445

Nature in Art
Wallsworth Hall Twigworth Gloucester Gloucestershire
One Child Free
With Every Full Paying Adult
Not to be used in conjunction with any other offer. One voucher per party. Not valid on Bank Hols or special events
Valid until end Feb 2005

Blue Reef Aquarium
Clarence Esplanade Southsea Portsmouth Hampshire
One Child Free
With One Full Paying Adult
Not to be used in conjunction with any other offer. One voucher per party. Not valid on Bank Hols or special events
Valid until end Feb 2005

D-Day Museum and Overlord Embroidery
Clarence Esplanade Southsea Hampshire PO5 3NT
20% Off Single Price Ticket
With Voucher
Not to be used in conjunction with any other offer. One voucher per party. Not valid on Bank Hols or special events
Valid until end Feb 2005

Explosion! The Museum of Naval Firepower
Priddy's Hard Heritage Way Gosport Hampshire
Two For The Price Of One
Not Valid On Special Rated Or Event Tickets
Free Ticket Will Be The Lowest Value
Not to be used in conjunction with any other offer. One voucher per party. Not valid on Bank Hols or special events
Valid until end Dec 2004

Longdown Activity Farm
Longdown Ashurst Southampton Hampshire
One Free Child
With Two Full Paying Adults
Not to be used in conjunction with any other offer. One voucher per party. Not valid on Bank Hols or special events
Valid until end Feb 2005

Milestones Living History Museum
Leisure Park Churchill Way West Basingstoke Hampshire
One Child Free When
Accompanied By One Full Paying Adult
Not to be used in conjunction with any other offer. One voucher per party. Not valid on Bank Hols or special events
Valid until end Feb 2005

1. Each voucher entitles the holder to the discount specified by the selected attraction.
2. Valid for use until 28/02/05 (unless otherwise specified, or if attraction season finishes prior to this). Vouchers are subject to the terms, conditions and restrictions of the selected attraction.
3. One voucher per party will be accepted, cannot be used in conjunction with any other offer, photocopies will not be accepted.
4. All attractions offering a discount have confirmed their willingness to participate. All information is subject to change without notice and should any attraction close or decline to accept a voucher for any reason, Days Out UK are not liable and cannot be held responsible.
5. Days Out UK shall not accept liability for any loss, accident or injury that may occur at a participating attraction and any dispute arising must be settled direct with the attraction concerned.
6. Cash redemption value of each voucher is 0.001p.
7. You are advised to check all relevant information with your chosen attraction before commencing your journey.

Days Out UK, PO Box 427, Northampton NN1 3YN. Tel: 01604 622445

1. Each voucher entitles the holder to the discount specified by the selected attraction.
2. Valid for use until 28/02/05 (unless otherwise specified, or if attraction season finishes prior to this). Vouchers are subject to the terms, conditions and restrictions of the selected attraction.
3. One voucher per party will be accepted, cannot be used in conjunction with any other offer, photocopies will not be accepted.
4. All attractions offering a discount have confirmed their willingness to participate. All information is subject to change without notice and should any attraction close or decline to accept a voucher for any reason, Days Out UK are not liable and cannot be held responsible.
5. Days Out UK shall not accept liability for any loss, accident or injury that may occur at a participating attraction and any dispute arising must be settled direct with the attraction concerned.
6. Cash redemption value of each voucher is 0.001p.
7. You are advised to check all relevant information with your chosen attraction before commencing your journey.

Days Out UK, PO Box 427, Northampton NN1 3YN. Tel: 01604 622445

1. Each voucher entitles the holder to the discount specified by the selected attraction.
2. Valid for use until 28/02/05 (unless otherwise specified, or if attraction season finishes prior to this). Vouchers are subject to the terms, conditions and restrictions of the selected attraction.
3. One voucher per party will be accepted, cannot be used in conjunction with any other offer, photocopies will not be accepted.
4. All attractions offering a discount have confirmed their willingness to participate. All information is subject to change without notice and should any attraction close or decline to accept a voucher for any reason, Days Out UK are not liable and cannot be held responsible.
5. Days Out UK shall not accept liability for any loss, accident or injury that may occur at a participating attraction and any dispute arising must be settled direct with the attraction concerned.
6. Cash redemption value of each voucher is 0.001p.
7. You are advised to check all relevant information with your chosen attraction before commencing your journey.

Days Out UK, PO Box 427, Northampton NN1 3YN. Tel: 01604 622445

1. Each voucher entitles the holder to the discount specified by the selected attraction.
2. Valid for use until 28/02/05 (unless otherwise specified, or if attraction season finishes prior to this). Vouchers are subject to the terms, conditions and restrictions of the selected attraction.
3. One voucher per party will be accepted, cannot be used in conjunction with any other offer, photocopies will not be accepted.
4. All attractions offering a discount have confirmed their willingness to participate. All information is subject to change without notice and should any attraction close or decline to accept a voucher for any reason, Days Out UK are not liable and cannot be held responsible.
5. Days Out UK shall not accept liability for any loss, accident or injury that may occur at a participating attraction and any dispute arising must be settled direct with the attraction concerned.
6. Cash redemption value of each voucher is 0.001p.
7. You are advised to check all relevant information with your chosen attraction before commencing your journey.

Days Out UK, PO Box 427, Northampton NN1 3YN. Tel: 01604 622445

1. Each voucher entitles the holder to the discount specified by the selected attraction.
2. Valid for use until 28/02/05 (unless otherwise specified, or if attraction season finishes prior to this). Vouchers are subject to the terms, conditions and restrictions of the selected attraction.
3. One voucher per party will be accepted, cannot be used in conjunction with any other offer, photocopies will not be accepted.
4. All attractions offering a discount have confirmed their willingness to participate. All information is subject to change without notice and should any attraction close or decline to accept a voucher for any reason, Days Out UK are not liable and cannot be held responsible.
5. Days Out UK shall not accept liability for any loss, accident or injury that may occur at a participating attraction and any dispute arising must be settled direct with the attraction concerned.
6. Cash redemption value of each voucher is 0.001p.
7. You are advised to check all relevant information with your chosen attraction before commencing your journey.

Days Out UK, PO Box 427, Northampton NN1 3YN. Tel: 01604 622445

DAYS OUT UK
The place to look for places to go

DISCOUNT VOUCHER

Museum of Army Flying
Middle Wallop Stockbridge Hampshire SO20 8DY
Two For The Price Of One
NOT Valid For Special Events & Air Shows

Please see page 171 for full attraction details

Not to be used in conjunction with any other offer. One voucher per party. Not valid on Bank Hols or special events

Valid until end Feb 2005

DAYS OUT UK
The place to look for places to go

DISCOUNT VOUCHER

Royal Marines Museum
Eastney Esplanade Southsea Hampshire PO4 9PX
Two For The Price Of One

Please see page 168 for full attraction details

Not to be used in conjunction with any other offer. One voucher per party. Not valid on Bank Hols or special events

Valid until end Feb 2005

DAYS OUT UK
The place to look for places to go

DISCOUNT VOUCHER

Watercress Line
The Railway Station Alresford Hampshire SO24 9JG
Two For The Price Of One
Valid On Bank Holidays, Not Valid On Dining Services, Daylight Rail Tours Or Footplate Experiences

Please see page 172 for full attraction details

Not to be used in conjunction with any other offer. One voucher per party. Not valid on special events

Valid until end Feb 2005

DAYS OUT UK
The place to look for places to go

DISCOUNT VOUCHER

Berrington Hall
Berrington Leominster Herefordshire HR6 0DW
Two For The Price Of One

Please see page 179 for full attraction details

Not to be used in conjunction with any other offer. One voucher per party. Not valid on Bank Hols or special events

Valid until end Feb 2005

DAYS OUT UK
The place to look for places to go

DISCOUNT VOUCHER

Hergest Croft Gardens
Kington Herefordshire HR5 3EG
Two For The Price Of One

Please see page 178 for full attraction details

Not to be used in conjunction with any other offer. One voucher per party. Not valid on Bank Hols or special events

Valid July-Oct 2004 (Except 17 Oct - Plant Fair)

DAYS OUT UK
The place to look for places to go

DISCOUNT VOUCHER

Hatfield House, Park and Gardens
Hatfield Hertfordshire AL9 5NQ
Two For The Price Of One
For Gardens Only. (Excludes Fri & Major Events)

Please see page 183 for full attraction details

Not to be used in conjunction with any other offer. One voucher per party. Not valid on Bank Hols, Fri & major events

Valid until end Feb 2005

1. Each voucher entitles the holder to the discount specified by the selected attraction.
2. Valid for use until 28/02/05 (unless otherwise specified, or if attraction season finishes prior to this). Vouchers are subject to the terms, conditions and restrictions of the selected attraction.
3. One voucher per party will be accepted, cannot be used in conjunction with any other offer, photocopies will not be accepted.
4. All attractions offering a discount have confirmed their willingness to participate. All information is subject to change without notice and should any attraction close or decline to accept a voucher for any reason, Days Out UK are not liable and cannot be held responsible.
5. Days Out UK shall not accept liability for any loss, accident or injury that may occur at a participating attraction and any dispute arising must be settled direct with the attraction concerned.
6. Cash redemption value of each voucher is 0.001p.
7. You are advised to check all relevant information with your chosen attraction before commencing your journey.

Days Out UK, PO Box 427, Northampton NN1 3YN. Tel: 01604 622445

1. Each voucher entitles the holder to the discount specified by the selected attraction.
2. Valid for use until 28/02/05 (unless otherwise specified, or if attraction season finishes prior to this). Vouchers are subject to the terms, conditions and restrictions of the selected attraction.
3. One voucher per party will be accepted, cannot be used in conjunction with any other offer, photocopies will not be accepted.
4. All attractions offering a discount have confirmed their willingness to participate. All information is subject to change without notice and should any attraction close or decline to accept a voucher for any reason, Days Out UK are not liable and cannot be held responsible.
5. Days Out UK shall not accept liability for any loss, accident or injury that may occur at a participating attraction and any dispute arising must be settled direct with the attraction concerned.
6. Cash redemption value of each voucher is 0.001p.
7. You are advised to check all relevant information with your chosen attraction before commencing your journey.

Days Out UK, PO Box 427, Northampton NN1 3YN. Tel: 01604 622445

1. Each voucher entitles the holder to the discount specified by the selected attraction.
2. Valid for use until 28/02/05 (unless otherwise specified, or if attraction season finishes prior to this). Vouchers are subject to the terms, conditions and restrictions of the selected attraction.
3. One voucher per party will be accepted, cannot be used in conjunction with any other offer, photocopies will not be accepted.
4. All attractions offering a discount have confirmed their willingness to participate. All information is subject to change without notice and should any attraction close or decline to accept a voucher for any reason, Days Out UK are not liable and cannot be held responsible.
5. Days Out UK shall not accept liability for any loss, accident or injury that may occur at a participating attraction and any dispute arising must be settled direct with the attraction concerned.
6. Cash redemption value of each voucher is 0.001p.
7. You are advised to check all relevant information with your chosen attraction before commencing your journey.

Days Out UK, PO Box 427, Northampton NN1 3YN. Tel: 01604 622445

1. Each voucher entitles the holder to the discount specified by the selected attraction.
2. Valid for use until 28/02/05 (unless otherwise specified, or if attraction season finishes prior to this). Vouchers are subject to the terms, conditions and restrictions of the selected attraction.
3. One voucher per party will be accepted, cannot be used in conjunction with any other offer, photocopies will not be accepted.
4. All attractions offering a discount have confirmed their willingness to participate. All information is subject to change without notice and should any attraction close or decline to accept a voucher for any reason, Days Out UK are not liable and cannot be held responsible.
5. Days Out UK shall not accept liability for any loss, accident or injury that may occur at a participating attraction and any dispute arising must be settled direct with the attraction concerned.
6. Cash redemption value of each voucher is 0.001p.
7. You are advised to check all relevant information with your chosen attraction before commencing your journey.

Days Out UK, PO Box 427, Northampton NN1 3YN. Tel: 01604 622445

1. Each voucher entitles the holder to the discount specified by the selected attraction.
2. Valid for use until 28/02/05 (unless otherwise specified, or if attraction season finishes prior to this). Vouchers are subject to the terms, conditions and restrictions of the selected attraction.
3. One voucher per party will be accepted, cannot be used in conjunction with any other offer, photocopies will not be accepted.
4. All attractions offering a discount have confirmed their willingness to participate. All information is subject to change without notice and should any attraction close or decline to accept a voucher for any reason, Days Out UK are not liable and cannot be held responsible.
5. Days Out UK shall not accept liability for any loss, accident or injury that may occur at a participating attraction and any dispute arising must be settled direct with the attraction concerned.
6. Cash redemption value of each voucher is 0.001p.
7. You are advised to check all relevant information with your chosen attraction before commencing your journey.

Days Out UK, PO Box 427, Northampton NN1 3YN. Tel: 01604 622445

1. Each voucher entitles the holder to the discount specified by the selected attraction.
2. Valid for use until 28/02/05 (unless otherwise specified, or if attraction season finishes prior to this). Vouchers are subject to the terms, conditions and restrictions of the selected attraction.
3. One voucher per party will be accepted, cannot be used in conjunction with any other offer, photocopies will not be accepted.
4. All attractions offering a discount have confirmed their willingness to participate. All information is subject to change without notice and should any attraction close or decline to accept a voucher for any reason, Days Out UK are not liable and cannot be held responsible.
5. Days Out UK shall not accept liability for any loss, accident or injury that may occur at a participating attraction and any dispute arising must be settled direct with the attraction concerned.
6. Cash redemption value of each voucher is 0.001p.
7. You are advised to check all relevant information with your chosen attraction before commencing your journey.

Days Out UK, PO Box 427, Northampton NN1 3YN. Tel: 01604 622445

1. Each voucher entitles the holder to the discount specified by the selected attraction.
2. Valid for use until 28/02/05 (unless otherwise specified, or if attraction season finishes prior to this). Vouchers are subject to the terms, conditions and restrictions of the selected attraction.
3. One voucher per party will be accepted, cannot be used in conjunction with any other offer, photocopies will not be accepted.
4. All attractions offering a discount have confirmed their willingness to participate. All information is subject to change without notice and should any attraction close or decline to accept a voucher for any reason, Days Out UK are not liable and cannot be held responsible.
5. Days Out UK shall not accept liability for any loss, accident or injury that may occur at a participating attraction and any dispute arising must be settled direct with the attraction concerned.
6. Cash redemption value of each voucher is 0.001p.
7. You are advised to check all relevant information with your chosen attraction before commencing your journey.

Days Out UK, PO Box 427, Northampton NN1 3YN. Tel: 01604 622445

1. Each voucher entitles the holder to the discount specified by the selected attraction.
2. Valid for use until 28/02/05 (unless otherwise specified, or if attraction season finishes prior to this). Vouchers are subject to the terms, conditions and restrictions of the selected attraction.
3. One voucher per party will be accepted, cannot be used in conjunction with any other offer, photocopies will not be accepted.
4. All attractions offering a discount have confirmed their willingness to participate. All information is subject to change without notice and should any attraction close or decline to accept a voucher for any reason, Days Out UK are not liable and cannot be held responsible.
5. Days Out UK shall not accept liability for any loss, accident or injury that may occur at a participating attraction and any dispute arising must be settled direct with the attraction concerned.
6. Cash redemption value of each voucher is 0.001p.
7. You are advised to check all relevant information with your chosen attraction before commencing your journey.

Days Out UK, PO Box 427, Northampton NN1 3YN. Tel: 01604 622445

1. Each voucher entitles the holder to the discount specified by the selected attraction.
2. Valid for use until 28/02/05 (unless otherwise specified, or if attraction season finishes prior to this). Vouchers are subject to the terms, conditions and restrictions of the selected attraction.
3. One voucher per party will be accepted, cannot be used in conjunction with any other offer, photocopies will not be accepted.
4. All attractions offering a discount have confirmed their willingness to participate. All information is subject to change without notice and should any attraction close or decline to accept a voucher for any reason, Days Out UK are not liable and cannot be held responsible.
5. Days Out UK shall not accept liability for any loss, accident or injury that may occur at a participating attraction and any dispute arising must be settled direct with the attraction concerned.
6. Cash redemption value of each voucher is 0.001p.
7. You are advised to check all relevant information with your chosen attraction before commencing your journey.

Days Out UK, PO Box 427, Northampton NN1 3YN. Tel: 01604 622445

1. Each voucher entitles the holder to the discount specified by the selected attraction.
2. Valid for use until 28/02/05 (unless otherwise specified, or if attraction season finishes prior to this). Vouchers are subject to the terms, conditions and restrictions of the selected attraction.
3. One voucher per party will be accepted, cannot be used in conjunction with any other offer, photocopies will not be accepted.
4. All attractions offering a discount have confirmed their willingness to participate. All information is subject to change without notice and should any attraction close or decline to accept a voucher for any reason, Days Out UK are not liable and cannot be held responsible.
5. Days Out UK shall not accept liability for any loss, accident or injury that may occur at a participating attraction and any dispute arising must be settled direct with the attraction concerned.
6. Cash redemption value of each voucher is 0.001p.
7. You are advised to check all relevant information with your chosen attraction before commencing your journey.

Days Out UK, PO Box 427, Northampton NN1 3YN. Tel: 01604 622445

Shanklin Chine

12 Pomona Road Shanklin Isle of Wight PO37 6PF

Two For The Price Of One

Not to be used in conjunction with any other offer. One voucher per party. Not valid on Bank Hols or special events

Valid until end Feb 2005

Waltzing Waters

Aqua Theatre Brading Road Ryde Isle of Wight

One Child Free

With Each Full Paying Adult

Not to be used in conjunction with any other offer. One voucher per party. Not valid on Bank Hols or special events

Valid until end Feb 2005

Biddenden Vineyards and Cider Works

Little Whatmans Gribble Bridge Lane Biddenden Kent

10% Discount On All Shop Purchases

Valid All Year Including Weekends & Bank Hols

Not to be used in conjunction with any other offer. One voucher per party.

Valid until end Feb 2005

Diggerland

Roman Way Medway Valley Leisure Park Strood Kent

1/2 Price Entry For Up To 6 People

(Voucher Applies To Entry Charge Only)

Not to be used in conjunction with any other offer. One voucher per party. Not valid on Bank Hols or special events

Valid until end Feb 2005

Hop Farm Country Park

Maidstone Road Paddock Wood Tonbridge Kent

Half Price Child Admission
With Full Paying Adult

Excludes Music Events And War & Peace Show

Not to be used in conjunction with any other offer. One voucher per party. Not valid on Bank Hols or special events

Valid until end Feb 2005

Kent and East Sussex Steam Railway

Tenterden Town Station Tenterden Kent TN30 6HE
£1.00 Off Adult & £0.50 Off Child's Fare
On Any Full Return Train Ride To Bodiam
Valid For Up To Four People

Not to be used in conjunction with any other offer. One voucher per party. Not valid on Bank Hols or special events

Valid until end Feb 2005

1. Each voucher entitles the holder to the discount specified by the selected attraction.
2. Valid for use until 28/02/05 (unless otherwise specified, or if attraction season finishes prior to this). Vouchers are subject to the terms, conditions and restrictions of the selected attraction.
3. One voucher per party will be accepted, cannot be used in conjunction with any other offer, photocopies will not be accepted.
4. All attractions offering a discount have confirmed their willingness to participate. All information is subject to change without notice and should any attraction close or decline to accept a voucher for any reason, Days Out UK are not liable and cannot be held responsible.
5. Days Out UK shall not accept liability for any loss, accident or injury that may occur at a participating attraction and any dispute arising must be settled direct with the attraction concerned.
6. Cash redemption value of each voucher is 0.001p.
7. You are advised to check all relevant information with your chosen attraction before commencing your journey.

Days Out UK, PO Box 427, Northampton NN1 3YN. Tel: 01604 622445

1. Each voucher entitles the holder to the discount specified by the selected attraction.
2. Valid for use until 28/02/05 (unless otherwise specified, or if attraction season finishes prior to this). Vouchers are subject to the terms, conditions and restrictions of the selected attraction.
3. One voucher per party will be accepted, cannot be used in conjunction with any other offer, photocopies will not be accepted.
4. All attractions offering a discount have confirmed their willingness to participate. All information is subject to change without notice and should any attraction close or decline to accept a voucher for any reason, Days Out UK are not liable and cannot be held responsible.
5. Days Out UK shall not accept liability for any loss, accident or injury that may occur at a participating attraction and any dispute arising must be settled direct with the attraction concerned.
6. Cash redemption value of each voucher is 0.001p.
7. You are advised to check all relevant information with your chosen attraction before commencing your journey.

Days Out UK, PO Box 427, Northampton NN1 3YN. Tel: 01604 622445

1. Each voucher entitles the holder to the discount specified by the selected attraction.
2. Valid for use until 28/02/05 (unless otherwise specified, or if attraction season finishes prior to this). Vouchers are subject to the terms, conditions and restrictions of the selected attraction.
3. One voucher per party will be accepted, cannot be used in conjunction with any other offer, photocopies will not be accepted.
4. All attractions offering a discount have confirmed their willingness to participate. All information is subject to change without notice and should any attraction close or decline to accept a voucher for any reason, Days Out UK are not liable and cannot be held responsible.
5. Days Out UK shall not accept liability for any loss, accident or injury that may occur at a participating attraction and any dispute arising must be settled direct with the attraction concerned.
6. Cash redemption value of each voucher is 0.001p.
7. You are advised to check all relevant information with your chosen attraction before commencing your journey.

Days Out UK, PO Box 427, Northampton NN1 3YN. Tel: 01604 622445

1. Each voucher entitles the holder to the discount specified by the selected attraction.
2. Valid for use until 28/02/05 (unless otherwise specified, or if attraction season finishes prior to this). Vouchers are subject to the terms, conditions and restrictions of the selected attraction.
3. One voucher per party will be accepted, cannot be used in conjunction with any other offer, photocopies will not be accepted.
4. All attractions offering a discount have confirmed their willingness to participate. All information is subject to change without notice and should any attraction close or decline to accept a voucher for any reason, Days Out UK are not liable and cannot be held responsible.
5. Days Out UK shall not accept liability for any loss, accident or injury that may occur at a participating attraction and any dispute arising must be settled direct with the attraction concerned.
6. Cash redemption value of each voucher is 0.001p.
7. You are advised to check all relevant information with your chosen attraction before commencing your journey.

Days Out UK, PO Box 427, Northampton NN1 3YN. Tel: 01604 622445

1. Each voucher entitles the holder to the discount specified by the selected attraction.
2. Valid for use until 28/02/05 (unless otherwise specified, or if attraction season finishes prior to this). Vouchers are subject to the terms, conditions and restrictions of the selected attraction.
3. One voucher per party will be accepted, cannot be used in conjunction with any other offer, photocopies will not be accepted.
4. All attractions offering a discount have confirmed their willingness to participate. All information is subject to change without notice and should any attraction close or decline to accept a voucher for any reason, Days Out UK are not liable and cannot be held responsible.
5. Days Out UK shall not accept liability for any loss, accident or injury that may occur at a participating attraction and any dispute arising must be settled direct with the attraction concerned.
6. Cash redemption value of each voucher is 0.001p.
7. You are advised to check all relevant information with your chosen attraction before commencing your journey.

Days Out UK, PO Box 427, Northampton NN1 3YN. Tel: 01604 622445

1. Each voucher entitles the holder to the discount specified by the selected attraction.
2. Valid for use until 28/02/05 (unless otherwise specified, or if attraction season finishes prior to this). Vouchers are subject to the terms, conditions and restrictions of the selected attraction.
3. One voucher per party will be accepted, cannot be used in conjunction with any other offer, photocopies will not be accepted.
4. All attractions offering a discount have confirmed their willingness to participate. All information is subject to change without notice and should any attraction close or decline to accept a voucher for any reason, Days Out UK are not liable and cannot be held responsible.
5. Days Out UK shall not accept liability for any loss, accident or injury that may occur at a participating attraction and any dispute arising must be settled direct with the attraction concerned.
6. Cash redemption value of each voucher is 0.001p.
7. You are advised to check all relevant information with your chosen attraction before commencing your journey.

Days Out UK, PO Box 427, Northampton NN1 3YN. Tel: 01604 622445

589

1. Each voucher entitles the holder to the discount specified by the selected attraction.
2. Valid for use until 28/02/05 (unless otherwise specified, or if attraction season finishes prior to this). Vouchers are subject to the terms, conditions and restrictions of the selected attraction.
3. One voucher per party will be accepted, cannot be used in conjunction with any other offer, photocopies will not be accepted.
4. All attractions offering a discount have confirmed their willingness to participate. All information is subject to change without notice and should any attraction close or decline to accept a voucher for any reason, Days Out UK are not liable and cannot be held responsible.
5. Days Out UK shall not accept liability for any loss, accident or injury that may occur at a participating attraction and any dispute arising must be settled direct with the attraction concerned.
6. Cash redemption value of each voucher is 0.001p.
7. You are advised to check all relevant information with your chosen attraction before commencing your journey.

Days Out UK, PO Box 427, Northampton NN1 3YN. Tel: 01604 622445

1. Each voucher entitles the holder to the discount specified by the selected attraction.
2. Valid for use until 28/02/05 (unless otherwise specified. or if attraction season finishes prior to this). Vouchers are subject to the terms, conditions and restrictions of the selected attraction.
3. One voucher per party will be accepted, cannot be used in conjunction with any other offer, photocopies will not be accepted.
4. All attractions offering a discount have confirmed their willingness to participate. All information is subject to change without notice and should any attraction close or decline to accept a voucher for any reason, Days Out UK are not liable and cannot be held responsible.
5. Days Out UK shall not accept liability for any loss, accident or injury that may occur at a participating attraction and any dispute arising must be settled direct with the attraction concerned.
6. Cash redemption value of each voucher is 0.001p.
7. You are advised to check all relevant information with your chosen attraction before commencing your journey.

Days Out UK, PO Box 427, Northampton NN1 3YN. Tel: 01604 622445

1. Each voucher entitles the holder to the discount specified by the selected attraction.
2. Valid for use until 28/02/05 (unless otherwise specified, or if attraction season finishes prior to this). Vouchers are subject to the terms, conditions and restrictions of the selected attraction.
3. One voucher per party will be accepted, cannot be used in conjunction with any other offer, photocopies will not be accepted.
4. All attractions offering a discount have confirmed their willingness to participate. All information is subject to change without notice and should any attraction close or decline to accept a voucher for any reason, Days Out UK are not liable and cannot be held responsible.
5. Days Out UK shall not accept liability for any loss, accident or injury that may occur at a participating attraction and any dispute arising must be settled direct with the attraction concerned.
6. Cash redemption value of each voucher is 0.001p.
7. You are advised to check all relevant information with your chosen attraction before commencing your journey.

Days Out UK, PO Box 427, Northampton NN1 3YN. Tel: 01604 622445

1. Each voucher entitles the holder to the discount specified by the selected attraction.
2. Valid for use until 28/02/05 (unless otherwise specified, or if attraction season finishes prior to this). Vouchers are subject to the terms, conditions and restrictions of the selected attraction.
3. One voucher per party will be accepted, cannot be used in conjunction with any other offer, photocopies will not be accepted.
4. All attractions offering a discount have confirmed their willingness to participate. All information is subject to change without notice and should any attraction close or decline to accept a voucher for any reason, Days Out UK are not liable and cannot be held responsible.
5. Days Out UK shall not accept liability for any loss, accident or injury that may occur at a participating attraction and any dispute arising must be settled direct with the attraction concerned.
6. Cash redemption value of each voucher is 0.001p.
7. You are advised to check all relevant information with your chosen attraction before commencing your journey.

Days Out UK, PO Box 427, Northampton NN1 3YN. Tel: 01604 622445

1. Each voucher entitles the holder to the discount specified by the selected attraction.
2. Valid for use until 28/02/05 (unless otherwise specified, or if attraction season finishes prior to this). Vouchers are subject to the terms, conditions and restrictions of the selected attraction.
3. One voucher per party will be accepted, cannot be used in conjunction with any other offer, photocopies will not be accepted.
4. All attractions offering a discount have confirmed their willingness to participate. All information is subject to change without notice and should any attraction close or decline to accept a voucher for any reason, Days Out UK are not liable and cannot be held responsible.
5. Days Out UK shall not accept liability for any loss, accident or injury that may occur at a participating attraction and any dispute arising must be settled direct with the attraction concerned.
6. Cash redemption value of each voucher is 0.001p.
7. You are advised to check all relevant information with your chosen attraction before commencing your journey.

Days Out UK, PO Box 427, Northampton NN1 3YN. Tel: 01604 622445

Manchester United Museum and Tour Centre
Sir Matt Busby Way Old Trafford Manchester
£2.00 Off Admission To Museum And Tour
Please Exchange Voucher At Ticket Office

Not to be used in conjunction with any other offer. One voucher per party. Not valid on Bank Hols or special events

Valid until end Feb 2005

DISCOUNT VOUCHER

People's History Museum
The Pum Hose Bridge Street Manchester
Two For The Price Of One

Not to be used in conjunction with any other offer. One voucher per party. Not valid on Bank Hols or special events

Valid until end Feb 2005

DISCOUNT VOUCHER

Battlefield Line Railway
Shackersone Station Shackerstone Nuneaton
Two Adults For The Price Of One

Not to be used in conjunction with any other offer. One voucher per party. Not valid on Bank Hols or special events

Valid until end Feb 2005

DISCOUNT VOUCHER

Market Rasen Racecourse
Legsby Road Market Rasen Lincolnshire LN8 3EA
£2.00 Off Tattersalls
(If Booked In Advance By Telephone Or Post
Voucher Must Be Sent With Payment)

Not to be used in conjunction with any other offer. One voucher per party. Not valid on Bank Hols or special events

Valid until end Feb 2005

DISCOUNT VOUCHER

Skegness Natureland Seal Sanctuary
North Parade Skegness Lincolnshire PE25 1DB
One Child Free
With Full Paying Adult

Not to be used in conjunction with any other offer. One voucher per party. Not valid on Bank Hols or special events

Valid until end Feb 2005

DISCOUNT VOUCHER

Apsley House, Wellington Museum
Hyde Park Corner 149 Piccadilly London W1J 7NT
Two For The Price Of One

Not to be used in conjunction with any other offer. One voucher per party. Not valid on Bank Hols or special events

Valid until end Feb 2005

DISCOUNT VOUCHER

1. Each voucher entitles the holder to the discount specified by the selected attraction.
2. Valid for use until 28/02/05 (unless otherwise specified, or if attraction season finishes prior to this). Vouchers are subject to the terms, conditions and restrictions of the selected attraction.
3. One voucher per party will be accepted, cannot be used in conjunction with any other offer, photocopies will not be accepted.
4. All attractions offering a discount have confirmed their willingness to participate. All information is subject to change without notice and should any attraction close or decline to accept a voucher for any reason, Days Out UK are not liable and cannot be held responsible.
5. Days Out UK shall not accept liability for any loss, accident or injury that may occur at a participating attraction and any dispute arising must be settled direct with the attraction concerned.
6. Cash redemption value of each voucher is 0.001p.
7. You are advised to check all relevant information with your chosen attraction before commencing your journey.

Days Out UK, PO Box 427, Northampton NN1 3YN. Tel: 01604 622445

1. Each voucher entitles the holder to the discount specified by the selected attraction.
2. Valid for use until 28/02/05 (unless otherwise specified, or if attraction season finishes prior to this). Vouchers are subject to the terms, conditions and restrictions of the selected attraction.
3. One voucher per party will be accepted, cannot be used in conjunction with any other offer, photocopies will not be accepted.
4. All attractions offering a discount have confirmed their willingness to participate. All information is subject to change without notice and should any attraction close or decline to accept a voucher for any reason, Days Out UK are not liable and cannot be held responsible.
5. Days Out UK shall not accept liability for any loss, accident or injury that may occur at a participating attraction and any dispute arising must be settled direct with the attraction concerned.
6. Cash redemption value of each voucher is 0.001p.
7. You are advised to check all relevant information with your chosen attraction before commencing your journey.

Days Out UK, PO Box 427, Northampton NN1 3YN. Tel: 01604 622445

1. Each voucher entitles the holder to the discount specified by the selected attraction.
2. Valid for use until 28/02/05 (unless otherwise specified, or if attraction season finishes prior to this). Vouchers are subject to the terms, conditions and restrictions of the selected attraction.
3. One voucher per party will be accepted, cannot be used in conjunction with any other offer, photocopies will not be accepted.
4. All attractions offering a discount have confirmed their willingness to participate. All information is subject to change without notice and should any attraction close or decline to accept a voucher for any reason, Days Out UK are not liable and cannot be held responsible.
5. Days Out UK shall not accept liability for any loss, accident or injury that may occur at a participating attraction and any dispute arising must be settled direct with the attraction concerned.
6. Cash redemption value of each voucher is 0.001p.
7. You are advised to check all relevant information with your chosen attraction before commencing your journey.

Days Out UK, PO Box 427, Northampton NN1 3YN. Tel: 01604 622445

1. Each voucher entitles the holder to the discount specified by the selected attraction.
2. Valid for use until 28/02/05 (unless otherwise specified, or if attraction season finishes prior to this). Vouchers are subject to the terms, conditions and restrictions of the selected attraction.
3. One voucher per party will be accepted, cannot be used in conjunction with any other offer, photocopies will not be accepted.
4. All attractions offering a discount have confirmed their willingness to participate. All information is subject to change without notice and should any attraction close or decline to accept a voucher for any reason, Days Out UK are not liable and cannot be held responsible.
5. Days Out UK shall not accept liability for any loss, accident or injury that may occur at a participating attraction and any dispute arising must be settled direct with the attraction concerned.
6. Cash redemption value of each voucher is 0.001p.
7. You are advised to check all relevant information with your chosen attraction before commencing your journey.

Days Out UK, PO Box 427, Northampton NN1 3YN. Tel: 01604 622445

1. Each voucher entitles the holder to the discount specified by the selected attraction.
2. Valid for use until 28/02/05 (unless otherwise specified, or if attraction season finishes prior to this). Vouchers are subject to the terms, conditions and restrictions of the selected attraction.
3. One voucher per party will be accepted, cannot be used in conjunction with any other offer, photocopies will not be accepted.
4. All attractions offering a discount have confirmed their willingness to participate. All information is subject to change without notice and should any attraction close or decline to accept a voucher for any reason, Days Out UK are not liable and cannot be held responsible.
5. Days Out UK shall not accept liability for any loss, accident or injury that may occur at a participating attraction and any dispute arising must be settled direct with the attraction concerned.
6. Cash redemption value of each voucher is 0.001p.
7. You are advised to check all relevant information with your chosen attraction before commencing your journey.

Days Out UK, PO Box 427, Northampton NN1 3YN. Tel: 01604 622445

DAYS OUT UK
The place to look for places to go

Please see page 250
for full attraction
details

Chislehurst Caves
Old Hill Chislehurst Kent BR7 5NB
One Free Admission
When A Second Admission Of Equal Or Greater
Value Is Purchased
Not to be used in conjunction with any other offer. One voucher per party. Not valid on Bank Hols or special events
Valid until end Feb 2005

DISCOUNT VOUCHER

DAYS OUT UK
The place to look for places to go

Please see page 275
for full attraction
details

City Cruises
Cherry Garden Pier Cherry Garden Street London
£1.50 Off Full Adult River Red Rover Ticket And
£0.75 Off Full Child River Red Rover Ticket
Valid On Westminster/Waterloo/Tower/Greenwich Sightseeing
Service. No Credit And Debit Card Booking Fee With This Voucher
Not to be used in conjunction with any other offer. One voucher per party. Not valid on Bank Hols or special events
Valid until end Feb 2005

DISCOUNT VOUCHER

DAYS OUT UK
The place to look for places to go

Please see page 244
for full attraction
details

Dulwich Picture Gallery
Gallery Road Dulwich London SE21 7AD
Two For The Price Of One
With This Voucher
Not to be used in conjunction with any other offer. One voucher per party. Not valid on Bank Hols or special events
Valid until end Feb 2005

DISCOUNT VOUCHER

DAYS OUT UK
The place to look for places to go

Please see page 268
for full attraction
details

Firepower! the Royal Artillery Museum
Royal Arsenal Woolwich London SE18 6ST
£1.00 Off A Full Paying Adult
Admission
Not to be used in conjunction with any other offer. One voucher per party. Not valid on Bank Hols or special events
Valid until end Feb 2005

DISCOUNT VOUCHER

DAYS OUT UK
The place to look for places to go

Please see page 281
for full attraction
details

London Aquarium
County Hall Westminster Bridge Road London
One Child Free
When Accompanied By A Full Paying Adult
(Child Aged 3-14 years)
Not to be used in conjunction with any other offer. One voucher per party. Not valid on Bank Hols or special events
Valid until end Feb 2005

DISCOUNT VOUCHER

DAYS OUT UK
The place to look for places to go

Please see page 272
for full attraction
details

London Wetland Centre
Queen Elizabeth's Walk Barnes London SW13 9WT
£0.50 Off Child Admission
With Full Paying Adult
Not to be used in conjunction with any other offer. One voucher per party. Not valid on Bank Hols or special events
Valid until end Feb 2005

DISCOUNT VOUCHER

1. Each voucher entitles the holder to the discount specified by the selected attraction.
2. Valid for use until 28/02/05 (unless otherwise specified, or if attraction season finishes prior to this). Vouchers are subject to the terms, conditions and restrictions of the selected attraction.
3. One voucher per party will be accepted, cannot be used in conjunction with any other offer, photocopies will not be accepted.
4. All attractions offering a discount have confirmed their willingness to participate. All information is subject to change without notice and should any attraction close or decline to accept a voucher for any reason, Days Out UK are not liable and cannot be held responsible.
5. Days Out UK shall not accept liability for any loss, accident or injury that may occur at a participating attraction and any dispute arising must be settled direct with the attraction concerned.
6. Cash redemption value of each voucher is 0.001p.
7. You are advised to check all relevant information with your chosen attraction before commencing your journey.

Days Out UK, PO Box 427, Northampton NN1 3YN. Tel: 01604 622445

1. Each voucher entitles the holder to the discount specified by the selected attraction.
2. Valid for use until 28/02/05 (unless otherwise specified. or if attraction season finishes prior to this). Vouchers are subject to the terms, conditions and restrictions of the selected attraction.
3. One voucher per party will be accepted, cannot be used in conjunction with any other offer, photocopies will not be accepted.
4. All attractions offering a discount have confirmed their willingness to participate. All information is subject to change without notice and should any attraction close or decline to accept a voucher for any reason, Days Out UK are not liable and cannot be held responsible.
5. Days Out UK shall not accept liability for any loss, accident or injury that may occur at a participating attraction and any dispute arising must be settled direct with the attraction concerned.
6. Cash redemption value of each voucher is 0.001p.
7. You are advised to check all relevant information with your chosen attraction before commencing your journey.

Days Out UK, PO Box 427, Northampton NN1 3YN. Tel: 01604 622445

1. Each voucher entitles the holder to the discount specified by the selected attraction.
2. Valid for use until 28/02/05 (unless otherwise specified, or if attraction season finishes prior to this). Vouchers are subject to the terms, conditions and restrictions of the selected attraction.
3. One voucher per party will be accepted, cannot be used in conjunction with any other offer, photocopies will not be accepted.
4. All attractions offering a discount have confirmed their willingness to participate. All information is subject to change without notice and should any attraction close or decline to accept a voucher for any reason, Days Out UK are not liable and cannot be held responsible.
5. Days Out UK shall not accept liability for any loss, accident or injury that may occur at a participating attraction and any dispute arising must be settled direct with the attraction concerned.
6. Cash redemption value of each voucher is 0.001p.
7. You are advised to check all relevant information with your chosen attraction before commencing your journey.

Days Out UK, PO Box 427, Northampton NN1 3YN. Tel: 01604 622445

1. Each voucher entitles the holder to the discount specified by the selected attraction.
2. Valid for use until 28/02/05 (unless otherwise specified, or if attraction season finishes prior to this). Vouchers are subject to the terms, conditions and restrictions of the selected attraction.
3. One voucher per party will be accepted, cannot be used in conjunction with any other offer, photocopies will not be accepted.
4. All attractions offering a discount have confirmed their willingness to participate. All information is subject to change without notice and should any attraction close or decline to accept a voucher for any reason, Days Out UK are not liable and cannot be held responsible.
5. Days Out UK shall not accept liability for any loss, accident or injury that may occur at a participating attraction and any dispute arising must be settled direct with the attraction concerned.
6. Cash redemption value of each voucher is 0.001p.
7. You are advised to check all relevant information with your chosen attraction before commencing your journey.

Days Out UK, PO Box 427, Northampton NN1 3YN. Tel: 01604 622445

1. Each voucher entitles the holder to the discount specified by the selected attraction.
2. Valid for use until 28/02/05 (unless otherwise specified, or if attraction season finishes prior to this). Vouchers are subject to the terms, conditions and restrictions of the selected attraction.
3. One voucher per party will be accepted, cannot be used in conjunction with any other offer, photocopies will not be accepted.
4. All attractions offering a discount have confirmed their willingness to participate. All information is subject to change without notice and should any attraction close or decline to accept a voucher for any reason, Days Out UK are not liable and cannot be held responsible.
5. Days Out UK shall not accept liability for any loss, accident or injury that may occur at a participating attraction and any dispute arising must be settled direct with the attraction concerned.
6. Cash redemption value of each voucher is 0.001p.
7. You are advised to check all relevant information with your chosen attraction before commencing your journey.

Days Out UK, PO Box 427, Northampton NN1 3YN. Tel: 01604 622445

595

1. Each voucher entitles the holder to the discount specified by the selected attraction.
2. Valid for use until 28/02/05 (unless otherwise specified, or if attraction season finishes prior to this). Vouchers are subject to the terms, conditions and restrictions of the selected attraction.
3. One voucher per party will be accepted, cannot be used in conjunction with any other offer, photocopies will not be accepted.
4. All attractions offering a discount have confirmed their willingness to participate. All information is subject to change without notice and should any attraction close or decline to accept a voucher for any reason, Days Out UK are not liable and cannot be held responsible.
5. Days Out UK shall not accept liability for any loss, accident or injury that may occur at a participating attraction and any dispute arising must be settled direct with the attraction concerned.
6. Cash redemption value of each voucher is 0.001p.
7. You are advised to check all relevant information with your chosen attraction before commencing your journey.

Days Out UK, PO Box 427, Northampton NN1 3YN. Tel: 01604 622445

1. Each voucher entitles the holder to the discount specified by the selected attraction.
2. Valid for use until 28/02/05 (unless otherwise specified, or if attraction season finishes prior to this). Vouchers are subject to the terms, conditions and restrictions of the selected attraction.
3. One voucher per party will be accepted, cannot be used in conjunction with any other offer, photocopies will not be accepted.
4. All attractions offering a discount have confirmed their willingness to participate. All information is subject to change without notice and should any attraction close or decline to accept a voucher for any reason, Days Out UK are not liable and cannot be held responsible.
5. Days Out UK shall not accept liability for any loss, accident or injury that may occur at a participating attraction and any dispute arising must be settled direct with the attraction concerned.
6. Cash redemption value of each voucher is 0.001p.
7. You are advised to check all relevant information with your chosen attraction before commencing your journey.

Days Out UK, PO Box 427, Northampton NN1 3YN. Tel: 01604 622445

1. Each voucher entitles the holder to the discount specified by the selected attraction.
2. Valid for use until 28/02/05 (unless otherwise specified. or if attraction season finishes prior to this). Vouchers are subject to the terms, conditions and restrictions of the selected attraction.
3. One voucher per party will be accepted, cannot be used in conjunction with any other offer, photocopies will not be accepted.
4. All attractions offering a discount have confirmed their willingness to participate. All information is subject to change without notice and should any attraction close or decline to accept a voucher for any reason, Days Out UK are not liable and cannot be held responsible.
5. Days Out UK shall not accept liability for any loss, accident or injury that may occur at a participating attraction and any dispute arising must be settled direct with the attraction concerned.
6. Cash redemption value of each voucher is 0.001p.
7. You are advised to check all relevant information with your chosen attraction before commencing your journey.

Days Out UK, PO Box 427, Northampton NN1 3YN. Tel: 01604 622445

1. Each voucher entitles the holder to the discount specified by the selected attraction.
2. Valid for use until 28/02/05 (unless otherwise specified, or if attraction season finishes prior to this). Vouchers are subject to the terms, conditions and restrictions of the selected attraction.
3. One voucher per party will be accepted, cannot be used in conjunction with any other offer, photocopies will not be accepted.
4. All attractions offering a discount have confirmed their willingness to participate. All information is subject to change without notice and should any attraction close or decline to accept a voucher for any reason, Days Out UK are not liable and cannot be held responsible.
5. Days Out UK shall not accept liability for any loss, accident or injury that may occur at a participating attraction and any dispute arising must be settled direct with the attraction concerned.
6. Cash redemption value of each voucher is 0.001p.
7. You are advised to check all relevant information with your chosen attraction before commencing your journey.

Days Out UK, PO Box 427, Northampton NN1 3YN. Tel: 01604 622445

1. Each voucher entitles the holder to the discount specified by the selected attraction.
2. Valid for use until 28/02/05 (unless otherwise specified, or if attraction season finishes prior to this). Vouchers are subject to the terms, conditions and restrictions of the selected attraction.
3. One voucher per party will be accepted, cannot be used in conjunction with any other offer, photocopies will not be accepted.
4. All attractions offering a discount have confirmed their willingness to participate. All information is subject to change without notice and should any attraction close or decline to accept a voucher for any reason, Days Out UK are not liable and cannot be held responsible.
5. Days Out UK shall not accept liability for any loss, accident or injury that may occur at a participating attraction and any dispute arising must be settled direct with the attraction concerned.
6. Cash redemption value of each voucher is 0.001p.
7. You are advised to check all relevant information with your chosen attraction before commencing your journey.

Days Out UK, PO Box 427, Northampton NN1 3YN. Tel: 01604 622445

1. Each voucher entitles the holder to the discount specified by the selected attraction.
2. Valid for use until 28/02/05 (unless otherwise specified, or if attraction season finishes prior to this). Vouchers are subject to the terms, conditions and restrictions of the selected attraction.
3. One voucher per party will be accepted, cannot be used in conjunction with any other offer, photocopies will not be accepted.
4. All attractions offering a discount have confirmed their willingness to participate. All information is subject to change without notice and should any attraction close or decline to accept a voucher for any reason, Days Out UK are not liable and cannot be held responsible.
5. Days Out UK shall not accept liability for any loss, accident or injury that may occur at a participating attraction and any dispute arising must be settled direct with the attraction concerned.
6. Cash redemption value of each voucher is 0.001p.
7. You are advised to check all relevant information with your chosen attraction before commencing your journey.

Days Out UK, PO Box 427, Northampton NN1 3YN. Tel: 01604 622445

The Charles Dickens Museum
48 Doughty Street London WC1N 2LX
Two For The Price Of One

Not to be used in conjunction with any other offer. One voucher per party. Not valid on Bank Hols or special events

Valid until end Feb 2005

DISCOUNT VOUCHER

Vinopolis, City of Wine
1 Bank End London SE1 9BU
£2.50 Off For Up To Four Guests

Not to be used in conjunction with any other offer. One voucher per party. Not valid on Bank Hols or special events

Valid until end Dec 2004

DISCOUNT VOUCHER

Wimbledon Lawn Tennis Museum and Tour
Centre Court All England Lawn Tennis & Croquet Club Church Road

Wimbledon London SW19 5AE
£1.00 Off Adult Admission

Not to be used in conjunction with any other offer. One voucher per party. Not valid on Bank Hols or special events

Valid until end Feb 2005

DISCOUNT VOUCHER

Beatles Story
Britannia Vaults Albert Dock Liverpool Merseyside
Two For The Price Of One

Not to be used in conjunction with any other offer. One voucher per party. Not valid on Bank Hols or special events

Valid until end Feb 2005

DISCOUNT VOUCHER

Fingerprints of Elvis
Units 17-19 The Colonnades Albert Dock Liverpool

Merseyside L3 4AA
£1.00 Off Admission

Not to be used in conjunction with any other offer. One voucher per party. Not valid on Bank Hols or special events

Valid until end Feb 2005

DISCOUNT VOUCHER

Historic Warships: HMS Plymouth and HMS Onyx
East Float Dock Road Birkenhead Wirral CH41 1DJ
One Child Free
With Full Paying Adult

Not to be used in conjunction with any other offer. One voucher per party. Not valid on Bank Hols or special events

Valid until end Feb 2005

DISCOUNT VOUCHER

1. Each voucher entitles the holder to the discount specified by the selected attraction.
2. Valid for use until 28/02/05 (unless otherwise specified, or if attraction season finishes prior to this). Vouchers are subject to the terms, conditions and restrictions of the selected attraction.
3. One voucher per party will be accepted, cannot be used in conjunction with any other offer, photocopies will not be accepted.
4. All attractions offering a discount have confirmed their willingness to participate. All information is subject to change without notice and should any attraction close or decline to accept a voucher for any reason, Days Out UK are not liable and cannot be held responsible.
5. Days Out UK shall not accept liability for any loss, accident or injury that may occur at a participating attraction and any dispute arising must be settled direct with the attraction concerned.
6. Cash redemption value of each voucher is 0.001p.
7. You are advised to check all relevant information with your chosen attraction before commencing your journey.

Days Out UK, PO Box 427, Northampton NN1 3YN. Tel: 01604 622445

1. Each voucher entitles the holder to the discount specified by the selected attraction.
2. Valid for use until 28/02/05 (unless otherwise specified, or if attraction season finishes prior to this). Vouchers are subject to the terms, conditions and restrictions of the selected attraction.
3. One voucher per party will be accepted, cannot be used in conjunction with any other offer, photocopies will not be accepted.
4. All attractions offering a discount have confirmed their willingness to participate. All information is subject to change without notice and should any attraction close or decline to accept a voucher for any reason, Days Out UK are not liable and cannot be held responsible.
5. Days Out UK shall not accept liability for any loss, accident or injury that may occur at a participating attraction and any dispute arising must be settled direct with the attraction concerned.
6. Cash redemption value of each voucher is 0.001p.
7. You are advised to check all relevant information with your chosen attraction before commencing your journey.

Days Out UK, PO Box 427, Northampton NN1 3YN. Tel: 01604 622445

1. Each voucher entitles the holder to the discount specified by the selected attraction.
2. Valid for use until 28/02/05 (unless otherwise specified, or if attraction season finishes prior to this). Vouchers are subject to the terms, conditions and restrictions of the selected attraction.
3. One voucher per party will be accepted, cannot be used in conjunction with any other offer, photocopies will not be accepted.
4. All attractions offering a discount have confirmed their willingness to participate. All information is subject to change without notice and should any attraction close or decline to accept a voucher for any reason, Days Out UK are not liable and cannot be held responsible.
5. Days Out UK shall not accept liability for any loss, accident or injury that may occur at a participating attraction and any dispute arising must be settled direct with the attraction concerned.
6. Cash redemption value of each voucher is 0.001p.
7. You are advised to check all relevant information with your chosen attraction before commencing your journey.

Days Out UK, PO Box 427, Northampton NN1 3YN. Tel: 01604 622445

1. Each voucher entitles the holder to the discount specified by the selected attraction.
2. Valid for use until 28/02/05 (unless otherwise specified, or if attraction season finishes prior to this). Vouchers are subject to the terms, conditions and restrictions of the selected attraction.
3. One voucher per party will be accepted, cannot be used in conjunction with any other offer, photocopies will not be accepted.
4. All attractions offering a discount have confirmed their willingness to participate. All information is subject to change without notice and should any attraction close or decline to accept a voucher for any reason, Days Out UK are not liable and cannot be held responsible.
5. Days Out UK shall not accept liability for any loss, accident or injury that may occur at a participating attraction and any dispute arising must be settled direct with the attraction concerned.
6. Cash redemption value of each voucher is 0.001p.
7. You are advised to check all relevant information with your chosen attraction before commencing your journey.

Days Out UK, PO Box 427, Northampton NN1 3YN. Tel: 01604 622445

1. Each voucher entitles the holder to the discount specified by the selected attraction.
2. Valid for use until 28/02/05 (unless otherwise specified, or if attraction season finishes prior to this). Vouchers are subject to the terms, conditions and restrictions of the selected attraction.
3. One voucher per party will be accepted, cannot be used in conjunction with any other offer, photocopies will not be accepted.
4. All attractions offering a discount have confirmed their willingness to participate. All information is subject to change without notice and should any attraction close or decline to accept a voucher for any reason, Days Out UK are not liable and cannot be held responsible.
5. Days Out UK shall not accept liability for any loss, accident or injury that may occur at a participating attraction and any dispute arising must be settled direct with the attraction concerned.
6. Cash redemption value of each voucher is 0.001p.
7. You are advised to check all relevant information with your chosen attraction before commencing your journey.

Days Out UK, PO Box 427, Northampton NN1 3YN. Tel: 01604 622445

599

1. Each voucher entitles the holder to the discount specified by the selected attraction.
2. Valid for use until 28/02/05 (unless otherwise specified, or if attraction season finishes prior to this). Vouchers are subject to the terms, conditions and restrictions of the selected attraction.
3. One voucher per party will be accepted, cannot be used in conjunction with any other offer, photocopies will not be accepted.
4. All attractions offering a discount have confirmed their willingness to participate. All information is subject to change without notice and should any attraction close or decline to accept a voucher for any reason, Days Out UK are not liable and cannot be held responsible.
5. Days Out UK shall not accept liability for any loss, accident or injury that may occur at a participating attraction and any dispute arising must be settled direct with the attraction concerned.
6. Cash redemption value of each voucher is 0.001p.
7. You are advised to check all relevant information with your chosen attraction before commencing your journey.

Days Out UK, PO Box 427, Northampton NN1 3YN. Tel: 01604 622445

1. Each voucher entitles the holder to the discount specified by the selected attraction.
2. Valid for use until 28/02/05 (unless otherwise specified, or if attraction season finishes prior to this). Vouchers are subject to the terms, conditions and restrictions of the selected attraction.
3. One voucher per party will be accepted, cannot be used in conjunction with any other offer, photocopies will not be accepted.
4. All attractions offering a discount have confirmed their willingness to participate. All information is subject to change without notice and should any attraction close or decline to accept a voucher for any reason, Days Out UK are not liable and cannot be held responsible.
5. Days Out UK shall not accept liability for any loss, accident or injury that may occur at a participating attraction and any dispute arising must be settled direct with the attraction concerned.
6. Cash redemption value of each voucher is 0.001p.
7. You are advised to check all relevant information with your chosen attraction before commencing your journey.

Days Out UK, PO Box 427, Northampton NN1 3YN. Tel: 01604 622445

1. Each voucher entitles the holder to the discount specified by the selected attraction.
2. Valid for use until 28/02/05 (unless otherwise specified. or if attraction season finishes prior to this). Vouchers are subject to the terms, conditions and restrictions of the selected attraction.
3. One voucher per party will be accepted, cannot be used in conjunction with any other offer, photocopies will not be accepted.
4. All attractions offering a discount have confirmed their willingness to participate. All information is subject to change without notice and should any attraction close or decline to accept a voucher for any reason, Days Out UK are not liable and cannot be held responsible.
5. Days Out UK shall not accept liability for any loss, accident or injury that may occur at a participating attraction and any dispute arising must be settled direct with the attraction concerned.
6. Cash redemption value of each voucher is 0.001p.
7. You are advised to check all relevant information with your chosen attraction before commencing your journey.

Days Out UK, PO Box 427, Northampton NN1 3YN. Tel: 01604 622445

1. Each voucher entitles the holder to the discount specified by the selected attraction.
2. Valid for use until 28/02/05 (unless otherwise specified, or if attraction season finishes prior to this). Vouchers are subject to the terms, conditions and restrictions of the selected attraction.
3. One voucher per party will be accepted, cannot be used in conjunction with any other offer, photocopies will not be accepted.
4. All attractions offering a discount have confirmed their willingness to participate. All information is subject to change without notice and should any attraction close or decline to accept a voucher for any reason, Days Out UK are not liable and cannot be held responsible.
5. Days Out UK shall not accept liability for any loss, accident or injury that may occur at a participating attraction and any dispute arising must be settled direct with the attraction concerned.
6. Cash redemption value of each voucher is 0.001p.
7. You are advised to check all relevant information with your chosen attraction before commencing your journey.

Days Out UK, PO Box 427, Northampton NN1 3YN. Tel: 01604 622445

1. Each voucher entitles the holder to the discount specified by the selected attraction.
2. Valid for use until 28/02/05 (unless otherwise specified, or if attraction season finishes prior to this). Vouchers are subject to the terms, conditions and restrictions of the selected attraction.
3. One voucher per party will be accepted, cannot be used in conjunction with any other offer, photocopies will not be accepted.
4. All attractions offering a discount have confirmed their willingness to participate. All information is subject to change without notice and should any attraction close or decline to accept a voucher for any reason, Days Out UK are not liable and cannot be held responsible.
5. Days Out UK shall not accept liability for any loss, accident or injury that may occur at a participating attraction and any dispute arising must be settled direct with the attraction concerned.
6. Cash redemption value of each voucher is 0.001p.
7. You are advised to check all relevant information with your chosen attraction before commencing your journey.

Days Out UK, PO Box 427, Northampton NN1 3YN. Tel: 01604 622445

1. Each voucher entitles the holder to the discount specified by the selected attraction.
2. Valid for use until 28/02/05 (unless otherwise specified, or if attraction season finishes prior to this). Vouchers are subject to the terms, conditions and restrictions of the selected attraction.
3. One voucher per party will be accepted, cannot be used in conjunction with any other offer, photocopies will not be accepted.
4. All attractions offering a discount have confirmed their willingness to participate. All information is subject to change without notice and should any attraction close or decline to accept a voucher for any reason, Days Out UK are not liable and cannot be held responsible.
5. Days Out UK shall not accept liability for any loss, accident or injury that may occur at a participating attraction and any dispute arising must be settled direct with the attraction concerned.
6. Cash redemption value of each voucher is 0.001p.
7. You are advised to check all relevant information with your chosen attraction before commencing your journey.

Days Out UK, PO Box 427, Northampton NN1 3YN. Tel: 01604 622445

DaYSOUtUK
he place to look for places to go

Please see page 318
for full attraction
details

Saint Patrick's Trian Visitor Complex
40 English Street Armagh County Armagh BT61 7BA
Two For The Price Of One
Not to be used in conjunction with any other offer. One voucher per party. Not valid on Bank Hols or special events
Valid until end Feb 2005

DISCOUNT VOUCHER

DaYSOUtUK
he place to look for places to go

Please see page 327
for full attraction
details

Bailiffgate Museum
14 Bailiffgate Alnwick Northumberland NE66 1LU
20% Off With Voucher
Not to be used in conjunction with any other offer. One voucher per party. Not valid on Bank Hols or special events
Valid until end Feb 2005

DISCOUNT VOUCHER

DaYSOUtUK
he place to look for places to go

Please see page 330
for full attraction
details

City of Caves
Upper Level Broad Marsh Shopping Centre Nottingham
One Child Free
With One Full Paying Adult
Not to be used in conjunction with any other offer. One voucher per party. Not valid on Bank Hols or special events
Valid until end Feb 2005

DISCOUNT VOUCHER

DaYSOUtUK
he place to look for places to go

Please see page 334
for full attraction
details

Galleries of Justice
Shire Hall High Pavement Lace Market Nottingham
Two For The Price Of One
Not to be used in conjunction with any other offer. One voucher per party. Not valid on Bank Hols or special events
Valid until end Feb 2005

DISCOUNT VOUCHER

DaYSOUtUK
he place to look for places to go

Please see page 332
for full attraction
details

Tales of Robin Hood
30-38 Maid Marian Way Nottingham NG1 6GF
Two For The Price Of One
Not to be used in conjunction with any other offer. One voucher per party. Not valid on Bank Hols or special events
Valid until end Feb 2005

DISCOUNT VOUCHER

DaYSOUtUK
he place to look for places to go

Please see page 338
for full attraction
details

Broughton Castle
Banbury Oxfordshire OX15 5EB
Two Adults For The Price Of One
Not to be used in conjunction with any other offer. One voucher per party. Not valid on Bank Hols or special events
Valid until end Feb 2005

DISCOUNT VOUCHER

1. Each voucher entitles the holder to the discount specified by the selected attraction.
2. Valid for use until 28/02/05 (unless otherwise specified, or if attraction season finishes prior to this). Vouchers are subject to the terms, conditions and restrictions of the selected attraction.
3. One voucher per party will be accepted, cannot be used in conjunction with any other offer, photocopies will not be accepted.
4. All attractions offering a discount have confirmed their willingness to participate. All information is subject to change without notice and should any attraction close or decline to accept a voucher for any reason, Days Out UK are not liable and cannot be held responsible.
5. Days Out UK shall not accept liability for any loss, accident or injury that may occur at a participating attraction and any dispute arising must be settled direct with the attraction concerned.
6. Cash redemption value of each voucher is 0.001p.
7. You are advised to check all relevant information with your chosen attraction before commencing your journey.

Days Out UK, PO Box 427, Northampton NN1 3YN. Tel: 01604 622445

1. Each voucher entitles the holder to the discount specified by the selected attraction.
2. Valid for use until 28/02/05 (unless otherwise specified, or if attraction season finishes prior to this). Vouchers are subject to the terms, conditions and restrictions of the selected attraction.
3. One voucher per party will be accepted, cannot be used in conjunction with any other offer, photocopies will not be accepted.
4. All attractions offering a discount have confirmed their willingness to participate. All information is subject to change without notice and should any attraction close or decline to accept a voucher for any reason, Days Out UK are not liable and cannot be held responsible.
5. Days Out UK shall not accept liability for any loss, accident or injury that may occur at a participating attraction and any dispute arising must be settled direct with the attraction concerned.
6. Cash redemption value of each voucher is 0.001p.
7. You are advised to check all relevant information with your chosen attraction before commencing your journey.

Days Out UK, PO Box 427, Northampton NN1 3YN. Tel: 01604 622445

1. Each voucher entitles the holder to the discount specified by the selected attraction.
2. Valid for use until 28/02/05 (unless otherwise specified, or if attraction season finishes prior to this). Vouchers are subject to the terms, conditions and restrictions of the selected attraction.
3. One voucher per party will be accepted, cannot be used in conjunction with any other offer, photocopies will not be accepted.
4. All attractions offering a discount have confirmed their willingness to participate. All information is subject to change without notice and should any attraction close or decline to accept a voucher for any reason, Days Out UK are not liable and cannot be held responsible.
5. Days Out UK shall not accept liability for any loss, accident or injury that may occur at a participating attraction and any dispute arising must be settled direct with the attraction concerned.
6. Cash redemption value of each voucher is 0.001p.
7. You are advised to check all relevant information with your chosen attraction before commencing your journey.

Days Out UK, PO Box 427, Northampton NN1 3YN. Tel: 01604 622445

1. Each voucher entitles the holder to the discount specified by the selected attraction.
2. Valid for use until 28/02/05 (unless otherwise specified, or if attraction season finishes prior to this). Vouchers are subject to the terms, conditions and restrictions of the selected attraction.
3. One voucher per party will be accepted, cannot be used in conjunction with any other offer, photocopies will not be accepted.
4. All attractions offering a discount have confirmed their willingness to participate. All information is subject to change without notice and should any attraction close or decline to accept a voucher for any reason, Days Out UK are not liable and cannot be held responsible.
5. Days Out UK shall not accept liability for any loss, accident or injury that may occur at a participating attraction and any dispute arising must be settled direct with the attraction concerned.
6. Cash redemption value of each voucher is 0.001p.
7. You are advised to check all relevant information with your chosen attraction before commencing your journey.

Days Out UK, PO Box 427, Northampton NN1 3YN. Tel: 01604 622445

1. Each voucher entitles the holder to the discount specified by the selected attraction.
2. Valid for use until 28/02/05 (unless otherwise specified, or if attraction season finishes prior to this). Vouchers are subject to the terms, conditions and restrictions of the selected attraction.
3. One voucher per party will be accepted, cannot be used in conjunction with any other offer, photocopies will not be accepted.
4. All attractions offering a discount have confirmed their willingness to participate. All information is subject to change without notice and should any attraction close or decline to accept a voucher for any reason, Days Out UK are not liable and cannot be held responsible.
5. Days Out UK shall not accept liability for any loss, accident or injury that may occur at a participating attraction and any dispute arising must be settled direct with the attraction concerned.
6. Cash redemption value of each voucher is 0.001p.
7. You are advised to check all relevant information with your chosen attraction before commencing your journey.

Days Out UK, PO Box 427, Northampton NN1 3YN. Tel: 01604 622445

1. Each voucher entitles the holder to the discount specified by the selected attraction.
2. Valid for use until 28/02/05 (unless otherwise specified, or if attraction season finishes prior to this). Vouchers are subject to the terms, conditions and restrictions of the selected attraction.
3. One voucher per party will be accepted, cannot be used in conjunction with any other offer, photocopies will not be accepted.
4. All attractions offering a discount have confirmed their willingness to participate. All information is subject to change without notice and should any attraction close or decline to accept a voucher for any reason, Days Out UK are not liable and cannot be held responsible.
5. Days Out UK shall not accept liability for any loss, accident or injury that may occur at a participating attraction and any dispute arising must be settled direct with the attraction concerned.
6. Cash redemption value of each voucher is 0.001p.
7. You are advised to check all relevant information with your chosen attraction before commencing your journey.

Days Out UK, PO Box 427, Northampton NN1 3YN. Tel: 01604 622445

Cholsey and Wallingford Railway

Hithercroft Road Wallingford Oxfordshire OX10 9GQ

One Child Free With Every Full Paying Adult

Valid For All Events, Excluding Santa Specials

Not to be used in conjunction with any other offer. One voucher per party. Not valid on Bank Hols or Santa Specials

Valid until end Feb 2005

Please see page 339 for full attraction details

Cogges Manor Farm Museum

Church Lane Witney Oxfordshire OX28 3LA

Two For The Price Of One

Not to be used in conjunction with any other offer. One voucher per party. Not valid on Bank Hols or special events

Valid until end Feb 2005

Please see page 344 for full attraction details

Didcot Railway Centre

Didcot Oxfordshire OX11 7NJ

One Adult Or Child Free

With Full Paying Adult

Not to be used in conjunction with any other offer. One voucher per party. Not valid on Bank Hols or special events

Valid until end Feb 2005

Please see page 340 for full attraction details

Archaeolink Prehistory Park

Oyne Insch Aberdeenshire AB52 6QP

Two For The Price Of One

Not to be used in conjunction with any other offer. One voucher per party. Not valid on Bank Hols or special events

Valid until end Feb 2005

Please see page 371 for full attraction details

Buckie Drifter Maritime Heritage Centre

Freuchny Road Buckie Moray AB56 1TT

One Child Free

With One Paying Adult

Not to be used in conjunction with any other offer. One voucher per party. Not valid on Bank Hols or special events

Valid Mar-Oct 2004

Please see page 372 for full attraction details

Galloway Wildlife Conservation Park

Lochfergus Plantation Kirkcudbright Dumfries and Galloway

One Child Free

With Two Full Paying Adults

Not to be used in conjunction with any other offer. One voucher per party. Not valid on Bank Hols or special events

Valid until end Feb 2005

Please see page 385 for full attraction details

1. Each voucher entitles the holder to the discount specified by the selected attraction.
2. Valid for use until 28/02/05 (unless otherwise specified, or if attraction season finishes prior to this). Vouchers are subject to the terms, conditions and restrictions of the selected attraction.
3. One voucher per party will be accepted, cannot be used in conjunction with any other offer, photocopies will not be accepted.
4. All attractions offering a discount have confirmed their willingness to participate. All information is subject to change without notice and should any attraction close or decline to accept a voucher for any reason, Days Out UK are not liable and cannot be held responsible.
5. Days Out UK shall not accept liability for any loss, accident or injury that may occur at a participating attraction and any dispute arising must be settled direct with the attraction concerned.
6. Cash redemption value of each voucher is 0.001p.
7. You are advised to check all relevant information with your chosen attraction before commencing your journey.

Days Out UK, PO Box 427, Northampton NN1 3YN. Tel: 01604 622445

1. Each voucher entitles the holder to the discount specified by the selected attraction.
2. Valid for use until 28/02/05 (unless otherwise specified, or if attraction season finishes prior to this). Vouchers are subject to the terms, conditions and restrictions of the selected attraction.
3. One voucher per party will be accepted, cannot be used in conjunction with any other offer, photocopies will not be accepted.
4. All attractions offering a discount have confirmed their willingness to participate. All information is subject to change without notice and should any attraction close or decline to accept a voucher for any reason, Days Out UK are not liable and cannot be held responsible.
5. Days Out UK shall not accept liability for any loss, accident or injury that may occur at a participating attraction and any dispute arising must be settled direct with the attraction concerned.
6. Cash redemption value of each voucher is 0.001p.
7. You are advised to check all relevant information with your chosen attraction before commencing your journey.

Days Out UK, PO Box 427, Northampton NN1 3YN. Tel: 01604 622445

1. Each voucher entitles the holder to the discount specified by the selected attraction.
2. Valid for use until 28/02/05 (unless otherwise specified, or if attraction season finishes prior to this). Vouchers are subject to the terms, conditions and restrictions of the selected attraction.
3. One voucher per party will be accepted, cannot be used in conjunction with any other offer, photocopies will not be accepted.
4. All attractions offering a discount have confirmed their willingness to participate. All information is subject to change without notice and should any attraction close or decline to accept a voucher for any reason, Days Out UK are not liable and cannot be held responsible.
5. Days Out UK shall not accept liability for any loss, accident or injury that may occur at a participating attraction and any dispute arising must be settled direct with the attraction concerned.
6. Cash redemption value of each voucher is 0.001p.
7. You are advised to check all relevant information with your chosen attraction before commencing your journey.

Days Out UK, PO Box 427, Northampton NN1 3YN. Tel: 01604 622445

1. Each voucher entitles the holder to the discount specified by the selected attraction.
2. Valid for use until 28/02/05 (unless otherwise specified, or if attraction season finishes prior to this). Vouchers are subject to the terms, conditions and restrictions of the selected attraction.
3. One voucher per party will be accepted, cannot be used in conjunction with any other offer, photocopies will not be accepted.
4. All attractions offering a discount have confirmed their willingness to participate. All information is subject to change without notice and should any attraction close or decline to accept a voucher for any reason, Days Out UK are not liable and cannot be held responsible.
5. Days Out UK shall not accept liability for any loss, accident or injury that may occur at a participating attraction and any dispute arising must be settled direct with the attraction concerned.
6. Cash redemption value of each voucher is 0.001p.
7. You are advised to check all relevant information with your chosen attraction before commencing your journey.

Days Out UK, PO Box 427, Northampton NN1 3YN. Tel: 01604 622445

1. Each voucher entitles the holder to the discount specified by the selected attraction.
2. Valid for use until 28/02/05 (unless otherwise specified, or if attraction season finishes prior to this). Vouchers are subject to the terms, conditions and restrictions of the selected attraction.
3. One voucher per party will be accepted, cannot be used in conjunction with any other offer, photocopies will not be accepted.
4. All attractions offering a discount have confirmed their willingness to participate. All information is subject to change without notice and should any attraction close or decline to accept a voucher for any reason, Days Out UK are not liable and cannot be held responsible.
5. Days Out UK shall not accept liability for any loss, accident or injury that may occur at a participating attraction and any dispute arising must be settled direct with the attraction concerned.
6. Cash redemption value of each voucher is 0.001p.
7. You are advised to check all relevant information with your chosen attraction before commencing your journey.

Days Out UK, PO Box 427, Northampton NN1 3YN. Tel: 01604 622445

1. Each voucher entitles the holder to the discount specified by the selected attraction.
2. Valid for use until 28/02/05 (unless otherwise specified, or if attraction season finishes prior to this). Vouchers are subject to the terms, conditions and restrictions of the selected attraction.
3. One voucher per party will be accepted, cannot be used in conjunction with any other offer, photocopies will not be accepted.
4. All attractions offering a discount have confirmed their willingness to participate. All information is subject to change without notice and should any attraction close or decline to accept a voucher for any reason, Days Out UK are not liable and cannot be held responsible.
5. Days Out UK shall not accept liability for any loss, accident or injury that may occur at a participating attraction and any dispute arising must be settled direct with the attraction concerned.
6. Cash redemption value of each voucher is 0.001p.
7. You are advised to check all relevant information with your chosen attraction before commencing your journey.

Days Out UK, PO Box 427, Northampton NN1 3YN. Tel: 01604 622445

607

1. Each voucher entitles the holder to the discount specified by the selected attraction.
2. Valid for use until 28/02/05 (unless otherwise specified, or if attraction season finishes prior to this). Vouchers are subject to the terms, conditions and restrictions of the selected attraction.
3. One voucher per party will be accepted, cannot be used in conjunction with any other offer, photocopies will not be accepted.
4. All attractions offering a discount have confirmed their willingness to participate. All information is subject to change without notice and should any attraction close or decline to accept a voucher for any reason, Days Out UK are not liable and cannot be held responsible.
5. Days Out UK shall not accept liability for any loss, accident or injury that may occur at a participating attraction and any dispute arising must be settled direct with the attraction concerned.
6. Cash redemption value of each voucher is 0.001p.
7. You are advised to check all relevant information with your chosen attraction before commencing your journey.

Days Out UK, PO Box 427, Northampton NN1 3YN. Tel: 01604 622445

1. Each voucher entitles the holder to the discount specified by the selected attraction.
2. Valid for use until 28/02/05 (unless otherwise specified, or if attraction season finishes prior to this). Vouchers are subject to the terms, conditions and restrictions of the selected attraction.
3. One voucher per party will be accepted, cannot be used in conjunction with any other offer, photocopies will not be accepted.
4. All attractions offering a discount have confirmed their willingness to participate. All information is subject to change without notice and should any attraction close or decline to accept a voucher for any reason, Days Out UK are not liable and cannot be held responsible.
5. Days Out UK shall not accept liability for any loss, accident or injury that may occur at a participating attraction and any dispute arising must be settled direct with the attraction concerned.
6. Cash redemption value of each voucher is 0.001p.
7. You are advised to check all relevant information with your chosen attraction before commencing your journey.

Days Out UK, PO Box 427, Northampton NN1 3YN. Tel: 01604 622445

1. Each voucher entitles the holder to the discount specified by the selected attraction.
2. Valid for use until 28/02/05 (unless otherwise specified, or if attraction season finishes prior to this). Vouchers are subject to the terms, conditions and restrictions of the selected attraction.
3. One voucher per party will be accepted, cannot be used in conjunction with any other offer, photocopies will not be accepted.
4. All attractions offering a discount have confirmed their willingness to participate. All information is subject to change without notice and should any attraction close or decline to accept a voucher for any reason, Days Out UK are not liable and cannot be held responsible.
5. Days Out UK shall not accept liability for any loss, accident or injury that may occur at a participating attraction and any dispute arising must be settled direct with the attraction concerned.
6. Cash redemption value of each voucher is 0.001p.
7. You are advised to check all relevant information with your chosen attraction before commencing your journey.

Days Out UK, PO Box 427, Northampton NN1 3YN. Tel: 01604 622445

1. Each voucher entitles the holder to the discount specified by the selected attraction.
2. Valid for use until 28/02/05 (unless otherwise specified, or if attraction season finishes prior to this). Vouchers are subject to the terms, conditions and restrictions of the selected attraction.
3. One voucher per party will be accepted, cannot be used in conjunction with any other offer, photocopies will not be accepted.
4. All attractions offering a discount have confirmed their willingness to participate. All information is subject to change without notice and should any attraction close or decline to accept a voucher for any reason, Days Out UK are not liable and cannot be held responsible.
5. Days Out UK shall not accept liability for any loss, accident or injury that may occur at a participating attraction and any dispute arising must be settled direct with the attraction concerned.
6. Cash redemption value of each voucher is 0.001p.
7. You are advised to check all relevant information with your chosen attraction before commencing your journey.

Days Out UK, PO Box 427, Northampton NN1 3YN. Tel: 01604 622445

1. Each voucher entitles the holder to the discount specified by the selected attraction.
2. Valid for use until 28/02/05 (unless otherwise specified, or if attraction season finishes prior to this). Vouchers are subject to the terms, conditions and restrictions of the selected attraction.
3. One voucher per party will be accepted, cannot be used in conjunction with any other offer, photocopies will not be accepted.
4. All attractions offering a discount have confirmed their willingness to participate. All information is subject to change without notice and should any attraction close or decline to accept a voucher for any reason, Days Out UK are not liable and cannot be held responsible.
5. Days Out UK shall not accept liability for any loss, accident or injury that may occur at a participating attraction and any dispute arising must be settled direct with the attraction concerned.
6. Cash redemption value of each voucher is 0.001p.
7. You are advised to check all relevant information with your chosen attraction before commencing your journey.

Days Out UK, PO Box 427, Northampton NN1 3YN. Tel: 01604 622445

Drayton Manor Family Theme Park
Tamworth Staffordshire B78 3TW
Buy 2 - Get 1 Free

One Adult (Age 12+) Or Child (4-11) Can Enjoy Drayton Manor Theme Park Absolutely FREE When You Purchase Two Full Price Adult Tickets. Present this voucher at Park entrance. Offer applies to car visitors only - coach rates do not apply. Call info line for opening times 08708 725252
Not to be used in conjunction with any other offer. One voucher per party. Not valid on Bank Hols, Bank Hol weekends or special events

Valid until end of 2004

Please see page 417 for full attraction details

Erasmus Darwin House
Beacon Street Lichfield Staffordshire WS13 7AD
Two For The Price Of One

Not to be used in conjunction with any other offer. One voucher per party. Not valid on Bank Hols or special events

Valid until end Feb 2005

Please see page 413 for full attraction details

Etruria Industrial Museum
Lower Bedford Street Etruria Staffordshire
Two For The Price Of One

Not to be used in conjunction with any other offer. One voucher per party. Not valid on Bank Hols or special events

Valid until end Feb 2005

Please see page 411 for full attraction details

Ford Green Hall
Ford Green Road Smallthorne Staffordshire
Two For The Price Of One

Excludes Evening Events And Children's Activities
Not to be used in conjunction with any other offer. One voucher per party. Not valid on Bank Hols or special events

Valid until end Feb 2005

Please see page 414 for full attraction details

Gladstone Working Pottery Museum
Uttoxeter Road Longton Stoke-On-Trent Staffordshire
One Child Free
With Every Full Paying Adult

Not to be used in conjunction with any other offer. One voucher per party. Not valid on Bank Hols or special events

Valid until end Feb 2005

Please see page 406 for full attraction details

Royal Doulton Visitor Centre
Nile Street Burslem Stoke-On-Trent Staffordshire
Two For The Price Of One
For The Visitor Centre Only

Not to be used in conjunction with any other offer. One voucher per party. Not valid on Bank Hols or special events

Valid until end Feb 2005

Please see page 409 for full attraction details

1. Each voucher entitles the holder to the discount specified by the selected attraction.
2. Valid for use until 28/02/05 (unless otherwise specified, or if attraction season finishes prior to this). Vouchers are subject to the terms, conditions and restrictions of the selected attraction.
3. One voucher per party will be accepted, cannot be used in conjunction with any other offer, photocopies will not be accepted.
4. All attractions offering a discount have confirmed their willingness to participate. All information is subject to change without notice and should any attraction close or decline to accept a voucher for any reason, Days Out UK are not liable and cannot be held responsible.
5. Days Out UK shall not accept liability for any loss, accident or injury that may occur at a participating attraction and any dispute arising must be settled direct with the attraction concerned.
6. Cash redemption value of each voucher is 0.001p.
7. You are advised to check all relevant information with your chosen attraction before commencing your journey.

Days Out UK, PO Box 427, Northampton NN1 3YN. Tel: 01604 622445

1. Each voucher entitles the holder to the discount specified by the selected attraction.
2. Valid for use until 28/02/05 (unless otherwise specified, or if attraction season finishes prior to this). Vouchers are subject to the terms, conditions and restrictions of the selected attraction.
3. One voucher per party will be accepted, cannot be used in conjunction with any other offer, photocopies will not be accepted.
4. All attractions offering a discount have confirmed their willingness to participate. All information is subject to change without notice and should any attraction close or decline to accept a voucher for any reason, Days Out UK are not liable and cannot be held responsible.
5. Days Out UK shall not accept liability for any loss, accident or injury that may occur at a participating attraction and any dispute arising must be settled direct with the attraction concerned.
6. Cash redemption value of each voucher is 0.001p.
7. You are advised to check all relevant information with your chosen attraction before commencing your journey.

Days Out UK, PO Box 427, Northampton NN1 3YN. Tel: 01604 622445

1. Each voucher entitles the holder to the discount specified by the selected attraction.
2. Valid for use until 28/02/05 (unless otherwise specified, or if attraction season finishes prior to this). Vouchers are subject to the terms, conditions and restrictions of the selected attraction.
3. One voucher per party will be accepted, cannot be used in conjunction with any other offer, photocopies will not be accepted.
4. All attractions offering a discount have confirmed their willingness to participate. All information is subject to change without notice and should any attraction close or decline to accept a voucher for any reason, Days Out UK are not liable and cannot be held responsible.
5. Days Out UK shall not accept liability for any loss, accident or injury that may occur at a participating attraction and any dispute arising must be settled direct with the attraction concerned.
6. Cash redemption value of each voucher is 0.001p.
7. You are advised to check all relevant information with your chosen attraction before commencing your journey.

Days Out UK, PO Box 427, Northampton NN1 3YN. Tel: 01604 622445

1. Each voucher entitles the holder to the discount specified by the selected attraction.
2. Valid for use until 28/02/05 (unless otherwise specified, or if attraction season finishes prior to this). Vouchers are subject to the terms, conditions and restrictions of the selected attraction.
3. One voucher per party will be accepted, cannot be used in conjunction with any other offer, photocopies will not be accepted.
4. All attractions offering a discount have confirmed their willingness to participate. All information is subject to change without notice and should any attraction close or decline to accept a voucher for any reason, Days Out UK are not liable and cannot be held responsible.
5. Days Out UK shall not accept liability for any loss, accident or injury that may occur at a participating attraction and any dispute arising must be settled direct with the attraction concerned.
6. Cash redemption value of each voucher is 0.001p.
7. You are advised to check all relevant information with your chosen attraction before commencing your journey.

Days Out UK, PO Box 427, Northampton NN1 3YN. Tel: 01604 622445

1. Each voucher entitles the holder to the discount specified by the selected attraction.
2. Valid for use until 28/02/05 (unless otherwise specified, or if attraction season finishes prior to this). Vouchers are subject to the terms, conditions and restrictions of the selected attraction.
3. One voucher per party will be accepted, cannot be used in conjunction with any other offer, photocopies will not be accepted.
4. All attractions offering a discount have confirmed their willingness to participate. All information is subject to change without notice and should any attraction close or decline to accept a voucher for any reason, Days Out UK are not liable and cannot be held responsible.
5. Days Out UK shall not accept liability for any loss, accident or injury that may occur at a participating attraction and any dispute arising must be settled direct with the attraction concerned.
6. Cash redemption value of each voucher is 0.001p.
7. You are advised to check all relevant information with your chosen attraction before commencing your journey.

Days Out UK, PO Box 427, Northampton NN1 3YN. Tel: 01604 622445

1. Each voucher entitles the holder to the discount specified by the selected attraction.
2. Valid for use until 28/02/05 (unless otherwise specified, or if attraction season finishes prior to this). Vouchers are subject to the terms, conditions and restrictions of the selected attraction.
3. One voucher per party will be accepted, cannot be used in conjunction with any other offer, photocopies will not be accepted.
4. All attractions offering a discount have confirmed their willingness to participate. All information is subject to change without notice and should any attraction close or decline to accept a voucher for any reason, Days Out UK are not liable and cannot be held responsible.
5. Days Out UK shall not accept liability for any loss, accident or injury that may occur at a participating attraction and any dispute arising must be settled direct with the attraction concerned.
6. Cash redemption value of each voucher is 0.001p.
7. You are advised to check all relevant information with your chosen attraction before commencing your journey.

Days Out UK, PO Box 427, Northampton NN1 3YN. Tel: 01604 622445

1. Each voucher entitles the holder to the discount specified by the selected attraction.
2. Valid for use until 28/02/05 (unless otherwise specified. or if attraction season finishes prior to this). Vouchers are subject to the terms, conditions and restrictions of the selected attraction.
3. One voucher per party will be accepted, cannot be used in conjunction with any other offer, photocopies will not be accepted.
4. All attractions offering a discount have confirmed their willingness to participate. All information is subject to change without notice and should any attraction close or decline to accept a voucher for any reason, Days Out UK are not liable and cannot be held responsible.
5. Days Out UK shall not accept liability for any loss, accident or injury that may occur at a participating attraction and any dispute arising must be settled direct with the attraction concerned.
6. Cash redemption value of each voucher is 0.001p.
7. You are advised to check all relevant information with your chosen attraction before commencing your journey.

Days Out UK, PO Box 427, Northampton NN1 3YN. Tel: 01604 622445

1. Each voucher entitles the holder to the discount specified by the selected attraction.
2. Valid for use until 28/02/05 (unless otherwise specified, or if attraction season finishes prior to this). Vouchers are subject to the terms, conditions and restrictions of the selected attraction.
3. One voucher per party will be accepted, cannot be used in conjunction with any other offer, photocopies will not be accepted.
4. All attractions offering a discount have confirmed their willingness to participate. All information is subject to change without notice and should any attraction close or decline to accept a voucher for any reason, Days Out UK are not liable and cannot be held responsible.
5. Days Out UK shall not accept liability for any loss, accident or injury that may occur at a participating attraction and any dispute arising must be settled direct with the attraction concerned.
6. Cash redemption value of each voucher is 0.001p.
7. You are advised to check all relevant information with your chosen attraction before commencing your journey.

Days Out UK, PO Box 427, Northampton NN1 3YN. Tel: 01604 622445

1. Each voucher entitles the holder to the discount specified by the selected attraction.
2. Valid for use until 28/02/05 (unless otherwise specified, or if attraction season finishes prior to this). Vouchers are subject to the terms, conditions and restrictions of the selected attraction.
3. One voucher per party will be accepted, cannot be used in conjunction with any other offer, photocopies will not be accepted.
4. All attractions offering a discount have confirmed their willingness to participate. All information is subject to change without notice and should any attraction close or decline to accept a voucher for any reason, Days Out UK are not liable and cannot be held responsible.
5. Days Out UK shall not accept liability for any loss, accident or injury that may occur at a participating attraction and any dispute arising must be settled direct with the attraction concerned.
6. Cash redemption value of each voucher is 0.001p.
7. You are advised to check all relevant information with your chosen attraction before commencing your journey.

Days Out UK, PO Box 427, Northampton NN1 3YN. Tel: 01604 622445

1. Each voucher entitles the holder to the discount specified by the selected attraction.
2. Valid for use until 28/02/05 (unless otherwise specified, or if attraction season finishes prior to this). Vouchers are subject to the terms, conditions and restrictions of the selected attraction.
3. One voucher per party will be accepted, cannot be used in conjunction with any other offer, photocopies will not be accepted.
4. All attractions offering a discount have confirmed their willingness to participate. All information is subject to change without notice and should any attraction close or decline to accept a voucher for any reason, Days Out UK are not liable and cannot be held responsible.
5. Days Out UK shall not accept liability for any loss, accident or injury that may occur at a participating attraction and any dispute arising must be settled direct with the attraction concerned.
6. Cash redemption value of each voucher is 0.001p.
7. You are advised to check all relevant information with your chosen attraction before commencing your journey.

Days Out UK, PO Box 427, Northampton NN1 3YN. Tel: 01604 622445

West Stow Anglo-Saxon Village

West Stow Country Park West Stow Suffolk

Two For The Price Of One

Does Not Apply To Family Ticket

Not to be used in conjunction with any other offer. One voucher per party. Not valid on Bank Hols or special events

Valid until end Feb 2005

Birdworld, Underwater World and Jenny Wren Farm

Farnham Road Holt Pound Farnham Surrey

One Child Free Valid With One Full Paying Adult

Not Valid For Santa Events Or Bank Holidays

Not to be used in conjunction with any other offer. One voucher per party. Not valid on Bank Hols or Santa events

Valid until end Feb 2005

Campaign Paintball Park

Old Lane Cobham Surrey KT11 1NH

£2.50 Off Per Person

With This Voucher

Not to be used in conjunction with any other offer. One voucher per party. Not valid on Bank Hols or special events

Valid until end Feb 2005

RHS Garden Wisley

RHS Garden Wisley Woking Surrey GU23 6QB

Two For The Price Of One

Excluding Bank Hol Weekends

Not to be used in conjunction with any other offer. One voucher per party. Not valid on Bank Hols or special events

Valid Oct 2004-Mar 2005 Mon-Sat only

Rural Life Centre

The Reeds Tilford Farnham Surrey GU10 2DL

Two For The Price Of One

Not Valid On Special Event Days

Not to be used in conjunction with any other offer. One voucher per party. Not valid on Bank Hols or special events

Valid until end Feb 2005

Arundel Castle

Arundel Sussex BN18 9AB

Two for the Price of One

Not Applicable To Family Tickets, Group Rates Or On Event Days When Special Ticket Price Applies

Not to be used in conjunction with any other offer. One voucher per party. Not valid on Bank Hols or special events

Valid until end Feb 2005

1. Each voucher entitles the holder to the discount specified by the selected attraction.
2. Valid for use until 28/02/05 (unless otherwise specified, or if attraction season finishes prior to this). Vouchers are subject to the terms, conditions and restrictions of the selected attraction.
3. One voucher per party will be accepted, cannot be used in conjunction with any other offer, photocopies will not be accepted.
4. All attractions offering a discount have confirmed their willingness to participate. All information is subject to change without notice and should any attraction close or decline to accept a voucher for any reason, Days Out UK are not liable and cannot be held responsible.
5. Days Out UK shall not accept liability for any loss, accident or injury that may occur at a participating attraction and any dispute arising must be settled direct with the attraction concerned.
6. Cash redemption value of each voucher is 0.001p.
7. You are advised to check all relevant information with your chosen attraction before commencing your journey.

Days Out UK, PO Box 427, Northampton NN1 3YN. Tel: 01604 622445

1. Each voucher entitles the holder to the discount specified by the selected attraction.
2. Valid for use until 28/02/05 (unless otherwise specified. or if attraction season finishes prior to this). Vouchers are subject to the terms, conditions and restrictions of the selected attraction.
3. One voucher per party will be accepted, cannot be used in conjunction with any other offer, photocopies will not be accepted.
4. All attractions offering a discount have confirmed their willingness to participate. All information is subject to change without notice and should any attraction close or decline to accept a voucher for any reason, Days Out UK are not liable and cannot be held responsible.
5. Days Out UK shall not accept liability for any loss, accident or injury that may occur at a participating attraction and any dispute arising must be settled direct with the attraction concerned.
6. Cash redemption value of each voucher is 0.001p.
7. You are advised to check all relevant information with your chosen attraction before commencing your journey.

Days Out UK, PO Box 427, Northampton NN1 3YN. Tel: 01604 622445

1. Each voucher entitles the holder to the discount specified by the selected attraction.
2. Valid for use until 28/02/05 (unless otherwise specified, or if attraction season finishes prior to this). Vouchers are subject to the terms, conditions and restrictions of the selected attraction.
3. One voucher per party will be accepted, cannot be used in conjunction with any other offer, photocopies will not be accepted.
4. All attractions offering a discount have confirmed their willingness to participate. All information is subject to change without notice and should any attraction close or decline to accept a voucher for any reason, Days Out UK are not liable and cannot be held responsible.
5. Days Out UK shall not accept liability for any loss, accident or injury that may occur at a participating attraction and any dispute arising must be settled direct with the attraction concerned.
6. Cash redemption value of each voucher is 0.001p.
7. You are advised to check all relevant information with your chosen attraction before commencing your journey.

Days Out UK, PO Box 427, Northampton NN1 3YN. Tel: 01604 622445

1. Each voucher entitles the holder to the discount specified by the selected attraction.
2. Valid for use until 28/02/05 (unless otherwise specified, or if attraction season finishes prior to this). Vouchers are subject to the terms, conditions and restrictions of the selected attraction.
3. One voucher per party will be accepted, cannot be used in conjunction with any other offer, photocopies will not be accepted.
4. All attractions offering a discount have confirmed their willingness to participate. All information is subject to change without notice and should any attraction close or decline to accept a voucher for any reason, Days Out UK are not liable and cannot be held responsible.
5. Days Out UK shall not accept liability for any loss, accident or injury that may occur at a participating attraction and any dispute arising must be settled direct with the attraction concerned.
6. Cash redemption value of each voucher is 0.001p.
7. You are advised to check all relevant information with your chosen attraction before commencing your journey.

Days Out UK, PO Box 427, Northampton NN1 3YN. Tel: 01604 622445

1. Each voucher entitles the holder to the discount specified by the selected attraction.
2. Valid for use until 28/02/05 (unless otherwise specified, or if attraction season finishes prior to this). Vouchers are subject to the terms, conditions and restrictions of the selected attraction.
3. One voucher per party will be accepted, cannot be used in conjunction with any other offer, photocopies will not be accepted.
4. All attractions offering a discount have confirmed their willingness to participate. All information is subject to change without notice and should any attraction close or decline to accept a voucher for any reason, Days Out UK are not liable and cannot be held responsible.
5. Days Out UK shall not accept liability for any loss, accident or injury that may occur at a participating attraction and any dispute arising must be settled direct with the attraction concerned.
6. Cash redemption value of each voucher is 0.001p.
7. You are advised to check all relevant information with your chosen attraction before commencing your journey.

Days Out UK, PO Box 427, Northampton NN1 3YN. Tel: 01604 622445

Bignor Roman Villa and Museum

Bignor Lane Bignor Pulborough West Sussex

20% Discount

On Production Of Voucher

Not to be used in conjunction with any other offer. One voucher per party. Not valid on Bank Hols or special events

Valid until end Feb 2005

DISCOUNT VOUCHER

Brighton Sea Life Centre

Marine Parade Brighton Sussex BN2 1TB

One Child Free

With One Full Paying Adult

Not to be used in conjunction with any other offer. One voucher per party. Not valid on Bank Hols or special events

Valid until end Feb 2005

DISCOUNT VOUCHER

Buckleys Yesterday's World

80-90 High Street Battle Sussex TN33 0AQ

£0.50 Off Each Admission

Valid For Up To 6 People

Not to be used in conjunction with any other offer. One voucher per party. Not valid on Bank Hols or special events

Valid until end Feb 2005

DISCOUNT VOUCHER

Denmans Garden

Clock House Denmans Lane Fontwell Arundel Sussex

Two Full Paying Adults For The Price Of One

Excluding Weekends And Bank Holidays

Not to be used in conjunction with any other offer. One voucher per party. Not valid on Bank Hols or special events

Valid 1 Mar-31 Oct 2004

DISCOUNT VOUCHER

Knockhatch Adventure Park

Hempstead Lane Hailsham Sussex BN27 3PR

50p Off Park Entry Per Person

Not to be used in conjunction with any other offer. One voucher per party. Not valid on Bank Hols or special events

Valid until end Feb 2005

DISCOUNT VOUCHER

Paradise Park

Avis Road Newhaven East Sussex BN9 0DH

Two For The Price Of One

Not to be used in conjunction with any other offer. One voucher per party. Not valid on Bank Hols or special events

Valid until end Feb 2005

DISCOUNT VOUCHER

1. Each voucher entitles the holder to the discount specified by the selected attraction.
2. Valid for use until 28/02/05 (unless otherwise specified, or if attraction season finishes prior to this). Vouchers are subject to the terms, conditions and restrictions of the selected attraction.
3. One voucher per party will be accepted, cannot be used in conjunction with any other offer, photocopies will not be accepted.
4. All attractions offering a discount have confirmed their willingness to participate. All information is subject to change without notice and should any attraction close or decline to accept a voucher for any reason, Days Out UK are not liable and cannot be held responsible.
5. Days Out UK shall not accept liability for any loss, accident or injury that may occur at a participating attraction and any dispute arising must be settled direct with the attraction concerned.
6. Cash redemption value of each voucher is 0.001p.
7. You are advised to check all relevant information with your chosen attraction before commencing your journey.

Days Out UK, PO Box 427, Northampton NN1 3YN. Tel: 01604 622445

1. Each voucher entitles the holder to the discount specified by the selected attraction.
2. Valid for use until 28/02/05 (unless otherwise specified. or if attraction season finishes prior to this). Vouchers are subject to the terms, conditions and restrictions of the selected attraction.
3. One voucher per party will be accepted, cannot be used in conjunction with any other offer, photocopies will not be accepted.
4. All attractions offering a discount have confirmed their willingness to participate. All information is subject to change without notice and should any attraction close or decline to accept a voucher for any reason, Days Out UK are not liable and cannot be held responsible.
5. Days Out UK shall not accept liability for any loss, accident or injury that may occur at a participating attraction and any dispute arising must be settled direct with the attraction concerned.
6. Cash redemption value of each voucher is 0.001p.
7. You are advised to check all relevant information with your chosen attraction before commencing your journey.

Days Out UK, PO Box 427, Northampton NN1 3YN. Tel: 01604 622445

1. Each voucher entitles the holder to the discount specified by the selected attraction.
2. Valid for use until 28/02/05 (unless otherwise specified, or if attraction season finishes prior to this). Vouchers are subject to the terms, conditions and restrictions of the selected attraction.
3. One voucher per party will be accepted, cannot be used in conjunction with any other offer, photocopies will not be accepted.
4. All attractions offering a discount have confirmed their willingness to participate. All information is subject to change without notice and should any attraction close or decline to accept a voucher for any reason, Days Out UK are not liable and cannot be held responsible.
5. Days Out UK shall not accept liability for any loss, accident or injury that may occur at a participating attraction and any dispute arising must be settled direct with the attraction concerned.
6. Cash redemption value of each voucher is 0.001p.
7. You are advised to check all relevant information with your chosen attraction before commencing your journey.

Days Out UK, PO Box 427, Northampton NN1 3YN. Tel: 01604 622445

1. Each voucher entitles the holder to the discount specified by the selected attraction.
2. Valid for use until 28/02/05 (unless otherwise specified, or if attraction season finishes prior to this). Vouchers are subject to the terms, conditions and restrictions of the selected attraction.
3. One voucher per party will be accepted, cannot be used in conjunction with any other offer, photocopies will not be accepted.
4. All attractions offering a discount have confirmed their willingness to participate. All information is subject to change without notice and should any attraction close or decline to accept a voucher for any reason, Days Out UK are not liable and cannot be held responsible.
5. Days Out UK shall not accept liability for any loss, accident or injury that may occur at a participating attraction and any dispute arising must be settled direct with the attraction concerned.
6. Cash redemption value of each voucher is 0.001p.
7. You are advised to check all relevant information with your chosen attraction before commencing your journey.

Days Out UK, PO Box 427, Northampton NN1 3YN. Tel: 01604 622445

1. Each voucher entitles the holder to the discount specified by the selected attraction.
2. Valid for use until 28/02/05 (unless otherwise specified, or if attraction season finishes prior to this). Vouchers are subject to the terms, conditions and restrictions of the selected attraction.
3. One voucher per party will be accepted, cannot be used in conjunction with any other offer, photocopies will not be accepted.
4. All attractions offering a discount have confirmed their willingness to participate. All information is subject to change without notice and should any attraction close or decline to accept a voucher for any reason, Days Out UK are not liable and cannot be held responsible.
5. Days Out UK shall not accept liability for any loss, accident or injury that may occur at a participating attraction and any dispute arising must be settled direct with the attraction concerned.
6. Cash redemption value of each voucher is 0.001p.
7. You are advised to check all relevant information with your chosen attraction before commencing your journey.

Days Out UK, PO Box 427, Northampton NN1 3YN. Tel: 01604 622445

DAYS OUT UK
The place to look for places to go

DISCOUNT VOUCHER

Royal Pavilion
Brighton Sussex BN1 1EE
One Free Admission
With One Full Paying Adult
Not to be used in conjunction with any other offer. One voucher per party. Not valid on Bank Hols or special events
Valid until end Feb 2005

Please see page 457 for full attraction details

DAYS OUT UK
The place to look for places to go

DISCOUNT VOUCHER

Story of Rye
Rye Heritage Centre Strand Quay Rye Sussex
Two For The Price Of One
For Either The Story of Rye Or The Personal Stereo Tour
Not to be used in conjunction with any other offer. One voucher per party. Not valid on Bank Hols or special events
Valid until end Feb 2005

Please see page 453 for full attraction details

DAYS OUT UK
The place to look for places to go

DISCOUNT VOUCHER

West Dean Gardens
West Dean Chichester West Sussex PO18 8QZ
One Child Free
When One Adult Or OAP Ticket Purchased
Not to be used in conjunction with any other offer. One voucher per party. Not valid on Bank Hols or special events
Valid until end Oct 2004

Please see page 452 for full attraction details

DAYS OUT UK
The place to look for places to go

DISCOUNT VOUCHER

Blue Reef Aquarium
Grand Parade Tynemouth Tyne & Wear NE30 4JF
One Child Free
With One Full Paying Adult
Not to be used in conjunction with any other offer. One voucher per party. Not valid on Bank Hols or special events
Valid until end Feb 2005

Please see page 473 for full attraction details

DAYS OUT UK
The place to look for places to go

DISCOUNT VOUCHER

National Glass Centre
Liberty Way Sunderland Tyne & Wear SR6 0GL
One Person Free
With Every Full Paying Adult
Not to be used in conjunction with any other offer. One voucher per party. Not valid on Bank Hols or special events
Valid until end Feb 2005

Please see page 470 for full attraction details

DAYS OUT UK
The place to look for places to go

DISCOUNT VOUCHER

New Metroland
39 Garden Walk Metrocentre Gateshead Tyne & Wear
Buy One Get One For £1.50
On A Gold All Day Pass
Not to be used in conjunction with any other offer. One voucher per party. Not valid on Bank Hols or special events
Valid until end Feb 2005

Please see page 474 for full attraction details

1. Each voucher entitles the holder to the discount specified by the selected attraction.
2. Valid for use until 28/02/05 (unless otherwise specified, or if attraction season finishes prior to this). Vouchers are subject to the terms, conditions and restrictions of the selected attraction.
3. One voucher per party will be accepted, cannot be used in conjunction with any other offer, photocopies will not be accepted.
4. All attractions offering a discount have confirmed their willingness to participate. All information is subject to change without notice and should any attraction close or decline to accept a voucher for any reason, Days Out UK are not liable and cannot be held responsible.
5. Days Out UK shall not accept liability for any loss, accident or injury that may occur at a participating attraction and any dispute arising must be settled direct with the attraction concerned.
6. Cash redemption value of each voucher is 0.001p.
7. You are advised to check all relevant information with your chosen attraction before commencing your journey.

Days Out UK, PO Box 427, Northampton NN1 3YN. Tel: 01604 622445

1. Each voucher entitles the holder to the discount specified by the selected attraction.
2. Valid for use until 28/02/05 (unless otherwise specified. or if attraction season finishes prior to this). Vouchers are subject to the terms, conditions and restrictions of the selected attraction.
3. One voucher per party will be accepted, cannot be used in conjunction with any other offer, photocopies will not be accepted.
4. All attractions offering a discount have confirmed their willingness to participate. All information is subject to change without notice and should any attraction close or decline to accept a voucher for any reason, Days Out UK are not liable and cannot be held responsible.
5. Days Out UK shall not accept liability for any loss, accident or injury that may occur at a participating attraction and any dispute arising must be settled direct with the attraction concerned.
6. Cash redemption value of each voucher is 0.001p.
7. You are advised to check all relevant information with your chosen attraction before commencing your journey.

Days Out UK, PO Box 427, Northampton NN1 3YN. Tel: 01604 622445

1. Each voucher entitles the holder to the discount specified by the selected attraction.
2. Valid for use until 28/02/05 (unless otherwise specified, or if attraction season finishes prior to this). Vouchers are subject to the terms, conditions and restrictions of the selected attraction.
3. One voucher per party will be accepted, cannot be used in conjunction with any other offer, photocopies will not be accepted.
4. All attractions offering a discount have confirmed their willingness to participate. All information is subject to change without notice and should any attraction close or decline to accept a voucher for any reason, Days Out UK are not liable and cannot be held responsible.
5. Days Out UK shall not accept liability for any loss, accident or injury that may occur at a participating attraction and any dispute arising must be settled direct with the attraction concerned.
6. Cash redemption value of each voucher is 0.001p.
7. You are advised to check all relevant information with your chosen attraction before commencing your journey.

Days Out UK, PO Box 427, Northampton NN1 3YN. Tel: 01604 622445

1. Each voucher entitles the holder to the discount specified by the selected attraction.
2. Valid for use until 28/02/05 (unless otherwise specified, or if attraction season finishes prior to this). Vouchers are subject to the terms, conditions and restrictions of the selected attraction.
3. One voucher per party will be accepted, cannot be used in conjunction with any other offer, photocopies will not be accepted.
4. All attractions offering a discount have confirmed their willingness to participate. All information is subject to change without notice and should any attraction close or decline to accept a voucher for any reason, Days Out UK are not liable and cannot be held responsible.
5. Days Out UK shall not accept liability for any loss, accident or injury that may occur at a participating attraction and any dispute arising must be settled direct with the attraction concerned.
6. Cash redemption value of each voucher is 0.001p.
7. You are advised to check all relevant information with your chosen attraction before commencing your journey.

Days Out UK, PO Box 427, Northampton NN1 3YN. Tel: 01604 622445

1. Each voucher entitles the holder to the discount specified by the selected attraction.
2. Valid for use until 28/02/05 (unless otherwise specified, or if attraction season finishes prior to this). Vouchers are subject to the terms, conditions and restrictions of the selected attraction.
3. One voucher per party will be accepted, cannot be used in conjunction with any other offer, photocopies will not be accepted.
4. All attractions offering a discount have confirmed their willingness to participate. All information is subject to change without notice and should any attraction close or decline to accept a voucher for any reason, Days Out UK are not liable and cannot be held responsible.
5. Days Out UK shall not accept liability for any loss, accident or injury that may occur at a participating attraction and any dispute arising must be settled direct with the attraction concerned.
6. Cash redemption value of each voucher is 0.001p.
7. You are advised to check all relevant information with your chosen attraction before commencing your journey.

Days Out UK, PO Box 427, Northampton NN1 3YN. Tel: 01604 622445

DAYSOUTUK
The place to look for places to go

Please see page 492
for full attraction
details

Anglesey Sea Zoo
Brynsiencyn Llanfairpwllgwyngyll Anglesey LL61 6TQ
One Child Free
For Every Two Full Paying Adults

Not to be used in conjunction with any other offer. One voucher per party. Not valid on Bank Hols or special events

Valid until end Feb 2005

DISCOUNT VOUCHER

DAYSOUTUK
The place to look for places to go

Please see page 478
for full attraction
details

Felinwynt Rainforest and Butterfly Centre
Felinwynt Cardigan Ceredigion SA43 1RT
Two For The Price Of One

Not to be used in conjunction with any other offer. One voucher per party. Not valid on Bank Hols or special events

Valid until end Feb 2005

DISCOUNT VOUCHER

DAYSOUTUK
The place to look for places to go

Please see page 483
for full attraction
details

Glansevern Hall Gardens
Berriew Welshpool Powys SY21 8AH
Three For The Price Of Two

Not to be used in conjunction with any other offer. One voucher per party. Not valid on Bank Hols or special events

Valid until end Feb 2005

DISCOUNT VOUCHER

DAYSOUTUK
The place to look for places to go

Please see page 476
for full attraction
details

Greenmeadow Community Farm
Greenforge Way Cwmbran Gwent NP44 5AJ
One Child Free
With A Full Paying Adult. One Discount Per Family

Not to be used in conjunction with any other offer. One voucher per party. Not valid on Bank Hols or special events

Valid until end Feb 2005

DISCOUNT VOUCHER

DAYSOUTUK
The place to look for places to go

Please see page 490
for full attraction
details

Gwili Steam Railway
Bronwydd Arms Station Bronwydd Carmarthen
One Child Free
With A Full Paying Adult

Not to be used in conjunction with any other offer. One voucher per party. Not valid on Bank Hols or special events

Valid until end Feb 2005

DISCOUNT VOUCHER

DAYSOUTUK
The place to look for places to go

Please see page 494
for full attraction
details

Judge's Lodging
Broad Street Presteigne Powys LD8 2AD
Two For The Price Of One

Not to be used in conjunction with any other offer. One voucher per party. Not valid on Bank Hols or special events

Valid until 22 Dec 2004

DISCOUNT VOUCHER

1. Each voucher entitles the holder to the discount specified by the selected attraction.
2. Valid for use until 28/02/05 (unless otherwise specified, or if attraction season finishes prior to this). Vouchers are subject to the terms, conditions and restrictions of the selected attraction.
3. One voucher per party will be accepted, cannot be used in conjunction with any other offer, photocopies will not be accepted.
4. All attractions offering a discount have confirmed their willingness to participate. All information is subject to change without notice and should any attraction close or decline to accept a voucher for any reason, Days Out UK are not liable and cannot be held responsible.
5. Days Out UK shall not accept liability for any loss, accident or injury that may occur at a participating attraction and any dispute arising must be settled direct with the attraction concerned.
6. Cash redemption value of each voucher is 0.001p.
7. You are advised to check all relevant information with your chosen attraction before commencing your journey.

Days Out UK, PO Box 427, Northampton NN1 3YN. Tel: 01604 622445

1. Each voucher entitles the holder to the discount specified by the selected attraction.
2. Valid for use until 28/02/05 (unless otherwise specified. or if attraction season finishes prior to this). Vouchers are subject to the terms, conditions and restrictions of the selected attraction.
3. One voucher per party will be accepted, cannot be used in conjunction with any other offer, photocopies will not be accepted.
4. All attractions offering a discount have confirmed their willingness to participate. All information is subject to change without notice and should any attraction close or decline to accept a voucher for any reason, Days Out UK are not liable and cannot be held responsible.
5. Days Out UK shall not accept liability for any loss, accident or injury that may occur at a participating attraction and any dispute arising must be settled direct with the attraction concerned.
6. Cash redemption value of each voucher is 0.001p.
7. You are advised to check all relevant information with your chosen attraction before commencing your journey.

Days Out UK, PO Box 427, Northampton NN1 3YN. Tel: 01604 622445

1. Each voucher entitles the holder to the discount specified by the selected attraction.
2. Valid for use until 28/02/05 (unless otherwise specified, or if attraction season finishes prior to this). Vouchers are subject to the terms, conditions and restrictions of the selected attraction.
3. One voucher per party will be accepted, cannot be used in conjunction with any other offer, photocopies will not be accepted.
4. All attractions offering a discount have confirmed their willingness to participate. All information is subject to change without notice and should any attraction close or decline to accept a voucher for any reason, Days Out UK are not liable and cannot be held responsible.
5. Days Out UK shall not accept liability for any loss, accident or injury that may occur at a participating attraction and any dispute arising must be settled direct with the attraction concerned.
6. Cash redemption value of each voucher is 0.001p.
7. You are advised to check all relevant information with your chosen attraction before commencing your journey.

Days Out UK, PO Box 427, Northampton NN1 3YN. Tel: 01604 622445

1. Each voucher entitles the holder to the discount specified by the selected attraction.
2. Valid for use until 28/02/05 (unless otherwise specified, or if attraction season finishes prior to this). Vouchers are subject to the terms, conditions and restrictions of the selected attraction.
3. One voucher per party will be accepted, cannot be used in conjunction with any other offer, photocopies will not be accepted.
4. All attractions offering a discount have confirmed their willingness to participate. All information is subject to change without notice and should any attraction close or decline to accept a voucher for any reason, Days Out UK are not liable and cannot be held responsible.
5. Days Out UK shall not accept liability for any loss, accident or injury that may occur at a participating attraction and any dispute arising must be settled direct with the attraction concerned.
6. Cash redemption value of each voucher is 0.001p.
7. You are advised to check all relevant information with your chosen attraction before commencing your journey.

Days Out UK, PO Box 427, Northampton NN1 3YN. Tel: 01604 622445

1. Each voucher entitles the holder to the discount specified by the selected attraction.
2. Valid for use until 28/02/05 (unless otherwise specified, or if attraction season finishes prior to this). Vouchers are subject to the terms, conditions and restrictions of the selected attraction.
3. One voucher per party will be accepted, cannot be used in conjunction with any other offer, photocopies will not be accepted.
4. All attractions offering a discount have confirmed their willingness to participate. All information is subject to change without notice and should any attraction close or decline to accept a voucher for any reason, Days Out UK are not liable and cannot be held responsible.
5. Days Out UK shall not accept liability for any loss, accident or injury that may occur at a participating attraction and any dispute arising must be settled direct with the attraction concerned.
6. Cash redemption value of each voucher is 0.001p.
7. You are advised to check all relevant information with your chosen attraction before commencing your journey.

Days Out UK, PO Box 427, Northampton NN1 3YN. Tel: 01604 622445

1. Each voucher entitles the holder to the discount specified by the selected attraction.
2. Valid for use until 28/02/05 (unless otherwise specified, or if attraction season finishes prior to this). Vouchers are subject to the terms, conditions and restrictions of the selected attraction.
3. One voucher per party will be accepted, cannot be used in conjunction with any other offer, photocopies will not be accepted.
4. All attractions offering a discount have confirmed their willingness to participate. All information is subject to change without notice and should any attraction close or decline to accept a voucher for any reason, Days Out UK are not liable and cannot be held responsible.
5. Days Out UK shall not accept liability for any loss, accident or injury that may occur at a participating attraction and any dispute arising must be settled direct with the attraction concerned.
6. Cash redemption value of each voucher is 0.001p.
7. You are advised to check all relevant information with your chosen attraction before commencing your journey.

Days Out UK, PO Box 427, Northampton NN1 3YN. Tel: 01604 622445

1. Each voucher entitles the holder to the discount specified by the selected attraction.
2. Valid for use until 28/02/05 (unless otherwise specified, or if attraction season finishes prior to this). Vouchers are subject to the terms, conditions and restrictions of the selected attraction.
3. One voucher per party will be accepted, cannot be used in conjunction with any other offer, photocopies will not be accepted.
4. All attractions offering a discount have confirmed their willingness to participate. All information is subject to change without notice and should any attraction close or decline to accept a voucher for any reason, Days Out UK are not liable and cannot be held responsible.
5. Days Out UK shall not accept liability for any loss, accident or injury that may occur at a participating attraction and any dispute arising must be settled direct with the attraction concerned.
6. Cash redemption value of each voucher is 0.001p.
7. You are advised to check all relevant information with your chosen attraction before commencing your journey.

Days Out UK, PO Box 427, Northampton NN1 3YN. Tel: 01604 622445

1. Each voucher entitles the holder to the discount specified by the selected attraction.
2. Valid for use until 28/02/05 (unless otherwise specified, or if attraction season finishes prior to this). Vouchers are subject to the terms, conditions and restrictions of the selected attraction.
3. One voucher per party will be accepted, cannot be used in conjunction with any other offer, photocopies will not be accepted.
4. All attractions offering a discount have confirmed their willingness to participate. All information is subject to change without notice and should any attraction close or decline to accept a voucher for any reason, Days Out UK are not liable and cannot be held responsible.
5. Days Out UK shall not accept liability for any loss, accident or injury that may occur at a participating attraction and any dispute arising must be settled direct with the attraction concerned.
6. Cash redemption value of each voucher is 0.001p.
7. You are advised to check all relevant information with your chosen attraction before commencing your journey.

Days Out UK, PO Box 427, Northampton NN1 3YN. Tel: 01604 622445

1. Each voucher entitles the holder to the discount specified by the selected attraction.
2. Valid for use until 28/02/05 (unless otherwise specified, or if attraction season finishes prior to this). Vouchers are subject to the terms, conditions and restrictions of the selected attraction.
3. One voucher per party will be accepted, cannot be used in conjunction with any other offer, photocopies will not be accepted.
4. All attractions offering a discount have confirmed their willingness to participate. All information is subject to change without notice and should any attraction close or decline to accept a voucher for any reason, Days Out UK are not liable and cannot be held responsible.
5. Days Out UK shall not accept liability for any loss, accident or injury that may occur at a participating attraction and any dispute arising must be settled direct with the attraction concerned.
6. Cash redemption value of each voucher is 0.001p.
7. You are advised to check all relevant information with your chosen attraction before commencing your journey.

Days Out UK, PO Box 427, Northampton NN1 3YN. Tel: 01604 622445

1. Each voucher entitles the holder to the discount specified by the selected attraction.
2. Valid for use until 28/02/05 (unless otherwise specified, or if attraction season finishes prior to this). Vouchers are subject to the terms, conditions and restrictions of the selected attraction.
3. One voucher per party will be accepted, cannot be used in conjunction with any other offer, photocopies will not be accepted.
4. All attractions offering a discount have confirmed their willingness to participate. All information is subject to change without notice and should any attraction close or decline to accept a voucher for any reason, Days Out UK are not liable and cannot be held responsible.
5. Days Out UK shall not accept liability for any loss, accident or injury that may occur at a participating attraction and any dispute arising must be settled direct with the attraction concerned.
6. Cash redemption value of each voucher is 0.001p.
7. You are advised to check all relevant information with your chosen attraction before commencing your journey.

Days Out UK, PO Box 427, Northampton NN1 3YN. Tel: 01604 622445

Teddy Bear Museum

19 Greenhill Street Stratford-Upon-Avon Warwickshire

One Child Free

With One Full Paying Adult

Not to be used in conjunction with any other offer. One voucher per party. Not valid on Bank Hols or special events

Valid until end Feb 2005

DISCOUNT VOUCHER

Twycross Zoo Park

Atherstone Warwickshire CV9 3PX

One Child Free

With Two Adults Paying Full Price

Not to be used in conjunction with any other offer. One voucher per party. Not valid on Bank Hols or special events

Valid until end Feb 2005

DISCOUNT VOUCHER

Birmingham Botanical Gardens and Glasshouses

Westbourne Road Edgbaston Birmingham B15 3TR

Admission At Group Rate With Voucher

Not to be used in conjunction with any other offer. One voucher per party. Not valid on Bank Hols or special events

Valid until end Feb 2005

DISCOUNT VOUCHER

Broadfield House Glass Museum

Compton Drive Kingswinford West Midlands DY6 9NS

10% Discount Off Shop Purchases

Not to be used in conjunction with any other offer. One voucher per party. Not valid on Bank Hols or special events

Valid until end Feb 2005

DISCOUNT VOUCHER

Castle Bromwich Hall Gardens

Chester Road Castle Bromwich West Midlands

Two For The Price Of One

NOT VALID On Event Days

Not to be used in conjunction with any other offer. One voucher per party. Not valid on Bank Hols or special events

Valid until end Oct 2004

DISCOUNT VOUCHER

National Sea Life Centre

The Waters Edge Brindleyplace Birmingham B1 2HL

Two Children Free

With One Full Paying Adult. Ref: DAYUK04

Not to be used in conjunction with any other offer. One voucher per party. Not valid on Bank Hols or special events

Valid until end Dec 2004

DISCOUNT VOUCHER

1. Each voucher entitles the holder to the discount specified by the selected attraction.
2. Valid for use until 28/02/05 (unless otherwise specified, or if attraction season finishes prior to this). Vouchers are subject to the terms, conditions and restrictions of the selected attraction.
3. One voucher per party will be accepted, cannot be used in conjunction with any other offer, photocopies will not be accepted.
4. All attractions offering a discount have confirmed their willingness to participate. All information is subject to change without notice and should any attraction close or decline to accept a voucher for any reason, Days Out UK are not liable and cannot be held responsible.
5. Days Out UK shall not accept liability for any loss, accident or injury that may occur at a participating attraction and any dispute arising must be settled direct with the attraction concerned.
6. Cash redemption value of each voucher is 0.001p.
7. You are advised to check all relevant information with your chosen attraction before commencing your journey.

Days Out UK, PO Box 427, Northampton NN1 3YN. Tel: 01604 622445

1. Each voucher entitles the holder to the discount specified by the selected attraction.
2. Valid for use until 28/02/05 (unless otherwise specified, or if attraction season finishes prior to this). Vouchers are subject to the terms, conditions and restrictions of the selected attraction.
3. One voucher per party will be accepted, cannot be used in conjunction with any other offer, photocopies will not be accepted.
4. All attractions offering a discount have confirmed their willingness to participate. All information is subject to change without notice and should any attraction close or decline to accept a voucher for any reason, Days Out UK are not liable and cannot be held responsible.
5. Days Out UK shall not accept liability for any loss, accident or injury that may occur at a participating attraction and any dispute arising must be settled direct with the attraction concerned.
6. Cash redemption value of each voucher is 0.001p.
7. You are advised to check all relevant information with your chosen attraction before commencing your journey.

Days Out UK, PO Box 427, Northampton NN1 3YN. Tel: 01604 622445

1. Each voucher entitles the holder to the discount specified by the selected attraction.
2. Valid for use until 28/02/05 (unless otherwise specified, or if attraction season finishes prior to this). Vouchers are subject to the terms, conditions and restrictions of the selected attraction.
3. One voucher per party will be accepted, cannot be used in conjunction with any other offer, photocopies will not be accepted.
4. All attractions offering a discount have confirmed their willingness to participate. All information is subject to change without notice and should any attraction close or decline to accept a voucher for any reason, Days Out UK are not liable and cannot be held responsible.
5. Days Out UK shall not accept liability for any loss, accident or injury that may occur at a participating attraction and any dispute arising must be settled direct with the attraction concerned.
6. Cash redemption value of each voucher is 0.001p.
7. You are advised to check all relevant information with your chosen attraction before commencing your journey.

Days Out UK, PO Box 427, Northampton NN1 3YN. Tel: 01604 622445

1. Each voucher entitles the holder to the discount specified by the selected attraction.
2. Valid for use until 28/02/05 (unless otherwise specified, or if attraction season finishes prior to this). Vouchers are subject to the terms, conditions and restrictions of the selected attraction.
3. One voucher per party will be accepted, cannot be used in conjunction with any other offer, photocopies will not be accepted.
4. All attractions offering a discount have confirmed their willingness to participate. All information is subject to change without notice and should any attraction close or decline to accept a voucher for any reason, Days Out UK are not liable and cannot be held responsible.
5. Days Out UK shall not accept liability for any loss, accident or injury that may occur at a participating attraction and any dispute arising must be settled direct with the attraction concerned.
6. Cash redemption value of each voucher is 0.001p.
7. You are advised to check all relevant information with your chosen attraction before commencing your journey.

Days Out UK, PO Box 427, Northampton NN1 3YN. Tel: 01604 622445

1. Each voucher entitles the holder to the discount specified by the selected attraction.
2. Valid for use until 28/02/05 (unless otherwise specified, or if attraction season finishes prior to this). Vouchers are subject to the terms, conditions and restrictions of the selected attraction.
3. One voucher per party will be accepted, cannot be used in conjunction with any other offer, photocopies will not be accepted.
4. All attractions offering a discount have confirmed their willingness to participate. All information is subject to change without notice and should any attraction close or decline to accept a voucher for any reason, Days Out UK are not liable and cannot be held responsible.
5. Days Out UK shall not accept liability for any loss, accident or injury that may occur at a participating attraction and any dispute arising must be settled direct with the attraction concerned.
6. Cash redemption value of each voucher is 0.001p.
7. You are advised to check all relevant information with your chosen attraction before commencing your journey.

Days Out UK, PO Box 427, Northampton NN1 3YN. Tel: 01604 622445

1. Each voucher entitles the holder to the discount specified by the selected attraction.
2. Valid for use until 28/02/05 (unless otherwise specified, or if attraction season finishes prior to this). Vouchers are subject to the terms, conditions and restrictions of the selected attraction.
3. One voucher per party will be accepted, cannot be used in conjunction with any other offer, photocopies will not be accepted.
4. All attractions offering a discount have confirmed their willingness to participate. All information is subject to change without notice and should any attraction close or decline to accept a voucher for any reason, Days Out UK are not liable and cannot be held responsible.
5. Days Out UK shall not accept liability for any loss, accident or injury that may occur at a participating attraction and any dispute arising must be settled direct with the attraction concerned.
6. Cash redemption value of each voucher is 0.001p.
7. You are advised to check all relevant information with your chosen attraction before commencing your journey.

Days Out UK, PO Box 427, Northampton NN1 3YN. Tel: 01604 622445

DISCOUNT VOUCHER

Lackham Country Park
Wiltshire College Lackham Lacock Wiltshire
Two Children Free
With Each Full Paying Accompanying Adult
Not to be used in conjunction with any other offer. One voucher per party. Not valid on Bank Hols or special events
Valid May-Aug 2004

Please see page 517 for full attraction details

DISCOUNT VOUCHER

Wilton House
Wilton Salisbury Wiltshire SP2 0BJ
Two For The Price Of One
Applies To Adult House & Grounds Tickets Only
Not to be used in conjunction with any other offer. One voucher per party. Not valid on Bank Hols or special events
Valid until end Feb 2005

Please see page 519 for full attraction details

DISCOUNT VOUCHER

Avoncroft Museum of Historic Buildings
Stoke Heath Bromsgrove Worcestershire
One Child Free With Full Paying Adult
OR £2.00 Off A 2nd Full Paying Adult
Not to be used in conjunction with any other offer. One voucher per party. Not valid on Bank Hols or special events
Valid until end Feb 2005

Please see page 524 for full attraction details

DISCOUNT VOUCHER

Burford House Gardens
Tenbury Wells Worcestershire WR15 8HQ
Two For The Price Of One
Into The Gardens
Not to be used in conjunction with any other offer. One voucher per party. Not valid on Bank Hols or special events
Valid until end Feb 2005

Please see page 526 for full attraction details

DISCOUNT VOUCHER

The Commandery
Sidbury Worcester Worcestershire WR1 2HU
One Child Free
With Every Full Paying Adult
Not to be used in conjunction with any other offer. One voucher per party. Not valid on Bank Hols or special events
Valid until end Feb 2005

Please see page 527 for full attraction details

DISCOUNT VOUCHER

Royal Worcester Visitor Centre
Severn Street Worcester Worcestershire WR1 2NE
Two For The Price Of One
Admission To Visitor Attractions, Pre-booking Advised For Tours
Not to be used in conjunction with any other offer. One voucher per party. Not valid on Bank Hols or special events
Valid until end Feb 2005

Please see page 524 for full attraction details

1. Each voucher entitles the holder to the discount specified by the selected attraction.
2. Valid for use until 28/02/05 (unless otherwise specified, or if attraction season finishes prior to this). Vouchers are subject to the terms, conditions and restrictions of the selected attraction.
3. One voucher per party will be accepted, cannot be used in conjunction with any other offer, photocopies will not be accepted.
4. All attractions offering a discount have confirmed their willingness to participate. All information is subject to change without notice and should any attraction close or decline to accept a voucher for any reason, Days Out UK are not liable and cannot be held responsible.
5. Days Out UK shall not accept liability for any loss, accident or injury that may occur at a participating attraction and any dispute arising must be settled direct with the attraction concerned.
6. Cash redemption value of each voucher is 0.001p.
7. You are advised to check all relevant information with your chosen attraction before commencing your journey.

Days Out UK, PO Box 427, Northampton NN1 3YN. Tel: 01604 622445

1. Each voucher entitles the holder to the discount specified by the selected attraction.
2. Valid for use until 28/02/05 (unless otherwise specified, or if attraction season finishes prior to this). Vouchers are subject to the terms, conditions and restrictions of the selected attraction.
3. One voucher per party will be accepted, cannot be used in conjunction with any other offer, photocopies will not be accepted.
4. All attractions offering a discount have confirmed their willingness to participate. All information is subject to change without notice and should any attraction close or decline to accept a voucher for any reason, Days Out UK are not liable and cannot be held responsible.
5. Days Out UK shall not accept liability for any loss, accident or injury that may occur at a participating attraction and any dispute arising must be settled direct with the attraction concerned.
6. Cash redemption value of each voucher is 0.001p.
7. You are advised to check all relevant information with your chosen attraction before commencing your journey.

Days Out UK, PO Box 427, Northampton NN1 3YN. Tel: 01604 622445

1. Each voucher entitles the holder to the discount specified by the selected attraction.
2. Valid for use until 28/02/05 (unless otherwise specified, or if attraction season finishes prior to this). Vouchers are subject to the terms, conditions and restrictions of the selected attraction.
3. One voucher per party will be accepted, cannot be used in conjunction with any other offer, photocopies will not be accepted.
4. All attractions offering a discount have confirmed their willingness to participate. All information is subject to change without notice and should any attraction close or decline to accept a voucher for any reason, Days Out UK are not liable and cannot be held responsible.
5. Days Out UK shall not accept liability for any loss, accident or injury that may occur at a participating attraction and any dispute arising must be settled direct with the attraction concerned.
6. Cash redemption value of each voucher is 0.001p.
7. You are advised to check all relevant information with your chosen attraction before commencing your journey.

Days Out UK, PO Box 427, Northampton NN1 3YN. Tel: 01604 622445

1. Each voucher entitles the holder to the discount specified by the selected attraction.
2. Valid for use until 28/02/05 (unless otherwise specified, or if attraction season finishes prior to this). Vouchers are subject to the terms, conditions and restrictions of the selected attraction.
3. One voucher per party will be accepted, cannot be used in conjunction with any other offer, photocopies will not be accepted.
4. All attractions offering a discount have confirmed their willingness to participate. All information is subject to change without notice and should any attraction close or decline to accept a voucher for any reason, Days Out UK are not liable and cannot be held responsible.
5. Days Out UK shall not accept liability for any loss, accident or injury that may occur at a participating attraction and any dispute arising must be settled direct with the attraction concerned.
6. Cash redemption value of each voucher is 0.001p.
7. You are advised to check all relevant information with your chosen attraction before commencing your journey.

Days Out UK, PO Box 427, Northampton NN1 3YN. Tel: 01604 622445

1. Each voucher entitles the holder to the discount specified by the selected attraction.
2. Valid for use until 28/02/05 (unless otherwise specified, or if attraction season finishes prior to this). Vouchers are subject to the terms, conditions and restrictions of the selected attraction.
3. One voucher per party will be accepted, cannot be used in conjunction with any other offer, photocopies will not be accepted.
4. All attractions offering a discount have confirmed their willingness to participate. All information is subject to change without notice and should any attraction close or decline to accept a voucher for any reason, Days Out UK are not liable and cannot be held responsible.
5. Days Out UK shall not accept liability for any loss, accident or injury that may occur at a participating attraction and any dispute arising must be settled direct with the attraction concerned.
6. Cash redemption value of each voucher is 0.001p.
7. You are advised to check all relevant information with your chosen attraction before commencing your journey.

Days Out UK, PO Box 427, Northampton NN1 3YN. Tel: 01604 622445

1. Each voucher entitles the holder to the discount specified by the selected attraction.
2. Valid for use until 28/02/05 (unless otherwise specified, or if attraction season finishes prior to this). Vouchers are subject to the terms, conditions and restrictions of the selected attraction.
3. One voucher per party will be accepted, cannot be used in conjunction with any other offer, photocopies will not be accepted.
4. All attractions offering a discount have confirmed their willingness to participate. All information is subject to change without notice and should any attraction close or decline to accept a voucher for any reason, Days Out UK are not liable and cannot be held responsible.
5. Days Out UK shall not accept liability for any loss, accident or injury that may occur at a participating attraction and any dispute arising must be settled direct with the attraction concerned.
6. Cash redemption value of each voucher is 0.001p.
7. You are advised to check all relevant information with your chosen attraction before commencing your journey.

Days Out UK, PO Box 427, Northampton NN1 3YN. Tel: 01604 622445

Blue-John Cavern and Mine

Buxton Road Castleton Sheffield Yorkshire S30 2WP

One Child Free

With Every Full Paying Adult

Please see page 535 for full attraction details

Not to be used in conjunction with any other offer. One voucher per party. Not valid on Bank Hols or special events

Valid until end Feb 2005

DISCOUNT VOUCHER

Castle Howard

York Yorkshire YO60 7DA

Two Children Free

When Accompanied By Two Full Paying Adults
To The House & Grounds

Please see page 543 for full attraction details

Not to be used in conjunction with any other offer. One voucher per party. Not valid on Bank Hols or special events

Valid 14 Feb-31 Oct 2004

DISCOUNT VOUCHER

Harewood House and Bird Garden

Harewood Leeds West Yorkshire LS17 9LQ

One Child Free

With A Full Paying Adult. Ref: 103

Please see page 544 for full attraction details

Not to be used in conjunction with any other offer. One voucher per party. Not valid on Bank Hols or special events

Valid Mon-Sat until 2 Nov 2004

DISCOUNT VOUCHER

Kirklees Light Railway

Park Mill Way Clayton West Huddersfield Yorkshire

One Free Child With One Full Paying Adult

Valid With One Voucher When You Take A 50min Return Trip On
Yorkshire's Great Little Steam Train. Not Valid For Special Events

Please see page 553 for full attraction details

Not to be used in conjunction with any other offer. One voucher per party. Not valid on Bank Hols or special events

Valid until end Dec 2004

DISCOUNT VOUCHER

Lightwater Valley Theme Park

North Stainley Ripon Yorkshire

One Guest Admitted Free When Accompanied By Two Full Paying Guests

Excludes Bank Holiday Weekends, August, Family Ticket &
Group Rates. Confirm Opening Times on 0870 458 0040

Please see page 558 for full attraction details

Not to be used in conjunction with any other offer. One voucher per party. Not valid on Bank Hols or special events

Valid until end Oct 2004

DISCOUNT VOUCHER

Metrodome Leisure Complex

Queens Ground Barnsley South Yorkshire

Two For One Swim

Please see page 557 for full attraction details

Not to be used in conjunction with any other offer. One voucher per party. Not valid on Bank Hols or special events

Valid Tues 16.00-21.00 until end Feb 2005

DISCOUNT VOUCHER

1. Each voucher entitles the holder to the discount specified by the selected attraction.
2. Valid for use until 28/02/05 (unless otherwise specified, or if attraction season finishes prior to this). Vouchers are subject to the terms, conditions and restrictions of the selected attraction.
3. One voucher per party will be accepted, cannot be used in conjunction with any other offer, photocopies will not be accepted.
4. All attractions offering a discount have confirmed their willingness to participate. All information is subject to change without notice and should any attraction close or decline to accept a voucher for any reason, Days Out UK are not liable and cannot be held responsible.
5. Days Out UK shall not accept liability for any loss, accident or injury that may occur at a participating attraction and any dispute arising must be settled direct with the attraction concerned.
6. Cash redemption value of each voucher is 0.001p.
7. You are advised to check all relevant information with your chosen attraction before commencing your journey.

Days Out UK, PO Box 427, Northampton NN1 3YN. Tel: 01604 622445

1. Each voucher entitles the holder to the discount specified by the selected attraction.
2. Valid for use until 28/02/05 (unless otherwise specified, or if attraction season finishes prior to this). Vouchers are subject to the terms, conditions and restrictions of the selected attraction.
3. One voucher per party will be accepted, cannot be used in conjunction with any other offer, photocopies will not be accepted.
4. All attractions offering a discount have confirmed their willingness to participate. All information is subject to change without notice and should any attraction close or decline to accept a voucher for any reason, Days Out UK are not liable and cannot be held responsible.
5. Days Out UK shall not accept liability for any loss, accident or injury that may occur at a participating attraction and any dispute arising must be settled direct with the attraction concerned.
6. Cash redemption value of each voucher is 0.001p.
7. You are advised to check all relevant information with your chosen attraction before commencing your journey.

Days Out UK, PO Box 427, Northampton NN1 3YN. Tel: 01604 622445

1. Each voucher entitles the holder to the discount specified by the selected attraction.
2. Valid for use until 28/02/05 (unless otherwise specified. or if attraction season finishes prior to this). Vouchers are subject to the terms, conditions and restrictions of the selected attraction.
3. One voucher per party will be accepted, cannot be used in conjunction with any other offer, photocopies will not be accepted.
4. All attractions offering a discount have confirmed their willingness to participate. All information is subject to change without notice and should any attraction close or decline to accept a voucher for any reason, Days Out UK are not liable and cannot be held responsible.
5. Days Out UK shall not accept liability for any loss, accident or injury that may occur at a participating attraction and any dispute arising must be settled direct with the attraction concerned.
6. Cash redemption value of each voucher is 0.001p.
7. You are advised to check all relevant information with your chosen attraction before commencing your journey.

Days Out UK, PO Box 427, Northampton NN1 3YN. Tel: 01604 622445

1. Each voucher entitles the holder to the discount specified by the selected attraction.
2. Valid for use until 28/02/05 (unless otherwise specified, or if attraction season finishes prior to this). Vouchers are subject to the terms, conditions and restrictions of the selected attraction.
3. One voucher per party will be accepted, cannot be used in conjunction with any other offer, photocopies will not be accepted.
4. All attractions offering a discount have confirmed their willingness to participate. All information is subject to change without notice and should any attraction close or decline to accept a voucher for any reason, Days Out UK are not liable and cannot be held responsible.
5. Days Out UK shall not accept liability for any loss, accident or injury that may occur at a participating attraction and any dispute arising must be settled direct with the attraction concerned.
6. Cash redemption value of each voucher is 0.001p.
7. You are advised to check all relevant information with your chosen attraction before commencing your journey.

Days Out UK, PO Box 427, Northampton NN1 3YN. Tel: 01604 622445

1. Each voucher entitles the holder to the discount specified by the selected attraction.
2. Valid for use until 28/02/05 (unless otherwise specified, or if attraction season finishes prior to this). Vouchers are subject to the terms, conditions and restrictions of the selected attraction.
3. One voucher per party will be accepted, cannot be used in conjunction with any other offer, photocopies will not be accepted.
4. All attractions offering a discount have confirmed their willingness to participate. All information is subject to change without notice and should any attraction close or decline to accept a voucher for any reason, Days Out UK are not liable and cannot be held responsible.
5. Days Out UK shall not accept liability for any loss, accident or injury that may occur at a participating attraction and any dispute arising must be settled direct with the attraction concerned.
6. Cash redemption value of each voucher is 0.001p.
7. You are advised to check all relevant information with your chosen attraction before commencing your journey.

Days Out UK, PO Box 427, Northampton NN1 3YN. Tel: 01604 622445

1. Each voucher entitles the holder to the discount specified by the selected attraction.
2. Valid for use until 28/02/05 (unless otherwise specified, or if attraction season finishes prior to this). Vouchers are subject to the terms, conditions and restrictions of the selected attraction.
3. One voucher per party will be accepted, cannot be used in conjunction with any other offer, photocopies will not be accepted.
4. All attractions offering a discount have confirmed their willingness to participate. All information is subject to change without notice and should any attraction close or decline to accept a voucher for any reason, Days Out UK are not liable and cannot be held responsible.
5. Days Out UK shall not accept liability for any loss, accident or injury that may occur at a participating attraction and any dispute arising must be settled direct with the attraction concerned.
6. Cash redemption value of each voucher is 0.001p.
7. You are advised to check all relevant information with your chosen attraction before commencing your journey.

Days Out UK, PO Box 427, Northampton NN1 3YN. Tel: 01604 622445

Middleton Railway Leeds

Moor Road Hunslet Leeds Yorkshire

Two Adults For The Price Of One

Not Valid On Special Event Days

Not to be used in conjunction with any other offer. One voucher per party. Not valid on Bank Hols or special events

Valid until end Feb 2005

DISCOUNT VOUCHER

Please see page 554 for full attraction details

Newby Hall and Gardens

Newby Hall Ripon Yorkshire HG4 5AE

One Child Free

When Accompanied By A Full Paying Adult

Not to be used in conjunction with any other offer. One voucher per party. Not valid on Bank Hols or special events

Valid until end Feb 2005

DISCOUNT VOUCHER

Please see page 548 for full attraction details

Thackray Museum

Beckett Street Leeds Yorkshire LS9 7LN

Buy One Full Price Adult Ticket And Receive

Another Free

Not to be used in conjunction with any other offer. One voucher per party. Not valid on Bank Hols or special events

Valid until end Feb 2005

DISCOUNT VOUCHER

Please see page 550 for full attraction details

World of James Herriot

23 Kirkgate Thirsk Yorkshire YO7 1PL

Two For The Price Of One Adult Admission

Not to be used in conjunction with any other offer. One voucher per party. Not valid on Bank Hols or special events

Valid until end Feb 2005

DISCOUNT VOUCHER

Please see page 540 for full attraction details

Creswell Crags

Crags Road Welbeck Worksop Nottinghamshire

One Free Adult/Child

When One Adult Pays Full Price

Not to be used in conjunction with any other offer. One voucher per party. Not valid on Bank Hols or special events

Valid until end Feb 2005

DISCOUNT VOUCHER

Please see page 330 for full attraction details

Days Out UK, PO Box 427, Northampton NN1 3YN. Tel: 01604 622445

1. Each voucher entitles the holder to the discount specified by the selected attraction.
2. Valid for use until 28/02/05 (unless otherwise specified, or if attraction season finishes prior to this). Vouchers are subject to the terms, conditions and restrictions of the selected attraction.
3. One voucher per party will be accepted, cannot be used in conjunction with any other offer, photocopies will not be accepted.
4. All attractions offering a discount have confirmed their willingness to participate. All information is subject to change without notice and should any attraction close or decline to accept a voucher for any reason, Days Out UK are not liable and cannot be held responsible.
5. Days Out UK shall not accept liability for any loss, accident or injury that may occur at a participating attraction and any dispute arising must be settled direct with the attraction concerned.
6. Cash redemption value of each voucher is 0.001p.
7. You are advised to check all relevant information with your chosen attraction before commencing your journey.

Days Out UK, PO Box 427, Northampton NN1 3YN. Tel: 01604 622445

1. Each voucher entitles the holder to the discount specified by the selected attraction.
2. Valid for use until 28/02/05 (unless otherwise specified, or if attraction season finishes prior to this). Vouchers are subject to the terms, conditions and restrictions of the selected attraction.
3. One voucher per party will be accepted, cannot be used in conjunction with any other offer, photocopies will not be accepted.
4. All attractions offering a discount have confirmed their willingness to participate. All information is subject to change without notice and should any attraction close or decline to accept a voucher for any reason, Days Out UK are not liable and cannot be held responsible.
5. Days Out UK shall not accept liability for any loss, accident or injury that may occur at a participating attraction and any dispute arising must be settled direct with the attraction concerned.
6. Cash redemption value of each voucher is 0.001p.
7. You are advised to check all relevant information with your chosen attraction before commencing your journey.

Days Out UK, PO Box 427, Northampton NN1 3YN. Tel: 01604 622445

1. Each voucher entitles the holder to the discount specified by the selected attraction.
2. Valid for use until 28/02/05 (unless otherwise specified, or if attraction season finishes prior to this). Vouchers are subject to the terms, conditions and restrictions of the selected attraction.
3. One voucher per party will be accepted, cannot be used in conjunction with any other offer, photocopies will not be accepted.
4. All attractions offering a discount have confirmed their willingness to participate. All information is subject to change without notice and should any attraction close or decline to accept a voucher for any reason, Days Out UK are not liable and cannot be held responsible.
5. Days Out UK shall not accept liability for any loss, accident or injury that may occur at a participating attraction and any dispute arising must be settled direct with the attraction concerned.
6. Cash redemption value of each voucher is 0.001p.
7. You are advised to check all relevant information with your chosen attraction before commencing your journey.

Days Out UK, PO Box 427, Northampton NN1 3YN. Tel: 01604 622445

1. Each voucher entitles the holder to the discount specified by the selected attraction.
2. Valid for use until 28/02/05 (unless otherwise specified, or if attraction season finishes prior to this). Vouchers are subject to the terms, conditions and restrictions of the selected attraction.
3. One voucher per party will be accepted, cannot be used in conjunction with any other offer, photocopies will not be accepted.
4. All attractions offering a discount have confirmed their willingness to participate. All information is subject to change without notice and should any attraction close or decline to accept a voucher for any reason, Days Out UK are not liable and cannot be held responsible.
5. Days Out UK shall not accept liability for any loss, accident or injury that may occur at a participating attraction and any dispute arising must be settled direct with the attraction concerned.
6. Cash redemption value of each voucher is 0.001p.
7. You are advised to check all relevant information with your chosen attraction before commencing your journey.

Days Out UK, PO Box 427, Northampton NN1 3YN. Tel: 01604 622445

notes

index

◉ index

█ index

![train icon] index

◉ index

index

⬤ index

▦ index

Numbers in italic refer to colour section

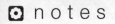

■ notes

notes